THE
unofficial GUIDE®

ᵀᴼ Disneyland

2016

COME CHECK US OUT!

Supplement your valuable guidebook with tips, news, and deals by visiting our website:

theunofficialguides.com

Also, while there, sign up for The Unofficial Guide newsletter for even more travel tips and special offers.

Join the conversation on social media:

 @theUGSeries

 theUnofficialGuides

 theUGSeries

 theUGSeries

#theUGseries

Other *Unofficial Guides*

Beyond Disney: The Unofficial Guide to Universal Orlando, SeaWorld, & the Best of Central Florida

The Disneyland Story: The Unofficial Guide to the Evolution of Walt Disney's Dream

Mini Mickey: The Pocket-Sized Unofficial Guide to Walt Disney World

Universal vs. Disney: The Unofficial Guide to American Theme Parks' Greatest Rivalry

The Unofficial Guide Color Companion to Walt Disney World

The Unofficial Guide to Disney Cruise Line

The Unofficial Guide to Las Vegas

The Unofficial Guide to Universal Orlando

The Unofficial Guide to Walt Disney World

The Unofficial Guide to Walt Disney World with Kids

The Unofficial Guide to Washington, D.C.

THE *unofficial* GUIDE®
TO Disneyland*

2016

BOB SEHLINGER *and* **SETH KUBERSKY**
with **GUY SELGA JR.**

*Disneyland® is officially known as the Disneyland Resort®.

keen
communications

Please note that prices fluctuate in the course of time and that travel information changes under the impact of many factors that influence the travel industry. We therefore suggest that you write or call ahead for confirmation when making your travel plans. Every effort has been made to ensure the accuracy of information throughout this book, and the contents of this publication are believed to be correct at the time of printing. Nevertheless, the publishers cannot accept responsibility for errors or omissions, for changes in details given in this guide, or for the consequences of any reliance on the information provided by the same. Assessments of attractions and so forth are based upon the author's own experience; therefore, descriptions given in this guide necessarily contain an element of subjective opinion, which may not reflect the publisher's opinion or dictate a reader's own experience on another occasion. Readers are invited to write the publisher with ideas, comments, and suggestions for future editions.

Published by:
Keen Communications, LLC
2204 First Avenue South, Suite 102
Birmingham. AL 35233

Cover design by Scott McGrew

Text design by Vertigo Design with updates by Annie Long

For information on our other products and services or to obtain technical support, please contact us from within the United States at 888-604-4537 or by fax at 205-326-1012.

Keen Communications, LLC, also publishes its books in a variety of electronic formats. Some content that appears in print may not be available in electronic formats.

ISBN: 978-1-62809-040-6; eISBN: 978-1-62809-041-3

Manufactured in the United States of America

5 4 3 2 1

CONTENTS

LIST of MAPS

ACKNOWLEDGMENTS

A BIG SALUTE TO OUR WHOLE UNOFFICIAL TEAM, who rendered a Herculean effort in what must have seemed like a fantasy version of Jean-Paul Sartre's *No Exit* to the tune of "It's a Small World." We hope you all recover to tour another day.

Special thanks to Disney historian Jim Hill; cartoonist Tami Knight; Unofficial Guide research director Len Testa; child psychologist Karen Turnbow, PhD; Unofficial Guide statistician Fred Hazleton; "Unheralded Treasures" writer Lani Teshima; and Unofficial friend Genevieve Bernard.

Lisa C. Bailey, Amber Kaye Henderson, Annie Long, Ryan Cardwell, and Darcie Vance all contributed energetically to shaping this latest edition. Much appreciation also goes to editorial-production manager Molly Merkle, cartographer Steve Jones, and indexer Rich Carlson.

—*Bob Sehlinger*

INTRODUCTION

WHY "UNOFFICIAL"?

DECLARATION OF INDEPENDENCE

THE AUTHORS AND RESEARCHERS OF THIS GUIDE specifically and categorically declare that they are and always have been totally independent of the Walt Disney Company, Inc., of Disneyland, Inc., of Walt Disney World Company, Inc., and of any and all other members of the Disney corporate family.

The material in this guide originated with the authors and researchers and has not been reviewed, edited, or in any way approved by Walt Disney Company, Inc., Disneyland, Inc., or Walt Disney World Company, Inc.

This guidebook represents the first comprehensive *critical* appraisal of Disneyland. Its purpose is to provide the reader with the information necessary to tour the theme parks with the greatest efficiency and economy and with the least amount of hassle and standing in line. The researchers of this guide believe in the wondrous variety, joy, and excitement of the Disney attractions. At the same time, we realistically recognize that Disneyland is a business, with the same profit motivations as businesses all over the world.

With no obligation to toe the Disney line, we represent and serve you, the reader. The contents were researched and compiled by a team of evaluators who are completely independent of the Walt Disney Company, Inc. If a restaurant serves bad food, if a gift item is overpriced, or if a ride isn't worth the wait, we say so. And in the process, we hope to make your visit more fun, efficient, and economical.

DANCE TO THE MUSIC

A DANCE HAS A BEGINNING AND AN END. But when you're dancing, you're not concerned about getting to the end or where on the dance floor you might wind up. In other words, you're totally in the moment. That's the way you should be on your Disneyland vacation.

You may feel a bit of pressure concerning your vacation. Vacations, after all, are very special events, and expensive ones to boot. So you work hard to make your vacation the best that it can be. Planning and organizing are essential to a successful Disneyland vacation, but if they become your focus, you won't be able to hear the music and enjoy the dance.

So think of us as your dancing coach. We'll teach you the steps to the dance in advance, so when you're on vacation and the music plays, you will dance with effortless grace and ease.

THE IMPORTANCE OF BEING GOOFY

THE DISNEYLAND CHARACTER PHYSICIAN was having lunch with the director of park operations when the doc's phone rang.

"Excuse me," the doctor said. "This is the fertility clinic. I'd better take it." He got up, exited the restaurant, and returned a few minutes later, looking concerned.

"This is weird," the doctor said, "but there's not a darn thing wrong with any of them."

"Any of whom?" the director asked.

"The Disney princes and princesses. They all checked out fine."

The director couldn't believe his ears. He stared at the doctor. "Wait a minute. Are you telling me that you sent all of the Disney princes and princesses to a fertility clinic?"

"Just the human ones who are married, plus Beast. I didn't send Mickey and Minnie, Donald and Daisy, Lady and Tramp, and a bunch of others who have been going together for decades but never got hitched."

Still stupefied, the director stammered, "Why? I didn't even know there was a problem."

"Well, the characters never complained, but most have been married for years and years, and . . . um . . . haven't you noticed that none of them have had children?" the doctor asked.

"I never gave it any thought," the director said, "but it means fewer high-earning characters on my payroll."

"I've given it plenty of thought. We're locked in a fierce competition with Universal, and their characters are having babies left and right. Shrek and Princess Fiona alone have been popping out little ogres like Martha White biscuits."

The director gave the doctor a hard look. "I could have told you that there's nothing wrong physically with the princes and princesses."

"If that's the case, why aren't they having children? Don't they know about the birds and the bees?" the doctor asked.

"The birds and the bees shall not be spoken of at Disneyland! But that's not why they don't have kids."

"Then why?"

The director leaned across the table to keep from being overheard. "Why do you think princes and princesses live happily ever after?"

And so it goes . . .

The Death of Spontaneity

One of our all-time favorite letters is from a man in Chapel Hill, North Carolina. He writes:

> *Your book reads like the operations plan for an amphibious landing: go here, do this, proceed to Step 15. You must think that everyone is a hyperactive, type-A theme park commando. What happened to the satisfaction of self-discovery or the joy of spontaneity? Next you will be telling us when to empty our bladders.*

As it happens, we at The Unofficial Guides are a pretty existential crew. We are big on self-discovery when walking in the woods or watching birds. Some of us are able to improvise jazz without reading music, while others can whip up a mean pot of chili without a recipe. When it comes to Disneyland, however, we all agree that you either need a good plan or a frontal lobotomy. The operational definition of self-discovery and spontaneity at Disneyland is the "pleasure" of heat prostration and the "joy" of standing in line.

It's easy to spot the free spirits at Disneyland Park and Disney California Adventure, particularly at opening time. While everybody else is stampeding to Splash Mountain or Radiator Springs Racers, they're the ones standing in a cloud of dust puzzling over the park map. Later, they're the folks running around like chickens in a thunderstorm trying to find an attraction with less than a 40-minute wait. Face it: Disneyland Resort is not a very existential place. In many ways it's the ultimate in mass-produced entertainment, the most planned and programmed environment imaginable. Self-discovery and spontaneity work about as well at Disneyland as they do on your tax return. One mother of two young boys had this to say about our book:

> *Your book was invaluable in giving us the tools to plan a great day. We had a magical day thanks to being able to prioritize our goals. Thank you for the full descriptions of rides—with only one day, you really need to pick your battles.*

We're not saying that you can't have a great time at Disneyland. Bowling isn't very spontaneous either, but lots of people love it. What we *are* saying is that you need a plan. You don't have to be inflexible about it. Just think about what you want to do—before you go. Don't delude yourself by rationalizing that the information in this modest tome is only for the pathological and superorganized.

HOW *This* GUIDE WAS RESEARCHED *and* WRITTEN

WHILE MUCH HAS BEEN WRITTEN CONCERNING Disneyland Resort, very little has been comparative or evaluative. In preparing this guide, nothing was taken for granted. The theme parks were visited at different times throughout the year by a team of trained observers who conducted detailed evaluations, rating the theme parks along with all of their component rides, shows, exhibits, services, and concessions according to formal, pretested rating criteria. Interviews with attraction patrons were conducted to determine what tourists of all age groups enjoyed most and least during their Disneyland visit.

*un**official* TIP
The Unofficial Guide to Disneyland maintains a researcher whose job it is to be in one of the two Disneyland Resort parks several days each week.

Though our observers are independent and impartial, we do not claim special expertise or scientific backgrounds relative to the types of exhibits, performances, or attractions viewed. Like you, we visit the Disneyland parks as tourists, noting our satisfaction or dissatisfaction. Disneyland offerings are marketed to the touring public, and it is as the public that we have experienced them.

The primary difference between the average tourist and the trained evaluator is that the latter approaches attractions equipped with professional skills in organization, preparation, and observation. The trained evaluator is responsible for much more than simply observing and cataloging. While the tourist is being entertained and delighted by the *Enchanted Tiki Room,* the professional evaluator seated nearby is rating the performance in terms of theme, pace, continuity, and originality. The evaluator also checks out the physical arrangements: Is the sound system clear and audible without being overpowering; is the audience shielded from the sun or rain; is seating adequate; can everyone in the audience clearly see the stage? Similarly, detailed and relevant checklists are prepared by observer teams and applied to rides, exhibits, and concessions, as well as to the theme park in general. Finally, observations and evaluator ratings are integrated with audience reactions and the opinions of patrons to compile a comprehensive profile of each feature and service.

In compiling this guide, we recognize the fact that a tourist's age, gender, background, and interests will strongly influence his or her taste in Disneyland offerings and will account for his or her preference of one ride or feature over another. Given this fact, we make no attempt at comparing apples with oranges. How, indeed, could a meaningful comparison be made between the serenity and beauty of the Storybook Land Canal Boats and the wild roller coaster ride of California Screamin'? Instead, our objective is to provide the reader with a critical evaluation and enough pertinent data to make knowledgeable decisions according to individual tastes.

The essence of this guide, then, consists of individual critiques and descriptions of each feature of the Disneyland parks, supplemented with some maps to help you get around and several detailed touring plans to help you avoid bottlenecks and crowds. Because so many Disneyland guests also visit Universal Studios Hollywood, we have included comprehensive coverage and a touring plan for that park as well.

A WORD TO OUR READERS
ABOUT ANNUAL REVISIONS

SOME OF YOU WHO PURCHASE EACH NEW EDITION of *The Unofficial Guide to Disneyland* have chastised us for retaining examples, comments, and descriptions from previous years' editions. This letter from a Grand Rapids, Michigan, reader is typical:

Your guidebook still has the same little example stories. When I got my new book, I expected a true update and new stuff, not the same old, same old!

First, *The Unofficial Guide to Disneyland* is a reference work. Though we are flattered that some readers read the guide from cover to cover, and that some of you find it entertaining, our objective is fairly straightforward: to provide information that enables you to have the best possible Disneyland vacation.

Each year during our revision research, we check every attraction, restaurant, hotel, shop, and entertainment offering. Though there are many changes, much remains the same from year to year. When we profile and critique an attraction, we try to provide the reader with the most insightful, relevant, and useful information, written in the clearest possible language. It is our opinion that if an attraction does not change, then it makes little sense to risk clarity and content for the sake of freshening up the prose. Disneyland guests who try the Mad Tea Party or Pinocchio's Daring Journey today, for example, experience the same presentation as guests who visited Disneyland in 2013, 1995, or 1986. Moreover, according to our extensive patron surveys (about 1,000 each year), today's guests still respond to these attractions in the same way as prior-year patrons.

The bottom line: We believe that our readers are better served if we devote our time to that which is changing and new as opposed to that which remains the same. The success or failure of this *Unofficial Guide* is determined not by the style of the writing but by the accuracy of the information and, ultimately, whether you have a positive experience at Disneyland. Every change to the guide we make (or don't make) is evaluated in this context.

WE'VE GOT ATTITUDE

SOME READERS DISAGREE with our attitude toward Disney. One, a 30-something woman from Golden, Colorado, lambasted us, writing:

I read your book cover to cover and felt you were way too hard on Disney. It's disappointing, when you're all enthused about going, to be slammed with all these criticisms and possible pitfalls.

A reader from Little Rock, Arkansas, also took us to task:

Your book was quite complimentary of Disney, perhaps too complimentary. Maybe the free trips you travel writers get at Disneyland are chipping away at your objectivity.

And from a Williamsport, Pennsylvania, mother of three:

Reading your book irritated me before we went because of all the warnings and cautions. I guess I'm used to having guidebooks pump me up about where I'm going. But once I arrived, I found that I was fully prepared and we had a great time. In retrospect, I have to admit you were right on the money. What I regarded as you being negative was just a good dose of reality.

A Vienna, Virginia, family chimed in with this:

After being at Disney for three days at the height of tourist season, I laughed out loud at your "Death of Spontaneity" section. We are definitely free spirit types who don't like to plan our days when we are on vacation. A friend warned us, and we got your guidebook. After skimming through it before we left, I was terrified that we had made a terrible mistake booking this vacation. Thanks to your book, we had a wonderful time. If it had not been for the book, we definitely would have been trampled by all the people stampeding to Space Mountain while we were standing there with our maps.

Finally, a reader from Phoenixville, Pennsylvania, prefers no opinions at all, writing:

Though each person has the right to his or her own opinion, I did not purchase the book for an opinion.

For the record, we've always paid our own way at Disneyland Resort: hotels, admissions, meals, the works. We don't dislike Disney, and we most definitely don't have an ax to grind. We're positive by nature and much prefer to praise than to criticize. Personally, we have enjoyed the Disney parks immensely over the years, both experiencing them and writing about them. Disney, however, as with all corporations (and all people, for that matter), is better at some things than others. Because our readers shell out big bucks to go to Disneyland, we believe that they have the right to know in advance what's good and what's not. For those who think we're overly positive, please understand that *The Unofficial Guide to Disneyland* is a guidebook, not an exposé. Our overriding objective is for you to enjoy your visit. To that end we try to report fairly and objectively. When readers disagree with our opinions, we, in the interest of fairness and balance, publish their point of view right alongside ours. To the best of our knowledge, The Unofficial Guides are the only travel guides in print that do this.

THE SUM OF ALL FEARS

EVERY WRITER WHO EXPRESSES an opinion is quite accustomed to readers who strongly agree or disagree. It comes with the territory. Troubling in the extreme, however, is the possibility that our efforts to be objective have frightened some readers away from Disneyland, or stimulated in others a state of apprehension. For the record, if you enjoy theme parks, Disneyland and Walt Disney World are as good as they get: absolute nirvana. They're upbeat, safe, fun, eye-popping, happy, and exciting. Even if you arrive knowing nothing about the place and make every possible touring mistake, chances are about 90% that you'll have a wonderful time anyway. In the end, guidebooks don't make or break great destinations. They are simply tools to help you enhance your experience and get the most vacation for your money.

As wonderful as Disneyland is, however, it is nevertheless a complex destination. Even so, it's certainly not nearly as challenging or difficult as visiting New York, San Francisco, Paris, Acapulco, or any other large city or destination. And, happily, there are numerous ways, if forewarned, to save money, minimize hassle, and make the most of your time. In large measure, that's what this guide is about: giving you a heads-up regarding potential problems and opportunities. Unfortunately, some folks reading *The Unofficial Guide* subconsciously add up the various warnings and critical advice and conclude that Disneyland is altogether too intimidating or, alternatively, too expensive or too much work. They lose track of the wonder of Disneyland and become focused instead on what might go wrong.

Our philosophy is that knowledge is power (and time and money too). You're free to follow our advice or not at your sole discretion. But you'd be denied the opportunity to exercise that discretion if we failed to fairly present the issues.

With or without a guidebook, you'll have a great time at Disneyland. If you let us, we'll help you smooth the potential bumps. We are certain that we can help you turn a great vacation into an absolutely superb one. Either way, once there, you will get the feel of the place and quickly reach a comfort level that will allay your apprehensions, as well as allow you to have a great experience.

THE *UNOFFICIAL GUIDE* PUBLISHING YEAR

WE RECEIVE MANY QUERIES each year asking when the next edition of *The Unofficial Guide to Disneyland* will be available. Usually our new editions are published and available in stores by late August or early September. Thus the 2017 edition will be on the shelves in the fall of 2016.

WHERE'S THE INDEX?

TO ELIMINATE YOUR HAVING TO CARRY THIS TOME around the theme parks, we've created quite a few tear-out pages with touring plans at the end of the book. Consequently, we've moved the index from its usual position as the last thing in the book to immediately precede the tear-out pages.

LETTERS, COMMENTS, AND QUESTIONS FROM READERS

MANY OF THOSE WHO USE *The Unofficial Guide to Disneyland* write to us, asking questions, making comments, or sharing their own strategies for visiting Disneyland. We appreciate all such input, both positive and critical, and encourage our readers to continue writing. Readers' comments and observations are frequently used in revised editions of *The Unofficial Guide to Disneyland* and have contributed immeasurably to its improvement.

Reader Survey

Please fill out our reader survey online by visiting **touringplans.com /disneyland-resort/survey.** You can rest assured that we won't release your name and address to any mailing-list companies, direct mail advertisers, or other third party. Unless you instruct us otherwise, we will assume that you do not object to being quoted in a future edition.

How to Contact the Author

Write to Seth Kubersky at this address:

> *The Unofficial Guide to Disneyland*
> 2204 First Ave. S, Ste. 102
> Birmingham, AL 35233

Or e-mail him at **unofficialguides@menasharidge.com.** When you write, put your address on both your letter and envelope; sometimes the two get separated. It is also a good idea to include your phone number and e-mail address. If you e-mail us, please tell us where you're from. Remember, as travel writers, we're often out of the office for long periods of time, so forgive us if our response is slow. Unofficial Guide e-mail is not forwarded to us when we're traveling, but we will respond as soon as possible when we return.

Questions from Readers

Questions frequently asked by readers are answered in an appendix at the back of this *Unofficial Guide.*

DISNEYLAND RESORT:
An OVERVIEW

IF YOU HAVEN'T BEEN TO DISNEYLAND for a while, you'll hardly know the place. First, of course, there is **Disneyland Park,** which in 2015 marked its 60th year as the original Disney theme park with a Diamond Anniversary celebration (complete with a jewel-encrusted Sleeping Beauty Castle) that continues through 2016; it's also the only park that Walt Disney saw completed in his lifetime. Much more than the Magic Kingdom at Walt Disney World, Disneyland Park embodies the quiet, charming spirit of nostalgia that so characterized Walt himself. The park is vast yet intimate, steeped in the tradition of its creator yet continually changing.

Disneyland was opened in 1955 on a 107-acre tract surrounded almost exclusively by orange groves, just west of the sleepy and little-known Southern California community of Anaheim. Constrained by finances and ultimately enveloped by the city it helped create, Disneyland operated on that same modest parcel of land until 2001.

Disneyland Park is a collection of adventures, rides, and shows symbolized by the Disney characters and Sleeping Beauty Castle. It's divided into eight subareas, or "lands," arranged around a central hub. First encountered is **Main Street, U.S.A.,** which connects the Disneyland entrance with the central hub. Moving clockwise around the hub, the other lands are **Adventureland, Frontierland, Fantasyland,** and **Tomorrowland.** Two major lands, **Critter Country** and **New Orleans Square,** are accessible via Adventureland and Frontierland but do not connect directly with the central hub. Another land, **Mickey's Toontown,** connects to Fantasyland. All eight lands will be described in detail later.

Growth and change at Disneyland (until 1996) had been internal, in marked contrast to the ever-enlarging development of Walt Disney World near Orlando, Florida. Until recently, when something new was added at Disneyland, something old had to go. The Disney engineers, to their credit, however, have never been shy about disturbing the status quo. Patrons of the park's earlier, modest years are amazed by the transformation. Gone are the days of the "magical little park" with the Monsanto House of the Future, donkey rides, and Captain Hook's Pirate Ship. Substituted in a process of continuous evolution and modernization are state-of-the-art fourth-, fifth-, and sixth-generation attractions and entertainment. To paraphrase Walt Disney, Disneyland will never stop changing as long as there are new ideas to explore.

Disneyland Park was arguably Walt Disney's riskiest venture. It was developed on a shoestring budget and made possible only through Disney's relationship with ABC Television and a handful of brave corporate sponsors. The capital available was barely sufficient to acquire the property and build the park; nothing was left over for the development of hotels or the acquisition and improvement of property adjoining the park. Even the Disneyland Hotel, connected to the theme park by monorail, was owned and operated by a third party until 1989.

Disneyland's success spawned a wave of development that rapidly surrounded the theme park with whimsically themed mom-and-pop motels, souvenir stands, and fast-food restaurants. Disney, still deep in debt, looked on in abject shock, powerless to intervene. In fact, the Disneyland experience was etched so deeply into the Disney corporate consciousness that Walt purchased 27,500 acres and established an autonomous development district in Florida (unaccountable to any local or county authority) when he was ready to launch Disney World.

Though the Florida project gave Disney the opportunity to develop a destination resort in a totally controlled environment, the steady decline of the area encircling Disneyland continued to rankle Walt. After tolerating the blight for 30 years, the Walt Disney Company (finally flush with funds and ready for a good fight) set about putting Disneyland Park right. Quietly at first, then aggressively, Disney began buying up the mom-and-pop motels, as well as the few remaining orange and vegetable groves near the park.

In June 1993 the City of Anaheim adopted a Disney plan that called for the development of a new Disney destination resort, including a second theme park situated in what was once the Disneyland parking lot; a Disney-owned hotel district with 4,600 hotel rooms; two new parking facilities; and improvements, including extensive landscaping of the streets that provide access to the complex. City of Anaheim, Orange County, and State of California infrastructure changes required to support the expanded Disney presence included widening I-5, building new interchanges, moving a major power line, adding new sewer systems, and expanding utilities capacity.

By the end of 2000, all of the changes, modifications, and additions were finished, and Disneyland began the new century as a complete multi–theme park resort destination. The second and newest park, **Disney California Adventure** (or DCA to the initiated), celebrated its grand opening on February 8, 2001.

DCA is an oddly shaped park built around a lagoon on one side and the Grand Californian Hotel on the other, with one of Disney's trademark mountains, **Grizzly Peak,** plopped down in the middle. **Buena Vista Street,** an entranceway evoking 1920s Los Angeles, leads to seven "lands." Inside the front gate and to the left is **Hollywood Land** (formerly Hollywood Pictures Backlot), a diminutive version of the Disney's Hollywood Studios theme park at Walt Disney World. Then there are Grizzly Peak (which absorbed the former Condor Flats area) and Pacific Wharf, a pair of lands (originally known collectively as Golden State) celebrating California's industry, cuisine, and natural resources. Next is **A Bug's Land,** with characters and attractions based on the Disney-Pixar film *a bug's life.* **Cars Land** is dedicated to the desert town of Radiator Springs from Disney-Pixar's *Cars.* Finally, **Paradise Pier** recalls the grand old seaside amusement parks of the early 20th century.

The entrances to Disneyland Park and DCA face each other across a palm-studded pedestrian plaza called the **Esplanade,** which begins at Harbor Boulevard and runs west, between the parks, passing into **Downtown Disney,** a dining, shopping, entertainment, and nightlife venue. From Downtown Disney, the Esplanade continues via an overpass across Downtown Drive and past the monorail station to the **Disneyland** and **Paradise Pier Hotels.**

Sandwiched between the Esplanade and Downtown Disney on the north and DCA on the south is the 945-room **Grand Californian Hotel** and the 50-unit **Grand Californian Villas.** Designed in the image of rustic national park lodges, the Grand Californian supplanted the Disneyland Hotel as Disneyland's prestigious lodging property.

North of the hotels and across West Street from Disneyland Park is a huge multistory parking garage that can be accessed directly from I-5. This is where most Disneyland guests park. Tram transport is provided from the garage, from the adjacent oversize-vehicle lot, and from outlying lots to the Esplanade. Kennels are located to the right of the Disneyland Park main entrance. Ticket booths are situated along the Esplanade.

SHOULD I GO TO DISNEYLAND PARK IF I'VE SEEN WALT DISNEY WORLD?

DISNEYLAND PARK IS ROUGHLY COMPARABLE to the Magic Kingdom theme park at Walt Disney World near Orlando, Florida. Both are arranged by "lands" accessible from a central hub and connected to the entrance by a main street. Both parks feature many rides and attractions of the same name: Space Mountain, Jungle Cruise, Pirates of the Caribbean, It's a Small World, and Dumbo the Flying Elephant, to name a few. Interestingly, however, the same name does not necessarily connote the same experience. Pirates of the Caribbean at Disneyland Park is much longer and more elaborate than its Walt Disney World counterpart. The Haunted Mansion is more elaborate in Florida, and the *Enchanted Tiki Room* is about the same in both places.

Disneyland Park is more intimate than the Magic Kingdom, not having the room for expansion enjoyed by the Florida park. Pedestrian thoroughfares are narrower, and everything from Big Thunder Mountain to the castle is scaled down somewhat. Large crowds are more taxing at Disneyland Park because there is less room for them to disperse. At Disneyland Park, however, there are dozens of little surprises, small unheralded attractions tucked away in crooks and corners of the park, which give Disneyland Park a special charm and variety that the Magic Kingdom lacks. And, of course, Disneyland Park has the stamp of Walt Disney's personal touch.

A Minnesota couple who have sampled Disney both east and west offered this observation:

> We have been to WDW in Florida several times. This was our first visit to Disneyland. For parents with children 10 years of age and younger, I highly recommend Disneyland instead of WDW. Its size is much more manageable. You can stay within walking distance of the front gate. That makes it practical and easy to get to the gates early in the morning (an absolute imperative) and get away in the afternoon for a break (always helpful). The size and scale of WDW make this impractical.

A Salem, Massachusetts, family who had visited WDW three years prior to their Disneyland trip, agreed:

> We heard from many that Disneyland was small and that the castle was underwhelming. But the Disney magic was there, and we had a great time exploring what was unique about each park. We spent three days at the parks and wished that we had planned to be there longer. The parks may be smaller, but there is still plenty to see and do.

Disneyland first-timers (along with honeymooners and birthday or anniversary celebrants) are rewarded with a special pin, as this Oregon mom relates:

> When I went to pick up something at Town Hall on Main Street, I realized that they had pins to proudly announce it was a first visit to DL. I don't recall reading anything about this in your book and

CRITICAL COMPARISON OF ATTRACTIONS FOUND AT BOTH PARKS

ADVENTURELAND

• *Enchanted Tiki Room* About the same at both parks.
• **Jungle Cruise** Updated Audio-Animatronic (robotic) animals and funnier narrators at Disneyland, but longer ride at Walt Disney World.

CRITTER COUNTRY

• **The Many Adventures of Winnie the Pooh** Longer and with more motion at the Magic Kingdom.
• **Splash Mountain** Longer ride and a bigger drop at Magic Kingdom, but California has more animatronic animals.

FANTASYLAND

• **Carrousels** About the same at both parks.
• **Castles** Far larger and more beautiful at Magic Kingdom; Disneyland has walk-through display.
• **Dumbo the Flying Elephant** About the same, but WDW version has double the capacity and an interactive circus-themed queue.
• **It's a Small World** Disneyland version is longer with hidden Disney characters, and it gets a holiday overlay.
• **Mad Tea Party** Disneyland's is open-air; otherwise the same at both parks.
• **Peter Pan's Flight** Shorter but with upgraded special effects at Disneyland.
• **Royal Hall at Fantasy Faire/Princess Fairytale Hall** About the same, but Disneyland doesn't have Anna and Elsa (or FastPass).

FRONTIERLAND

• **Big Thunder Mountain Railroad** More monumental mountain and an interactive queue at Magic Kingdom; smoother track and upgraded effects at Disneyland.
• **Tom Sawyer Island** Comparable; pirate theme with more elaborate effects at Disneyland, but more caves and play structures to explore at Magic Kingdom.
• **Various river cruises (canoes, boats, and such)** More interesting sights at Disneyland, and only Disneyland offers canoes.

MAIN STREET, U.S.A.

• **Railroads** The Disneyland Railroad is far more entertaining by virtue of the Grand Canyon diorama and the primeval world components not found at the Magic Kingdom.

NEW ORLEANS SQUARE

• **The Haunted Mansion** Longer ride and hitchhiking ghosts give Magic Kingdom the edge. Holiday version is offered only at Disneyland.
• **Pirates of the Caribbean** Far superior at Disneyland.

TOMORROWLAND

• **Astro Orbitor** About the same at both parks, but much higher in the air at the Magic Kingdom.
• **Autopia/Tomorrowland Speedway** Disneyland version is superior.
• **Buzz Lightyear** More mobile guns and better game play at Disneyland.
• **Space Mountain** Much better effects and smoother track at Disneyland, but a wilder ride with sharper drops at Magic Kingdom.

*It should be noted that several of the attractions at Disney California Adventure, such as *Disney Junior, It's Tough to Be a Bug!, Muppet-Vision 3-D,* Toy Story Midway Mania!, The Twilight Zone Tower of Terror, and *Turtle Talk with Crush,* appeared first at one of the Walt Disney World theme parks. Versions of Ariel's Undersea Adventure, Soarin' Over California, and Star Tours have been exported to Walt Disney World. None of the remaining DCA attractions are found at Disney World.

*would have taken advantage of it with my older son's first visit. For-
tunately, there is no date on it, so I got one for each son and told them
that no one would know it was the older one's second time.*

To allow for a meaningful comparison, we have provided a summary of those features found at Disneyland Park and not WDW's
Magic Kingdom (listed alphabetically below), accompanied by a critical look at the attractions found at both parks on the preceding page.

ATTRACTIONS FOUND ONLY AT DISNEYLAND PARK

ADVENTURELAND

- Indiana Jones Adventure   • Tarzan's Treehouse

CRITTER COUNTRY

- Davy Crockett's Explorer Canoes

FANTASYLAND

- Alice in Wonderland   • Casey Jr. Circus Train   • Fantasyland Theatre
- Matterhorn Bobsleds   • Mr. Toad's Wild Ride   • Pinocchio's Daring Journey
- Royal Theatre at Fantasy Faire   • Sleeping Beauty Castle Walk-Through
- Snow White's Scary Adventures   • Storybook Land Canal Boats

FRONTIERLAND

- *Fantasmic!* (at Disney's Hollywood Studios)   • The Golden Horseshoe
- Sailing Ship *Columbia*

MAIN STREET, U.S.A.

- *The Disneyland Story,* presenting *Great Moments with Mr. Lincoln*

MICKEY'S TOONTOWN

- Chip 'n Dale Treehouse   • Gadget's Go Coaster   • Goofy's Playhouse
- Mickey's House   • Minnie's House   • *Miss Daisy,* Donald's Boat
- Roger Rabbit's Car Toon Spin

TOMORROWLAND

- Disneyland Monorail System   • Finding Nemo Submarine Voyage   • *Jedi
Training Academy* (at Disney's Hollywood Studios)   • Star Tours—The
Adventures Continue (at Disney's Hollywood Studios)   • Tomorrowland
Theater

PART ONE

PLANNING *Before* YOU LEAVE HOME

▎█ GATHERING INFORMATION

IN ADDITION TO THIS GUIDE, we recommend that you first visit our website, **touringplans.com,** which offers essential tools for planning your trip and saving you time and money. Our blog, **blog.touringplans .com,** lists breaking news for the Disneyland Resort and Disney theme parks worldwide.

The site also offers computer-optimized touring plans for Disneyland and DCA. With these, you choose the attractions you want to experience, including character greetings, parades, fireworks, meals, and midday breaks, and we'll give you a step-by-step itinerary for your specific dates of travel, showing you how to see everything with minimal waits in line. The touring plans can incorporate any FastPasses you retrieve.

You can update the touring plans when you're in the parks, too. Let's say that your touring plan calls for riding The Haunted Mansion next, but your family really needs an ice cream break and 30 minutes out of the sun. Get the ice cream and take the break. When you're done, click the OPTIMIZE button on your plan, and it will be updated with what to do next. The ability to redo your plan allows you to recover from any situation while still minimizing your waits for the rest of the day.

Another really popular part of **touringplans.com** is our Crowd Calendar, which shows crowd projections for Disneyland and DCA for every day of the year. Look up the dates of your visit, and the calendar will not only show the projected wait times for each day but will also indicate for each day which theme park will be the least crowded. Historical wait times are also available, so you can see how crowded the parks were last year for your upcoming trip dates.

The website also has complete dining menus, including wine lists, for every food cart, stand, kiosk, counter-service restaurant, and sitdown restaurant in the Disneyland Resort. The whole thing is searchable, too, so you can find every restaurant in DCA that serves steak (and its prices), or see which snacks are available in New Orleans Square. Updated constantly, these menus represent the most accurate collection of Disney dining information available anywhere.

The touring plans, menus, Crowd Calendar, and more are available in Lines, our mobile application, which provides continuous real-time updates on wait times at Disneyland. Using in-park staff and updates sent in by readers, Lines shows you the current wait and FastPass distribution times at every attraction in every park, as well as our estimated actual waits for these attractions for the rest of today. For example, Lines will tell you that the posted wait time for Space Mountain is 60 minutes, and that based on what we know about how Disney manages Space Mountain's queue, the actual time you'll probably wait in line is 48 minutes. Lines is the only Disney app that shows you both posted and actual wait times.

Lines also has an online chat feature, where folks can ask questions and give travel tips. Hundreds of "Liners" interact every day in discussions that stay remarkably on-topic for an Internet forum, and the group organizes regular in-park meets. We're thrilled with it. One couple from Easton, Pennsylvania, found Lines especially useful:

> *I don't know what we would have done without* The Unofficial Guide to Disneyland *and the Lines app. This was our first and possibly only trip to Disneyland. We were able to do everything we wanted and ride many big attractions like the Matterhorn several times. We also enjoyed using the menu feature on the site and app. I was able to plan all our meals before arriving at a restaurant instead of realizing later that there were no good vegetarian options.*

Lines is available free to **touringplans.com** subscribers for the Apple iPhone and iPad at the iTunes Store (search for "TouringPlans") and for Android devices at the Google Play Store. Owners of other phones can use the Web-based version at **m.touringplans.com.**

As long as you have that smartphone handy while visiting the parks, we and your fellow *Unofficial Guide* readers would love it if you could report on the actual wait times you get while you're there. Run Lines, log in to your user account, and click +TIME in the upper right corner to help everyone out. We'll use that information to update the wait times for everyone in the park, and make everyone's lives just a little bit better.

Much of our Web content—including the menus, resort photos and video, and errata for this book—is completely free for anyone to use. Access to part of the site, most notably the Crowd Calendar, additional touring plans, and in-park wait times, requires a small subscription fee (current-book owners get a substantial discount). This nominal charge helps keep us online and costs less than lunch at the French Market restaurant in Disneyland. Plus **touringplans.com** offers a 45-day money-back guarantee.

In addition we recommend that you obtain copies of the following publications:

1. DISNEYLAND RESORT VACATION PLANNING DVD Moving boldly into the post-paper digital era, Disney has largely done away with its full-color booklets describing Disneyland and listing vacation package rates. Instead, it offers free vacation-planning toolkits, featuring DVDs documenting the resort's offerings. To get it, call the Walt Disney Resort Travel Sales Center at ☎ 714-520-5060 or visit **disneyvacations.com /vacation-planning-tools.** You can also get DVDs for Walt Disney World, Disney Cruise Line, and other Disney destinations delivered from the same site. This is a good way to get your name on Disney's mailing list for discount offers.

2. *DISNEYLAND GUIDEBOOK FOR GUESTS WITH DISABILITIES* If members of your party are sight- or hearing-impaired or partially or wholly nonambulatory, you will find this small guide very helpful. Disney does not mail them, but copies are readily available at the park. You can also download the guide at **disneyland.disney.go.com/guest-services/guests -with-disabilities**.

3. *HOTELCOUPONS.COM SOUTHWEST GUIDE* A good source of lodging discounts throughout the state of California, the *HotelCoupons.com Southwest Guide* can be obtained by calling ☎ 800-222-3948, Monday–Friday, 8:30 a.m.–5:30 p.m. Eastern time, or visiting **hotel coupons.com.** The guide is free, but you will be charged $4 ($6 Canadian) for postage and handling. Similar guides to other states are available at the same number.

Disneyland Main Information Phone and Website

The following website and phone numbers provide general information. Inquiries may be expedited by using phone numbers specific to the nature

IMPORTANT DISNEYLAND RESORT PHONE NUMBERS	
ANAHEIM TRAVEL INFORMATION	☎ 714-765-8888
ASK OTTO AUTOMATED ATTRACTION INFO	☎ 714-520-7090
DINING RESERVATIONS	☎ 714-781-3463, Option 4
DISABILITY SERVICES	☎ 407-560-2547
DISNEY CRUISE LINE	☎ 800-951-3532
DISNEY GUIDED TOURS	☎ 714-781-8687
DISNEYLAND HOTEL	☎ 714-778-6600
DISNEYLAND RESORT ROOM RESERVATIONS	☎ 714-956-6425
DISNEYLAND VACATION PACKAGES	☎ 714-520-5060
FANTASMIC! PREMIUM VIEWING	☎ 714-781-7469
FOREIGN LANGUAGE ASSISTANCE	☎ 714-781-7290
GRAND CALIFORNIAN HOTEL	☎ 714-635-2300
LOST & FOUND	☎ 714-781-4765
PARADISE PIER HOTEL	☎ 714-999-0990

of the inquiry (other phone numbers are listed elsewhere in this chapter, under their relevant topics, and in the table on the preceding page). If you don't mind interacting with an AI, you can call ☎ 714-520-7090 and Ask Otto, Disneyland's automated information hot line, about ride wait times and upcoming shows.

Disneyland Guest Relations
☎ 714-781-4565 for recorded information;
☎ 714-781-7290 for live operator; **disneyland.com**

The Phone from Hell

Sometimes it is virtually impossible to get through on the Disneyland information numbers listed above. When you get through, you will get a recording that offers various information options. If none of the recorded options answer your question, you will have to hold for a live person. Eat before you call—you may have a long wait. If, after repeated attempts, you get tired of a busy signal in your ear or, worse, 20 minutes' worth of singing mice warbling "Cinderelly" in alto falsettos while you are on hold, call the Disneyland Hotel at ☎ 714-778-6600.

RECOMMENDED WEBSITES

A NUMBER OF GOOD Disneyland information sources are on the Web. The following are brief profiles of our favorites:

BEST OFFICIAL THEME PARK SITES The official Disneyland website, **disneyland.com,** is so loaded with videos, photos, and gimmicks that it's slow to load and cumbersome to search unless you have a fast computer and high-speed Internet. For those who do, there's a ton of information to be had, but even so it usually takes a lot of clicks to find what you're looking for. **Disneyland.com** has been upgraded in recent years to finally catch up with its sister site, **disneyworld.com,** in areas such as online dining reservations. The Universal Studios website is **universalstudios hollywood.com.** Like the Disneyland site, it has a lot of bells and whistles. As far as your computer's concerned, be new, be fast, or be gone.

BEST OFFICIAL AREA WEBSITE Anaheimoc.org is the official website of the Anaheim–Orange County Visitor & Convention Bureau. You'll find everything from hotels and restaurants to weather and driving directions on this site.

BEST GENERAL UNOFFICIAL WEBSITES We recommend the following websites for general information related to the Disneyland Resort.

Mouseplanet.com is a comprehensive resource for Disneyland data, offering features and reviews by guest writers, information on the Disney theme parks, discussion groups, and news. The site includes an interactive Disney restaurant and hotel review page, where users can voice opinions on their Disney dining and lodging experiences. We particularly enjoy the weekly Disneyland update column.

Intercotwest.com (Internet Community of Tomorrow–West) is filled with detailed information on every corner of Disneyland Resort.

Featured are frequent news updates, as well as descriptions, reviews, and ratings of every attraction, restaurant, and shop at the resort.

Deb Wills's **allears.net,** which maintains a fantastic site for Walt Disney World, also has a growing Disneyland sister site. It includes extensive information about the Disney resorts and attractions, including reader reviews. The site is updated several times a week and includes Disney restaurant menus, ticketing information, maps, and more.

Wdwinfo.com has a vibrant Disneyland section that can be found at **wdwinfo.com/disneyland.** It includes up-to-date dining menus, attraction reviews, touring tips, and more.

BEST DISNEYLAND HISTORY WEBSITE At **yesterland.com** you can visit the Disneyland of the past, where retired Disneyland attractions are brought back to life through vivid descriptions and historical photographs. Yesterland attraction descriptions relate what it was once like to experience the Flying Saucers, the Mine Train through Nature's Wonderland, the Tahitian Terrace, and dozens of other rides, shows, parades, and restaurants.

BEST WEBSITE FOR RUMORS AND THE INSIDE SCOOP **Jimhillmedia.com** is perfectly attuned to what's going on behind the scenes—Jim Hill always has good gossip. He works with The Unofficial Guides as our resident historian and contributes sidebars and anecdotes to our Disney titles.

BEST DISNEYLAND NEWS SITES **Micechat.com,** with a dedicated group of local editors, is the definitive on-the-ground coverage of the Disneyland Resort. Be sure to check out "Dateline Disneyland" and "In The Parks," two weekly columns that stay on the pulse of the parks, complete with photos. **Mouseplanet.com** and Robert Niles's **themeparkinsider.com** are other great sources for breaking Southern California theme park news. For official news, the Disney Parks Blog (**disneyparks.com/blog**) covers news from all Disney resorts.

BEST MONEY-SAVING SITE **Mousesavers.com** specializes in finding you the deepest discounts on hotels, park admissions, and rental cars. Mouse-Savers does not actually sell travel but rather unearths and publishes special discount codes that you can use to obtain the discounts. It's the first place we look for deals when we go to Disneyland Resort.

BEST DISNEY DISCUSSION BOARDS The best online discussion of all things Disney can be found at **micechat.com/forums, mousepad.mouseplanet .com,** and **disboards.com.** With tens of thousands of members and millions of posts, they are the most active and popular discussion boards on the Web. There is also a rousing chat room inside our own mobile application, Lines (learn more at **touringplans.com/lines**).

BEST DISNEY PODCASTS Our favorite Disneyland-centric podcast is *Mousetalgia,* found at **mousetalgia.com,** which covers Disneyland, Disney California Adventure, and everything else Disney. The hosts appreciate the history of the resort while maintaining balanced coverage of new Disneyland developments. **Seasonpasspodcast.com** has breaking news and in-depth interviews with theme park designers and executives from Disneyland and parks around the world. Hosted by industry veterans (and fans!), the show provides detailed discussions about how and why theme parks work. And if you want warts-and-all tales from behind the scenes of Mickey's kingdoms, don't miss *The Unofficial Guide's Disney Dish with Jim Hill,* hosted by coauthor Len Testa. For Universal Studios Hollywood updates, check out **insideuniversal.net.**

BEST DISNEY TWITTER FEEDS If you want your Disney news and rumors in 140 character bites, follow these prolific park Tweeters:

@thedisneyblog	@disneyland	@disneylandtoday	@disneyparks
@dlandnewslive	@latimesfunland	@micechat	@ocregister
@touringplans	@guyselga	@skubersky	

ADMISSION OPTIONS

THEME PARK ADMISSION OPTIONS are pretty straightforward at Disneyland Resort. You have only two things to decide:

1. How many days admission you'll need.
2. Whether you want to go to both Disneyland Park and Disney California Adventure on the same day. This is known as park hopping.

Multiday tickets expire 13 days after the first use, so you don't want to buy more days than you'll need. Needless to say, tickets expire after you've used the number of days purchased even if 13 days haven't passed yet.

All admissions can be purchased at the park entrance, at the Disneyland Resort hotels, from the Walt Disney Travel Sales Center, on the Disneyland website, and at most Disney stores in the western United States. One- and 2-year-olds are exempt from admission fees.

Admission Costs and Available Discounts

It's possible to obtain discounts on all multiday tickets, but only in the 1%–7% range. You can purchase tickets in advance with Magic Morning Hours for full gate prices at **disneyland.com.** These tickets allow you to enter only Disneyland Park on select days 1 hour earlier than the general public one time during your visit. The feature is offered only on three-, four-, and five-day tickets purchased in advance of your visit. If any special seasonal discounts are being offered directly from Disney, you can learn about them at **disneyland .disney.go.com/offers-discounts.**

unofficial **TIP**
The money you can save makes researching Disney's dizzying array of ticket options worthwhile.

If you purchase tickets on the Disneyland website, you can choose between "hard" tickets, which will be shipped to you, or e-tickets, which can be downloaded as PDF files and printed at home or scanned from your mobile device. An e-ticket printed from your home computer will show two bar codes. A cast member will scan these at the turnstiles. Once the bar codes are read, the cast member can issue your actual ticket. You can also now purchase one-day tickets through your smartphone at **m.disneyland.com**

ADMISSION OPTIONS	ADULT (age 10 and up)	CHILD (ages 3–9)
One-Day, One Park	$99	$93
One-Day Park Hopper	$139	$133
Two-Day, One Park Per Day	$185	$172
Two-Day Park Hopper	$225	$212
Three-Day, One Park Per Day with Magic Morning	$235	$224
Three-Day Park Hopper with Magic Morning	$275	$264
Four-Day, One Park Per Day with Magic Morning	$260	$245
Four-Day Park Hopper with Magic Morning	$300	$285
Five-Day, One Park Per Day with Magic Morning	$275	$259
Five-Day Park Hopper with Magic Morning	$315	$299
Southern California Select Annual Passport *(many blackout dates; only available to residents of certain zip codes)*	$299	$299
Deluxe Annual Passport *(some blackout dates)*	$549	$549
Premium Annual Passport *(no blackout dates; parking included)*	$779	$779
Disney Premier Passport *(no blackout dates; valid at all California and Florida parks)*	$1,099	$1,099

without needing to print anything, but these passes don't include any discounts or bonuses.

The deepest discounts we've found are from **ARES Travel** (**ares travel.com**). ARES usually beats the Disney advance purchase price by $4–$18 per ticket and also includes the Magic Morning feature. Guests may pick up their tickets at any main entrance window; a $2-per-ticket convenience fee applies. You can order online or call ☎ 800-434-7894. You must provide the first date you intend to visit when purchasing the ticket, and exchanging the voucher for your ticket can be a bit of a hassle.

If you plan to visit other Southern California attractions in addition to Disneyland, you might want to consider a **CityPass.** CityPass includes a Three-Day Park Hopper for Disneyland Park and DCA, including early entry to a designated park for one day. Also included are one day's admission each to Legoland California and SeaWorld San Diego. Costing $329 for adults and $286 for children ages 3–9, the pass is valid for 14 days from first use. If you plan to visit all these parks, it will save you about 25% on admissions. If you don't use all of the admissions, however, you will save little or nothing by purchasing the CityPass. The pass does not include dining or shopping discounts. Details concerning other CityPass destinations are available at **citypass.com.**

Military discounts are available for all Disney theme parks, usually in the 7%–25% range; in 2015 a Three-Day Park Hopper was offered for less than the regular price of a One-Day Park Hopper. Check with your base Morale, Welfare, & Recreation office for info. Military ID may be required at the gate. Many readers report buying military tickets for friends and relatives who used them without problems. Learn about current military discount offers at **disneyland.disney.go.com /offers-discounts/military-park-tickets.**

Disneyland Resort and other area attractions sometimes offer discounted afternoon and evening tickets for convention goers. See **disneyconventiontickets.com.**

Admission prices increase from time to time. For planning your budget, however, the table on page 20 provides a fair estimate. Note that Walt Disney World tickets are *not* valid for admission to Disneyland, with the sole exception of bicoastal Premier Annual Passports.

One-Day, One Park

This pass is good for one day's admission at your choice of Disneyland Park or Disney California Adventure. As the name implies, you cannot "hop" from park to park.

Park Hopper Tickets

These are good for one, two, three, four, or five days, respectively, and allow you to visit both parks on the same day. These multiday tickets do not have to be used on consecutive days, but they do expire 13 days after their first use. If you mistakenly bought multiday tickets because you were not aware of the 13-day expiration, call ☎ 714-781-7290 or ☎ 714-781-4565 and ask to be connected to Guest Communications, which has the authority to issue you a voucher for the unused days on your ticket.

We are lukewarm on the value of Park Hopper tickets at Walt Disney World during visits of fewer than five days, but if you are spending more than two days at Disneyland Resort, we strongly encourage you to spring for the park-to-park access. The ease of walking from one park to the other, and the potential for doubling up on FastPass opportunities in the process, makes the Park Hopper premium more than worth it.

Any time before a pass expires, you can apply the full original value of the ticket toward the cost of a higher priced ticket. If you buy a Four-Day Park Hopper ticket, for example, and then decide you'd rather have an Annual Passport, you can apply the full original value of the former toward the purchase of the latter. Unlike at Walt Disney World, which sells up to 10-day tickets, the maximum number of days you can purchase on a standard Disneyland ticket is 5. After that you have to upgrade to an annual pass or buy another ticket, which makes a six- or seven-day visit extremely cost-ineffective. Upgraded passes expire on the same 13-day deadline date as the original ticket; annual passes expire one year from the first usage of the original ticket. To restrict the reselling of half-used passes, Disneyland photographs every multiday pass holder upon first entry for identification purposes; be prepared to have your pass (and face) scanned shortly before passing the turnstiles.

Annual Passports

The Disneyland Resort offers a few annual passports. The Premium Annual Passport is good for an entire year with no blackout dates and is the only Disneyland passport that includes parking. The pass costs $779 and is good for admission to both parks during normal operating hours with use of all attractions (excluding arcades), up to 15% discounts at most resort dining locations, and 20% off most merchandise. Deluxe Passports ($549) are valid 315 days per year (after preselected peak season blackout dates) and offer 10% discounts. Prices for children are the same as those for adults on annual passports. If you purchase your annual passport in July of this year and schedule your visit next year for June, you'll cover two years' vacations with a single pass.

Admission passes can be ordered by calling ☎ 714-781-4565 or visiting the Disneyland website. They can also be purchased in advance from Disneyland Resort hotels, Disney Stores in the western United States, and the Walt Disney Travel Sales Center at ☎ 800-854-3104.

unofficial **TIP**
If you are a local who visits Disneyland five or more days each year, or a tourist making at least two five-day trips, an Annual Pass is a potential money saver.

Disneyland offers a Southern California Select Annual Passport ($299) valid 170 days per year to residents in qualifying zip codes.

Rides and Shows Closed for Repairs or Maintenance

Rides and shows at Disneyland parks are sometimes closed for maintenance or repairs. If a certain attraction is important to you, call ☎ 714-781-7290 before your visit to make sure that it will be operating. We also maintain an unofficial schedule of current and upcoming closures at **touringplans.com/disneyland-resort/closures.** A mother from Dover, Massachusetts, wrote us, lamenting:

> We were disappointed to find Space Mountain and the Riverboat closed for repairs. We felt that a large chunk [of the park] was not working, yet the tickets were still full price and expensive!

TOP 10 AMERICAN THEME PARKS		
THEME PARK	**ANNUAL ATTENDANCE**	**AVERAGE DAILY ATTENDANCE**
WALT DISNEY WORLD'S MAGIC KINGDOM	19.3 million	52,964
DISNEYLAND	16.8 million	45,942
WALT DISNEY WORLD'S EPCOT	11.5 million	31,381
WALT DISNEY WORLD'S ANIMAL KINGDOM	10.4 million	28,499
DISNEY'S HOLLYWOOD STUDIOS	10.3 million	28,252
DISNEY CALIFORNIA ADVENTURE	8.8 million	24,025
UNIVERSAL STUDIOS FLORIDA	8.3 million	22,638
UNIVERSAL ORLANDO'S ISLANDS OF ADVENTURE	8.1 million	22,304
UNIVERSAL STUDIOS HOLLYWOOD	6.8 million	18,696
SEAWORLD FLORIDA	4.7 million	12,830

Source: Themed Entertainment Association

Even if an attraction isn't on the disabled list, unplanned outages may prevent you from riding, as a woman from Antioch, Illinois, discovered:

The biggest drawback of the whole trip was the numerous break-downs of the rides. We were aware of Big Thunder Mountain and a few other rides closed for long-term scheduled maintenance, but a lot of the rides broke down as soon as we headed to them! The only thing that didn't have any breakdowns were the cash registers!

HOW MUCH DOES IT COST TO GO TO DISNEYLAND FOR A DAY?

LET'S SAY THAT WE HAVE A FAMILY OF FOUR—Mom, Dad, Tim (age 12), and Tami (age 8)—driving their own car. Because they plan to be in the area for a few days, they intend to buy the Three-Day Park Hopper tickets. A typical day would cost $616.11, excluding lodging and transportation. See the table below for a breakdown of expenses.

HOW MUCH DOES A DAY COST?	
Breakfast for four at Denny's with tax and tip	$37.82
Disneyland parking fee	$17.00
One day's admission for four on a Three-Day Park Hopper Pass	$363.00
Dad: *Adult three-day with tax is $275 divided by three days = $91.67*	
Mom: *Adult three-day with tax is $275 divided by three days = $91.67*	
Tim: *Adult three-day with tax is $275 divided by three days = $91.67*	
Tami: *Child three-day with tax is $264 divided by three days = $88.00*	
Morning break (soda or coffee)	$13.78
Fast-food lunch (burger, fries, and soda), no tip	$49.38
Afternoon break (soda and popcorn)	$32.40
Dinner in park at counter-service restaurant with tax	$55.32
Souvenirs (Mickey T-shirts for Tim and Tami) with tax*	$47.41
One-day total (without lodging or transportation)	**$616.11**

* *Cheer up—you won't have to buy souvenirs every day.*

▌ TIMING *Your* VISIT

SELECTING THE TIME OF YEAR FOR YOUR VISIT

CROWDS ARE LARGEST at Disneyland during the summer (Memorial Day–Labor Day) and during specific holiday periods throughout the rest of the year. The busiest time of all is December 25–January 1. Thanksgiving weekend, the week of George Washington's birthday, spring break for schools and colleges, and the two weeks around Easter are also extremely busy. To give

unofficial **TIP**
You can't pick a less crowded time to visit Disneyland than the period following Thanksgiving weekend and leading up to Christmas.

you some idea of what *busy* means at Disneyland, more than 88,000 people have toured Disneyland Park in one day! While this level of attendance is far from typical, the possibility of its occurrence should prevent all but the ignorant and the foolish from challenging this mega-attraction at its busiest periods.

The least-busy time of all is from after Thanksgiving weekend until the week before Christmas. The next slowest times are September through the weekend preceding Thanksgiving, January 4 through the first week of March, and the week following Easter up to Memorial Day weekend. At the risk of being blasphemous, our research team was so impressed with the relative ease of touring in the fall and other off-season periods that we would rather take our children out of school for a few days than do battle with the summer crowds. Though we strongly recommend going to Disneyland in the fall or in the spring, it should be noted that there are certain trade-offs. The parks often close earlier on fall, winter, and spring days, sometimes early enough to eliminate evening parades, fireworks, and other live-entertainment offerings such as *Fantasmic!* Also, because these are slow times of the year at Disneyland, you can anticipate that some rides and attractions may be closed for maintenance or renovation. Finally, if the parks open late and close early, it's tough to see everything, even if the crowds are light.

unofficial **TIP**
In our opinion, the risk of encountering colder weather and closed attractions during an off-season visit to Disneyland is worth it.

Most readers who have tried Disney parks at varying times of the year concur. A wintertime visitor from Sacramento, California, agrees:

> *Though there was a torrential storm on two days of our four-day visit, I can safely say that I will never visit in high season again. Yes, we were wet. Yes, there were attractions and rides closed for refurb. BUT, the longest line we waited in was 25 minutes to see the princesses. There were characters EVERYWHERE, and access to them was easy as pie. There were no issues with heat or sunburn. And we saved a boatload of money.*

Not to overstate the case: We want to emphasize that you can have a great time at the Disneyland parks regardless of the time of year or crowd level. In fact, a primary objective of this guide is to make the parks fun and manageable for those readers who visit during the busier times of year.

Of course, crowds are not the only consideration when deciding what time of year to visit Disneyland. Holidays are celebrated at Disneyland like nowhere else, and the festive decor is almost worth the price of admission. The parks are decked out for Halloween from late September until the end of October. Be aware that after-hours extra-cost Halloween parties (tickets are $69–$84) cause Disneyland to close early to day-guests on several evenings in the fall, as a Tucson, Arizona, family found:

The Halloween event from mid-September to the end of October changes the low season to a zoo. Every local with an annual pass showed up in the afternoon. The park closed early for this event, and DCA backed up because of the early closure of Disneyland Park.

Christmas trappings transform Disneyland Park from mid-November until after New Year's Day. There's also a Christmas parade, and several attractions such as The Haunted Mansion and It's a Small World offer a special holiday version. Some holiday entertainment (such as the special parade and fireworks) may require a special ticket to an after-hours event, if long-running rumors of Orlando's popular Mickey's Very Merry Christmas Party migrating westward ever pan out. Finally, beware of Grad Night late-night parties for high school seniors on select days each May and June. The kids have after-hours access to Disney California Adventure, but they also get admission to both parks during the daytime and make their presence known in the crowded queues starting midafternoon.

*un**official* **TIP**
If it's not your first trip to Disneyland and you must join the holiday-weekend crowds, you may have just as much fun enjoying Disney's fantastic array of shows, parades, and fireworks as you would riding the rides.

THE SPOILER

SO YOU CHOOSE YOUR OFF-SEASON DATES and then find it almost impossible to find a hotel room. What gives? In all probability you've been foiled by a mammoth convention or trade show at the Anaheim Convention Center. One of the largest and busiest convention venues in the country, the convention center hosts meetings with as many as 75,000 attendees. The sheer numbers alone guarantee that hotel rooms will be hard to find. Compounding the problem is the fact that most business travelers don't have roommates. Thus a trade show with 8,000 people registered might suck up 13,000 rooms (including people who registered late)! The final straw as you might expect is that room rates climb into the stratosphere based on the high demand and scarcity of supply. In regard to increased crowds at the theme parks, it's estimated that less than 10% of convention attendees will find time to enjoy the parks. It's also true, however, that business travelers are more likely to bring their spouse and even kids to a convention held in Anaheim. The bottom line is that you don't want to schedule your vacation while a major event is going on at the convention center. To help you avoid major trade shows and conventions, we've created a calendar of meetings scheduled through February 2017, showing the number of expected attendees of each (see page 27). As if that wasn't enough, the City of Anaheim has approved a $180-million expansion project to add 200,000 square feet to the convention center, which is certain to draw larger events impacting hotel availability when it opens in 2016.

SELECTING THE DAY OF THE WEEK FOR YOUR VISIT

THE CROWDS AT WALT DISNEY WORLD in Florida comprise mostly out-of-state visitors. Not necessarily so at Disneyland Resort, which, along with Six Flags Magic Mountain, serves as an often-frequented recreational resource for the greater Los Angeles and San Diego communities. To many Southern Californians, Disneyland Park and Disney California Adventure are their private theme parks. Yearly passes are available at less cost than a year's membership to the YMCA.

What all this means is that weekends are usually packed. Sunday is the busiest day of the week because many locals have annual passes that are blocked out on Saturdays. Saturday, particularly Saturday morning, is the best bet if you have to go on a weekend, but it is also extremely busy.

During the summer, Monday and Friday are very busy, Tuesday and Wednesday are usually less so, and Thursday is normally the slowest day of all. During the off-season (September–May, holiday periods excepted), Thursday is usually the least crowded day, followed by Tuesday.

In Florida, there are four Disney theme parks with a substantial daily variance in attendance from park to park. At Disneyland Resort, Disneyland Park usually hosts crowds 50% larger than those at Disney California Adventure, but because DCA is smaller, crowd conditions are comparable. Expressed differently, the most crowded and least crowded days are essentially the same for both Disneyland parks. However, if you are ineligible for early admission (see below), we advise visiting the park that does not offer early entry, as the other will be busy by the time ordinary guests arrive.

EARLY ENTRY

ANYONE WHO BUYS in advance a three-or-more-day ticket with Magic Morning admission may enter Disneyland Park 1 hour before the park is opened to the general public on one morning of their vacation. You can exercise your early-entry privilege on Tuesday, Thursday, or Saturday. Guests at the Paradise Pier, Grand Californian, and Disneyland Hotels can also enter on any early-entry day, as long as they have any valid ticket; this privilege is referred to as Extra Magic Hour. During this early-entry hour, most of the Fantasyland attractions—along with Astro Orbitor, Buzz Lightyear Astro Blasters, Finding Nemo Submarine Voyage, Space Mountain, and Star Tours: The Adventures Continue in Tomorrowland—will usually be open. The rest of the park's attractions (and all FastPass machines) will remain off-limits until the official opening time. Disney California Adventure (DCA) also offers its own Extra Magic Hour exclusively for hotel guests, offering access to all of Cars Land, along with select attractions in Hollywood Land, Paradise Pier, and Grizzly Peak, on four mornings (Sunday, Monday, Wednesday, and Friday).

OPERATING HOURS

DISNEYLAND RESORT RUNS a dozen or more different operating schedules during the year, making it advisable to visit **disneyland.disney**

ANAHEIM CONVENTION and SPECIAL EVENTS CALENDAR

DATES	CONVENTION/ EVENT	NUMBER OF ATTENDEES
2015		
Oct. 4-8	Technology Marketing Corporation IT Expo	7,000
Oct. 4-11	Industrial Fabrics Association Intl. Meeting & Expo	8,000
Oct. 20-28	AABB Annual Meeting	7,000
Nov. 10-16	West Coast Franchise Expo	5,000
Nov. 12-15	RunDisney Avengers Super Heroes Half Marathon	51,000
2016		
Jan. 7-13	Craft & Hobby Assn. Winter Conv. & Trade Show	12,000
Jan. 20-26	The NAMM Show	97,000
Feb. 4-13	UBM Canon Medical Design & Mfg. Expo	35,000
Feb. 15-21	American Physical Therapy Assn. Combined Sections Mtg.	9,700
Feb. 24-29	Archdiocese of Los Angeles Religious Education Congress	40,000
Mar. 6-15	Natural Products Expo West Annual Trade Show	70,000
Mar. 17-21	Varsity USA, Inc., Spirit Nationals	33,000
Mar. 19-25	OSA The Optical Society Conference & Expo	12,000
Mar. 19-22	Varsity USA, Inc., College Nationals	6,000
Mar. 21-26	Confidential Group	36,000
Mar. 29-Apr. 9	Association of PeriOperative Registered Nurses Conf.	14,000
Mar. 31-Apr. 3	Varsity USA, Inc., Dance & Drill Nationals	10,500
Apr. 11-17	Society for Industrial & Organizational Psychology Conf.	4,000
Apr. 14-18	Varsity Spirit Corporation American Championships	22,000
Apr. 24-May 1	Pri-Med West Conf. Exhibition	6,500
May 10-15	California Dental Assn. The Art & Science of Dentistry	30,000
July 4-9	LifeVantage Corp. Elite Academy Convention	7,000
July 20-31	Confidential Group	25,000
Aug. 4-16	Confidential Group	5,000
Aug. 4-10	Academy of Management Annual Meeting	10,000
Sept. 23-Oct. 1	Soc. for the Advancement of Material & Process Engineers	8,500
Oct. 15-22	National Safety Council Congress & Expo	20,000
Oct. 21-28	EDUCAUSE Annual Convention	5,800
Nov. 7-12	Confidential Group	4,000
2017		
Jan. 14-22	The NAMM Show	93,000
Feb. 3-11	UBM Canon Medical Design & Mfg. Expo	42,000
Feb. 21-27	Archdiocese of Los Angeles Religious Education Congress	40,000
Feb. 27-Mar. 2	PennWell Corporation Strategies in Light	5,500

.**go.com/calendar** or call ☎ 714-781-4565 the day before you arrive for exact hours of operation.

PACKED-PARK COMPENSATION PLAN

THE THOUGHT OF TEEMING, jostling throngs jockeying for position in endless lines under the baking Fourth of July sun is enough to wilt the will and ears of the most ardent Mouseketeer. Why would anyone go to Disneyland Park or DCA on a summer Saturday or during a major holiday period? Indeed, if you have never been to the parks, and you thought you would just drop in for a few rides and a look-see on such a day, you might be better off shooting yourself in the foot. The Disney folks, however, being Disney folks, feel kind of bad about those interminably long lines and the basically impossible touring conditions on packed days and compensate patrons with a no-less-than-incredible array of first-rate live entertainment and happenings throughout the park.

Throughout the day, the party goes on with shows, parades, concerts, and pageantry. In the evening, there is so much going on that you have to make some tough choices. Big-name musical groups perform on the Tomorrowland Terrace stage. Other concerts are produced concurrently in Hollywood Land at DCA. There are always parades and fireworks, and the Disney characters make frequent appearances. No question about it—you can go to the Disneyland parks on the Fourth of July (or any other crowded extended-hours day), never get on a ride, and still get your money's worth. Even on the busiest days, there are attractions at each park that rarely require more than a 15-minute wait: *Great Moments with Mr. Lincoln,* the *Enchanted Tiki Room,* the railroad and monorail, and Tomorrowland's Marvel and *Star Wars* exhibits at Disneyland Park, as well as Disney Animation and the sourdough factory at DCA.

If you decide to go on one of the parks' big days, we suggest that you arrive 1 hour and 20 minutes before the stated opening time. Use the touring plan of your choice until about 1 p.m., and then take the monorail to Downtown Disney for lunch and relaxation. Southern Californian visitors often chip in and rent a room for the group (make reservations well in advance) at the Disneyland Resort hotels, thus affording a place to meet, relax, have a drink, or change clothes before enjoying the pools at the hotel. A comparable arrangement can be made at other nearby hotels as long as they are within walking distance or furnish a shuttle service to and from the park. After an early dinner, return to the park for the evening's festivities, which really crank up at about 8 p.m.

GETTING THERE

DISNEY PATRONS CAN drive directly into and out of parking facilities without becoming enmeshed in surface street traffic. To avoid traffic problems, we recommend the following:

1. Stay as close to Disneyland as possible. If you are within walking distance, leave your car at the hotel and walk to the park using the pedestrian entrance on the east side of the resort, along Harbor Boulevard between Disney Way and Manchester Avenue, or through the Grand Californian Hotel into Downtown Disney if walking from the west side along Disneyland Drive. If your hotel provides efficient shuttle service (that is, will get you to the parks at least 30 minutes before opening), use the shuttle.

2. If your hotel is more than 5 miles from Disneyland and you intend to drive your car, leave for the park extra early, say 1 hour or more.

3. If you must use the Santa Ana Freeway (I-5), give yourself lots of extra time.

4. Any time you leave the park just before, at, or just after closing time, you can expect considerable congestion in the parking lots and in the loading area for hotel shuttles. The easiest way to return to your hotel (if you do not have a car in the Disneyland Resort parking lot) is to take the monorail to the Disneyland Hotel or walk to the Grand Californian Hotel, and then take a cab to your own hotel. While cabs in Anaheim are a little pricey, they are usually available in ample numbers at the Disneyland hotels and at the taxi stand in Downtown Disney behind ESPN Zone. When you consider the alternatives of fighting your way onto a hotel shuttle or trudging back to your hotel on worn-out feet, spending $5–$10 for a cab often sounds pretty reasonable. Ride-share services (such as **Uber** and **Lyft**) are also readily available to and from the hotels, as well as to and from Los Angeles International and John Wayne Airports, though they're currently barred from Long Beach Airport.

5. The Orange County Transit District provides very efficient bus service to Disneyland with several different long-distance lines. Running about every 30 minutes during the day and evening, service runs 10 a.m.–midnight, depending on the season and your location. Buses drop off and pick up passengers at the east shuttle loop off Harbor Boulevard. From there, guests can walk to the park entrance. Bus fare is about $2 and children age 5 and under ride free. A bus day pass is available for $5; seven-day passes are $25. For additional information, call ☎ 714-636-7433 or visit **octa.net.** For public transportation in the immediate area surrounding Disneyland, see our discussion of the Anaheim Resort Transit (ART) system starting on page 33.

DISNEYLAND PARKING

DISNEYLAND HAS FOUR PARKING AREAS. The main parking facility, the Mickey & Friends parking garage, can be accessed directly from I-5, Disneyland Drive, or Ball Road. One of the largest parking structures in the world, the garage is connected to Downtown Disney and the theme parks by Disney tram. Noncollapsible strollers are permitted on trams only in the first or last car where there are extra-large sections for strollers and wheelchairs. If you'd rather hoof it, the walking distance to the park gates is just less than 1 mile along a paved outdoor path.

The secondary parking areas are the Simba lot behind the Paradise Pier Hotel, the Pumbaa lot off Disney Way across from the Anaheim GardenWalk, and the Toy Story lot south of the corner of Katella

unofficial **TIP**

Warning: Most shuttles don't add vehicles at park-opening or park-closing times. In the mornings, you may not get a seat.

Southern California at a Glance

Avenue and Harbor Boulevard (a favorite of local pass holders and our top pick for the most convenient place to park). From Simba you can walk through Downtown Disney to the parks or alternatively walk to the Downtown Disney Monorail stop and take the monorail into Disneyland Park (not Disney California Adventure). Toy Story (and sometimes Pumbaa) offers shuttles to and from the bus loop east of the Esplanade, or you can walk (about 0.5 mile for each). The Pinocchio parking lot between the main parking structure and Disneyland Hotel is used for overflow and for oversize vehicles and buses. Parking fees for all lots are $17 for cars, $22 for RVs and oversize vehicles. After parking your car, save yourself a frantic search at the end of your day by taking a digital photo of the lot name and section number.

You can park for free for up to 3 hours in the Downtown Disney parking lot and get 2 additional free hours with validation from AMC Theatres or select table-service dining restaurants. Additional hours cost $6 each (charged in $2/20-minute increments) up to a $30 daily maximum. Valet parking is available after 5 p.m. at Downtown Disney ($6 plus $6 per hour, up to $36 daily) or any time at the resort hotels ($25 plus $9 per hour, up to $61 daily for non-guests). If you have money to burn, valet parking at the Grand Californian puts you closest to the parks.

TAKING A TRAM OR SHUTTLE BUS FROM YOUR HOTEL

TRAMS AND SHUTTLE BUSES are provided by many hotels and motels in the vicinity of Disneyland. Usually without charge, they represent a fairly carefree means of getting to and from the theme parks, letting you off near the entrances and saving you the cost of parking. The rub is that they might not get you there as early as you desire (a critical point if you take our touring advice) or be available at the time you wish to return to your lodging. Also, some shuttles are direct to Disneyland, while others make stops at other motels and hotels in the vicinity. Each shuttle service is a little bit different, so check out the particulars before you book your hotel. If the shuttle provided by your hotel runs regularly throughout the day to and from Disneyland and if you have the flexibility to tour the parks over two or three days, the shuttle provides a wonderful opportunity to tour in the morning and return to your lodging for lunch, a swim, or perhaps a nap; then you can head back to Disneyland refreshed in the early evening for a little more fun.

Be forewarned that most hotel shuttle services do not add more vehicles at the parks' opening or closing times. In the mornings, your biggest problem is that you might not get a seat on the first shuttle. This occurs most frequently if your hotel is the last stop for a shuttle that serves several hotels. Because hotels that share a shuttle service are usually located close together, you can improve your chances of getting a seat by simply walking to the hotel preceding yours on the pickup route. At closing time, and sometimes following a hard rain, you can expect a mass exodus from the parks. The worst-case scenario in this event is that more people will be waiting for the shuttle to your hotel than the bus will hold and that some will be left. While most (but not all) hotel shuttles return for stranded guests, you may suffer a wait of 15 minutes–1 hour. Our suggestion, if you are depending on hotel shuttles, is to exit the park at least 45 minutes before closing. If you stay in a park until closing and lack the energy to deal with the shuttle or hike back to your hotel, go to the Disneyland Hotel and catch a cab from there. A cab stand is also

Around Disneyland

W. Ball Rd.

Santa Ana Fwy.

I-5

Disneyland Dr.

S. Walnut Rd.

Mickey & Friends Parking

Pinocchio Parking

ART loading

DISNEYLAND PARK

Magic Way

Disneyland Hotel Self-Parking

Downtown Disney Self-Parking and Valet

DOWNTOWN DISNEY

Harbor Blvd.

Fantasy Tower

Adventure Tower

DISNEYLAND HOTEL

Grand Californian Hotel Self-Parking

Frontier Tower

GRAND CALIFORNIAN HOTEL

hotel shuttle loading

ART stop

main pedestrian entrance

DISNEY CALIFORNIA ADVENTURE

DISNEY'S PARADISE PIER HOTEL

Downtown Disney Parking

Disneyland Dr.

W. Katella Ave.

ANAHEIM CONVENTION CENTER

0   0.25 mi

0   0.25 km

N

behind the ESPN Zone in Downtown Disney and another is at the Grand Californian Hotel.

The shuttle-loading area is located on the Harbor Boulevard side of the Disneyland Park's main entrances. The loading area connects to a pedestrian corridor that leads to the park entrances. Each hotel's shuttle bus is color-coded yellow, blue, red, silver, or white. Signs of like color designate where the shuttles load and unload. You'll also find a passenger drop-off loop (parking strictly prohibited) off Harbor; taxis may deposit here, but they are not supposed to pick up. If you are staying near the corner of Harbor and Katella, you can walk into the Toy Story parking lot and use its park shuttle for free.

Anaheim Resort Transit

Anaheim Resort Transit (ART) provides shuttle service to the Disneyland Resort, Anaheim GardenWalk, and the convention center. The service operates 20 routes designated 1–21 (excluding 13). There are just three to nine well-marked stops on each route, so a complete circuit on any given route usually takes about 20 minutes, but some take up to 1 hour. All of the routes originate and terminate at Disneyland's bus loop east of the Esplanade near Harbor Boulevard. There is also service from Disneyland to Knott's Berry Farm, Discovery Cube Orange County, and Angel Stadium in case you want to catch an afternoon ballgame. To continue on to the convention center, you must transfer at Disneyland to Route 1, 3–6, 9, 12, or 17–20.

The colorful buses are wheelchair accessible. They ideally run every 10 minutes on peak days during morning and evening periods but can take up to 30 minutes when it's really busy, every 20 minutes during the less busy middle part of the day, and every 20 minutes all day long on off-peak days. Service begins 100 minutes before park opening and ends 30–90 minutes after park closing (may vary seasonally). If you commute to Disneyland on ART and then head to Downtown Disney after the parks close, you'll have to find your own way home if you stay at Downtown Disney more than 90 minutes. All shuttle vehicles and respective stops are clearly marked with the route designation.

Vending kiosks and hotels served by ART sell one-day, three-day, and five-day passes for $5, $12, and $20, respectively. You'll also find an ART vending kiosk at the Disneyland bus loop. Children age 2 years and under ride free with a paying adult. Day passes for children can be purchased for $2, a three-day pass for $3, and a five-day pass for $5. One-way cash fares are $3 for adults, $1 for children. Children must be taken out of strollers to ride. Passes cannot be purchased from the driver. For more information, call ☎ 888-364-ARTS (2787) or check **rideart.org.** Passes are also available at ART's website.

 # *A* **WORD** *About* **LODGING**

TRAFFIC AROUND DISNEYLAND, and in the Anaheim–Los Angeles area in general, is so terrible that we advocate staying in accommodations within 2–3 miles of the park. Included in this radius are many expensive hotels as well as a considerable number of moderately priced establishments and a small number of bargain motels.

READERS' DISNEYLAND RESORT REPORT CARD

BELOW IS THE READERS' DISNEYLAND RESORT REPORT CARD. Room quality indicates cleanliness, bed comfort, and room size. Check-in efficiency rates how quickly and accurately the hotel staff get you into your room. Quietness of room considers soundproofing from neighbors and exterior noise. The pool rating includes the size of the pool, how crowded it gets, and how clean the pool and pool area are. The staff category assesses how friendly and effective the hotel staff are at handling problems and special requests. Our hotel dining rating applies to any on-site counter-service dining, and the overall rating is the summary for every category.

Readers continue to rate Disneyland hotels better than neighboring hotels. (The same was again true this year for Disney's Orlando hotels.) Much of the lodging in the immediate vicinity of Disneyland are motels with aging rooms, many in need of refurbishment, content to trade on their proximity to the park rather than the quality of their rooms. But for Disney to charge a premium on its rooms, it needs to have a substantially better product.

As far as off-site hotels go, no single property stood out in this year's survey results. Among those that did well are Desert Inn & Suites (also favored by our Disneyland guy, Guy); Park Vue Inn (the pick of Tom Bricker, our photographer); and Ramada Anaheim Maingate at the Park (consistently recommended by our Lines community). The Hilton Anaheim, near the Anaheim Convention Center, also gets high marks, but it's a substantially farther walk to the theme parks.

HOTEL	ROOM QUALITY	CHECK-IN EFFICIENCY	QUIETNESS OF ROOM	POOL	STAFF	HOTEL DINING	OVERALL RATING
READERS' DISNEYLAND RESORT REPORT CARD							
DISNEYLAND HOTEL	A	A	B	B+	A	B-	B+
GRAND CALIFORNIAN	B+	B+	A	B-	B	B-	B
PARADISE PIER	B+	B-	D+	D+	B-	C-	C

WALKING TO DISNEYLAND FROM NEARBY HOTELS

WHILE IT IS TRUE THAT MOST DISNEYLAND area hotels provide shuttle service, or are on the ART routes, it is equally true that an ever-increasing number of guests walk to the parks from their hotels. Shuttles are not always available when needed, and parking in the Disneyland lot has become pretty expensive. A pedestrian walkway from Harbor Boulevard provides safe access to Disneyland for guests on foot. This pedestrian corridor extends from Harbor Boulevard west to the

Disneyland Hotel, connecting Disneyland Park, Disney California Adventure, and Downtown Disney.

Close proximity to the theme parks figures prominently in the choice of a hotel. Harbor Boulevard borders Disneyland Resort on the east, and Katella Avenue runs along the resort's southern boundary. The closest non-Disney hotels, and the only ones really within walking distance, are on Harbor Boulevard from just south of I-5 to the north to just south of the intersection of Katella Avenue, and along Katella Avenue near Harbor. Farther south on Harbor are some of the best hotels in the area, but they are a little far removed for commuting to the parks on foot. Additionally, these hotels are close to the Anaheim Convention Center and tend to cater, though certainly not exclusively, to business travelers. While the hotels near Disneyland Drive appear close to Disney property on a map, there is no easy pedestrian access to the park from the west. If staying along Katella Avenue, you can walk north on Disneyland Drive and cut through the Grand Californian Hotel. From West Ball Road, you can take a long and somewhat scary walk south along Disneyland Drive to Downtown Disney; the Mickey & Friends garage may seem a short walk away, but pedestrian access for guests is forbidden from the north. Neither walk is particularly convenient, and we can't recommend it for families with children.

For families, a second important consideration is the quality of the hotel swimming pool. We mention this because, unfortunately, many of the non-Disney hotels closest to the theme parks have really crummy pools, sometimes just a tiny rectangle on a stark slab of concrete surrounded on four sides by a parking lot. To bring pool quality and proximity to the theme parks together, we've developed a table (see the next page) that lists the hotels, both Disney and non-Disney, within walking distance of the theme parks.

The table shows the walking time from each hotel to the theme park entrances. The times provided are averages—a couple of fit adults might cover the distance in less time, and a family with small children will likely take longer. Also on the table we rate the swimming areas of the hotels listed on a scale of 1–10, with 10 being best. As a rule of thumb, any pool with a rating less than 5 is not a place where most folks would want to spend much time. Any hotel not listed is, in our opinion, too far away for walking. Note that several non-Disney hotels are closer than the Disneyland Resort hotels, except for the Grand Californian.

The table and the above discussion might lead you to wonder whether there's any real advantage to staying in a Disney-owned hotel. The Disney hotels, of course, are very expensive, but if you can handle the tariff, here are the primary benefits of staying in one:

1. You are eligible for early entry at Disneyland Park three days each week and DCA on the other four days.

2. Dozens of full- and counter-service restaurants are within walking distance.

3. The Disney hotels offer the nicest rooms of any of the hotels within walking distance.

4. The Disney hotels offer the nicest swimming pools of any of the hotels within walking distance.

5. Numerous entertainment and shopping options are in Downtown Disney.

WALKING TIMES TO THE THEME PARK ENTRANCES AND SWIMMING POOL RATINGS

HOTEL	MAP NUMBER (pgs. 64–65)	OVERALL QUALITY RATING	COST ($=$50)	WALKING TIME	POOL RATING
Alpine Inn	3	★★½	$$$+	13:00	2
The Anabella	5	★★★	$+ x 5	14:30	6
Anaheim Camelot Inn & Suites	6	★★★½	$$$+	7:15	2
Anaheim Plaza Hotel & Suites	13	★★★	$$$+	11:00	7
Anaheim Quality Inn & Suites	14	★★½	$$$+	13:30	2
Best Western Plus Anaheim Inn	17	★★½	$$$$-	7:15	2
Best Western Plus Park Place Inn	18	★★★	$$$+	5:45	2
Best Western Plus Stovall's Inn	21	★★★½	$$$	15:00	6
Candy Cane Inn	23	★★★½	$$$+	10:30	4
Carousel Inn & Suites	24	★★★	$$$$	6:45	2
Castle Inn & Suites	25	★★★½	$$$+	12:30	1
del Sol Inn Anaheim Resort	33	★★½	$$$+	7:00	3
Desert Inn & Suites	34	★★★½	$$$$-	6:40	3
Desert Palms Hotel & Suites	35	★★★½	$- x 5	13:00	2
Disneyland Hotel	36	★★★★	$+ x 9	10:00 –12:00	10
Disney's Grand Californian Hotel**	37	★★★★½	$+ x 10	4:00*	10
Disney's Paradise Pier Hotel**	38	★★★★	$- x 7	7:00	7
Fairfield Inn Anaheim Resort	44	★★★½	$$$$+	9:30	4
Hotel Indigo Anaheim	51	★★★½	$$$$+	15:00	2
Howard Johnson Anaheim Hotel & Water Playground	53	★★★½	$$$$+	10:15	8
Park Vue Inn	59	★★½	$$$+	6:40	6
Portofino Inn & Suites	61	★★★★	$$$+	16:30	7
Ramada Maingate at the Park	66	★★★	$+ x 5	8:20	8
Ramada Plaza Anaheim Hotel	67	★★★½	$$$$-	14:30	2
Red Lion Hotel Anaheim	68	★★★★	$$$$+	16:45	4
Residence Inn Anaheim-Maingate	69	★★★½	$- x 5	16:30	4
Sheraton Park Hotel at Anaheim Resort	70	★★★★	$$$+	17:00	7
SpringHill Suites at Anaheim Resort/ Convention Center	72	★★★★	$- x 6	15:30	5
Super 8 Anaheim Near Disneyland	76	★★½	$$$+	15:30	2
Tropicana Inn & Suites	80	★★★	$$$+	6:15	3

* To Disneyland Park. The Grand Californian has an on-site entrance to DCA.
** Requires crossing Disneyland Drive and cutting though the Grand Californian Hotel.

6. It's easy to retreat to your hotel for a meal, a nap, or a swim.

7. You don't need a car.

8. You can charge purchases at most Disney-owned shops and restaurants to your hotel account, and have packages delivered to your room.

DISNEYLAND RESORT HOTELS

DISNEY OFFERS THREE ON-SITE HOTELS: the **Grand Californian Hotel,** the **Disneyland Hotel,** and the **Paradise Pier Hotel.** The Grand Californian, built in the rustic stone-and-timber style of the grand national park lodges, is the flagship property. Newer, more elaborately themed, and closer to the theme parks and Downtown Disney than the other two on-property hotels, the Grand Californian is without a doubt the best place to stay . . . if you can afford it.

The next most convenient is the sprawling Disneyland Hotel, the oldest, but most recently renovated, of the three. Comprising three guest-room towers, the hotel is lushly landscaped with a new vintage Disneyana theme and offers large, luxurious guest rooms. Walking time to the monorail station, with transportation to Disneyland Park, is about 3–6 minutes. The Grand Californian and Disneyland Hotels both offer club-level rooms with luxury amenities, such as nightly turndown service and access to a private club, but one reader from Ontario, Canada, didn't feel that it was worth the extra money:

The club lounge was open 6:30 a.m.–8:30 p.m. each day. The early-morning park hours began at 7 a.m., and one needs to be at the park at least 45 minutes before park opening, so breakfast in the lounge was not possible. The lounge was also closed too early in the evening, not allowing us to stop and pick up a water or soda on our way back from the parks.

The east side of the third Disney hotel overlooks the Paradise Pier section of Disney California Adventure theme park, hence the name Paradise Pier Hotel. Though the guest rooms and public areas have a beach-and-boardwalk flavor, the hotel is not themed. The guest rooms here are large. Walking to the monorail station and Downtown Disney takes about 5–10 minutes.

Guests at all three Disney-owned hotels can use their keys to charge dining and shopping within the resort to their room. Third-party vendors (including most Downtown Disney restaurants) are excluded, and you'll need to show photo ID along with your room key. Parking at any of the Disney-owned hotels is $17 a day for self-parking (free for Disney Vacation Club members) or $25 for valet (☎ 714-635-2300). On the plus side, none of the hotels charge a resort fee, and all provide safes, mini-fridges, coffeemakers, and free Wi-Fi (supposedly high-speed, but don't plan on streaming Netflix) in rooms and public areas.

Disney's Grand Californian Hotel & Spa

The Grand Californian Hotel is the crown jewel of Disneyland Resort's three hotels. With its shingle siding, rock foundations, cavernous hewn-beam lobby, polished hardwood floors, and cozy hearths, the hotel is a stately combination of elements from Western national park lodges. Designed by architect Peter Dominick (who also designed the Wilderness Lodge at Walt Disney World), the Grand Californian is rendered in the Arts & Crafts style of the early 20th century, with such classic features as "flying" roofs, projecting beams, massive buttresses, and an earth-tone color palette. We strongly encourage visitors with an interest in architecture to take the fascinating (and free) hour-long Art of the Craft walking tour of the resort, offered several times each week through the Guest Services desk. Most reminiscent of the Ahwahnee Hotel at Yosemite National Park, the Grand Californian combines rugged craftsmanship and grand scale with functional design and intimate spaces. Pull up a vintage rocker in front of a blazing fire, and the bustling lobby instantly becomes a snug cabin.

The hotel's main entrance off Downtown Drive is primarily for vehicular traffic. Two pedestrian-only entrances open into Downtown Disney and DCA; this last makes it a cinch to return to the hotel from DCA for a nap, a swim, or lunch.

The features we like in the 751 guest rooms include excellent light for reading in bed, more than adequate storage space, a two-sink vanity outside the toilet and bath, and, in some rooms, a balcony. Views from the guest rooms overlook the swimming pool, Downtown Disney, or Disney California Adventure theme park. Ranging $379 (for a standard view) to more than $1,800 (for a three-bedroom suite) per night, guest rooms are the most expensive at Disneyland Resort.

Disney's time-share condo enterprise, the Disney Vacation Club, premiered its first West Coast property as part of the 2009 expansion of the Grand Californian. The Villas at Disney's Grand Californian consist of 48 two-bedroom equivalent villas and two Grand Villas. Equivalent is the term used to describe single units that can be sold (or rented) as studio suites or combined to make two- and three-bedroom villas. All villas except studio suites include kitchens, living rooms, and dining areas, as well as washers and dryers. Master bedrooms offer a king bed, while other bedrooms provide two queen beds. Studio suites come with a single queen bed. All bedrooms have a flat-panel TV, private bath, and private balcony. Though studio suites don't have full kitchens, they do include a small fridge, a microwave, and a coffeemaker. Two-bedroom villas consist of a one-bedroom villa joined to a studio suite. Three-bedroom Grand Villas are two-story affairs with the living area, kitchen, and master bedroom on the lower level and two bedrooms on the upper level. Rates for various villas range from $238 for a studio suite during the off-season to more than $2,500 for a three-bedroom Grand Villa on New Year's weekend. Other elements of the Grand Californian include a swimming pool for the villas and an underground parking garage.

The resort's pool complex, beautifully landscaped with rocks and conifers in a High Sierra theme, includes a lap pool, a Mickey-shaped pool, and a kids' pool with a 100-foot-long twisting slide. The on-site

Mandara Spa is one of Disney's best, offering a wide selection of treatments and a state-of-the-art fitness facility. Rounding out the Grand Californian's amenity mix are two clubby lounges and a child-care center for children ages 5–12.

The Disneyland Hotel

Walt Disney barely managed to finance the construction of the Disneyland theme park. He certainly didn't have the funds to purchase adjacent property or build hotels, though on-site hotels were central to his overall concept. So he cut a deal with petroleum engineer and TV producer Jack Wrather to build and operate Disneyland Hotel. The deal not only gave Wrather the rights to the Disneyland Hotel but also allowed him to build other Disneyland Hotels within the state of California until 2054. It always irked Walt that he didn't own the hotel that bore his name, but Wrather steadfastly refused to renegotiate the rights. After Jack Wrather died in 1984, the Walt Disney Company bought the entire Wrather Corporation, which among other things held the rights to the *Lone Ranger* and *Lassie* TV series and, improbably, the RMS *Queen Mary*, docked at Long Beach. By acquiring the whole corporation, the Walt Disney Company brought Disneyland Hotel under Disney ownership in 1988.

Disneyland Hotel consists of three towers facing each other across a verdant landscaped plaza, as well as a swimming complex, restaurants, and shops. The hotel was originally connected to Disneyland Park by monorail, but a portion of the hotel was demolished during the construction of DCA and Downtown Disney, and the station was rebuilt on its original location. Guest registration for all three towers is situated in the Fantasy Tower (previously called the Magic Tower, and the Marina Tower before that), which is connected to the Disneyland Convention Center and Disneyland Hotel's self-parking garage. Though all three towers share restaurants, shopping, and recreational amenities, the Fantasy Tower is most conveniently located. It and the Adventure Tower (formerly Dreams, née Sierra) are closest to Downtown Disney and the theme parks. The Frontier Tower (formerly Wonder, formerly Bonita) is the farthest from the action.

Rack rates for the Disneyland Hotel range from around $329 for a city view in the off-season to $579 for a theme park view during holiday periods (and more than $1,250 for a three-bedroom suite). The best views can be had from the east-west-facing Adventure Tower, which overlooks the hotel's inner plaza and pool area on the west and Downtown Disney and the theme parks to the east. The most lackluster views are the north-facing vistas of the Fantasy Tower.

Disneyland Hotel embraces the retro-nostalgia of baby boomer Disneyland devotees with decorative elements evoking the park's early years; look for 1950s-style signage outside each tower and a tribute to Frontierland's long-gone Old Unfaithful geysers. The main lobby evokes Mary Blair's It's a Small World designs and features a blown-up fun map of the original park. The check-in area sports early attraction concept artwork and seating styled after the spinning tea-cups, whimsical touches that stand in stark contrast with the ultra-modern sculpted steel behind the front desk. Peek inside the Fron-tier Tower lobby to see an amazingly detailed model of Big Thunder Mountain. Large windows, specially designed to filter outside noise, give the facade a glistening sky-blue tint.

The rooms have a sleek monochromatic contemporary look. Each room has one king-size or two queen-size beds, along with a pullout couch; one-bedroom suites with a wet bar and living room are also available. Features include a headboard with a carving of Sleeping Beauty Castle; fiber optics in the headboard create a skyline with fire-works (accompanied by a tinny rendition of "When You Wish Upon a Star") at the flick of a switch. Other decorative touches include black-and-white photography depicting the history of Disneyland and hidden Mickey designs in the carpet, though the overall feel is more business modern than Disney whimsy. Each room has a flat-panel HDTV, per-fect for connecting a laptop or video game console. Other room ame-nities include mini-refrigerators, coffeemakers, safes large enough for laptops, and high-tech phone, cable, and wireless Internet connections.

If the standard rooms aren't pixie-dusted (or pricey) enough for you, five different elaborately themed Signature Suites allow big spend-ers to sleep in a pirate's lair, the Big Thunder mine, or Mickey's pent-house. A night in one of these rooms can easily run into the mid-four figures; if you have to ask how much, you probably can't afford it.

The bathrooms are small for an upscale hotel, but there is a sink and vanity outside the bathrooms. As in most family hotels built in the 1950s and '60s, a connecting door, situated by the closet and the aforementioned single sink, leads to an adjoining room. Soundproof-ing around the connecting doors is nonexistent, so be prepared to revel in the sounds of your neighbors brushing their teeth, coping with indigestion, and arguing over what to wear. Fortunately, these sounds don't carry into the sleeping area.

The swimming complex's centerpiece is a pair of waterslides (187 feet and 112 feet long, respectively) themed to resemble vintage mono-rail trains, topped by the classic Disneyland block-letter logo. There's also a 19-foot kiddie slide and bubble jets for the little ones. A 4-foot-deep pool separates the 4,800-square-foot E-Ticket Pool and the water-slides, with a footbridge allowing easy passage from one side of the water to the other. On sunny days expect long inefficient lines for the slides, as well as a severe shortage of lounge chairs and elbow room.

During the 2009 renovation, the fan-favorite tropical gardens—with walking paths, waterfalls, and koi ponds—disappeared. In their place is Tangaroa Terrace and Trader Sam's, a casual restaurant and bar that banks on fond memories of Adventureland's 1960s-era *Tahitian Terrace* dinner show. Disneyland Hotel's other restaurants include Steakhouse 55 and Goofy's Kitchen, the hotel's character-meal headquarters. (All Disneyland Hotel restaurants are profiled in full in Part Four.)

As concerns practical matters, parking is a royal pain at the Disneyland Hotel. The self-parking garage is convenient only to the Fantasy Tower, and even there you'll probably have a long walk. To reach the other two towers, you must pass through the Fantasy Tower and navigate across the hotel's inner plaza and pool area. The Frontier Tower on the southern end of the property has a small parking lot to the rear, accessible via Downtown Drive and Paradise Way. Unfortunately, many of the already limited spaces are reserved for the adjacent Disney Vacation Club time-share sales office. Even so, if you're staying at the Frontier Tower, it's your best bet. If there's no room in the Frontier lot, you're better off parking in the Paradise Pier Hotel's lot than in the Disneyland Hotel parking garage. The only valet parking is at the Fantasy Tower, so even if you valet park, you'll still have to hoof it to the other towers.

Paradise Pier Hotel

Disney acquired the independent Pan Pacific Hotel just south of the Disneyland Hotel in 1997 and changed its name to the Disneyland Pacific Hotel. Just before Disney California Adventure opened in 2001, the hotel was rechristened as the Paradise Pier Hotel in recognition of the Paradise Pier district of DCA that the hotel overlooks.

The 481-room property makes a mostly successful attempt to merge the hotel's original South Seas flavor with a vintage seaside amusement theme inspired by the attractions across the street. Guest rooms are furnished with blond wood furniture and the usual Disney-pastel soft goods, including bedspreads with a hidden Mickey pattern. Somewhat more whimsical than rooms at the Disneyland Hotel or the Grand Californian, Paradise Pier rooms include accents such as Mickey Mouse table lamps, beach ball pillows, and seashell-patterned carpets. Guest room picture windows on the hotel's east side offer the best vistas of any of the Disneyland Resort hotels, with a perfect view of the lights and attractions of Paradise Pier inside DCA. From rooms on the other side of the hotel you can see, well, parking lots. Rates range $259–$982, depending on season and view.

For dining, the informal Disney's PCH Grill serves a breakfast (with characters) and dinner daily. Amenities include a fitness center and an often breezy rooftop pool complete with a waterslide (the view from the top of the slide is killer). Self-parking in Paradise Pier's on-site garage is fast and convenient. Somewhat isolated on the Disneyland Resort property, the hotel is a 14-minute hike to the theme park entrances, farther away than most non-Disney hotels lining Harbor Boulevard on the east side of the resort, if you walk through Downtown Disney. Crossing Disneyland Drive and going through Grand Californian Hotel cuts the walk in half, or even shorter if entering DCA.

HOW TO GET DISCOUNTS ON LODGING AT DISNEYLAND RESORT HOTELS

SO MANY GUEST ROOMS ARE in and around Disneyland Resort that competition is brisk, and everyone, including Disney, wheels and deals to keep them filled. The recession only compounded this. It has led to a more flexible discount policy for Disneyland Resort hotels. Here are tips for getting price breaks:

1. DISNEYLAND RESORT WEBSITE Disney has become more aggressive about offering deals on its website. Go to **disneyland.com** and check the page for "Special Offers." When booking rooms on Disney's or any other site, be sure to click on "Terms and Conditions" and read the fine print *before* making reservations.

2. SEASONAL SAVINGS You can save $15 to more than $200 per night on a Disneyland Resort hotel room by visiting during the slower times of the year. Disney uses so many adjectives (regular, holiday, peak, value, and such) to describe its seasonal calendar, however, that it's hard to keep up without a scorecard. To confuse matters more, the dates for each season vary from hotel to hotel. Understand that Disney seasonal dates are not sequential like spring, summer, fall, and winter. For any specific resort, there are sometimes several seasonal changes in a month. This is important because your room rate per night is determined by the season prevailing when you check in. Let's say that you checked in to the Disneyland Hotel on April 10 for a five-night stay. April 10 is in the more expensive peak season that ends April 11, followed by the less pricey regular season beginning April 12. Because you arrived during peak season, the peak season rate will be applied for your entire stay, even though more than half of your stay will be in regular season. Your strategy, therefore, is to shift your dates (if possible) to arrive during a less expensive season.

3. ASK ABOUT SPECIALS When you talk to Disney reservationists, inquire specifically about special deals. Ask, for example, "What special rates or discounts are available at Disney hotels during the time of our visit?" Being specific and assertive paid off for an Illinois reader:

> I called Disney's reservations number and asked for availability and rates. [Because] of The Unofficial Guide *warning about Disney reservationists answering only the questions posed, I specifically asked, "Are there any special rates or discounts for that room during the month of October?" She replied, "Yes, we have that room available at a special price." [For] the price of one phone call, I saved $440.*

Along similar lines, a Warren Township, New Jersey, dad chimed in with this:

> Your tip about asking Disney employees about discounts was invaluable. They will not volunteer this information, but by asking we saved almost $500 on our hotel room.

4. LEARN ABOUT DEALS OFFERED TO SPECIFIC MARKETS The folks at **mousesavers.com** keep an updated list of discounts for use at Disney resorts. The discounts are separated into categories such as "for anyone," "for residents of certain states," "for Annual Passport holders," and so on. For example, the site once listed a deal targeted to residents of the San

Diego area published in an ad in a San Diego newspaper. Dozens of discounts are usually listed on the site, covering almost all Disneyland Resort hotels. Usually anyone calling the Disneyland Resort Reservations Office (call ☎ 714-956-6425 and press 1 on the menu) can cite the referenced ad and get the discounted rate.

You should be aware that Disney has moved away from room-discount codes that anyone can use. Instead, Disney is targeting people with pin codes in e-mails and direct mailings. Pin-code discounts are offered to specific individuals and are correlated with that person's name and address. Pin-code offers are nontransferable. When you try to make a reservation using the code, Disney will verify that the street or e-mail address to which the pin code was sent is yours.

unofficial **TIP**
For the best rates and least crowded conditions, try to avoid visiting Disneyland Resort when a major convention or trade show is in progress.

To enhance your chances of receiving a pin-code offer, you need to get your name and street or e-mail address into the Disney system. One way is to call the Disney Resort Travel Sales Center at ☎ 714-520-5060 and request that info be sent to you. If you've been to Disneyland previously, your name and address will already be on record, but you won't be as likely to receive a pin-code offer as you would by calling and requesting to be sent information. The latter is regarded as new business. Or, expressed differently, if Disney smells blood, they're more likely to come after you. On the Web, go to **disneyland.com,** click on "Sign Up for Updates" at the bottom, and have offers and news sent automatically to your e-mail address.

Mousesavers.com also features a great links page with short descriptions and URLs of the best Disney-related websites and a current-year seasonal rates calendar.

5. KAYAK.COM This search engine compares discounts offered by hotel chains and Internet travel sellers. With Kayak's help you can see photos and descriptions of Disneyland-area hotels and determine which seller is offering the best discounts.

6. ANNUAL PASSPORT HOLDER DISCOUNTS Annual Passport holders are eligible for discounts on dining, shopping, and lodging. If you visit Disneyland Resort once a year or more, or if you plan on a visit of five or more days, you might save money overall by purchasing an Annual Passport. We've seen resort discounts as deep as 30% offered to Annual Passport holders. It doesn't take long to recoup the extra bucks you spent on an Annual Passport when you're saving that kind of money on lodging. Discounts in the 10%–15% range are more the norm.

7. TRAVEL AGENTS Travel agents are active players in the market and are particularly good sources of information on time-limited special programs and discounts. In our opinion, a good travel agent is the best friend a traveler can have. And though we at The Unofficial Guides know a thing or two about the travel industry, we always give our agent a chance to beat any deal we find. If our agent can't beat the deal, we let her book it if she can receive commission from it. In other words, we create a relationship that gives her plenty of incentive to really roll up her sleeves and work on our behalf.

As you might expect, some travel agents and agencies specialize, sometimes exclusively, in selling Disneyland and Walt Disney World. These agents have spent an incredible amount of time at both resorts and have completed extensive Disney education programs. They are usually the most Disney-knowledgeable agents in the travel industry. Most of these specialists and their agencies display the "Earmarked" logo indicating that they are Authorized Disney Vacation Planners. These Disney specialists are so good that we use them ourselves. They save us time and money, sometimes lots of both. The best of the best include **Sue Pisaturo,** whom we've used many times and who is a contributor to this guide **(sue@wdwvacations.com),** and **Tracy Desjardin (tracy@smallworldvacations.com).**

8. ROOM UPGRADES Sometimes a room upgrade is as good as a discount. If you're visiting Disneyland Resort during a slower time, book the least expensive room your discounts will allow. Checking in, ask very politely about being upgraded to a pool view room. A fair percentage of the time, you will get one at no additional charge.

NON-DISNEY HOTELS

WHEN WALT DISNEY BUILT DISNEYLAND, he did not have the funding to include hotels or to purchase the property surrounding his theme park. Consequently, the area around the park developed in an essentially uncontrolled manner. Many of the hotels and motels near Disneyland were built in the early 1960s, and they are small and sometimes unattractive by today's standards. Quite a few motels adopted adventure or fantasy themes in emulation of Disneyland. As you might imagine, these themes from five decades ago seem hokey and irrelevant today. There is a disquieting (though rapidly diminishing) number of seedy hotels near Disneyland, and even some of the chain properties fail to live up to their national standards.

If you consider a non-Disney-owned hotel in Anaheim, check its quality as reported by a reliable independent rating system such as those offered by The Unofficial Guides, AAA Directories, Forbes Guides, or Frommer's guides. Also, before you book, ask how old the hotel is and when the guest rooms were last refurbished. Be aware that almost any hotel can be made to look good on a website, so don't depend on websites alone. Locate the hotel on our street map (see pages 64–65) to verify its proximity to Disneyland. If you will not have a car, make sure that the hotel has a shuttle service that will satisfy your needs.

GOOD NEIGHBOR HOTELS

A GOOD NEIGHBOR HOTEL is a hotel that has paid Disney a marketing fee to display that designation. Usually a ticket shop in the lobby will sell full-price Disney tickets. Other than that, the Good Neighbor designation means little to nothing for the consumer. It does not guarantee quality or proximity to Disneyland. Unlike at Walt Disney World, Disneyland does not require Good Neighbor hotels to provide free shuttle service to the park, though many do. You can book Good Neighbor hotels in a package with park tickets through the Walt Disney Travel Co.; prices are the same as if booked à la carte, though they toss in a free on-attraction photo, a $10 credit to play in ESPN Zone's sports arcade, and some free collectible pins (woo-hoo). In our opinion, you shouldn't let the presence or absence of the Good Neighbor designation influence your hotel choice.

GETTING A GOOD DEAL AT NON-DISNEY HOTELS

FOLLOWING ARE SOME TIPS and strategies for getting a good deal on a hotel room near Disneyland. Though the following list may seem a bit intimidating and may refer to players in the travel market that are unfamiliar to you, acquainting yourself with the strategies will serve you well in the long run. Simply put, the tips we provide for getting a good deal near Disneyland will work equally well at just about any other place where you need a hotel. Once you have invested a little time and have experimented with these strategies, you will be able to routinely obtain rooms at the best hotels and at the lowest possible rates.

Remember that Disneyland Resort is right across the street from the Anaheim Convention Center, one of the largest and busiest convention centers in the country. Room availability, as well as rates, are affected significantly by trade shows and other events at the convention center. To determine whether such an event will be going on during your projected dates, check out the convention calendar on page 27.

1. MOUSESAVERS.COM is a site dedicated to finding great deals on hotels, admissions, and more at Disneyland Resort and Walt Disney World. The site covers discounts on both Disney and non-Disney hotels and is especially effective at keeping track of time-limited deals and discounts offered in a select market—San Diego, for example. However, the site does not sell travel products.

2. KAYAK.COM AND MOBISSIMO.COM are travel search engines that search the better hotel-discount sites, as well as chain and individual hotel websites. (As an aside, Kayak used to be purely a search engine but now sells travel products, raising the issue of whether products not sold by Kayak are equally likely to come up in a search. Mobissimo, on the other hand, only links potential buyers to provider websites.)

3. EXPEDIA.COM AND TRAVELOCITY.COM sometimes offer good discounts on area hotels. We find that Expedia offers the best deals if you're booking within two weeks of your visit. In fact, some of Expedia's last-minute deals are amazing, really rock-bottom rates. Travelocity frequently beats Expedia, however, if you reserve two weeks to three months out. Neither site offers anything to get excited about if you book more than three months from the time of your visit. If you use either site, be sure to take into consideration the demand for rooms during the season of your visit, and check to see if any big conventions or trade shows are scheduled for the convention center.

4. PRICELINE.COM allows you to tender a bid for a room. You can't bid on a specific hotel, but you can specify location ("Disneyland Vicinity") and the quality rating expressed in stars. If your bid is accepted, you will be assigned to a hotel consistent with your location and quality requirements, and your credit card will be charged in a nonrefundable transaction for your entire stay. Notification of acceptance usually takes less than an hour. We recommend bidding $35–$55 per night for a three-star hotel and $55–$80 per night for a four-star property. To gauge your chances of success, check to see if any major conventions or trade shows are scheduled during your preferred dates.

5. *HOTELCOUPONS.COM SOUTHWEST GUIDE* is a book of discount coupons for hotels throughout California and is available free of charge at many restaurants and motels along the main interstates in and leading to California. However, because most folks make reservations before leaving home, picking up the coupon book en route does not help much. But for $4 ($6 Canadian) the company will mail you a copy, allowing you to examine the discounts offered before you make your reservations. The guide is free; the charge is for the postage. To order call ☎ 800-222-3948, Monday–Friday, 8:30 a.m.–5:30 p.m. Eastern time. You can also download the guide from **hotelcoupons.com** or have it e-mailed to you at no charge.

6. SPECIAL WEEKEND RATES If you are not averse to about an hour's drive to Disneyland, you can get a great weekend rate on rooms in downtown Los Angeles. Most hotels that cater to business, government, and convention travelers offer special weekend discounts that range 15%–40% below normal weekday rates. You can find out about weekend specials by calling the hotel or by consulting your travel agent.

7. WHOLESALERS, CONSOLIDATORS, AND RESERVATION SERVICES Wholesalers and consolidators buy rooms, or options on rooms (room blocks), from hotels at a low negotiated rate. They then resell the rooms at a profit through travel agents, tour packagers, or directly to the public. Most wholesalers and consolidators have a provision for returning unsold rooms to participating hotels, but they are disinclined to do so. The wholesaler's or consolidator's relationship with any hotel is predicated on volume. If they return rooms unsold, the hotel might not make as many rooms available to them the next time around. Thus, wholesalers and consolidators often offer rooms at bargain rates, anywhere from 15%–50% off rack, occasionally sacrificing their profit margin to avoid returning the rooms to the hotel unsold.

When wholesalers and consolidators deal directly with the public, they frequently represent themselves as reservation services. When you call, you can ask for a rate quote for a particular hotel or, alternatively, ask for their best available deal in the area where you prefer to stay. If there is a maximum amount you are willing to pay, say so. Chances are that the service will find something that will work for you, even if they have to shave a dollar or two off their own profit. Sometimes you will have to prepay for your room with your credit card when

DISNEY LODGING FOR LESS

The people at **mousesavers.com** (see page 18) know more about Disney hotel packages than anyone on the planet. Here are their money-saving suggestions.

• **BOOK ROOM-ONLY.** It's frequently a better deal to book a room-only reservation instead of buying a vacation package. When you buy a package, you're typically paying a premium for convenience. You can often save money by putting together your own package—just book room-only at a resort and buy passes, meals, and extras separately.

Disney prices its standard packages at the same rates as if you had purchased individual components separately at full price. However, what Disney doesn't tell you is that components can usually be purchased separately at a discount—and those discounts are not reflected in the brochure prices of Disney's packages. (Sometimes you can get special-offer packages that do include discounts; see below.)

Disney's packages often include extras you are unlikely to use. Also, packages require a $200 deposit and full payment 45 days in advance; plus, they have stringent change and cancellation policies. Generally, booking room-only requires a deposit of one night's room rate with the remainder due at check-in. Your reservation can be changed or canceled for any reason until five days before check-in.

Whether you decide to book a Disney vacation package or create your own, there are a number of ways to save:

• **BE FLEXIBLE.** Buying a room or package with a discount code is a little like shopping for clothes at a discount store: If you wear size XX-small or XXXX-large, or you like green when everyone else is wearing pink, you're a lot more likely to score a bargain. Likewise, resort discounts are available only when Disney has excess rooms. You're more likely to get a discount during less-popular times (such as value season) and at larger or less-popular resorts.

• **BE PERSISTENT.** This is the most important tip. Disney allots a certain number of rooms to each discount. Once the discounted rooms are gone, you won't get that rate unless someone cancels. Fortunately, people change and cancel reservations all the time. If you can't get your preferred dates or hotel with one discount code, try another one (if available) or keep calling back first thing in the morning to check for cancellations—the system resets overnight, and any reservations with unpaid deposits are automatically released for resale.

you make your reservation. Most often, you will pay when you check out. Listed below are two services that frequently offer substantial discounts in the Anaheim area.

ANAHEIM AREA WHOLESALERS AND CONSOLIDATORS

California reservations ☎ 800-780-5733 cheap-discount-hotels.com
hotels.com ☎ 800-246-8357 hotels.com

8. CLUBS AND ORGANIZATIONS If you belong to AAA, AARP, or a number of other organizations, you can obtain lodging discounts. Usually the discounts are modest, 5%–15%, but occasionally higher.

9. IF YOU MAKE YOUR OWN RESERVATION As you poke around trying to find a good deal, there are several things you should know. First, always call the hotel in question as opposed to the hotel chain's national toll-free number. Quite often, the reservationists at the national numbers are unaware of local specials. Always ask about specials before you inquire about corporate rates. Do not be reluctant to bargain. If you are buying a hotel's weekend package, for example, and want to extend your stay into the following week, you can often obtain at least the corporate rate for the extra days. Do your bargaining before you check in, however, preferably when you make your reservations. Work far enough in advance to receive a confirmation.

HOW TO GET THE ROOM YOU WANT

MOST HOTELS, INCLUDING DISNEY'S, won't guarantee a specific room when you book but will post your request on your reservations record and try to accommodate you. Our experience indicates that if you give them your first, second, and third choices, you'll probably get one of the three.

*un*official **TIP**
Request a renovated room at your hotel—these can be much nicer than the older rooms.

When speaking to the reservationist or your travel agent, it's important to be specific. If you want a room overlooking the pool, say so. Similarly, be sure to clearly state such preferences as a particular floor, a corner room, a room close to restaurants, a room away from elevators and ice machines, a nonsmoking room, a room with a balcony, or any other preference. If you have a list of preferences, type it up in order of importance, and e-mail or fax it to the hotel or to your travel agent. Keep in mind that Disney's reservations computer is limited to storing a short block of text, so keep your request as brief and specific as possible. Be sure to include your own contact information and, if you've already booked, your reservation confirmation number. If it makes you feel better, call back in a few days to make sure that your preferences were posted to your reservations record.

About Hotel Renovations

We have inspected almost 100 hotels in the Disneyland Resort area to compile the lodging choices presented here. Each year we phone each hotel to verify contact information and inquire about renovations or refurbishments. If a hotel has been renovated or has refurbished its guest rooms, we reinspect that hotel along with new hotels for the next edition of this book.

Most hotels more than five years old refurbish 10%–20% of their guest rooms each year. This incremental approach minimizes disruption of business but makes your room assignment a crapshoot. You might luck into a newly renovated room or be assigned a threadbare room. Disney resorts will not guarantee a recently renovated room but will note your request and try to accommodate you. Non-Disney hotels will often guarantee an updated room when you book.

Our hotel ratings are provided starting on page 55.

TRAVEL PACKAGES

PACKAGE TOURS THAT INCLUDE LODGING, park admission, and other features are routinely available. Some packages are very good deals if you make use of the features you are paying for.

Finally, here's a helpful source of regional travel information:

ANAHEIM-ORANGE COUNTY VISITOR & CONVENTION BUREAU
☎ 714-765-8888; **anaheimoc.org**

How to Evaluate a Disneyland Travel Package

Hundreds of Disneyland package vacations are offered to the public each year. Some are created by the Disney Resort Travel Sales Center, others by airline touring companies, and some by independent travel agents and wholesalers. Almost all Disneyland packages include lodging at or near Disneyland and theme park admission. Packages offered by the airlines include air transportation.

Package prices vary seasonally, with mid-June to mid-August and holiday periods being the most expensive. During the off-season, forget packages; there are plenty of empty rooms, and you can negotiate great discounts (at non-Disney properties) yourself. Similarly, airfares and rental cars are cheaper at off-peak times.

When considering a package, choose one that includes features that you are sure to use. Whether you use all the features or not, you will most certainly pay for them. Second, if cost is of greater concern than convenience, make a few phone calls and see what the package would cost if you booked its individual components (such as airfare, rental car, and lodging) on your own. If the package price is less than the à la carte cost, the package is a good deal. If the costs are about the same, the package is probably worth it for the convenience.

If you buy a package from Disney, do not expect Disney reservationists to offer suggestions or help you sort out your options. As a rule they will not volunteer information but will only respond to specific questions you pose, adroitly ducking any query that calls for an opinion. A reader from North Riverside, Illinois, wrote to *The Unofficial Guide,* complaining:

> *I have received various pieces of literature from Disney, and it is very confusing to try and figure everything out. My wife made two telephone calls, and the [Disney] representatives were very courteous. However, they answered only the questions posed and were not very eager to give advice on what might be most cost-effective. The reps would not say if we would be better off doing one thing over the other. I feel that a person could spend 8 hours on the phone with [Disney] reps and not have any more input than you get from reading the literature.*

If you cannot get the information you need from the Disney people, try a good travel agent. Chances are that the agent will be more forthcoming in helping you sort out your options.

Information Needed for Evaluation

For quick reference, visit **disneyland.com** or call the Disney Resort Travel Sales Center at ☎ 714-520-5060 and ask that it mail you a current Disneyland Resort Vacation Planning DVD containing video footage and descriptions for all Disneyland lodging properties. In addition, ask for a rate sheet listing admission options and prices for the theme parks. With this in hand, you are ready to evaluate any package that appeals to you. Remember that all packages are quoted on a per-person basis, two to a room (double occupancy). Good luck.

ONE MORE THING

If your travel plans include a stay in the area of more than two or three days, lodge near Disneyland Resort only just before and on the days you visit the parks. The same traffic you avoid by staying close to the park will eat you alive when you begin branching out to other Los Angeles–area attractions. Also, the area immediately around Disneyland is uninspiring, and there is a marked scarcity of decent restaurants.

VACATION HOMES

SOME OF THE BEST LODGING DEALS in the Disneyland Resort area are vacation homes. Prices range from about $195 a night for two-bedroom condos and town homes to $200–$600 a night for three- to five-bedroom vacation homes.

Forgetting about taxes to keep things simple, let's compare renting a vacation home with staying at a three-star hotel near Disneyland. A family of two parents, two teens, and two grandparents would need three hotel rooms at the Fairfield Inn Anaheim Resort. At the lowest rate obtainable, they'd be spending $179 per night per room, or $645.98 total with tax and parking. Rooms are 228 square feet each, so they'd have a total of 684 square feet. Each room has a private bath, TV, and mini-fridge. The hotel has a pool and whirlpool tub, but parking costs extra.

At the same time of year, they can rent a 1,350-square-foot, three-bedroom, two-bath vacation home with a private pool within easy walking distance of Disneyland for $357.65—a saving of $288.33 per night over the Fairfield Inn rate (a total saving of $1441.64 on a five-night stay). But that's not all: The home comes with a washer and dryer; an outdoor hot tub; a large, grassy play area; a barbecue grill; lounge chairs; a game room with pool table; a family room with a 52-inch high-definition TV, DVD player, and surround sound; a stereo system; a dining room with seating for eight, plus a covered patio dining area; and off-street parking. The only trade-off for our hypothetical family would be having two bathrooms instead of three.

You can see the specific home described above at **vrbo.com/175261.** VRBO stands for **Vacation Rental by Owner,** a listing service for owners of vacation properties nationwide. One thing we like about the VRBO website is that it offers detailed information, including a good number of photos of each specific home. When you book, the home you've been looking at is the actual one you're reserving. On the other hand, some vacation-home rental companies, like rental car agencies, don't assign you a specific home until the day you arrive—these companies provide photos of a "typical" home instead of making information available on each of the individual homes in their inventory. In this case, you have to take the company's word that the typical home pictured is representative and that the property you'll be assigned will be just as nice.

Location is everything, especially in Southern California with its legendary traffic. Before renting a home, contact the owner and get the address. Then, using **google.com/maps,** obtain exact directions from the home to Disneyland. This will tell you how long and how complicated your commute will be. Avoid homes for which it's necessary to drive on a freeway for more than a couple of miles. Don't worry if the home isn't in Anaheim per se; it's the distance to Disneyland that counts.

The only practical way to shop for a rental home is on the Web. Going online makes it relatively easy to compare different properties and rental companies. The best sites are easy to navigate, let you see what you're interested in without having to log in or divulge any personal information, and list memberships in such organizations as the Better Business Bureau. Before you book, ask about minimum stays, damage deposits, cleaning charges, pets, and how any problems will be addressed once you're in the home.

HOTELS *and* **MOTELS:**
Rated and Ranked

WHAT'S IN A ROOM?

EXCEPT FOR CLEANLINESS, STATE OF REPAIR, and decor, most travelers do not pay much attention to hotel rooms. There is, of course, a discernible standard of quality and luxury that differentiates Motel 6 from Holiday Inn, Holiday Inn from Marriott, and so on. In general, however, hotel guests fail to appreciate that some rooms are better engineered than others.

Contrary to what you might suppose, designing a hotel room is (or should be) a lot more complex than picking a bedspread to match the carpet and drapes. Making the room usable to its occupants is an art, a planning discipline that combines both form and function.

Decor and taste are important, certainly. No one wants to spend several days in a room where the decor is dated, garish, or even ugly. But beyond the decor, there are variables that determine how livable a hotel room is. In Anaheim, for example, we have seen some beautifully appointed rooms that are simply not well designed for human habitation. The next time you stay in a hotel, pay attention to the details and design elements of your room. Even more than decor, these are the things that will make you feel comfortable and at home.

ROOM RATINGS

TO SEPARATE PROPERTIES ACCORDING to the relative quality, tastefulness, state of repair, cleanliness, and size of their standard rooms, we have grouped the hotels and motels into classifications denoted by stars. Star ratings in this guide apply to Anaheim properties only and do not necessarily correspond to ratings awarded by Forbes, AAA, or other travel critics. Because stars have little relevance when awarded in the absence of commonly recognized standards of comparison, we have tied our ratings to expected levels of quality established by specific American hotel corporations.

Star ratings apply to *room quality only* and describe the property's standard accommodations. For most hotels and motels, a standard accommodation is a hotel room with either one king bed or two queen beds. In an all-suite property, the standard accommodation is either a studio or one-bedroom suite. In addition to standard accommodations, many hotels offer luxury rooms and special suites that are not rated in this guide. Star ratings for rooms are assigned without regard to whether a property has a restaurant, recreational facilities, entertainment, or other extras.

In addition to stars (which delineate broad categories), we also employ a numerical rating system. Our rating scale is 0–100, with 100 as the best possible rating. Numerical ratings are presented to show the difference we perceive between one property and another. Rooms at the Desert Palms Hotel & Suites and Howard Johnson Hotel are both rated as three and a half stars (★★★½). In the supplemental numerical ratings, the Desert Palms is rated an 82 and the Howard Johnson a 79. This means that within the three-and-a-half-star category, the Desert Palms has slightly nicer rooms than the Howard Johnson.

OVERALL STAR RATINGS		
★★★★★	Superior rooms	Tasteful and luxurious by any standard
★★★★	Extremely nice rooms	What you'd expect at a Hyatt Regency or Marriott
★★★	Nice rooms	Holiday Inn or comparable quality
★★	Adequate rooms	Clean, comfortable, and functional without frills—like a Motel 6

HOW THE HOTELS COMPARE

COST ESTIMATES ARE BASED on the hotel's published rack rates for standard rooms. Each "$" represents $50. Thus, a cost symbol of "$$$" means a room (or suite) at that hotel will be about $150 a night (it may be less for weekdays or more on weekends).

On pages 55–57, we list a hit parade of the nicest rooms in town. We've focused strictly on room quality and have excluded any consideration of location, services, recreation, or amenities. In some instances, a one- or two-room suite can be had for the same price or less than that of a hotel room.

If you used an earlier edition of this guide, you will notice that many of the ratings and rankings have changed. In addition to the inclusion of new properties, these changes are occasioned by such positive developments as guest room renovation or improved maintenance and housekeeping. A failure to properly maintain guest rooms or a lapse in housekeeping standards can negatively affect the ratings.

Finally, before you begin to shop for a hotel, take a hard look at this letter we received from a couple in Hot Springs, Arkansas:

We canceled our room reservations to follow the advice in your book [and reserved a hotel highly ranked by The Unofficial Guide*]. We wanted inexpensive but clean and cheerful. We got inexpensive but dirty, grim, and depressing. I really felt disappointed in your advice and the room. It was the pits. That was the one real piece of information I needed from your book!*

Needless to say, this letter was as unsettling to us as the bad room was to our reader. Our integrity as travel journalists, after all, is based on the quality of the information we provide to our readers. Even with the best of intentions and the most conscientious research, however, we cannot inspect every room in every hotel. What we do, in statistical terms, is take a sample: We check out several rooms selected at random in each hotel and base our ratings and rankings on those rooms. Though it would be unusual, it is certainly possible that the rooms we randomly inspect are not representative of the majority of rooms at a particular hotel. Another possibility is that the rooms we inspect in a given hotel are representative but that by bad luck a reader is assigned to an inferior room. When we rechecked the hotel that our reader disliked so intensely, we discovered that our rating was correctly representative but that he and his wife had unfortunately been assigned to one of a small number of threadbare rooms scheduled for renovation.

The key to avoiding disappointment is to do some snooping around in advance. We recommend that you ask to get a photo of a hotel's standard guest room before you book, or at least a copy of the hotel's promotional brochure. Be forewarned, however, that some hotel chains use the same guest room photo in their promotional literature for all hotels in the chain, and that the guest room in a specific property may not resemble the photo in the brochure. When you or your travel agent call, ask how old the property is and when the guest room you are being assigned was last renovated. If you arrive and are assigned a room inferior to that which you had been led to expect, demand to be moved to another room.

THE TOP 30 BEST DEALS

IN ADDITION TO LISTING THE BETTER ROOMS in town, we also take a look at the best combinations of quality and value in a room. The rankings are made without consideration of location or the availability of restaurants, recreational facilities, entertainment, or amenities.

The Disneyland Hotel, you may notice, is not one of the best deals. This is because you can get more for your money at other properties. The Disneyland and Grand Californian Hotels, however, are two of the most popular hotels in the area, and many guests are willing to pay a higher rate for their convenience, service, and amenities.

Continued on page 57

THE TOP 30 BEST DEALS

RANK	HOTEL	MAP NUMBER (pgs. 64–65)	OVERALL QUALITY RATING	ROOM QUALITY RATING	COST ($ = $50)	PHONE
1.	Sheraton Park Hotel at the Anaheim Resort	70	★★★★	85	$$$+	714-750-1811
2.	Majestic Garden Hotel	57	★★★★	87	$$$+	714-778-1700
3.	Ramada Anaheim Maingate North	64	★★★½	80	$$$-	714-999-0684
4.	Hyatt Regency Orange County	54	★★★★	89	$$$$-	714-750-1234
5.	DoubleTree by Hilton Hotel Anaheim-Orange County	39	★★★★	83	$$$+	714-634-4500
6.	TownePlace Suites Anaheim Maingate Near Angel Stadium	77	★★★★	88	$$$+	714-939-9700
7.	Portofino Inn & Suites	61	★★★★	84	$$$+	714-782-7600
8.	Best Western Plus Stovall's Inn	21	★★★½	82	$$$	714-778-1880
9.	Ayres Hotel Anaheim	15	★★★★	85	$$$$-	714-634-2106
10.	DoubleTree Suites by Hilton Hotel Anaheim Resort-Convention Center	40	★★★★	86	$$$$-	714-750-3000
11.	Greenwood Suites Anaheim Resort	45	★★★½	82	$$$+	714-808-9000
12.	Ramada Anaheim South	65	★★★	72	$$+	714-971-3553
13.	Holiday Inn-Anaheim Resort Area	48	★★★★	83	$$$$-	714-748-7777
14.	Wyndham Anaheim Garden Grove	81	★★★★	86	$$$$-	714-867-5555
15.	Staybridge Suites Anaheim Resort	74	★★★★	84	$$$$-	714-748-7700
16.	Holiday Inn Hotel & Suites Anaheim	49	★★★½	82	$$$+	714-535-0300
17.	La Quinta Inn & Suites Anaheim	56	★★★½	76	$$$+	714-635-5000
18.	Peacock Suites	60	★★★½	82	$$$+	714-535-8255
19.	Park Vue Inn	59	★★★½	78	$$$+	714-772-3691
20.	Anaheim Camelot Inn & Suites	6	★★★½	80	$$$+	714-635-7275
21.	Extended Stay America Orange County-Anaheim Convention Center	43	★★★	69	$$+	714-502-9988
22.	Anaheim Marriott	11	★★★½	82	$$$+	714-750-8000
23.	Candy Cane Inn	23	★★★½	78	$$$+	714-774-5284
24.	Ramada Plaza Anaheim Hotel	67	★★★½	81	$$$$-	714-991-6868
25.	Homewood Suites by Hilton Anaheim-Main Gate Area	50	★★★★	85	$$$$+	714-740-1800
26.	Desert Inn & Suites	34	★★★½	81	$$$$-	714-772-5050
27.	Red Lion Hotel Anaheim	68	★★★★	85	$$$$+	714-750-2801
28.	Budget Inn	22	★★½	57	$$-	714-535-5524
29.	Travelodge Anaheim Inn & Suites	78	★★★	65	$$$-	714-774-7600
30.	Embassy Suites Anaheim-Orange	41	★★★★	87	$- x 5	714-938-1111

HOW THE HOTELS COMPARE

HOTEL	MAP NUMBER (pgs. 64-65)	OVERALL QUALITY RATING	ROOM QUALITY RATING	COST ($ = $50)
DISNEYLAND AREA				
Disney's Grand Californian Hotel & Spa	37	★★★★½	90	$+ x 10
Hyatt Regency Orange County	54	★★★★	89	$$$$-
Disneyland Hotel	36	★★★★	89	$+ x 9
TownePlace Suites Anaheim Maingate Near Angel Stadium	77	★★★★	88	$$$+
SpringHill Suites at Anaheim Resort/ Convention Center	72	★★★★	88	$- x 6
Majestic Garden Hotel	57	★★★★	87	$$$+
Embassy Suites Anaheim-Orange	41	★★★★	87	$- x 5
SpringHill Suites Anaheim Maingate	71	★★★★	87	$+ x 6
DoubleTree Suites by Hilton Hotel Anaheim Resort-Convention Center	40	★★★★	86	$$$$-
Wyndham Anaheim Garden Grove	81	★★★★	86	$$$$-
Disney's Paradise Pier Hotel	38	★★★★	86	$- x 7
Sheraton Park Hotel at the Anaheim Resort	70	★★★★	85	$$$+
Ayres Hotel Anaheim	15	★★★★	85	$$$$-
Homewood Suites by Hilton Anaheim-Main Gate Area	50	★★★★	85	$$$$+
Red Lion Hotel Anaheim	68	★★★★	85	$$$$+
Anaheim Marriott Suites	12	★★★★	85	$- x 5
Portofino Inn & Suites	61	★★★★	84	$$$+
Staybridge Suites Anaheim Resort	74	★★★★	84	$$$$-
DoubleTree by Hilton Hotel Anaheim-Orange County	39	★★★★	83	$$$+
Holiday Inn-Anaheim Resort Area	48	★★★★	83	$$$$-
Embassy Suites Anaheim-South	42	★★★★	83	$- x 5
Best Western Plus Stovall's Inn	21	★★★½	82	$$$
Greenwood Suites Anaheim Resort	45	★★★½	82	$$$+
Holiday Inn Hotel & Suites Anaheim	49	★★★½	82	$$$+
Peacock Suites	60	★★★½	82	$$$+
Anaheim Marriott	11	★★★½	82	$$$+
Desert Palms Hotel & Suites Anaheim Resort	35	★★★½	82	$- x 5
Ramada Plaza Anaheim Hotel	67	★★★½	81	$$$$-
Desert Inn & Suites	34	★★★½	81	$$$$-
Hilton Anaheim	46	★★★½	81	$$$$
Ramada Anaheim Maingate North	64	★★★½	80	$$$-
Anaheim Camelot Inn & Suites	6	★★★½	80	$$$+
Hilton Garden Inn Anaheim-Garden Grove	47	★★★½	79	$$$$-
Howard Johnson Anaheim Hotel & Water Playground	53	★★★½	79	$$$$+
Park Vue Inn	59	★★★½	78	$$$+
Candy Cane Inn	23	★★★½	78	$$$+

HOW THE HOTELS COMPARE *(continued)*

HOTEL	MAP NUMBER (pgs. 64-65)	OVERALL QUALITY RATING	ROOM QUALITY RATING	COST ($ = $50)
DISNEYLAND AREA				
Residence Inn Anaheim–Maingate	69	★★★½	78	$- x 5
La Quinta Inn & Suites Anaheim	56	★★★½	76	$$$+
Fairfield Inn Anaheim Resort	44	★★★½	75	$$$$+
Hotel Indigo Anaheim	51	★★★½	75	$$$$+
Courtyard by Marriott Anaheim	29	★★★½	75	$- x 5
Alo Hotel	2	★★★	73	$$$$-
Ramada Anaheim South	65	★★★	72	$$+
Cortona Inn & Suites	28	★★★	72	$$$$-
The Anabella	5	★★★	72	$+ x 5
Castle Inn & Suites	25	★★★	71	$$$+
Clarion Hotel Anaheim	26	★★★	70	$$$$-
Ramada Maingate at the Park	66	★★★	70	$+ x 5
Extended Stay America Orange County–Anaheim Convention Center	43	★★★	69	$$+
Comfort Inn & Suites	27	★★★	69	$$$$-
Stanford Inn & Suites	73	★★★	68	$$$+
Best Western Plus Raffles Inn & Suites	20	★★★	67	$$$$-
Carousel Inn & Suites	24	★★★	66	$$$$
Travelodge Anaheim Inn & Suites	78	★★★	65	$$$-
Tropicana Inn & Suites	80	★★★	65	$$$+
Anaheim Plaza Hotel & Suites	13	★★★	65	$$$+
Best Western Plus Park Place Inn & Mini-Suites	18	★★★	65	$$$+
Days Inn Anaheim West	31	★★½	64	$$+
Anaheim Carriage Inn	7	★★½	64	$$+
Alpine Inn	3	★★½	64	$$$+
Best Western Plus Pavilions	19	★★½	63	$$$
Hotel Menage	52	★★½	63	$$$$-
del Sol Inn Anaheim Resort	33	★★½	62	$$$+
Super 8 Anaheim Near Disneyland	76	★★½	62	$$$+
Motel 6 Anaheim Maingate	58	★★½	61	$$+
America's Best Value Astoria Inn & Suites	4	★★½	61	$$+
Best Western Plus Anaheim Inn	17	★★½	61	$$$$-
Quality Inn Maingate	63	★★½	60	$$$-
Best Western Courtesy Inn	16	★★½	60	$$$+
Days Inn Anaheim Maingate	30	★★½	59	$$+
Knights Inn Anaheim	55	★★½	59	$$$$-
Budget Inn	22	★★½	57	$$-
Anaheim Maingate Inn	10	★★½	57	$$
Anaheim Quality Inn & Suites	14	★★½	57	$$$+
Anaheim Express Inn Maingate	8	★★½	57	$$$$-

HOW THE HOTELS COMPARE (continued)

HOTEL	MAP NUMBER (pgs. 64-65)	OVERALL QUALITY RATING	ROOM QUALITY RATING	COST ($ = $50)
DISNEYLAND AREA				
Days Inn & Suites Anaheim at Disneyland Park	32	★★½	56	$$+
Quality Inn & Suites Anaheim at the Park	62	★★½	56	$$$+
Super 8 Anaheim-Disneyland Drive	75	★★	55	$$+
Alamo Inn & Suites Anaheim	1	★★	52	$$$+
Travelodge Anaheim International Inn	79	★★	50	$$-
Anaheim Hacienda Inn & Suites Disneyland	9	★★	46	$$$-
UNIVERSAL AREA	**MAP NUMBER (pg. 66)**			
Hilton Los Angeles at Universal City	4	★★★★	87	$- x 8
Sheraton Universal Hotel	7	★★★★	85	$+ x 5
Chamberlain West Hollywood	2	★★★½	81	$- x 9
Marriott Los Angeles Burbank Airport	6	★★★½	80	$ x 5
Holiday Inn Burbank-Media Center	5	★★★	71	$$$$+
Best Western Hollywood Plaza Inn	1	★★½	62	$+ x 5
Colony Inn	3	★★½	60	$$$$+

Continued from page 53

We once had a reader complain to us that he had booked one of our top-ranked rooms for value and had been very disappointed in the room. On checking we noticed that the room the reader occupied had a quality rating of ★★½. We would remind you that the value ratings are intended to give you some sense of value received for your lodging dollar spent. A ★★½ room at $35 may have the same value rating as a ★★★★ room at $85, but that does not mean that the rooms will be of comparable quality. Regardless of whether it's a good deal or not, a ★★½ room is still a ★★½ room.

Listed on page 54 are the top 30 room buys for the money, regardless of location or star classification, based on rack rates. Note that sometimes a suite can cost less than a hotel room.

Continued on page 66

HOTEL INFORMATION CHART

Alamo Inn & Suites Anaheim ★★
1140 W. Katella Ave.
Anaheim 92802
☎ 714-635-8070
thealamoinn.com

ROOM RATING	52
COST	$$$+
POOL	●
ON-SITE DINING	—
BREAKFAST	—
WI-FI	Free
PARKING	Free

Alo Hotel ★★★
3737 W. Chapman Ave.
Orange 92868
☎ 714-978-9168
ayreshotels.com/alo-hotel

ROOM RATING	73
COST	$$$$−
POOL	●
ON-SITE DINING	●
BREAKFAST	Free
WI-FI	Free
PARKING	Paid

Alpine Inn ★★½
715 W. Katella Ave.
Anaheim 92802
☎ 714-535-2186
alpineinnanaheim.com

ROOM RATING	64
COST	$$$+
POOL	●
ON-SITE DINING	—
BREAKFAST	Free
WI-FI	Free
PARKING	Free

Anaheim Carriage Inn ★★½
2125 S. Harbor Blvd.
Anaheim 92802
☎ 714-740-1440
anaheimcarriageinnhotel.com

ROOM RATING	64
COST	$$+
POOL	●
ON-SITE DINING	—
BREAKFAST	Free
WI-FI	Free
PARKING	Free

Anaheim Express Inn Maingate ★★½
620 W. Orangewood Ave.
Anaheim 92802
☎ 714-971-9000
anainn.com

ROOM RATING	57
COST	$$$$−
POOL	●
ON-SITE DINING	—
BREAKFAST	Free
WI-FI	Free
PARKING	Free

Anaheim Hacienda Inn & Suites Disneyland ★★
2176 S. Harbor Blvd.; Anaheim 92802
☎ 714-750-2101
magnusonhotels.com/anaheim-hacienda-inn-suites-disneyland

ROOM RATING	46
COST	$$$−
POOL	—
ON-SITE DINING	—
BREAKFAST	—
WI-FI	Free
PARKING	Free

Anaheim Plaza Hotel & Suites ★★★
1700 S. Harbor Blvd.
Anaheim 92802
☎ 714-772-5900
anaheimplazahotel.com

ROOM RATING	65
COST	$$$+
POOL	●
ON-SITE DINING	●
BREAKFAST	Paid
WI-FI	Paid
PARKING	Paid

Anaheim Quality Inn & Suites ★★½
1441 S. Manchester Ave.
Anaheim 92802
☎ 714-991-8100
anaheimqualityinn.com

ROOM RATING	57
COST	$$$+
POOL	●
ON-SITE DINING	—
BREAKFAST	Free
WI-FI	Free
PARKING	Paid

Ayres Hotel Anaheim ★★★★
2550 E. Katella Ave.; Anaheim 92806
☎ 714-634-2106
ayreshotels.com/ayres-hotel-anaheim

ROOM RATING	85
COST	$$$$−
POOL	●
ON-SITE DINING	—
BREAKFAST	Free
WI-FI	Free
PARKING	Paid

Best Western Plus Park Place Inn & Mini-Suites ★★★
1544 S. Harbor Blvd.; Anaheim 92802
☎ 714-776-4800
parkplaceinnandminisuites.com

ROOM RATING	65
COST	$$$+
POOL	●
ON-SITE DINING	—
BREAKFAST	Free
WI-FI	Free
PARKING	Paid

Best Western Plus Pavilions ★★½
1176 W. Katella Ave.
Anaheim 92802
☎ 714-776-0140
pavilionshotel.com

ROOM RATING	63
COST	$$$
POOL	●
ON-SITE DINING	—
BREAKFAST	Free
WI-FI	Free
PARKING	Free

Best Western Plus Raffles Inn & Suites ★★★
2040 S. Harbor Blvd.; Anaheim 92802
☎ 714-750-6100
bestwesternrafflesinn.com

ROOM RATING	67
COST	$$$$−
POOL	●
ON-SITE DINING	—
BREAKFAST	Free
WI-FI	Free
PARKING	Paid

Carousel Inn & Suites ★★★
1530 S. Harbor Blvd.
Anaheim 92802
☎ 714-758-0444
carouselinnandsuites.com

ROOM RATING	66
COST	$$$$
POOL	●
ON-SITE DINING	●
BREAKFAST	—
WI-FI	Paid
PARKING	Paid

Castle Inn & Suites ★★★
1734 S. Harbor Blvd.
Anaheim 92802
☎ 714-774-8111
castleinn.com

ROOM RATING	71
COST	$$$+
POOL	●
ON-SITE DINING	—
BREAKFAST	—
WI-FI	Free
PARKING	Free

Chamberlain West Hollywood ★★★½
1000 Westmount Drive
West Hollywood 90069
☎ 310-657-7400
chamberlainwesthollywood.com

ROOM RATING	81
COST	$- x 9
POOL	●
ON-SITE DINING	●
BREAKFAST	Paid
WI-FI	Free
PARKING	Paid

America's Best Value Astoria Inn & Suites ★★½
426 W. Ball Rd.; Anaheim 92805
☎ 714-774-3882
anaheimastoriainn.com

ROOM RATING	61
COST	$$+
POOL	—
ON-SITE DINING	—
BREAKFAST	Free
WI-FI	Free
PARKING	Free

The Anabella ★★★
1030 W. Katella Ave.
Anaheim 92802
☎ 714-905-1050
anabellahotel.com

ROOM RATING	72
COST	$+ x 5
POOL	●
ON-SITE DINING	●
BREAKFAST	Paid
WI-FI	Free
PARKING	Paid

Anaheim Camelot Inn & Suites ★★★½
1520 S. Harbor Blvd.; Anaheim 92802
☎ 714-635-7275
camelotinn-anaheim.com

ROOM RATING	80
COST	$$$+
POOL	●
ON-SITE DINING	—
BREAKFAST	—
WI-FI	Free
PARKING	Paid

Anaheim Maingate Inn ★★½
1211 West Pl.
Anaheim 92802
☎ 714-533-2500
anaheimmaingateinn.com

ROOM RATING	57
COST	$$
POOL	—
ON-SITE DINING	—
BREAKFAST	Free
WI-FI	Free
PARKING	Free

Anaheim Marriott ★★★½
700 W. Convention Way
Anaheim 92802
☎ 714-750-8000
tinyurl.com/anamarriott

ROOM RATING	82
COST	$$$+
POOL	●
ON-SITE DINING	●
BREAKFAST	Paid
WI-FI	Paid
PARKING	Paid

Anaheim Marriott Suites ★★★★
12015 Harbor Blvd.
Anaheim 92802
☎ 714-750-1000
tinyurl.com/anamarriottste

ROOM RATING	85
COST	$- x 5
POOL	●
ON-SITE DINING	●
BREAKFAST	Paid
WI-FI	Paid
PARKING	Paid

Best Western Courtesy Inn ★★½
1070 W. Ball Rd.
Anaheim 92802
☎ 714-772-2470
bestwesternanaheimhotel.com

ROOM RATING	60
COST	$$$+
POOL	●
ON-SITE DINING	—
BREAKFAST	Free
WI-FI	Free
PARKING	Free

Best Western Hollywood Plaza Inn ★★½
2011 N. Highland Ave.; Hollywood 90068
☎ 323-851-1800
bestwesternhollywoodhotel.com

ROOM RATING	62
COST	$+ x 5
POOL	●
ON-SITE DINING	●
BREAKFAST	Paid
WI-FI	Free
PARKING	Paid

Best Western Plus Anaheim Inn ★★½
1630 S. Harbor Blvd.
Anaheim 92802
☎ 714-774-1050
anaheiminn.com

ROOM RATING	61
COST	$$$$-
POOL	●
ON-SITE DINING	—
BREAKFAST	Free
WI-FI	Free
PARKING	Free

Best Western Plus Stovall's Inn ★★★½
1110 W. Katella Ave.; Anaheim 92802
☎ 714-778-1880
stovallsinn.com

ROOM RATING	82
COST	$$$
POOL	●
ON-SITE DINING	●
BREAKFAST	Free
WI-FI	Free
PARKING	Paid

Budget Inn ★★½
1042 W. Ball Rd.
Anaheim 92802
☎ 714-535-5524
anaheimbudgetinn.com

ROOM RATING	57
COST	$$-
POOL	●
ON-SITE DINING	—
BREAKFAST	—
WI-FI	Free
PARKING	Free

Candy Cane Inn ★★★½
1747 S. Harbor Blvd.
Anaheim 92802
☎ 714-774-5284
candycaneinn.net

ROOM RATING	78
COST	$$$+
POOL	●
ON-SITE DINING	—
BREAKFAST	Free
WI-FI	Free
PARKING	Free

Clarion Hotel Anaheim ★★★
616 Convention Way
Anaheim 92802
☎ 714-750-3131
clarionanaheim.com

ROOM RATING	70
COST	$$$$-
POOL	●
ON-SITE DINING	●
BREAKFAST	Paid
WI-FI	Free
PARKING	Paid

Colony Inn ★★½
4917 Vineland Ave.
North Hollywood 91601
☎ 818-763-2787
colonyinn.com

ROOM RATING	60
COST	$$$$+
POOL	—
ON-SITE DINING	—
BREAKFAST	Free
WI-FI	Free
PARKING	Free

Comfort Inn & Suites ★★★
300 E. Katella Way
Anaheim 92802
☎ 866-488-4858
comfortinnsuitesanaheim.com

ROOM RATING	69
COST	$$$$-
POOL	●
ON-SITE DINING	—
BREAKFAST	Free
WI-FI	Free
PARKING	Free

HOTEL INFORMATION CHART *(continued)*

Cortona Inn & Suites ★★★
2029 S. Harbor Blvd.
Anaheim 92802
☎ 714-971-5000
cortonainn.com

ROOM RATING	72
COST	$$$$-
POOL	●
ON-SITE DINING	—
BREAKFAST	Free
WI-FI	Free
PARKING	Free

Courtyard by Marriott Anaheim
★★★½
2045 S. Harbor Blvd.; Anaheim 92802
☎ 714-740-2645
courtyardanaheim.com

ROOM RATING	75
COST	$- x 5
POOL	●
ON-SITE DINING	●
BREAKFAST	Paid
WI-FI	Free
PARKING	Paid

Days Inn Anaheim Maingate ★★½
2200 S. Harbor Blvd.
Anaheim 92802
☎ 714-750-5211
daysinnanaheimmaingate.com

ROOM RATING	59
COST	$$+
POOL	●
ON-SITE DINING	—
BREAKFAST	Free
WI-FI	Free
PARKING	Free

Desert Inn & Suites ★★★½
1600 S. Harbor Blvd.
Anaheim 92802
☎ 714-772-5050
anaheimdesertinn.com

ROOM RATING	81
COST	$$$$-
POOL	●
ON-SITE DINING	—
BREAKFAST	Free
WI-FI	Free
PARKING	Paid

Desert Palms Hotel & Suites Anaheim Resort ★★★½
631 W. Katella Ave.; Anaheim 92802
☎ 714-535-1133
desertpalmshotel.com

ROOM RATING	82
COST	$- x 5
POOL	●
ON-SITE DINING	—
BREAKFAST	Free
WI-FI	Free
PARKING	Free

Disneyland Hotel ★★★★
1150 W. Magic Way; Anaheim 92802
☎ 714-778-6600
disneyland.disney.go.com/hotels/disneyland-hotel

ROOM RATING	89
COST	$+ x 9
POOL	●
ON-SITE DINING	●
BREAKFAST	Paid
WI-FI	Free
PARKING	Paid

DoubleTree Suites by Hilton Hotel Anaheim Resort-Convention Center ★★★★
2085 S. Harbor Blvd.
Anaheim 92802
☎ 714-750-3000
tinyurl.com/doubletreeanaconv

ROOM RATING	86
COST	$$$$-
POOL	●
ON-SITE DINING	●
BREAKFAST	Paid
WI-FI	Free
PARKING	Paid

Embassy Suites Anaheim–Orange
★★★★
400 N. State College Blvd.
Orange 92862; ☎ 714-938-1111
embassysuitesanaheimorange.com

ROOM RATING	87
COST	$- x 5
POOL	●
ON-SITE DINING	●
BREAKFAST	Free
WI-FI	Paid
PARKING	Paid

Embassy Suites Anaheim–South
★★★★
11767 Harbor Blvd.; Garden Grove 92840
☎ 714-539-3300
anaheimsouth.embassysuites.com

ROOM RATING	83
COST	$- x 5
POOL	●
ON-SITE DINING	●
BREAKFAST	Free
WI-FI	Paid
PARKING	Paid

Hilton Anaheim ★★★½
777 W. Convention Way
Anaheim 92802
☎ 714-750-4321
hiltonanaheimhotel.com

ROOM RATING	81
COST	$$$$
POOL	●
ON-SITE DINING	●
BREAKFAST	Paid
WI-FI	Free
PARKING	Paid

Hilton Garden Inn Anaheim–Garden Grove ★★★½
11777 Harbor Blvd.; Garden Grove 92840
☎ 714-703-9100
tinyurl.com/hiltonana

ROOM RATING	79
COST	$$$$-
POOL	●
ON-SITE DINING	—
BREAKFAST	Paid
WI-FI	Free
PARKING	Paid

Hilton Los Angeles at Universal City
★★★★
555 Universal Hollywood Dr.
Universal City 91608; ☎ 818-506-2500
tinyurl.com/hiltonuniversal

ROOM RATING	87
COST	$- x 8
POOL	●
ON-SITE DINING	●
BREAKFAST	Paid
WI-FI	Paid
PARKING	Paid

Homewood Suites by Hilton Anaheim-Main Gate Area ★★★★
12005 Harbor Blvd
Garden Grove 92840; ☎ 714-740-1800
homewoodsuitesanaheim.com

ROOM RATING	85
COST	$$$$+
POOL	●
ON-SITE DINING	—
BREAKFAST	Free
WI-FI	Free
PARKING	Paid

Hotel Indigo Anaheim ★★★½
435 W. Katella Ave.
Anaheim 92802
☎ 714-772-7755
tinyurl.com/hotelindigoana

ROOM RATING	75
COST	$$$$+
POOL	●
ON-SITE DINING	●
BREAKFAST	Paid
WI-FI	Free
PARKING	Free

Hotel Menage ★★½
1221 S. Harbor Blvd.
Anaheim 92805
☎ 714-758-0900
hotelmenage.com

ROOM RATING	63
COST	$$$$-
POOL	●
ON-SITE DINING	●
BREAKFAST	Paid
WI-FI	Free
PARKING	Paid

Days Inn Anaheim West ★★½
1030 W. Ball Rd.
Anaheim 92802
☎ 714-520-0101
tinyurl.com/daysinnanawest

ROOM RATING	64
COST	$$+
POOL	●
ON-SITE DINING	—
BREAKFAST	Free
WI-FI	Free
PARKING	Free

Days Inn & Suites Anaheim at Disneyland Park ★★½
1111 S. Harbor Blvd.; Anaheim 92805
☎ 714-533-8830
tinyurl.com/daysinndland

ROOM RATING	56
COST	$$+
POOL	●
ON-SITE DINING	—
BREAKFAST	Free
WI-FI	Free
PARKING	Free

del Sol Inn Anaheim Resort ★★½
1604 S. Harbor Blvd.
Anaheim 92802
☎ 714-234-3411
delsolinn.com

ROOM RATING	62
COST	$$$+
POOL	●
ON-SITE DINING	●
BREAKFAST	Free
WI-FI	Free
PARKING	Paid

Disney's Grand Californian Hotel & Spa ★★★★½
1600 S. Disneyland Dr.; Anaheim 92802
☎ 714-635-2300
disneyland.disney.go.com/hotels/grand-californian-hotel

ROOM RATING	90
COST	$+ x 10
POOL	●
ON-SITE DINING	●
BREAKFAST	Paid
WI-FI	Free
PARKING	Paid

Disney's Paradise Pier Hotel ★★★★
1717 S. Disneyland Dr.; Anaheim 92802
☎ 714-999-0990
disneyland.disney.go.com/hotels/paradise-pier-hotel

ROOM RATING	86
COST	$- x 7
POOL	●
ON-SITE DINING	●
BREAKFAST	Paid
WI-FI	Free
PARKING	Paid

DoubleTree by Hilton Hotel Anaheim-Orange County ★★★★
100 The City Dr.; Orange 92868
☎ 714-634-4500
tinyurl.com/doubletreeana

ROOM RATING	83
COST	$$$+
POOL	●
ON-SITE DINING	●
BREAKFAST	Paid
WI-FI	Paid
PARKING	Paid

Extended Stay America Orange County-Anaheim Convention Center ★★★
1742 S. Clementine St.
Anaheim 92802
☎ 714-502-9988
tinyurl.com/exstayorangeco

ROOM RATING	69
COST	$$+
POOL	●
ON-SITE DINING	—
BREAKFAST	Free
WI-FI	Free
PARKING	Free

Fairfield Inn Anaheim Resort ★★★½
1460 S. Harbor Blvd.
Anaheim 92802
☎ 714-772-6777
tinyurl.com/fairfieldinnana

ROOM RATING	75
COST	$$$$+
POOL	●
ON-SITE DINING	●
BREAKFAST	Paid
WI-FI	Free
PARKING	Paid

Greenwood Suites Anaheim Resort ★★★½
1733 S. Anaheim Blvd.
Anaheim 92805
☎ 714-808-9000
greenwoodsuitesanaheimresort.com

ROOM RATING	82
COST	$$$+
POOL	—
ON-SITE DINING	—
BREAKFAST	—
WI-FI	Free
PARKING	Paid

Holiday Inn-Anaheim Resort Area ★★★★
1915 S. Manchester Ave.
Anaheim 92802; ☎ 714-748-7777
tinyurl.com/holidayanaresort

ROOM RATING	83
COST	$$$$-
POOL	●
ON-SITE DINING	●
BREAKFAST	Paid
WI-FI	Free
PARKING	Free

Holiday Inn Burbank-Media Center ★★★
150 E. Angeleno Ave.; Burbank 91502
☎ 818-841-4770
tinyurl.com/holidayinnburbank

ROOM RATING	71
COST	$$$$+
POOL	●
ON-SITE DINING	●
BREAKFAST	Paid
WI-FI	Free
PARKING	Free

Holiday Inn Hotel & Suites Anaheim ★★★½
1240 S. Walnut Ave.; Anaheim 92802
☎ 714-535-0300
tinyurl.com/holidayinnana

ROOM RATING	82
COST	$$$+
POOL	●
ON-SITE DINING	●
BREAKFAST	Paid
WI-FI	Free
PARKING	Paid

Howard Johnson Anaheim Hotel & Water Playground ★★★½
1380 S. Harbor Blvd.; Anaheim 92802
☎ 714-776-6120
hojoanaheim.com

ROOM RATING	79
COST	$$$$+
POOL	●
ON-SITE DINING	●
BREAKFAST	Paid
WI-FI	Free
PARKING	Free

Hyatt Regency Orange County ★★★★
11999 Harbor Blvd.
Garden Grove 92840; ☎ 714-750-1234
orangecounty.hyatt.com

ROOM RATING	89
COST	$$$$-
POOL	●
ON-SITE DINING	●
BREAKFAST	Paid
WI-FI	Paid
PARKING	Paid

Knights Inn Anaheim ★★½
414 W. Ball Rd.
Anaheim 92805
☎ 714-533-2570
knightsinnanaheim.com

ROOM RATING	59
COST	$$$$-
POOL	●
ON-SITE DINING	—
BREAKFAST	—
WI-FI	Free
PARKING	Free

HOTEL INFORMATION CHART *(continued)*

La Quinta Inn & Suites Anaheim
★★★½
1752 S. Clementine St.; Anaheim 92802
☎ 714-635-5000
laquintaanaheim.com

ROOM RATING	76
COST	$$$+
POOL	●
ON-SITE DINING	—
BREAKFAST	Free
WI-FI	Free
PARKING	Paid

Majestic Garden Hotel ★★★★
900 S. Disneyland Dr.
Anaheim 92802
☎ 714-778-1700
majesticgardenhotel.com

ROOM RATING	87
COST	$$$+
POOL	●
ON-SITE DINING	●
BREAKFAST	Free
WI-FI	Free
PARKING	Free

Marriott Los Angeles Burbank Airport ★★★½
2500 N. Hollywood Way
Burbank 91505; ☎ 818-843-6000
marriottburbankairport.com

ROOM RATING	80
COST	$ x 5
POOL	●
ON-SITE DINING	●
BREAKFAST	Paid
WI-FI	Paid
PARKING	Paid

Portofino Inn & Suites ★★★★
1831 S. Harbor Blvd.
Anaheim 92802
☎ 714-782-7600
portofinoinnanaheim.com

ROOM RATING	84
COST	$$$+
POOL	●
ON-SITE DINING	—
BREAKFAST	—
WI-FI	Free
PARKING	Free

Quality Inn & Suites Anaheim at the Park ★★½
1166 W. Katella Ave.; Anaheim 92805
☎ 714-774-7817
tinyurl.com/qualityinnana

ROOM RATING	56
COST	$$$+
POOL	●
ON-SITE DINING	—
BREAKFAST	Free
WI-FI	Free
PARKING	Free

Quality Inn Maingate ★★½
871 S. Harbor Blvd.
Anaheim 92802
☎ 714-535-7878
anaheimresortqualityinn.com

ROOM RATING	60
COST	$$$-
POOL	●
ON-SITE DINING	—
BREAKFAST	Free
WI-FI	Free
PARKING	Paid

Ramada Plaza Anaheim Hotel ★★★½
515 W. Katella Ave.
Anaheim 92802
☎ 714-991-6868
ramadaanaheim.com

ROOM RATING	81
COST	$$$$-
POOL	●
ON-SITE DINING	●
BREAKFAST	Free
WI-FI	Free
PARKING	Free

Red Lion Hotel Anaheim ★★★★
1850 S. Harbor Blvd.
Anaheim 92802
☎ 714-750-2801
redlion.com/anaheim

ROOM RATING	85
COST	$$$$+
POOL	●
ON-SITE DINING	●
BREAKFAST	—
WI-FI	Free
PARKING	Paid

Residence Inn Anaheim–Maingate
★★★½
1700 S. Clementine St.; Anaheim 92802
☎ 714-533-3555
tinyurl.com/residencemaingate

ROOM RATING	78
COST	$- x 5
POOL	●
ON-SITE DINING	—
BREAKFAST	Free
WI-FI	Free
PARKING	Free

SpringHill Suites at Anaheim Resort/ Convention Center ★★★★
1801 S. Harbor Blvd.; Anaheim 92802
☎ 714-533-2101
springhillanaheim.com

ROOM RATING	88
COST	$- x 6
POOL	●
ON-SITE DINING	●
BREAKFAST	Free
WI-FI	Free
PARKING	Paid

Stanford Inn & Suites ★★★
2171 S. Harbor Blvd.
Anaheim 92802
☎ 714-703-1220
stanfordinnanaheim.com

ROOM RATING	68
COST	$$$+
POOL	●
ON-SITE DINING	—
BREAKFAST	Free
WI-FI	Free
PARKING	Free

Staybridge Suites Anaheim Resort
★★★★
1855 S. Manchester Ave.
Anaheim 92802; ☎ 714-748-7700
sbsanaheim.com

ROOM RATING	84
COST	$$$$-
POOL	●
ON-SITE DINING	—
BREAKFAST	Free
WI-FI	Free
PARKING	Free

Travelodge Anaheim Inn & Suites
★★★
1057 W. Ball Rd.; Anaheim 92802
☎ 714-774-7600
travelodgedisneyland.com

ROOM RATING	65
COST	$$$-
POOL	●
ON-SITE DINING	—
BREAKFAST	Free
WI-FI	Free
PARKING	Free

Travelodge Anaheim International Inn
★★
2060 S. Harbor Blvd.; Anaheim 92802
☎ 714-971-9393
tinyurl.com/travelodgeintana

ROOM RATING	50
COST	$$-
POOL	●
ON-SITE DINING	—
BREAKFAST	Free
WI-FI	Free
PARKING	Free

Tropicana Inn & Suites ★★★
1540 S. Harbor Blvd.
Anaheim 92802
☎ 714-635-4082
tropicanainn-anaheim.com

ROOM RATING	65
COST	$$$+
POOL	●
ON-SITE DINING	●
BREAKFAST	Paid
WI-FI	Free
PARKING	Paid

Motel 6 Anaheim Maingate ★★½
100 W. Disney Way
Anaheim 92802
☎ 714-520-9696
motel6-anaheim.com

ROOM RATING	61
COST	$$+
POOL	●
ON-SITE DINING	—
BREAKFAST	—
WI-FI	Paid
PARKING	Free

Park Vue Inn ★★★½
1570 S. Harbor Blvd.
Anaheim 92802
☎ 714-772-3691
parkvueinn.com

ROOM RATING	78
COST	$$$+
POOL	●
ON-SITE DINING	—
BREAKFAST	Free
WI-FI	Free
PARKING	Free

Peacock Suites ★★★½
1745 S. Anaheim Blvd.
Anaheim 92805
☎ 714-535-8255
shellhospitality.com/peacock-suites

ROOM RATING	82
COST	$$$+
POOL	●
ON-SITE DINING	—
BREAKFAST	—
WI-FI	Free
PARKING	Paid

Ramada Anaheim Maingate North ★★★½
921 S. Harbor Blvd.; Anaheim 92802
☎ 714-999-0684
tinyurl.com/ramadamgnorth

ROOM RATING	80
COST	$$$-
POOL	●
ON-SITE DINING	—
BREAKFAST	Free
WI-FI	Free
PARKING	Free

Ramada Anaheim South ★★★
2141 S. Harbor Blvd.
Anaheim 92802
☎ 714-971-3553
tinyurl.com/ramadamainnorth

ROOM RATING	72
COST	$$+
POOL	●
ON-SITE DINING	—
BREAKFAST	Free
WI-FI	Free
PARKING	Free

Ramada Maingate at the Park ★★★
1650 S. Harbor Blvd.
Anaheim 92802
☎ 714-772-0440
ramadamaingate.com

ROOM RATING	70
COST	$+ x 5
POOL	●
ON-SITE DINING	—
BREAKFAST	Free
WI-FI	Free
PARKING	Paid

Sheraton Park Hotel at the Anaheim Resort ★★★★
1855 S. Harbor Blvd.; Anaheim 92802
☎ 714-750-1811
sheratonparkanaheim.com

ROOM RATING	85
COST	$$$+
POOL	●
ON-SITE DINING	●
BREAKFAST	Paid
WI-FI	Paid
PARKING	Paid

Sheraton Universal Hotel ★★★★
333 Universal Hollywood Dr.
Universal City 91608
☎ 818-980-1212
sheratonuniversal.com

ROOM RATING	85
COST	$+ x 5
POOL	●
ON-SITE DINING	●
BREAKFAST	Paid
WI-FI	Paid
PARKING	Paid

SpringHill Suites Anaheim Maingate ★★★★
1160 W. Ball Rd.; Anaheim 92802
☎ 714-215-4000
shsanaheim.com

ROOM RATING	87
COST	$+ x 6
POOL	●
ON-SITE DINING	—
BREAKFAST	Free
WI-FI	Free
PARKING	Paid

Super 8 Anaheim–Disneyland Drive ★★
915 S. Disneyland Dr.; Anaheim 92802
☎ 714-778-0350
tinyurl.com/super8dlanddr

ROOM RATING	55
COST	$$+
POOL	●
ON-SITE DINING	—
BREAKFAST	Free
WI-FI	Free
PARKING	Free

Super 8 Anaheim Near Disneyland ★★½
415 W. Katella Ave.; Anaheim 92802
☎ 714-778-6900
tinyurl.com/super8nrdland

ROOM RATING	62
COST	$$$+
POOL	●
ON-SITE DINING	—
BREAKFAST	Free
WI-FI	Free
PARKING	Free

TownePlace Suites Anaheim Maingate Near Angel Stadium ★★★★
1730 S. State College Blvd.
Anaheim 92806; ☎ 714-939-9700
tinyurl.com/towneplacemaingate

ROOM RATING	88
COST	$$$+
POOL	●
ON-SITE DINING	—
BREAKFAST	Free
WI-FI	Free
PARKING	Free

Wyndham Anaheim Garden Grove ★★★★
12021 Harbor Blvd.; Garden Grove 92840
☎ 714-867-5555
anaheimwyndham.com

ROOM RATING	86
COST	$$$$-
POOL	●
ON-SITE DINING	●
BREAKFAST	Paid
WI-FI	Free
PARKING	Free

Disneyland-Area Hotels

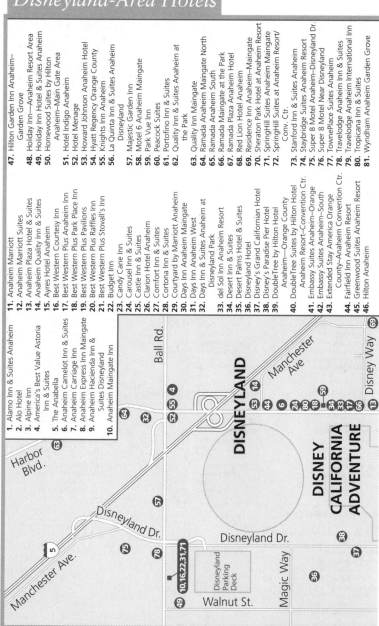

1. Alamo Inn & Suites Anaheim
2. Alo Hotel
3. Alpine Inn
4. America's Best Value Astoria Inn & Suites
5. The Anabella
6. Anaheim Camelot Inn & Suites
7. Anaheim Carriage Inn
8. Anaheim Express Inn Maingate
9. Anaheim Hacienda Inn & Suites Disneyland
10. Anaheim Maingate Inn
11. Anaheim Marriott
12. Anaheim Marriott Suites
13. Anaheim Plaza Hotel & Suites
14. Anaheim Quality Inn & Suites
15. Ayres Hotel Anaheim
16. Best Western Courtesy Inn
17. Best Western Plus Anaheim Inn
18. Best Western Plus Park Place Inn
19. Best Western Plus Pavilions
20. Best Western Plus Raffles Inn
21. Best Western Plus Stovall's Inn
22. Budget Inn
23. Candy Cane Inn
24. Carousel Inn & Suites
25. Castle Inn & Suites
26. Clarion Hotel Anaheim
27. Comfort Inn & Suites
28. Cortona Inn & Suites
29. Courtyard by Marriott Anaheim
30. Days Inn Anaheim Maingate
31. Days Inn Anaheim West
32. Days Inn & Suites Anaheim at Disneyland Park
33. del Sol Inn Anaheim Resort
34. Desert Inn & Suites
35. Desert Palms Hotel & Suites
36. Disneyland Hotel
37. Disney's Grand Californian Hotel
38. Disney's Paradise Pier Hotel
39. DoubleTree by Hilton Hotel Anaheim—Orange County
40. DoubleTree Suites by Hilton Hotel Anaheim Resort-Convention Ctr.
41. Embassy Suites Anaheim—Orange
42. Embassy Suites Anaheim—South
43. Extended Stay America Orange County—Anaheim Convention Ctr.
44. Fairfield Inn Anaheim Resort
45. Greenwood Suites Anaheim Resort
46. Hilton Anaheim
47. Hilton Garden Inn Anaheim—Garden Grove
48. Holiday Inn—Anaheim Resort Area
49. Holiday Inn Hotel & Suites Anaheim
50. Homewood Suites by Hilton Anaheim–Main Gate Area
51. Hotel Indigo Anaheim
52. Hotel Menage
53. Howard Johnson Anaheim Hotel
54. Hyatt Regency Orange County
55. Knights Inn Anaheim
56. La Quinta Inn & Suites Anaheim Disneyland
57. Majestic Garden Inn
58. Motel 6 Anaheim Maingate
59. Park Vue Inn
60. Peacock Suites
61. Portofino Inn & Suites
62. Quality Inn & Suites Anaheim at the Park
63. Quality Inn Maingate
64. Ramada Anaheim Maingate North
65. Ramada Anaheim South
66. Ramada Maingate at the Park
67. Ramada Plaza Anaheim Hotel
68. Red Lion Hotel Anaheim
69. Residence Inn Anaheim–Maingate
70. Sheraton Park Hotel at Anaheim Resort
71. SpringHill Suites Anaheim Maingate
72. SpringHill Suites at Anaheim Resort/Conv. Ctr.
73. Stanford Inn & Suites Anaheim
74. Staybridge Suites Anaheim Resort
75. Super 8 Motel Anaheim–Disneyland Dr.
76. Super 8 Motel Near Disneyland
77. TownePlace Suites Anaheim
78. Travelodge Anaheim Inn & Suites
79. Travelodge Anaheim International Inn
80. Tropicana Inn & Suites
81. Wyndham Anaheim Garden Grove

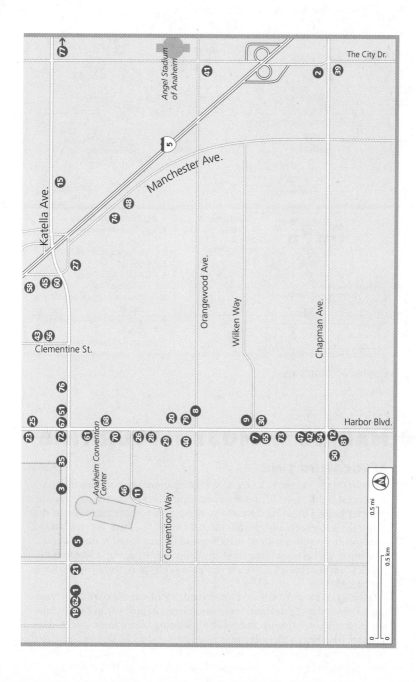

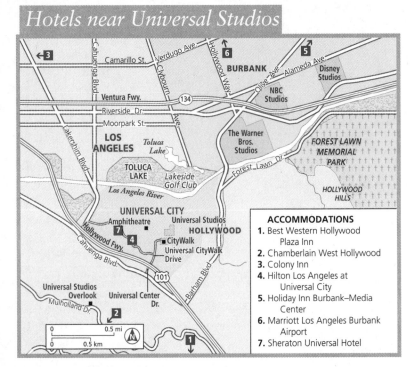

Hotels near Universal Studios

ACCOMMODATIONS

1. Best Western Hollywood Plaza Inn
2. Chamberlain West Hollywood
3. Colony Inn
4. Hilton Los Angeles at Universal City
5. Holiday Inn Burbank–Media Center
6. Marriott Los Angeles Burbank Airport
7. Sheraton Universal Hotel

Continued from page 57

MAKING *the* MOST *of* YOUR TIME

ALLOCATING TIME

THE DISNEY PEOPLE RECOMMEND spending two to four full days at Disneyland Resort. While this may seem a little self-serving, it is not without basis. Disneyland Resort is *huge*, with something to see or do crammed into every conceivable space. In addition, there are two parks, and touring requires a lot of walking, and often a lot of waiting in line. Moving in and among large crowds all day is exhausting, and often the unrelenting Southern California sun zaps even the most hardy, making tempers short.

During our many visits to Disneyland, we observed, particularly on hot summer days, a dramatic transition from happy, enthusiastic touring on arrival to almost zombielike plodding along later in the day. Visitors who began their day enjoying the wonders of Disney imagination ultimately lapsed into an exhausted production mentality ("We have two more rides in Fantasyland; then we can go to the hotel").

OPTIMUM TOURING SITUATION

WE DON'T BELIEVE THAT THERE IS ONE IDEAL ITINERARY. Tastes, energy levels, and perspectives on what constitutes entertainment and relaxation vary. This understood, here are some considerations for developing your own ideal itinerary.

Optimum touring at Disneyland requires a good game plan, a minimum of three to five days on-site (excluding travel time), and a fair amount of money. It also requires a fairly prodigious appetite for Disney entertainment. The essence of optimum touring is to see the attractions in a series of shorter, less-exhausting visits during the cooler, less-crowded times of day, with plenty of rest and relaxation between excursions.

Because optimum touring calls for leaving and returning to the theme parks, it makes sense to stay in one of the Disney hotels or in one of the non-Disney hotels within walking distance. If you visit Disneyland during busy times, you need to get up early to beat the crowds. Short lines and stress-free touring are incompatible with sleeping in. If you want to sleep in *and* enjoy your touring, visit Disneyland when attendance is lighter.

THE CARDINAL RULES FOR SUCCESSFUL TOURING

MANY VISITORS DON'T HAVE THREE DAYS to devote to Disneyland Resort. For these visitors, efficient touring is a must. Even the most time-effective plan, however, won't allow you to cover both Disney theme parks in one day. Plan to allocate at least an entire day to each park. If your schedule permits only one day of touring, concentrate on one theme park and save the other for another visit.

One-Day Touring

A comprehensive one-day tour of Disneyland Park or Disney California Adventure is possible, but it requires knowledge of the parks, good planning, and plenty of energy and endurance. One-day touring doesn't leave much time for full-service meals, prolonged shopping, or lengthy breaks. One-day touring can be fun and rewarding, but allocating two days per park, especially for Disneyland Park, is always preferable if possible.

Successful touring of Disneyland Park or Disney California Adventure hinges on three rules:

1. DETERMINE IN ADVANCE WHAT YOU REALLY WANT TO SEE What rides and attractions most appeal to you? Which additional rides and attractions would you like to experience if you have any time left? What are you willing to forgo?

To help you establish your touring priorities, we have described every attraction in detail. In each description, we include the author's critical evaluation of the attraction as well as the opinions of Disneyland Resort guests expressed as star ratings. Five stars is the highest (best) rating possible.

Finally, because Disneyland Resort attractions range in scope from midway-type rides and horse-drawn trolleys to colossal, high-tech extravaganzas spanning the equivalent of whole city blocks, we have developed a hierarchy of categories for attractions to give you some sense of their order of magnitude:

SUPER-HEADLINERS The best attractions that the theme park has to offer. They are mind-boggling in size, scope, and imagination and represent the cutting edge of modern attraction technology and design.

HEADLINERS Full-blown, multimillion-dollar, full-scale, themed adventure experiences and theater presentations. They are modern in their technology and design and employ a full range of special effects.

MAJOR ATTRACTIONS Themed adventure experiences on a more modest scale but incorporating state-of-the-art technologies, or larger-scale attractions of older design.

MINOR ATTRACTIONS Midway-type rides, small-scale dark rides (spook house–type rides), minor theater presentations, transportation rides, and elaborate walk-through attractions.

DIVERSIONS Exhibits, both passive and interactive. Also include playgrounds, video arcades, and street theater.

Though not every attraction fits neatly into the above categories, the categories provide a relative comparison of attraction size and scope. Remember, however, that bigger and more elaborate does not always mean better. Peter Pan's Flight, a minor attraction, continues to be one of the park's most beloved rides. Likewise, for many small children, there is no attraction, regardless of size, that can surpass Dumbo the Flying Elephant.

2. ARRIVE EARLY! ARRIVE EARLY! ARRIVE EARLY! This is the single most important key to touring efficiently and avoiding long lines. With your admission pass in hand, be at the gate ready to go at least 30 minutes before the theme park's stated opening time. There are no lines and relatively few people first thing in the morning. The same four rides you can experience in 1 hour in the early morning will take more than 3 hours to see after 11 a.m. Have breakfast before you arrive, so you will not have to waste prime touring time sitting in a restaurant. This advice is especially important at Disneyland Resort, where locals arriving after work tend to swell queues in the afternoon and evening, the opposite of typical attendance patterns at Walt Disney World.

From a Cincinnati, Ohio, mom:

Arriving early made a tremendous difference. But I'll admit that at 6:15 in the morning when I was dragging our children out of bed, I thought that we'd lost our minds. But we had so much fun that morning riding rides with no waiting in line. It was worth the early arrival.

A couple from Austin, Texas, waxed enthusiastically:

I am telling everyone about your book. It saved my girlfriend and me hours and hours of waiting in line (during spring break no less!). We were first in line for the parks every morning, and boy was it worth it.

Be aware that all park guests must pass through security, set up in open tents in the Esplanade between the two parks. If you arrive before security screening begins and go straight to the turnstiles to await admittance, you will ultimately be directed to abandon your position to go through security. If this occurs, you'll find yourself behind people who arrived 20–30 minutes after you. Therefore, if you arrive before security is set up, wait in one of the open tents for the security folks to arrive.

3. AVOID BOTTLENECKS Helping you avoid bottlenecks is what this guide is all about. Bottlenecks occur as a result of crowd concentrations and/ or less-than-optimal traffic engineering. Concentrations of hungry people create bottlenecks at restaurants during the lunch and dinner hours; concentrations of people moving toward the exit near closing time create bottlenecks in the gift shops en route to the gate; concentrations of visitors at new and unusually popular rides create bottlenecks and long waiting lines; rides slow to load and unload passengers create bottlenecks and long waiting lines. Avoiding bottlenecks involves being able to predict where, when, and why they occur. To this end, we provide field-tested touring plans to keep you ahead of the crowd or out of its way (see discussion following). In addition, we provide critical data on all rides and shows that helps you estimate how long you may have to wait in line, compares rides in terms of their capacity to accommodate large crowds, and rates the rides according to our opinions and the opinions of other Disneyland visitors.

TOURING PLANS

OF UTMOST IMPORTANCE: READ THIS!

IN ANALYZING READER SURVEYS we were astonished by the percentage of readers who do not use our touring plans. Scientifically tested and proven, these plans can save you 4 entire hours or more of waiting in line. Four hours! Four fewer hours of standing, 4 hours freed up to do something fun. Our groundbreaking research that created the touring plans has been the subject of front-page articles in the *Dallas Morning News* and *The New York Times* and has been cited in numerous scholarly journals. So the question is, why would you not use them?

We get a ton of e-mail from both our Disneyland and Walt Disney World readers—98% of it positive—commenting on our touring plans. First, from a Puyallup, Washington, woman:

> *We flew through all the attractions, only waiting in 10- to 15-minute lines all day. The longest line was for Toy Story Midway Mania!, but only because we chose to deviate from the plan and left it until the very end of the day. It proved to my group that the planning really works. (I think they initially thought I was a little loco!)*

A family from Stockton, California, descended on Disneyland Park over the Easter holiday:

> *We're not much for plans and regimentation, so we winged it the first day. It was so awful that the next day we gave one of your itineraries a shot. It worked so well that I was telling strangers about it that night like [I was] some kind of Bible thumper.*

A mom from Aurora, Colorado, offered this:

> *We went to WDW in 2007, and I didn't use the touring plans provided because, with my kids, I didn't think the extra walking would be worth it. I decided to try out the plans in Disneyland when it was just my mom and me. I was amazed that when I got to the point*

*where it said, "Now might be a good time to grab lunch," it was
11:15 a.m. We are going to WDW in November with the kids, and
I have already put together all our touring plans from your book!*

From a Salt Lake City, Utah, family of five:

I credit this book for a whine-free, fun-filled, four-day vacation. Several people noticed the book we were using; one man even asked if he could take a picture of the cover so he could use the book next time. I seriously felt like we would be lost without it.

A mom from Scottsdale, Arizona:

Your book was INCREDIBLE. On our first visit to Disney, I read it from cover to cover and felt totally prepared! The tips and knowledge you provided were really the difference in making a good trip a GREAT trip! Our relatives, who live in California and go to Disney often, couldn't believe all the stuff they didn't know about that I did, all thanks to your book!

From a mom in South Jordan, Utah:

I especially loved your daily itineraries and your Cars Land advice. Thanks to FastPasses and baby switch passes, my kids were able to ride Radiator Springs twice every day for the three days we were at the parks. I appreciated your recommendation to run over for Fast-Passes for Radiator Springs at Cars Land while the rest of my family was at Disneyland in the morning.

From a Chicago mom:

I feel strongly that you have to go into a Disney trip with a firm plan or else all you will remember of your vacation will be the squabbles and the long lines! The daily touring plans not only allowed me to see everything that I wanted but also allowed me time to revisit my favorite attractions multiple times! Those who complain that the touring plans are too rigid need a serious reality check. Yes, they are structured, but they save you mountains of time! RELAX and use the touring plans if you are going during a busy part of the year. Not only will it save you the time that you are spending complaining about the plans in the first place, but it will also save you the complaining you will be doing when you are in line for Space Mountain for 90 minutes!

A family of six from Sacramento, California:

The Unofficial Guide was a godsend! I was not so sure how the touring plans would work, but they went over and beyond my expectations. We went to Disneyland during spring break, a very busy time, very crowded, and we hardly spent any time at all in lines for rides (as long as we stuck to the touring plans)! At one point we would get off a ride and get right on another. We did six rides within a half hour. This trip was the first time EVER that my family and I got to do everything we wanted at Disneyland!

From a Portland, Oregon, man:

I followed the Two-Day Plan A. I hadn't been to Disneyland in 30 years, and it was fantastic and painless to just follow a plan. The Fast-Pass tips were awesome.

WHAT'S A QUEUE?

THOUGH IT'S NOT COMMONLY used in the United States, *queue* (pronounced "cue") is the universal English word for a line, such as one in which you wait to cash a check at the bank or to board a ride at a theme park. There's a mathematical area of specialization within the field of operations research called queuing theory, which studies and models how lines work. Because The Unofficial Guides draw heavily on this discipline, we use some of its terminology. In addition to the noun, the verb *to queue* means "to get in line," and a queuing area is a waiting area that accommodates a line.

TOURING PLANS: WHAT THEY ARE AND HOW THEY WORK

WHEN WE INTERVIEWED DISNEYLAND VISITORS who toured the theme park(s) on slow days, they invariably waxed eloquent about the sheer delight of their experience. When we questioned visitors who toured on moderate or busy days, however, they talked at length about the jostling crowds and how much time they stood in line. What a shame, they said, that so much time and energy are spent fighting crowds in a place as special as Disneyland.

Given this complaint, our researchers descended on Disneyland to determine whether a touring plan could be devised that would liberate visitors from the traffic flow and allow them to see any theme park in one day with minimal waiting in line. On some of the busiest days of the year, our team monitored traffic into and through Disneyland Park, noting how it filled and how patrons were distributed among the attractions. We also observed which rides and attractions were most popular and where bottlenecks were most likely to occur.

After many years of collecting data, we devised preliminary touring plans, which we tested during one of the busiest weeks of the year. Each day, our researchers would tour the park using one of the preliminary plans, noting how long it took to walk from place to place and how long the wait in line was for each attraction. Combining the information gained on trial runs, we devised a master plan that we retested and fine-tuned. This plan, with very little variance from day to day, allowed us to experience all major rides and attractions and most lesser ones in one day, with an average wait in line of less than 10 minutes at each.

From this master plan, we developed alternative plans that took into account the varying tastes and personal requirements of different Disneyland patrons. Each plan operated with the same logic as the master plan but addressed the special needs and preferences of its intended users.

Finally, after all of the plans were tested by our staff, we selected (using convenience sampling) Disneyland visitors to test the plans. The only prerequisite for being chosen to test the plans was that the guests must have been visiting a Disney park for the first time. A second group of patrons was chosen for a control group. These were first-time visitors who would tour the park according to their own plans but who would make notes about what they did and how much time they spent in lines.

When the two groups were compared, the results were amazing. On days when major theme park attendance exceeded 42,000, visitors touring without our plans *averaged* 2 hours and 36 minutes more waiting in line per day than the patrons touring with our plans, and they experienced 33% fewer attractions. In 2004 the application of a cutting-edge algorithm to our touring plan software increased the waiting time saved to an average of 4 hours. Our latest advancement, introduced in 2012, gives subscribers to **touringplans.com** the ability to build personalized plans online, and then use the Lines smartphone app while inside the parks to optimize their itineraries with real-time wait time data. We expect additional research to continue to improve the performance of the touring plans in future editions.

General Overview of the Touring Plans

Our touring plans are step-by-step guides for seeing as much as possible with a minimum of standing in line. They're designed to help you avoid crowds and bottlenecks on days of moderate to heavy attendance. On days of lighter attendance (see "Selecting the Time of Year for Your Visit," page 23), the plans still save time but aren't as critical to successful touring.

What You Can Realistically Expect from the Touring Plans

Though we present one-day touring plans for both of the theme parks, you should understand that Disneyland Park has more attractions than you can see in one day, even if you never wait in line. If you must cram your visit to Disneyland Park into a single day, the one-day touring plans will allow you to see as much as is humanly possible. Under certain circumstances you may not complete the plan, and you definitely won't be able to see everything. For Disneyland Park, the most comprehensive, efficient, and relaxing touring plans are the two-day plans. Though Disney California Adventure has grown recently, you should be able to see everything in one day by following our touring plans.

Variables That Will Affect the Success of the Touring Plans

How quickly you move from one ride to another; when and how many refreshment and restroom breaks you take; when, where, and how you eat meals; and your ability (or lack thereof) to find your way around will all have an impact on the success of the plans. Smaller groups almost always move faster than larger groups, and parties of adults generally can cover more ground than families with young children.

Switching off (see page 145), among other things, prohibits families with little ones from moving expeditiously among attractions. Plus, some children simply cannot conform to the "early to rise" conditions of the touring plans. A mom from Nutley, New Jersey, writes:

> [Though] the touring plans all advise getting to parks at opening, we just couldn't burn the candle at both ends. Our kids (10, 7, and 4) would not go to sleep early and couldn't be up at dawn and still stay relatively sane. It worked well for us to let them sleep a little later, go out and bring breakfast back to the room while they slept, and still get a relatively early start by not spending time on eating breakfast out. We managed to avoid long lines with an early morning and by hitting popular attractions during parades, mealtimes, and late evenings.

And a family from Centerville, Ohio, says:

> The toughest thing about your tour plans was getting the rest of the family to stay with them, at least to some degree. Getting them to pass by attractions to hit something across the park was no easy task (sometimes impossible).

A multigenerational family wonders how to know if you are on track or not, writing:

> It seems like the touring plans were very time dependent, yet there were no specific times attached to the plan outside of the early morning. On more than one day, I often had to guess as to whether we were on track.

There is no objective measurement for being on track. Each group's experience will differ to some degree. Regardless of whether your group is large or small, fast or slow, the sequence of attractions in the touring plans will allow you to enjoy the greatest number of attractions in the least possible time. Two quickly moving adults will probably take in more attractions in a specific time period than will a large group comprised of children, parents, and grandparents. However, given the characteristics of the respective groups, each will maximize their touring time and experience as many attractions as possible. That said, if you really want specific times for each step of your touring plan, use the online versions and customize them for your specific day of travel.

Finally, if you have young children in your party, be prepared for character encounters. The appearance of a Disney character is usually sufficient to stop a touring plan dead in its tracks. What's more, while some characters continue to stroll the parks, it is becoming more the rule to assemble characters in some specific venue (such as at Mickey's Toontown), where families must queue for photos of and autographs from Mickey. Meeting characters, posing for photos, and collecting autographs can burn hours of touring time. If your kids are into character-autograph collecting, you will need to anticipate these interruptions to the touring plan and negotiate some understanding with your children about when you will follow the plan and when you will collect autographs. Our advice is to either go with the flow or alternatively set aside a certain morning or afternoon for photos and autographs. Be aware, however, that queues for autographs, especially in Fantasy Faire and Pixie Hollow at Disneyland Park, are every bit as long as the queues for major attractions. The only time-efficient way to collect autographs is to line up at the character-greeting areas first thing in the morning. Because this is also the best time to experience the more popular attractions, you may have some tough decisions to make.

While we realize that following the touring plans is not always easy, we nevertheless recommend continuous, expeditious touring until around noon. After that hour, breaks and diversions won't affect the plans significantly.

Some variables that can profoundly affect the touring plans are beyond your control. Chief among these is the manner and timing of bringing a particular ride to capacity. For example, Big Thunder Mountain Railroad, a roller coaster in Disneyland Park, has five trains. On a given morning it may begin operation with two of the five, and then add the other three if and when they are needed. If the waiting line builds rapidly before operators decide to go to full capacity, you could have a long wait, even in early morning.

Another variable relates to the time you arrive for a show. Usually your wait will be the length of time from your arrival to the end of the presentation in progress. Thus, if the *Enchanted Tiki Room* show is 15 minutes long and you arrive 1 minute after a show has begun, your wait for the next show will be 14 minutes. Conversely, if you arrive as the show is wrapping up, your wait will be only 1 or 2 minutes.

What to Do If You Lose the Thread

Anything from a blister to a broken attraction can throw off a touring plan. If unforeseen events interrupt a plan:

1. If you're following a printed touring plan, skip one step on the plan for every 20 minutes' delay. If, for example, you lose your billfold and spend an hour hunting for it, skip three steps and pick up from there, or

2. Forget the plan; organize the remainder of your day using the standby wait times listed in Lines or the recommended attraction visitation times in each attraction profile.

3. If you're following a touring plan in our **Lines** app (**touringplans.com/lines**), just press the OPTIMIZE button when you're ready to start touring again. Lines will figure out the best possible plan for the remainder of your day.

Flexibility

The attractions included in the touring plans are the most popular attractions as determined by more than 19,500 reader surveys. Even so, your favorite attractions might be different. Fortunately, the touring plans are flexible. If the touring plan calls for an attraction that you don't wish to experience, simply skip it and move on to the next attraction on the plan.

Additionally, you can substitute similar attractions in the same area of the park. If the plan calls for riding Dumbo, for example, and you're not interested but would enjoy the Mad Tea Party (which is not on the plan), then substitute the Mad Tea Party for Dumbo. As long as the substitution is a similar attraction (it won't work to substitute a show for a ride) and located pretty close to the attraction called for in the plan, you won't compromise the overall effectiveness of the touring plan.

For the ultimate in flexibility and efficiency, use our Lines smartphone app to check off steps on your plan as you complete them (or delete ones you decide to skip), and then click the OPTIMIZE button to update your itinerary's ideal next destination using the most recent wait times.

A family of four from South Slocan, British Columbia, found that they could easily tailor the touring plans to meet their needs:

We amended your touring plans by taking out the attractions we didn't want to do and just doing the remainder in order. It worked great, and by arriving before the parks opened, we got to see everything we wanted, with virtually no waits! The best advice by far was to get there early!

A multigenerational family from South Jordan, Utah, found it helpful to use this book in conjunction with **touringplans.com**:

We didn't follow an exact touring plan, but I used the tips in your book and touring plans to make our own. We decided to see all the major attractions first to do them before the crowds came. We arrived at about 8:05 a.m., and by 11 we were walking on to our eighth attraction. We were able to see all we wanted and then take a more relaxed pace the rest of the day. A downside was that after getting on so many rides so quickly, we didn't want to wait in line for even 20 minutes the rest of the day.

Clip-Out Pocket Outlines of Touring Plans

Select the plan appropriate for your party, and then clip the pocket version from the back of this guide and carry it with you as a quick reference at the theme park.

Will the Plans Continue to Work Once the Secret Is Out?

Yes! First, all of the plans require that a patron be there when the theme parks open. Many Disneyland patrons simply refuse to get up early while on vacation. Second, less than 1% of any day's attendance has been exposed to the plans, too little to affect results. Last, most groups tailor the plans, skipping rides or shows according to personal taste.

How Frequently Are the Touring Plans Revised?

Because Disney is always adding new attractions and changing operations, we revise the touring plans every year. Most complaints we receive about them come from readers who are using out-of-date editions of

The Unofficial Guide. Be prepared, however, for surprises. Opening procedures and showtimes, for example, may change, and you never know when an attraction might break down. Touring plans inside our Lines app are updated even more often and can instantly adapt to any refurbishments or breakdowns during your visit.

Tour Groups from Hell

We have discovered that tour groups of up to 200 people sometimes use our plans. Unless your party is as large as that tour group, this development shouldn't alarm you. Because tour groups are big, they move slowly and have to stop periodically to collect stragglers. The tour guide also has to accommodate the unpredictability of five dozen or so bladders. In short, you should have no problem passing a group after the initial encounter.

Bouncing Around

Many readers object to crisscrossing a theme park, as our touring plans sometimes require. A woman from Decatur, Georgia, said she "got dizzy from all the bouncing around" and that the "running back and forth reminded [her] of a scavenger hunt." We empathize, but here's the rub.

In Disneyland Park, the most popular attractions are positioned across the park from one another. This is no accident. It's good planning, a method of more equally distributing guests throughout the park. If you want to experience the most popular attractions in one day without long waits, you can arrive before the park fills and see those attractions first thing (which requires crisscrossing the park), or you can enjoy the main attractions on one side of the park first thing in the morning, and then use FastPass for the popular attractions on the other side. All other approaches will subject you to awesome waits at some attractions if you tour during busy times of the year.

The best way to minimize bouncing around at Disneyland Park is to use one of our two-day touring plans, which spread the more popular attractions over two mornings and work beautifully even when the park closes at 8 p.m. or earlier. Using FastPass will decrease your waiting time but will increase bouncing around because you must first go to the attraction to obtain your FastPass and then backtrack later to the same attraction to use your pass.

Disney California Adventure is configured in a way that precludes an orderly approach to touring, or to a clockwise or counterclockwise rotation. Orderly touring is further frustrated by the limited guest capacity of the midway rides in the Paradise Pier district of the park. At DCA, therefore, you're stuck with bouncing around, whether you use the touring plan or not, if you want to avoid horrendous waits.

We suggest that you follow the touring plans religiously, especially in the mornings, if you're visiting Disneyland during busy, more crowded times. The consequence of touring spontaneity in peak season is hours of otherwise avoidable standing in line. During quieter times of year, there's no need to be compulsive about following the plans.

Touring Plan Rejection

We've discovered that you can't implant a touring plan in certain personalities without vehement rejection. Some folks just do not respond well to regimentation. If you bump into this problem with someone in your party, it's best to roll with the punches, as did this couple:

> *The rest of the group was not receptive to the use of the touring plans. They all thought I was being a little too regimented about planning this vacation. Rather than argue, I left the touring plans behind as we ventured off for the parks. You can guess the outcome. We took our camcorder with us, and when we returned home, we watched the movies. About every 5 minutes there is a shot of us all gathered around a park map trying to decide what to do next.*

Finally, as a Connecticut woman alleges, the touring plans are incompatible with some readers' bladders as well as their personalities:

> *When you write those day schedules next year, can you schedule bathroom breaks in there too? You expect us to be at a certain ride at a certain time and with no stops in between. The schedules are a problem if you are a laid-back, slow-moving, careful detail noticer. What were you thinking when you made these schedules?*

Before you injure your urinary tract, feel free to deviate from the touring plan as necessary to heed the call of nature. If you are using a customized plan in Lines, you can build in as many breaks (bathroom or otherwise) as you like, and the optimizer will plan around them.

A Clamor for Customized Touring Plans

We're inundated by letters urging us to create additional touring plans. These include a plan for 9th- and 10th-graders, a plan for rainy days, a seniors' plan, a plan for folks who sleep late, a plan omitting rides that "bump, jerk, and clonk," a plan for gardening enthusiasts, and a plan for single women.

The touring plans in this book are intended to be flexible. Adapt them to your preferences. If you don't like rides that bump and jerk, skip them when they come up in a touring plan. If you want to sleep in and go to the park at noon, use the afternoon part of a plan. If you're a ninth-grader and want to ride Space Mountain three times in a row, do it. Will it decrease the touring plan's effectiveness? Sure, but the plan was created only to help you have fun. It's your day.

If you really want to tailor your itinerary, we highly recommend subscribing to **touringplans.com,** where you can customize your day's to-do list down to the last snack cart. Our computers will evaluate the efficiency of your chosen attraction order, and try to suggest a better path through the park. For a truly personalized experience, some of our team members (including this book's coauthor) offer professional tour-planning services; visit **touringplans.com /disneyland-resort/touring-plans/faq** for details.

WHAT TO EXPECT WHEN YOU ARRIVE AT THE PARKS

BECAUSE EACH TOURING PLAN IS BASED on being present when the theme park opens, you need to know a little about opening procedures. Disney transportation to the parks, and the respective theme park parking lots, open 1–2 hours before official opening time.

Each park has an entrance plaza just outside the turnstiles. Usually you will be held outside the turnstiles until 30 minutes before official opening time. If you are admitted before the official opening time, you will usually be held at the turnstiles. Sometimes you might be confined in a small section of the park until the official opening time. At Disneyland Park you might be admitted to Main Street, U.S.A.; at Disney California Adventure to Buena Vista Street. If you proceed farther into a park, you will encounter a rope barrier manned by Disney cast members who will keep you from entering the remainder of the park. You will remain here until the rope drop, when the rope barrier is removed and the park and all (or most) of its attractions are opened at the official opening time.

A Word About the Rope Drop

Disney has a number of cast members supervising the rope drop in order to suppress the mayhem of anxiously waiting guests. A pleasantly parental prerecorded "Please walk; don't run" announcement seems to have a somewhat subduing effect on the straining crowds. In some cases, the rope is not even dropped. Instead, it's walked back. In other words, Disney cast members lead you with the rope at a fast walk toward the attraction you're straining to reach, forcing you (and everyone else) to maintain their pace. Not until they come within close proximity of the attraction do the cast members step aside.

So here's the scoop. If cast members persist in walking the rope back, the only way you can gain an advantage over the rest of the crowd is to arrive early enough to be one of those close to the rope. Be alert, though; sometimes the Disney folks will step out of the way after about 50 yards or so. If this happens, you can fire up the afterburners and speed the remaining distance to your destination.

FASTPASS

FASTPASS IS A SYSTEM for moderating the waiting time for popular attractions. Here's how it works.

Your handout park map, as well as signs at respective attractions, will tell you which attractions are included. Attractions that use Fast-Pass will have a regular line and a FastPass line. A sign at the entrance will tell you how long the wait is in the regular line. If the wait is acceptable, hop in line. If the wait seems too long, you can insert your park admission pass into a FastPass machine and receive an appointment (for a time later in the day) to come back and ride. When you return at the appointed time, you will enter the FastPass line and proceed directly to the attraction's preshow or boarding area with minimal further wait. There is no extra charge to use FastPass, but you can get an appointment for only one attraction per park at a time (with a few exceptions, noted below).

FastPass works remarkably well, primarily because FastPass holders get amazingly preferential treatment. The effort to accommodate FastPass holders makes anyone in the regular line feel like an illegal immigrant. As a telling indication of their status, Disney (borrowing a term from the airlines) refers to those in the regular line as standby guests. Indeed, we watched guests in the regular line stand by and stand by, shifting despondently from foot to foot while dozens and sometimes hundreds of FastPass holders were ushered into the boarding area ahead of them. Clearly Disney is sending a message here, to wit: FastPass is heaven; anything else is limbo at best and probably purgatory. In either event, you'll think you've been in purgatory if you get stuck in the regular line during the hot, crowded part of the day.

FASTPASS ATTRACTIONS	
DISNEYLAND PARK	**DISNEY CALIFORNIA ADVENTURE**
Big Thunder Mountain Railroad	Anna & Elsa's Royal Welcome
Buzz Lightyear Astro Blasters	California Screamin'
Fantasmic!	*For the First Time in Forever—A Frozen Sing-Along Celebration*
The Haunted Mansion Holiday (seasonal)	Goofy's Sky School*
Indiana Jones Adventure	Grizzly River Run
Roger Rabbit's Car Toon Spin*	Radiator Springs Racers*
Royal Theatre Presents *Frozen* (seasonal)	Soarin' Over California*
Space Mountain*	The Twilight Zone Tower of Terror
Splash Mountain*	*World of Color*
Star Tours—The Adventures Continue*	

*Denotes rides that routinely issue FastPasses for redemption 3–7 hours later.

FastPass, however, doesn't eliminate the need to arrive at the theme park early. Because each park offers at most 10 FastPass attractions, you still need to get an early start if you want to see as much as possible in a single day. Plus, as we'll discuss later, there's only a limited supply of FastPasses available for each attraction on a given day. So if you don't show up until the middle of the afternoon, you might discover that all the FastPasses have been distributed to other guests. FastPass does, happily, make it possible to see more with less waiting than ever before, and it's a great benefit to those who like to sleep late or who enjoy an afternoon or evening at the theme parks on their arrival day. It also enables you to postpone wet rides such as the Grizzly River Run at Disney California Adventure or Splash Mountain at Disneyland Park until the warmer part of the day.

Understanding the FastPass System

The purpose of the FastPass system is to reduce the waiting time for designated attractions by more equally distributing the arrival of guests at those attractions over the course of the day. This is accomplished by providing a shorter wait in line for guests who are willing to postpone experiencing the attraction until sometime later in the day. The system also, in effect, imposes a penalty—that is, being relegated to standby status—to those who opt not to use it (though spreading guest arrivals more equally decreases waiting time for standby guests too).

When you insert your admission pass into a FastPass machine, it spits out a small slip of paper about two-thirds the size of a credit card, small enough to fit in your wallet (but also small enough to lose easily). Printed on the paper will be the name of the attraction and a specific 1-hour time window—for example, 1:15–2:15 p.m. You can return to enjoy the ride any time from 1:15 to 2:15 p.m. Disneyland Resort strictly enforces the 1-hour FastPass windows, allowing an unpublicized 15-minute grace period and exceptions for ride break-downs. Pay close attention to the printed time when you receive your FastPass, and plan your return accordingly. Each person in your party must have his or her own FastPass.

When you report back to the attraction later, you'll enter a line marked FASTPASS RETURN that will route you more or less directly to the boarding area or preshow area. Each person in your party must have his or her own FastPass and be ready to show it to the Disney cast member at the entrance of the FastPass return line. Before you enter the boarding area, another cast member will collect your FastPass.

You may show up at any time within the period printed on your FastPass begins, and from our observation, no specific time is better or worse. This holds true because cast members are instructed to minimize waits for FastPass holders. Thus, if the FastPass return line is suddenly inundated (something that occurs more or less by chance), cast members rapidly intervene to reduce the FastPass line. This is done by admit-ting as many as 25 FastPass holders for each standby guest until the FastPass line is down to an acceptable length. Though FastPass will lop off as much as 80% of the wait you'd experience in the regular line, you can still expect a short wait, but usually less than 20 minutes.

You can obtain a FastPass any time after a park officially opens (not counting early entry), though the FastPass return lines do not begin operating until about 35–50 minutes after opening. Thus, if the attractions at Disneyland Park open at 9 a.m., the FastPass machines will also be available at 9 a.m., and the FastPass line will begin operating at about 9:35 a.m.

unofficial **TIP**
Use FastPass if the wait in the regular line is more than 30 minutes.

Whatever time you obtain a FastPass, you can be assured of a period of time between when you receive your FastPass and the beginning of your return window. The interval can be as short as 30 minutes or as long as 7 hours depending on park attendance, the popularity of the attraction, and the attraction's hourly capacity. As a general rule, the earlier in the day you secure a FastPass, the shorter the interval between time of issue and the beginning of your return window. On a day that the park opens at 9 a.m., if you pick up a

FastPass for Splash Mountain at, say, 9:25 a.m., your recommended window for returning to ride would be something like 10–11 a.m., or perhaps 10:10–11:10 a.m. The exact time will be determined by how many other guests have obtained FastPasses before you.

To more effectively distribute guests over the course of a day, the FastPass machines bump the 1-hour return period back 5 minutes for a specific number of passes issued (usually the number is equal to about 6% of the attraction's hourly capacity). When Splash Mountain opens at 9 a.m., for example, the first 125 people to obtain a Fast-Pass will get a 10–11 a.m. recommended return window. The next 125 guests are issued FastPasses that can be used between 10:05–11:05 a.m., with the next 125 assigned a 10:10–11:10 a.m. time slot. And so it goes, with the time window dropping back 5 minutes for every 125 guests. The fewer guests who obtain FastPasses for an attraction, the shorter the interval between the receipt of your pass and the return window. Conversely, the more guests issued FastPasses, the longer the interval. If an attraction is exceptionally popular and/or its hourly capacity is relatively small, the return window might be pushed back all the way to park closing time. When this happens, the FastPass machines stop issuing passes. It would not be unusual, for example, for Radiator Springs Racers at Disney California Adventure to distribute an entire day's allocation of FastPasses by 10 a.m. When this happens, the machines simply shut down and a sign is posted saying that FastPasses are all gone for the day.

FASTPASS GUIDELINES

- Park tickets must be activated at the front turnstiles (or Downtown Disney monorail station) before being used to obtain FastPasses, so you can't send one family member into the park while the others snooze. However, once everyone has entered, you can send one person across to the other park with everyone's tickets to retrieve FastPasses there.

- Don't use FastPass unless it can save you 30 minutes or more at an attraction.

- If you arrive after a park opens, obtain a FastPass for your preferred FastPass attraction first thing.

- Always check the FastPass return period before obtaining your FastPass.

- Obtain FastPasses for Star Tours, *Fantasmic!,* Space Mountain, and Splash Mountain at Disneyland Park and for Soarin' Over California, Radiator Springs Racers, Anna & Elsa's Royal Welcome, *World of Color,* and Goofy's Sky School at DCA as early in the day as practical.

- Try to obtain FastPasses for rides not mentioned above by 1 p.m.

- Don't depend on FastPasses being available for ride attractions after 2 p.m. during busier times of the year.

- Make sure that everyone in your party has his or her own FastPass.

- You can obtain a second FastPass as soon as you enter the return period for your first FastPass or after 2 hours from issuance, whichever comes first.

- Maximize efficiency by always obtaining a new FastPass for the next attraction before using the first FastPass you already hold.

- Be mindful of your FastPass return time, and plan intervening activities accordingly.

- Rides don't dispense FastPasses during early entry, nor while they are closed for technical difficulties or special events.

Disconnected FastPass Attractions

Some attractions' FastPass kiosks are not hooked up to the park-wide FastPass distribution system. Because a disconnected attraction has no way of knowing if you have a FastPass for another attraction, it will issue you a FastPass at any time. In Disneyland Park, Roger Rabbit's Car Toon Spin has been disconnected in the past (but wasn't at press time), and Anna & Elsa's Royal Welcome meet-and-greet at DCA is disconnected, as is California Screamin' at times. *World of Color*'s and *Fantasmic!*'s FastPasses are always disconnected from the other attractions. Disney can connect and disconnect FastPass attractions at will, so the disconnected lineup may vary somewhat during your visit. The use of disconnected FastPass attractions is incorporated in our touring plans. Finally, Disneyland Park's and DCA's FastPass systems are not connected. You can obtain a FastPass at one park and then immediately walk to the other park and obtain another FastPass.

When to Use FastPass

Except as discussed below, there's no reason to use FastPass during the first 30–40 minutes a park is open. Lines for most attractions are quite manageable during this period. In addition, this is the only time of the day when the FastPass attractions exclusively serve those in the regular line. Regardless of time of day, however, if the wait in the regular line at a FastPass attraction is 25–30 minutes or less, we recommend joining the regular line.

Think about it. Using FastPass requires two trips to the same attraction: one to obtain the pass and one to use it. This means that you must invest time to secure the pass (by the way, sometimes there are lines at the FastPass machines!) and then later interrupt your touring and backtrack in order to use your FastPass. The additional time, effort, and touring modification required, therefore, are justified only if you can save more than 30 minutes. And don't forget: Even in the FastPass line, you must endure some waiting.

Tricks of the Trade

Though Disney stipulates that you can hold a FastPass to only one attraction at a time, it's possible to acquire a second FastPass before using the first. Let's say you obtain a FastPass to Star Tours at Disneyland Park with a return time slot of 10:15–11:15 a.m. Any time after your FastPass window begins (anytime after 10:15 a.m.), you will be able to obtain another FastPass, for Splash Mountain, for example. This is possible because the

FastPass computer system monitors only the distribution of passes, ignoring whether or when a FastPass is used. Finally, don't forget that you can obtain a second FastPass 2 hours after the time of issuance of the first FastPass if that's sooner than the return time on your first FastPass.

When obtaining FastPasses, it's faster and more considerate of other guests if one person obtains passes for your entire party. This means entrusting one individual with both your valuable park admission passes and your FastPasses, so choose wisely.

FastPass Runners

If you've ever taken a walk with a dog that runs and darts all over the place while you plod along in a straight line, you'll appreciate the concept of FastPass running. First you choose a high-energy, inexhaustible member of your party who is quick on his feet and mature and responsible enough not to lose everyone's admission passes. Second, you give him all the passes (after you enter the park) and dispatch him to the first attraction to obtain FastPasses for the whole group. Then, about once each hour, the FastPass runner will split from the group to get the next FastPasses. Rinse, repeat. In Disneyland Park, for example, he would speed off to Space Mountain. Because the return time is usually 1 hour or less, it won't be long until he can scoot off again to obtain FastPasses at Splash Mountain. And so it goes. You can even send the runner across the Esplanade to get FastPasses at the other park, provided you have Park Hopper tickets. Collecting FastPasses this way allows the group to spend the less-crowded early-morning time visiting popular slow-loading attractions that don't offer FastPass. A father from Petaluma, California, shares his technique:

> The trick is to always be holding FastPasses for the next headliner ride. Sending a runner to get the FastPasses is easy to do, as a solo adult can quickly and easily make his/her way across the park and back to rejoin the group. A time-saving maneuver I call the FastPass Daddy Limbo works like this: The main group gets in line for a ride (the line must be at least 15–20 minutes long) while Dad takes off to get FastPasses for another ride. Dad returns 10–15 minutes later and rejoins his group in line by going under/over/through the railing (unclasping a chain if necessary). The dad may need to wait a few minutes to rejoin his group until they are positioned at an easily accessible point. This should be possible at other accessible lines such as Star Tours and Splash Mountain, provided that the line outside is long enough.

FastPass+

In 2014 Walt Disney World completed the rollout of a new iteration of FastPass that is expected to eventually migrate west to Disneyland. Currently, Walt Disney World guests can reserve three FastPass+ experiences per day up to 60 days in advance of their visit; Annual Pass holders not staying on-property also get to make up to 7 days of FastPass+ reservations within a rolling 30-day window. Rather than retrieve timed

FastPass tickets from kiosks inside the park, guests use their smartphones and radio-frequency-identification-enabled electronic wristbands to pre-arrange FastPass times days or weeks before arriving at the resort. The rocky implementation of FastPass+ in Orlando sparked significant controversy, and no time line for its transfer to Anaheim has been officially announced yet. However, our Lines app is ready to address any impact to your touring plans once FastPass+ arrives on the West Coast.

SAVING TIME IN LINE BY UNDERSTANDING THE RIDES

THERE ARE MANY DIFFERENT TYPES of rides in Disneyland. Some rides, such as It's a Small World, are engineered to carry several thousand people every hour. At the other extreme, rides such as Dumbo the Flying Elephant can accommodate only around 500 people in an hour. Most rides fall somewhere in between. Lots of factors figure into how long you will have to wait to experience a particular ride: the popularity of the ride, how it loads and unloads, how many people can ride at one time, how many units (cars, rockets, boats, flying elephants, or whatever) of those available are in service at a given time, and how many staff personnel are available to operate the ride. Let's take them one by one:

1. HOW POPULAR IS THE RIDE? Newer rides such as Star Tours—The Adventures Continue or Radiator Springs Racers attract a lot of people, as do longtime favorites such as the Jungle Cruise. If you know a ride is popular, you need to learn a little more about how it operates to determine when might be the best time to ride. But a ride need not be especially popular to form long lines. The lines can be the result of less-than-desirable traffic engineering; that is, it takes so long to load and unload that a line builds up. This is the situation at the Mad Tea Party and Dumbo. Only a small percentage of the visitors to Disneyland Park (mostly kids) ride Dumbo, for instance, but because it takes so long to load and unload, this ride can form long waiting lines.

2. HOW DOES THE RIDE LOAD AND UNLOAD? Some rides never stop. They are like a circular conveyor belt that goes around and around. We call these continuous loaders. The Haunted Mansion is a continuous loader. The more cars or ships or whatever on the conveyor, the more people can be moved through in an hour. The Haunted Mansion has lots of cars on the conveyor belt and consequently can move more than 2,400 people an hour.

Other rides are interval loaders. This means that cars are unloaded, loaded, and dispatched at certain set intervals (sometimes controlled manually and sometimes by a computer). Matterhorn Bobsleds is an interval loader. It has two separate tracks (in other words, the ride has been duplicated in the same facility). Each track can run up to 10 sleds, released at 23-second or greater intervals (the bigger the crowd, the shorter the interval). In another kind of interval loader, such as the Jungle Cruise, empty boats return to the starting point, where they line up waiting to be reloaded. In a third type of interval loader, one group of riders enters the vehicle while the last group of riders departs. We call these in-and-out interval loaders. Indiana Jones Adventure is a good example of an in-and-out interval loader. As a troop transport pulls up to the loading station, those who have just completed their ride exit to the left. At almost the same time, those waiting to ride enter the troop transport from the right. The troop transport is released to the dispatch point a few yards down the line where it is launched according to whatever second interval is being used. Interval loaders of all three types can be very efficient at moving people if (1) the release (launch) interval is relatively short and (2) the ride can accommodate a large number of vehicles in the system at one time. Because many boats can be floating through Pirates of the Caribbean at a given time and the release interval is short, almost 2,300 people an hour can see this attraction.

A third group of rides are cycle rides. Another name for these same rides is stop-and-go rides; those waiting to ride exchange places with those who have just ridden. The main difference between in-and-out interval rides and cycle rides is that with a cycle ride, the whole system shuts down when loading and unloading is in progress. While one boat is loading and unloading in It's a Small World, many other boats are proceeding through the ride. But when Dumbo the Flying Elephant touches down, the whole ride is at a standstill until the next flight is launched.

In discussing a cycle ride, the amount of time the ride is in motion is called ride time. The amount of time that the ride is idle while loading and unloading is called load time. Load time plus ride time equals cycle time, or the time expended from the start of one run of the ride until the start of the succeeding run. Cycle rides are the least efficient of all the Disneyland rides in terms of traffic engineering. Disneyland Park has 6 cycle rides, while Disney California Adventure has 10, an astonishing number for a modern park.

CYCLE RIDES AT DISNEYLAND PARK		
FANTASYLAND	**MICKEY'S TOONTOWN**	**TOMORROWLAND**
• Casey Jr. Circus Train • Dumbo the Flying Elephant • King Arthur Carrousel • Mad Tea Party	• Gadget's Go Coaster	• Astro Orbitor
CYCLE RIDES AT DISNEY CALIFORNIA ADVENTURE		
A BUG'S LAND	**PARADISE PIER**	**CARS LAND**
• Flik's Flyers • Francis' Ladybug Boogie • Mickey's Fun Wheel • Tuck and Roll's Drive 'Em Buggies	• Golden Zephyr • Jumpin' Jellyfish • King Triton's Carousel • Silly Symphony Swings	• Luigi's Rollickin' Roadsters • Mater's Junkyard Jamboree

3. HOW MANY PEOPLE CAN RIDE AT ONE TIME? This figure is defined in terms of per-ride capacity or system capacity. Either way, the figures refer to the number of people who can ride at the same time. Our discussion above illustrates that the greater a ride's carrying capacity (all other things being equal), the more visitors it can accommodate in an hour.

4. HOW MANY UNITS ARE IN SERVICE AT A GIVEN TIME? A unit is simply a term for the vehicle you sit in during your ride. At the Mad Tea Party the unit is a teacup, and at Alice in Wonderland it's a caterpillar. On some rides (mostly cycle rides), the number of units in operation at a given time is fixed. Thus, there are always 16 elephant units operating on the Dumbo ride, 72 horses on King Arthur Carrousel, and so on. What this fixed number of units means to you is that there is no way to increase the carrying capacity of the ride by adding more units. On a busy day, therefore, the only way to carry more people each hour on a fixed-unit cycle ride is to shorten the loading time (which, as we will see in number 5 below, is sometimes impossible) or by decreasing the riding time, the actual time the ride is in motion. The bottom line on a busy day for a cycle ride is that you will wait longer and be rewarded for your wait with a shorter ride. This is why we try to steer you clear of the cycle rides unless you are willing to ride them early in the morning or late at night.

Other rides at Disneyland can increase their carrying capacity by adding units to the system as the crowds build. The Big Thunder Mountain Railroad is a good example. If attendance is very light, Big Thunder can start the day by running one of five available mine trains. When lines start to build, more mine trains can be placed into operation. At full capacity, a total of five trains can carry about 2,400 people an hour. Sometimes a long line will disappear almost instantly when new units are brought online. On the other hand, the queue may stop altogether for a few minutes while new units are added, extending the wait for guests who were about to board. When an interval-loading ride places more units into operation, it usually shortens the dispatch interval, so more units are being dispatched more often.

5. HOW MANY CAST MEMBERS ARE AVAILABLE TO OPERATE THE RIDE? Allocation of additional staff to a given ride can allow extra units to be placed in operation, or additional loading areas or holding areas to be opened. Pirates of the Caribbean and It's a Small World can run two separate waiting lines and loading zones. The Haunted Mansion has a short preshow, which is staged in a "stretch room." On busy days a second stretch room can be activated, thus permitting a more continuous flow of visitors to the actual loading area. Additional staff make a world of difference on some cycle rides. Often, if not usually, one attendant will operate the Golden Zephyr. This single person must clear the visitors from the ride just completed, admit and seat visitors for the upcoming ride, check that all zephyrs are properly secured (which entails an inspection of each zephyr), return to the control panel, issue instructions to the riders, and finally, activate the ride (whew!). A second attendant allows for the division of these responsibilities and has the effect of cutting loading time by 25%–50%.

BEWARE OF THE DARK, WET, ROUGH, AND SCARY

 ALMOST FORGOT: There's a member of our team you need to meet. Called a Wuffo, she's our very own character. She'll warn you when rides are too scary, too dark, or too wet. You'll bump into her throughout the book doing, well, what characters do. Pay attention to her—she knows what she's talking about.

SAVING TIME IN LINE BY UNDERSTANDING THE SHOWS

MANY OF THE FEATURED ATTRACTIONS at Disneyland are theater presentations. While they're not as complex as rides from a traffic-engineering viewpoint, a little enlightenment concerning their operation may save some touring time.

Most Disneyland theater attractions operate in three distinct phases:

1. First, there are the visitors who are in the theater viewing the presentation.

2. Next, there are the visitors who have passed through the turnstile into a holding area or waiting lobby. These people will be admitted to the theater as soon as the current presentation is concluded. Several attractions offer a pre-show in their waiting lobby to entertain the crowd until they are admitted to the main show.

3. Finally, there is the outside line. Visitors waiting here will enter the waiting lobby when there is room and then move into the theater when the audience turns over (is exchanged) between shows.

The theater capacity and popularity of the presentation, along with the level of attendance in the park, determine how long the lines will be at a given theater attraction. Except for holidays and other days of especially heavy attendance, the longest wait for a show usually does not exceed the length of one complete performance.

Because almost all Disneyland theater attractions run continually, only stopping long enough for the previous audience to leave and the waiting audience to enter, a performance will already be in progress when you arrive. If the *Enchanted Tiki Room* show lasts 15 minutes, the wait under normal circumstances should be 15 minutes if you were to arrive just after the show began.

All Disneyland theaters (except the Main Street Cinema and some amphitheater productions) are very strict when it comes to controlling access. Unlike at a regular movie theater, you can't just walk in during the middle of a performance; you will always have at least a short wait.

GUIDED TOURS AT DISNEYLAND PARK AND DCA

FIVE GUIDED GROUP TOURS are offered year-round, in addition to ultra-expensive private VIP tours. All require a valid park admission in addition to the price of the tour. All Disneyland Resort tours can be booked up to 30 days in advance by calling ☎ 714-781-8687 for the standard tours or ☎ 714-300-7710 for the VIP treatment. All tours are subject to change without notice, and some tours are offered only on

certain days, so call ahead. During the Halloween and Christmas seasons, special tours highlighting holiday decorations may be available in addition to the following year-round offerings. All Disneyland Park tours begin at the Tour Gardens kiosk to the left of City Hall on Main Street, U.S.A. Annual Pass holders get a 20% discount on guided tours.

CULTIVATING THE MAGIC TOUR This 2-hour introduction to the resort's horticultural treasures features an insider's peek at the park's remarkable landscaping efforts. You'll also get express entry into three classic rides, with exclusive narration pointing out their often-overlooked agricultural elements. The tour is a photographer's paradise, and even if you don't have a green thumb, we think this is one of the most entertaining and educational ways to experience a unique aspect of Disneyland Park. The tour is offered Saturday and Sunday at 9 a.m. and Monday at 10 a.m.; the cost is $49 per guest and includes a souvenir pin and seed packet.

DISCOVER THE MAGIC TOUR Kids interact with Disney characters in a sort of treasure hunt to find clues to the treasure and avoid villainous characters. Designed for ages 3–9, the frenetic, fast-paced family program lasts approximately 2½ hours and includes a frozen treat and souvenir Disney pin. Prices are $59 for the first two tickets, $49 for the third and subsequent tickets. The tour is offered Friday–Sunday at 10 a.m.

DISNEY CALIFORNIA STORY TOUR The resort's newest guided tour is a 3-hour stroll through the story of Walt Disney's arrival in California during the early 1900s. The tour departs Friday–Sunday at 10 a.m.; the cost is $109 for guests age 3 and older. The tour includes three attraction experiences and a look into the exclusive 1901 Lounge, plus a collectible pin and private lunch. Check in at the Chamber of Commerce on Buena Vista Street. While the tour is informative and respectful of Walt's legacy, there is no backstage access, and the visit to 1901 is very brief. Considering the cost, we don't think it's as good a value as Walk in Walt's Footsteps.

A WALK IN WALT'S FOOTSTEPS This 3½-hour tour offers a historical perspective on both Disneyland Park and the man who created it. It provides a lot of detail as it covers Disney's vision and the challenges in bringing the groundbreaking theme park to life. The tour includes a light lunch. You'll take a trip on the Disneyland Railroad (with a look inside the *Lilly Belle* private car if you're lucky), and ride two other 1955-vintage attractions. Highlights of the tour are an exclusive visit to the interior of the Dream Suite in New Orleans Square (sadly, Walt's original private apartment above the Main Street firehouse has been retired from the tour) and a glimpse of the lobby of Club 33, where Disney was to entertain his friends and dignitaries. Unfortunately, he died five months before the club was finished. Cost is $109 for all ages, and the tour is offered every day at 9:30 a.m., regardless of the park's opening time. (The tour is considered inappropriate for younger children and those who can't walk on their own.) A reader from Superior, Colorado, tried the tour for her birthday and gave a mixed review:

> We took our first guided Disneyland tour ever (Walk in Walt's Footsteps) and tried several new things. The tour was good, but I wouldn't do it more than once. Our guide was a little too rehearsed (read: memorization), and several people on the tour (including my husband and I) knew things she didn't know.

WELCOME TO DISNEYLAND TOUR This 2½-hour tour for first-time visitors provides a warp-speed look at pretty much the entire Disneyland Resort. Guides provide background and history of the parks, attractions, and sights as you tour both theme parks, Downtown Disney, and the Disney-owned hotels. Suffice it to say, you'll do a lot of walking. The tour includes expedited access to two selected attractions, reserved viewing for performances of a select show (such as the *Aladdin* stage musical), dining reservations, and two FastPasses per person for use after the tour. The tour, offered Friday–Monday at 10:30 a.m., is reasonably priced at $25.

VIP TOURS For the well-heeled, exclusive VIP tours are available for an eye-popping $360 per hour for up to 10 guests ($500 during peak season) with a 6-hour minimum; park admission is required but not included. VIP guides will arrange special parade and show seating, make dining reservations, dispense Disneyland trivia, and (most crucially) "back door" you past the queues for unlimited expedited boarding at most attractions. You must make reservations 72 hours in advance and cancel at least 48 hours in advance or face a 2-hour cancellation fee.

PART TWO

ESSENTIALS

 The **BARE NECESSITIES**

CREDIT CARDS

AMERICAN EXPRESS, MASTERCARD, VISA, Discover, and Japan Credit Bureau credit cards are accepted for theme park admission. Disneyland shops, fast-food and counter-service restaurants, sit-down restaurants, and the Disneyland Resort hotels also accept all the cards listed above. Some vendor carts accept credit cards while others do not—ask before you order. Disney Visa cardholders can get a private character meet-and-greet in Disney California Adventure's (DCA's) Hollywood Land 10:30 a.m.–1:30 p.m.; the voucher you receive (one per card per day) is valid for a free 5-by-7-inch print of your private character encounter from the Kingswell Camera Shop near the park entrance. Disney Visa cardholders also save 10% on merchandise ($50 minimum purchase) and dining at select resort locations and 15% on guided tours. Instant application kiosks can be found in Downtown Disney, with $50 gift cards sometimes offered as an incentive to approved applicants.

Apple Pay is a wireless payment method currently found on the iPhone 6, 6 Plus, and newer models, as well as Apple Watch. By the end of 2015, Disney is scheduled to start rolling out support for Apple Pay in most of its ticket booths, stores, quick-service restaurants, and outdoor vending carts. Locations that support Apple Pay will have a small black pad with a Contactless Indicator symbol (also known as an EMVCo symbol, which looks like a Wi-Fi symbol turned sideways). When it works, Apple Pay is the swiftest way to pay, even quicker than swiping a hotel key.

RAIN

IF IT RAINS, GO ANYWAY; the bad weather will diminish the crowds. Additionally, most of the rides and attractions at the parks are under cover. Likewise, all but a few of the waiting areas are protected from inclement weather. Some outdoor attractions—such as Tom Sawyer's Island, Mad Tea Party, Alice in Wonderland, Tarzan's Treehouse, and Gadget's Go Coaster at Disneyland Park, and Radiator Springs Racers, Redwood Creek Challenge Trail, and Golden Zephyr at DCA—may close for safety reasons in inclement weather. Radiator Springs Racers may require hours of downtime after a storm before safely reopening. Roller coasters such as Big Thunder Mountain Railroad and California Screamin' can operate in a drizzle but will close down if lightning is nearby. Fireworks are rarely canceled solely due to rain but may be scuttled by strong winds, and parades may be shortened or modified for safety. A father from Petaluma, California, recommends some supplemental supplies for wet weather, writing:

> Ride operators make a token effort to use a shop vac or towels, but it's good to have your own towel even on sunny days for the water ride seats. For multiday park touring in the rain, it is good to have a second pair of shoes to switch off every night at the hotel, allowing 24 hours to dry. . . . Bringing a small fan to the room also paid off, drying shoes and jackets that got wet on Splash Mountain and Grizzly River Run.

If you get caught in an unexpected downpour, raingear can be purchased at a number of shops. Whatever you do, don't flee for the parking trams during a sudden thunderstorm, or you may find yourself in an unpleasant scene, like this mother of two from Los Angeles:

> It was pouring rain and the park rapidly emptied out, with everyone heading for the trams that take you to the parking structure. There was complete chaos by the tram loading area [with] hundreds of people pushing and shoving—desperate to get on a tram and get out of there. The trams were arriving very sporadically and tempers were rising.

Instead, wait out the storm inside a self-paced indoor attraction, such as *Great Moments with Mr. Lincoln,* Main Street Cinema, or Tomorrowland's Marvel and Star Wars exhibits at Disneyland Park, and Boudin bakery tour or Disney Animation at DCA.

VISITORS WITH SPECIAL NEEDS

DISABLED VISITORS Rental wheelchairs are available just inside both parks' main gates. Daily wheelchair rentals are $12 (manual) or $50 (electric); a $20 refundable deposit is required. Note that wheelchairs and electric convenience vehicles rented inside the parks are not permitted beyond the Esplanade. A limited supply of nonelectric wheelchairs which may be taken through the Downtown Disney district are available to rent at the three Disneyland Resort hotels.

Most rides, shows, attractions, restrooms, and restaurants are engineered to accommodate the disabled. For specific inquiries call ☎ 714-781-7290. If you have an impairment that makes it difficult for you to stand in line and navigate stairs, or otherwise need special assistance, go to City Hall on Main Street in Disneyland Park or Guest

Relations in the entrance plaza at DCA and ask to register for Disability Access Service (DAS), which will be electronically attached to your admission ticket. This program is free and available for the disabled visitor and up to five additional guests. You should not have to show a doctor's note or proof of disability.

The DAS system replaced the former Guest Assistance Card program in 2013. Under the current system, instead of being immediately admitted to an attraction's entrance, users are issued return times based on the current standby wait (minus 10 minutes) from designated kiosks strategically scattered around the parks. In effect, DAS is a special FastPass for disabled guests and can be used in conjunction with the regular FastPass service. The DAS Card is valid for 60 days, after which it must be renewed in person, which should be fine for most visitors but can be annoying for local Annual Pass holders. The current system was intended to reduce rampant abuse of the system, which sometimes had hundreds of able-bodied guests skipping the standby line for limited-capacity attractions, but it has proven controversial among autism activists whose children may have meltdowns when told they must wait for their ride. Additional services, such as rider switch and break areas, are available for guests with cognitive disabilities. If you feel you may need the DAS Card or other accommodations, be sure to read up on your options in advance at **disneyland.disney.go.com /guest-services/guests-with-disabilities.** A Southern California mom with an autistic daughter had this suggestion:

> *Anyone staying any length of time should get their DAS Card at DCA—the lines are always shorter there, unless you are in the gates of Disneyland at opening.*

Guests in wheelchairs who do not have additional cognitive or sensory issues do not need to sign up for DAS because all attraction standby queues in Disney California Adventure, and most in Disneyland, are fully wheelchair accessible. At those in Disneyland that are not fully accessible, guests in wheelchairs will go to the ride's main entrance and be issued a return time based on the current wait time (minus 10 minutes), at which point they can report to an alternate accessible entrance. Though similar to DAS, this program is independent of it and does not require preregistration.

For guests with visual or auditory impairments, digital audio and Braille guides, assistive listening devices, captioning, and sign language services are also available through City Hall and Guest Relations. Trained service animals are welcome but must be kept on a leash at all times. Note the special symbol on park maps designating service animal relief areas in both parks.

Close-in parking is available for the disabled; inquire when you pay your parking fee. Parking trams can accommodate guests who bring their own wheelchairs, and a special transportation van is also available (ask a parking lot cast member). Curbside drop-off is only available at the Harbor Boulevard entrance, near the stops for hotel shuttles and local buses. It may be challenging for disabled guests who don't bring their own wheelchairs to walk from there into the parks. If you don't think that you can travel the necessary distance, consider renting a chair or scooter for the length of your vacation from a third-party vendor who can deliver it to your hotel. Even with all of Disneyland's accommodations for disabled guests, one Claremont, California, woman says that the resort still has a ways to go:

> For disabled guests, restrooms are terrible. Usually there is only one handicapped stall, and it is OFTEN used by teens and even cast members, as well as moms taking strollers or multiple kids into the stall.
>
> There are only two companion restrooms in each park (outside of first aid). Other theme parks in Southern California have staff who assist and tell guests not to use these stalls, and other parks have added many more family and companion restroom facilities.
>
> There still are not enough handicapped parking spaces on more crowded days, not enough handicapped restroom stalls, nor adequate seating at many restaurants to accommodate the various types of need.

VISITORS WITH DIETARY RESTRICTIONS Guests on special or restricted diets, including those requiring kosher meals, can arrange for assistance at City Hall at Disneyland Park or at Guest Relations at DCA. These locations can also provide information on gluten-free menu options at restaurants in the resort. For special service at Disneyland Resort restaurants, call the restaurant one day in advance for assistance. See page 162 in Part Four for more details on allergies and dietary restrictions at Disneyland Resort.

FOREIGN-LANGUAGE ASSISTANCE Translation services are available to guests who do not speak English. Inquire by calling ☎ 714-781-7290 or visiting City Hall at Disneyland Park or at Guest Relations at DCA.

LOST ADULTS Arrange a plan for regrouping with those in your party should you become separated. Failing this, you can leave a message at City Hall or Guest Relations for your missing person. For information concerning lost children, see page 150.

MESSAGES Messages for your fellow group members can be left at City Hall in Disneyland Park or at DCA Guest Relations.

CAR TROUBLE If you elected to decrease the chance of losing your keys by locking them in your car, or decided that your car might be easier to find if you left your lights on, you may have a little problem to deal with when you return to the parking lot. Fortunately, the security patrols that continually cruise the parking lots are equipped to handle these types of situations and can quickly put you back in business.

LOST AND FOUND The lost-and-found office is located in the Guest Services building in the Esplanade to the west of the park entrances. This location services both theme parks and the Downtown Disney complex. If you do not discover your loss until you have left the parks, call ☎ 714-817-2166 between 8 a.m. and 8 p.m. daily.

EXCUSE ME, BUT WHERE CAN I FIND . . .

SOME PLACE TO PUT ALL THESE PACKAGES? Lockers are available at both parks for $7–$15 per day, depending on size. A more convenient solution, if you plan to spend 2 or more hours in the park, is to have the salesperson forward your purchases to Package Pickup. When you leave the park, your purchases will be there waiting for you.

GROCERIES? Several convenience stores are on Harbor Boulevard near Disneyland, but no supermarkets are within easy walking distance. The closest store with a good selection is **Food-4-Less** (**food4less.com**) at 1616 W. Katella Ave. about a mile west of Disneyland Resort. **Target** is about a 5-minute drive south of Disneyland on Harbor. The adjacent **Viva Bargain Center** is a good place for cheap supplies.

A MIXED DRINK OR BEER? If you are in Disneyland Park, you are out of luck unless you're fortunate enough to have an ultraexpensive membership to the exclusive Club 33 hidden in New Orleans Square. You will have to exit the park and try one of the hotels or Downtown Disney. At DCA alcoholic beverages are readily available.

SOME RAINGEAR? At Disneyland, raingear is available at most shops but is not always displayed. You have to ask for it. Ponchos are $9.50 for adults and $8.50 for kids, and umbrellas are $20 and up.

A CURE FOR THIS HEADACHE? Aspirin and various other sundries can be purchased on Main Street at the Emporium in Disneyland Park and at Elias and Co. at the DCA entrance plaza (they keep them behind the counter, so you have to ask). You'll also find basic medical supplies in each hotel's gift shop.

A PRESCRIPTION FILLED? Unfortunately, there is no place in Disneyland Resort to have a prescription filled. The nearest full-service pharmacy is the **Walgreens** on Harbor Boulevard at Chapman Avenue, about 1.5 miles south of Disneyland.

A DOCTOR? HouseCall Physicians (☎ 800-362-7911) will make house calls to your hotel room 24/7. The fee is $350 per house call plus incidentals (such as medications dispensed), payable at the time of the visit. The closest hospital to Disneyland is the **University California Irvine Medical Center,** which is about 2 miles distant at Chapman Avenue and City Drive. For dental emergencies, there is **7 Day Dental** at 637 N. Euclid St. in Anaheim, ☎ 866-856-4335.

If you are staying at a Disneyland on-site hotel, dial 911 on the in-house phone to connect with the resort's medical services, who can send a registered nurse to your room free of charge.

SUNTAN LOTION? Suntan lotion and various other sundries can be purchased in Disneyland Park on Main Street at the Emporium and at Elias and Co. at the DCA entrance plaza (they keep them behind the counter, so you have to ask).

A SMOKE? You won't find cigarettes for sale at Disneyland parks, and you'll have a hard time finding a place to smoke any that you bring with you. Smoking is strongly discouraged throughout the parks and resorts, though there are a few designated smoking areas.

FEMININE-HYGIENE PRODUCTS? These are available in most women's restrooms at Disneyland Resort.

CASH? Basic banking services and foreign currency exchange are provided at City Hall in Disneyland Park, Guest Relations at DCA, Travelex in Downtown Disney, and the front desks of Disneyland hotels. At Travelex you can also exchange travelers' checks or receive cash advances on MasterCard and Visa credit cards. ATMs can be found in the following places:

AT DISNEYLAND PARK

- Outside the main entrance
- On Main Street, next to the *Disneyland Story* at the Town Square end
- At the entrance to Frontierland on the left
- Near Fantasyland Theatre
- In Tomorrowland, near Starcade

AT DOWNTOWN DISNEY

- Next to Häagen-Dazs
- At the Lego Imagination Center

AT DISNEY CALIFORNIA ADVENTURE

- Outside the main entrance
- At the phone and locker complex just inside the main entrance and to the right
- Near the restrooms at Hollywood Land
- Near the restrooms on Pacific Wharf
- Near the restrooms behind Flo's V8 Cafe in Cars Land
- Near Mickey's Fun Wheel at Paradise Pier
- Near the restrooms across from The Little Mermaid: Ariel's Undersea Adventure entrance
- Outside the restrooms near Paradise Gardens Grill

A PLACE TO LEAVE MY PET? Pets are not allowed in the parks (except for service dogs). Kennels and holding facilities are provided for the temporary care of your pets and are located at the parking garage. If you are adamant, the folks at the kennels will accept custody of just about any type of animal. Owners of pets, exotic or otherwise, must themselves place their charge in the assigned cage. Small pets (mice, hamsters, birds, snakes, turtles, alligators, and the like) must arrive in their own escape-proof quarters. Kennels cost $20 per pet, per day and are located to the right of the Disneyland Park main entrance. For more information, call ☎ 714-781-4565. There are several other details you may need to know:

- Advance reservations for animals are not accepted.
- Kennel employees are not permitted to handle your pet, so you will need to

transfer your pet to and from its enclosure and return during the day to walk him or her.

- Cash, credit, or Disney dollars are accepted.
- Kennels open 30 minutes before and close 30 minutes after theme park operating hours.
- Pets may not be boarded overnight.
- Guests leaving exotic pets should supply food for their pet.
- On busy days, there is a 1- to 2-hour bottleneck at the kennel, beginning 30 minutes before the park opens. If you need to use the kennels on such a day, arrive at least 1 hour before the park's stated opening time.
- Pets are fed on request only (yours, not your pet's), and there is no additional charge for food.
- For dogs over 4 months old, proof of current rabies, distemper, and hepatitis vaccines is required. For cats over 4 months old, proof of rabies, panleukopenia, rhinotracheitis, and calicivirus vaccines is required.

A PLACE TO CHARGE MY CELL PHONE? Disneyland Park offers cell phone charging lockers in the locker facility near Main Street's Market House. They cost $2 per hour, and you can pick one with common connectors built-in (iPhone, Android, and BlackBerry) or a standard power outlet to use with your own charger. A few free accessible power outlets can be found around the parks (our favorites are along the stage in *Great Moments with Mr. Lincoln,* inside Miss Chris's Cabin at Big Thunder Ranch, and in the balcony in the Golden Horseshoe); just be sure not to block traffic or remove any installed plugs or covers.

CAMERAS AND MEMORY CARDS? You can buy a disposable camera, with or without a flash, in both parks. You can buy film, digital memory cards, and batteries throughout the parks. If you'd rather let professionals take the pictures, Disney PhotoPass photographers are stationed at scenic spots around the parks. They'll take your snapshot with their camera (and yours, if you request) for free, and then hand you a PhotoPass identification card, which you can continue using during your vacation. Then stop by Main Street Photo Supply in Disneyland Park or Kingswell Camera Shop in DCA (go at midafternoon to avoid long lines), or log onto **disneyphotopass.com** within 30 days of your visit to preview and purchase all your pictures. You can purchase prints individually ($15 and up), along with books, mugs, and mouse pads. Or order a photo CD with all of your high-resolution pictures for about $70, and print them at your local drugstore for less. For $100 ($70 if ordered online at least 14 days in advance of your trip) PhotoPass+ combines your photo CD (including select attraction photos) with a CD of stock images and free printed photos at character restaurants. This package is a great bargain if you take full advantage of the ride and dinner photos.

PART THREE

DISNEYLAND *with* KIDS

I am very grateful for the help your book gave me. The best part was that there were no surprises that spoiled the fun. I was ready for rain, wind, cold, expensive food, small child meltdowns, and 40-minute potty stops for the grandparents (well, maybe not quite ready for the 40-minute potty stops). I did need an hour alone in the Grand Californian bar after the third day.

—Mom from Lompoc, California

The BRUTAL TRUTH About FAMILY VACATIONS

IT HAS BEEN SUGGESTED that the phrase *family vacation* is a bit of an oxymoron because you can never take a vacation from the responsibilities of parenting if your children are traveling with you. Though you leave work and normal routine far behind, your children require as much attention, if not more, when traveling as they do at home.

Parenting on the road requires imagination and organization. You have to do all the usual stuff (feed, dress, bathe, supervise, comfort, discipline, and so on) in an atmosphere where your children are hyperstimulated, without the familiarity of place and the resources available at home. Though not impossible—and possibly even fun—parenting on the road is not something you want to learn on the fly.

The point is that preparation, or the lack thereof, can make or break your Disneyland vacation. Believe us: You don't want to leave the success of your expensive Disney vacation to chance. Your preparation can be organized into several categories: mental, emotional, physical, organizational, and logistical. You also need a basic understanding of the two theme parks and a well-considered plan for how to go about seeing them.

MENTAL *and* EMOTIONAL PREPARATION

MENTAL PREPARATION BEGINS with realistic expectations about your Disney vacation and consideration of what each adult and child in your party most wants and needs from his or her Disneyland experience. Getting in touch with this aspect of planning requires a lot of introspection and good, open family communication.

DIVISION OF LABOR

TALK ABOUT WHAT YOU AND YOUR PARTNER NEED and what you expect to happen on the vacation. This discussion alone can pre-empt some unpleasant surprises mid-trip. If you are a two-parent family, do you have a clear understanding of how the parenting workload will be distributed? We've seen some distinctly disruptive misunderstandings in two-parent households in which one parent is (pardon the legalese) the primary caregiver. Often, the other parent expects the primary care-giver to function on vacation as she (or he) does at home. The primary caregiver, on the other hand, is ready for a break. She expects her part-ner to either shoulder the load equally or perhaps even assume the lion's share so she can have a real vacation. However you divide the respon-sibility, of course, is up to you. Just make sure that you negotiate a clear understanding before you leave home.

TOGETHERNESS

ANOTHER DIMENSION TO CONSIDER is how much togetherness seems appropriate to you. For some parents, a vacation represents a rare opportunity to really connect with their children, to talk, exchange ideas, and get reacquainted. For others, a vacation affords the time to get a little distance, to enjoy a round of golf while the kids are enjoying the theme park. The point here is to think about your and your chil-dren's preferences and needs concerning your time together. A typical day at a Disney theme park provides the structure of experiencing attractions together, punctuated by periods of waiting in line, eating, and so on, which facilitate conversation and sharing. Most attractions can be enjoyed together by the whole family, regardless of age ranges. This allows for more consensus and less dissent when it comes to decid-ing what to see and do. For many parents and children, however, the rhythms of a Disneyland day seem to consist of passive entertainment experiences alternated with endless discussions of where to go and what to do next. As a mother from Winston-Salem, North Carolina, reported:

> Our family mostly talked about what to do next with very little shar-ing or discussion about what we had seen. [The conversation] was pretty task-oriented.

Two observations: First, fighting the crowds and keeping the family moving along can easily escalate into a pressure-driven outing. Having a plan or itinerary eliminates moment-to-moment guesswork and decision making, thus creating more time for savoring and connecting. Second, external variables such as crowd size, noise, and weather, among others, can be so distracting as to preclude any meaningful togetherness. These negative impacts can be moderated, as previously discussed in Part One, by being selective concerning the time of year, day of the week, and the time of day you visit the theme parks, as well as the number of days of your visit. The bottom line is that you can achieve the degree of connection and togetherness you desire with a little advance planning and a realistic awareness of the distractions you will encounter.

LIGHTEN UP

PREPARE YOURSELF MENTALLY to be a little less compulsive on vacation about correcting small behavioral deviations and pounding home the lessons of life. Certainly, little Mildred will have to learn eventually that it's very un-Disney-like to take off her top at the pool. But there's plenty of time for that later. So what if Matt eats hamburgers for breakfast, lunch, and dinner every day? You can make him eat peas and broccoli when you get home. Roll with the little stuff, and remember when your children act out that they are wired to the max. At least some of that adrenaline is bound to spill out in undesirable ways. Coming down hard will send an already frayed little nervous system into orbit.

SOMETHING FOR EVERYONE

unofficial **TIP**
Try to schedule some time alone with each of your children—if not each day, then at least a couple of times during the trip.

IF YOU TRAVEL WITH AN INFANT, toddler, or any child who requires a lot of special attention, make sure that you have some energy and time remaining for the rest of your brood. In the course of your planning, invite each child to name something special to do or see at Disneyland with Mom or Dad alone. Work these special activities into your trip itinerary. Whatever else, if you commit, write it down so that you don't forget. Remember that a casually expressed willingness to do this or that may be perceived as a promise.

WHOSE IDEA *WAS* THIS, ANYWAY?

THE DISCORD THAT MANY VACATIONING families experience arises from the kids being on a completely different wavelength from Mom and Dad. Parents and grandparents are often worse than children when it comes to conjuring fantasy scenarios of what a Disneyland vacation will be like. It can be many things, but believe us when we tell you that there's a lot more to it than just riding Dumbo and seeing Mickey.

In our experience, most parents and nearly all grandparents expect children to enter a state of rapture at Disneyland, bouncing from attraction to attraction in wide-eyed wonder, appreciative beyond words to their adult benefactors. What they get, more often than not, is not even in the same ballpark. Preschoolers will, without a doubt, be wide-eyed, often with delight but also with a general sense of being overwhelmed by noise, crowds, and Disney characters as big as tool-sheds. We've substantiated through thousands of interviews and surveys that the best part of a Disney vacation for a preschooler is the hotel swimming pool. With some grade-schoolers and pre-driving-age teens, you get near-manic hyperactivity coupled with periods of studied nonchalance. This last phenomenon, which relates to the importance of being cool at all costs, translates into a maddening display of boredom and a "been there, done that" attitude. Older teens are frequently the exponential version of the younger teens and grade-schoolers, except without the manic behavior.

As a function of probability, you may escape many—but most likely not all—of the above behaviors. Even in the event that they are all visited on you, however, take heart; there are antidotes.

unofficial **TIP**
The more information your kids have before arriving at Disneyland, the less likely they'll be to act out.

For preschoolers, you can keep things light and happy by limiting the time you spend in the theme parks. The most critical point is that the overstimulation of the parks must be balanced by adequate rest and more-mellow activities. For grade-schoolers and early teens, you can moderate the hyperactivity and false ennui by

enlisting their help in planning the vacation, especially by allowing them to take a leading role in determining the itinerary for days at the theme parks. Putting them in charge of specific responsibilities that focus on the happiness of other family members also works well. For example, one reader turned a 12-year-old liability into an asset by asking him to help guard against attractions that might frighten his 5-year-old sister. Knowledge enhances anticipation and at the same time affords a level of comfort and control that helps kids understand the big picture. The more they feel in control, the less they will act out of control.

BASIC CONSIDERATIONS:
Is Disneyland for You?

ALMOST ALL VISITORS ENJOY Disneyland on some level and find things to see and do that they like. In fact, for many, the theme park attractions are just the tip of the iceberg. The more salient question, then (since this is a family vacation), is whether the members of your family basically like the same things. If you do, fine. If not, how will you handle the differing agendas?

A mother from Toronto wrote a few years ago describing her husband's aversion to Disney's (in his terms) "phony, plastic, and idealized version of life." Touring the theme parks, he was a real cynic and managed to diminish the experience for the rest of the family. As it happened, however, Dad's pejorative point of view didn't extend to the area golf courses. So Mom packed him up and sent him golfing while the family enjoyed the theme parks.

If you have someone in your family who doesn't like theme parks or, for whatever reason, doesn't care for Disney's brand of entertainment, it helps to get the attitude out in the open. We recommend dealing with the person up front. Glossing over or ignoring the contrary opinion and hoping that "Tom will like it once he gets there" is naive and unrealistic. Either leave Tom at home or help him discover and plan activities that he will enjoy, resigning yourself in the process to the fact that the family won't be together at all times.

DIFFERENT FOLKS, DIFFERENT STROKES

IT'S NO SECRET THAT we at The Unofficial Guides believe that thorough planning is an essential key to a successful Disneyland vacation. It's also no secret that our emphasis on planning rubs some folks the wrong way. Bob's sister and her husband, for example, are spontaneous people and do not appreciate the concept of detailed planning or, more particularly, following one of our touring plans when they visit the theme parks. To them the most important thing is to relax, take things as they come, and enjoy the moment. Sometimes they arrive at 10:30 in the morning (impossibly late for us Unofficial Guide types), walk around enjoying the landscaping and architecture, and then sit with a cup of espresso, watching other guests race around the park like maniacs. They would be the first to admit that they don't see many attractions, but experiencing attractions is not what lights their sparklers.

Not coincidentally, most of our readers are big on planning. When they go to the theme park, they want to experience the attractions, and the shorter the lines, the better. In a word, they are willing to sacrifice some spontaneity for touring efficiency.

We want you to have the best possible time, whatever that means to you, so plan (or not) according to your preference. The point here is that most families are not entirely in agreement on this planning versus spontaneity issue. If you are a serious planner and your oldest daughter and husband are free spirits, you have the makings of a problem. In practice, the way this and similar scenarios shake out is that the planner (usually the more assertive or type-A person) just takes over. Sometimes daughter and husband go along and everything works out, but just as often they feel resentful. There are as many ways of developing a win-win compromise as there are well-intentioned people on different sides of this situation. How you settle it is up to you. We're simply suggesting that you examine the problem and work out the solution before you go on vacation.

THE NATURE OF THE BEAST

THOUGH MANY PARENTS DON'T REALIZE IT, there is no law that says you must take your kids to Disneyland or Walt Disney World. Likewise, there's no law that says you will enjoy Disneyland. And though we will help you make the most of any visit, we can't change the basic nature of the beast—er, mouse. A Disneyland vacation is an active and physically demanding undertaking. Regimentation, getting up early, lots of walking, waiting in lines, fighting crowds, and (often) enduring the hot California sun are as intrinsic to a Disneyland vacation as stripes are to a zebra. Especially if you're traveling with children, you'll need a sense of humor, more than a modicum of patience, and the ability to roll with the punches.

KNOW THYSELF AND NOTHING TO EXCESS

THIS GOOD ADVICE WAS made available to ancient Greeks courtesy of the oracle of Apollo at Delphi. First, concerning the "know thyself" part, do some serious thinking about what you want in a vacation. Entertain the notion that having fun and deriving pleasure from your vacation may be very different indeed from doing and seeing as much as possible.

unofficial **TIP**
You can have a perfectly wonderful time at Disneyland if you're realistic, organized, and prepared.

Because Disneyland Resort is expensive, many families confuse seeing everything to get your money's worth with having a great time. Sometimes the two are compatible, but more often they're not. So if sleeping in, relaxing with the paper over coffee, sunbathing by the pool, or taking a nap rank high on your vacation hit parade, you need to give them due emphasis on your Disney visit (are you listening?), even if it means that you see less of the theme parks.

Which brings us to the "nothing to excess" part. At the Disneyland parks, especially if you're touring with children, less is definitely more. Trust us: It's tough to go full tilt from dawn to dusk in the theme parks. First you'll get tired, then you'll get cranky, and then you'll adopt a production mentality ("We have three more rides, and then we can go back to the hotel"). Finally, you'll hit the wall because you just can't maintain the pace.

This mom had a great vacation, but not exactly the vacation she had been expecting:

> I was unprepared for traveling with a 2-year-old. All the indoor rides were deemed too dark and scary, and all she wanted to do was see the characters (which I thought she'd be petrified of!). We had a great trip once I threw all my maps and plans out the window and just went with the flow! . . . We all would have appreciated more pool time. Think twice before bringing a 2-year-old. It is one exhausting trip!

unofficial **TIP**
Get a grip on your needs and preferences before you leave home, and develop an itinerary that incorporates all the things that make you happiest.

Plan on seeing the Disneyland parks in bite-size chunks with plenty of swimming, napping, and relaxing in between. Most Disneyland vacations are short. Even if you have to stay an extra day to build in some relaxation, you'll be happier while you're there and more rested when you get home. Ask yourself over and over in both the planning stage and while you are at Disneyland: What will contribute the greatest contentedness, satisfaction, and harmony? Trust your instincts. If stopping for ice cream or returning to the hotel for a dip feels like more fun than seeing another attraction, do it—even if it means wasting the remaining hours of an expensive admissions pass.

The AGE THING

THERE'S A LOT OF SERIOUS COGITATION among parents and grandparents in regard to how old a child should be before embarking on a trip to Disneyland. The answer, not always obvious, stems from the personalities and maturity of the children, and the personalities and parenting style of the adults.

Disneyland for Infants and Toddlers

We believe that traveling with infants and toddlers is a great idea. Developmentally, travel is a stimulating learning experience for even the youngest of children. Infants, of course, won't know Mickey Mouse from a draft horse but will respond to sun and shade, music, bright colors, and the extra attention they receive from you. From first steps to full mobility, toddlers respond to the excitement and spectacle of the Disneyland parks, though of course in a much different way than you do. Your toddler will prefer splashing in fountains and clambering over curbs and benches to experiencing most attractions, but no matter: He or she will still have a great time.

An Iowa City, Iowa, mother of three says, "Get over it!":

> Get over it! In my opinion, people think too much about the age thing. If taking your 3-year-old would make you happy, that's all that counts. It doesn't matter if the trip is really for you or your child. You shouldn't have to jump through hoops to give yourself permission to go.

Somewhere between 4 and 6 years of age, your child will experience the first vacation that he or she will remember as an adult. Though more likely to remember the coziness of the hotel room than the theme parks, the child will be able to experience and comprehend many attractions. Even so, his or her favorite activity is likely to be swimming in the hotel pool.

unofficial **TIP**
Traveling with infants and toddlers sharpens parenting skills and makes the entire family more mobile and flexible, resulting in a richer, fuller life for all.

As concerns infants and toddlers, there are good reasons and bad reasons for vacationing at Disneyland. A good reason for taking your little one to Disneyland Resort is that you want to go and there's no one available to care for your child during your absence. Philosophically, we are very much against putting your life (including your vacation) on hold until your children are older.

Especially if you have children of varying ages (or plan to, for that matter), it's better to take the show on the road than to wait until the youngest reaches the perceived ideal age. If your family includes a toddler or infant, you will find everything from private facilities for breast-feeding to changing tables in both men's and women's rest-rooms to facilitate baby's care.

unofficial TIP
Baby supplies—including disposable diapers, for-mula, and baby food—are for sale, and rockers and special chairs are available for nursing mothers at each park's Baby Care Center.

An illogical reason, however, for taking an infant or toddler to Disneyland Resort is that you think Disneyland is the perfect vacation des-tination for babies. It's not, so think again if you are contemplating Disneyland Resort primarily for your child's enjoyment. For starters, attrac-tions are geared more toward older children and adults. Even designer play areas such as the Pirate's Lair on Tom Sawyer Island in Disneyland Park are developed with older children in mind.

Remember when you were little and you got that nifty electric train for Christmas, the one with which Dad wouldn't let you play? Did you ever wonder for whom that train was really? Ask yourself the same question about your vacation to Disneyland Resort. Whose dream are you trying to make come true: yours or your child's?

That said, let us stress that for the well prepared, taking a tod-dler to Disneyland Resort can be a totally glorious experience. There's truly nothing like watching your child respond to the color, the sound, the festivity, and, most of all, the characters. You'll return home with scrapbooks of photos that you will treasure forever. Your little one won't remember much, but your memories will be unforgettable.

If you elect to take your infant or toddler to Disneyland Resort, rest assured that their needs have been anticipated. The theme parks have centralized facilities for infant and toddler care. Everything necessary for changing diapers, preparing formula, and warming bottles and food is available. At the Disneyland Park, the Baby Care Center is next to the Plaza Inn at the end of Main Street and to the right. At DCA the Baby Care Center is tucked out of the way next to the Ghirardelli Chocolate Factory in the Pacific Wharf area of the park. Dads in charge of little ones are welcome at the centers and can use most services offered. In addition, men's rooms in the parks have changing tables.

Infants and toddlers are allowed to experience any attraction that doesn't have minimum height or age restrictions. A mother of three from Utah wrote to us, saying:

> We traveled with my 9-month-old, so we did the switching-off option a lot. However, I would appreciate it if you listed in the guide a complete list of all the rides that babies can be carried on. I was there alone with all three kids while my husband had to work for part of the time, and it would've been really nice to just look at a list of all the rides that we could've gone on with a baby.

It's actually far easier to list the attractions that you *can't* take a baby on at Disneyland. Unless a minimum height or age requirement is explicitly posted, children of any size—even handheld infants—are welcome on any ride. That includes all the family dark rides, kid-die carnival attractions, and slow-moving boats. On the next page

ATTRACTION MINIMUM HEIGHT REQUIREMENTS

DISNEYLAND PARK

AUTOPIA 32" minimum height (54" to drive unassisted)

BIG THUNDER MOUNTAIN RAILROAD 40" minimum height

GADGET'S GO COASTER 35" minimum height

INDIANA JONES ADVENTURE 46" minimum height

MATTERHORN BOBSLEDS 42" minimum height

SPACE MOUNTAIN 40" minimum height

SPLASH MOUNTAIN 40" minimum height

STAR TOURS—THE ADVENTURES CONTINUE 40" minimum height

DISNEY CALIFORNIA ADVENTURE

CALIFORNIA SCREAMIN' 48" minimum height

GOOFY'S SKY SCHOOL 42" minimum height

GRIZZLY RIVER RUN 42" minimum height

JUMPIN' JELLYFISH 40" minimum height

LUIGI'S ROLLICKIN' ROADSTERS 32" minimum height

MATER'S JUNKYARD JAMBOREE 32" minimum height

RADIATOR SPRINGS RACERS 40" minimum height

REDWOOD CREEK CHALLENGE TRAIL 42" minimum height *(rock wall and zip line only)*

SILLY SYMPHONY SPRINGS 40" minimum height (tandem swing) 48" minimum height (single swing)

SOARIN' OVER CALIFORNIA 40" minimum height

TUCK AND ROLL'S DRIVE 'EM BUGGIES 36" minimum height

THE TWILIGHT ZONE TOWER OF TERROR 40" minimum height

is a table of all the rides that do impose a height restriction; if a ride isn't listed, you can bring the young 'uns along. But as a Minneapolis mother reports, some attractions are better for babies than others:

> *Shows and boat rides are easier for babies (ours was almost 1 year old, not yet walking). Rides where a bar comes down are doable but harder. Peter Pan's Flight was our first encounter with this type, and we had barely gotten situated when I realized that he might fall out of my grasp. The 3-D films are too intense; the noise level is deafening and the images inescapable.*
>
> *You don't have a rating system for babies, and I don't expect to see one, but I thought you might want to know what a baby thought (based on his reactions). At Disneyland Park: Jungle Cruise: didn't get into it. Pirates of the Caribbean: slept through it. Mark Twain River-boat: the horn made him cry. It's a Small World: wide-eyed, took it all in. Peter Pan's Flight: couldn't really sit on the seat. A bit danger-ous. He didn't get into it. Disneyland Railroad: liked the motion and scenery. Enchanted Tiki Room: loved it. Danced, clapped, sang along.*

The same mom also advises:

We used a baby sling on our trip and thought it was great when standing in the lines—much better than a stroller, which you have to park before getting in line and navigate through crowds. It is impractical to go to the Baby Care Center every time your baby needs to nurse, so moms should be comfortable nursing in public situations.

The rental strollers at the parks are designed for toddlers and children up to 4 and 5 years old but definitely not for infants. Still, if you bring pillows and padding, the strollers can be made to work. You can alternatively bring your own stroller, but only a limited number of noncollapsible strollers fit on each parking tram, and large strollers may not fit on the Toy Story lot's shuttle buses.

unofficial **TIP**
In addition to providing an alternative to carrying your child, a stroller serves as a handy cart for diaper bags, water bottles, and other necessary items.

Even if you opt for a stroller (your own or a rental), we also recommend that you also bring a baby sling or baby/child backpack. Simply put, there will be many times in the theme parks when you will have to park the stroller and carry your child.

One point that needs addressing is the perception that there are not many good places in the theme parks for breast-feeding. Many nursing moms recommend breast-feeding during a dark Disney theater presentation. This only works, however, if the presentation is long enough for the baby to finish nursing. Shows at the Hyperion Theater at DCA are long enough at about 45 minutes, but the theater is not as dark as those that show films. Tomorrowland Theater at Disneyland Park is way too loud, as is *Muppet-Vision 3-D* at DCA.

unofficial **TIP**
Infants are easy travelers. As long as they are fed and comfortable, there is really no limit to what you can do when on the road with little ones. Food plus adequate rest is the perfect formula for happy babies.

Many Disney shows run back-to-back with only 1 or 2 minutes in between to change the audience. If you want to breast-feed and require more time than the length of the show, tell the cast member on entering that you want to breast-feed and ask if you can remain in the theater while your baby finishes.

If you can adjust to nursing in more public places with your breast and the baby's head covered with a shawl or some such, nursing will not be a problem at all. Even on the most crowded days, you can always find a back corner of a restaurant or a comparatively secluded park bench or garden spot to nurse.

Disneyland for 4-, 5-, and 6-year-olds

Kids in this age group vary immensely in their capacity to comprehend and enjoy Disneyland Resort. With this age group, the go/no-go decision is a judgment call. If your child is sturdy, easygoing, and fairly adventuresome, and demonstrates a high degree of independence, the trip will probably work. On the other hand, if your child tires easily, is temperamental, or is a bit timid or reticent in embracing new experiences, you're much better off waiting a few years. Whereas the travel and sensory-overload problems of infants and toddlers can be addressed and (usually) remedied on the go, discontented 4- to 6-year-olds have the ability to stop a family dead in its tracks, as this mother of three from Cape May, New Jersey, attests:

> My 5-year-old was scared pretty badly on Snow White's Scary Adventures our first day. For the rest of the trip, we had to coax and reassure her before each and every ride before she would go.

If you have a retiring, clinging, and/or difficult 4- to 6-year-old who, for whatever circumstances, will be part of your group, you can sidestep or diminish potential problems with a bit of preparation. Even if your preschooler is plucky and game, the same prep measures (described later in this section) will enhance his or her experience and make life easier for the rest of the family.

Parents who understand that a visit with 4- to 6-year-old children is going to be more about the cumulative experience than about seeing it all will have wonderful memories of their children's amazement.

The Ideal Age

Though our readers report successful trips as well as disasters with children of all ages, the consensus is that children's ages ideal for family compatibility and togetherness at Disneyland are 8–12 years. This age group is old enough, tall enough, and sufficiently stalwart to experience, understand, and appreciate practically all Disney attractions. Moreover, they are developed to the extent that they can get around the parks on their own steam without being carried or collapsing. Best of all, they are still young enough to enjoy being with Mom and Dad. From our experience, ages 10–12 are better than 8–9, though what you gain in maturity is at the cost of that irrepressible, wide-eyed wonder so prevalent in the 8- and 9-year-olds.

Disneyland for Teens

Teens love Disneyland, and for parents of teens, Disneyland Resort is a nearly perfect, albeit expensive, vacation choice. Though your teens might not be as wide-eyed and impressionable as their younger sibs, they are at an age where they can sample, understand, and enjoy practically everything Disneyland Resort has to offer.

For parents Disneyland Resort is a vacation destination where you can permit your teens an extraordinary amount of freedom. The entertainment is wholesome, the venues are safe, and the entire complex of hotels, theme parks, restaurants, and shopping is easily accessible on foot. Because most adolescents relish freedom, you may have difficulty keeping your teens with the rest of the family. Thus, if one of your objectives is to spend time with your teenage children during your Disneyland vacation, you will need to establish some clear-cut guidelines regarding togetherness and separateness before you leave home. Make your teens part of the discussion and try to meet them halfway in crafting a decision with which everyone can live. For your teens, touring on their own at Disneyland is tantamount to being independent in an exotic city. It's intoxicating, to say the least, and can be an excellent learning experience, if not a rite of passage. In any event, we're not suggesting that you just turn them loose. Rather, we are just attempting to sensitize you to the fact that, for your teens, some transcendent issues are involved. (Children must be at least 14 years old to enter a Disneyland Resort park without an accompanying parent or guardian.)

Most teens crave the company of other teens. If you have a solitary teen in your family, do not be surprised if he or she wants to invite a friend on your vacation. If you are invested in sharing intimate, quality time with your solitary teen, the presence of a friend will make this more difficult, if not impossible. However, if you turn down the request to bring a friend, be prepared to go the extra mile to be a companion to your teen at Disneyland. If you're a teen, it's not much fun to ride Space Mountain by yourself.

One specific issue that absolutely should be addressed before you leave home is what assistance (if any) you expect from your teen in regard to helping with younger children in the family. Once again, try to carve out a win-win compromise. Consider the case of the mother from Indiana who had a teenage daughter from an earlier marriage and two children under age 10 from a second marriage. After a couple of vacations where she thrust the unwilling teen into the position of being a surrogate parent to her half sisters, the teen declined henceforth to participate in family vacations.

Some parents have written *The Unofficial Guide* asking if there are unsafe places at Disneyland Resort or places where teens simply should not be allowed to go. Though the answer depends more on your family values and the relative maturity of your teens than on Disneyland Resort, the basic answer is no. Though it's true that teens (or adults, for that matter) who are looking for trouble can find it anywhere, there is absolutely nothing at Disneyland Resort that could be construed as a precipitant or a catalyst. Be advised, however, that adults consume alcohol at most Disneyland Resort restaurants outside of Disneyland Park. Also, be aware that some of the movies available at the cinemas at Downtown Disney demand the same discretion you exercise when allowing your kids to see movies at home.

About INVITING *Your* CHILDREN'S FRIENDS

IF YOUR CHILDREN WANT TO INVITE FRIENDS on your Disneyland vacation, give your decision careful thought. First, consider the logistics of numbers. Is there room in the car? Will you have to leave something at home that you had planned on taking to make room in the trunk for the friend's luggage? Will additional hotel rooms or a larger suite be required? Will the increased number of people in your group make it hard to get a table at a restaurant?

If you determine that you can logistically accommodate one or more friends, the next step is to consider how the inclusion of the friend will affect your group's dynamics. Generally speaking, the presence of a friend will make it harder to really connect with your own children. So if one of your vacation goals is an intimate bonding experience with your children, the addition of friends will possibly frustrate your attempts to realize that objective.

If family relationship building is not necessarily a primary objective of your vacation, it's quite possible that the inclusion of a friend will make life easier for you. This is especially true in the case of only children, who may otherwise depend exclusively on you to keep them happy and occupied. Having a friend along can take the pressure off and give you some much-needed breathing room.

If you decide to allow a friend to accompany you, limit the selection to children you know really well and whose parents you also know. Your Disneyland vacation is not the time to include "my friend Eddie from school" whom you've never met. Your children's friends who have spent time in your home will have a sense of your parenting style, and you will have a sense of their personality, behavior, and compatibility with your family. Assess the prospective child's potential to fit in well on a long trip. Is he or she polite, personable, fun to be with, and reasonably mature? Does he or she relate well to you and to the other members of your family?

Because a Disneyland vacation is not, for most of us, a spur-of-the-moment thing, you should have adequate time to evaluate potential candidate friends. A trip to the mall including a meal in a sit-down restaurant will tell you volumes about the friend. Likewise, inviting the friend to share dinner with the family and then spend the night will provide a lot of relevant information. Ideally this type of evaluation should take place early on in the normal course of family events, before you discuss the possibility of a friend joining you on your vacation. This will allow you to size things up without your child (or the friend) realizing that an evaluation is taking place.

By seizing the initiative, you can guide the outcome. For example, Ann, a Redding, California, mom, anticipated that her 12-year-old son would ask to take a friend on their vacation. As she pondered the various friends her son might propose, she came up with four names. One, an otherwise sweet child, had a medical condition that Ann felt unqualified to monitor or treat. A second friend was overly aggressive with younger children and was often socially inappropriate for his age. Two other friends, Chuck and Marty, with whom she had had a generally positive experience, were good candidates for the trip. After orchestrating some opportunities to spend time with each of the boys, she made her decision and asked her son, "Would you like to take Marty with us to Disneyland?" Her son was delighted, and Ann had diplomatically preempted having to turn down friends her son might have proposed.

We recommend that you do the inviting, instead of your child, and that the invitation be extended parent to parent (to avoid disappointment, you might want to sound out the friend's parent before broaching the issue with your child). Observing this recommendation will allow you to query the friend's parents concerning food preferences, any medical conditions, how discipline is administered in the friend's family, how the friend's parents feel about the way you administer discipline, and the parents' expectation regarding religious observations while their child is in your care.

unofficial **TIP**
We suggest that you arrange for the friend's parents to reimburse you after the trip for things such as restaurant meals and admissions. This is much easier than trying to balance the books after every expenditure.

Before you extend the invitation, give some serious thought to who pays for what. Make a specific proposal for financing the trip a part of your invitation; for example: "There's room for Marty in the hotel room, and transportation's no problem because we're driving. So we'll just need you to pick up Marty's meals, theme park admissions, and spending money."

A **FEW WORDS** *for* **SINGLE PARENTS**

BECAUSE SINGLE PARENTS ARE GENERALLY also working parents, planning a special getaway with your children can be the best way to spend some quality time together. But remember, the vacation is not just for your child—it's for you too. You might invite a grandparent or a favorite aunt or uncle along; the other adult provides nice company for you, and your child will benefit from the time with family members. You might likewise consider inviting an adult friend.

Though bringing along another adult is the best option, the reality is that many single parents don't have friends, grandparents, or favorite aunts or uncles who can make the trip. And while spending time with your child is wonderful, it is very difficult to match the energy level of your child if you are the sole focus of his or her world.

One alternative: Try to meet other single parents at Disneyland. It may seem odd, but most of them are in the same boat as you; besides, all you have to do is ask. Another option, albeit expensive, is to take along a trustworthy babysitter (18 or up) to travel with you.

The easiest way to meet other single parents is to hang out at the hotel pool. Make your way there on the day you arrive, after traveling by car or plane and without enough time to blow a full admission ticket at a theme park. In any event, a couple of hours spent poolside is a relaxing way to start your vacation.

If you visit Disneyland Resort with another single parent, get adjoining rooms; take turns watching all the kids; and, on at least one night, get a sitter and enjoy an evening out.

Throughout this book we mention the importance of good planning and touring. For a single parent, this is an absolute must. In addition, make sure that every day you set aside downtime back at the hotel.

Finally, don't try to spend every moment with your children on vacation. Instead, plan some activities for your children with other children. Then take advantage of your free time to do what you want to do: Read a book, have a massage, take a long walk, or enjoy a catnap.

"He Who Hesitates Is Launched!"
TIPS *and* WARNINGS
for GRANDPARENTS

SENIORS OFTEN GET INTO PREDICAMENTS caused by touring with grandchildren. Run ragged and pressured to endure a blistering pace, many seniors just concentrate on surviving Disneyland rather than enjoying it. The theme parks have as much to offer older visitors as they do children, and seniors must either set the pace or dispatch the young folks to tour on their own. An older reader writes:

> Being a senior is not for wusses. At Disney [parks] particularly, it requires courage and pluck. Things that used to be easy take a lot of effort, and sometimes your brain has to wait for your body to catch up. Half the time, your grandchildren treat you like a crumbling ruin, and then turn around and trick you into getting on a roller coaster in the dark. Seniors have to be alert and not trust anyone. Not their children or even the Disney people, and especially not their grandchildren. When your grandchildren want you to go on a ride, don't follow along blindly like a lamb to the slaughter. Make sure you know what the ride is all about. Stand your ground and do not waffle. He who hesitates is launched!

If you don't get to see much of your grandchildren, you might think that Disneyland is the perfect place for a little bonding and togetherness. Wrong! Disneyland can potentially send children into system overload and precipitates behaviors that pose a challenge even to adoring parents, never mind grandparents. You don't take your grandchildren straight to Disneyland for the same reason you don't buy your 16-year-old son a Ferrari: Handling it safely and well requires some experience.

Begin by spending time with your grandchildren in an environment that you can control. Have them over one at a time for dinner and to spend the night. Check out how they respond to your oversight and discipline. Most of all, zero in on whether you are compatible, enjoy each other's company, and have fun together. Determine that you can set limits and that they will accept those limits. When you reach this stage, you can contemplate some outings to the zoo, the mall, or the state fair. Gauge how demanding your grandchildren are when you are out of the house. Eat a meal or two in a full-service restaurant to get a sense of their social skills and their ability to behave appropriately. Don't expect perfection, and be prepared to modify your behavior a little too. As a senior friend of mine told her husband (none too decorously), "You can't see Disneyland sitting on a stick."

If you have a good relationship with your grandchildren and have had a positive one-on-one experience taking care of them, you might consider a trip to Disneyland. If you do, we have two recommendations. Visit Disneyland without them to get an idea of what you're getting into. A scouting trip will also provide you an opportunity to enjoy some of the attractions that won't be on the itinerary when you return with the grandkids.

Tips for Grandparents

1. It's best to take one grandchild at a time, two at the most. Cousins can be better than siblings because they don't fight as much. To preclude sibling jealousy, try connecting the trip to a child's milestone, such as finishing the sixth grade.

2. Let your grandchildren help plan the vacation, and keep the first one short. Be flexible, and don't overplan.

3. Discuss mealtimes and bedtime. Fortunately, many grandparents are on an early dinner schedule, which works nicely with younger children.

4. Gear plans to your grandchildren's age levels, because if they're not happy, you won't be happy.

5. Create an itinerary that offers some supervised activities for children in case you need a rest.

6. If you're traveling by car, this is the one time we highly recommend earphones or earbuds. Kids' musical tastes are vastly different from most grandparents'. It's simply more enjoyable when everyone can listen to his or her own preferred style of music, at least for some portion of the trip.

7. Take along a night-light.

8. Carry a notarized statement from parents for permission for medical care in case of an emergency. Also be sure that you have insurance information and copies of any prescriptions for medicines the kids may take. Ditto for eyeglass prescriptions.

9. Tell your grandchildren about any medical problems you may have, so they can be prepared if there's an emergency.

10. Many attractions and hotels offer discounts for seniors, so be sure to check ahead of time for bargains.

11. Plan your evening meal early to avoid long waits. And make reservations if you're dining in a popular spot, even if it's early. Take some crayons and paper to keep kids occupied. If planning a family-friendly trip seems overwhelming, try a tour operator–travel agent aimed at kids and their grandparents.

HOW *to* CHILDPROOF
a HOTEL ROOM

TODDLERS AND SMALL CHILDREN up to 3 years of age (and sometimes older) can wreak mayhem if not outright disaster in a hotel room. They're mobile, curious, and amazingly fast, and they have a penchant for turning the most seemingly innocuous furnishing or decoration into a lethal weapon. Here's what to look for.

Always begin by checking the room for hazards that you cannot neutralize, such as balconies, chipping paint, cracked walls, sharp surfaces, shag carpeting, and windows that can't be secured shut. If you encounter anything that you don't like or is too much of a hassle to fix, ask for another room.

If you use a crib supplied by the hotel, make sure the mattress is firm and covers the entire bottom of the crib. If there is a mattress cover, it should fit tightly. Slats should be 2⅜ inches (about the width of a soda can) or less apart. Test the drop sides to ensure that they work properly and that your child cannot release them accidentally. Examine the crib from all angles (including from underneath) to make sure that it has been assembled correctly and that there are no sharp edges. Check for potentially toxic substances that your child might ingest. Wipe down surfaces that your child might touch to diminish the potential of infection transmitted from a previous occupant. Finally, position the crib away from drape cords, heaters, wall sockets, and air conditioners.

If your infant can turn over, we recommend changing him or her on a pad on the floor. Likewise, if you have a child seat of any sort, place it where it cannot be knocked over, and always strap your child in.

If your child can roll, crawl, or walk, you should bring about eight electrical outlet covers and some cord to tie cabinets shut and to bind drape cords and the like out of reach. Check for appliances, lamps, ashtrays, ice buckets, and anything else that your child might pull down on him- or herself. Have the hotel remove coffee tables with sharp edges and both real and artificial plants that are within your child's reach. Round up items from tables and countertops such as matchbooks, courtesy toiletries, and drinking glasses and store them out of reach.

If the bathroom door can be accidentally locked, cover the locking mechanism with duct tape or a doorknob cover. Use the security chain or upper latch on the room's entrance door to ensure that your child doesn't open it without your knowledge.

Inspect the floor and remove pins, coins, and other foreign objects that your child might find. Don't forget to check under beds and furniture. One of the best tips we've heard came from a Fort Lauderdale, Florida, mother who crawls around the room on her hands and knees in order to see possible hazards from her child's perspective.

If you rent a suite, you'll have more territory to childproof and will have to deal with the possible presence of cleaning supplies, a stove, a refrigerator, cooking utensils, and low cabinet doors, among other things. Sometimes the best option is to seal off the kitchen with a folding safety gate.

PHYSICAL PREPARATION

YOU'LL FIND THAT SOME PHYSICAL CONDITIONING, coupled with a realistic sense of the toll that Disneyland takes on your body, will preclude falling apart in the middle of your vacation. As one of our readers put it, "If you pay attention to eat, heat, feet, and sleep, you'll be OK."

As you contemplate the stamina of your family, it's important to understand that somebody is going to run out of steam first, and when they do, the whole family will be affected. Sometimes a cold drink or a snack will revive the flagging member. Sometimes, however, no amount of cajoling or treats will work. In this situation it's crucial that you recognize that the child, grandparent, or spouse is at the end of his or her rope. The correct decision is to get them back to the hotel. Pushing the exhausted beyond their capacity will spoil the day for them—and you. Accept that stamina and energy levels vary, and be prepared to administer to members of your family who poop out. One more thing: No guilt trips. "We've driven 300 miles to take you to Disneyland, and now you're going to ruin everything!" is not an appropriate response.

unofficial **TIP**
If your children (or you, for that matter) think that wearing socks isn't cool, get over it! Bare feet, whether encased in Nikes, Weejuns, Docksides, or Crocs, will turn into lumps of throbbing red meat if you tackle a Disney park without socks.

THE AGONY OF THE FEET

IF YOU SPEND A DAY AT DISNEYLAND PARK, you will walk 3–6 miles! If you walk to the park from your hotel, you can add 1–2 miles, and another couple of miles if you park-hop to DCA. The walking, however, will be nothing like a 5-mile hike in the woods. At Disneyland Park and DCA, you will be in direct sunlight most of the time, navigate through huge jostling crowds, walk on hot pavement, and endure waits in line between bursts of walking. The bottom line, if you haven't figured it out, is that Disney theme parks (especially in the summer) are not for wimps!

unofficial **TIP**
Be sure to give your kids adequate recovery time between training walks (48 hours will usually be enough), however, or you'll make the problem worse.

Though most children are active, their normal play usually doesn't condition them for the exertion of touring a Disney theme park. We recommend starting a program of family walks six weeks or more before your trip. A Pennsylvania mom who did just that offers the following:

We had our 6-year-old begin walking with us a bit every day one month before leaving. When we arrived, her little legs could carry her, and she had a lot of stamina.

A father of two had this to say:

My wife walked with my son to school every day when it was nice. His stamina was outstanding.

A Riverside, Utah, dad forgot to train this year:

I think you really need to stress the importance of starting a walking regimen before going to Disneyland. Last year we had a five-day hopper, and I started walking a month ahead and ran around that place like a champ. This year I didn't walk much at all and was worn out the first day, and we only had a four-day hopper!

The first thing you need to do, immediately after making your hotel reservation, is to get thee to a footery. Take the whole family to a shoe store, and buy each member the best pair of walking, hiking, or running shoes you can afford. When trying on the shoes, wear exactly the kind of socks that you will wear when using them to hike. Do not under any circumstances attempt to tour Disneyland shod in plastic sandals, cheap flip-flops, loafers, or any kind of high heel or platform shoe (though one of our authors swears by high-quality leather sandals or river-rafting footwear, especially for water rides).

Good socks are as important as good shoes. When you walk, your feet sweat like a mule in a peat bog, and moisture increases friction. To minimize friction, wear a pair of SmartWool or Coolmax hiking socks, available at most outdoor retail (camping equipment) stores, as well as Target and online retailers. To further combat moisture, dust your feet with some antifungal talcum powder.

unofficial **TIP**
If your child is age 8 or younger, we recommend regular foot inspections whether he or she understands the hot spot idea or not. Even the brightest child will fail to sound off when distracted.

Now that you have some good shoes and socks, the next thing to do is to break the shoes in. You can accomplish this painlessly by wearing the shoes in the course of normal activities for about three weeks.

Once the shoes are broken in, it's time to start walking. The whole family will need to toughen up their feet and build endurance. As you begin, remember that little people have little strides, and though your 6-year-old may create the appearance of running circles around you, consider that (1) he won't have the stamina to go at that pace very long, and (2) more to the point, he probably has to take two strides or so to every one of yours to keep up.

Start by taking short walks around the neighborhood, walking on pavement, and increasing the distance about 0.25 mile on each outing. Older children will shape up quickly. Younger children should build endurance more slowly and incrementally. Increase distance until you can manage a 6- or 7-mile hike without requiring CPR. And remember, you're not training to be able to walk 6–7 miles just once; at Disneyland you will be hiking 5–7 miles or more almost every day of your visit. So unless you plan to crash after the first day, you need to prepare your feet to walk long distances for three to five consecutive days.

Not all feet are created equal. Some folks are blessed with really tough feet, whereas the feet of others sprout blisters if you look at them sideways. Assuming that there's nothing wrong with either shoes or socks, a few brisk walks will clue you in to what kind of feet your family members have. If you have a tenderfooted family member, walks of incrementally increased distances will usually toughen up his or her feet to some extent. For those whose feet refuse to toughen, your only alternative is preventive care. After several walks, you will know where your tenderfoot tends to develop blisters. If you can anticipate where blisters will develop, you can cover sensitive spots in advance with moleskin, a friction-resistant adhesive dressing.

When you initiate your walking program, teach your children to tell you if they feel a hot spot on their feet. This is the warning that a blister is developing. If your kids are too young, oblivious, or preoccupied, or don't understand the concept, your best bet is to make regular foot checks. Have your children remove their shoes and socks and present their feet for inspection. Look for red spots and blisters, and ask if they have any places on their feet that hurt.

During your conditioning, and also at Disneyland, carry a foot emergency kit in your day pack or hip pack. The kit should contain gauze, antibiotic ointment, an assortment of Band-Aid Blister Bandages, a sewing needle or some such to drain blisters, as well as matches to sterilize the needle. An extra pair of dry socks and talc are optional.

If you discover a hot spot, dry the foot and cover the spot immediately with a blister bandage. If a blister has fully or partially developed, first air out and dry the foot. Next, using a sterile needle, drain the fluid but do not remove the top skin. Clean the area with antibiotic ointment, and place a Band-Aid Blister Bandage over the blister. If you do not have Band-Aid Blister Bandages, do not try to cover the hot spot or blister with regular Band-Aids. Regular Band-Aids slip and wad up. Head to First Aid instead.

*un*official **TIP**
If you have a child who will physically fit in a stroller, rent one, no matter how well conditioned your family is.

A stroller will provide the child the option of walking or riding, and, if he poops out, you won't have to carry him. Even if your child hardly uses the stroller, it serves as a convenient place for water bottles and other stuff you may not feel like carrying. Strollers at Disneyland are covered in detail on beginning on page 133.

SLEEP, REST, AND RELAXATION

OK, WE KNOW THAT THIS DISCUSSION is about physical preparation before you go, but this concept is so absolutely critical that we need to tattoo it on your brain right now.

Physical conditioning is important but is not a substitute for rest. Even marathon runners need recovery time. If you push too hard and try to do too much, you'll either crash or, at a minimum, turn what should be fun into an ordeal. Rest means plenty of sleep at night and, if possible, naps during the afternoon and planned breaks in your vacation itinerary. And don't forget that the brain, as well as the body, needs rest and relaxation. The stimulation inherent in touring a Disney theme park is enough to put many children and some adults into system overload. It is imperative that you remove your family from this unremitting assault on the senses and do something relaxing and quiet such as swimming or reading.

The theme parks are pretty big, so don't try to see everything in one day. Even during the off-season, when the crowds are smaller and the temperatures more pleasant, the size of the theme parks will exhaust most children under age 8 by lunchtime. A Texas family underscores the importance of naps and rest:

Despite not following any of your tours, we did follow the theme of visiting a specific park in the morning, leaving midafternoon for either a nap back at the room or a trip to the pool, and then returning to one of the parks in the evening. On the few occasions when we skipped your advice, I was muttering to myself by dinner. I can't tell you what I was muttering.

When it comes to naps, this mom does not mince words:

One last thing for parents of small kids—take the book's advice and get out of the park and take the nap, take the nap, TAKE THE NAP! Never in my life have I seen so many parents screaming at, ridiculing, or slapping their kids. (What a vacation!) Disney [parks are] overwhelming for kids and adults.

A mom from Rochester, New York, was equally adamant:

You absolutely must rest during the day. Kids went from 8 a.m. to 9 p.m. in the park. Kids did great that day, but we were all completely worthless the next day. Definitely must pace yourself.

If you plan to return to your hotel at midday and would like your room made up, let housekeeping know before you leave in the morning.

Routines That Travel

If when at home you observe certain routines—for example, reading a book before bed or having a bath first thing in the morning—try to incorporate these familiar activities into your vacation schedule. They will provide your children with a sense of security and normalcy.

Maintaining a normal routine is especially important with toddlers, as a mother of two from Lawrenceville, Georgia, relates:

The first day, we tried an early start, so we woke the children (ages 2 and 4) and hurried them to get going. BAD IDEA with toddlers. This put them off schedule for naps and meals the rest of the day. It is best to let young ones stay on their regular schedule and see Disney at their own pace, and you'll have much more fun.

DEVELOPING *a* GOOD PLAN

ALLOW YOUR CHILDREN to participate in the planning of your time at Disneyland. Guide them diplomatically through the options, establishing advance decisions about what to do each day. Begin with your trip to Disneyland, deciding what time to depart, who sits by the window, whether to stop for meals or eat in the car, and so on. For the Disneyland part of your vacation, build consensus for wake-up call, bedtime, and building naps into the itinerary, and establish ground rules for eating, buying refreshments, and shopping. Determine the order for visiting the two theme parks and make a list of must-see attractions. To help you fill in the blanks of your days, and especially to prevent you from spending most of your time standing in line, we offer a number of field-tested touring plans. The plans are designed to minimize your waiting time at each park by providing step-by-step itineraries that route you counter to the flow of traffic. The plans are explained in greater detail starting on page 265.

*un*official **TIP**

To keep your thinking fresh and to adequately cover all bases, develop your plan in two or three family meetings no longer than 40 minutes each. You'll discover that all members of the family will devote a lot of thought to the plan both in and between meetings. Don't try to anticipate every conceivable contingency, or you'll end up with something as detailed and unworkable as the tax code.

Generally, it's better to just sketch in the broad strokes on the master plan. The detail of what to do when you actually arrive at the park can be decided the night before you go, or with the help of one of our touring plans once you get there. Above all, be flexible. One important caveat: Make sure that you keep any promises or agreements that you make when planning. They may not seem important to you, but they will to your children, who will remember for a long, long time if you let them down.

The more you can agree to and nail down in advance, the less potential you'll have for disagreement and confrontation once you arrive. Because children are more comfortable with the tangible than the conceptual, and also because they sometimes have short memories, we recommend typing up all of your decisions and agreements and providing a copy to each child. Create a fun document, not a legalistic one. You'll find that your children will review it in anticipation of all the things they will see and do, will consult it often, and will even read it to their younger siblings.

By now you're probably wondering what one of these documents looks like, so we've provided a sample on pages 121–122. Incidentally, this itinerary reflects the preferences of its creators, the Shelton family, and is not meant to be offered as an example of an ideal itinerary. It does, however, incorporate many of our most basic and strongly held recommendations, such as setting limits and guidelines in advance, getting enough rest, getting to the theme parks early, and saving time and money by having a cooler full of food for breakfast. As you will see, the Sheltons go pretty much full tilt without much unstructured time and will probably be exhausted by the time they get home, but

THE GREAT DISNEYLAND EXPEDITION

COCAPTAINS Mary and Jack Shelton

TEAM MEMBERS Lynn and Jimmy Shelton

EXPEDITION FUNDING The main Expedition Fund will cover everything except personal purchases. Each team member will receive $40 for souvenirs and personal purchases. Anything above $40 will be paid for by team members with their own money.

EXPEDITION GEAR Each team member will wear an official expedition T-shirt and carry a hip pack.

PREDEPARTURE Jack makes dining reservations at Disneyland restaurants. Mary, Lynn, and Jimmy make up trail mix and other snacks for the hip packs.

SHELTON FAMILY ITINERARY

DAY 1: FRIDAY

- **6:30 p.m.** Dinner • **After dinner** Pack car • **10 p.m.** Lights out

DAY 2: SATURDAY

- **7 a.m.** Wake up! • **7:15 a.m.** Breakfast
- **8 a.m.** Depart Portland for Hampton Inn Oakland-Hayward; Confirmation #DE56432; Lynn rides shotgun
- **About noon** Stop for lunch; Jimmy picks restaurant • **7 p.m.** Dinner
- **9:30 p.m.** Lights out

DAY 3: SUNDAY

- **7 a.m.** Wake up! • **7:30 a.m.** Breakfast
- **8:15 a.m.** Depart Oakland for Disneyland, Disneyland Hotel; Confirmation #L124532; Jimmy rides shotgun
- **About noon** Stop for lunch; Lynn picks restaurant
- **5 p.m.** Check in, buy park admissions, and unpack
- **6–7 p.m.** Mary and Jimmy shop for breakfast food for cooler
- **7:15 p.m.** Dinner at Rainforest Cafe at Downtown Disney
- **After dinner** Explore Downtown Disney • **10 p.m.** Lights out

DAY 4: MONDAY

- **7 a.m.** Wake up! Cold breakfast from cooler in room
- **8 a.m.** Depart room for Disneyland Park
- **Noon** Lunch at park • **1 p.m.** Return to hotel for swimming and a nap
- **5 p.m.** Return to park for touring, dinner, and *Fantasmic!*
- **9:30 p.m.** Return to hotel • **10:30 p.m.** Lights out

DAY 5: TUESDAY

- **7 a.m.** Wake up! Cold breakfast from cooler in room
- **7:45 a.m.** Depart room for DCA • **Noon** Lunch at park
- **2:30 p.m.** Return to hotel for swimming and a nap
- **6 p.m.** Drive to dinner at Outback Steakhouse
- **7:30 p.m.** Return to DCA for touring
- **10 p.m.** Return to hotel • **11 p.m.** Lights out

Continued on next page

SHELTON FAMILY ITINERARY *(continued)*

DAY 6: WEDNESDAY

- **ZZZZZZ!** Lazy morning—sleep in! • **10:30 a.m.** Late-morning swim
- **Noon** Check out of Disneyland Hotel • **1 p.m.** Fast-food lunch
- **1:45 p.m.** Depart Anaheim for Hollywood; Sheraton Universal Hotel; Confirmation #3542986X; Lynn rides shotgun
- **7:30 p.m.** Dinner at Universal CityWalk
- **9:15 p.m.** Return to hotel • **10:30 p.m.** Lights out

DAY 7: THURSDAY

- **7 a.m.** Wake up! Cold breakfast from cooler in room
- **7:45 a.m.** Depart for Universal Studios • **11:30 a.m.** Lunch at park
- **4:45 p.m.** Return to hotel for downtime
- **7:30 p.m.** Dinner at Asakuma Rice, 848 N. La Cienga Blvd., West Hollywood
- **10 p.m.** Return to hotel • **11:45 p.m.** Lights out

DAY 8: FRIDAY

- **7:30 a.m.** Wake up!
- **8:30 a.m.** After fast-food breakfast, depart for Vagabond Inn Executive, Old Town Sacramento; Confirmation #SD234; Jimmy rides shotgun
- **About noon** Stop for lunch; Lynn picks restaurant
- **7 p.m.** Dinner • **10 p.m.** Lights out

DAY 9: SATURDAY

- **7 a.m.** Wake up!
- **7:45 a.m.** Depart for home after fast-food breakfast; Lynn rides shotgun
- **About noon** Stop for lunch; Jimmy picks restaurant
- **5:30 p.m.** Home, sweet home!

that's their choice. One more thing—the Sheltons visited Disneyland in late June, when all of the theme parks stay open late.

Notice that the Sheltons' itinerary provides minimum structure and maximum flexibility. It specifies which park the family will tour each day without attempting to nail down exactly what the family will do there. No matter how detailed your itinerary is, be prepared for surprises at Disneyland, both good and bad. If an unforeseen event renders part of the plan useless or impractical, just roll with it. And always remember that it's your itinerary; you created it, and you can change it. Just try to make any changes the result of family discussion and be especially careful not to scrap an element of the plan that your children perceive as something you promised them.

LOGISTIC PREPARATION

WHEN WE RECENTLY LAUNCHED into our spiel about good logistic preparation for a Disneyland vacation, a friend from Phoenix said, "Wait, what's the big deal? You pack clothes, a few games for the car, and then go!" So OK, we confess, that will work, but life can be sweeter and the vacation smoother (as well as less expensive) with the right gear.

CLOTHING

LET'S START WITH CLOTHES. We recommend springing for vacation uniforms. Buy for each child several sets of jeans (or shorts) and T-shirts, all matching, and all the same. For a one-week trip, for example, get each child three pairs of khaki shorts, three light-yellow T-shirts, and three pairs of SmartWool or Coolmax hiking socks. What's the point? First, you don't have to play fashion designer, coordinating a week's worth of stylish combos. Each morning the kids put on their uniform. It's simple, it saves time, and there are no decisions to make or arguments about what to wear. Second, uniforms make your children easier to spot and keep together in the theme parks. Third, the uniforms give your family, as well as the vacation itself, some added identity. If you're like the Shelton family who created the sample itinerary in the previous section, you might go so far as to create a logo for the trip to be printed on the shirts.

unofficial **TIP**
Give your teens the job of coming up with the logo for your shirts. They will love being the family designers.

When it comes to buying your uniforms, we have a few suggestions. Purchase well-made, durable shorts or jeans that will serve your children well beyond the vacation. Active children can never have too many pairs of shorts or jeans. As far as the T-shirts go, buy short-sleeve shirts in light colors for warm weather, or long-sleeve, darker-colored T-shirts for cooler weather. We suggest that you purchase your colored shirts from a local T-shirt printing company. These firms will be happy to sell you either printed T-shirts or unprinted T-shirts (called blanks) with long or short sleeves. You can select from a wide choice of colors not generally available in retail clothing stores and will not have to worry about finding the sizes you need. Plus, the shirts will cost a fraction of what a clothing retailer would charge. Most shirts come in the more durable 100% cotton or in the more wrinkle-resistant 50% cotton and 50% polyester (50–50s). The cotton shirts are a little cooler and more comfortable in hot, humid weather. The 50–50s dry a bit faster if they get wet.

unofficial **TIP**
Equip each child with a big bandanna. Though bandannas come in handy for wiping noses, scouring ice cream from chins and mouths, and dabbing sweat from the forehead, they can also be tied around the neck to protect from sunburn.

LABELS A great idea, especially for younger children, is to attach labels with your family name, hometown, the name of your hotel, the dates of your stay, and your cell phone number inside the shirt—for example:

HODDER FAMILY OF DENVER, CO.;
CAMELOT INN; MAY 5–12; 303-555-2108

Instruct your smaller children to show the label to an adult if they get separated from you. Elimination of the child's first name (which most children of talking age can articulate in any event) allows you to order labels that are all the same, that can be used by anyone in the family, and that can also be affixed to such easily lost items as caps, hats, jackets, hip packs, ponchos, and umbrellas. If fooling with labels sounds like too much of a hassle, check out "Lost Children" (see page 150) for some alternatives.

DRESSING FOR COOLER WEATHER Southern California experiences temperatures all over the scale November–March, so it could be a bit chilly if you visit during those months. Our suggestion is to layer: for example, a breathable, waterproof or water-resistant Windbreaker over a light, long-sleeve polypropylene shirt over a long-sleeve T-shirt. As with the baffles of a sleeping bag or down coat, it is the air trapped between the layers that keeps you warm. If all the layers are thin, you won't be left with something bulky to cart around if you want to pull off one or more. Later in this section, we'll advocate wearing a hip pack. Each layer should be sufficiently compatible to fit easily in that hip pack along with whatever else is in it.

ACCESSORIES

BOB WANTED TO CALL THIS PART "Belts and Stuff," but our editor (who obviously spends a lot of time at Macy's) thought "Accessories" put a finer point on it. In any event, for your children we recommend pants with reinforced elastic waistbands; this eliminates the need to wear a belt (one less thing to find when you're trying to leave). If your children like belts or want to carry an item suspended from their belts, buy them military-style 1½-inch-wide web belts at any Army–Navy surplus or camping-equipment store. The belts weigh less than half as much as leather, are cooler, and are washable.

SUNGLASSES Smog notwithstanding, the California sun is so bright and the glare so blinding that we recommend sunglasses for each family member. For children and adults of all ages, a good accessory item is an eyeglass strap for spectacles or sunglasses. The best models have a little device for adjusting the amount of slack in the strap. This allows your child to comfortably hang sunglasses from his or her neck when indoors or, alternately, to secure them fast to his or her head while experiencing a fast ride outdoors.

HIP PACKS AND WALLETS Unless you are touring with an infant or toddler, the largest thing anyone in your family should carry is a hip pack or fanny pack. Each person should have one. The pack should be large enough to carry at least a half-day's worth of snacks and other items deemed necessary (lip balm, bandanna, antibacterial hand gel, and so on) and still have enough room left to stash a hat, poncho, or light Windbreaker. We recommend buying full-size hip packs at outdoor retailers as opposed to small, child-size hip packs. The packs are light; can be made to fit any child large enough to tote a hip pack; have slip-resistant, comfortable, wide belting; and will last for years.

Do not carry billfolds or wallets, car keys, Disney Resort IDs, or room keys in your hip packs. We usually give this advice because hip packs are vulnerable to thieves (who snip them off and run), but pickpocketing and theft are not all that common at Disneyland. In this instance, the advice stems from a tendency of children to inadvertently drop their wallet in the process of rummaging around in their hip packs for snacks and other items.

You should weed through your billfold and remove to a safe place anything that you will not need on your vacation (photos, library card, department store credit cards, business cards, and so on). In addition to having a lighter wallet to lug around, you will decrease your exposure in the event that your wallet is lost or stolen. When we are working at Disneyland, we carry a small profile billfold with a driver's license, a credit card, our room key, and a small amount of cash. You don't need anything else.

DAY PACKS We see a lot of folks at Disneyland carrying day packs (that is, small, frameless backpacks) and/or water bottle belts that strap around your waist. Day packs might be a good choice if you plan to carry a lot of camera equipment or if you need to carry baby supplies on your person. Otherwise, try to travel as light as possible. Packs are hot, cumbersome, and not very secure, and they must be removed every time you get on a ride or sit down for a show. Hip packs, by way of contrast, can simply be rotated around the waist from your back to your abdomen if you need to sit down. Additionally, our observation has been that the contents of one day pack can usually be redistributed to two or so hip packs (except in the case of camera equipment).

CAPS Kids pull caps on and off as they enter and exit attractions, restrooms, and restaurants, and—big surprise—they lose them. In fact, they lose them by the thousands.

If your children are partial to caps, a device sold at ski and camping supply stores might increase the likelihood of the cap returning home with the child. Essentially, it's a short, light cord with little alligator clips on both ends. Hook one clip to the shirt collar and the other to the hat. It's a great little invention. Bob uses one when he skis in case his cap blows off.

RAINGEAR Rain is a fact of life, though persistent rain day after day is unusual. Check out the Weather Channel or weather forecasts on the Internet for three or so days before you leave home to see if any major storm systems are heading for Southern California. Weather predictions concerning systems and fronts four to seven days out are pretty reliable. If it appears that you might see some rough weather during your visit,

unofficial **TIP**
If your kids are little and don't mind a hairdo change, consider getting them a short haircut before you leave home. Not only will they be cooler and more comfortable, but—especially with your girls—you'll save them (and yourselves) the hassle of tangles and about 20 minutes of foo-fooing a day.

you're better off bringing raingear from home. If, however, nothing big is on the horizon weather wise, you can take your chances.

We at The Unofficial Guides usually do not bring raingear. Ponchos sell for about $9.50 adults, $8.50 child, and are available in seemingly every retail shop; they're even cheaper at local discount stores (such as Target).

If you do find yourself in a big storm, you'll want to have both a poncho and an umbrella. As one Unofficial reader puts it, "Umbrellas

RESPECT FOR THE SUN

Health and science writer **Avery Hurt** sheds some light on the often confusing products and methods for avoiding sunburn. Here's the basic advice from the medical experts.

- **Choose a sunscreen that is convenient for you to use.** Some prefer sprays, others lotions. The form of sunscreen doesn't matter as much as the technique of applying it.
- **Apply sunscreen a half hour before going out,** and be sure to get enough on you. One ounce per application is recommended—that means a full shot glass worth each time you apply. The 1-ounce amount was calculated for average adults in swimsuits; an average 7-year-old will probably take two-thirds of an ounce (20 cc). It's a good idea to measure that ounce in your hands at home, so you'll be familiar with what an ounce looks like in your palms. It's far more sunscreen than you tend to think.
- **Get a generous covering on all exposed skin.** Then reapply (another full shot glass) every 2 hours or after swimming or sweating. No matter what it says on the label, water resistance of sunscreen is limited. And none of them last all day.
- **There is very little difference in protection** between 30 or so SPF and 45 or 50 or greater. There is no need to spend more for higher SPF numbers. In fact, it is much safer to choose a lower (and typically less expensive) SPF (as long as it is at least 30) and apply it more often. However, do be sure to choose a product that has broad-spectrum coverage, meaning that it filters out both UVA and UVB rays. As long as the SPF is at least 30 and offers broad-spectrum protection, one brand can serve the whole family. There's no need to pay extra for special formulas made for children.
- **It is best to keep babies under 6 months old covered** and out of the sun. However, the American Academy of Pediatrics condones a small amount of sunscreen on vulnerable areas, such as the nose and chin, when you have your baby out. Be very careful to monitor your baby even if he is wearing a hat and sitting under an umbrella.
- **Use a lip balm** with an SPF of 15 and reapply often to your own lips and those of your kids. Again, the brand is less important than choosing something that you will use—and remembering to use it.
- **Sunglasses are also a must.** Too much sun exposure can contribute to age-related macular degeneration (among other things). Not all sunglasses filter out damaging rays. Be sure to choose shades (for adults and kids) that have 99% UV protection. Large lenses and wraparound styles might not look as cool, but they offer much better protection. You may have to spend a little more to be sure you are getting adequate protection, but you don't want to skimp on this.
- **If you do get a burn,** cool baths, aloe gels, and ibuprofen (or for adults, aspirin) usually help ease the suffering. Occasionally sunburns can be as dangerous in the short term as they are in the long term. If you or your child experience nausea, vomiting, high fever, severe pain, confusion, or fainting, seek medical care immediately.

make the rain much more bearable. When rain isn't beating down on your ponchoed head, it's easier to ignore."

And consider this tip from a Memphis, Tennessee, mom:

Scotchgard your shoes. The difference is unbelievable.

MISCELLANEOUS ITEMS

MEDICATION Some parents of hyperactive children on medication discontinue or decrease the child's normal dosage at the end of the school year. If you have such a child, be aware that the Disneyland parks might overly stimulate him or her. Consult your physician before altering your child's medication regimen. Also, if your child has attention-deficit disorder, remember that especially loud sounds can drive him or her right up the wall. Unfortunately, some Disney theater attractions are almost unbearably loud.

SUNSCREEN Overheating and sunburn are among the most common problems of younger children at Disneyland. Carry and use sunscreen of SPF 15 or higher. Be sure to put some on kids in strollers, even if the stroller has a canopy. Some of the worst cases of sunburn we've seen were on the exposed foreheads and feet of toddlers and infants in strollers. Protect skin from overexposure. To avoid overheating, rest regularly in the shade or in an air-conditioned restaurant or show.

WATER BOTTLES Don't count on keeping young children hydrated with soft drinks and water fountains. Long lines may impede buying refreshments, and fountains may not be handy. Furthermore, excited children may not realize or tell you that they're thirsty or hot. We recommend renting a stroller for children age 6 and younger and carrying bottles of water and sports drinks. Bottled water runs about $3 in all major parks, or bring your own water bottle and strap from home.

COOLERS AND MINI-FRIDGES If you drive to Disneyland, bring two coolers: a small one for drinks in the car and a large one for the hotel room. If you fly and rent a car, stop and purchase a large Styrofoam cooler, which can be discarded at the end of the trip. If you will be without a car, book a hotel with mini-fridges in each room. All on-site Disneyland hotels provide free mini-fridges and coffeemakers. If mini-fridges aren't provided, rent one from the hotel.

Coolers and mini-fridges allow you to have breakfast in your hotel room, store snacks and lunch supplies to take to the theme parks, and supplant expensive vending machines for snacks and beverages at the hotel. To keep the contents of your cooler cold, freeze a 2-gallon milk jug full of water before you head out. In a good cooler, it will take the jug five or more days to thaw. If you buy a Styrofoam cooler, you can use bagged ice and ice from the ice machine at your hotel. Even if you have to rent a mini-fridge, you will save a bundle of cash as well as significant time by reducing dependence on restaurant meals and expensive snacks and drinks purchased from vendors.

*un*official **TIP**
About two weeks before arriving, ship a box to your hotel containing food, plastic cutlery, and toiletries, plus pretty much any other consumables that might come in handy during your stay. If you fly, this helps avoid overweight fees and problems with liquid restrictions for carry-on luggage.

FOOD-PREP KIT If you plan to make sandwiches, bring along condiments and seasonings from home. A typical travel kit will include mayonnaise, ketchup, mustard, salt and pepper, and packets of artificial sweetener or sugar. Also throw in some plastic knives and spoons, napkins, plastic cups, and zip-top plastic bags. For breakfast you will need some plastic bowls for cereal. Of course, you can buy this stuff in Anaheim, but you probably won't consume it all, so why waste the money? If you drink bottled beer or wine, bring a bottle opener and corkscrew.

ENERGY BOOSTERS Kids get cranky when they're hungry, and when that happens, your entire group has a problem. Like many parents you might, for nutritional reasons, keep a tight rein on snacks available to your children at home. At Disneyland, however, maintaining energy and equanimity trumps between-meal snack discipline. For maximum zip and contentedness, give your kids snacks containing complex carbohydrates (fruits, crackers, nonfat energy bars, and the like) before they get hungry or show signs of exhaustion. You should avoid snacks that are high in fats and proteins because these foods take a long time to digest and will tend to unsettle your stomach if it's a hot day.

An experienced and wise grandma underscores the point:

> *Children who get cranky during a visit often do so from all that time and energy expended without food. Feed them! A snack at any price goes a long way to keeping the little kids happy and enjoying the parks, and keeping parents sane. Oh, and the security people are very nice about you taking snacks or drinks in, but DO NOT bring glass containers! That is apparently what they are really looking for.*

ELECTRONICS Regardless of your children's ages, always bring a nightlight. Flashlights are also handy for finding stuff in a dark hotel room after the kids are asleep.

MP3 players and iPods with earphones, as well as some electronic games, are often controversial gear for a family outing. We recommend compromise. Earbuds allow kids to create their own space even when they're with others, and that can be a safety valve. That said, try to agree before the trip on some earphone parameters, so you don't begin to feel as if they're being used to keep other family members and the trip itself at a distance. If you're traveling by car, take turns choosing the radio station or playlist for part of the trip.

Likewise, mobile phones are a mixed blessing. On the one hand, they can be invaluable in an emergency or if your party wants to split up, and if you have a smartphone, you can use our Lines app to see current wait times in the parks. Unfortunately, they also lead to guests missing out on what's around them and bumping into each other because they're glued to a tiny screen. Unlike Walt Disney World, Disneyland does not yet offer free Wi-Fi, and when local cell towers are overloaded on busy days, you can drain your phone in a matter of hours. Consider disabling high-speed data, Wi-Fi, and Bluetooth to save on batteries.

Be especially cautious about taking expensive iPads or other tablets into the parks, and for Mickey's sake, beware while using them as cameras during shows and parades, lest you blind or block everyone behind you. Also, be aware that Disney banned selfie sticks from all its parks in 2015, though collapsible monopods and tripods are still OK. Fear not, any friendly cast member will be happy to take your photo for you the old-fashioned way.

DON'T FORGET THE TENT This is not a joke and has nothing to do with camping. When Bob's daughter was preschool age, he almost went crazy trying to get her to sleep in a shared hotel room. She was accustomed to having her own room at home and was hyperstimulated whenever she traveled. Bob tried makeshift curtains and room dividers and even rearranged the furniture in a few hotel rooms to create the illusion of a more private, separate space for her. It was all for naught. It wasn't until she was around 4 years old and Bob took her camping that he seized on an idea that had some promise. She liked the cozy, secure, womblike feel of a backpacking tent and quieted down much more readily than she ever had in hotel rooms. So the next time the family stayed in a hotel, he pitched his backpacking tent in the corner of the room. In she went, nested for a bit, and fell asleep.

Since the time of Bob's daughter's childhood, there has been an astounding evolution in tent design. Tent manufacturers have developed a broad range of tents with self-supporting frames that can be erected virtually anywhere without ropes or stakes. Affordable and sturdy, many are as simple to put up as opening an umbrella. So if your child is too young for a room of his or her own or you can't afford a second hotel room, try pitching a small tent. Modern tents are self-contained with floors and an entrance that can be zipped up for privacy but cannot be locked. Kids appreciate having their own space and enjoy the adventure of being in a tent, even one set up in the corner of a hotel room. Sizes range from children's play tents with a 2- to 3-foot base to models large enough to sleep two or three husky teens. Light and compact when stored, a two-adult-size tent in its own storage bag (called a stuff sack) will take up about one-tenth or less of a standard overhead bin on a commercial airliner. Another option for infants and toddlers is to drape a sheet over a portable crib or playpen to make a tent.

> *un**official* **TIP**
> Often little ones fall asleep in their strollers (hallelujah!). Bring a large lightweight cloth to drape over the stroller to cover your child from the sun. A few clothespins will keep it in place.

THE BOX Bob here: On one memorable Disneyland excursion when my children were younger, we began each morning with an immensely annoying, involuntary scavenger hunt. Invariably, seconds before our scheduled departure to the theme park, we discovered that some combination of shoes, billfolds, sunglasses, hip packs, or other necessities were missing. For the next 15 minutes we would root through the room like pigs hunting truffles in an attempt to locate the absent items. When my kids lost something, they always searched where it was easiest to look, as opposed to where the lost article was most likely to be. I would be jammed under a bed feeling around while my children stood in the middle of the room intently inspecting the ceiling. As my friends will tell you, I'm as open to a novel theory as the next guy, but we never did find any shoes on the ceiling. Anyway, here's what I finally did: I swung by a local store and mooched a big empty box. From then on, every time we returned to the room, I had the kids deposit shoes, hip packs, and other potentially wayward items in the box. After that the box was off-limits until the next morning, when I doled out the contents.

PLASTIC GARBAGE BAGS At the Grizzly River Run raft ride at DCA and Splash Mountain in Disneyland Park, you are certain to get wet and possibly soaked. If it's really hot and you don't care, then fine. But if it's cool or you're just not up for a soaking, bring a large plastic trash bag or a cheap poncho to the park. By cutting holes in the top and on the sides of a trash bag, you can fashion a sack poncho that will keep your clothes from getting wet. On the raft ride, you will also get your feet wet. If you're not up for walking around in squishing, soaked shoes, bring a second, smaller plastic bag to wear over your feet while riding.

SUPPLIES FOR INFANTS AND TODDLERS

BASED ON RECOMMENDATIONS from hundreds of Unofficial Guide readers, here's what we suggest that you carry with you when touring with infants and toddlers:

- A disposable diaper for every hour you plan to be away from your hotel
- A cloth diaper or kitchen towel to put over your shoulder for burping
- Two receiving blankets: one to wrap the baby and one to lay the baby on or to drape over you when you nurse
- Ointment for diaper rash
- A package of wipes
- Prepared formula in bottles if you are not breast-feeding
- A washable bib, baby spoon, and baby food if your infant is eating solids
- For toddlers, a small toy for comfort and to keep them occupied during attractions

Baby Care Centers at the theme parks will sell you just about anything that you forget or run out of. Like all things Disney, prices will be higher than elsewhere, but at least you won't need to detour to a drugstore in the middle of your touring day.

REMEMBERING *Your* TRIP

1. Purchase a notebook for each child and spend time each evening recording the day's events. If your children have trouble getting motivated or don't know what to write about, start a discussion; otherwise, let them write or draw whatever they want to remember from the day.

2. Collect mementos along the way and create a treasure box in a small tin or cigar box. Months or years later, it's fun to look at postcards, pins, or ticket stubs to jump-start a memory.

3. Add inexpensive postcards to your photographs to create an album; then write a few words on each page to accompany the images.

4. Give each child a disposable camera to record his or her version of the trip. One 5-year-old snapped an entire series of photos that never showed anyone above the waist—his view of Disneyland (and the photos were priceless).

5. Nowadays, many families travel with a video camera, digital camera, or camera phone, though we recommend using one sparingly—parents end up viewing the trip through the lens rather than being in the moment. If you must, take it along, but only record a few moments of major sights (too much is boring anyway). And let the kids record and narrate. On the topic of narration, speak loudly so as to be heard over the not-insignificant background noise of the parks. Make use of lockers at all of the parks when the camera becomes a burden or when you're going to experience an attraction that might damage it or get it wet. Unless you have a camera designed for underwater shots or a waterproof carrying case, leave it behind on Splash Mountain, the Grizzly River Run, and any other ride where water is involved. Don't forget extra batteries.

6. Another inexpensive way to record memories is a palm-size voice recorder. Let all family members describe their experiences. Hearing a small child's voice years later is so endearing, and those recorded descriptions will trigger an album's worth of memories, far more focused than what many novices capture with a camcorder.

7. Consider using Disney's PhotoPass service for some professional-quality pictures; it's free to use and you only pay for the images you want to keep (see page 98 for details).

Finally, when it comes to taking photos and collecting mementos, don't let the tail wag the dog. You are not going to Disneyland to build the biggest scrapbook in history. Or as this Houston mom put it:

Tell your readers to get a grip on the photography thing. We were so busy shooting pictures that we kind of lost the thread. We had to get our pictures developed when we got home to see what all we did [while on vacation].

TRIAL RUN

IF YOU GIVE THOUGHTFUL CONSIDERATION to all areas of mental, physical, organizational, and logistical preparation discussed in this chapter, what remains is to familiarize yourself with the Disneyland parks and, of course, to conduct your field test. Yep, that's right, we want you to take the whole platoon on the road for a day to see if you are combat ready. No joke—this is important. You'll learn who tuckers out first, who's prone to developing blisters, who has to pee every 11 seconds, who keeps losing her cap and, given the proper forum, how compatible your family is in terms of what you like to see and do.

For the most informative trial run, choose a local venue that requires lots of walking, dealing with crowds, and making decisions on how to spend your time. Regional theme parks and state fairs are your best bets, followed by large zoos and museums. Devote the whole day. Kick off the morning with an early start, just like you will at Disneyland, paying attention to who's organized and ready to go and who's dragging his or her butt and holding up the group. If you have to drive 1 or 2 hours to get to your test venue, no big deal. You may have to do some commuting at Disneyland too. Spend the whole day, eat a couple of meals, and stay late.

Don't bias the sample (that is, mess with the outcome) by telling everyone that you are practicing for Disneyland. Everyone behaves differently when they know that they are being tested or evaluated. Your objective is not to run a perfect drill but to find out as much as you can about how the individuals in your family, as well as the family as a group, respond to and deal with everything they experience during the day. Pay attention to who moves quickly and who is slow; who is adventuresome and who is reticent; who keeps going and who needs frequent rest breaks; who sets the agenda and who is content to follow; who is easily agitated and who stays cool; who tends to dawdle or wander off; who is curious and who is bored; who is demanding and who is accepting. You get the idea.

Discuss the findings of the test run with your spouse the next day. Don't be discouraged if your test day wasn't perfect; few (if any) are. Distinguish between problems that are remediable and problems that are intrinsic to your family's emotional or physical makeup (no amount of hiking, for example, will toughen up some people's feet).

Establish a plan for addressing remediable problems (further conditioning, setting limits before you go, trying harder to achieve family consensus) and develop strategies for minimizing or working around problems that are a fact of life (waking sleepyheads 15 minutes early, placing moleskin on likely blister sites before setting out, or packing familiar food for the toddler who balks at restaurant fare). If you are an attentive observer, a fair diagnostician, and a creative problem solver, you'll be able to work out many of the problems you're likely to encounter at Disneyland before you leave home.

ABOUT THE UNOFFICIAL GUIDE TOURING PLANS Parents who embark on one of our touring plans are often frustrated by the various interruptions and delays occasioned by their small children. In case you haven't given the subject much thought, here is what to expect:

1. Many small children will stop dead in their tracks whenever they see a Disney character. Our advice: Live with it. An attempt to haul your children away before they have satisfied their curiosity is likely to precipitate anything from whining to a full-scale revolt.

2. The touring plans call for visiting attractions in a specified sequence, often skipping certain attractions along the way. Children do not like skipping anything! If they see something that attracts them, they want to experience it now. Some children can be persuaded to skip attractions if parents explain things in advance. Other kids severely flip out at the threat of skipping something, particularly something in Fantasyland. A mom from Charleston, South Carolina, had this to say:

Following the touring plans turned out to be a train wreck. The main problem with the plan is that it starts in Fantasyland. When we were on Dumbo, my 5-year-old saw eight-dozen other things in Fantasyland she wanted to see. The long and the short is that, after Dumbo, there was no getting her out of there.

3. Children seem to have a genetic instinct when it comes to finding restrooms. We have seen perfectly functional adults equipped with all manner of maps search interminably for a restroom. Small children, on the other hand, including those who cannot read, will head for the nearest restroom with the certainty of a homing pigeon. While you may skip certain attractions, you can be sure that your children will ferret out (and want to use) every restroom in the park.

STROLLERS

unofficial **TIP**
Strollers are also great for older kids who tire easily.

STROLLERS ARE AVAILABLE for about $15 per day for a single, $25 per day for two; the rental covers the entire day and is good at both parks. If you rent a stroller and later decide to go back to your hotel for lunch, a swim, or a nap, turn in your stroller but hang on to your rental receipt. When you return to either park later in the day, present your receipt. You will be issued another stroller at no additional charge. The rental procedure is fast and efficient, and a central stroller rental facility is in the Main Entrance Plaza between Disneyland and DCA, to the right of the Disneyland Park entrance. Likewise, returning the stroller is a breeze. Even in the evening, when several hundred strollers are turned in following the fireworks or water show, there is no wait or hassle. *Note:* Rented strollers are not permitted in Downtown Disney.

The strollers come with sun canopies and small cargo compartments under the seat. For infants and toddlers, strollers are a must, and we recommend a small pillow or blanket to help make the stroller more comfortable for your child during what may be long periods in the seat. We have also observed many sharp parents renting strollers for somewhat older children. Strollers prevent parents from having to carry children when they run out of steam and provide an easy, convenient way to carry water, snacks, diaper bags, and the like.

When you enter a show or board a ride, you will have to park your stroller, usually in an open, unprotected area. If it rains before you return, you'll need a cloth, towel, or spare diaper to dry off the stroller.

Bringing Your Own Stroller

You are allowed to bring your own stroller to the theme parks. However, only collapsible strollers are allowed on the monorail and parking-lot trams. Your stroller is unlikely to be stolen, but mark it with your name. We strongly recommend bringing your own stroller. In addition to the parks there is the walk from and to your hotel, the parking-lot tram, or the bus/hotel-shuttle boarding area, not to mention many other occasions at your hotel or during shopping when you will be happy to have a stroller handy.

If you do not want to bring your own stroller, you may consider buying one of the umbrella-style collapsible strollers. You may even consider ordering online at places such as **walmart.com, toysrus.com,** or **sears.com** and shipping it right to your hotel. Make sure you leave enough time between your order and arrival dates.

Having her own stroller was indispensable to this mother of two toddlers:

> *How I was going to manage to get the kids from the parking lot to the park was a big worry for me before I made the trip. I found that, for me personally, since I have two kids ages 1 and 2, it was easier to walk to the entrance of the park from the parking lot with the kids in my own stroller than to take the kids out of the stroller, fold the stroller (while trying to control the two kids and associated gear), load the stroller and the kids onto the tram, etc. No matter where I was parked, I could always just walk to the entrance. It sometimes took a while, but it was easier for me.*

An Oklahoma mom, however, reports a bad experience with bringing her own stroller:

> *The first time we took our kids we had a large stroller (big mistake). It is so much easier to rent one in the park. The large [personally owned] strollers are nearly impossible to get on [airport shuttle] buses and are a hassle at the airport. I remember feeling dread when a bus pulled up that was even semifull of people. People look at you like you have a cage full of live chickens when you drag heavy strollers onto the bus.*

Stroller Wars

Sometimes strollers disappear while you are enjoying a ride or a show. Do not be alarmed. You won't have to buy the missing stroller, and you will be issued a new stroller for your continued use. Lost strollers can be replaced at the main rental facility near the park entrances.

unofficial **TIP**
Beware of stroller stealers. With so many identical strollers, it's easy to grab the wrong one. Mark yours with a bandanna or some other easily identifiable flag.

While replacing a ripped-off stroller is not a big deal, it is an inconvenience. One family complained that their stroller had been taken six times in one day. Even with free replacements, larceny on this scale represents a lot of wasted time. Through our own experiments and suggestions from readers, we have developed several techniques for hanging on to your rented stroller:

1. Write your name in permanent marker on a 6-by-9-inch card, put the card in a transparent freezer bag, and secure the bag to the handle of the stroller with masking or duct tape.

2. Affix something personal (but expendable) to the handle of the stroller. Evidently most strollers are pirated by mistake (because they all look the same) or because it's easier to swipe someone else's stroller (when yours disappears) than to troop off to the replacement center. Because most stroller theft is a function of confusion, laziness, or revenge, the average pram-pincher will balk at hauling off a stroller bearing another person's property. After trying several items, we concluded that a bright, inexpensive scarf or bandanna tied to the handle works well, and a sock partially stuffed with rags or paper works even better (the weirder and more personal the object, the greater the deterrent). Best of all is a dead mackerel dangling from the handle, though in truth, the kids who ride in the stroller prefer the other methods.

A multigenerational family tried this:

We "decorated" our stroller with electrical tape to make it stand out. We also zip-tied an unused, small, insulated diaper bag to the handle to make carrying things easier. One of your readers mentioned using a bike chain or cable lock to insure their stroller was not stolen but said the Disney cast members were a little disturbed. So I took an extra firearm lock (looks like a mini-bike lock) to lock a wheel to the frame while parked. My son added a small cowbell to make it clang if moved. The stroller could then be moved easily for short distances by lifting the back, but trying to go farther would be uncomfortable and noisy.

We receive quite a few letters from readers debating the pros and cons of bringing your own stroller versus renting one of Disney's. A mother with two small children opted for her own pram:

I took my own stroller because the rented strollers aren't appropriate for infants (we had a 5-year-old and a 5-month-old). No one said anything about me using a bike lock to secure our brand-new Aprica stroller. However, an attendant came over and told us not to lock it anywhere because it's a fire hazard! (Outside?) When I politely asked the attendant if she wanted to be responsible for my $300 stroller, she told me to go ahead and lock it but not tell anyone! I observed the attendants constantly moving the strollers. This seems very confusing—no wonder people think their strollers are getting ripped off!

As the reader mentioned, Disney cast members often rearrange strollers parked outside an attraction. Sometimes this is done simply to tidy up. At other times the strollers are moved to make additional room along a walkway. In any event, do not assume that your stroller is stolen because it is missing from the exact place you left it. Check around. Chances are that it will be neatly arranged just a few feet away.

BABYSITTING

CHILD-CARE SERVICES ARE UNAVAILABLE in the Disney parks. The services of Pinocchio's Workshop, a child-care facility at the Grand Californian Hotel, are available only to guests of the three Disneyland Resort hotels. Children ages 5–12 can be left for up to 4 hours at a cost of $13 per hour, per child. Pinocchio's Workshop requires a minimum of 2 hours, and its hours are 5 p.m.–midnight. Dinner is available for an additional fee.

Fullerton Child Care Agency, an independent organization, provides in-room sitting for infants and children. If you pay the tab, Fullerton sitters will even take your kids to Disneyland. All sitters are experienced and licensed to drive, and the Fullerton Child Care Agency is fully insured. The basic rate for in-room sitting for one or two children is $48 for the first 4 hours, with a 4-hour minimum, and $10 each hour thereafter. The charge for each additional child varies with the sitter. There is no transportation fee, but the client is expected to pay for parking when applicable. All fees and charges must be paid in cash at the end of the assignment. To reserve a sitter, one or two days' advance notice is requested. They fill up quickly, so a couple of weeks' notice is ideal. You can reach the Fullerton Child Care Agency by calling ☎ 714-528-1640.

DISNEY, KIDS, *and* SCARY STUFF

DISNEYLAND PARK and Disney California Adventure are family theme parks. Yet some of the Disney adventure rides can be intimidating to small children. On certain rides, such as Splash Mountain and the roller coasters (California Screamin', Space Mountain, Matterhorn Bobsleds, and Big Thunder Mountain Railroad), the ride itself may be frightening. On other rides, such as The Haunted Mansion and Snow White's Scary Adventures, it is the special effects. We recommend a little parent-child dialogue coupled with a "testing the water" approach. A child who is frightened by Peter Pan's Flight should not have to sit through The Haunted Mansion. Likewise, if Big Thunder Mountain Railroad is too much, don't try Space Mountain or California Screamin'. Just because a child in your party isn't ready for a ride doesn't mean that the grown-ups have to miss out; learn about Disney's "baby swap" system on page 145.

Disney rides and shows are adventures. They focus on the substance and themes of all adventure, and indeed of life itself: good and evil, beauty and the grotesque, fellowship and enmity, quest, and death. Though the endings are all happy, the impact of the adventures, with Disney's gift for special effects, is often intimidating and occasionally frightening to small children.

There are rides with menacing witches, rides with burning towns, and rides with ghouls popping out of their graves, all done tongue in cheek and with a sense of humor, provided you are old enough to understand the joke. And there are bones, lots of bones—human bones, cattle bones, and whole skeletons are everywhere you look. There have to be more bones at Disneyland Park than at the Smithsonian and the UCLA Medical School combined. A stack of skulls is at the headhunter's camp on the Jungle Cruise; a veritable platoon of skeletons sails ghost ships in Pirates of the Caribbean; a macabre assemblage of skulls and skeletons are in The Haunted Mansion; and more skulls, skeletons, and bones punctuate Snow White's Scary Adventures, Peter Pan's Flight, and Big Thunder Mountain Railroad.

One reader wrote us after taking his preschoolers on Star Tours:

> We took a 4-year-old and a 5-year-old, and they had the *#%^! scared out of them at Star Tours. We did this first thing in the morning, and it took hours of Tom Sawyer Island and It's a Small World to get back to normal.
>
> Our kids were the youngest by far in Star Tours. I assume that either other adults had more sense or were not such avid readers of your book. Preschoolers should start with Dumbo and work up to the Jungle Cruise in the late morning, after being revved up and before getting hungry, thirsty, or tired. Pirates of the Caribbean is out for preschoolers. You get the idea.

The reaction of young children to the inevitable system overload of Disney parks should be anticipated. Be sensitive, alert, and prepared for almost anything, even behavior that is out of character for your child at home. Most small children take Disney's variety of macabre trappings in stride, and others are quickly comforted by an arm around the shoulder or a little squeeze of the hand. For parents who have observed a tendency in their kids to become upset, we recommend taking it slowly and easily by sampling more benign adventures such as the Jungle Cruise, gauging reactions, and discussing with children how they felt about the things they saw. A mother of two reported this:

> The one thing I regret is taking my 4-year-old on the Tower of Terror—the drops and jolts didn't bother him, but the holographic "ghosts" sure did!

Sometimes, small children will rise above their anxiety in an effort to please their parents or siblings. This behavior, however, does not necessarily indicate a mastery of fear, much less enjoyment. If children come off a ride in ostensibly good shape, we recommend asking if they would like to go on the ride again (not necessarily right now, but sometime). The response to this question will usually give you a clue as to how much they actually enjoyed the experience. There is a lot of difference between having a good time and mustering the courage to get through something.

Evaluating a child's capacity to handle the visual and tactile effects of the Disney parks requires patience, understanding, and experimentation. Each of us, after all, has his own demons. If a child balks at or is frightened by a ride, respond constructively. Let your children know that lots of people, adults as well as children, are scared by what they see and feel. Help them understand that it is OK if they get frightened. Take pains not to compound the discomfort by making a child feel inadequate; try not to undermine self-esteem, impugn courage, or subject a child to ridicule. Most of all, do not induce guilt, as if your child's trepidation is ruining the family's fun. When older siblings are present, it is sometimes necessary to restrain their taunting and teasing.

A visit to a Disney park is more than an outing or an adventure for a small child. It is a testing experience, a sort of controlled rite of passage. If you help your little one work through the challenges, the time can be immeasurably rewarding and a bonding experience for both of you.

The Fright Factor

While each youngster is different, there are essentially seven attraction elements that alone or combined can push a child's buttons:

1. THE NAME OF THE ATTRACTION Small children will naturally be apprehensive about something called The Haunted Mansion or Snow White's Scary Adventures.

2. THE VISUAL IMPACT OF THE ATTRACTION FROM OUTSIDE Splash Mountain, The Twilight Zone Tower of Terror, and Big Thunder Mountain Railroad look scary enough to give even adults second thoughts. To many small kids, the rides are visually terrifying.

3. THE VISUAL IMPACT OF THE INDOOR QUEUING AREA Pirates of the Caribbean with its dark bayou scene and The Haunted Mansion with its "stretch rooms" are capable of frightening small children before they even board the ride.

4. THE INTENSITY OF THE ATTRACTION Some attractions are so intense as to be overwhelming; they inundate the senses with sights, sounds, movement, and even smell. *Muppet-Vision 3-D* and *It's Tough to Be a Bug!,* for instance, combine loud music, tactile effects, lights, and 3-D cinematography to create a total sensory experience. For some pre-schoolers, this is two or three senses too many.

5. THE VISUAL IMPACT OF THE ATTRACTION ITSELF As previously discussed, the sights in various attractions range from falling boulders to lurking buzzards, from underwater volcanoes to attacking hippos. What one child calmly absorbs may scare the owl poop out of another child the same age.

6. DARK Many Disneyland attractions are dark rides—that is, they operate indoors in a dark environment. For some children, this fact alone is sufficient to trigger significant apprehension. A child who is frightened on one dark ride, for example Snow White's Scary Adventures, may be unwilling to try other indoor rides.

7. THE RIDE ITSELF; THE TACTILE EXPERIENCE Some Disney rides are downright wild—wild enough to induce motion sickness, wrench backs, and generally discombobulate patrons of any age.

A Bit of Preparation

We receive many tips from parents relating how they prepared their children for the Disneyland experience. A common strategy is to acquaint kids with the characters and the stories behind the attractions by reading Disney books and watching Disney DVDs at home.

Thanks to half the population of California walking around the parks with video cameras, you can view a clip of every attraction and show on **youtube.com.** Videos of dark rides aren't stellar but are good enough to get a sense of what you're in for. The mother of a 7-year-old found YouTube quite effective:

We watched every ride and show on YouTube before going, so my timid 7-year-old daughter would be prepared, and we cut out all the ones that looked too scary to her. She still did not like, and cried at, It's Tough to Be a Bug.

A mother from Gloucester, Massachusetts, handled her son's preparation a bit more extemporaneously:

The 3½-year-old liked It's a Small World but was afraid of The Haunted Mansion. We just pulled his hat over his face and quietly talked to him while we enjoyed the ride.

A Word about Height Requirements

A number of attractions require children to meet minimum height and age requirements, usually 40 inches tall to ride with an adult, or at least 40 inches and 7 years of age or older to ride alone. If you have children too short or too young to ride, you have several options, including switching off (described on page 145). Though the alternatives may resolve some practical and logistical issues, be forewarned that your smaller children might nonetheless be resentful of their older (or taller) siblings who qualify to ride. A mom from Virginia bumped into just such a situation, writing:

You mention height requirements for rides but not the intense sibling jealousy this can generate. Frontierland was a real problem in that respect. Our very petite 5-year-old, to her outrage, was stuck hanging around while our 8-year-old went on Splash Mountain and Big Thunder Mountain with Grandma and Granddad, and the nearby alternatives weren't helpful [too long a line for rafts to Tom Sawyer Island, and so on]. If we had thought ahead, we would have left the younger kid back in Mickey's Toontown with one of the grown-ups for another roller coaster or two and then met up later at a designated point. The best areas had a playground or other quick attractions for short people near the rides with height requirements.

The reader makes a valid point, though splitting the group and then meeting later can be more complicated in practical terms than she might imagine. If you choose to split up, ask the Disney greeter at the entrance to the height-restricted attraction(s) how long the wait is. If you tack 5 minutes for riding onto the anticipated wait, and then add 5 or so minutes to exit and reach the meeting point, you'll have an approximate sense of how long the younger kids (and their supervising

Continued on page 142

SMALL-CHILD FRIGHT-POTENTIAL TABLE

As a quick reference, we provide this table to warn you which attractions to be wary of and why. The table represents a generalization, and all kids are different. It relates specifically to kids 3–7 years of age. On average, as you would expect, children at the younger end of the age range are more likely to be frightened than children in their 6th or 7th year.

Disneyland Park

MAIN STREET, U.S.A.

- **DISNEYLAND RAILROAD** Tunnel with dinosaur display frightens some small children.
- *THE DISNEYLAND STORY,* PRESENTING *GREAT MOMENTS WITH MR. LINCOLN* Brief battle sound effects may surprise small children.

ADVENTURELAND

- *ENCHANTED TIKI ROOM* A small thunderstorm momentarily surprises very young children.
- **INDIANA JONES ADVENTURE** Visually intimidating, with intense effects and a jerky ride. Switching-off option (see page 145).
- **JUNGLE CRUISE** Moderately intense, with some macabre sights; a good test attraction for little ones.
- **TARZAN'S TREEHOUSE** Not frightening in any respect.

NEW ORLEANS SQUARE

- **THE HAUNTED MANSION** Name of attraction raises anxiety, as do sights and sounds of waiting area. An intense attraction with humorously presented macabre sights. The ride itself is gentle.
- **PIRATES OF THE CARIBBEAN** Slightly intimidating queuing area; an intense boat ride with gruesome (though humorously presented) sights and two short, unexpected slides down flumes.

CRITTER COUNTRY

- **DAVY CROCKETT'S EXPLORER CANOES** Not frightening in any respect.
- **THE MANY ADVENTURES OF WINNIE THE POOH** Not frightening in any respect.
- **SPLASH MOUNTAIN** Visually intimidating from the outside. Moderately intense visual effects. The ride itself, culminating in a 52-foot plunge down a steep chute, is somewhat hair-raising for all ages. Switching-off option (see page 145).

FRONTIERLAND

- **BIG THUNDER MOUNTAIN RAILROAD** Visually intimidating from the outside; moderately intense visual effects. The roller coaster may frighten many adults, particularly seniors. Switching-off option (see page 145).
- *FANTASMIC!* Loud and intense with fireworks and some scary villains, but most young children like it.
- **THE GOLDEN HORSESHOE—LAUGHING STOCK CO.** Not frightening in any respect.
- *MARK TWAIN* RIVERBOAT Not frightening in any respect.
- **PIRATE'S LAIR ON TOM SAWYER ISLAND** Some very small children are intimidated by dark walk-through tunnels that can be easily avoided.
- **SAILING SHIP** *COLUMBIA* Not frightening in any respect.

FANTASYLAND

- **ALICE IN WONDERLAND** Pretty benign but frightens a small percentage of preschoolers.
- **CASEY JR. CIRCUS TRAIN** Not frightening in any respect.
- **DUMBO THE FLYING ELEPHANT** A tame midway ride; a great favorite of most small children.

SMALL-CHILD FRIGHT-POTENTIAL TABLE

FANTASYLAND (continued)

- **FANTASYLAND THEATRE** Not frightening in any respect.
- **IT'S A SMALL WORLD** Not frightening in any respect.
- **KING ARTHUR CARROUSEL** Not frightening in any respect.
- **MAD TEA PARTY** Midway-type ride can induce motion sickness in all ages.
- **MATTERHORN BOBSLEDS** The ride itself is wilder than Big Thunder Mountain Railroad but not as wild as Space Mountain. Switching-off option (see page 145).
- **MR. TOAD'S WILD RIDE** Name of ride intimidates some. Moderately intense spook house–genre attraction with jerky ride. Frightens only a small percentage of preschoolers.
- **PETER PAN'S FLIGHT** Not frightening in any respect.
- **PINOCCHIO'S DARING JOURNEY** Less frightening than Alice in Wonderland but scares a few very young preschoolers.
- **ROYAL HALL AT FANTASY FAIRE** Not frightening in any respect.
- **ROYAL THEATRE AT FANTASY FAIRE** Not frightening in any respect.
- **SNOW WHITE'S SCARY ADVENTURES** Moderately intense spook housegenre attraction with some grim characters. Absolutely terrifying to many preschoolers.
- **STORYBOOK LAND CANAL BOATS** Not frightening in any respect.

MICKEY'S TOONTOWN

- **CHIP 'N DALE TREEHOUSE** Not frightening in any respect.
- **GADGET'S GO COASTER** Tame as far as coasters go; frightens some small children.
- **GOOFY'S PLAYHOUSE** Not frightening in any respect.
- **MICKEY'S HOUSE AND MEET MICKEY** Not frightening in any respect.
- **MINNIE'S HOUSE** Not frightening in any respect.
- **MISS DAISY, DONALD'S BOAT** Not frightening in any respect.
- **ROGER RABBIT'S CAR TOON SPIN** Intense special effects, coupled with a dark environment and wild ride; frightens many preschoolers.

TOMORROWLAND

- **ASTRO ORBITOR** Waiting area is visually intimidating to preschoolers. The ride is a lot higher, but just a bit wilder, than Dumbo.
- **AUTOPIA** The noise in the waiting area slightly intimidates preschoolers; otherwise, not frightening.
- **BUZZ LIGHTYEAR ASTRO BLASTERS** Intense special effects plus a dark environment frighten some preschoolers.
- **DISNEYLAND MONORAIL SYSTEM** Not frightening in any respect.
- **FINDING NEMO SUBMARINE VOYAGE** Being enclosed, as well as certain ride effects, may frighten preschoolers.
- **JEDI TRAINING ACADEMY** Not frightening in any respect.
- **SPACE MOUNTAIN** Very intense roller coaster in the dark; Disneyland's wildest ride and a scary roller coaster by anyone's standards. Switching-off option (see page 145).
- **STAR TOURS—THE ADVENTURES CONTINUE** Extremely intense visually for all ages; one of the wildest in Disney's repertoire. Switching-off option (see page 145).
- **TOMORROWLAND THEATER** Extremely intense visual effects and the loud volume scare many preschoolers. Stationary seating is offered.

Disney California Adventure

A BUG'S LAND

- **FLIK'S FUN FAIR** Not frightening in any respect.
- **IT'S TOUGH TO BE A BUG!** Loud and extremely intense with special effects that will terrify children under 8 years or anyone with a fear of insects.

SMALL-CHILD FRIGHT-POTENTIAL TABLE

Disney California Adventure (continued)

GRIZZLY PEAK

- **GRIZZLY RIVER RUN** Frightening to guests of all ages. Wet too!
- **REDWOOD CREEK CHALLENGE TRAIL AND WILDERNESS EXPLORER CAMP** Trail is a bit overwhelming to preschoolers but not frightening.
- **SOARIN' OVER CALIFORNIA** Frightens some children 7 years and under. Really a very sweet ride.

HOLLYWOOD LAND

- **ANNA & ELSA'S ROYAL WELCOME** Not frightening in any respect.
- **DISNEY ANIMATION** Not frightening in any respect.
- *DISNEY JUNIOR—LIVE ON STAGE!* Not frightening in any respect.
- *FOR THE FIRST TIME IN FOREVER: A FROZEN SING-ALONG CELEBRATION* Not frightening in any respect.
- **HYPERION THEATER/***DISNEY'S ALADDIN: A MUSICAL SPECTACULAR* Very intense and loud; otherwise, not frightening.
- **MONSTERS, INC. MIKE & SULLEY TO THE RESCUE** May frighten children under 7 years of age.
- *MUPPET-VISION 3-D* Intense and loud with a lot of special effects. Frightens some preschoolers.
- *TURTLE TALK WITH CRUSH* Not frightening in any respect.
- **THE TWILIGHT ZONE TOWER OF TERROR** Frightening to guests of all ages.

PACIFIC WHARF

- **BAKERY TOUR** Not frightening in any respect.

PARADISE PIER

- **CALIFORNIA SCREAMIN'** Frightening to guests of all ages.
- **GOLDEN ZEPHYR** Frightening to a small percentage of preschoolers.
- **GOOFY'S SKY SCHOOL** Frightening to the under-8 crowd.
- **JUMPIN' JELLYFISH** The ride's appearance frightens some younger children. The ride itself is exceedingly tame.
- **KING TRITON'S CAROUSEL** Not frightening in any respect.
- **THE LITTLE MERMAID: ARIEL'S UNDERSEA ADVENTURE** Moderately intense effects; Ursula may frighten children under 7 years of age.
- **MICKEY'S FUN WHEEL** The ride in the stationary cars is exceedingly tame. The ride in the swinging cars is frightening to guests of all ages.
- **SILLY SYMPHONY SWINGS** Height requirement keeps preschoolers from riding. Moderately intimidating to younger grade-schoolers.
- **TOY STORY MIDWAY MANIA!** Loud and intense but not frightening.

CARS LAND

- **LUIGI'S ROLLICKIN' ROADSTERS** Not frightening in any respect.
- **MATER'S JUNKYARD JAMBOREE** Midway-type ride can induce motion sickness in all ages.
- **RADIATOR SPRINGS RACERS** Moderately intense effects, with high-speed sections that may frighten younger children. Switching-off option (see page 145).

Continued from page 139

adult) will have to do other stuff. Our guess is that even with a long line for the rafts, the reader would have had more than sufficient time to take her daughter to Tom Sawyer Island while the sibs rode Splash

Mountain and Big Thunder Mountain with the grandparents. For sure she had time to tour Tarzan's Treehouse in adjacent Adventureland.

Additionally, children under age 7 must be accompanied on all attractions by another guest age 14 or older, who must sit in the same ride vehicle in the same row or an adjacent one. While this shouldn't pose a problem on most attractions, some with small vehicles (such as Gadget's Go Coaster) may require use of a baby swap (see page 145) if your party has an uneven ratio of little members to big ones; ask a cast member at the ride entrance for assistance if you have questions.

Attractions that Eat Adults

You may spend so much energy worrying about Junior's welfare that you forget to take care of yourself. If the ride component of the attraction (that is, the actual motion and movement of the conveyance itself) is potentially disturbing, persons of any age may be adversely affected. Several attractions likely to cause motion sickness or other problems for older children and adults are listed in the table below. Fast, jerky rides are also noted with icons in the attraction profiles.

POTENTIALLY PROBLEMATIC ATTRACTIONS FOR ADULTS
DISNEYLAND PARK
ADVENTURELAND Indiana Jones Adventure
CRITTER COUNTRY Splash Mountain
FANTASYLAND Mad Tea Party | Matterhorn Bobsleds
FRONTIERLAND Big Thunder Mountain Railroad
TOMORROWLAND Space Mountain | Star Tours—The Adventures Continue
DISNEY CALIFORNIA ADVENTURE
CARS LAND Mater's Junkyard Jamboree | Radiator Springs Racers
GRIZZLY PEAK Grizzly River Run
HOLLYWOOD LAND The Twilight Zone Tower of Terror
PARADISE PIER California Screamin' | Goofy's Sky School Mickey's Fun Wheel (swinging)

WAITING-LINE STRATEGIES *for* ADULTS *with* SMALL CHILDREN

CHILDREN HOLD UP BETTER through the day if you minimize the time they have to spend in lines. Arriving early and using the touring plans in this guide will reduce waiting time immensely. There are, however, additional measures you can employ to reduce stress on little ones.

1. LINE GAMES Smart parents anticipate how restless children become waiting in line and know that a little structured activity can relieve the stress and boredom. In the morning, kids handle the inactivity of waiting in line by discussing what they want to see and do during the course of the day. Later, however, as events wear on, they need a little help. Watching for, and counting, Disney characters is a good diversion. Simple guessing games such as 20 Questions also work well. Lines for rides move so continuously that games requiring pen and paper are cumbersome and impractical. Waiting in the holding area of a theater attraction, however, is a different story. Here, tic-tac-toe, hangman, drawing, and coloring can really make the time go by.

2. LAST-MINUTE ENTRY If a ride or show can accommodate an unusually large number of people at one time, it is often unnecessary to stand in line. The *Mark Twain* Riverboat in Frontierland is a good example. The boat holds about 450 people, usually more than are waiting in line to ride. Instead of standing uncomfortably in a crowd with dozens of other guests, grab a snack and sit in the shade until the boat arrives and loading is well under way. After the line has all but disappeared, go ahead and board.

In large-capacity theaters, such as Tomorrowland Theater, ask the entrance greeter how long it will be until guests are admitted to the theater for the next show. If the answer is 15 minutes or more, use the time for a restroom break or to get a snack; you can return to the attraction just a few minutes before the show starts. You will not be permitted to carry any food or drink into the attraction, so make sure you have time to finish your snack before entering.

To help you determine which attractions to target for last-minute entry, we provide the table below.

ATTRACTIONS YOU CAN USUALLY ENTER AT THE LAST MINUTE
DISNEYLAND PARK
• **FRONTIERLAND** *Mark Twain* Riverboat | Sailing Ship *Columbia*
• **MAIN STREET, U.S.A.** *Disneyland Story,* presenting *Great Moments with Mr. Lincoln*
• **TOMORROWLAND** Tomorrowland Theater
DISNEY CALIFORNIA ADVENTURE
• **HOLLYWOOD LAND** Disney Animation | *Muppet-Vision 3-D*

3. THE HAIL MARY PASS Certain waiting lines are configured in such a way that you and your smaller children can pass under the rail to join your partner just before boarding or entry. This technique allows the kids and one adult to rest, snack, cool off, or tinkle, while another adult or older sibling does the waiting. Other guests are understanding when it comes to using this strategy to keep small children content. You are likely to meet hostile opposition, however, if you try to pass older children or more than one adult under the rail. Attractions where it is usually possible to complete a Hail Mary pass are listed on the table below.

ATTRACTIONS WHERE YOU CAN USUALLY COMPLETE A HAIL MARY PASS
DISNEYLAND PARK
• **FANTASYLAND** Casey Jr. Circus Train | Dumbo the Flying Elephant King Arthur Carrousel | Mad Tea Party | Mr. Toad's Wild Ride | Peter Pan's Flight Snow White's Scary Adventures | Storybook Land Canal Boats
• **TOMORROWLAND** Autopia
DISNEY CALIFORNIA ADVENTURE
• **PARADISE PIER** Golden Zephyr | Jumpin' Jellyfish | King Triton's Carousel
• **CARS LAND** Luigi's Rollickin' Roadsters | Mater's Junkyard Jamboree

4. SWITCHING OFF (ALSO KNOWN AS RIDER SWAP, BABY SWAP, OR CHILD SWAP) Several attractions have minimum height and/or age requirements (see the table on page 107). In addition, all children must be at least 7 years old and 40 inches tall to ride any attraction without an accompanying adult. Some couples with children too short or too young forgo these attractions, while others take turns riding. Missing some of Disneyland's best rides is an unnecessary sacrifice, and waiting in line twice for the same ride is a tremendous waste of time.

Instead, take advantage of the switching-off option, also called the Rider Swap, Baby Swap, or Child Swap. To switch off, there must be at least two adults. At a few attractions, adults and children wait in line together. When you approach the queue, tell the first ride attendant you see (known as a greeter) that you want to switch off. The worker will allow everyone, including young children, to enter the attraction. When you reach the loading area, one adult rides while the other stays with the kids. Attractions at some parks offer waiting areas for this purpose. Then the riding adult disembarks and takes charge of the children while the other adult rides. A third adult (or a child who meets the minimum height or age requirement) in the party can ride twice, once with each switching-off adult, so the switching-off adults don't have to ride alone.

On FastPass attractions, the park may handle switching off somewhat differently. When you tell the worker that you want to switch off, he or she may issue you a special rider-exchange pass good for up to three people. One parent and the nonriding child (or children) will, at that point, be asked to leave the line and are free to do other things while the riding adult is waiting in line and experiencing the attraction. When those riding reunite with the waiting adult, the waiting adult and two other persons from the party can ride using the special ticket. This system eliminates confusion and congestion at the boarding area while sparing the nonriding adult and child the tedium and physical exertion of waiting in line.

There is no cost to use the switching-off option. The attractions where switching off is routinely practiced, often oriented to more mature guests, are listed on page 147. Sometimes it takes a lot of courage for a child just to move through the queue holding Dad's hand. In the boarding area, many children suddenly fear abandonment when one parent leaves to ride. Prepare your children for switching off, or you might have an emotional crisis on your hands. A mom from Edison, New Jersey, writes:

Once my son understood that the switch off would not leave him abandoned, he did not seem to mind. I would recommend practicing the switch off at home, so your child is not concerned that he will be left behind. At the very least, explain the procedure in advance, so little ones know what to expect.

A Philadelphia, Pennsylvania, mother discovered that the switching-off procedure varies among attractions. She says:

Most rides did not require the entire group to stand in line together. Some rider-switch passes were handed out by the first attendant, others by the last attendant. The most common procedure involved me holding a lanyard and giving it to the very last attendant we saw (the one loading the cars) in exchange for a rider-switch pass.

In addition, the rider-switch pass was good for up to three riders and did not have a time restriction like FastPasses. There were two babies in our party (two separate families), so each time we requested two rider-switch passes, we split up to return later. Because we also got a FastPass for each person with a ticket, we had two leftover FastPasses (because of the two adults who waited outside with the babies). Therefore, we could ride the ride, and then eight of us could reenter the ride immediately via the two switch passes (good for three people each) and the two extra FastPasses. This was a good alternative to the Chuck-Bubba Relay [see below] since we had several children in our group.

Finally, there's no rule that you have to ride an attraction once you reach the boarding station. Older children and adults who are unable or unwilling to ride an attraction but still want to experience the queue with their party can simply ask an attendant for the exit.

ATTRACTIONS WHERE SWITCHING OFF IS COMMON

DISNEYLAND PARK

- **ADVENTURELAND**   Indiana Jones Adventure
- **CRITTER COUNTRY**   Splash Mountain
- **FANTASYLAND**   Matterhorn Bobsleds
- **FRONTIERLAND**   Big Thunder Mountain Railroad
- **TOMORROWLAND**   Space Mountain | Star Tours—The Adventures Continue

DISNEY CALIFORNIA ADVENTURE

- **CARS LAND**   Radiator Springs Racers
- **GRIZZLY PEAK**   Grizzly River Run | Soarin' Over California
- **HOLLYWOOD LAND**   The Twilight Zone Tower of Terror
- **PARADISE PIER**   California Screamin' | Goofy's Sky School

---

5. HOW TO RIDE TWICE IN A ROW WITHOUT WAITING Many small children like to ride a favorite attraction two or more times in succession. Riding the second time often gives the child a feeling of mastery and accomplishment. Unfortunately, repeat rides can be time-consuming, even in the early morning. If you ride Dumbo as soon as Disneyland Park opens, for instance, you will only have a 1- or 2-minute wait for your first ride. When you come back for your second ride, your wait will be about 12 minutes. If you want to ride a third time, count on a 20-minute or longer wait.

The best way for getting your child on the ride twice (or more) without blowing your whole morning is by using the Chuck-Bubba Relay (named in honor of a reader from Kentucky):

1. Mom and little Bubba enter the waiting line.
2. Dad lets a certain number of people go in front of him (32 in the case of Dumbo) and then gets in line.
3. As soon as the ride stops, Mom exits with little Bubba and passes him to Dad to ride the second time.
4. If everybody is really getting into this, Mom can hop in line again, no less than 32 people behind Dad.

The Chuck-Bubba Relay will not work on every ride because of differences in the way the waiting areas are configured (that is, it is impossible in some cases to exit the ride and make the pass). The rides where the Chuck-Bubba Relay does work, along with the number of people to count off, appear on the table below.

When practicing the Chuck-Bubba Relay, if you are the second adult in line, you will reach a point in the waiting area that is obviously the easiest place to make the handoff. Sometimes this point is where those exiting the ride pass closest to those waiting to board. In any event, you will know it when you see it. Once there, if the first parent has not arrived with little Bubba, just let those behind you slip past until Bubba shows up.

ATTRACTIONS WHERE THE CHUCK-BUBBA RELAY USUALLY WORKS
DISNEYLAND PARK *Number of people between adults*
• ALICE IN WONDERLAND (tough, but possible) 38 people
• CASEY JR. CIRCUS TRAIN 34 people, if 2 trains are operating
• DAVY CROCKETT'S EXPLORER CANOES 94 people, if 6 canoes are operating
• DUMBO THE FLYING ELEPHANT 32 people
• KING ARTHUR CAROUSEL 70 people • MAD TEA PARTY 53 people
• MR. TOAD'S WILD RIDE 32 people • PETER PAN'S FLIGHT 25 people
• SNOW WHITE'S SCARY ADVENTURES 30 people
DISNEY CALIFORNIA ADVENTURE *Number of people between adults*
• GOLDEN ZEPHYR 64 people • JUMPIN' JELLYFISH 16 people
• KING TRITON'S CAROUSEL 64 people

6. LAST-MINUTE COLD FEET If your small child gets cold feet at the last minute after waiting for a ride (where there is no age or height requirement), you can usually arrange with the loading attendant for a switch-off; see the table on page 147. This situation arises frequently at Pirates of the Caribbean—small children lose their courage en route to the loading area.

There is no law that says you have to ride. If you get to the boarding area and someone is unhappy, just tell a Disney attendant that you have changed your mind, and one will show you the way out.

7. THROW YOURSELF ON THE GRENADE, MILDRED! For by-the-book, do-the-right-thing parents who are determined to sacrifice themselves on behalf of their children, we provide a one-day touring plan for Disneyland Park called the Dumbo-or-Die-in-a-Day Touring Plan for Parents with Small Children. This plan, detailed on page 269, will ensure that you run yourself ragged. Designed to help you forfeit everything of personal interest for the sake of your children's pleasure, the plan is guaranteed to send you home battered and exhausted with extraordinary stories of devotion and heroic perseverance. Anyone under 8 years old will love it.

8. DISNEY CALIFORNIA ADVENTURE This is not a great park for little ones. With the exception of Flik's Fun Fair, The Little Mermaid: Ariel's Undersea Adventure, three play areas, and a carousel, the remaining attractions are either boring or too frightening for most preschoolers. Elementary

school–age children will fare better but will probably be captivated by the low-capacity/long-line rides at the Paradise Pier district of the park. Though designed to be appealing to the eye, these attractions are simply gussied-up versions of midway rides your kids can enjoy less expensively and with a fraction of the wait at a local amusement park or state fair.

9. AUTOPIA Though Autopia at Disneyland Park is a great treat for small children, they must be 54 inches tall to drive unassisted. To work around the height requirement issues, go on the ride with your small child. After getting into the car, shift your child over behind the steering wheel. From your position you will still be able to control the foot pedals. To your child, it will feel like driving. Because the car travels on a self-guiding track, there is no way your child can make a mistake while steering.

LOST CHILDREN

LOST CHILDREN NORMALLY do not present much of a problem at Disneyland Resort. All Disney employees are schooled in handling such situations. If you lose a child while touring, report the situation to a Disney employee; then check in at City Hall (Disneyland Park) or Guest Relations (DCA) where lost-children logs are maintained. In an emergency, an alert can be issued throughout the park through internal communications. If a Disney cast member encounters a lost child, the cast member will escort the child to the Baby Care Center located at the central-hub end of Main Street in Disneyland Park and at the entrance plaza in DCA. Guests age 11 or under are taken to the Baby Care Center in the Pacific Wharf area at DCA. Guests age 12 and older may leave a written message at City Hall or the Guest Relations lobby or wait there.

unofficial **TIP**
We suggest that children younger than 8 years be color coded by dressing them in purple T-shirts or equally distinctive clothes.

It is amazingly easy to lose a child (or two) at a Disney park. It is a good idea to sew a label into each child's shirt that states his or her name, your name, and the name of your hotel. The same task can be accomplished by writing the information on a strip of masking tape; hotel security professionals suggest that the information be printed in small letters, and that the tape be affixed to the outside of the child's shirt 5 inches or so below the armpit.

HOW KIDS GET LOST

CHILDREN GET SEPARATED FROM PARENTS every day at the Disney parks under remarkably similar (and predictable) circumstances.

1. PREOCCUPIED SOLO PARENT In this scenario the only adult in the party is preoccupied with something such as buying refreshments, adjusting the camera settings, or using the restroom. Junior is there one moment and gone the next.

2. THE HIDDEN EXIT Sometimes parents wait on the sidelines while allowing two or more young children to experience a ride together. As it usually happens, the parents expect the kids to exit the attraction in one place, and, lo and behold, the young ones pop out somewhere else. The exits of some Disney attractions are considerably distant from the entrances. Make sure that you know exactly where your children will emerge before letting them ride by themselves.

3. AFTER THE SHOW At the completion of many shows and rides, a Disney staffer will announce, "Check for personal belongings and take small children by the hand." When dozens, if not hundreds, of

TIPS FOR KEEPING TRACK OF YOUR BROOD

- Same-colored T-shirts for the whole family will help you gather your troops in an easy and fun way. Opt for just a uniform color or have the T-shirts printed with a logo such as "The Brown Family's Assault on the Mouse." You might also include the date or the year of your visit. Light-colored T-shirts can even be autographed by the Disney characters.

- Clothing labels are great, of course. If you don't sew, buy labels that you can iron on the garment. If you own a cell phone, be sure to include the number on the label. If you do not own a cell phone, put in the phone number of the hotel where you'll be staying.

- An easier option is a temporary tattoo with your child's name and your phone number. Unlike other methods, the tattoos cannot fall off or be lost. Temporary tattoos last about two weeks, won't wash or sweat off, and are not irritating to the skin. They can be purchased online at **safetytat.com** or **tattooswithapurpose .com**. Special tattoos are available for children with food allergies or cognitive impairment such as autism.

- In pet stores you can have name tags printed for a very reasonable price. These are great to add to necklaces and bracelets, or attach them to your child's shoelaces or a belt loop.

- When you check into the hotel, take a business card of the hotel for each member in your party, especially those old enough to carry wallets and purses.

- Always agree on a meeting point before you see a parade, fireworks, or nighttime spectacles. Make sure the meeting place is in the park (as opposed to the car or some place outside the front gate).

- If you have a digital camera or camera phone, you may elect to take a picture of your kids every morning. If they get lost, the picture will show what they look like and what they are wearing.

- If all members of your party have cell phones, it's easy to locate each other. However, the noise in the parks is so loud that you probably won't hear your cell phone ring. Carry your phone in a front pants pocket and program the phone to vibrate. Or communicate via text message. If any of your younger kids carry cell phones, secure the phones with a strap.

- Save key tags and luggage tags for use on items you bring to the parks, including your stroller, diaper bag, and backpack or hip pack.

- Don't underestimate the power of the permanent marker, such as a Sharpie. They are great for labeling pretty much anything. Mini-Sharpies are great for collecting character autographs.

people leave an attraction at the same time, it is easy for parents to temporarily lose contact with their children unless they have them directly in tow.

4. RESTROOM PROBLEMS Mom tells 6-year-old Tommy, "I'll be sitting on this bench when you come out of the restroom." Three situations: One, Tommy exits through a different door and becomes disoriented (Mom may not know there is another door). Two, Mom decides belatedly that she will also use the restroom, and Tommy emerges to find her absent. Three, Mom pokes around in a shop while keeping an eye on the bench but misses Tommy when he comes out. A restroom adjacent to the Rancho del Zocalo Restuarante in Frontierland accounts for many lost children. Because it's located in a passageway connecting Frontierland and Fantasy Faire, children can wander into a totally different area of the park from where they came by simply making a wrong turn out of the restroom.

If you can't be with your child in the restroom, make sure that there is only one exit. Designate a meeting spot more distinctive than a bench, and be specific in your instructions: "I'll meet you by this flagpole. If you get out first, stay right here." Have your child repeat the directions back to you.

5. PARADES There are many special parades and shows at the theme park during which the audience stands. Children, because they are small, tend to jockey around for a better view. By moving a little this way and a little that way, it is amazing how much distance kids can put between themselves and you before anyone notices.

6. MASS MOVEMENTS Another situation to guard against is when huge crowds disperse after shows, fireworks, or parades, or at park closing. With 5,000–12,000 people suddenly moving at once, it is very easy to get separated from a small child or others in your party. Extra caution is recommended following the evening parades, fireworks, and *Fantasmic!* Families should develop specific plans for what to do and where to meet in the event they are separated.

7. CHARACTER GREETINGS A fair amount of activity and confusion is commonplace when the Disney characters are on the scene. See the next section on meeting the Disney characters.

The DISNEY CHARACTERS

FOR YEARS THE COSTUMED, walking versions of Mickey, Minnie, Donald, Goofy, and others have been a colorful supporting cast at Disneyland and Walt Disney World. Known unpretentiously as the Disney characters, these large and friendly figures help provide a link between Disney animated films and the Disney theme parks.

Audiences, it has been observed, cry during the sad parts of Disney animated films and cheer when the villain is vanquished. To the emotionally invested, the characters in these features are as real as next-door neighbors; never mind that they are simply cartoons. In recent years, the theme park personifications of Disney characters have likewise become real to us. For thousands of visitors, it is not just some person in a mouse costume they see—it is really Mickey. Similarly, running into Goofy or Snow White in Fantasyland is a memory to be treasured, an encounter with a real celebrity.

About 250 of the Disney animated-film characters have been brought to life in costume. Of these, a relatively small number (about 50) are greeters (the Disney term for characters who mix with the patrons). The remaining characters are relegated exclusively to performing in shows or participating in parades. Some appear only once or twice a year, usually in holiday parades or Disney anniversary celebrations.

CHARACTER ENCOUNTERS

CHARACTER WATCHING has developed into a pastime. Where families were once content to stumble across a character occasionally, they now pursue them armed with autograph books and cameras. For those who pay attention, some characters are more frequently encountered than others. Mickey, Minnie, and Goofy, for example, are seemingly everywhere, while Thumper rarely appears. Other characters are seen regularly but limit themselves to a specific location.

The fact that some characters are seldom seen has turned character watching into character collecting. Mickey Mouse may be the best-known and most-loved character, but from a collector's perspective, he is also the most common. To get an autograph from Mickey is no big deal, but Daisy Duck's signature is a real coup. Commercially tapping into the character-collecting movement, Disney sells autograph books throughout the parks. One *Unofficial Guide* reader offers this suggestion regarding character autographs:

> *Young children learn very quickly! If they see another child get an autograph, then they will want an autograph book as well. I recommend buying an autograph book right away. My 4-year-old daughter saw a child get Goofy's autograph, and right away she wanted to join the fun.*

PREPARING YOUR CHILDREN TO MEET THE CHARACTERS Because most small children are not expecting Minnie Mouse to be the size of a forklift, it's best to discuss the characters with your kids before you go. Almost all of the characters are quite large, and several, such as Br'er Bear, are huge! All of them can be extremely intimidating to a preschooler.

On first encounter, it is important not to thrust your child upon the character. Allow the little one to come to terms with this big thing from whatever distance the child feels safe. If two adults are present, one should stay close to the youngster while the other approaches the character and demonstrates that the character is safe and friendly. Some kids warm to the characters immediately, while some never do. Most take a little time, and often require several different encounters.

There are two kinds of characters: those whose costume includes a face-covering headpiece (animal characters plus some human characters such as Captain Hook), and face characters, or actors who resemble the cartoon characters to such an extent that no mask or headpiece is necessary. Face characters include Mary Poppins, Ariel, Jasmine, Aladdin, Cinderella, Mulan, Tarzan, Jane, Belle, Snow White, and Prince Charming, to name a few.

Only the face characters are allowed to speak. Headpiece characters, called furs in Disney-speak, do not talk or make noises of any kind. Because

unofficial **TIP**
Don't underestimate your child's excitement at meeting the Disney characters—but also be aware that very small kids may find the large, costumed characters a little frightening.

the cast members could not possibly imitate the distinctive voice of the characters, the Disney folks have determined that it is more effective to keep them silent. Lack of speech notwithstanding, the headpiece characters are extremely warm and responsive, and they communicate very effectively with gestures. As with the characters' size, children need to be forewarned that the characters do not talk. The only exceptions are the costumed stars of some newer shows and parades, who boast articulated facial features that blink and flap in sync with the sound tracks.

Parents need to understand that some of the character costumes are very cumbersome and that cast members often suffer from very poor visibility. You have to look closely, but the eyeholes are frequently in the mouth of the costume or even down on the neck. What this means in practical terms is that the characters are sort of clumsy and have a limited field of vision. Children who approach the character from the back or the side may not be noticed, even if the child is touching the character. It is perfectly possible in this situation for the character to accidentally step on the child or knock him or her down. The best way for a child to approach a character is from the front, and occasionally not even this works. For example, the various duck characters (Donald, Daisy, Uncle Scrooge, and so on) have to peer around their bills. If it appears that the character is ignoring your child, pick your child up and hold her in front of the character until the character responds.

It is OK to touch, pat, or hug the character if your child is so inclined. Understanding the unpredictability of children, the characters will keep their feet very still, particularly refraining from moving backward or to the side. Most of the characters will sign autographs or pose for pictures. Once again, be sure to approach from the front so that the character will understand your intentions. If your child collects autographs, it is a good idea to carry a big, fat pen about the size of a Magic Marker. The costumes make it exceedingly difficult for the characters to wield a smaller pen, so the bigger the better.

unofficial **TIP**
Explain to your children that the headpiece characters do not talk. Keep in mind, too, that the characters are clumsy and have a limited field of vision.

THE BIG HURT Many children expect to bump into Mickey the minute they enter a park and are disappointed when he is not around. If your children are unable to settle down and enjoy things until they see Mickey, simply ask a Disney cast member where to find him. If the cast member does not know Mickey's whereabouts, he or she can find out for you in short order.

"THEN SOME CONFUSION HAPPENED" Be forewarned that character encounters give rise to a situation during which small children sometimes get lost. There is usually a lot of activity around a character, with both adults and children touching the character or posing for pictures. In the most common scenario, the parents stay in the crowd while their child marches up to get acquainted. With the excitement of the encounter, all the milling people, and the character moving around, a child may get turned around and head off in the wrong direction. In the words of a Salt Lake City mom:

> *Milo was shaking hands with Dopey one moment, then some confusion happened, and he [Milo] was gone.*

Families with several small children, and parents who are busy fooling around with cameras, can lose track of a youngster in a heartbeat. Our recommendation for parents of preschoolers is to stay with the kids when they meet the characters, stepping back only long enough to take a picture, if necessary.

MEETING CHARACTERS You can *see* the Disney characters in live shows and in parades. For times, consult your *Times Guide*. If you have the time and money, you can share a meal with the characters (more about this later). But if you want to *meet* the characters, get autographs, and take photos, it's helpful to know where the characters hang out.

Disneyland Resort includes information about characters in its handout park maps and entertainment *Times Guide*. A listing specifies where and when certain characters will be available and also provides information on character dining. On the maps of the parks themselves, Mickey's gloved hand is used to denote locations where characters can be found.

At DCA, look for characters in Hollywood Land near the Animation Building, in parades, and in shows at the Hyperion Theater. In Cars Land, you'll find interactive incarnations of the series' automotive stars. Anna and Elsa from *Frozen* hold court inside the Disney Animation attraction. Elsewhere around the park, characters will be less in evidence than at Disneyland Park, but they will make periodic appearances at Flik's Fun Fair and Buena Vista Street (the central hub).

The last few years have seen a number of Disney initiatives aimed at satisfying guests' inexhaustible desire to meet the characters. At

Disneyland Park, Disney relegated four (Mickey, Minnie, Pluto, and Donald) of the "fab five" to all-day tours of duty in Mickey's Toontown. The fifth "fab," Goofy, works a similar schedule most days in Frontierland but also spends plenty of time in Toontown. Likewise, Pooh and Tigger can usually be found in Critter Country, and Aladdin and Jasmine in Adventureland. The Fantasy Faire plaza adjacent to Sleeping Beauty Castle is the prime place to meet Aurora, Ariel, Cinderella, Belle, Mulan, Tiana, Merida, and Rapunzel. Tinker Bell and her fairy friends draw long lines at their Pixie Hollow area off the central hub between Tomorrowland and the Matterhorn. Characters less in demand may pop up at the Big Thunder Ranch Jamboree in Frontierland or roam the "lands" consistent with their image (Br'er Bear and Br'er Fox in Critter Country, for example). Oswald the Lucky Rabbit (a long-lost forerunner of Mickey Mouse) meets guests near the park entrance, and Olaf the Snowman from *Frozen* gives warm hugs in Hollywood Land.

unofficial **TIP**
Characters make appearances in all the "lands" but are especially thick in Fantasyland, Mickey's Toontown, and Town Square on Main Street.

While making the characters routinely available has taken the guesswork out of finding them, it has likewise robbed character encounters of much of their surprise and spontaneity. Instead of chancing on a character as you turn a corner, it is much more common now to wait in a queue to meet the character. Be aware that lines for face characters move much more slowly than lines for nonspeaking characters do, as you might surmise. Because face characters are allowed to talk, they do, often engaging children in lengthy conversations, much to the consternation of the families stuck in the queue.

If you believe that Disneyland Park already has quite enough lines, and, furthermore, if you prefer to bump into your characters on the run, here's a quick rundown of where the bears and chipmunks roam. There will almost always be a character in Town Square on Main Street and often at the central hub. Snow White hangs out near her wishing well in the courtyard of the castle; the aforementioned Br'ers cruise Critter Country; and Alice and her Wonderland friends wander around Fantasyland. Any characters whom we haven't specifically mentioned generally continue to turn up randomly throughout the park. Character selection can vary seasonally, with some (such as Jack Skellington) appearing only around Halloween or Christmas.

Characters are also featured in the afternoon and evening parades, Frontierland waterfront shows, *Fantasmic!,* and Fantasy Faire. Performance times for all of the shows and parades are listed in the Disneyland Park's daily *Times Guide* entertainment listings. After the shows, characters will sometimes stick around to greet the audience.

Mickey Mouse is available to meet guests and pose for photos all day long in his dressing room at Mickey's Movie Barn in Mickey's Toontown. To reach the Movie Barn, proceed through the front door of Mickey's House and follow the crowd. If the line extends back to the entrance of Mickey's House, it will take you about 25–30 minutes to actually reach Mickey. When you finally get to his dressing room, one or two families at a time are admitted for a short personal audience with Mickey.

Many children are so excited about meeting Mickey that they cannot relax to enjoy the other attractions. If Mickey looms large in your child's day, board the Disneyland Railroad at the Main Street Station as soon as you arrive at the park, and proceed directly to Mickey's Toontown (half a circuit). If you visit Mickey within an hour of Toontown's opening, your wait will be short.

Minnie receives guests at her house in Toontown most of the day as well, and Donald and Pluto are frequently available for photographs and autographs in the gazebo in front of the Toontown Town Hall. There is, of course, a separate line for each character. Also, be aware that the characters bug out for parades and certain other special performances. Check the daily *Times Guide* entertainment listings for performance times and plan your visit to Toontown accordingly.

CHARACTER DINING

FRATERNIZING WITH DISNEY CHARACTERS has become so popular that Disney offers character breakfasts, brunches, and dinners where families can dine in the presence of Minnie, Goofy, and other costumed versions of animated celebrities. Character meals provide a familiar, controlled setting in which young children can warm gradually to the characters. All meals are attended by several characters. Adult prices apply to persons age 10 or older, children's prices to ages 3–9. Little ones under age 3 eat free. Because character dining is very popular, we recommend that you arrange reservations as far in advance (up to 60 days) as possible.

CHARACTER DINING: WHAT TO EXPECT Character meals are bustling affairs, held in hotels' or theme parks' largest table-service or "buffeteria" restaurants. Character breakfasts (there are five) offer a fixed menu served family-style or as a buffet. The typical family-style breakfast includes scrambled eggs; bacon, sausage, and ham; hash browns; waffles, pancakes, or French toast; biscuits, rolls, or pastries; and fruit. The meal is served in large skillets or platters at your table. If you run out of something, you can order seconds (or thirds) at no additional charge. Buffets offer much the same fare, but you have to fetch it yourself.

Whatever the meal, characters circulate around the room while you eat. During your meal, each of the three to five characters present will visit your table, arriving one at a time to cuddle the kids (and sometimes the adults), pose for photos, and sign autographs. Keep autograph books (with pens) and cameras handy. For the best photos, adults should sit across the table from their children. Always seat the children where characters can reach them most easily. If a table is against a wall, for example, adults should sit with their backs to the wall and children should sit nearest the aisle.

You will not be rushed to leave after you've eaten. Remember, however, lots of eager children and adults might be waiting not so patiently to be admitted.

You can dine with Disney characters at the Plaza Inn in Disneyland Park, Goofy's Kitchen at the Disneyland Hotel, Ariel's Grotto at DCA, the Storytellers Café at the Grand Californian Hotel, and Disney's PCH Grill at the Paradise Pier Hotel. For information about character meals and to make dining reservations up to 60 days in advance, call ☎ 714-781-DINE (3463).

*un**official* **TIP**
Arrange dining reservations as far in advance as possible. Your wait for a table will usually be less than 15 minutes.

ARIEL'S DISNEY PRINCESS CELEBRATION Overlooking Paradise Bay, Ariel's Grotto hosts breakfast, lunch, and dinner (until 5 p.m.) with Ariel and friends daily. Breakfast costs $37 for adults and $22 for kids, and lunch (or early dinner) is $40 for adults and $24 for kids. Fixed-price dinners include *World of Color* reservations, but the characters aren't present.

DISNEY'S PCH (PACIFIC COAST HIGHWAY) GRILL PCH Grill at the Paradise Pier Hotel serves a Surf's Up! Breakfast with Mickey & Friends buffet 7–11 a.m. that features traditional Mexican breakfast items such as *chilaquiles* in addition to the usual American fare. Prices are $33 for adults and $19 for kids. Mickey (wearing beach togs), along with Stitch, Minnie, and Pluto, entertains you. This is usually the least crowded of the hotel character meals.

GOOFY'S KITCHEN Located at the Disneyland Hotel, Goofy's Kitchen serves a character breakfast buffet 7–11:30 a.m. (until 1:15 p.m. Saturday–Sunday) and a character dinner buffet 5–8:45 p.m. Breakfast is $34 for adults and $20 for kids. Dinners run $39 and $23, respectively. Goofy, of course, is the head character, but he's usually joined by Minnie, Pluto, and others.

PLAZA INN Located at the end of Main Street and to the right, the Plaza Inn character buffet is usually packed because it hosts character breakfasts that are included in vacation packages sold by the Disney Resort Travel Sales Center. Served from opening until 11 a.m., the buffet costs $31 for adults and $18 for children. Characters present usually include Minnie, Goofy, Pluto, and Chip 'n' Dale.

STORYTELLERS CAFÉ Storytellers Café, located at the Grand Californian Hotel, is the most attractive of the character-meal venues. A breakfast buffet is served 7–11:25 a.m. The buffet costs $31 for adults and $18 for children. Chip 'n' Dale, the featured characters, are usually assisted by critters from *Tarzan, Brother Bear,* and *Pocahontas.*

PART FOUR

DINING *and* SHOPPING *In and Around* DISNEYLAND

▌ DINING *in* DISNEYLAND RESORT

IN THIS SECTION, we aim to help you find good food without going broke or tripping over one of Disneyland Resort's many culinary land mines. More than 50 restaurants operate in Disneyland Resort, including about 20 full-service restaurants, several of which are inside the theme parks. Collectively, Disney restaurants offer reasonable variety, serving everything from Louisiana Creole to Texas barbecue, but sadly, international cuisines other than Mexican, Asian, Mediterranean, and Italian are not represented.

On the upside, we've seen a dramatic improvement in Disneyland Resort restaurant quality since 2010, though the gains have leveled off lately. Ingredients are fresher, preparation is more careful, and even steam tables and buffets are under almost constant supervision. As a whole, the culinary team has definitely stepped up their game, and we are the winners. Many establishments have undergone complete menu makeovers, with terrific results. Unlike other attractions and shops inside the resort, the food and beverage operation remains in constant flux. Venues open and close, add and delete menu items, and change decor throughout the year. We strive to provide you with the most accurate information possible; however, we do eventually have to go to press with the most current information we have at the time. Keep this in mind when using the guide.

You can expect to pay hefty prices for food within Disneyland Resort. Nearly every entrée, snack, and drink purchased inside the theme parks and resort hotels will cost anywhere from 50% to 300% more than similar items at your hometown eateries. On the concession markup scale, Disneyland falls just behind airports and sports stadiums. However, its food is a bargain compared to some regional theme parks, and you can find munchies at more moderate (or at least mall-like) prices in Downtown Disney.

With fine dining offered at California Adventure, you can enjoy a glass of wine, a mug of beer, or even a cocktail inside the resorts without having to exit the park. Downtown Disney offers a wide variety of dining options, from mediocre to awesome, from intimate and adult to wild and kid-friendly. The Grand Californian Hotel is home to **Napa Rose,** one of the finest dining spots in all of Southern California, and even character meals at eateries such as **Ariel's Grotto** and **Disney's PCH Grill** offer better, healthier food than ever before.

Note: Disneyland dining reservations are the Disney-restaurant equivalent of FastPass. This feature is available where noted and gives you the option of picking a time and cutting to the head of the line. You may still have to wait, but it's from the front of the line instead of the back.

DISNEY DINING 101

DISNEYLAND RESORT RESTAURANT RESERVATIONS: WHAT'S IN A NAME

DISNEY TINKERS CEASELESSLY with its restaurant-reservations policy. Disneyland dining reservations issues reservations that aren't exactly reservations. When you call Disney Dining at ☎ 714-781-3463, option 4, or visit **disneyland.disney.go.com/dining,** your name and essential information are taken, well, as if you were making a reservation. The Disney representative then tells you that you have dining reservations for the restaurant on the date and time you requested, usually explaining that you will be seated ahead of walk-ins—that is, those guests without reservations. Frequent eaters will be thrilled to discover that Disneyland's online dining reservations system has finally caught up with its Orlando sibling and now allows you to book a table without any pesky human interaction. Visit **disneyland.disney.go.com/dining** on your computer or smartphone to see restaurant availability up to 60 days out. You will need to create a **disney.com** login account (if you don't already have one) and supply a credit card and phone number to secure a booking (see below).

Travelers who have experienced Walt Disney World's Advanced Dining Reservations system will be relieved to discover that Disneyland's dining reservations scheme is far less stress-inducing, largely because the Disney Dining Plan is not nearly as popular in Anaheim. Unlike in Orlando, there is no need to hit the phones at 7 a.m. on the 180th day before your Disneyland vacation; except on the busiest days, most restaurants in the parks and hotels offer same-day availability.

unofficial **TIP**
Dining reservations are available to all Disneyland visitors—not just guests of the resort hotels. In the theme parks, you can make reservations for later in the day at the door of the restaurant.

BEHIND THE SCENES AT DISNEYLAND RESORT DINING

DISNEY RESTAURANTS OPERATE on what they call a template system. Instead of scheduling reservations for actual tables, reservationists fill time slots. The number of slots available is based on the average observed length of time that guests occupy a table at a particular restaurant.

Here's a rough example of how it works: Let's say that the Blue Bayou Restaurant at Disneyland Park has 38 tables for four and 10 tables for six, and that the average length of time for a family to be seated, order, eat, pay, and depart is 40 minutes. Add 5 minutes to bus the table and set it up for the next guests, and the tables are turning every 45 minutes. The restaurant provides Disneyland Resort Dining (DRD) with a computer template of its capacity, along with the average time the table is occupied. Thus, when DRD makes reservations for four people at 6:15 p.m., the system removes one table for four from overall capacity for 45 minutes. The template on the reservationist's computer indicates that the table will not be available for reassignment until 7 p.m. (45 minutes later). And so it goes for all the tables in the restaurant, each being subtracted from overall capacity for 45 minutes, then listed as available again, then assigned to other guests and subtracted again, and so on, throughout the meal period. DRD tries to fill every time slot for every seat in the restaurant, or come as close to filling every slot as possible. No seats—repeat, none—are *reserved* for walk-ins, though all restaurants accommodate such customers on a space-available basis.

With dining reservations, your waiting time will almost always be less than 20 minutes during peak hours, and often less than 10 minutes. If you just walk in, especially during busier seasons, expect to wait 40–75 minutes.

GETTING YOUR ACT TOGETHER

IF YOU WANT TO PATRONIZE ANY of the Disneyland Resort full-service restaurants, especially buffets or character-dining eateries, you should consider dining reservations (call ☎ 714-781-3463, option 4, up to 60 days in advance). DRD handles reservations for both Disney-owned and independent restaurants at the theme parks, Disney hotels, and Downtown Disney. The sole exception is the **Rainforest Cafe** at Downtown Disney, which makes its own reservations at ☎ 714-772-0413.

If you fail to make dining reservations before you leave home, or if you want to make your dining decisions spontaneously, your chances of getting a table at the restaurant of your choice are good. Blue Bayou at Disneyland Park, Napa Rose at the Grand Californian Hotel, and the various character-meal venues are the most likely to sell out. If, however, you visit Disneyland during a very busy time of year, it's to your advantage to make dining reservations.

Disneyland collects a credit card number with every dining reservation. If you poop out in the theme park and are a no-show for your meal, you will be charged $10 per person. Your reservation will be voided 15 minutes after the scheduled time, and the penalty will apply unless you call DRD at least 24 hours before your seating. This same cancellation policy also applies to makeover appointments at Bibbidi Bobbidi Boutique, as well as cabanas at the hotel pools. If you've lined up many seatings, it's a good idea to phone DRD a few days before you arrive to make sure that everything is in order. If you stay at a Disney resort, Guest Services can print out a summary of all your dining reservations. If you have a seating for a theme park restaurant at a time before park opening, as is sometimes the case for a character breakfast, simply proceed to the turnstiles and inform a cast member, who will admit you to the park.

DRESS

DRESS IS INFORMAL at all theme park restaurants, but dressy casual is appropriate for resort restaurants such as Napa Rose. That means dress slacks (or dress shorts) with a collared shirt for men and slacks, skirts, or dress shorts with a blouse or sweater (or a dress) for women. You may be surprised how comfortable you feel when you're dressed appropriately.

FOOD ALLERGIES AND SPECIAL REQUESTS

WITH MILLIONS OF AMERICANS now reporting sensitivity to certain foods or following specific diets, the restaurants at Disneyland Resort are receiving a record number of special dietary requests. Happily, Disney has responded to this trend and is now able to accommodate most guests' gustatory needs. If you have dietary concerns, call ☎ 714-781-3463 to discuss any special requests when making dining reservations, and ask to speak with a chef or manager before your meal whenever arriving at a restaurant to confirm that your needs can be met.

In 2015, both Disneyland and Walt Disney World rolled out new allergy-friendly menus at many of their table- and quick-service restaurants, both inside and outside the theme parks. These new menus explicitly call out dishes without ingredients such as gluten, dairy, peanuts, tree nuts, eggs, soy, or shellfish. If you have one of these common allergies or are vegetarian, you can be confident of finding something to eat almost anywhere without needing to make special arrangements ahead of time. However, if you have an uncommon or complicated allergy or a metabolic disorder, e-mail **DLRSpecialDiets@ email.disney.com** with your needs at least two weeks before your visit.

Kosher meals are available on request at Plaza Inn, Rancho del Zocalo, and Tomorrowland Terrace at Disneyland Park, and at Smokejumpers Grill at Disney California Adventure (DCA). Kosher meals can also be delivered to table-service locations with 24 hours' notice (call the above number). About the only diet that can still be challenging to accommodate is vegan. While all locations have vegetarian dishes, they often don't alert you to incidental animal products in things such as cooking oil.

Be warned that, while the Disney folks do their best to meet guests' needs, they don't have separate allergen-free kitchen facilities or dining areas, and inadvertent contamination is always a possibility. If your dietary issue is a matter of life or death, you are allowed to bring your own food and medication into the parks. Glass containers are still prohibited, but edibles and EpiPens are OK; just know that Disney employees aren't allowed to hold or heat up your personal food.

Do Disney's attempts at dietary accommodation work? Well, a Phillipsburg, New Jersey, mom reports her family's experience:

My 6-year-old has many food allergies, and we often have to bring food with us to restaurants when we go out to eat. I was able to make reservations at the Disney restaurants in advance and indicate these allergies to the reservation clerk. When we arrived at the restaurants, the staff was already aware of my child's allergies and assigned our table a chef who double-checked the list of allergies with us. Each member of the waitstaff was also informed of the allergies. The chefs were very nice and made my son feel very special (to the point where my other family members felt a little jealous).

A FEW CAVEATS

BEFORE YOU BEGIN EATING YOUR WAY through Disneyland, take our advice:

1. However creative and enticing the menu descriptions, avoid fancy food at full-service restaurants in the theme parks. Order dishes that the kitchen is unlikely to botch. Stick with what's familiar in most cases and you won't be disappointed.

2. Don't order baked, broiled, poached, or grilled seafood unless the restaurant specializes in seafood or rates at least ★★★½ in our dining profiles.

3. Theme park restaurants rush their customers to make room for the next group of diners. Eating at high speed may appeal to a family with young, restless children, but for people wanting to relax, it's more like dining in a pressure chamber. The exceptions to this rule may be Wine Country Trattoria and Carthay Circle Restaurant inside DCA, upscale venues that encourage a respite over a glass or bottle of premium wine. But, sadly, you may feel pressure even there in peak season.

   If you want to linger over your expensive meal, don't order your entire dinner at once. Order drinks, study the menu while you sip, and then order appetizers. Tell the waiter you need more time to decide among entrées. Order your main course only after appetizers have been served. Dawdle over coffee and dessert.

4. If you're dining in a theme park and cost is an issue, make lunch your main meal. Entrées are similar to those on the dinner menu, but prices may be slightly lower.

DISNEYLAND RESORT RESTAURANT CATEGORIES

IN GENERAL, food and beverage offerings at Disneyland Resort are defined by service, price, and convenience:

FULL-SERVICE RESTAURANTS Full-service restaurants are in all Disneyland Resort hotels, both parks, and Downtown Disney. Disney operates most of the restaurants in the theme parks and its hotels; contractors or franchisees operate those at Downtown Disney. The restaurants accept Visa, MasterCard, American Express, Discover, and Diners Club.

BUFFETS AND FIXED-PRICE MEALS With set-price character meals, such as Ariel's Grotto at DCA, you can choose one item each from a limited selection of appetizers, salads, main courses, and desserts. Character buffets, such as the one at Goofy's Kitchen in the Disneyland Hotel, have a separate children's menu featuring kid favorites such as hot dogs, burgers, chicken nuggets, pizza, macaroni and cheese, and spaghetti and meatballs, as well as healthier options such as sliced fruit, yogurt, and whole-grain baked goods. Dining reservations are highly recommended for all character meals.

COUNTER SERVICE Counter-service fast food is available at both theme parks and Downtown Disney. The food compares in quality with McDonald's, Captain D's, Pizza Hut, or Taco Bell but is more expensive, though it's often served in larger portions.

HARD CHOICES

DINING DECISIONS will definitely affect your Disneyland Resort experience. If you're short on time and you want to see the theme parks, avoid full service. Ditto if you're short on funds. If you want to try a Disney full-service restaurant, arrange dining reservations—this won't reserve you a table, but it will minimize your wait.

Integrating Meals into *The Unofficial Guide* Touring Plans

Arrive before the park of your choice opens. Tour expeditiously, using your chosen plan (taking as few breaks as possible) until about 11–11:30 a.m. Once the park becomes crowded around midday, meals and other breaks won't affect the plan's efficiency. If you intend to stay in the park for evening parades, fireworks, or other events, eat dinner early enough to be finished in time for the festivities.

Character Dining

A number of restaurants, primarily those that serve all-you-can-eat buffets or family-style meals, offer character dining. At character meals, you pay a fixed price and dine in the presence of one to five Disney characters who circulate throughout the restaurant, hugging children, posing for photos, and signing autographs. Character breakfasts, lunches, and dinners are served at restaurants in and out of the theme parks. For an extensive discussion of character dining, see page 157.

FULL-SERVICE DINING FOR FAMILIES WITH YOUNG CHILDREN

NO MATTER HOW FORMAL a restaurant appears, the staff is accustomed to wiggling, impatient, and often boisterous children. In Disneyland Resort's finest dining rooms, it's not unusual to find at least two dozen young diners attired in basic black . . . mouse ears.

unofficial **TIP**
Bottom line: Young children are the rule, not the exception, at Disney restaurants.

Almost all Disney restaurants offer children's menus, and all have booster seats and high chairs. Waiters will supply little ones with crackers and rolls and serve your dinner much faster than in comparable restaurants elsewhere. In fact, letters from readers suggest that being served too quickly is much more common than having a long wait.

QUIET, ROMANTIC PLACES TO EAT

RESTAURANTS WITH GOOD FOOD *and* a couple-friendly ambience are rare in the theme parks. **Blue Bayou** at Disneyland Park satisfies both requirements. In Disney California Adventure, **Wine Country Trattoria** offers one of the quietest and more relaxed environments, along with a California wine country–inspired menu, while the elegant **Carthay Circle Restaurant** ranks as one of the best restaurants in any theme park. Among the hotels at the resort, **Napa Rose** at the Grand Californian Hotel & Spa is the leading candidate for a romantic adult dining experience. At Downtown Disney, try **Ralph Brennan's Jazz Kitchen**; ask for a quiet table, though, if you're not interested in the jazz music. **Catal** in Downtown Disney also offers a quiet ambience and an ambitious gourmet menu geared mostly to adults.

Eating later in the evening and choosing a restaurant we've mentioned will improve your chances for intimate dining; nevertheless, know that children, well behaved or otherwise, are everywhere at Disneyland, and you can't escape them.

FAST FOOD IN THE THEME PARKS

BECAUSE MOST MEALS during a Disneyland vacation are consumed on the run while touring, we'll tackle counter-service and vendor foods first. Plentiful at all theme parks are hot dogs, hamburgers, chicken sandwiches, salads, and pizza. They're augmented by special items that relate to the park's theme or the part of the park you're touring. In the alpine village setting of Fantasyland, for example, counter-service bratwurst and apple strudel are sold; in New Orleans Square, Cajun and Creole dishes are available. Counter-service prices are fairly consistent from park to park. Expect to pay the same amount for your coffee or hot dog at DCA that you would at Disneyland Park.

If you are used to counter-service food at Walt Disney World, the quality and variety in Anaheim may catch you off guard, as it did a Cottleville, Missouri, reader:

> *I was surprised that the counter-service food was so excellent. Plaza Inn, Flo's V8 Cafe, and French Market were superb. Selection and quality were clearly better than even table service at WDW.*

Getting your act together in regard to counter service is more a matter of courtesy than necessity. Rude guests rank fifth among reader complaints. A mother from Fort Wayne, Indiana, points out that indecision can be as maddening as outright discourtesy, especially when you're hungry:

> *Every fast-food restaurant has menus the size of billboards, but do you think anybody reads them? People waiting in line spend enough time in front of these menus to memorize them and still don't have a clue what they want when they finally get to the order taker. Tell your readers to PULEEEZ get their orders together ahead of time!*

Another reader offers a tip about counter-service food lines:

Many counter-service registers serve two queues each, one to the left and one to the right of each register. People are not used to this and will instinctively line up in one queue per register. We had register operators wave us up to the front several times to start a left queue instead of waiting behind others on the right.

Healthful Food at Disneyland Resort

One of the most commendable developments in food service at Disneyland has been the introduction of healthier foods and snacks. Diabetics, vegetarians, weight watchers, those requiring kosher meals, and guests on restricted diets should have no trouble finding something to eat. The same goes for anyone seeking wholesome, nutritious food. Health-conscious choices (including gluten-free bread) are available at most fast-food counters and even from vendors. A simple request is likely to get you what you need even if it doesn't necessarily appear on the menu.

Cutting Your Dining Time at the Theme Parks

Even if you confine your meals to vendor and counter-service fast food, you lose a lot of time getting sustenance in the theme parks. At Disneyland Park and DCA, everything begins with a line and ends with a cash register. When it comes to fast food, *fast* may apply to the time you spend eating it, not the time invested in obtaining it.

Here are suggestions for minimizing the time you spend hunting and gathering food:

1. Don't waste touring time on breakfast at the parks. Restaurants outside Disneyland offer some outstanding breakfast specials. Many hotels furnish small refrigerators in their guest rooms, or you can rent one. If you can get by on cold cereal, rolls, fruit, and juice, having a fridge in your room will save a ton of time. If you can't get a fridge, bring a cooler.

2. After a good breakfast, buy snacks from vendors in the parks as you tour, or stuff some snacks in a hip pack. This is very important if you're on a tight schedule and can't spend a lot of time waiting in line for food.

3. All theme park restaurants are busiest 11:30 a.m.–2:15 p.m. for lunch and 6–9 p.m. for dinner. For shorter lines and faster service, don't eat during these hours, especially 12:30–1:30 p.m.

4. Many counter-service restaurants sell cold sandwiches. Buy a cold lunch (except for drinks) before 11:30 a.m., and carry it until you're ready to eat. Ditto for dinner. Bring small plastic bags in which to pack the food; purchase drinks at the appropriate time from any convenient vendor.

5. Most fast-food eateries have more than one service window. Regardless of the time of day, check the lines at all windows before queuing. Sometimes a window that's staffed but out of the way will have a much shorter line or none at all. Note, however, that some windows may offer only certain items.

6. If you're short on time and the park closes early, stay until closing and eat dinner outside Disneyland before returning to your hotel. If the park stays open late, eat dinner about 4 or 4:30 p.m. at the restaurant of your choice. You should miss the last wave of lunchers and sneak in just ahead of the dinner crowd. Be warned, however, that most eateries at Downtown Disney and the Disneyland Resort hotels stop serving at 10 p.m., even when the parks are open until midnight.

7. Crowds pack nearby eateries before, during, and immediately after special events, parades, and shows such as the wildly popular *World of Color* in DCA. Conversely, dining venues far from the action are almost empty during their run times, and you can typically walk right up to the counter without any wait at all.

Beyond Counter Service: Tips for Saving Money on Food

Though buying food from counter-service restaurants and vendors will save you time and money compared with full-service dining, additional strategies can bolster your budget and maintain your waistline. Over the years, our readers have offered the following suggestions:

1. Go to Disneyland during a period of fasting and abstinence. You can save a fortune *and* save your soul!

2. Wear clothes that are slightly too small and make you feel like dieting. (No spandex allowed!)

3. Whenever you're feeling hungry, ride the Mad Tea Party, California Screamin', or other attractions that can induce motion sickness.

4. Leave your cash and credit cards at your hotel. Buy food only with money your children fish out of fountains and wishing wells.

Cost-conscious readers also have volunteered ideas for stretching food dollars. A Missouri mom writes:

unofficial **TIP**
Restaurants with a **Mickey Check** logo on their menus (showing Mickey's head with a check mark) offer special meals for kids ages 3–9. Menu items (including roast turkey, meat loaf, and mac and cheese) are designed to meet balanced nutritional guidelines with zero saturated and trans fats, less sugar, and reduced sodium.

We arrived with our cooler well stocked with milk and sandwich fixings. I froze a block of ice in a milk bottle, and we replenished it daily from the resort ice machine. I also froze small packages of deli meats for later in the week. We ate cereal, milk, and fruit each morning, with boxed juices. I also had a hot pot to boil water for instant coffee, oatmeal, and soup.

Each child had a belt bag of his own, which he filled from a special box of goodies each day. I made a great mystery of filling the box in the weeks before the trip. Some things were actual food, such as packages of crackers and cheese or peanuts and raisins. Some were worthless junk, such as candy and gum. They grazed from their bags at will throughout the day, with no interference from Mom and Dad. Each also had a small, rectangular plastic water bottle that could hang on the belt. We filled these at water fountains before getting into lines and were the envy of many.

We left the park before noon; ate sandwiches, chips, and soda in the room; and napped. We purchased our evening meal in the park at a counter-service eatery. We budgeted for morning and evening snacks from a vendor but often did not need them. It made the occasional treat all the more special. Our cooler had been pretty much emptied by the end of the week, but the block of ice was still there.

A mom from Whiteland, Indiana, who purchases drinks in the parks, offers this suggestion:

One must-take item if you're traveling with younger kids is a supply of small cups to split drinks, which are both huge and expensive.

We interviewed one woman who brought a huge picnic for her family of five packed in a large diaper–baby paraphernalia bag. She stowed the bag in a locker on Main Street and retrieved it when the family was hungry.

Note: Disney prohibits glass containers and alcoholic beverages, as well as coolers and backpacks of a certain size.

READERS' RESTAURANT-SURVEY RESPONSES

FOR EACH DISNEYLAND RESTAURANT PROFILED, we include the results of last year's Reader-Survey Responses. Results are expressed as a percentage of readers who liked the restaurant well enough to eat there again (thumbs-up 👍) versus the percentage who didn't (thumbs-down 👎). (Readers tend to be less critical than we are, for what it's worth.) If you'd like to participate in the ratings, go to **touringplans.com /disneyland-resort/survey.**

Remember that our survey results report overall reader satisfaction, not just food quality. Also, the star ratings of the full-service restaurants represent the opinions of our research team and our dining insider—your experience may vary.

THEME PARK COUNTER-SERVICE RESTAURANT
Mini-Profiles

TO HELP YOU FIND palatable fast-service foods that suit your taste, we have developed mini-profiles of Disneyland Park and DCA counter-service restaurants. The restaurants are listed alphabetically by park. Detailed profiles of all Disneyland full-service restaurants follow this section, beginning on page 176.

The restaurants profiled in the following pages are rated for quality and portion size as well as value. The value rating ranges from A to F as follows:

A	Exceptional value; a real bargain
B	Good value
C	Fair value; you get exactly what you pay for
D	Somewhat overpriced
F	Extremely overpriced

Note: Because they offer special or unusual dishes, the following counter-service restaurants are profiled in full and are listed with the full-service restaurants:

The French Market *Disneyland Park*

River Belle Terrace *Disneyland Park*

Rancho del Zocalo Restaurante *Disneyland Park*

DISNEYLAND PARK
Bengal Barbecue

QUALITY Good-Excellent	VALUE B-	PORTION Small	LOCATION Adventureland
Reader-Survey Responses 86% 👍 14% 👎			

Selections Beef, chicken, or veggie skewers; jalapeño cheese–stuffed pretzels.

Comments Skewers are small, but nothing costs more than $5. The bacon-wrapped asparagus and Polynesian chicken skewers are best, proving the old adage that everything tastes better on a stick. Portions have shrunk noticeably over the years, but this is still a good fast-food alternative to the dine-in options inside the park.

Daisy's Diner

QUALITY Fair	VALUE C-	PORTION Medium	LOCATION Mickey's Toontown
Reader-Survey Responses 17% 👍 83% 👎			

Selections Pepperoni and cheese pizzas.

Comments Subpar pizza for eating on the run—there's no convenient place to sit.

The Golden Horseshoe

QUALITY Fair	VALUE C	PORTION Medium	LOCATION Frontierland
Reader-Survey Responses 77% 👍 23% 👎			

Selections Chicken nuggets, fish-and-chips, crispy chicken salad, chili, and ice cream sundaes.

Comments The Golden Horseshoe hosts live interactive entertainment and fair fried food. Meaty chili is a tribute to Walt and available in an unadvertised side portion perfect for a snack, if you don't want it on a pile of fries or in a bread bowl. Service can be slow; the leftmost open register often has the shortest line. Gazebo-style seating next to the stage is best.

Harbour Galley

QUALITY Good	VALUE B	PORTION Medium	LOCATION Critter Country
Reader-Survey Responses 92% 👍 8% 👎			

Selections Broccoli-and–Cheddar cheese soup, clam chowder, or seasonal soup, all served in a sourdough bread bowl; roast beef salad or shrimp salad; stuffed baked potatoes. Kids' meal includes string cheese, yogurt, and fruit.

Comments The broccoli-and-cheese soup is really good on cool days. Limited seating, but other seats are available along the dock around the back of the restaurant. The popular overstuffed baked potatoes (with broccoli, bacon, or barbecue chicken) formerly found at Troubadour Tavern are now served here. The lobster roll is skimpy and overseasoned with Old Bay.

BEST SNACKS AT DISNEYLAND RESORT

We share our snacking insights on keeping your tummy happy at The Happiest Place on Earth. Call ☎ 714-781-0112 for a recorded message that reveals what candy will be made that week.

DISNEYLAND PARK

- Frozen lemonade *(vending cart)* • Caramel apple pie *(Plaza Inn)*
- Stuffed baked potatoes *(Harbour Galley)* • Taffy *(Candy Palace)*
- Honey-pot krispie *(Pooh's Hunny Spot)* • Turkey legs *(vending cart)*
- DL Tigger tails *(Pooh's Hunny Spot)* • Pommes frites *(Café Orléans)*
- Pickles *(fruit cart near Hungry Bear)* • English toffee *(Candy Palace)*
- Fritter trio *(New Orleans Square)* • Peanut brittle *(Main Street, Candy Palace)*
- Apple pie apple *(Pooh's Hunny Spot)* • Pumpkin fudge *(Candy Palace)*
- Chicken on a stick *(Bengal Barbecue)* • Snickerdoodles *(Pooh's Hunny Spot)*
- Mint juleps *(nonalcoholic; Mint Julep Bar)* • Bratwurst *(Troubadour Tavern)*
- Chocolate-dipped Oreos *(Pooh's Hunny Spot)*
- Bacon-wrapped asparagus *(Bengal Barbecue)*
- Mickey-shaped waffles *(breakfast at Carnation Café)*
- Mickey-shaped pancakes *(breakfast at River Belle Terrace)*
- Chili-lime corn on the cob *(Edelweiss Snacks)*
- Coconut macaroons shaped like the Matterhorn *(Jolly Holiday Bakery)*
- Ice cream in a freshly made, chocolate-dipped waffle cone *(Gibson Girl)*
- Pretzels stuffed with jalapeño cheese *(Refreshment Corner, Bengal Barbecue)*
- Pineapple—Dole whips, Dole whip floats, pineapple spears *(Tiki Juice Bar near Tiki Room)*

DISNEY CALIFORNIA ADVENTURE

- Red's Apple Freeze *(Cozy Cone Motel)* • Orange sorbet *(Wine Country Trattoria)*
- Hand-dipped ice cream bars *(Clarabelle's)*
- Character-inspired candy apples *(Trolley Treats)*
- Funky flavored popcorn *(Cozy Cone Motel)*
- Ugly crust apple-Cheddar pie *(Flo's V8 Cafe)*
- Edamame with sriracha *(Lucky Fortune Cookery)*
- Chocolate-covered pineapple skewer *(Trolley Treats)*

DOWNTOWN DISNEY

- Chunky strawberry *(Jamba Juice)* • Candy unique to Disneyland *(Marceline's)*
- Fried shrimp po'boy *(Ralph Brennan's Jazz Kitchen Express)*
- Churro ice cream sandwich *(vending cart)*
- Coconut ice cream with hot fudge *(Häagen-Dazs)*

RESORT RESTAURANTS

- Carnitas burger *(Whitewater Snacks at Grand Californian)*
- Panko-crusted long beans *(Trader Sam's at Disneyland Hotel)*
- Bananas Foster French toast *(breakfast character meal at Storytellers Café at Grand Californian)*

Hungry Bear Restaurant

QUALITY Good–Excellent   **VALUE** B+   **PORTION** Medium–Large   **LOCATION** Critter Country   **READER-SURVEY RESPONSES** 98% 👍 2% 👎

Selections A huge, one-third-pound chili cheeseburger topped with a fried onion ring (skip the chili; it's pasty and bland), a fried green tomato sandwich with a side of jicama coleslaw, and a fried chicken sandwich with honey mustard. Healthier choices include a turkey and provolone sandwich on a multigrain roll and Big Al's smoked chicken salad with lettuce, watermelon, candied pecans, dried cherries, and pickled red onions with a sweet-tart honey-lime vinaigrette. Kids can feast on healthier meals with string cheese, nonfat yogurt, sliced apples, and whole-grain fish crackers.

Comments The sweet potato fries are really tasty. Popular and crowded during busier times of the year. During slower times, grab a snack and sit on the deck overlooking the Rivers of America. We highly recommend the heirloom tomato sandwich (with Havarti and rémoulade on hearty whole grain) to lacto-ovo vegetarians and carnivores alike. The lemon cupcakes and seasonal berry pies are also really good.

Jolly Holiday Bakery

QUALITY Good–Excellent   **VALUE** B   **PORTION** Medium   **LOCATION** Main Street, U.S.A.   **Reader-Survey Responses** 95% 👍 5% 👎

Selections Broccoli-cheese quiche; house salad with pecans and Feta; toasted cheese sandwich with tomato soup; turkey, Italian, pastrami, or caprese sandwich; grilled vegetable salad; assorted pastries.

Comments Themed to *Mary Poppins,* with stained glass windows featuring penguin waiters, this is a good spot for a light breakfast or lunch, though lines can grow long at peak mealtimes. Seating is outdoors only, and soup and quiche portions are small, but the salads and sandwiches are substantial and savory. Don't miss the massive Matterhorn coconut macaroons.

Market House

QUALITY Good   **VALUE** B–   **PORTION** Medium   **LOCATION** Main Street, U.S.A.   **Reader-Survey Responses** 100% 👍 0% 👎

Selections Starbucks coffee drinks, cocoa, tea, juice, pastries, and breakfast sandwiches.

Comments Starbucks's usual vast array of blended beverages is available (including seasonal flavors), accompanied by its trademark long lines. You can also get a selection of hot breakfast sandwiches in the morning and sweets all day. Starbucks loyalty cards are valid for payment, but you can't earn rewards or redeem freebies here. The expanded coffee shop features a seating area themed after a vintage bookshop. Look for the potbellied stove, checkerboard, and antique party line telephones, all holdovers from the former decor.

Pluto's Dog House

QUALITY Fair–Good   **VALUE** C   **PORTION** Medium   **LOCATION** Mickey's Toontown   **Reader-Survey Responses** 40% 👍 60% 👎

Selections Hot dog basket, kids' turkey dog, and mac and cheese.

Comments Food's not bad, but there's really no place to sit and eat it.

Redd Rockett's Pizza Port

QUALITY Good	VALUE C	PORTION Medium–Large	LOCATION Tomorrowland
Reader-Survey Responses 78% 👍 22% 👎			

Selections Large slices of pizza; pasta with meatballs or chicken; Caesar, Asian chicken, Italian, or cranberry salads.

Comments Redd Rockett's is set up cafeteria-style, so all hot items sit under heat lamps until someone grabs them, but servers will be happy to mix up a fresh bowl of pasta or a pizza on request (a much better choice). The Asian chicken salad is slightly spicy with good flavor. Free drink refills are available. The cafeteria-style setup usually means less waiting. The A/C system is on steroids, making it a really cool place on a hot day. Even on the busiest days, there's ample room to sit on the outdoor patio.

Refreshment Corner

QUALITY Fair-Good	VALUE C	PORTION Medium	LOCATION Main Street, U.S.A.
Reader-Survey Responses 85% 👍 15% 👎			

Selections Hot dogs, chili-cheese dogs, and chili in a bread bowl.

Comments Some of the topping selections sound strange (Pulled pork? Mac and cheese?), but the dogs are good. Limited seating; time it right to catch the ragtime pianist or Dapper Dans performing on the patio.

Royal Street Veranda

QUALITY Good	VALUE B	PORTION Medium	LOCATION New Orleans Square
Reader-Survey Responses 86% 👍 14% 👎			

Selections Steak gumbo, vegetarian gumbo, and clam chowder, all served in a sourdough bread bowl; coffee, espresso, cappuccino, and fritters (fried dough balls) for dessert.

Comments Usually not crowded except around *Fantasmic!* showings. Veggie gumbo and clam chowder are the best, though all are seasoned well. You have to look hard to find any steak in the steak gumbo. Don't miss the fritters with fruit dipping sauce.

Stage Door Café

QUALITY Good	VALUE C	PORTION Medium	LOCATION Frontierland
Reader-Survey Responses 88% 👍 13% 👎			

Selections Chicken nuggets, fish-and-chips, funnel cakes, and corn dogs.

Comments The corn dogs are nearly as good as those from the Main Street cart, with a shorter line. The fish is edible (albeit previously frozen), but the fries and nuggets are bland. Try the funnel cakes.

Tomorrowland Terrace

QUALITY Fair	VALUE C+	PORTION Large	LOCATION Tomorrowland
Reader-Survey Responses 79% 👍 21% 👎			

Selections Breakfast burrito, scrambled egg platter, or French toast; one-third-pound Angus burgers, chicken sandwich, chopped salad, or grilled veggie or baked fish sandwich.

Comments The food isn't anything special, though the bread is fresh. Seating is available outdoors overlooking the Tomorrowland Terrace stage, which hosts live music and the popular *Jedi Training Academy.*

Troubadour Tavern

QUALITY	Fair–Good	VALUE	C+	PORTION	Medium	LOCATION	Fantasyland
Reader-Survey Responses	88% 👍	12% 👎					

Selections Bratwurst with sauerkraut, pretzel bites with cheese sauce, tavern nachos, apple slices with caramel sauce, cinnamon-apple pastry twists, and ice cream bites.

Comments Built as a concession stand for Fantasyland Theatre, Troubadour Tavern is overwhelmed during shows but overlooked the rest of the day. This and the Village Haus are the only quick-service sausage vendors serving spicy brown mustard. The menu's newest addition, tavern nachos, consists of kettle-style potato chips topped with cheese, sour cream, bacon, and green onions. We dare you to try it. For a quick snack, try Maurice's Treats, close to Fantasy Faire; it serves sweet (if overpriced) strawberry or chocolate pastry twists, as well as a boysenberry apple freeze. Its Cheddar garlic bagel twist is tough and tasteless.

Vendor Treats

LOCATIONS	Throughout the park	READER-SURVEY RESPONSES	83% 👍	17% 👎

Selections Popcorn, fries, smoked turkey legs, ice cream, churros, chimichangas, and more.

Comments We love the smoked turkey legs—big enough for a whole meal. Plus, there's something delightfully Neanderthal about tucking into a huge, meaty bone as you stroll the park.

Village Haus

QUALITY	Good	VALUE	B–	PORTION	Medium	LOCATION	Fantasyland
Reader-Survey Responses	75% 👍	25% 👎					

Selections Premium cheeseburger, chicken sausage sandwich, veggie burger, pepperoni and cheese pizzas, apple Cheddar salad, and mac and cheese kids' meals. Seasonal cupcake or apple strudel for dessert.

Comments The flatbread pizzas and heart-stopping pastrami cheeseburger are actually pretty good. Kids love the Pinocchio-themed seating area. Try the salad with fruit and cheese in a tangy yogurt-honey dressing.

DISNEY CALIFORNIA ADVENTURE
Award Wieners

QUALITY	Fair–Good	VALUE	C	PORTION	Medium	LOCATION	Hollywood Land
Reader-Survey Responses	86% 👍	14% 👎					

Selections Chili-cheese dogs, grilled sausages, and hot dogs; grilled mushroom, onion, and pepper sandwich.

Comments The grilled sausages are moderately spicy and good. It's a shame it only serves yellow mustard.

Boardwalk Pizza & Pasta

QUALITY	Good	VALUE	B+	PORTION	Medium–Large	LOCATION	Paradise Pier
Reader-Survey Responses	86% 👍	14% 👎					

Selections Pizzas run the gamut from a traditional cheese or pepperoni to a portobello mushroom and spinach. Pasta offerings include spaghetti and meatballs, chicken pasta in a sun-dried tomato cream sauce, or pesto ravioli. Freshly tossed salads include a chicken Caesar and a Mediterranean chef salad with provolone, salami, fresh mozzarella, ham, roasted peppers, and olives in a red-wine vinaigrette.

Comments Part of Paradise Garden, a Victorian-era outdoor courtyard with freestanding beer and corn dog stands outside the plaza. Salads are large enough to split three ways; say "hold the olives" (or another ingredient) for a fresh-mixed serving.

Cocina Cucamonga Mexican Grill

QUALITY	Good	VALUE	B-	PORTION	Large	LOCATION	Pacific	Wharf
Reader-Survey Responses	85% 👍	15% 👎						

Selections Tacos, burritos, tamales, grilled chicken, fajita salad, and chicken Caesar salad. Kids' choices include arroz con pollo (chicken with rice), bean and cheese burrito, and chicken tacos.

Comments Salads are a safe choice. The chicken is marinated with cumin, garlic, cilantro, and citrus, and it comes with flour tortillas. Very tasty. The carne asada has improved but still lacks the full flavor and texture that you would expect. The burritos include a lot of beans.

Cozy Cone Motel

QUALITY	Fair-Good	VALUE	B-	PORTION	Small-Medium	LOCATION	Cars	Land
Reader-Survey Responses	90% 👍	10% 👎						

Selections Chili, ice cream, churros, mac and cheese, and pretzel bites. Cone #5 coats popcorn in unusual favors such as dill pickle and bacon Cheddar, with two rotating varieties offered daily. Signature beverages include a syrupy pomegranate limeade and Red's Apple Freeze, a curiously addictive blend of tart frozen apple juice and sweet toasted marshmallow.

Comments Each conical commissary in this food court, based on Sally's construction-cone motel from the film, serves different snacks and drinks with punny names such as "chili cone queso" and "route beer floats." Check the selections before you line up because each of the five cones vends a different menu.

Fiddler, Fifer & Practical Café

QUALITY	Good	VALUE	B-	PORTION	Medium	LOCATION	Buena	Vista	St.
Reader-Survey Responses	79% 👍	21% 👎							

Selections Starbucks coffee, hot breakfast sandwiches, cinnamon rolls with cream cheese icing, premade cold sandwiches, and salads.

Comments This quick-service eatery, named after both the Three Little Pigs and an imaginary songstress trio whose manufactured mementos hang inside, boasts a large open dining area in the Arts & Crafts style. You can get your morning jolt of Starbucks-brand joe and grab-and-go breakfast pastries here, but expect long waits around opening. Starbucks loyalty cards can be used for payment but not for free refills or other rewards.

Flo's V8 Cafe

QUALITY	Good	VALUE	B	PORTION	Medium-Large	LOCATION	Cars	Land
Reader-Survey Responses	90% 👍	10% 👎						

Selections At breakfast, try the French toast. Lunch and dinner offer citrus turkey breast, pork ribs with cola barbecue sauce, roast beef, vegetarian shepherd's pie, and fruit pies.

Comments Cars Land's largest eatery serves classic American comfort food with a Southwestern twist. Signature lunch and dinner choices include a vegetarian casserole, with apple-Cheddar and chocolate pies for dessert. Try the pork ribs with a side of mashed potatoes. The veggie bake is tasty enough to attract meat eaters. The portions are decent and served on real plates but similarly priced to other counter service. Kids' meals come in a Lightning McQueen car. Memorabilia from proprietor Flo's past as a famous Motown singer is featured in the decor. Sit on the back patio for a spectacular view of Radiator Springs Racers' high-speed finale.

Lucky Fortune Cookery

QUALITY	Fair-Good	VALUE	C+	PORTION	Medium	LOCATION	Pacific	Wharf
Reader-Survey Responses	65% 👍	35% 👎						

Selections Steamed rice bowls with vegetables and your choice of chicken, beef, or tofu, all with your choice from a variety of pan-Asian sauces, including a popular teriyaki and a sweet, tangy Korean sauce; edamame; mango slices; teriyaki chicken and rice for kids.

Comments The tofu bowl is good, the chicken and beef are average, and the coconut curry sauce is bland. Edamame makes a nice side to share, especially dipped in spicy sriracha sauce.

Pacific Wharf Café

QUALITY	Good	VALUE	A	PORTION	Medium	LOCATION	Pacific	Wharf
Reader-Survey Responses	86% 👍	14% 👎						

Selections Fresh soups and salads served in hollowed-out sourdough loaves from San Francisco's famous Boudin bakery, plus turkey wraps and macaroni for the kids. The Chinese chicken salad and broccoli-and-cheese soup are both good, as is the clam chowder, with heaps of clams in a creamy, slightly salty base.

Comments Adults will appreciate the food and ambience as well as the very kid-friendly menu (nonfat yogurt, sliced apples, and whole-grain fish crackers). For dessert, try the candy, hot cocoa, ice cream sundae, or milk shake at Ghirardelli Soda Fountain & Chocolate Shop nearby.

Paradise Garden Grill

QUALITY	Good-Excellent	VALUE	A	PORTION	Medium	LOCATION	Paradise	Pier
Reader-Survey Responses	89% 👍	11% 👎						

Selections Variety of skewers (beef, chicken, and tofu) served with rice pilaf and a pita, beef gyro on pita bread, and classic Greek salad. For kids, there's a grilled chicken or beef skewer, served with choice of sauce.

Comments This open-air venue, with a Victorian beer garden theme, shares seating with Boardwalk Pizza. A selection of sauces are offered with the skewers, and you can request more than one; the *kefta* with Moroccan chili or *tzatziki* is especially flavorful. During Hispanic festivals such as ¡Viva Navidad!, the menu may be swapped for some excellent Latin entrées.

Smokejumpers Grill

QUALITY	Fair	VALUE	C	PORTION	Medium-Large	LOCATION	Grizzly	Peak
Reader-Survey Responses	85% 👍	15% 👎						

Selections Choose from American comfort food such as burgers, chicken sandwiches, and grilled chicken salad.

Comments The burgers come with a variety of toppings and sauces, and a separate toppings bar is available in case you need to stack on more. The onion rings are decent, and this is the only place in DCA that serves them. Formerly known as Taste Pilots' Grill, this eatery received a 2015 makeover inspired by "brave men and women who fight wildfires in our California forests." The handsome location features ample seating surrounded by lush pine trees, but the uninspired menu is unchanged.

DISNEYLAND RESORT RESTAURANTS:
Rated and Ranked

TO HELP YOU MAKE YOUR DINING CHOICES, we've developed profiles of full-service restaurants at Disneyland Resort. Each profile lets you quickly check the restaurant's cuisine, location, star rating, cost range, quality rating, and value rating. Profiles are listed alphabetically by restaurant. In addition to all full-service restaurants, we also list and profile a couple of delis and self-serve restaurants in the theme parks that transcend basic burgers, hot dogs, and pizza. All of the restaurants listed here have disabled access.

STAR RATING The star rating represents the entire dining experience: style, service, and ambience, in addition to taste, presentation, and food quality. Five stars, the highest rating, indicates that the restaurant offers the best of everything. Four-star restaurants are above average, and three-star restaurants offer good, though not necessarily memorable, meals. Two-star restaurants serve mediocre fare, and one-star restaurants are below average. Our star ratings don't correspond to ratings awarded by AAA, Forbes, Zagat, or other restaurant reviewers.

COST RANGE The next rating tells how much an entrée (or, depending on the restaurant, an entrée and side dish) will cost. Appetizers, desserts, drinks, and tips aren't included. We've rated the cost as inexpensive, moderate, or expensive.

INEXPENSIVE	$15 or less per person
MODERATE	$15–$28 per person
EXPENSIVE	More than $28 per person

QUALITY RATING The food quality is rated on a scale of one to five stars, five being the best. The quality rating is based on the taste, freshness of ingredients, preparation, presentation, and creativity of food. There is no consideration of price. If you want the best food available and cost is no issue, look no further than the quality ratings.

VALUE RATING If, on the other hand, you are looking for both quality and value, check the value rating, also expressed as stars.

★★★★★	Exceptional value; a real bargain
★★★★	Good value

★★★	Fair value; you get exactly what you pay for
★★	Somewhat overpriced
★	Significantly overpriced

PAYMENT All Disney restaurants accept American Express, MasterCard, Visa, Diners Club, Discover, and Japanese Credit Bureau.

Ariel's Grotto ★★★½

CHARACTER DINING/AMERICAN   EXPENSIVE   QUALITY ★★★½ VALUE ★★★½
Reader-Survey Responses   85% 👍 15% 👎

Disney California Adventure; ☎ 714-781-DINE

Reservations Recommended. **When to go** Anytime. **Entrée range** Fixed-price meals, $22–$50. **Service ★★★★**. **Friendliness ★★★★★**. **Bar** The Cove bar is upstairs. **Dress** Casual. **Hours** Daily, 9 a.m.–10 p.m.

SETTING AND ATMOSPHERE You're "under the sea" with bright 3-D ocean-themed murals, jellyfish lanterns, and seashell tables, all with views of the wharf, Paradise Bay, and Paradise Pier. The overstuffed semicircular booths along the back wall are the best seats in the house and well worth waiting for. At night, outdoor tables provide picturesque views of the illuminated Fun Wheel.

HOUSE SPECIALTIES At breakfast, Belgian waffles, spinach-artichoke frittatas, and steak and eggs. At lunch and dinner, oak-smoked tri-tip steak, lobster salad, citrus-glazed chicken, corn cakes, and shrimp pasta. Each meal includes soup or salad and finishes with a dessert trio featuring crème brûlée and s'mores.

OTHER RECOMMENDATIONS Surf and turf for dinner and a kids' menu featuring octopus-shaped hot dogs and angel-hair pasta.

SUMMARY AND COMMENTS Ariel's Grotto is *fun* but very pricey; it's also one of the most popular dining spots in DCA. Kids will love the fact that Ariel and two to four other Disney princesses—Snow White, Cinderella, Aurora, or Belle—are on hand for pictures and autographs at breakfast and lunch. One set price buys adults a cup of bacon-topped crab chowder or spring mix salad with dried cranberries and blue cheese (ask your server for one of each), a main course, and shared dessert; the evening-only combo of thinly sliced steak with honey-whiskey glaze and whole grilled lobster tail is the clear winner. Kids' meals are child-friendly standards with cutesy cartoonish presentations, like clam-shaped sandwich rolls. Even toddlers will enjoy the bright surroundings and nonthreatening character visits. Evening diners don't get to meet princesses, but they do receive reserved viewing passes for *World of Color* ($48.60 for adults, $27 for kids ages 3–9, including tax). Demand is high here for obvious reasons, so book your reservations early. Adults can escape upstairs to The Cove alfresco bar for a cocktail, glass of wine, or bottle of beer. The Cove also serves a small selection of appetizers, including enormous lobster nachos. This is a good spot for catching *World of Color* without a FastPass; views of the fountains from here are great, but the oblique angle to the projection screens isn't ideal.

Continued on page 179

DISNEYLAND RESORT RESTAURANTS BY CUISINE

CUISINE	LOCATION	OVERALL RATING	COST	QUALITY RATING	VALUE RATING
AMERICAN					
BIG THUNDER RANCH BARBECUE	Disneyland Park	★★★½	Mod	★★★½	★★★★
THE RIVER BELLE TERRACE*	Disneyland Park	★★★½	Mod	★★★½	★★★½
ARIEL'S GROTTO*	DCA	★★★½	Exp	★★★½	★★★½
PLAZA INN*	Disneyland Park	★★★	Mod	★★★	★★★½
TANGAROA TERRACE*	Disneyland Hotel	★★★	Mod	★★★	★★★½
CARNATION CAFÉ*	Disneyland Park	★★★	Mod	★★★	★★★
DISNEY'S PCH GRILL*	Paradise Pier Hotel	★★★	Mod	★★★	★★½
ESPN ZONE	Downtown Disney	★★½	Mod	★★★	★★★
RAINFOREST CAFE*	Downtown Disney	★★½	Mod	★★★	★★½
GOOFY'S KITCHEN*	Disneyland Hotel	★★	Exp	★★	★★½
CALIFORNIA/FUSION					
NAPA ROSE	Grand Californian	★★★★★	V. Exp	★★★★★	★★★½
CARTHAY CIRCLE RESTAURANT	DCA	★★★★½	Exp	★★★★½	★★★½
STORYTELLERS CAFÉ*	Grand Californian	★★★★	Exp	★★★★	★★★½
WINE COUNTRY TRATTORIA	DCA	★★★★	Mod	★★★★	★★★
CAJUN/CREOLE					
THE FRENCH MARKET	Disneyland Park	★★★½	Mod	★★★★	★★★★
CAFÉ ORLÉANS	Disneyland Park	★★★½	Mod	★★★½	★★★
RALPH BRENNAN'S JAZZ KITCHEN*	Downtown Disney	★★★½	Mod	★★★½	★★½
BLUE BAYOU	Disneyland Park	★★★½	Exp	★★★½	★★½
CROSSROADS AT HOUSE OF BLUES	Downtown Disney	★★★	Mod	★★★½	★★½
CHARACTER DINING					
STORYTELLERS CAFÉ*	Grand Californian	★★★★	Exp	★★★★	★★★½
ARIEL'S GROTTO*	DCA	★★★½	Exp	★★★½	★★★½
PLAZA INN*	Disneyland Park	★★★	Mod	★★★	★★★½
DISNEY'S PCH GRILL*	Paradise Pier Hotel	★★★	Mod	★★★	★★½
GOOFY'S KITCHEN*	Disneyland Hotel	★★	Exp	★★	★★½
DELI/BAKERY					
LA BREA BAKERY CAFÉ*	Downtown Disney	★★★	Inexp	★★½	★★★
NAPOLINI	Downtown Disney	★★½	Inexp	★★½	★★½

*Serves breakfast

DISNEYLAND RESORT RESTAURANTS BY CUISINE

CUISINE	LOCATION	OVERALL RATING	COST	QUALITY RATING	VALUE RATING
ITALIAN					
NAPLES RISTORANTE E PIZZERIA	Downtown Disney	★★★	Mod	★★★	★★★
NAPOLINI	Downtown Disney	★★½	Inexp	★★½	★★½
MEDITERRANEAN					
CATAL RESTAURANT & UVA BAR*	Downtown Disney	★★★½	Mod/Exp	★★★½	★★★
MEXICAN					
TORTILLA JO'S	Downtown Disney	★★★	Mod/Exp	★★½	★★½
RANCHO DEL ZOCALO RESTAURANTE	Disneyland Park	★★	Mod	★★	★★½
POLYNESIAN					
TANGAROA TERRACE*	Disneyland Hotel	★★★	Mod	★★★	★★★½
STEAK HOUSE					
STEAKHOUSE 55*	Disneyland Hotel	★★★★	V. Exp	★★★★½	★★★

Serves breakfast

Continued from page 177

Big Thunder Ranch Barbecue ★★★½

AMERICAN   MODERATE   QUALITY ★★★½ VALUE ★★★★
Reader-Survey Responses 95% 👍 5% 👎

Disneyland Park; ☎ 714-781-DINE

Reservations Available. **When to go** Lunch or dinner. **Entrée range** $15–$30. **Service** ★★★★. **Friendliness** ★★★★. **Dress** Casual. **Hours** Daily, 11:30 a.m.–8 p.m.

SETTING AND ATMOSPHERE Outdoor, family-style seating on long wooden tables and benches with lots of Western Americana touches such as hurricane lamps and checkered tablecloths.

HOUSE SPECIALTIES Family-style, all-you-can-eat barbecue featuring buckets of pork ribs and chicken in a sweet but nicely balanced barbecue sauce, a tangy citrus coleslaw, warm corn bread with sweet butter, and smoked sausages. The skillet chocolate-chip cookie with vanilla ice cream and hot fudge will definitely put you over the edge.

OTHER RECOMMENDATIONS Vegetarians can request a barbecue skewer with potatoes, squash, bell peppers, mushrooms, and tofu.

SUMMARY AND COMMENTS Prices may surprise you, but if the family is ready to pound some serious grub, this never-ending, all-you-can-eat palace to excess is just the spot. Drinks (served in Mason jars) and dessert are à la carte. The dinner menu is the same as lunch, plus smoked sausage and corncob wheels. A charming couple of singing cowpokes in Dale Evans and Roy Rogers costumes, accompanied by a honky-tonk piano player, perform kid-friendly comedic skits while you eat, improvising special occasion telegrams and leading sing-alongs of "Rocky Top" and "The Ballad of Davy Crockett." You can often get a seat here (especially for lunch) without advance reservations, even on busy days.

Blue Bayou ★★★½

CAJUN/CREOLE	EXPENSIVE	QUALITY ★★★½ VALUE ★★½
Reader-Survey Responses	94% 👍	6% 👎

Disneyland Park; ☎ 714-781-DINE

Reservations Required. **When to go** Early or late lunch, early evening. **Entrée range** $27–$48. **Service** ★★★. **Friendliness** ★★★. **Dress** Casual. **Hours** Daily, 11 a.m.–10:15 p.m.

SETTING AND ATMOSPHERE The Blue Bayou overlooks Pirates of the Caribbean and maintains an appropriately dark, moist ambience. The best tables ring the perimeter and afford a view of the faux bayou, replete with fireflies flickering among the weeping willows and mangroves, dilapidated houseboats, and soft lantern lights. If you're not lucky enough to get a table bayou-side, there's still enough wrought iron, uneven lighting, and twilight allure to soften the most hardened soul.

HOUSE SPECIALTIES Pan-seared salmon, filet mignon, and Le Special de Monte Cristo sandwich.

OTHER RECOMMENDATIONS Jambalaya, Tesoro Island chicken, or fork-tender short ribs. Spring for the saffron-infused bouillabaisse if offered as a seasonal special. Entrées include a cup of mild gumbo or a superb side salad with candied pecans and dried cranberries.

SUMMARY AND COMMENTS Easily the best restaurant in Disneyland Park, Blue Bayou is as close to fine dining as you'll get here. The restaurant fills quickly and stays busy, so make reservations before you leave home (up to 60 days in advance) or obtain a same-day reservation at the restaurant door as soon as you get to the park. Though there's a children's menu, this isn't the place to bring wound-up or tired kids for a leisurely meal; they'll be bored. Tables are tightly packed, and nothing disrupts the busy servers more than wild kids up and out of their seats. Blue Bayou is more of a place where adults can escape the noise and happy chaos in the rest of the park without having to exit the gates. For lunch, we love the Monte Cristo sandwich, a deep-fried turkey, ham, and cheese creation that you don't find on many menus these days. Side dishes—including the Blue Bayou potatoes, a house gratin, and fresh vegetables—are quite good as well. The crème brûlée is also a crowd-pleaser. Servers are Disney-pleasant, if a tad harried, but they're more than happy to accommodate the random request. And the dinner rolls are great! If seated at an unromantically over-lit table near the kitchen, don't be shy about requesting a relocation. On nights when *Fantasmic!* is shown, Blue Bayou offers a dining package for $66.96 per adult ($27 for kids 3–9), including tax, that includes a starter, entrée, and dessert, plus a FastPass to *Fantasmic!*'s center viewing section and a seat cushion to ease your wait. Unless you order the most expensive items on the prix fixe menu (shrimp cocktail, surf and turf), you'll be paying a lot for that souvenir pillow.

La Brea Bakery Café ★★★

DELI/BAKERY	INEXPENSIVE	QUALITY ★★½ VALUE ★★★
Reader-Survey Responses	89% 👍	11% 👎

Downtown Disney; ☎ 714-490-0233 or 714-781-DINE; labreabakery.com

Reservations Available. **When to go** Breakfast. **Entrée range** $9–$28. **Service** ★★★. **Friendliness** ★★★. **Bar** Limited. **Dress** Casual. **Hours** Sunday–Friday, 8 a.m.–10 p.m., Saturday, 8 a.m.–11 p.m. Open 1 hour later in summer.

SETTING AND ATMOSPHERE This indoor-outdoor space is rich with the yeasty aromas of breads and cakes, plus whiffs of herbs and spices. Hardwood floors and large glass display counters distinguish the dining room. A pleasant patio with colorful umbrellas fronting the café is the perfect perch for a quick cappuccino and pastry while you people-watch.

HOUSE SPECIALTIES For breakfast, nothing beats a large fruit muffin and your coffee drink of choice. The panini at lunch and dinner are better than the ones at Napolini.

OTHER RECOMMENDATIONS Take home one or more loaves of the artisanal breads. Or try this sandwich on for size: thick sourdough layered with Gruyère cheese, smoked ham, and a fried egg.

SUMMARY AND COMMENTS It's all about the bread . . . and the muffins, pastries, desserts, and anything else containing baked flour and yeast. Breakfast is the obvious time to enjoy La Brea, and if you must supplement your carbohydrate fix, add some smoked salmon or a veggie omelet. At lunch and dinner, the salads, sandwiches, and flatbread pizzas take over. Service has improved markedly in recent years; servers are more attentive and pleasant. Get there early—it's the first eatery at the east end of the resort entrance, and a popular starting (and ending) place for tourists and locals alike. You can get Starbucks-branded coffee here, usually with a shorter queue than you'll find inside the parks.

Café Orléans ★★★½

CAJUN/CREOLE	MODERATE	QUALITY ★★★½	VALUE ★★★
Reader-Survey Responses	96% 👍	4% 👎	

Disneyland Park; ☎ 714-781-DINE

Reservations Recommended. **When to go** Early or late lunch, early evening. **Entrée range** $16–$21. **Service** ★★★★. **Friendliness** ★★★★. **Dress** Casual. **Hours** Daily, 11:30 a.m.–park closing.

SETTING AND ATMOSPHERE Across the alley from Blue Bayou, Café Orléans overlooks the Rivers of America. There's a small patio and limited inside seating, but the table-side service offers a nice break from the serve-yourself and buffet options in the same price range. After a day of traipsing around the park, it's nice to kick back amid the wrought iron and scrolled-wood accents.

HOUSE SPECIALTIES The chef's *pommes frites* have to be among the best sides in the park: traditional thick-cut fries tossed with Parmesan cheese, garlic, and parsley and served with a mildly spicy Cajun rémoulade sauce. If they aren't served piping hot, send them back. Mickey-shaped beignets are also a treat for dessert.

OTHER RECOMMENDATIONS A decent French onion soup with melted Gruyère cheese; an artery-clogging Monte Cristo sandwich in two versions, traditional and three-cheese; and a nice selection of sweet and savory crêpes.

SUMMARY AND COMMENTS The *pommes frites* are worth the price of admission. If you don't eat anything else in the park your entire visit, try these. We like to hit Café Orléans for a midafternoon break, kick our feet up for a soda or sweet tea, and pick through a plate of the fries while we people-watch. The small menu makes ordering easy, provided you bring a big appetite and aren't afraid of a little cholesterol and trans fat. The Monte Cristo sandwiches are as good as Blue Bayou's and a few bucks cheaper. Kids will love the three-cheese version: Swiss, mozzarella, and double-cream Brie between thick slices of deep-fried, egg-battered bread. The gumbo is passable, if a little bland, while the salads, including a blackened-chicken Caesar and the Crescent City salad (a mix of baby spinach, field greens, caramelized pecans, roasted corn, grapes, orange slices, and pan-seared salmon in an orange-cilantro vinaigrette), are very good. For something different, try the crêpes—paper-thin pancakes stuffed with a variety of fillings, including chicken gumbo or beef. A Dixieland jazz band periodically provides lively entertainment.

Carnation Café ★ ★ ★

AMERICAN **MODERATE** **QUALITY** ★ ★ ★ **VALUE** ★ ★ ★
Reader-Survey Responses 84% 👍 16% 👎

Disneyland Park; ☎ 714-781-DINE

Reservations Recommended. **When to go** Breakfast or late lunch. **Entrée range** $6–$19. **Service** ★ ★ ★ ★. **Friendliness** ★ ★ ★ ★. **Dress** Casual. **Hours** Daily, 7:30 a.m.–9 p.m.

SETTING AND ATMOSPHERE A Main Street staple since the park opened in 1955, the Carnation Café serves up an American menu heavy with traditional favorites—hamburgers and meat loaf, eggs Benedict and Mickey-shaped waffles, and fried chicken—in a parlor circa 1890. For those in the know, Oscar Martinez, Disneyland's longest-tenured employee (nearly 60 years at the park), is the café's ambassador.

HOUSE SPECIALTIES The loaded baked potato soup (a hot, creamy concoction with Cheddar cheese, chives, and large chunks of baked potato) is a favorite. Other specialties include a spinach and tomato frittata at breakfast and a sourdough bacon melt (with pepper Jack, grilled onions, and spicy sauce) for lunch. Oscar recommends the catch of the day, pan-seared with edamame succotash. Guy thinks the meat loaf is one of the best entrées in the park.

OTHER RECOMMENDATIONS For starters, try the deep-fried dill pickle spears, dipped in a rémoulade-style sauce. The menu features a beef-and-pork meat loaf, roasted turkey sandwich on a multigrain roll, and warm spinach salad topped with grilled chicken and portobello mushrooms.

SUMMARY AND COMMENTS Despite its relatively low score from readers, we think the Carnation Café is still a place where the adults can find a decent plate, the kids can choose from their favorites, and it's easy on the wallet. Because of its location along Main Street, close to bathrooms and across from the locker facility, it gets busy—expect to see waiting lines stretching down the street. Service is friendly and unusually patient; someone's briefed these young cast members on how an hour's wait and low blood sugar can quickly erode a diner's mood. Once you're seated, the order comes quickly and with a smile.

Carthay Circle Restaurant ★ ★ ★ ★ ½

CALIFORNIA **EXPENSIVE** **QUALITY** ★ ★ ★ ★ ½ **VALUE** ★ ★ ★ ½
Reader-Survey Responses 95% 👍 5% 👎

Disney California Adventure; ☎ 714-781-DINE

Reservations Recommended. **When to go** Lunch or dinner. **Entrée range** $24–$47. **Service** ★★★. **Friendliness** ★★★★. **Bar** Full bar. **Dress** Dressy casual. **Hours** Daily, 11:30 a.m.–10 p.m.

SETTING AND ATMOSPHERE Intimate booths, wood paneling, and candle sconces evoke the setting of the opening night in 1937 of *Snow White and the Seven Dwarfs.*

HOUSE SPECIALTIES Crispy firecracker duck wings with chili sauce, grilled Angus steak, Skuna Bay salmon, and fried biscuits with Cheddar, bacon, and jalapeño.

OTHER RECOMMENDATIONS For lunch, try the "ultimate" beef sandwich or chicken and spinach ravioli; for dinner, start with fish ceviche with avocado or heirloom tomato salad. Salmon is served mid-rare with "forbidden" black rice. The signature biscuits (more like cheese-filled fritters) are heavy but have built a fanatical cult following, as have the surprisingly meaty sriracha-laced duck wings. For dessert, order the creamy citrus cheesecake. The kids' menu offers fresh fish with veggies, mini crispy tacos, or pasta.

SUMMARY AND COMMENTS The chefs of Napa Rose developed the Southern Californian menu. A downstairs lounge serves appetizers and quick meals, while the larger upstairs restaurant takes reservations. A three-course fixed-price *World of Color* menu is also offered (Lunch: $44.28 adults, $23.76 children ages 3–9; Dinner: $66.96 adults, $27 children ages 3–9), which includes access to the prime center-stage viewing section. Terrace seating is available. Though service is sometimes unexpectedly inattentive, this is among the finest restaurants found inside the gates of any American theme park (including the vaunted Club 33) and one of the best dining experiences at Disneyland Resort outside of its sibling at the Grand Californian, at a slightly less astronomical price point. If you don't want an entire meal, stop in the downstairs lounge for a classic craft cocktail and short rib tacos or charcuterie tray; it's just a shame duck wings aren't served downstairs. Or for an educational look at the historic photographs that festoon the wall, take the free guided tour offered daily at 10:30 a.m.

Catal Restaurant & Uva Bar ★★★½

MEDITERRANEAN   MODERATE–EXPENSIVE   QUALITY ★★★½ VALUE ★★★
Reader-Survey Responses 91% 👍 9% 👎

Downtown Disney; ☎ 714-774-4442; patinagroup.com/catal

Reservations Recommended. **When to go** Anytime. **Entrée range** $9–$41. **Service** ★★★. **Friendliness** ★★★. **Bar** Full bar and extensive wine list. **Dress** Dressy casual. **Hours** *Catal:* Daily, 8 a.m.–3 p.m. and 5–10 p.m. *Uva Bar:* Daily, 11 a.m.–3 p.m. and 5–10 p.m.

SETTING AND ATMOSPHERE Uva Bar, a circular open-air lounge, sits immediately outside the restaurant and is a good place for a quick bite (sans line) or a leisurely cocktail while you watch the crowds go by. The outside bistro features a menu focused on Cal-Mediterranean gastropub cuisine. Inside is an elegant Art Deco–inspired restaurant with hardwood floors, spacious dining areas, and fine accoutrements. There are two fireplaces and a large central bar; a narrow balcony with tables wraps around the entire top floor.

HOUSE SPECIALTIES Corn beef hash or *chilaquiles* for breakfast, house-made charcuterie, suckling pig with tart apples and quinoa, lamb shank in braising jus, and Skuna Bay salmon with beets and farro. Sample the *a la plancha* entrées, such as the lamb burger with *piquillo* peppers, Feta, arugula, lemon-dill aioli, and pickled red onion; or the market fish with asparagus, preserved lemon purée, and applewood bacon at Uva.

OTHER RECOMMENDATIONS Try a huge and very tasty plate of paella with chicken, chorizo Bilbao, saffron rice, and lemon-garlic aioli; the classic Uva street fries with chorizo Bilbao, spicy *crema,* pickled garlic, and melted cheese; or the Txakolí steamed mussels with chorizo.

SUMMARY AND COMMENTS Catal & Uva Bar are a Patina Group pairing, one in a chain of eateries operated by celebrity chef Joachim Splichal. Despite overblown descriptions, the menu is pretty straightforward. The small plates—mainly appetizers, salads, and a few pasta dishes—are better than the rest of the menu and a real value for the money. When the weather cooperates, Uva is the better of the two venues. Be cautious when ordering some of the more complex or unusual offerings; they can be very inconsistent. Side dishes shine though. Price notwithstanding, this is a very adult experience.

Crossroads at House of Blues ★★★

CAJUN/CREOLE	MODERATE	QUALITY ★★★½	VALUE ★★½
Reader-Survey Responses 100% 👍 0% 👎			

Downtown Disney; ☎ 714-778-BLUE; houseofblues.com/anaheim

Reservations Recommended. **When to go** Dinner. **Entrée range** $8–$40. **Service** ★★★. **Friendliness** ★★★. **Bar** Wine list and full bar. **Dress** Casual. **Hours** Daily, 11 a.m.–9 p.m.

SETTING AND ATMOSPHERE Think rustic-but-trendy blues club somewhere along the Mississippi River, maybe St. Louis. It's dark except for outside patios and a second-story terrace, with hardwood floors, small intimate tables, and indirect lighting. The walls feature a fantastic collection of American folk artists, some of whom (such as Missionary Mary Proctor) have works that hang in prestigious museums.

HOUSE SPECIALTIES Jambalaya, St. Louis–style ribs, pulled pork sandwich, and build-your-own burgers.

OTHER RECOMMENDATIONS Jamaican jerk chicken wings and steak "street" tacos with tomatillo salsa.

SUMMARY AND COMMENTS House of Blues is first and foremost a major concert site, with marquee names, up-and-comers, and strong local talent taking the stage every night. Unless stated otherwise, the separately ticketed concert hall is strictly an adult venue (18 and older), though children are always welcome in the restaurant. Food Network celebrity chef Aaron Sanchez created the menu, which bursts with bold flavors befitting a blend of Southern soul food with Sanchez's Latino background. Happy hour (Monday–Friday, 2–5 p.m., and daily, 10 p.m.–close) offers discounted drinks and cut-price appetizers.

Disney's PCH Grill ★★★

CHARACTER DINING/AMERICAN	MODERATE	QUALITY ★★★	VALUE ★★½
Reader-Survey Responses 92% 👍 8% 👎			

Disneyland Paradise Pier Hotel; ☎ 714-781-DINE

Reservations Accepted. **When to go** Breakfast and dinner. **Entrée range** $16–$28. **Service** ★★★★. **Friendliness** ★★★★. **Bar** Wine and beer. **Dress** Casual. **Hours** Daily, 7–11 a.m. and 5:30–9 p.m.

SETTING AND ATMOSPHERE A taste of Southern California beach life: bright primary colors, potted palms, and decorative elements such as surfboards and beach chairs.

HOUSE SPECIALTIES Banana caramel French toast and Mickey-shaped waffles at breakfast; shrimp Alfredo with cavatappi pasta and the s'mores bar at dinner.

OTHER RECOMMENDATIONS Breakfasts are your best bet, with an omelet station for the grown-ups and a kids' buffet. For dinner, the buffet has some surprisingly good tri-tip beef and baby back ribs.

SUMMARY AND COMMENTS If you can take one more character breakfast, this time with Mickey and friends, get the kids up early and hit the beach. In recent years the food has improved.

ESPN Zone ★★½

AMERICAN	MODERATE		QUALITY	★★★	VALUE	★★★
Reader-Survey Responses 83% 👍	17% 👎					

Downtown Disney; ☎ 714-781-DINE; espnzone.com

Reservations Recommended. **When to go** Lunch or dinner. **Entrée range** $12–$26. **Service** ★★★. **Friendliness** ★★★. **Bar** Full bar. **Dress** Casual. **Hours** Sunday–Thursday, 11 a.m.–11 p.m.; Friday–Saturday, 11 a.m.–midnight.

SETTING AND ATMOSPHERE Maybe the most entertaining place outside the park walls, with a little something for everyone except the very youngest, the ESPN Zone is a massive, two-story sports enthusiast's dream. Huge flat-panel TVs are everywhere, and there's not a bad seat in the house. There's also a TV and radio broadcast facility inside (from which you can catch live broadcasts, especially when local teams are playing), as well as a massive game and interactive sports arcade.

HOUSE SPECIALTIES A variety of sliders (three little sandwiches such as cheeseburgers and barbecued pork) and the barbecued baby back ribs. Salads are fresher and livelier than they have been in the past.

OTHER RECOMMENDATIONS Most of what comes off the grill or as a sandwich or appetizer is a safe bet. The more complicated the dish, the more likely it won't measure up to expectations. Wings, burgers, sliders, and a surprisingly good mahimahi tostada rank as your best options.

SUMMARY AND COMMENTS The ESPN Zone is a three-ring circus—food and beverages oozing from every corner, more televised sports feeds than you can count, and an interactive game zone. Kids will love the manic pace and endless ways to spend more of your money, as well as the kid-friendly fare. Even teens will have a reason to smile here (hoops, a batting cage, and a climbing wall). And adults won't feel guilty over letting the youngsters run amok while they soak up quite possibly the largest televised sports feed on the planet. The food's improved, the service is steady (patient if not a little distracted at times), and you may find yourself in the studio audience for one of the many taped and live sports broadcasts produced right in front of you. When local teams (Lakers, Dodgers, Kings, Angels, Clippers, or Galaxy) are being televised, waits for tables can be excruciatingly long, even with reservations.

The French Market ★★★½

CAJUN/CREOLE   MODERATE   QUALITY ★★★★ VALUE ★★★★
Reader-Survey Responses 90% 👍 10% 👎

Disneyland Park; ☎ 714-781-DINE

Reservations Not accepted. **When to go** Lunch and dinner. **Entrée range** $10–$15.
Service ★★★. **Friendliness** ★★★. **Dress** Casual. **Hours** Daily, 11 a.m.–10:30 p.m.

SETTING AND ATMOSPHERE In the heart of New Orleans Square, The French
Market suggests a laid-back Southern vibe with lots of wrought iron
under the shade of large, mature ficus trees. There's a small indoor dining area, but the best seating is outdoors on a large patio, covered with
umbrellas and shadowed further by the trees.

HOUSE SPECIALTIES The menu features a roasted half chicken with citrus and
Cajun spices, panko-crusted red snapper, and Cajun meat loaf. The jambalaya is a savory alternative that hits the spot on cooler winter days. Most
meals come with a side of rice or mashed potatoes and corn bread.

OTHER RECOMMENDATIONS Hearty soups; a few fresh and flavorful salads
(including a yam and apple salad).

SUMMARY AND COMMENTS The French Market features comfort food with a
Cajun-Creole flair and periodic entertainment from one or more of the
roving park musicians or groups.

Goofy's Kitchen ★★

CHARACTER DINING/AMERICAN   EXPENSIVE   QUALITY ★★ VALUE ★★½
Reader-Survey Responses 91% 👍 9% 👎

Disneyland Hotel; ☎ 714-781-DINE

Reservations Available. **When to go** Breakfast. **Entrée range** $16–$37. **Service**
★★★★. **Friendliness** ★★★★. **Bar** Wine, beer, and cocktails. **Dress** Casual. **Hours**
Daily, 7–11:30 a.m. and 5–8:45 p.m.

SETTING AND ATMOSPHERE Bright, fun, and modern, but also very loud. Goofy,
Pluto, and other characters always put a smile to kids' faces.

HOUSE SPECIALTIES It's a buffet and your chef is Goofy . . . which should tell
you everything that you need to know. Breakfast features Mickey-shaped
waffles, sausages, pancakes, bacon, scrambled eggs, and other traditional breakfast items. Dinner offers everything from prime rib to premium salads.

OTHER RECOMMENDATIONS The kids love Goofy's peanut butter pizza.

SUMMARY AND COMMENTS You come for two reasons: 1) It's convenient,
especially if you're staying at the resort, and 2) the youngsters haven't
yet had their fill of dining with a rotating cast of Disney characters.
Breakfast is your best option for both food and wait times. Goofy's
Kitchen has many fans, including this Alpine, Utah, grandmother:

*Goofy's Kitchen, even at the staggering price, was well worth it. The
food was really good, a lot of the menu is designed for children,
and the character visits are worth the price. What a thrill to see
my grandchildren's delight at being visited by Minnie, Pluto, Chip,
and Snow White (with whom my 2-year-old grandson flirted
brazenly!).*

Napa Rose ★★★★★

CALIFORNIA/FUSION   VERY EXPENSIVE   QUALITY ★★★★★   VALUE ★★★½
Reader-Survey Responses 86% 👍 14% 👎

Grand Californian Hotel; ☎ 714-781-DINE

Reservations Recommended. **When to go** Dinner. **Entrée range** $40–$45; $100 for four courses. **Service ★★★★★. Friendliness ★★★★. Bar** Impressive wine list. **Dress** Dressy casual. **Hours** Daily, 5:30–9:15 p.m.

SETTING AND ATMOSPHERE Napa Rose is Disneyland Resort's flagship fine-dining experience. The Grand Californian's Craftsman theme is carried into this premier room with sweeping views of Disney California Adventure from virtually every table. A large, open demonstration kitchen lets you watch the magic happen, and wine, in all of its glory, is displayed at every turn. Fine linens and china are the norm. This is an absolutely gorgeous room with food and service to match.

HOUSE SPECIALTIES The menu, rotated seasonally, focuses on the cuisine of California's wine region, ranchlands, farm belts, and coastline. Wine finds its way onto most of the menu in sauces, reductions, infusions, and dressings. Dishes include sautéed portobello mushroom bisque "cappuccino," cedar-roasted duck breast, grilled wild monkfish, and braised Angus beef short rib, as well as warm butterscotch bread pudding for dessert.

OTHER RECOMMENDATIONS Game meat, ranch and free-range beef and poultry, and the chef's prix fixe Vintner's Table are constantly changing and always exciting.

SUMMARY AND COMMENTS Napa Rose may be the best restaurant in Orange County and has been at the top of most critics' lists since its debut. Top talent in the kitchen (award-winning chef Andrew Sutton leads the charge) and in the dining room—a beautiful space with panoramic views and a wine cellar second to none—make this an incomparable gustatory experience. Every server has earned sommelier status, a designation that takes years of study and practical experience with wine and winemaking, easing the chore of choosing a wine from its cellar of more than 16,000 bottles. The waitstaff brings the whole experience, from wine rookies to experts, to match your level of knowledge and tastes. Look for unusual ingredients (Tahitian vanilla, smoked sturgeon, truffled quail eggs, lemongrass, almond oil) married to top-notch staples (Colorado lamb, Berkshire pork, pheasant breast, sustainable fresh fish), all deftly handled by a world-class kitchen crew. And though staff are very accommodating in the usual Disney manner, this is definitely not an adventure for the kids. Napa Rose should be on every adult's Disney bucket list, a must-do at least once. If the full menu is too rich for your blood, sit in the cozy lounge and order appetizers. An Albuquerque, New Mexico, woman tried both Napa Rose and Steakhouse 55 (in the Disneyland Hotel) and offers this comparison:

Prices were quite high, but we had a very good time. Napa Rose was the highlight of the trip, and our waiter was very good. Steakhouse 55 was the biggest letdown. We were expecting to repeat our experience at Napa Rose, but the staff and food didn't come close.

Naples Ristorante e Pizzeria ★★★

ITALIAN	MODERATE		QUALITY	★★★	VALUE	★★★

Reader-Survey Responses 91% 👍 9% 👎

Downtown Disney; ☎ 714-776-6200 or 714-781-DINE;
patinagroup.com/naples

Reservations Recommended. **When to go** Late lunch or early dinner. **Entrée range** $14–$45. **Service** ★★. **Friendliness** ★★★. **Bar** Extensive wine list and full bar. **Dress** Casual. **Hours** Sunday–Thursday, 11 a.m.–10:15 p.m.; Friday–Saturday, 11 a.m.–11 p.m.

SETTING AND ATMOSPHERE Food aside, this is a really fun restaurant: modern, colorful, and spacious, with tile floors, an open demonstration kitchen, and whimsical design touches that mirror nearby Disneyland. It's also noisy and crowded, typically filled with families. During peak hours, it's difficult to hear yourself think, let alone carry on a meaningful conversation. Nonetheless, it's a great gathering place, and there's something to appeal to everyone from small children to adults.

HOUSE SPECIALTIES Wood-fired Neapolitan-style pizzas: thin, crispy crusts with a hearty, almost spicy red sauce; handmade mozzarella cheese; and fresh toppings of choice.

OTHER RECOMMENDATIONS Some of the non-pasta entrées—pan-seared salmon with roasted tomatoes and green beans and a citrus-and-herb-rubbed chicken, for example—are the real highlights.

SUMMARY AND COMMENTS Another Patina–Joachim Splichal venture where most of the effort went into the design. While the menu seems sophisticated, the recipes are rather bland and uninspired with a few exceptions. The kids will enjoy the colorful decor and activities; adults can get a good glass of wine or a cocktail and feed the entire crew for less than $100.

Napolini ★★½

ITALIAN/DELI	INEXPENSIVE		QUALITY	★★½	VALUE	★★½

Reader-Survey Responses 87% 👍 13% 👎

Downtown Disney; ☎ 714-781-DINE

Reservations Not accepted. **When to go** Lunch or a quick dinner. **Entrée range** $6–$18. **Service** ★★. **Friendliness** ★★★. **Bar** Wine and beer only. **Dress** Casual. **Hours** Sunday–Thursday, 11 a.m.–10 p.m.; Friday–Saturday, 11 a.m.–midnight.

SETTING AND ATMOSPHERE This is next-door Naples's cousin—a quick-in, quick-out deli with most of what you'd expect, from swinging salamis to large jars of peppers. Counter and table service continue to improve, but expect a lapse in attitude once in awhile. They want to get it right, but when frustrated, servers lose patience.

HOUSE SPECIALTIES Wood-fired Neapolitan-style pizzas, panini, salads.

OTHER RECOMMENDATIONS Best bets are the panini—grilled sandwiches on thick Italian bread, loaded to order with salami, veggies, peppers, onions, and such.

SUMMARY AND COMMENTS Don't set your expectations too high and you won't be disappointed here. Servers get flustered easily, and order mistakes are common (our guess is that Napolini serves as a training ground for Naples). Noise spills over from Naples on busy nights, as do impatient diners who don't want to wait for a table next door, making for a volatile mix that can have you feeling very uncomfortable in a hurry. But maybe that's the plan: to get you in with the sweet, spicy aromas of Italian cooking and then out quickly.

Plaza Inn ★★★

CHARACTER DINING/AMERICAN   MODERATE   QUALITY ★★★   VALUE ★★★½
Reader-Survey Responses   93% 👍 7% 👎

Disneyland Park; ☎ 714-781-DINE

Reservations Recommended. **When to go** When you need a compromise, the kids insist, or you arrive right at the meal switch. **Entrée range** $12–$27. **Service** ★★★. **Friendliness** ★★★. **Dress** Casual. **Hours** Daily, 8 a.m.–midnight.

SETTING AND ATMOSPHERE Probably the high point of your meal at Plaza Inn is the gorgeous Victorian B&B ambience—comfortable, widely spaced tables in a spacious dining room with lots of brocade and brass. The large patio commands a great view of Main Street, where parades, strolling musicians, and the massive variety of visitors endlessly entertain us.

HOUSE SPECIALTIES The menu has been revamped with new items, but it's still a buffeteria that can be hit or miss; see if you can catch something being freshly delivered. Timing is everything. Best bets are the pot roast or the fried chicken (which some claim is better than Knott's famous birds), two items that rarely suffer from sitting on the steam table.

OTHER RECOMMENDATIONS The little ones will love the daily character breakfast (reservations strongly suggested) hosted by Minnie Mouse and two to four other characters. Adults will suffer through rubbery pancakes and soggy bacon.

SUMMARY AND COMMENTS Don't expect fine dining when you eat at the Plaza Inn, but strides have been made in the quality of the food and the steam table's maintenance, and portions are very generous. Hit this place right when everything comes fresh, during the transitions from breakfast to lunch and from lunch to dinner, but it's still your basic been-in-the-steam-table-too-long scenario.

Rainforest Cafe ★★½

AMERICAN   MODERATE   QUALITY   ★★★   VALUE   ★★½
Reader-Survey Responses   80% 👍 20% 👎

Downtown Disney; ☎ 714-772-0413; rainforestcafe.com

Reservations Available. **When to go** Lunch or dinner. **Entrée range** $9–$29. **Service** ★★. **Friendliness** ★★★. **Bar** Full bar. **Dress** Casual. **Hours** Sunday–Thursday, 8 a.m.–10:30 p.m.; Friday–Saturday, 8 a.m.–midnight.

SETTING AND ATMOSPHERE Couldn't get enough of the Jungle Cruise next door *and* you're starving? Exit the park and head to the Rainforest Cafe, a lush tropical experience that attracts a few thousand of your fellow diners on a daily basis. Take a safari through the winding sections of greenery, faux wildlife, and piped-in jungle sounds, and wade through a menu as large as the Orinoco Basin.

HOUSE SPECIALTIES Stick to the basics: burgers, simple sandwiches, and salads. The Volcanic Cobb Salad—a huge mix of romaine and iceberg greens, olives, crumbled blue cheese, chopped egg, bacon, and grilled chicken in a balsamic vinaigrette—is arguably the best one on the menu.

OTHER RECOMMENDATIONS The Mojo Bones (barbecued baby back ribs) are passable; the Volcano chocolate dessert (complete with sparkler top) is gargantuan and irresistible, so invite your posse because you'll never find the bottom of the bowl alone. The sandwich wraps are also a good alternative with some tasty meat and sauce mixes.

SUMMARY AND COMMENTS If the Adventureland experience just doesn't satisfy your lust for all things green, lush, and wildlike, this is the place for you. The menu is massive (maybe a little too large) and mostly palatable, but none of it is truly great. They do make up in quantity for any lack of quality; plates are enough for two in most circumstances. Children love the rain forest theme, and you can count on any number of the chain's signature animal characters to show up during the meal for photo ops and a little interaction with the kiddies. All in all, a bit distracting—but maybe that's the point.

Ralph Brennan's Jazz Kitchen ★★★½

CAJUN/CREOLE	MODERATE	QUALITY ★★★½ VALUE ★★½
Reader-Survey Responses 93% 👍 7% 👎		

Downtown Disney; ☎ 714-776-5200; rbjazzkitchen.com

Reservations Available. **When to go** Lunch or dinner. **Entrée range** $12–$38. **Service** ★★★. **Friendliness** ★★½. **Bar** Full bar. **Dress** Casual. **Hours** Monday–Thursday, 11 a.m.–10 p.m., Friday–Saturday, 11 a.m.–11 p.m.; Sunday, 10 a.m.–10 p.m. (*Jazz Kitchen Express:* Daily, 8 a.m.–10 p.m.)

SETTING AND ATMOSPHERE Take a step back in time and space to the 19th-century French Quarter of New Orleans. Almost half the seating area is an open-air courtyard surrounded by wrought iron, hanging ferns, and milled hardwood. Above a small stage where live jazz plays daily, there's a pounded-copper ceiling; to stage left is a beautiful enamel-finished grand piano. You can people-watch from a balcony dining area, but no matter where you sit, you're going to enjoy the ambience and music.

HOUSE SPECIALTIES Gumbo Ya-Ya, blackened fish, and New York steak with horseradish Madeira demi-glace.

OTHER RECOMMENDATIONS Barbecue shrimp and grits, grilled filet mignon medallions, and pasta jambalaya are all good.

SUMMARY AND COMMENTS This used to be one of our favorite restaurants in or immediately around the resort, but it seems to have suffered a little through the recession. The Brennan family is still intimately involved with every aspect of the menu, but both quality and presentation suffer between visits from the New Orleans crew. Servers, including actual Southerners and even a smattering of Louisiana natives, exude a laid-back (sometimes too laid-back), gracious attitude most of the time but have been known to get a little testy and impatient during the restaurant's busy times. This is a dining experience best suited to adults. Add live jazz to the mix (the zydeco brunch is especially fun), and, all things considered, you have one of Disneyland's better dining experiences. For a quick breakfast after 8 a.m., the sugar-dusted beignets and chicory coffee from the adjoining quick-service counter can't be beat. The N'awlins Brunch Fest menu (featuring chicken and waffles and Cajun omelets) is offered every Sunday morning 10 a.m.–3 p.m., accompanied by a made-to-order Bloody Mary bar and table-side card tricks.

Rancho del Zocalo Restaurante ★★

MEXICAN   MODERATE   QUALITY   ★★   VALUE   ★★½
Reader-Survey Responses 75% 👍 25% 👎

Disneyland Park; ☎ 714-781-DINE

Reservations Not accepted. When to go Early lunch or early dinner. Entrée range $11–$14. Service ★★★. Friendliness ★★★. Dress Casual. Hours Daily, 11 a.m.–9:30 p.m.

SETTING AND ATMOSPHERE Welcome to the hacienda! Faux adobe, wooden beams, and Mexican tile ring a dark interior and covered outdoor patio. Tucked away from the throngs in the northeast area of Frontierland, this can be a nice, quiet place for a meal.

HOUSE SPECIALTIES The enchiladas are your best bet, probably because they lend themselves to the buffet-style dining here.

OTHER RECOMMENDATIONS Hit or miss: If you can catch a tray of soft tacos, burritos, or grilled chicken fresh from the commissary, you score.

SUMMARY AND COMMENTS Three words sum up the Zocalo: Mexican, cafeteria style. On the bright side, most of the cuisine holds up well under the heat lamps and over the steam tables, the enchiladas and grilled chicken in particular. The rest of the menu—the typical tacos, burritos, Mexican rice, and refried beans—is resolutely average, except at opening or right before the dinner rush, when the food is fresh and uncorrupted. The tortillas, both corn and flour, are consistently good. Anybody not intimately familiar with really good Mexican cuisine may rate this place higher. Zocalo is also a great choice when you can't possibly choke down another hot dog, burger, or pizza slice. And because it's off the beaten path, it tends to be quiet and restful.

The River Belle Terrace ★★★½

AMERICAN   MODERATE   QUALITY   ★★★½   VALUE   ★★★½
Reader-Survey Responses 75% 👍 25% 👎

Disneyland Park; ☎ 714-781-DINE

Reservations Not accepted. When to go Breakfast and lunch. Entrée range $6–$12. Service ★★★. Friendliness ★★★. Dress Casual. Hours Daily, 9 a.m.–10:30 p.m.

SETTING AND ATMOSPHERE Situated between New Orleans Square and Frontierland, The River Belle Terrace has an Old South–style exterior replete with wrought iron and wood siding. Large shuttered windows belie a small indoor-dining area; most of the seating is outdoors on a large patio covered with colorful umbrellas.

HOUSE SPECIALTIES Mickey-shaped pancakes, country potatoes, and bacon are breakfast favorites. At lunch, chopped salads and steak, pork, or chicken sandwiches. At dinner, prix fixe packages with choice of New York strip and Cajun shrimp, rosemary chicken, or pasta primavera.

OTHER RECOMMENDATIONS *Fantasmic!* dining experience packages, including a FastPass to that evening's show, begin at 3 p.m. and cost $45.36 per adult ($23.76 children ages 3–9). The food is warmed-over wedding banquet fare at best, but the access to the premium viewing area is almost worth it.

SUMMARY AND COMMENTS This 1955 Disneyland original has switched from an all-day counter-service restaurant to counter service for breakfast and lunch, and *Fantasmic!* table-service dinner packages after 3 p.m. Disney lore places Walt here every morning for Mickey-shaped pancakes, scrambled eggs, bacon and sausage, and large, buttery cinnamon rolls dripping with buttercream frosting (a staff favorite). The outdoor seating area is good to people-watch or just take in the view of Rivers of America from the patio.

Steakhouse 55 ★★★★

STEAK HOUSE	VERY EXPENSIVE	QUALITY ★★★★½ VALUE ★★★
Reader-Survey Responses 91% 👍 9% 👎		

Disneyland Hotel; ☎ 714-781-DINE

Reservations Recommended. **When to go** Breakfast or dinner. **Entrée range** $8–$54. **Service** ★★★★. **Friendliness** ★★★★. **Bar** Wine list and full bar. **Dress** Business casual. **Hours** Daily, 7–11 a.m. and 5:30–10 p.m.

SETTING AND ATMOSPHERE At Steakhouse 55, stylishly Art Deco–inspired hardwood tables, sleek leather chairs, and smaller banquettes decorate this updated classic American steak house. The indirect lighting casts a warm glow over everything, including an impressive collection of black-and-white photographs from Disney's storied past.

HOUSE SPECIALTIES Breakfast is a good value and features eggs Benedict and New York steak and eggs. At dinner it's all about the meat—grilled certified Angus beef seasoned with the restaurant's signature rub—but you can also order one of the fresh seafood choices or delectable lamb, pork, or chicken. Choose a bottle of wine from an impressive wine cellar, or simply engage one of the numerous sommeliers to choose a wine to complement your meal.

OTHER RECOMMENDATIONS The lobster and steak combination is actually very good, but the price can catch you by surprise; always ask up front before ordering unless you have very deep pockets.

SUMMARY AND COMMENTS This underrated eatery has been a well-kept secret for years and matches many of the more well-known steak houses in the area (Morton's and Ruth's Chris) steak for steak. It's alluring and comfortable, a perfect place to spend a grown-up evening over a leisurely meal matched to premium wines. Longtime chef Jason Martin has had years to refine his menu and has been consistently recognized by local and visiting critics as a bona fide culinary talent. Best to leave the kids behind for this experience; they'll bore easily and may disrupt what could be one of the best adult nights you're likely to have during your stay.

Storytellers Café ★★★★

CHARACTER DINING/CALIFORNIA	EXPENSIVE	QUALITY ★★★★ VALUE ★★★½
Reader-Survey Responses 84% 👍 16% 👎		

Grand Californian Hotel; ☎ 714-781-DINE

Reservations Recommended. **When to go** Breakfast or dinner. **Entrée range** $15–$30. **Service** ★★★★★. **Friendliness** ★★★★. **Bar** Extensive wine list and full bar. **Dress** Casual. **Hours** Daily, 7 a.m.–9:45 p.m.

SETTING AND ATMOSPHERE The Storytellers Café carries the Grand Californian's Arts & Crafts theme throughout with large, open beams; natural wood and wood carvings; milled stone; and stained glass. The walls are adorned with impressive murals depicting the state's rich literary history, from Mark Twain's "The Celebrated Jumping Frog of Calaveras County" to Scott O'Dell's *Island of the Blue Dolphins.*

HOUSE SPECIALTIES Children under age 10 will love the character breakfast buffet. Hosted by Chip 'n' Dale, the meal features a complement of woodland friends who visit the tables, sing songs, and pose for photos between bites of omelets, waffles, and hotcakes. The Sonoma Valley braised chicken and lemon prawns are dinner favorites.

OTHER RECOMMENDATIONS Health-conscious diners will love the café's salads, such as the Lobster Cobb Salad (with avocado, bacon, tomato, and blue cheese topped by a low-fat citrus-chive vinaigrette). The grilled chicken sandwich, with caramelized onion, tomato, and cheese, is great.

SUMMARY AND COMMENTS You may experience a little sticker shock at first, but there's real value here. It's not quite on par with Napa Rose across the way, but the same dedication to quality and originality is evident from the menu to the service. Kids will find lots to like about the food, while the adults enjoy California wine country–inspired menu options (from pastas to steaks to fresh fish) and a leisurely cocktail or glass of wine. Dinner gives diners the option to order from the menu or visit the buffet. You'll want to save some room for dessert too—who could pass up warm seasonal-fruit cobbler heaped with vanilla ice cream or a warm chocolate brownie? A Manitowoc, Wisconsin, reader recommends the café as an alternative to dining inside DCA, writing:

We ended up eating at Storytellers Café on a spur-of-the-moment decision, and it was one of the best places at which we ate at the park, as far as food, price, and atmosphere. Can share meals too, which costs less than eating in the park. The lemonade with the foam on top was AMAZING!

Tangaroa Terrace ★★★

AMERICAN/POLYNESIAN	MODERATE	QUALITY ★★★	VALUE ★★★½
Reader-Survey Responses	80% 👍 20% 👎		

Disneyland Hotel; ☎ 714-781-DINE

Reservations Not accepted. **When to go** Anytime. **Entrée range** $4–$12. **Service** ★★★★. **Friendliness** ★★★★. **Bar** Beer, wine, and cocktails. **Dress** Casual. **Hours** Daily, 7 a.m.–10 p.m.

SETTING AND ATMOSPHERE This is Disneyland Hotel's poolside tropical retreat. Tiki torches and South Seas music are a dead giveaway that they want to evoke that island feeling.

HOUSE SPECIALTIES Breakfast starts with French toast with bacon and banana-caramel sauce or grilled cinnamon-spiced oatmeal cakes. Lunch and dinner feature a one-third-pound Hawaiian cheeseburger with teriyaki sauce, bacon, and grilled pineapple on a multigrain bun, or try the Asian chicken salad with red and yellow bell peppers, cashews, and rice noodles in sesame vinaigrette.

OTHER RECOMMENDATIONS Specials get a little more involved with sushi-grade ahi tuna *poke* and shrimp tacos. *Caution:* The sweet potato fries may be habit forming. Tangaroa Terrace also serves most of the same bar snacks as Trader Sam's next door, with the exception of the exquisite long beans.

SUMMARY AND COMMENTS This eatery has something for everyone, as long as everyone enjoys food with an Asian-Polynesian flare. Adults can enjoy a cocktail (maybe something a little exotic with a fruit garnish and little pink umbrellas) while kids frolic in the nearby pool in between bites. The adjoining Trader Sam's Enchanted Tiki Bar serves exotic cocktails and Asian-inspired appetizers in an intimate and elaborately decorated environment reminiscent of Walt Disney World's extinct Adventurers Club. Order an Uh Oa, Krakatoa Punch, or Shipwreck on the Rocks to see some explosive special effects. The best bet for late-night snacks are Sam's panko-crusted long beans or sweet and spicy Asian wings. If the interior is at capacity (a frequent occurrence on weekends), try the patio, which has live music and a cozy fireplace.

Tortilla Jo's ★★★

MEXICAN   MODERATE-EXPENSIVE   QUALITY ★★½ VALUE ★★½
Reader-Survey Responses 84% 👍 16% 👎

Downtown Disney; ☎ 714-535-5000; patinagroup.com/tortillajos

Reservations Available. **When to go** Lunch or dinner. **Entrée range** $13–$25. **Service** ★★★. **Friendliness** ★★★. **Bar** Full bar. **Dress** Casual. **Hours** Sunday–Thursday, 11 a.m.–10 p.m., Friday–Saturday, 11 a.m.–11 p.m.; *taqueria:* Sunday–Thursday, 11 a.m.–11:30 p.m., Friday–Saturday, 11 a.m.–1 a.m.

SETTING AND ATMOSPHERE Old Mexico meets California modern. Mexican touchstones such as glazed tiles; thick, crude glass; and wrought iron accent an open dining room with modern, eclectic touches. You can grab a quick bite at the taqueria, and the bartender pours from a huge selection of more than 100 premium and super-premium tequilas at an outdoor cantina. The place goes crazy on the weekends, so gird yourself for a raucous, booze-shooting, beer-chasing good time.

HOUSE SPECIALTIES Start with guacamole made fresh at your table. For an entrée, any one of the gigantic burritos, especially the signature Fajitas Burrito, are good.

OTHER RECOMMENDATIONS Try the gorditas or the mahimahi taco.

SUMMARY AND COMMENTS Another Patina Group eatery from überchef Joachim Splichal, Tortilla Jo's is upscale Mexican with a culinary twist. You can customize any taco or burrito. The eclectic, hybrid menu (and the loosey-goosey crowd) may be too much for the kids, but adults will appreciate a shot of Sauza Silver tequila and a tall glass of Corona beer, complete with a lime wedge. Strolling mariachi musicians fill the dining room and bar with foot-stomping traditional Mexican music.

Wine Country Trattoria ★★★★

CALIFORNIA NOUVELLE   MODERATE   QUALITY ★★★★ VALUE ★★★
Reader-Survey Responses 86% 👍 14% 👎

Disney California Adventure; ☎ 714-781-DINE

Reservations Recommended. **When to go** Lunch or dinner. **Entrée range** $14–$23. **Service** ★★★. **Friendliness** ★★. **Bar** Wine, beer, and cocktails. **Dress** Casual. **Hours** Daily, 11:30 a.m.–9:15 p.m.

SETTING AND ATMOSPHERE Arguably one of the better dining options at either park, the trattoria is a leisurely place to park yourself and family away from the frenetic crowds. Whether you choose one of three themed patios outside or the "patio" inside, this spacious bistro captures the California-casual mood with plenty of tile, wood, and trellised greenery, whisking you away from downtown Anaheim and positing you in the middle of California wine country.

HOUSE SPECIALTIES Try the Pasta Your Way: spaghetti, *campanelle,* or fettuccine with five sauces from which to choose.

OTHER RECOMMENDATIONS Wine Country shrimp on polenta with a lemon-caper butter sauce and the herb-roasted chicken breast.

SUMMARY AND COMMENTS The trattoria is a popular spot for a Mediterranean-style or California-inspired meal, paired with a glass of wine from its extensive cellar. Braised lamb shank and sustainable fish with citrus pesto is delicious. The Wine Country shrimp and fritto misto qualify as full-blown entrées. And to finish: Authentic tiramisu with sweetened Italian mascarpone is an exotic treat for adults among the more kid-friendly sweets that dominate in the rest of the resort. Wine Country Trattoria appeals more to adults without children, though an improved kids' menu and *World of Color* fixed-price dining packages has made this a more attractive option for families (Lunch: $34.56 for adults, $22.68 for kids; Dinner: $48.60 for adults, $27 for kids; all including tax). Note that *World of Color* lunch and dinner patrons each receive a center-section viewing ticket. Also note that the fixed-price *World of Color* menu is separate from the posted à la carte selections. The soup or salad and dessert sampler included in the viewing package are all excellent, but some of the entrées can be inconsistent. For a refreshing late-afternoon break, order a glass of wine and plate of fritto misto at the Alfresco Tasting Terrace on the upstairs patio. From a Richfield, Ohio, mom:

One place we all agreed on was the Wine Country Trattoria at DCA. The service was a bit on the slow side, but the food from start to finish was delicious and fresh. We arrived around 1:30 and enjoyed lunch and the parade, which passed by at 2. Delicious meal and a parade too!

DINING *Outside*
DISNEYLAND RESORT

UNOFFICIAL GUIDE RESEARCHERS LOVE GOOD FOOD and invest a fair amount of time scouting new places to eat. And because food at Disneyland Resort (all of the Disney complex including the theme parks, hotels, and Downtown Disney) is so expensive, we (like you) have an economic incentive for finding palatable meals off campus. Redevelopment of the surrounding real estate has attracted a whole new glut of fine-dining and fast-casual options. Choices abound from the familiar (**Cheesecake Factory, Roy's Hawaiian Fusion Cuisine, Ruth's Chris Steak House**) to local favorites (**Yard House, Umami Burger, The Catch**). Unique dining experiences abound. While the average Disneyland visitor stays for only two to four nights, there are more than enough fine-dining and fast-casual venues outside Disneyland Resort to keep you happy, if not confused, for that amount of time. Good ethnic dining, however, is woefully underrepresented. Especially hard to find are high-quality Thai, Chinese, Mexican, Japanese, Korean, and Greek restaurants. We've confined our coverage to restaurants that you can reach by car or cab in 15 minutes or less. If you're willing to range farther afield, your choices increase exponentially.

Among specialty restaurants in and out of Disneyland Resort, location and price will determine your choice. There is, for example, a decent Italian restaurant in Downtown Disney and several independent Italian eateries within 5 miles of the Disney complex. Which one you select depends on how much you want to spend and how convenient the place is.

Better restaurants outside Disneyland Resort cater primarily to adults and aren't as well equipped to deal with children. This is a plus, however, if you're looking to escape children and eat in peace and quiet.

The Anaheim GardenWalk retail and entertainment complex is east of the park. Popular chains such as **The Cheesecake Factory, Roy's Restaurant, California Pizza Kitchen,** and **Bubba Gump Shrimp Co.** are doing brisk business. The best of the lot is probably **McCormick & Schmick's Grille,** which serves well-prepared fresh seafood at outrageous prices.

BUFFETS AND MEAL DEALS
OUTSIDE DISNEYLAND RESORT

BUFFETS, RESTAURANT SPECIALS, AND DISCOUNT DINING abound in the area surrounding Disneyland Resort, especially on Harbor Boulevard and Katella Avenue. The local visitor magazines, which are distributed free at non-Disney hotels, among other places, are packed with advertisements and discount coupons for seafood feasts, buffets (Chinese, Indian, and the like), and a host of combination specials for everything from lobster to barbecue. For a family trying to economize on meals, some of the come-ons are mighty attractive. But are these places any good? Is the food fresh, tasty, and appealing? Are the restaurants clean and inviting? Armed with little more than a roll of Tums, the Unofficial research team tried all the eateries that advertise heavily in the tourist publications. Here's what we discovered.

Chinese Super Buffets

Talk about an oxymoron. If you've ever tried preparing Chinese food, especially a stir-fry, you know that split-second timing is required to avoid overcooking. So it should come as no big surprise that Chinese dishes languishing on a buffet lose their freshness, texture, and flavor in a hurry. On the bright side, however, the super buffets are so cheap that you really can't go wrong. So what if it's not the best Chinese food you've ever had if you can scarf down all you want for $10? All the Chinese buffets serve chicken prepared a dozen different ways but also offer such goodies as peel-and-eat shrimp, various fish and shellfish, the occasional carved meat, salads, soups, and sometimes sushi. Desserts are usually lackluster, but most folks are too stuffed to eat them anyway. The best Chinese buffet within a 15-minute drive of Disneyland Resort is as follows:

HARBOR SEAFOOD BUFFET   12761 Harbor Blvd., Ste. I1, Garden Grove; ☎ 714-636-3338; **theharborseafoodbuffet.net.** Dinner: $14.99 adults, Monday–Thursday; $15.99 adults, Friday–Sunday; $1.40 per year old for children ages 2–10, free for children under age 2. Seniors and military receive 10% off. Discount coupons available. Features Japanese food, sushi, and Mongolian barbecue in addition to Chinese dishes.

Indian Buffets

Indian food survives the ravages of heat lamps and steam tables much better on a buffet than Chinese food does. The mainstays of Indian buffets are curries. *Curry,* you may be surprised to know, is essentially the Indian word for "stew." In India each curry is prepared with a different combination of spices (dominated by cumin). The salient point about Indian buffets is that curries, unlike stir-fries, actually improve with a little aging. If you've ever reheated a leftover stew at home and noticed that it tasted better the second time, it's because the flavors and ingredients continued to marry during the storage period, making the stew richer and tastier.

In the Disneyland Resort area, most Indian restaurants offer buffets at lunch only—not too convenient if you plan on spending your day at the theme parks. If you're out shopping or taking a day off, here is one Indian buffet worth trying:

GANDHI PALACE   Ramada Plaza Hotel, 515 W. Katella Ave., Anaheim; ☎ 714-808-6777; **gandhipalaceanaheim.com.** Lunch buffet: Monday–Saturday, $12. Discount coupons available.

Salad Buffets

The most popular of these in the Disneyland Resort area is **Souplantation** (5939 W. Chapman Ave., Garden Grove; ☎ 714-895-1314; **souplantation.com**). The buffet features prepared salads and an extensive array of ingredients to build your own. Souplantation also offers a variety of soups, a modest pasta bar, a baked potato bar, an assortment of fresh fruit, and ice cream sundaes. Dinner runs $11.59 for adults, $5.99 for children ages 6–12, and $2.99 for children ages 3–5. Lunch is $9.99 for adults during the week and $9.59 on weekends; kids eat for the same price as at dinner.

ANAHEIM-AREA FULL-SERVICE RESTAURANTS

SOUTHERN CALIFORNIA IS A MOTHER LODE of wonderful dining, and if we directed you to Newport Beach, La Jolla, or LA, we could guarantee you a fantastic eating experience every night. In that you've chosen Disneyland as your destination, however, we've elected to profile only solid restaurants that you can reach by car or cab in 15 minutes or less. That said, here are our picks; all of them offer disabled access.

Anaheim White House ★★★★½

ITALIAN   EXPENSIVE   QUALITY ★★★★½   VALUE ★★★★

887 S. Anaheim Blvd., Anaheim; ☎ 714-772-1381; anaheimwhitehouse.com

Reservations Recommended. **When to go** Dinner. **Entrée range** $12–$97. **Service** ★★★★★. **Friendliness** ★★★★. **Bar** Full bar; plentiful wine list. **Dress** Business casual. **Hours** Monday–Friday, 11:30 a.m.–2 p.m. and 5–10 p.m.; Saturday, 5–10 p.m.; Sunday, 11 a.m.–3 p.m. and 5–10 p.m.

SETTING AND ATMOSPHERE A local institution, the Anaheim White House sits in a restored Victorian originally built in 1909. It has nine dining rooms, all with thick gold-and-white drapes and bright-gold accents against a white background. Tables are set with fine bone china and the best flatware. Service is extremely gracious and knowledgeable.

HOUSE SPECIALTIES Italian seafood recipes from northern Italy highlight an extensive menu. Braised boneless beef short ribs, steamed salmon (served with a Belgian white chocolate mashed potato purée), and lobster-and-basil ravioli in a ginger-citrus sauce are its signature dishes.

OTHER RECOMMENDATIONS Chicken stuffed with ham and mozzarella cheese in a light mushroom sauce.

SUMMARY AND COMMENTS The White House only seems to get better. The menu of northern Italian recipes is kept fresh and timely, and service is spot-on. This is an elegant restaurant—leave the kids with a sitter.

Bierstube German Pub at the Phoenix Club ★★★½

GERMAN   MODERATE   QUALITY ★★★½   VALUE ★★★★

1340 S. Sanderson Ave., behind Honda Center, Anaheim;
☎ 714-563-4166; thephoenixclub.com

Reservations Recommended. **When to go** Lunch or dinner. **Entrée range** $9–$18. **Service** ★★★. **Friendliness** ★★★★. **Bar** Wine list, extensive draft beer offerings, and full bar. **Dress** Casual. **Hours** Tuesday–Thursday and Sunday, 11 a.m.–9 p.m.; Friday–Saturday, 11 a.m.–10 p.m.

SETTING AND ATMOSPHERE Once a private club reserved for family members of the original German settlers of Anaheim and more recent émigrés, this famous landmark is now open to the public (members are still welcome and enjoy a few extra privileges). The boisterous Bierstube has more than a half dozen German beers on tap. Its menu is somewhat limited, trending toward less-fancy preparations, but it's these basic dishes that keep folks coming back. The Bierstube is conducive to raucous eating, drinking, and carousing. Live music seems omnipresent, from local and guest polka bands to renowned accordion artists.

HOUSE SPECIALTIES Wursts, kraut, pork roast, mixed platters, and sauerbraten are the best in a 100-mile radius.

OTHER RECOMMENDATIONS Pork in a creamy mushroom sauce.

SUMMARY AND COMMENTS The bastion of Anaheim's founding families and subsequent waves of German immigrants, The Phoenix Club offers a little taste of the *Mutterland* far from home. The food is good, occasionally great; the beer is always cold; and the help is always ready to show you a good time, German or not. During Oktoberfest, the place rocks. The kids will love the early reminders of a rough and rural Anaheim and the

ANAHEIM-AREA RESTAURANTS BY CUISINE

CUISINE/LOCATION	OVERALL RATING	COST	QUALITY RATING	VALUE RATING
AMERICAN				
CLANCY'S AMERICAN GRILL S. Harbor Blvd.	★★★	Mod	★★★	★★★
ROSCOE'S HOUSE OF CHICKEN & WAFFLES S. Harbor Blvd.	★★★★½	Inexp	★★★★	★★★½
CHINESE				
MAS' CHINESE ISLAMIC RESTAURANT E. Orangethorpe Ave.	★★★½	Mod	★★★	★★★½
GASTROPUB				
HAVEN GASTROPUB S. Glassell St.	★★★	Mod	★★★★	★★★½
GERMAN				
BIERSTUBE GERMAN PUB AT THE PHOENIX CLUB S. Sanderson Ave.	★★★½	Mod	★★★½	★★★★
JÄGERHAUS E. Ball Rd.	★★★	Inexp	★★★½	★★★
ITALIAN				
ANAHEIM WHITE HOUSE S. Anaheim Blvd.	★★★★½	Exp	★★★★½	★★★★
LUIGI'S D'ITALIA S. State College Blvd.	★★★½	Inexp/ Mod	★★★½	★★★★
CAROLINA'S ITALIAN RESTAURANT Chapman Ave.	★★★	Inexp	★★★	★★★½
MEXICAN				
GABBI'S MEXICAN KITCHEN S. Glassell St.	★★★	Mod	★★★★	★★★½
SEAFOOD				
THE CATCH E. Katella Ave.	★★★½	Exp	★★★★	★★★½
MCCORMICK & SCHMICK'S GRILLE W. Katella Ave.	★★★	Mod	★★★	★★★
STEAK				
PARK AVE STEAKS & CHOPS Beach Blvd.	★★★★½	Exp	★★★★	★★★★
MORTON'S S. Harbor Blvd.	★★★★	Exp	★★★½	★★★½
THE CATCH E. Katella Ave.	★★★½	Exp	★★★★	★★★½
PRIME CUT CAFÉ & WINE BAR W. Katella Ave.	★★★	Mod	★★★	★★★½

oompah bands, Mom and Dad will love the German beers, and everyone will love the sweet-and-sour flavors of German cuisine.

Carolina's Italian Restaurant ★★★

SOUTHERN ITALIAN   INEXPENSIVE   QUALITY ★★★   VALUE ★★★½

12045 Chapman Ave., Garden Grove; ☎ 714-971-5551; carolinasitalianrestaurant.com

Reservations Recommended. **When to go** Dinner. **Entrée range** $10–$23. **Service** ★★½. **Friendliness** ★★★½. **Bar** Extensive beer and wine lists. **Dress** Casual. **Hours** Sunday–Thursday, 11 a.m.–10 p.m.; Friday–Saturday, 11 a.m.–midnight.

SETTING AND ATMOSPHERE A classic Italian family restaurant replete with wall murals of the motherland, comfortable seating, and the overwhelming aroma of garlic and olive oil. It's like walking through a time warp.

HOUSE SPECIALTIES You can't go wrong with any one of more than three dozen hearty pasta dishes, from a very traditional meat sauce to an outstanding lasagna. The kitchen's showcase is a slab of fresh Atlantic salmon in a butter-garlic-mustard sauce.

OTHER RECOMMENDATIONS The Taste of Italy features the colors of Italy's flag with a combination of chicken penne pesto, shrimp fettuccine Alfredo, and spaghetti with meatballs. The house-made tiramisu, if you can manage more food after the large plates, is a treat.

SUMMARY AND COMMENTS Family owned and operated for three generations, Carolina's also features more than 200 beers from around the globe and a rather well-selected wine list for such a place. Portions tend toward the gigantic, so bring your appetite.

The Catch ★★★½

SEAFOOD/STEAK   EXPENSIVE   QUALITY ★★★★   VALUE ★★★½

2100 E. Katella Ave., Ste. 104, Anaheim; ☎ 714-935-0101; catchanaheim.com

Reservations Recommended. **When to go** Lunch or dinner. **Entrée range** $12–$48. **Service** ★★★. **Friendliness** ★★★½. **Bar** Full bar. **Dress** Business casual. **Hours** Monday–Friday, 11:30 a.m.–10 p.m.; Saturday, 11:30 a.m.–4 p.m. and 5–10 p.m.; Sunday, 11:30 a.m.–4 p.m. and 5–9 p.m.

SETTING AND ATMOSPHERE Clean, contemporary take on a steak house classic, The Catch exudes urban chic with a comfortable blend of hardwood, glass, and tile. Expect to see dozens of young urban professionals; old, die-hard loyalists; and even a smattering of professional athletes who play for the local Angels baseball and Anaheim Ducks hockey teams dallying at the bar and/or enjoying dinner with friends and family.

HOUSE SPECIALTIES Grilled fresh fish, premium meats, and chops dominate the menu. The Drunken Mahimahi, a lightly blackened fresh fillet splashed with tequila, is as good as it is simple. And for steak lovers, the top sirloin may be the best cut you're likely to sample anywhere.

OTHER RECOMMENDATIONS Lunch features butcher-block sandwiches: piles of thinly sliced meats or fish piled high on fresh slabs of bread, accompanied by all the usual condiments and some not-so-common spreads such as lemon aioli. For dinner, try the terrific bone-in rib eye.

SUMMARY AND COMMENTS The Catch reopened in 2010 under new leadership and in a brand-new location. Yes, the place is very expensive, but you're not likely to find a more beautiful yet comfortable room, attentive service, or high-quality food prepared with love and care anywhere close by. It has a vibrant bar scene favored by local luminaries, a beautiful dining room, and even a nicely appointed patio.

Clancy's American Grill ★★★

AMERICAN   MODERATE   QUALITY ★★★   VALUE ★★★

2191 S. Harbor Blvd., Anaheim; ☎ 714-750-7500; clancysamericangrill.com

Reservations Available. **When to go** Lunch or dinner. **Entrée range** $10–$25. **Service** ★★. **Friendliness** ★★★. **Bar** Full bar. **Dress** Casual. **Hours** Daily, 4–11 p.m.

GREAT EATS IN AND AROUND ANAHEIM

BEST BURGER

Umami Burger 338 S. Anaheim Blvd., Anaheim; ☎ 714-991-8626; **umamiburger** **.com.** Juicy house-ground burgers served mid-rare and topped with truffle cheese, shii-take mushrooms, fried eggs, or other fancy fixin's. Try the homemade pickles.

BEST CHINESE

Grand China Restaurant 575 W. Chapman Ave., Anaheim; ☎ 714-740-1888. Really outstanding service differentiates this spot from its nearby competitors. The menu's pretty standard, but what it does, it does well. The broccoli with beef and sweet-and-sour chicken are first-rate.

BEST INDIAN

Punjabi Tandoor 327 S. Anaheim Blvd., Ste. A, Anaheim; ☎ 714-635-3155; **punjabi** **tandoor.com.** The fresh tandoori in the evening is exceptional. Offers original dishes and excellent naan.

BEST JAPANESE

Sushi Pop 1105 Euclid St., Fullerton; ☎ 714-278-1062; **sushipopus.com.** An unpretentious strip-mall eatery offering all-you-can-eat nigiri and unusual maki rolls at reasonable prices.

BEST MEDITERRANEAN

Zankou Chicken 2424 W. Ball Rd., Anaheim; ☎ 714-229-2060; **zankouchicken** **.com.** Forget that this place is a chain, disregard the cheesy ambience, and go for the spit-roasted chicken, hummus, and shawarma beef. Inexpensive and delicious.

BEST MEXICAN

La Casa Garcia 531 W. Chapman Ave., Anaheim; ☎ 714-740-1108; **lacasagarcia** **.com.** Carnitas, *barbacoa* (beef slow-cooked in a red-chile sauce), and three-flavor chimichangas, all with a Tex-Mex twist, are not to be missed.

Los Sanchez 11906 Garden Grove Blvd., Garden Grove; ☎ 714-590-9300; **lossanchez** **.com.** This locals-only gem serves authentic Sonoran cuisine at reasonable prices. Fish ceviche, *lengua* (tongue) tacos, seafood soup, and the best chicken mole you've ever had.

BEST PIZZA

Pizza Press 1534 S. Harbor Blvd., Anaheim; ☎ 714-323-7134; **thepizzapress** **.com.** Excellent artisanal thin-crust pies with upscale toppings for a very reasonable $10—plus tossed-to-order salads, craft beers, and a 1 a.m. closing time—make this tiny independent pizzeria across from Disneyland a perfect post-park pit stop.

SETTING AND ATMOSPHERE Pure sports bar with full, high-definition flat-panel TVs in every direction, a few booths, and several rooms of tables, all with a view of the televised action.

HOUSE SPECIALTIES Wings marinated, baked, fried, and broiled to perfection with all the usual sauces, as well as a very different mango habañero. The pulled pork sandwich swims in a signature barbecue sauce.

OTHER RECOMMENDATIONS The steaks, including a baseball-cut top sirloin (a ball of meat with all the flavor of a sirloin and the tenderness of a filet mignon), are surprisingly good for a sports bar.

SUMMARY AND COMMENTS Clancy's is a great alternative to the crammed insanity of the ESPN Zone in Downtown Disney. The expansive menu has sports bar staples such as chicken wings and a decent cut of beef. Lots of locals and a friendly vibe; service can be sporadic.

Gabbi's Mexican Kitchen ★★★

GOURMET MEXICAN   MODERATE   QUALITY ★★★★   VALUE ★★★½

141 S. Glassell St., Orange; ☎ 714-633-3038; gabbipatrick.com

Reservations Recommended. **When to go** Lunch or dinner. **Entrée range** $14–$26. **Service** ★★★. **Friendliness** ★★★. **Bar** Full bar. **Dress** Casual. **Hours** Daily, 11 a.m.–11 p.m.

SETTING AND ATMOSPHERE Locals flock to Gabbi's vintage storefront that has no sign (look for the *poquito* patio next door to the Army surplus store). Just steps south of Orange's beloved plaza in charming Old Town, Gabbi's adds style to the narrow space with tall ceilings, exposed brick, and giant, colorful Mexican urns.

HOUSE SPECIALTIES Puerco Poc-Chuc (a Mayan recipe of grilled pork, onions, and habañero salsa), quesadillas with *cuitlacoche* and a poblano cream sauce, and squash blossom chiles rellenos.

OTHER RECOMMENDATIONS Chicken enchiladas and signature margaritas made from a tequila collection that would make a desperado blush.

SUMMARY AND COMMENTS In this county teeming with taco stands and burrito counters, chef-owner Gabbi Patrick stands apart with her more refined, regional takes on Mexican food that reflect both her Napa training and her Latino family's roots in the restaurant business.

Haven Gastropub ★★★

GASTROPUB   MODERATE   QUALITY ★★★★   VALUE ★★★½

190 S. Glassell St., Orange; ☎ 714-221-0680; havengastropub.com

Reservations Recommended. **When to go** Lunch or dinner. **Entrée range** $12–$42. **Service** ★★★. **Friendliness** ★★★½. **Bar** Beer and wine. **Dress** Casual. **Hours** Daily, 11 a.m.–2 a.m.

SETTING AND ATMOSPHERE The restaurant is in Old Town Orange, a historic area of preserved homes and businesses including this little gem. Like its neighbor, Gabbi's, Haven is housed in a restored brick building. Inside, you'll find a large open dining room packed with tables and booths, framed by a massive bar on one side and an open kitchen on the other.

HOUSE SPECIALTIES House-made potato chips are first soaked in beer, fried, and served with a sprinkling of herbs and a side of garlic aioli. Try the lamb burger with onion jam, *tzatziki,* and onion sprouts on a squishy brioche bun.

OTHER RECOMMENDATIONS Braised lamb neck served poutine style with Dijon gravy, Cheddar cheese curds, and *pommes frites*; a whole roasted suckling pig served family style for parties of eight or more (reserve one week in advance).

SUMMARY AND COMMENTS Think beer, anything made with beer, and all the food that goes with beer, and you have a grasp of what executive chef Greg Daniels has put together here. More than 200 craft beers on tap and in a bottle—and a service crew who knows every one of them intimately—together with an adventurous menu of faux familiar and exotic foods, and you have Haven. The place is a favorite for the local college students and fills quickly on weekends but stays open late every night until 2 a.m.

Jägerhaus ★★★

GERMAN   INEXPENSIVE   QUALITY ★★★½   VALUE ★★★

2525 E. Ball Rd., Anaheim; ☎ 714-520-9500; jagerhaus.net

Reservations Recommended only for large parties. **When to go** Breakfast. **Entrée range** $5–$21. **Service** ★★½. **Friendliness** ★★★★. **Bar** Wine list and extensive imported draft beer offerings. **Dress** Casual. **Hours** Monday–Friday, 7 a.m.–9 p.m.; Saturday–Sunday, 8 a.m.–9 p.m.

SETTING AND ATMOSPHERE We don't think that anything has changed since this restaurant opened decades ago. Wood paneling dominates. Pictures of alpine meadows and picturesque Old World villages hang beneath shelves of kitschy accoutrements, from delicate porcelain teapots to hearty beer steins—but it's clean and neat.

HOUSE SPECIALTIES The German pancakes, dense, doughy, platter-size egg cakes flavored with everything from lemon and powdered sugar to fruit jams and even fresh fruit; fat, juicy bratwursts.

OTHER RECOMMENDATIONS Omelets, corn beef hash, and house-made sausage patties.

SUMMARY AND COMMENTS Everyone from recent German émigrés and tourists to descendants of the original German settlers gather here to eat fat, fluffy German pancakes and sausage and gossip over coffee. The huge menu offers something for everyone, from burgers to bratwurst and bagels to Wiener schnitzel.

Luigi's D'Italia ★★★½

ITALIAN   INEXPENSIVE–MODERATE   QUALITY ★★★½   VALUE ★★★★

801 S. State College Blvd., Anaheim; ☎ 714-490-0990; italianoc.com

Reservations Recommended. **When to go** Lunch or dinner. **Entrée range** $8–$26. **Service** ★★★. **Friendliness** ★★★. **Bar** Wine and beer. **Dress** Casual. **Hours** Monday–Friday, 11 a.m.–10 p.m.; Saturday–Sunday, noon–10 p.m.

SETTING AND ATMOSPHERE The classic tacky Italian decor (think faux grapevines, funky murals, and Chianti-bottle candleholders) was renovated by celebrity chef Gordon Ramsay for an episode of *Kitchen Nightmares* and replaced by a trendy postage-stamp motif, but the generally good food and warm and friendly service are still the same.

HOUSE SPECIALTIES Better-than-average hand-tossed pizzas with all the familiar toppings (pepperoni, mushroom, sausage, and such); a very tasty (and hearty) eggplant Sorrentino.

OTHER RECOMMENDATIONS The pastas, including a superb spaghetti Bolognese, are commendable.

SUMMARY AND COMMENTS When the pocketbook can't take another huge hit no matter how good the menu looks, head to Luigi's. Old-fashioned Italian fare, a welcoming ambience, and friendly smiles await. The pizzas and pastas, Italian staples, are all familiar, hearty, and tasty, if not overly generous in their portions. The kids will love watching the pizzas get tossed, and your credit card will breathe a sigh of relief.

Mas' Chinese Islamic Restaurant ★★★½

NORTHERN CHINESE   MODERATE   QUALITY ★★★   VALUE ★★★½

601 E. Orangethorpe Ave., Anaheim; ☎ 714-446-9553

Reservations Recommended. **When to go** Lunch or dinner. **Entrée range** $8–$26. **Service** ★★★. **Friendliness** ★★★½. **Dress** Casual but modest (no shorts). **Hours** Monday and Wednesday–Thursday, 11 a.m.–3 p.m. and 5–9:30 p.m.; Friday–Sunday, 11 a.m.–3 p.m. and 5–10 p.m.

SETTING AND ATMOSPHERE One of a small chain of Islamic Chinese restaurants, this is the real deal. Mas' Islamic's dining room is spacious, with comfortable booths and large tables. The decor blends Middle Eastern and Chinese motifs with lots of tile, repetitive patterned mosaics, and lofty arches.

HOUSE SPECIALTIES Get the thick sesame bread with green onions as a starter. Any lamb dish is a sure bet, especially the one served with *sa cha*, a spicy brown sauce.

OTHER RECOMMENDATIONS The warm pots—northern-Chinese stews—are great, as is the beef with green onions.

SUMMARY AND COMMENTS This is a veritable institution among local Muslims (Arabs and East and Southeast Asians), so expect to see women in veils and burkas and men dressed very conservatively; also, note that no alcohol is served. Service is gracious, if a bit English-challenged. Stick to the northern-Chinese specialties—the more familiar Chinese side of the menu is less exciting.

McCormick & Schmick's Grille ★★★

SEAFOOD MODERATE QUALITY ★★★ VALUE ★★★

321 W. Katella Ave., Anaheim; ☎ 714-535-9000;
mccormickandschmicks.com

Reservations Recommended. **When to go** Lunch or dinner. **Entrée range** $11–$39. **Service** ★★★. **Friendliness** ★★★★. **Bar** Full bar and extensive wine list. **Dress** Business casual. **Hours** Monday–Wednesday and Sunday, 11:30 a.m.–10 p.m.; Thursday–Saturday, 11:30 a.m.–11 p.m.

SETTING AND ATMOSPHERE This large chain of seafood eateries designs each of its units differently to match its local surroundings. In addition to lots of dark hardwoods and spacious booths, the decor here takes its cues from the rich agricultural history of the area.

HOUSE SPECIALTIES Fish—fresh and infinitely variable. Each chef is free to choose from among 80 different preparations, and there's an abundance of fresh selections. You can't miss with king crab, lobster, fresh salmon, or killer fresh swordfish.

SUMMARY AND COMMENTS This is a very popular spot with local business types, and waits without reservations can be long. The menu can be overwhelming; on the other hand, there's something for everyone, even folks who don't eat fish. Happy hour specials (Monday–Friday, 4–7 p.m.) somewhat soften the sting of expensive entrées; the $5 steamed mussels are an especially good deal.

Morton's ★★★★

STEAK HOUSE EXPENSIVE QUALITY ★★★½ VALUE ★★★½

1895 S. Harbor Blvd., Anaheim; ☎ 714-621-0101; mortons.com

Reservations Recommended. **When to go** Dinner. **Entrée range** $24–$88. **Service** ★★★★. **Friendliness** ★★★★. **Bar** Extensive wine list and full bar. **Dress** Dressy casual. **Hours** Monday–Saturday, 5:30–11 p.m.; Sunday, 5–10 p.m.

SETTING AND ATMOSPHERE Classic steak house with overstuffed booths, soft lighting, and dark hardwoods.

HOUSE SPECIALTIES Try the center-cut filet mignon Oscar-style (with lump crab, asparagus, and béarnaise sauce).

OTHER RECOMMENDATIONS The bone-in rib eye is a Chicago staple and beef-eater's dream: 22 ounces of prime steak, grilled to order.

SUMMARY AND COMMENTS Morton's is a carnivore's delight—beef, lamb, and chicken dominate the menu. Of course, there's a smattering of fish options, including shrimp in several different iterations, but this place is really about the beef.

Park Ave Steaks & Chops ★★★★½

STEAK HOUSE   EXPENSIVE   QUALITY ★★★★   VALUE ★★★★

11200 Beach Blvd., Stanton; ☎ 714-901-4400; parkavedining.com

Reservations Recommended. **When to go** Dinner. **Entrée range** $18–$32. **Service** ★★★. **Friendliness** ★★★½. **Bar** Full bar. **Dress** Dressy casual/business. **Hours** Tuesday–Friday, 11 a.m.–midnight; Saturday–Sunday, 4 p.m.–midnight.

SETTING AND ATMOSPHERE From the flagstone walls and Sputnik-like lighting to red leather booths, this place exudes 1950s modern chic. There's also an expansive terrace and meticulously maintained grounds, where the chef grows his own herbs, vegetables, and fruit.

HOUSE SPECIALTIES Bone-in rib eye and the five-spiced baked salmon drizzled with honey.

OTHER RECOMMENDATIONS The chef does a marvelous job with a salad featuring marinated skirt steak, dripping with a ginger, molasses, and soy sauce.

SUMMARY AND COMMENTS Park Ave is a throwback to all things mid-20th century—except the menu. The proprietors have managed to avoid the kitsch and concentrate on those things that evoke a simpler, less complicated era—down to a friendly bar shaking up some of the meanest martinis in Orange County. The food is exceptionally good (award winning), but service gets a little sloppy, especially on slower nights. A more casual garden restaurant on the same grounds offers a compact menu of Italian classics.

Prime Cut Café & Wine Bar ★★★

STEAK HOUSE   MODERATE   QUALITY ★★★   VALUE ★★★½

1547 W. Katella Ave. (Stadium Promenade Center), Ste. 101, Orange; ☎ 714-532-4300; primecutcafe.com

Reservations Recommended. **When to go** Lunch or dinner. **Entrée range** $11–$33. **Service** ★★★. **Friendliness** ★★★. **Bar** Wine and cocktails. **Dress** Casual. **Hours** Sunday–Thursday, 11 a.m.–9:30 p.m.; Friday–Saturday, 11 a.m.–10:30 p.m.

SETTING AND ATMOSPHERE Polished but laid-back, this dapper newcomer is a welcome independent in a sea of chain operations. A massive granite bar anchors the attractive space that also offers a roomy patio overlooking the center's water fountain.

HOUSE SPECIALTIES Slow-roasted prime rib is offered in two sizes, both partnered with good Yorkshire pudding and rich creamed spinach. A huge pork chop is another winner, paired with pistachios, butter-braised bacon, and apple cider reduction.

OTHER RECOMMENDATIONS Prime rib may hog the spotlight, but steaks, burgers, and entrée salads often outshine the showy star of the menu. Sides such as potato gratin are scene-stealers, as are from-scratch desserts.

SUMMARY AND COMMENTS Prime Cut Café does a good job of making first-rate dining affordable and approachable. Eighty-plus wines sold by the glass, taste, or bottle is an attraction for wine lovers, though wine snobs might find the list a bit lowbrow. The menu offers lots of appetizers and snacks that pair well with wine, making this a great option for a quick bite or grown-up get-together. The central location means that crowds swell or recede according to events at nearby Anaheim Stadium, Honda Pond, or even what's hot at the adjacent multiplex cinema.

Roscoe's House of Chicken & Waffles ★★★★½

AMERICAN INEXPENSIVE QUALITY ★★★★ VALUE ★★★½

2110 S. Harbor Blvd., Anaheim; ☎ 714-823-4130;
roscoeschickenandwaffles.com

Reservations Not accepted. When to go Anytime. Entrée range $7–$15. Service ★★★. Friendliness ★★★. Dress Casual. Hours Daily, 8 a.m.–11 p.m.

SETTING AND ATMOSPHERE The outside is a plain, almost featureless, building surrounded by palm trees. The decorations inside are also sparse, save for the occasional cheap painting or neon sign. Going on only looks, you'll wonder why there's a huge line to get in, especially on nights and weekends.

HOUSE SPECIALTIES It's right there in the name: chicken and waffles.

OTHER RECOMMENDATIONS We love the Jeanne Jones Omelette and the macaroni and cheese side dish.

SUMMARY AND COMMENTS Roscoe's is a longtime Los Angeles institution that finally made its way to Orange County in 2014. Like all the other locations, locals flock to Roscoe's for its delicious Southern-style comfort food, including the signature chicken and waffles. While the fried chicken is good, it may not be the best you'll ever have. But the waffles are excellent, and the macaroni and cheese is a must-try.

▮▮ SHOPPING *at* DISNEYLAND

SHOPS ADD REALISM AND ATMOSPHERE to the various theme settings and offer souvenirs, clothing, novelties, jewelry, decorator items, and more. Much of the merchandise displayed (with the exception of Disney trademark souvenir items), though, is available back home and elsewhere, so we recommend bypassing the shops on a one-day visit. If you have two or more days to spend at Disneyland Resort, browse in the early afternoon, when many attractions are crowded.

Our recommendations notwithstanding, we realize that for many guests, Disney souvenirs and memorabilia are irresistible. One of our readers writes:

People have a compelling need to buy Disney stuff at Disneyland. When you get home, you wonder why you ever got a cashmere sweater with Mickey Mouse embroidered on the breast, or a tie with tiny Goofys all over it. Maybe they put something in the food?

If you don't want to lug your packages around, you can leave them at the information stand just inside the front gate and pick them up as you exit the park. Retrieving your purchases might take a while if you depart after a parade or fireworks show or at closing, when guests exit en masse. If you're staying at a Disneyland Resort hotel, your loot will be delivered directly to your resort's bellhop desk (by 7 a.m. the following day) on request. If you have a problem with your purchases or need to make a return, call Disneyland Exclusive Merchandise at ☎ 800-760-3566, Monday–Friday, 8 a.m.–5 p.m. PST. If you return home and realize that you forgot to buy those Rastafarian mouse ears or some similarly essential tchotchke, a large selection of park-exclusive merchandise is available to order at **disneyparks.com/store.**

DOWNTOWN DISNEY

DOWNTOWN DISNEY, verdant and landscaped by day, pops alive with neon and glitter at night. The complex offers more than 300,000 square feet of specialty shopping, clubs, restaurants, and movie theaters. Many of the restaurants offer entertainment in addition to dining, including **Crossroads at House of Blues** and **Ralph Brennan's Jazz Kitchen.** The **ESPN Zone** is a sports bar and restaurant with dozens of giant TV screens. Other restaurant options include **Naples Ristorante e Pizzeria, Tortilla Jo's** Mexican restaurant, **Earl of Sandwich,** and jungle-themed dining at the **Rainforest Cafe.** An elegant **Starbucks** serves all the chain's beverages and sandwiches and offers free Wi-Fi, phone-charging stations, and full loyalty card benefits (though it doesn't accept Disney gift cards).

If you're not hungry, there's always shopping and a 12-theater **AMC Movieplex** with IMAX 3-D to keep you occupied. A 40,000-square-foot **World of Disney** store, the second largest on the planet, anchors the shopping scene. Other retailers include **Sanuk,** a shoe store; **Little-MissMatched,** selling socks that don't match (for more than you'd pay for socks that do); **Disney Vault 28,** with fashion apparel, jewelry, handbags, and accessories; **Anna & Elsa's Boutique,** offering hairstyling, braiding, and princess makeovers, as well as a selection of *Frozen* merchandise; **Sephora,** featuring cosmetics; and **Something Silver,** specializing in jewelry. **D-Street** is where you'll find merchandise from Disney's films and TV shows that are targeted at teenagers and adults, such as Marvel or *Star Wars.* **Quiksilver** is home to a large assortment of surfing and skateboard apparel. If expensive designer sunglasses are your thing, head to **Sunglass Icon** for a large variety of shades. For an artistic memento, **WonderGround Gallery** showcases edgy (and expensive) reinterpretations of classic Disney images, often signed by their creators. **LEGO Imagination Center** features interactive play tables with LEGO bricks and life-size statues of Disney characters made entirely of LEGOs. At **Build-A-Bear Workshop,** you can customize a teddy bear, starting from scratch with the bearskin, stuffing it,

Downtown Disney

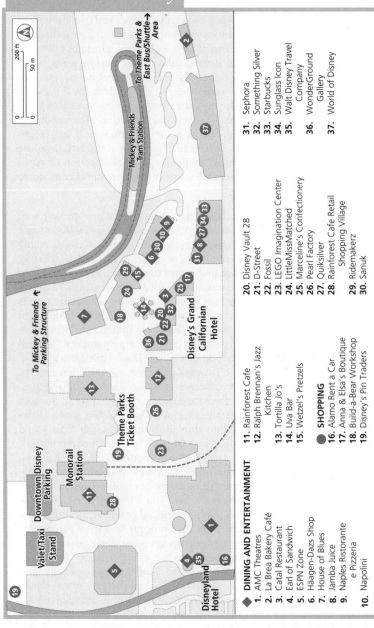

◆ DINING AND ENTERTAINMENT

1. AMC Theatres
2. La Brea Bakery Café
3. Catal Restaurant
4. Earl of Sandwich
5. ESPN Zone
6. Häagen-Dazs Shop
7. House of Blues
8. Jamba Juice
9. Naples Ristorante e Pizzeria
10. Napolini
11. Rainforest Cafe
12. Ralph Brennan's Jazz Kitchen
13. Tortilla Jo's
14. Uva Bar
15. Wetzel's Pretzels

● SHOPPING

16. Alamo Rent a Car
17. Anna & Elsa's Boutique
18. Build-a-Bear Workshop
19. Disney's Pin Traders
20. Disney Vault 28
21. D-Street
22. Fossil
23. LEGO Imagination Center
24. LittleMissMatched
25. Marceline's Confectionery
26. Pearl Factory
27. Quiksilver
28. Rainforest Cafe Retail Shopping Village
29. Ridemakerz
30. Sanuk
31. Sephora
32. Something Silver
33. Starbucks
34. Sunglass Icon
35. Walt Disney Travel Company
36. WonderGround Gallery
37. World of Disney

and then accessorizing it. In the same vein as Build-A-Bear, next door there's **Ridemakerz.** But instead of teddy bears, guests can build custom remote-control cars and trucks. During the winter months, look for a holiday village of treat and gift vendors and an extra-charge ice skating rink set up near the Disneyland Hotel.

Our map of Downtown Disney, listing storefronts and restaurants, appears on the opposite page.

ANAHEIM GARDENWALK

ANAHEIM GARDENWALK is a shopping, dining, and entertainment venue that stretches from West Katella Avenue to Disney Way. Built on three levels and nicely landscaped, the GardenWalk effectively doubles the restaurant, lounge, and shopping choices for Disneyland Resort visitors and attendees of conventions at nearby Anaheim Convention Center. Restaurants include **Bubba Gump Shrimp Co., California Pizza Kitchen, The Cheesecake Factory, Fire + Ice, McCormick & Schmick's Grille, McFadden's Irish Pub, P.F. Chang's Chinese Bistro,** and **Roy's Hawaiian Fusion Cuisine.**

For entertainment, there's an UltraLuxe 14-screen movie theater with D-Box motion seats and in-seat beverage service, a 41-lane bowling complex and nightspot combo, a 24-hour fitness center, and an ultra lounge. The complex changed hands a few years back, and the current backers were banking on a new Toby Keith–branded bar to revitalize it, but little construction progress has been made in months. A handful of venues, such as **Lush Cosmetics** and an indoor family-entertainment center, are still hanging on, but there are far more shuttered storefronts than open ones, giving the entire venue a depressing *Dawn of the Dead* vibe. For additional information, see **anaheim gardenwalk.com** or call ☎ 714-635-7410.

PART FIVE

DISNEYLAND PARK

ARRIVING *and*
GETTING ORIENTED

IF YOU DRIVE, you will probably be directed to the massive Mickey
& Friends parking garage on West Street near Ball Road. Parking costs
$17 for cars, $22 for RVs. Be sure to make a note of your section, row,
and space. A tram will transport you to a loading/unloading area connected to the entrance by a pedestrian corridor. Many locals prefer to
park in the Toy Story surface lot on Harbor Boulevard south of Katella
Avenue, which offers shuttle service to the east side of the resort
entrance Esplanade. Most pedestrians enter the resort from Harbor
Boulevard to the east, passing though the bus drop-off area on their
way to the ticket booths; on-site hotel guests approach from the west
through Downtown Disney. Because security screening is conducted
just before passing through the turnstiles, the lines to enter the park
are often quite lengthy, and there is no bypass for those without bags
(as found at Walt Disney World). When entering the resort from the
east, the far-left security line is often the shortest. Two entrance gates,
14 and 19, are blocked by trees situated in the entrance plaza about
10 feet from the security checkpoint. The trees sometimes inhibit the
formation of a line in front of both of the obstructed gates. Gates 14
and 19 are staffed nonetheless and draw guests from adjacent lines 13
or 15 and 18 or 20. When this happens, it significantly speeds up the
entry process for guests waiting in lines 13 and 20. Our advice on
arriving, therefore, is to inspect the lines leading to gates 14 and 19
and join whichever looks to be shortest. Later in the day, the outside
gates (1 and 32) tend to be fastest for reentry. Stroller and wheelchair
rentals are available in the Main Entrance Plaza between Disneyland
and Disney California Adventure. As you enter Main Street, City Hall
is to your left, serving as the center for general information, lost and
found, and entertainment information.

To combat rampant resales of unexpired tickets, Disneyland Resort has implemented a policy of photographing all multiday pass holders upon their first park entry. Have your ticket ready for scanning by a cast member just before you enter the turnstiles; if your mug isn't yet in Mickey's mainframe, you'll be asked to pose before proceeding. These added steps can sometimes slow the line at the start of the day, and there's no express lane for single-day guests or Annual Pass holders. As long as this plan is imposed, we suggest that you arrive 5 minutes earlier than you otherwise would have, and bring extra patience.

Be sure to pick up a park map as you pass through the turnstiles. Maps are also available in the passages connecting the park entrance to Main Street, U.S.A.; at City Hall; and at a number of shops throughout the park. Also, pick up a *Times Guide*. This pamphlet contains the daily entertainment schedule for live shows, parades, fireworks, and other events and tells you where you can find the characters. If a *Times Guide* is not available for the day you visit (a very rare occurrence), the daily entertainment schedule will be included in the park map. The park map lists all the attractions, shops, and eateries and provides helpful information about first aid, baby care, assistance for the disabled, and more.

Notice on your map that Main Street ends at a central hub from which branch the entrances to four other sections of Disneyland: **Adventureland, Frontierland, Fantasyland,** and **Tomorrowland.** Two other "lands," **New Orleans Square** and **Critter Country,** can be reached through Adventureland and Frontierland. **Mickey's Toontown** is located on the far side of the railroad tracks from It's a Small World in Fantasyland. **Sleeping Beauty Castle,** the entrance to Fantasyland, is a focal landmark and the visual center of the park. The castle is a great place to meet if your group decides to split up for any reason during the day, and it can serve as an emergency meeting place if you are accidentally separated. Keep in mind, however, that the castle covers a lot of territory, so be specific about *where* to meet at the castle. Also be forewarned that parades and live shows sometimes make it difficult to access the entrance of the castle fronting the central hub. Another good meeting spot is the *Partners* statue of Mickey and Walt in the central hub.

DISNEY DISH WITH JIM HILL

WILL THERE BE A THIRD PARK? Real estate in and around Disneyland Resort comes at a premium. So when people ask when the Imagineers will get serious about building a third theme park in Anaheim, I say, "When you see a multistory parking garage, similar to the Mickey & Friends parking garage (which holds more than 10,000 cars), you'll know for certain that Theme Park No. 3 (which is rumored to be built in the Toy Story parking lot, near the Anaheim Convention Center) is finally on its way." That's the first domino that has to fall before Disneyland Resort can expand beyond Disneyland Park and Disney California Adventure.

Continued on page 214

Disneyland Park

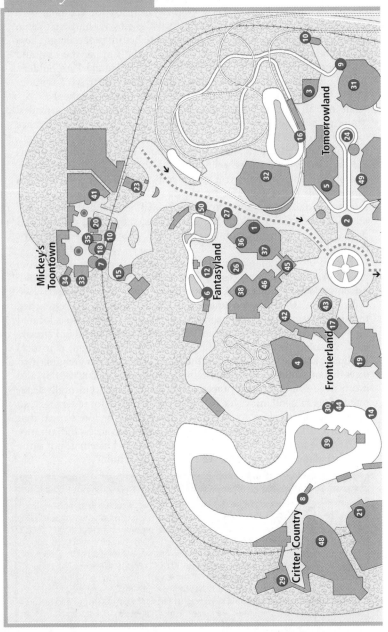

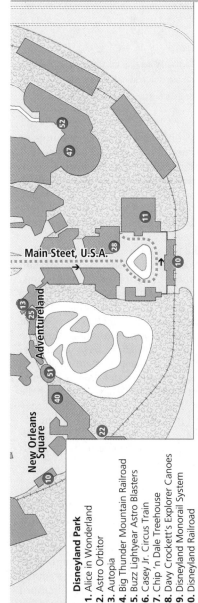

Main Steet, U.S.A.

New Orleans Square

Adventureland

Disneyland Park
1. Alice in Wonderland
2. Astro Orbitor
3. Autopia
4. Big Thunder Mountain Railroad
5. Buzz Lightyear Astro Blasters
6. Casey Jr. Circus Train
7. Chip 'n Dale Treehouse
8. Davy Crockett's Explorer Canoes
9. Disneyland Monorail System
10. Disneyland Railroad
11. *The Disneyland Story,*
    presenting *Great Moments*
    with Mr. Lincoln
12. Dumbo the Flying Elephant
13. *Enchanted Tiki Room*
14. *Fantasmic!*
15. Fantasyland Theatre/*Mickey and*
    the Magical Map
16. Finding Nemo Submarine Voyage
17. Frontierland Shootin' Exposition
18. Gadget's Go Coaster
19. The Golden Horseshoe–Laughing
    Stock Co.
20. Goofy's Playhouse
21. The Haunted Mansion
22. Indiana Jones Adventure

23. It's a Small World
24. *Jedi Training Academy*
25. Jungle Cruise
26. King Arthur Carrousel
27. Mad Tea Party
28. Main Street Cinema
29. The Many Adventures
    of Winnie the Pooh
30. *Mark Twain Riverboat*
31. Marvel and Star Wars Exhibits
32. Matterhorn Bobsleds
33. Mickey's House and Meet Mickey
34. Minnie's House
35. *Miss Daisy, Donald's Boat*
36. Mr. Toad's Wild Ride
37. Peter Pan's Flight

38. Pinocchio's Daring Journey
39. Pirate's Lair on Tom Sawyer Island
40. Pirates of the Caribbean
41. Roger Rabbit's Car Toon Spin
42. Royal Hall at Fantasy Faire
43. Royal Theatre at Fantasy Faire
44. Sailing Ship *Columbia*
45. Sleeping Beauty Castle
46. Snow White's Scary Adventures
47. Space Mountain
48. Splash Mountain
49. Star Tours–The Adventures Continue
50. Storybook Land Canal Boats
51. Tarzan's Treehouse
52. Tomorrowland Theater
    Parade Route ▪ ▪ ▪ ▪

Continued from page 211

NOT TO BE MISSED AT DISNEYLAND PARK
ADVENTURELAND Indiana Jones Adventure
CRITTER COUNTRY Splash Mountain
FRONTIERLAND Big Thunder Mountain Railroad
NEW ORLEANS SQUARE The Haunted Mansion	Pirates of the Caribbean
TOMORROWLAND Space Mountain	Star Tours—The Adventures Continue
LIVE ENTERTAINMENT *Disneyland Forever*	*Fantasmic!*	Paint the Night

STARTING THE TOUR

EVERYONE WILL SOON FIND his or her own favorite and not-so-favorite attractions in Disneyland Park. Be open-minded and adventuresome. Don't dismiss a particular ride or show as not being for you until *after* you have tried it. Our personal experience as well as our research indicates that each visitor is different in terms of which Disney offerings he or she most enjoys. So don't miss seeing an attraction because a friend from home didn't like it; that attraction may turn out to be your favorite.

We do recommend that you take advantage of what Disney does best—the fantasy adventures such as Indiana Jones Adventure and The Haunted Mansion and the Audio-Animatronics (talking robots, that is) attractions such as Pirates of the Caribbean. Unless you have almost unlimited time, don't burn a lot of daylight browsing through the shops. Except for some special Disney souvenirs, you can find much of the same merchandise elsewhere. Try to minimize the time you spend on midway-type rides, as you probably have an amusement park, carnival, or state fair close to your hometown. Don't, however, mistake rides such as Splash Mountain and the Big Thunder Mountain Railroad for amusement park rides. They may be of the flume ride or roller coaster genre, but they represent pure Disney genius. Similarly, do not devote a lot of time to waiting in line for meals. Eat a good early breakfast before you come, snack on vendor-sold foods during the touring day, or follow the suggestions for meals incorporated into the various touring plans presented.

SINGLE-RIDER LINES

YOU CAN OFTEN SAVE TIME WAITING IN LINE by taking advantage of single-rider lines, a separate line for people who are alone or don't mind riding alone or with a stranger. The objective of single-rider lines is to fill odd spaces left by groups who don't quite fill the entire ride vehicle. Because there aren't many singles and most groups aren't willing to split up, single-rider lines are usually much shorter than the regular line. In Disneyland Park, Indiana Jones Adventure, Matterhorn Bobsleds, and Splash Mountain have single-rider lines. Ask an attraction employee how to enter the single-rider queue; you'll usually be given a paper pass and directed up the exit.

DISNEYLAND PARK SERVICES

Baby Care Center At the central-hub end of Main Street

Banking Services/Currency Exchange At City Hall at the railroad station end of Main Street

Disneyland and Local Attraction Information At City Hall

First Aid Two doors down from Plaza Inn at the central-hub end of Main Street

Live Entertainment and Parade Information At City Hall

Lost Adults and Messages At City Hall

Lost and Found Lost and Found for the entire resort is located west of the entrance to Disneyland Park

Lost Children At the central-hub end of Main Street

Storage Lockers Down Main Street one block (as you walk toward the castle) and to the right

MAIN STREET, U.S.A.

THIS SECTION OF DISNEYLAND PARK is where you'll begin and end your visit. The Disneyland Railroad stops at the Main Street Station, and you can board here for a grand circle tour of the park, or you can get off the train in New Orleans Square, Mickey's Toontown/ Fantasyland, or Tomorrowland.

Main Street is an idealized version of a turn-of-the-20th-century American small-town street. Many visitors are surprised to discover that all the buildings are real, not elaborate props. Attention to detail is exceptional—interiors, furnishings, and fixtures conform to the period. As with any real Main Street, the Disney version is essentially a collection of shops and eating places, with a city hall, a fire station, and an old-time cinema. A mixed-media attraction combines static exhibits recalling the life of Walt Disney with a patriotic remembrance of Abraham Lincoln. Horse-drawn trolleys, fire engines, and horseless carriages give rides along Main Street and transport visitors to the central hub.

Disneyland Railroad ★★★½

APPEAL BY AGE	PRESCHOOL ★★★★½	GRADE SCHOOL ★★★★	TEENS ★★★★
YOUNG ADULTS ★★★★	OVER 30 ★★★★		SENIORS ★★★★

What it is Scenic railroad ride around the park's perimeter; also transportation to New Orleans Square, Mickey's Toontown, Fantasyland, and Tomorrowland. **Scope and scale** Major attraction. **When to go** After 11 a.m. or when you need transportation. **Special comment** The Main Street and Tomorrowland Stations are usually the least-congested boarding points. **Duration of ride** About 22 minutes for a complete circuit. **Average wait in line per 100 people ahead of you** 8 minutes. **Assumes** 3 trains operating. **Loading speed** Fast.

Thumbs Up for the Whole Family

DESCRIPTION AND COMMENTS A transportation ride that blends an eclectic variety of sights and experiences with an energy-saving way of getting around the park. In addition to providing a glimpse of all the lands except Adventureland, the train passes through the Grand Canyon Diorama (between Tomorrowland and Main Street), a three-dimensional replication of the canyon, complete with wildlife, as it appears from the southern rim. Another sight on the train circuit is Primeval World, a depiction of a prehistoric peat bog and rain forest populated by Audio-Animatronic (robotic) dinosaurs. Opened in 1966 Primeval World uses animatronics recycled from the Disney-designed Ford's Magic Skyway pavilion for the 1964 World's Fair, and it was a precursor to a similar presentation at Epcot's Universe of Energy.

TOURING TIPS Save the train ride until after you have seen the featured attractions, or use it when you need transportation. It can also be a helpful way to relax during the peak times of the day when the crowds are swelling. You can get a good estimate of how long you'll wait for the next train by using the posted wait time sign outside each station. It will either list 5 minutes (three trains operating), 10 minutes (two trains), or 20 minutes (only one train). If you have small children who are hell-bent on seeing Mickey first thing in the morning, you might consider taking the train to Mickey's Toontown (a half circuit) and visiting Mickey in his dressing room as soon as you enter the park. Many families find that this tactic puts the kids in a more receptive frame of mind for the other attractions. On busy days, lines form at the New Orleans Square and Mickey's Toontown/Fantasyland Stations but rarely at the Main Street or Tomorrowland Stations.

The Disneyland Story, presenting *Great Moments with Mr. Lincoln* ★★★½

| APPEAL BY AGE | PRESCHOOL ★★★ | GRADE SCHOOL ★★★ | TEENS ★★★½ |
| YOUNG ADULTS ★★★ | | OVER 30 ★★★★ | SENIORS ★★★★★ |

Thumbs Up for the Whole Family

What it is Nostalgic exhibits documenting the Disney success story followed by an Audio-Animatronics patriotic presentation. **Scope and scale** Minor attraction. **When to go** During the hot, crowded period of day. **Duration of show** 15 minutes including preshow of Disney exhibits. **Probable waiting time** Usually none.

DESCRIPTION AND COMMENTS A warm and well-presented remembrance of the man who started it all. Well worth seeing; especially touching for those old enough to remember Walt Disney himself. The attraction lobby consists of a museum of Disney memorabilia. Especially interesting are rotating Disney Gallery displays of concept artwork and historical artifacts, most recently featuring formative sketches from the early days of Disneyland by Disney Legends such as John Hench, Sam McKim, and Harper Goff. A short film starring comedian (and former Disneyland cast member) Steve Martin and Donald Duck, originally created to celebrate the park's 50th anniversary in 2005, screens in the lobby as a preshow. Beyond the Disney memorabilia, guests are admitted to a large theater where *Great Moments with Mr. Lincoln* is presented. A patriotic performance, *Great Moments* stars an extremely lifelike and sophisticated Audio-Animatronics Abe Lincoln delivering an amalgamation of his notable speeches (though the over-familiar "Gettysburg Address" is not recited in full) as originally recorded by actor Royal Dano for the 1964 World's Fair. Lincoln's head is stunningly emotive, capable of wrinkling his brow and pursing his lips with unrivaled realism. Surround sound effects and songs borrowed from Epcot's *American Adventure* add to this brief but inspiring biography of America's 16th president.

TOURING TIPS You usually do not have to wait long for this show, so see it during the busy times of day when lines are long elsewhere or as you are leaving the park. Sit up close to best see the detail on the Lincoln figure, or sit a few rows back for a more comfortable view of the screen.

Main Street Cinema ★★

APPEAL BY AGE	PRESCHOOL ★★½		GRADE SCHOOL ★★		TEENS ★★
YOUNG	ADULTS ★½		OVER 30 ★★		SENIORS ★★

What it is Vintage Disney cartoons. **Scope and scale** Diversion. **When to go** Whenever you want. **Special comment** Wonderful selection of old-time flicks. **Duration of show** Runs continuously. **Probable waiting time** None.

DESCRIPTION AND COMMENTS An opening-day attraction, this small theater shows six classic Disney cartoons simultaneously. Early black-and-white Mickey Mouse shorts such as "Steamboat Willie" and "Plane Crazy" are screened, along with the celebrity caricature–stocked oddity "Mickey's Polo Team." The films are played at a low enough volume that the theater remains a quiet respite from the rest of the park.

TOURING TIPS Good place to get out of the sun or rain or to kill time while others in your group shop on Main Street. Fun, but not something you can't afford to miss. Audience stands.

Transportation Rides

DESCRIPTION AND COMMENTS Trolleys, buses, and the like add color to Main Street. One-way only.

TOURING TIPS The rides will save you a walk to the central hub. Not worth waiting in line. If you catch the first trolley of the morning, you may be serenaded onboard by the Dapper Dans.

ADVENTURELAND

ADVENTURELAND IS THE FIRST "LAND" to the left of Main Street and somehow manages to seamlessly combine South Pacific island, Middle Eastern bazaar, and African safari themes. Transitions from one part of Adventureland to another feel quite natural, and the identity crisis inherent in the mixed-theme cocktail never registers in the minds of most guests. Space is tight in Adventureland, however, making for some of the worst pedestrian congestion in any of the Disney theme parks. If you're just passing through Adventureland, say on your way to Splash Mountain, you can avoid the congestion by transiting Frontierland instead.

Enchanted Tiki Room ★★★½

APPEAL BY AGE	PRESCHOOL ★★★½	GRADE SCHOOL ★★★★	TEENS ★★★★
YOUNG	ADULTS ★★★	OVER 30 ★★★★	SENIORS ★★★★½

What it is Audio-Animatronics Pacific island musical show. **Scope and scale** Minor attraction. **When to go** Anytime. **Duration of show** 14½ minutes plus preshow of talking totem poles. **Probable waiting time** 11 minutes.

DESCRIPTION AND COMMENTS An unusual sit-down theater performance in which more than 200 birds, flowers, and tiki-god statues sing and whistle through a Polynesian-style musical program. One of Walt's first large-scale uses of Audio-Animatronics, *Tiki Room* might be more impressive for the technology it took to get the show (ahem) flying in 1963. Beloved by Disneyland fans for its detail and immersive setting, the current version of the show is only slightly altered from the original.

TOURING TIPS One of the most bizarre (yet endearing) of the Disneyland Park entertainments and rarely very crowded. We like it in the late afternoon, when we can especially appreciate sitting for a bit in an air-conditioned theater. Back row seats provide the broadest view with the least neck strain.

The Tiki Juice Bar that straddles the *Tiki Room* entrance dispenses Dole Whip, a delectable blend of pineapple slush and vanilla soft-serve ice cream, one of the park's most popular snacks. Dole sponsors the attraction, so you can enjoy your Tiki Juice Bar treats while watching the show. There are service windows both inside and outside the attraction's waiting area. The line outside may look longer, but it often moves much faster.

Indiana Jones Adventure *(FastPass)* ★★★★★

**APPEAL BY AGE PRESCHOOL ★★★★   GRADE SCHOOL ★★★½ TEENS ★★★★½
YOUNG ADULTS ★★★★★   OVER 30 ★★★★½   SENIORS ★★★★½**

What it is Motion-simulator dark ride. **Scope and scale** Super-headliner. **When to go** Before 9:30 a.m. or use FastPass. **Special comments** Not to be missed. Must be 46″ tall to ride; switching-off option provided (see page 145). **Duration of ride** 3⅓ minutes. **Average wait in line per 100 people ahead of you** 3 minutes. **Assumes** Full-capacity operation with 18-second dispatch interval. **Loading speed** Fast.

DESCRIPTION AND COMMENTS This is a combination track ride and motion simulator. In addition to moving along its path, the military troop–transport vehicle bucks and pitches (the simulator part) in sync with the visuals and special effects. Though the plot is complicated and not altogether clear, the bottom line is that if you look into the Forbidden Eye, you're in big trouble. The Forbidden Eye, of course, stands out like Rush Limbaugh in a diaper, and *everybody* stares at it. The rest of the ride consists of a mad race to escape the temple as it collapses around you. In the process, you encounter snakes, spiders, lava pits, rats, swinging bridges, and the house-size granite bowling ball that everyone remembers from *Raiders of the Lost Ark.*

The Indiana Jones ride is a Disney masterpiece—nonstop action from beginning to end with brilliant visual effects. Elaborate even by Disney standards, the attraction provides a level of detail and variety of action that make use of the entire Imagineering arsenal of high-tech gimmickry. Recently, the attraction was upgraded with dazzling digital projection effects that bring the idol in the opening chamber to life.

Sophisticated in its electronic and computer applications, Indiana Jones purports to offer a different experience on each ride. According to the designers, there are veritable menus of special effects that the computer can mix and match. In practice, however, we could not see much difference from ride to ride. There are, no doubt, subtle variations, but the ride is so wild and frenetic that it's hard to apprehend subtlety.

The adventure begins in the queue, which sometimes extends out the entrance of the attraction and over the bridge leading to Adventureland! When you ultimately work your way into the attraction area, you find yourself at the site of an archaeology expedition with the Temple of the Forbidden Eye entrance beckoning only 50 feet away. After crossing a wooden bridge, you finally step into the temple. The good news is that you are out of the California sun. The bad news is that you have just entered Indiana Jones's indoor queuing area, a system of tunnels and passageways extending to within 50 yards of the Santa Monica Pier.

Fortunately, the queuing area is interesting. You wind through caves, down the interior corridors of the temple, and into subterranean rotundas where the archaeologists have been hard at work. Along the way there are various surprises (be sure to disregard any DO NOT TOUCH signs you see on supporting poles or safety ropes), as well as a succession of homilies etched in an "ancient" language on the temple walls. You will eventually stumble into a chamber where a short movie will explain the plot. From there it's back into the maze and finally on to the loading area.

TOURING TIPS Indiana Jones stays fairly mobbed all day. Try to ride during the first hour the park is open or use FastPass. Another alternative, if you don't mind riding alone, is to take advantage of the single-rider line, where the wait is generally about one-third that of guests in the regular queue. Be forewarned that the single-rider line at Indiana Jones is a bit of a maze, requiring you to negotiate your way up the exit ramp, up one elevator, across a walkway over the track, and then down another elevator to the loading area.

During the first hour or so the park is open, Indiana Jones cast members often employ a line-management technique known as stacking. Simply stated, they allow the line for Indiana Jones to form outside the attraction, leaving the cavernous inside queuing area virtually empty. Guests, of course, assume that the attraction is packed to the gills and that the outside line is overflow. Naturally, this discourages guests from getting in line. The reality is that the wait is not nearly as bad as it looks, and that it is probably as short as it will be all day. If you arrive in the park early and the Indiana Jones line appears huge, have the rest of your party get in line while you enter Indiana Jones *through the attraction exit* and check out the inside queue. If it is empty or sparsely populated, stacking is being practiced. Join your party in line and enjoy the attraction; your wait will be comparatively short. If the inside queue is bumper to bumper, try Indiana Jones later or use FastPass or the single-rider line. Stacking is also sometimes practiced during the hour just before the park closes.

There is one other thing you should know. Indiana Jones, because it is high-tech, breaks down a lot. The Disney people will announce that the ride is broken but usually will not estimate how long repairs will take. From our experience, most glitches are resolved in approximately 15–30 minutes, and probably the best advice is to stick it out.

If you miss Indiana Jones in the early morning and the FastPasses are all gone, use the single-rider line or try again during a parade or *Fantasmic!*, or during the hour before the park closes. Regarding the latter, the Disney folks will usually admit to the attraction anyone in line at closing time. During one visit to Indiana Jones, Disneyland Park closed at 8 p.m. We hopped in the line for Indiana Jones at 7:45 p.m. and actually got on the ride at 8:30 p.m.

Though the Indiana Jones ride is wild and jerky, the motion has been somewhat toned down since its debut, and it is primarily distinguished by its visual impact and realistic special effects. Thus, we encourage the over-50 crowd to give it a chance: We think you'll like it. As for children, most find the ride extremely intense and action-packed but not particularly frightening. We encountered very few children who met the 46-inch minimum-height requirement who were in any way intimidated.

Jungle Cruise ★★★

APPEAL BY AGE   PRESCHOOL ★★★★   GRADE SCHOOL ★★★★   TEENS ★★★★
YOUNG ADULTS ★★★½   OVER 30 ★★★★   SENIORS ★★★★

Thumbs Up for the Whole Family

What it is A Disney outdoor-adventure boat ride. **Scope and scale** Major attraction. **When to go** Before 10 a.m. or after 6 p.m. **Special comment** A Disney standard. **Duration of ride** 7½ minutes. **Average wait in line per 100 people ahead of you** 3½ minutes. **Assumes** 10 boats operating. **Loading speed** Moderate–slow.

DESCRIPTION AND COMMENTS On this boat ride through jungle waterways, passengers encounter elephants, lions, hostile natives, and a menacing hippo. It's a long-enduring Disney favorite with the boatman's spiel adding measurably to the fun.

As more technologically advanced attractions have been added to the park over the years, the Jungle Cruise has, by comparison, lost some of its luster. Though still a good attraction, it offers few thrills and no surprises for Disneyland Park veterans, many of whom can rattle off the ride's narration right along with the guide. For park first-timers, however, the Jungle Cruise continues to delight.

A "Jingle Cruise" holiday makeover runs early November–early January. The seasonal attraction features holiday-themed jokes in the skipper's script, a few holiday items in the queue and around the attraction, and substantially longer waits.

TOURING TIPS This ride loads slowly, and long lines form as the park fills. To compound problems, guests exiting Indiana Jones tend to head for the Jungle Cruise. Go early, or during a parade or *Fantasmic!* Be forewarned that the Jungle Cruise has an especially deceptive line: Just when you think that you are about to board, you are shunted into yet another queuing maze (not visible outside the ride). Regardless of how short the line *looks* when you approach the Jungle Cruise, inquire about the length of the wait—at least you will know what you are getting into. If the second floor of the queue building is in use, you're in for at least a 20-minute wait. When the queue splits before the loading dock, the left lane is often quicker. Finally, many readers consider the Jungle Cruise much better at night.

Tarzan's Treehouse ★★★

APPEAL BY AGE   PRESCHOOL ★★★★★   GRADE SCHOOL ★★★½   TEENS ★★½
YOUNG ADULTS ★★★   OVER 30 ★★★   SENIORS ★★½

What it is Walk-through tree house exhibit. **Scope and scale** Minor attraction. **When to go** Anytime. **Special comments** Requires climbing a lot of stairs; a very creative exhibit. **Duration of tour** 8–12 minutes. **Average wait in line per 100 people ahead of you** 7 minutes.

DESCRIPTION AND COMMENTS Inspired by Disney's 1999 animated film *Tarzan,* Tarzan's Treehouse replaced the venerable Swiss Family Treehouse that had been an Adventureland icon for 37 years. To enter the attraction, you climb a rus-

Thumbs Up for the Whole Family

tic staircase and cross a suspension bridge. From there, as they say, it's all downhill. Pages from Jane's sketchbook scattered about tell the Tarzan story and provide insights into the various rooms and levels of the tree house. At the base of the tree is an interactive play area.

TOURING TIPS This self-guided, walk-through tour involves a lot of climbing up and down stairs but with no ropes or ladders or anything fancy. People who stop during the walk-through to look extra-long or to rest sometimes create bottlenecks that slow crowd flow. We recommend visiting this attraction in the late afternoon or early evening if you are on a one-day tour schedule.

NEW ORLEANS SQUARE

ACCESSIBLE VIA ADVENTURELAND AND FRONTIERLAND, New Orleans Square is one of three "lands" that don't emanate from the central hub. The architecture and setting are Caribbean Colonial, like New Orleans itself, with exceptional attention to detail.

Disneyland Railroad

DESCRIPTION AND COMMENTS The Disneyland Railroad stops in New Orleans Square on its circle tour around the park. See the description starting on page 215 for additional details regarding the sights en route.

TOURING TIPS This is a pleasant and feet-saving way to commute to Mickey's Toontown/Fantasyland, Tomorrowland, or Main Street. Be advised, however, that the New Orleans Square Station is usually the most congested.

The Haunted Mansion *(seasonal FastPass)* ★★★★

| APPEAL BY AGE | PRESCHOOL ★★★½ | GRADE SCHOOL ★★★★ | TEENS ★★★★½ |
| YOUNG ADULTS ★★★★½ | | OVER 30 ★★★★½ | SENIORS ★★★★★ |

What it is Indoor haunted-house ride. **Scope and scale** Major attraction. **When to go** Before 11:30 a.m. or after 6:30 p.m. **Special comments** Not to be missed; some of Disneyland's best special effects. Frightens some small children. **Duration of ride** 5½-minute ride plus a 2-minute preshow. **Average wait in line per 100 people ahead of you** 2½ minutes. **Assumes** Both "stretch rooms" operating. **Loading speed** Fast.

Dark   Scary

DESCRIPTION AND COMMENTS The Haunted Mansion is a fun attraction more than it is a scary one. An ingenious preshow serves as a vehicle to deliver guests to the ride's boarding area, where they board "doom buggies" for a ride through the mansion's parlor, dining room, library, halls, and attic before descending to an uncommonly active graveyard. Disney employs almost every special effect in its repertoire in The Haunted Mansion, making it one of the most inventive and different of all Disney attractions. Be warned that some youngsters build a lot of anxiety concerning what they think they will see. The actual attraction scares almost nobody. Though this mansion is the original, the ride is somewhat shorter and lacks the interactive queue and some high-tech upgrades that the Walt Disney World version has; however, Disneyland does have the infamous Hat Box Ghost, an impressive new animatronic that "rematerialized" in the mansion's attic in 2015, nearly 45 years after appearing briefly during the attraction's opening days and sparking generations of urban legends. The reimagined figure employs digital projection trickery to make his leering skull vanish from his shoulders and reappear hanging from his outstretched hand, adding an effectively eerie punctuation to the ride's second act.

The Haunted Mansion is one of veteran Unofficial Guide writer Eve Zibart's favorite attractions. She warns:

Don't let the childishness of the old-fashioned Haunted Mansion put you off: This is one of the best attractions in the park. It's jam-packed with visual puns, special effects, hidden Mickeys, and really lovely Victorian-spooky sets. It's not scary, except in the sweetest of ways, but it will remind you of the days before ghost stories gave way to slasher flicks.

Each September, The Haunted Mansion substitutes a special holiday version of the attraction that runs through early January. Inspired by Tim Burton's 1993 stop-motion musical *The Nightmare Before Christmas,* the overlay features characters such as Jack Skellington and Oogie Boogie cavorting among the familiar mansion haunts to songs from Danny Elfman's classic score. *Note:* The attraction will be closed for several weeks before and after the holiday season to install and remove the overlay.

TOURING TIPS This attraction would be more at home in Fantasyland, but no matter—it's Disney at its best: another not-to-be-missed attraction. Because The Haunted Mansion is in an especially high-traffic corridor (between Pirates of the Caribbean and Splash Mountain), it stays busy all day. Try to see The Haunted Mansion before 11:30 a.m., after 6:30 p.m., or during a parade. In the evening, crowds for *Fantasmic!* gather in front of The Haunted Mansion, making it very difficult to access. The holiday version of this attraction (which may offer Fast-Pass) is very popular and draws quite a queue, so make it a higher priority than during the rest of the year. FastPass is offered intermittently for the Haunted Mansion, mostly during peak periods or when new upgrades boost its popularity.

Pirates of the Caribbean ★★★★★

APPEAL BY AGE	PRESCHOOL ★★★½	GRADE SCHOOL ★★★★½	TEENS ★★★★½
YOUNG ADULTS ★★★★★	OVER 30 ★★★★½	SENIORS ★★★★½	

What it is A Disney indoor-adventure boat ride. **Scope and scale** Major attraction. **When to go** Before 11:30 a.m. or after 4:30 p.m. **Special comments** Our pick as one of Disneyland's very best. Frightens some small children. **Duration of ride** Approximately 14 minutes. **Average wait in line per 100 people ahead of you** 3 minutes. **Assumes** 42 boats operating. **Loading speed** Fast.

Dark   Loud   Scary

DESCRIPTION AND COMMENTS Another boat ride, this time indoors, Pirates of the Caribbean takes you through a series of sets depicting a pirate raid on an island settlement, from the bombardment of the fortress to the debauchery that follows the victory. The attraction includes characters Jack Sparrow and Barbossa in animatronic form, as well as a high-tech mist projection of Davy Jones, from the *Pirates of the Caribbean* movies.

TOURING TIPS Another not-to-be-missed attraction. Undoubtedly one of the most elaborate and imaginative attractions in Disneyland Park. Though engineered to move large crowds, this ride sometimes gets overwhelmingly busy in the early and midafternoon. Try to ride before noon or while a parade or *Fantasmic!* is in progress. If you have only experienced the Walt Disney World version of Pirates, don't bypass Disneyland's version thinking that it's more of the same: The original ride is far longer, more detailed, and better maintained than its Floridian cousin.

CRITTER COUNTRY

CRITTER COUNTRY, situated at the end of a cul-de-sac and accessible via New Orleans Square, sports a pioneer appearance not unlike that of Frontierland.

Davy Crockett's Explorer Canoes *(open seasonally)* ★★★

APPEAL BY AGE	PRESCHOOL ★★	GRADE SCHOOL ★★★½	TEENS ★★★★½
YOUNG ADULTS ★		OVER 30 ★★½	SENIORS ★

What it is Scenic canoe ride. **Scope and scale** Minor attraction. **When to go** As soon as it opens, usually 11 a.m. **Special comments** Skip if the lines are long; closes at sunset. Most fun way to see Rivers of America. **Duration of ride** 8–10 minutes, depending on how fast you paddle. **Average wait in line per 100 people ahead of you** 12½ minutes. **Assumes** 6 canoes operating. **Loading speed** Slow.

DESCRIPTION AND COMMENTS Paddle-powered ride (you do the paddling) around Tom Sawyer Island and Fort Wilderness. Runs the same route with the same sights as the steamboat and the sailing ship. According to newspaper accounts, when the 9-million-gallon river was drained in 2010 for refurbishment, workers found half a canoe, scores of Mickey Mouse ears, and hundreds of cell phones at the bottom. The lesson here is to always keep a tight grip on your canoe. The canoes operate only on busier days and close at sunset. The sights are fun and the ride is a little different in that the patrons paddle the canoe. Those with tender rotator cuffs be warned: The trip can give your shoulders quite a workout, unless you slack off and let your fellow passengers handle the hard rowing. Long lines from about 11 a.m. on reflect the popularity of this attraction.

TOURING TIPS The canoes represent one of three ways to see the same waterways. Because the canoes are slower in loading, we usually opt for the larger steamboat or sailing ship. If you're not up for a boat ride, a different view of the same sights can be had by hoofing around Tom Sawyer Island. Try to ride at 11 a.m. or shortly thereafter. The canoes operate on selected days and seasonal periods only. If the canoes are a big deal to you, call ahead to make sure that they are operating.

The Many Adventures of Winnie the Pooh ★★★½

APPEAL BY AGE **PRESCHOOL** ★★★★½ **GRADE SCHOOL** ★★★★ **TEENS** ★★★½
YOUNG ADULTS ★★★½ **OVER 30** ★★★½ **SENIORS** ★★★½

Thumbs Up for the Whole Family

What it is Indoor track ride. **Scope and scale** Minor attraction. **When to go** Before 11 a.m. or the late afternoon or evening. **Duration of ride** About 3 minutes. **Average wait in line per 100 people ahead of you** 5 minutes. **Assumes** Normal staffing. **Loading speed** Moderate.

DESCRIPTION AND COMMENTS Pooh is sunny, upbeat, and fun—more in the image of Peter Pan's Flight or Splash Mountain. You ride a "hunny pot" through the pages of a huge picture book into the Hundred Acre Wood, where you encounter Pooh, Eeyore, Owl, Rabbit, Tigger, Kanga, Roo, and Piglet too as they contend with a blustery day. There's even a dream sequence with Heffalumps and Woozles, a favorite of this 30-something couple from Lexington, Massachusetts, who think Pooh has plenty to offer adults:

The attention to detail and special effects on this ride make it worth seeing even if you don't have children in your party. The Pooh dream sequence was great!

TOURING TIPS Though well done, The Many Adventures of Winnie the Pooh is not wildly popular. There is rarely more than a 15-minute wait, and it's typically less than 5. The only exceptions are on supercrowded days or when Splash Mountain is temporarily closed, which then causes crowds to swarm Winnie the Pooh.

Splash Mountain *(FastPass)* ★★★★½

APPEAL BY AGE **PRESCHOOL** ★★★★½ † **GRADE SCHOOL** ★★★★★ **TEENS** ★★★★½
YOUNG ADULTS ★★★★½ **OVER 30** ★★★★½ **SENIORS** ★★★½

†*Many preschoolers are too short to meet the height requirement, while others are intimidated by watching the ride while standing in line. Of those preschoolers who actually ride, most give the attraction high marks.*

What it is Water-flume adventure boat ride. **Scope and scale** Headliner. **When to go** Before 9:45 a.m. or use FastPass. **Special comments** A wet winner, not to be missed. Must be 40" tall to ride; those age 7 or younger must ride with an adult; switching-off option provided (see page 145). **Duration of ride** About 10 minutes. **Average wait in line per 100 people ahead of you** 3½ minutes. **Assumes** Operation at full capacity. **Loading speed** Moderate.

Scary Lose Things Queasy Muss Your 'Do

DESCRIPTION AND COMMENTS Splash Mountain is a Disney-style amusement park flume ride. The ride combines steep chutes with a variety of Disney's best special effects. Covering more than 0.5 mile, the ride splashes through swamps, caves, and backwoods bayous before climaxing in a 52-foot plunge and Br'er Rabbit's triumphant return home. The entire ride is populated by more than 100 Audio-Animatronics, including Br'er Rabbit, Br'er Bear, and Br'er Fox, all regaling riders with songs, including "Zip-A-Dee-Doo-Dah."

TOURING TIPS This is the most popular ride in Disneyland Park for patrons of all ages—happy, exciting, and adventuresome all at once. Though eclipsed somewhat by newer attractions, Splash Mountain nevertheless builds crowds quickly during the morning, and waits of more than 70 minutes are not uncommon once Disneyland Park fills up on a busy day. Lines persist throughout the day until a few minutes before closing. These words are particularly true on hotter days, as weather affects the wait times significantly.

There are five ways to experience Splash Mountain without a long wait. The first is to be on hand when the park opens and to sprint over and get in line before anyone else. The second way is to allow the initial mob of Splash cadets to be processed through and to arrive at Splash Mountain about 20–40 minutes after the park opens or after riding Peter Pan's Flight and/or Space Mountain. A third strategy is to get in line for Splash Mountain during a parade and/or a performance of *Fantasmic!* Be advised, however, that huge crowds gathering along the New Orleans Square and Frontierland water-fronts for *Fantasmic!* make getting to Splash Mountain very difficult (if not impossible) just before, during, and just after performances. Fourth, use FastPass, and fifth, use the single-rider line by entering through the exit.

A Disneyland veteran from Layton, Utah, offers this suggestion:

Use FastPass to experience Splash. This lets you visit non-FastPass, slow-loading attractions in the golden early morning. Also, who wants to get wet first thing in the morning?

A Suffolk, Virginia, mom contends that there are more important considerations than beating crowds:

The only recommendation I have is to definitely wait to do Splash Mountain at the end of the day. We were seated in the front of the ride, and needless to say we were drenched to the bone. If we had ridden first thing in the morning, I personally would have been miserable for the rest of the day. Parents, beware! It says you will get wet, not drowned.

It is almost a certainty that you will get wet, though probably not drenched, riding Splash Mountain. During the summer months, the water jets are cranked up to 11, practically guaranteeing that you'll get soaked. If you visit on a cool day, you may want to carry a plastic garbage bag. By tearing holes in the bottom and sides, you can fashion a sort of raincoat. Be sure to tuck the bag under your bottom. Though you can get splashed regardless of where you sit, riders in the front seat generally get the worst of it. If you have a camera, either leave it with a nonriding member of your party or wrap it in a plastic bag.

One final word: This is not just a fancy flume ride—it is a full-blown Disney adventure. The scariest part by far is the big drop into the pool (visible from the sidewalk in front of Splash Mountain), and even this plunge looks worse than it really is. Despite reassurances, however, many children wig out after watching it from the sidewalk. A Grand Rapids, Michigan, mother recalls her kids' rather unique reaction:

We discovered after the fact that our children thought they would go underwater after the five-story drop and tried to hold their breath throughout the ride in preparation. They were really too preoccupied to enjoy the clever Br'er Rabbit story.

FRONTIERLAND

FRONTIERLAND ADJOINS NEW ORLEANS SQUARE as you move clockwise around the theme park. The focus here is on the Old West, with log stockades and pioneer trappings. Big Thunder Ranch, on the walkway to Fantasyland, features pungent pygmy petting goats, a jamboree of character meet and greets, and Miss Chris's cabin of coloring activities and equestrian Disney memorabilia.

Big Thunder Mountain Railroad (*FastPass*) ★★★★

APPEAL BY AGE   PRESCHOOL ★★★★   GRADE SCHOOL ★★★★½   TEENS ★★★★★
YOUNG ADULTS ★★★★½   OVER 30 ★★★★½   SENIORS ★★★★½

What it is Tame roller coaster with exciting special effects. **Scope and scale** Headliner. **When to go** Before 10:30 a.m., after 6:30 p.m., or use FastPass. **Special comments** Great effects, though a relatively tame ride. Must be 40" tall to ride; those age 8 and younger must ride with an adult; switching-off option provided (see page 145). **Duration of ride** 3½ minutes. **Average wait in line per 100 people ahead of you** 3 minutes. **Assumes** 5 trains operating. **Loading speed** Moderate–fast.

Scary   Lose Things   Queasy   Rough   Muss Your 'Do

DESCRIPTION AND COMMENTS A roller coaster through and around a Disney "mountain." The idea is that you're on a runaway mine train during gold rush days. Along with the usual thrills of a roller coaster (about a 5 on a "scary scale" of 10), the ride showcases some first-rate examples of Disney creativity: lifelike scenes depicting a mining town, colorful caverns, and a dynamite-chewing goat, all humorously animated.

In 2014 Disneyland replaced the aging track and trains and reconstructed the ramshackle Rainbow Ridge buildings, which dated to 1956. The track layout and vehicle stylings remain the same, but visitors appreciate the smoother ride and enhanced final lift hill, which supplanted the unconvincing old earthquake effects with an explosive fog-fueled finale.

TOURING TIPS A superb Disney experience but not too wild a roller coaster. The emphasis here is much more on the sights than on the thrill of the ride itself. Regardless, it's a not-to-be-missed attraction. Finally, give Big Thunder a try after dark. The lighting gives the attraction a whole new feel.

As an example of how differently guests experience Disney attractions, consider this letter from a reader in Brookline, Massachusetts:

As senior citizens with limited time, my friend and I confined our activities to those attractions rated as 4 or 5 stars for seniors. Because you listed it as not to be missed, we waited an hour to board Big Thunder Mountain Railroad, which you rated a 5 on a scary scale of 10. After living through 3½ minutes of pure terror, I rate that attraction a 15 on a scary scale of 10. We were so busy holding on and screaming and even praying for our safety that we did not see any falling rocks or a mining town. In our opinion it should not be recommended for seniors or preschool children.

A woman from New England discovered that there's more to consider about Big Thunder than being scared:

I won't say it warranted a higher scare rating, but it was much higher on the lose-your-lunch meter. One more sharp turn and the kids in front of me would have needed a dip in Splash Mountain!

Frontierland Shootin' Exposition   ★★

What it is Electronic shooting gallery. **Scope and scale**
Diversion. **When to go** Whenever convenient. **Special
comment** Costs extra; a nifty shooting gallery.

Thumbs Up for the Whole Family

DESCRIPTION AND COMMENTS A very elaborate
   electronic shooting gallery that costs $1 to
   play. One of the few attractions in Disneyland
   Park not included in the admission pass.

TOURING TIPS Good fun for those who like to shoot, but definitely not a
   place to blow time if you are on a tight schedule. Try it on your second
   day if time allows.

The Golden Horseshoe—Laughing Stock Co.   ★★★

What it is Western dance hall with improvisation comedy show. **Scope and scale**
Minor attraction. **When to go** Catch a show and lunch at the same time; check the
Times Guide for schedule. **Special comment** Zany show. **Duration of show** 12 minutes.

DESCRIPTION AND COMMENTS The Golden Horseshoe has always offered a
   decent show, hearty snacks, and a nice air-conditioned respite from the
   sun. At the end of 2013, Disneyland foolishly put Billy Hill and the Hillbil-
   lies, a comic bluegrass fiddling quartet (and fan favorite here for more
   than two decades), out to premature pasture. Billy and the boys were
   quickly snatched up by nearby Knott's Berry Farm. Disneyland bumped up
   their day-off substitutes, The Laughing Stock Co., to the headlining spot.

   Each interactive, semi-improvised Laughing Stock Co. show is different
   and includes a set of zany Wild West–style characters. A particular favorite of ours is "find a suitor," where three unsuspecting members of the
   crowd are selected to answer questions from the Mayor of Frontierland's
   less-than-handsome daughter (played by a man). It's an amusing diversion
   when you want a break from big rides, but it won't erase memories of Billy
   Hill, whose genius can be relived through their album *The Billys—Live!* on
   Amazon and iTunes.

TOURING TIPS The Golden Horseshoe has first-come, first-serve seating. We
   recommend arriving 30 minutes early if you want to find a table and grab
   some grub. Food service can be slow; look for the shortest of the open
   service lines, usually on the far left. Absurdly oversize safety railings now
   ruin sight lines from the balcony (curse you, OSHA!), so the best view is
   from the floor, front and center, but Walt liked the opera box seats best.

Mark Twain Riverboat   ★★★

What it is Scenic boat ride. **Scope and scale** Minor attraction. **When to go**
11 a.m.–5 p.m. **Special comment** Provides an excellent vantage point. **Duration of
ride** About 14 minutes. **Average wait to board** 10 minutes. **Assumes** Normal operations. **Loading speed** Fast—en masse.

DESCRIPTION AND COMMENTS This large-capacity paddle-wheel riverboat navigates the waters around Tom Sawyer Island and Fort Wilderness. A beautiful craft, the riverboat provides a lofty perch from which to see Frontierland and New Orleans Square. The *Mark Twain,* Sailing Ship *Columbia,* and Davy Crockett's Explorer Canoes travel through the Rivers of America. The show scenes include a home for Mike Fink (and one of his keelboats, a former Disneyland attraction) and 26 Audio-Animatronic animals; the audio spiel includes a musical nod to the New Orleans–set *The Princess and the Frog.*

TOURING TIPS One of three boat rides that survey the same real estate. Because the Explorer Canoes are slower in loading and the *Columbia* operates seasonally, we think the riverboat makes more efficient use of touring time. If you're not in the mood for a boat ride, many of the same sights can be seen by hiking around Tom Sawyer Island. The riverboat typically operates until 75 minutes before the park closes, except on *Fantasmic!* performance nights, when the voyages end at 5:45 p.m. If you're looking for a new experience aboard the *Mark Twain,* try asking a cast member if you can enjoy the trip from the pilothouse.

Pirate's Lair on Tom Sawyer Island   ★★★

**APPEAL BY AGE PRESCHOOL ★★★★★   GRADE SCHOOL ★★★★★   TEENS ★★★★½
YOUNG   ADULTS   ★★★   OVER   30   ★★★½   SENIORS   ★★**

What it is Walk-through exhibit and rustic playground. **Scope and scale** Minor attraction. **When to go** Midmorning–late afternoon. **Special comments** The place for rambunctious kids; closes at sunset.

DESCRIPTION AND COMMENTS Pirate's Lair on Tom Sawyer Island manages to impart a sense of isolation from the rest of the park. It has hills to climb, tipsy bridges to cross, paths to follow, and a "rock-climbing" play area. It's a delight for adults but a godsend for children who have been in tow all day. Sadly, safety and maintenance issues have closed a few of the island's play elements, including the tree house, somewhat diminishing the attraction's entertainment value.

As an aside, a mother of four from Duncan, South Carolina, found Tom Sawyer Island as much a refuge as an attraction, writing:

In the afternoon, when the crowds were at their peak, the weather was hottest, and the kids started lagging behind, our organization began to suffer. We then retreated over to Tom Sawyer Island, which proved to be a true haven. My husband and I found a secluded bench and regrouped. Meanwhile, the kids were able to run freely in the shade. Afterward, we were ready to tackle the park again refreshed and with direction once more.

The island has sets from the *Pirates of the Caribbean* films, such as William Turner's blacksmith shop, and story artifacts, such as Elizabeth Swann's love letters, tucked into every nook and cranny. Kids exploring the caverns of Dead Man's Grotto will encounter spooky voices, ghostly apparitions, and buried treasure. Elsewhere, a sunken chest can be discovered by operating a hoist.

Evidently, you can't have a pirate's lair without a bunch of gore. A pop-up head and moving skeletal arm are just the beginning. There's also a "bone cage" and, our favorite, a treasure chest containing Davy Jones's beating heart. The Bootstrappers pirate band occasionally rides the rafts over to administer pirate oaths and lead sing-alongs.

TOURING TIPS Pirate's Lair on Tom Sawyer Island is not one of Disneyland Park's more celebrated attractions, but it's certainly one of the most well done. Attention to detail is excellent, and kids particularly revel in its adventuresome atmosphere. We think it's a must for families with children ages 5–15. If your party has only adults, visit the island on your second day, or stop by on your first day if you have seen the attractions you most wanted to see. We like the island from about noon until the island closes at sunset. Access is by raft from Frontierland, and you may have to stand in line to board both coming and going. Two or three rafts operate simultaneously, however, and the round-trip is usually pretty time efficient. Tom Sawyer Island takes about 30 minutes or so to see, but many children could spend a whole day there.

Raft to and from Tom Sawyer Island

What it is Transportation ride to Tom Sawyer Island. **Scope and scale** Minor attraction. **Duration of ride** A little more than 1 minute one way. **Average wait in line per 100 people ahead of you** 4½ minutes. **Assumes** 3 rafts operating. **Loading speed** Moderate.

Sailing Ship *Columbia*
(open seasonally) ★★★½

APPEAL BY AGE	PRESCHOOL ★★½	GRADE SCHOOL ★★★½	TEENS ★★★½
YOUNG ADULTS ★★★		OVER 30 ★★★★	SENIORS ★★★★

Thumbs Up for the Whole Family

What it is Scenic boat ride. **Scope and scale** Minor attraction. **When to go** 11 a.m.–5 p.m. **Special comments** Pirates on extremely busy days; a stunning piece of workmanship. **Duration of ride** About 14 minutes. **Average wait to board** 10 minutes. **Assumes** Normal operations. **Loading speed** Fast—en masse.

DESCRIPTION AND COMMENTS The *Columbia* is a stunning replica of a three-masted 18th-century merchant ship. Both its above- and belowdecks are open to visitors, with belowdecks outfitted to depict the life and work environment of the ship's crew in 1787. The *Columbia* operates only on busier days and runs the same route as the canoes and the riverboat. As with the other rivercraft, the *Columbia* suspends operations at sunset.

TOURING TIPS The *Columbia,* along with the *Mark Twain* Riverboat, provides a short-wait, high-carrying-capacity alternative for cruising the Rivers of America. We found the beautifully crafted *Columbia* by far the most aesthetically pleasing and historically interesting of any of the three choices of boat rides on the Rivers of America. If you have time to be choosy, ride aboard the *Columbia.* After boarding, while waiting for the cruise to begin, tour below. Once the ride begins, come topside and stroll the deck, taking in the beauty and complexity of the rigging.

The *Columbia* does not usually require a long wait, which makes it a good bet during the crowded afternoon hours.

FANTASYLAND

TRULY AN ENCHANTING PLACE, spread gracefully like a miniature alpine village beneath the towers of Sleeping Beauty Castle, Fantasyland is the heart of the park. Fantasyland is the backbone of the Magic Mornings early-entry program, with nine rides open. If your group consists of older kids and adults, ride Peter Pan's Flight first during the early-entry period, followed by Alice in Wonderland and Matterhorn Bobsleds. If you have younger children in your group, start with Peter Pan's Flight and Alice in Wonderland and then ride Dumbo. Certain Fantasyland attractions close for fireworks and may not reopen until the fire marshal gives the all clear, as this Calgary dad discovered:

A significant number of Disneyland's Fantasyland attractions close before fireworks, and of these, some reopen several minutes later while others remain closed for the night. We arrived at Fantasyland immediately after the fireworks and found very little open.

Alice in Wonderland ★★★½

APPEAL BY AGE	PRESCHOOL ★★★★		GRADE SCHOOL ★★★★	TEENS ★★★½
YOUNG ADULTS ★★★½		OVER 30 ★★★½		SENIORS ★★★½

What it is Track ride in the dark. **Scope and scale** Minor attraction. **When to go** Before 11 a.m. or after 5 p.m. **Special comment** Good characterization and story line. **Duration of ride** Almost 4 minutes. **Average wait in line per 100 people ahead of you** 12 minutes. **Assumes** 16 cars operating. **Loading speed** Slow.

DESCRIPTION AND COMMENTS This attraction recalls the story of *Alice in Wonderland* with some nice surprises and colorful effects. Guests ride nifty caterpillar cars in this Disney spook-house adaptation. Though not a spring chicken, Alice is a third-generation Disney dark ride with more vibrant, evocative, and three-dimensional sets and characters than Pinocchio's Daring Journey or Mr. Toad's Wild Ride. This is also the only two-story Disney dark ride with an outdoor section. In 2014 an extensive refurbishment brought the elevated outdoor track up to modern safety standards; advanced new projection effects utilize original hand-drawn animation to bring the static sets to life, reinvigorating the ride without ruining its classic charm.

TOURING TIPS This is a well-done ride in the best Disney tradition, with familiar characters, good effects, and a theme you can follow—too bad it loads very slowly. Do not confuse it with the Mad Tea Party ride. This very popular attraction can build quite a lengthy line as the morning progresses, so we like to ride this as early in the day as possible, usually right after Peter Pan's Flight.

Bibbidi Bobbidi Boutique

This pricey beauty salon for little girls is located in Sleeping Beauty Castle. Here, Fairy Godmothers–in-training make would-be princesses look like prom queens (or vice versa). A range of packages is offered, including everything from hair styling and makeup to princess gowns and accessories (cha-ching). The top-of-the-line package includes skip-the-line VIP access to the nearby Royal Hall princess meet and greet, which may be worth its *wait* in gold. If you have the bucks, the girls love it. For reservations, call ☎ 714-781-7895. A Winston, Oregon, mom thinks highly of Bibbidi Bobbidi:

> *Bibbidi Bobbidi Boutique is a must if traveling with little girls. Our party had three girls ages 4, 4, and 6, and this was their favorite and most memorable event of the trip. Even though we traveled during the off-season, it was hectic and a little unorganized. We made reservations and still had to wait 30 minutes, but once the girls were matched with their Fairy Godmother–in-training, we were absolutely pleased with the service. It is a little spendy (I think around $55 for a princess hairdo, even more if you want the full service), but it was completely worth it. The hair survived the rest of the day and looked perfect when they put their princess gowns on at night for the fireworks.*

Casey Jr. Circus Train ★★½

APPEAL BY AGE	PRESCHOOL ★★★★★	GRADE SCHOOL ★★★½	TEENS ★★½
YOUNG ADULTS ★★½	OVER 30 ★★½		SENIORS ★

What it is Miniature train ride. **Scope and scale** Minor attraction. **When to go** Before 11 a.m. or after 5 p.m. **Special comment** A quiet, scenic ride. **Duration of ride** A little under 4 minutes. **Average wait in line per 100 people ahead of you** 12 minutes. **Assumes** 2 trains operating. **Loading speed** Slow.

DESCRIPTION AND COMMENTS A long-standing attraction and a pet project of Walt Disney, Casey Jr. circulates through a landscape of miniature towns, farms, and lakes. Visible from this ride are some stunning bonsai specimens, as well as some of the most manicured landscaping you are ever likely to see.

TOURING TIPS This ride covers the same sights as the Storybook Land Canal Boats but does it faster and with less of a wait. Accommodations for adults, however, are less than optimal on this ride, with some passengers having to squeeze into diminutive caged cars (after all, it is a circus train). If you do not have children in your party, you can enjoy the same sights more comfortably by riding the Storybook Land Canal Boats, which also benefit from live narration instead of Casey Jr.'s canned sound track.

A father of two toddlers from Menlo Park, California, explains that issues of redundancy were not uppermost in his children's minds.

> *Contrary to your advice, the Casey Jr. Circus Train and Storybook Land Canal Boats are totally different experiences—if you are 4 or younger. Hey, one is a boat, and one is a train! Seems obvious to the mind of a 4-year-old! We did both, and the kids loved both.*

Disneyland Railroad

DESCRIPTION AND COMMENTS The Disneyland Railroad stops in Fantasyland/Mickey's Toontown on its circuit around the park. The station is located to the left of It's a Small World, next to the Fantasyland Theatre. From this often-crowded boarding point, transportation is available to Tomorrowland, Main Street, and New Orleans Square.

Dumbo the Flying Elephant ★★½

APPEAL BY AGE	PRESCHOOL ★★★★½	GRADE SCHOOL ★★★★	TEENS ★★★
YOUNG ADULTS ★★	OVER 30 ★★★	SENIORS ★★½

What it is Disneyfied midway ride. **Scope and scale** Minor attraction. **When to go**

Before 10 a.m. or during late evening parades, fireworks, or *Fantasmic!* performances. **Duration of ride** 1⅔ minutes. **Average wait in line per 100 people ahead of you** 12 minutes. **Assumes** Normal staffing. **Loading speed** Slow.

DESCRIPTION AND COMMENTS A nice, tame, happy children's ride based on the lovable Disney flying elephant, this is an upgraded rendition of a ride that can be found at state fairs and amusement parks across the country. Shortcomings notwithstanding, Dumbo is the favorite Disneyland Park attraction of most preschoolers. A lot of readers take us to task for lumping Dumbo in with state-fair midway rides. These comments from a reader in Armdale, Nova Scotia, are representative:

I think you have acquired a jaded attitude. I know Dumbo is not for everybody, but when we took our oldest child (then just 4), the sign at the end of the line said there would be a 90-minute wait. He knew and he didn't care, and he and I stood in the hot afternoon sun for 90 blissful minutes waiting for his 90-second flight. Anything that a 4-year-old would wait for that long and that patiently must be pretty special.

TOURING TIPS This is a slow-loading ride that we recommend you bypass unless you are on a very relaxed touring schedule. If your kids are excited about Dumbo, try to get them on the ride before 10 a.m., during the parades or *Fantasmic!,* or just before the park closes. Also, consider this advice from an Arlington, Virginia, mom:

Grown-ups, beware! Dumbo is really a tight fit with one adult and two kids. My kids threw me out of their Dumbo, and I had to sit in a Dumbo all by myself. Pretty embarrassing, and my husband got lots of pictures.

Fantasyland Theatre / *Mickey and the Magical Map*
★★★½

APPEAL BY AGE PRESCHOOL ★★★★★	**GRADE SCHOOL ★★★★**	**TEENS ★★★½**	
YOUNG ADULTS ★★★★	**OVER 30 ★★★★½**	**SENIORS ★★★★**	

What it is Musical stage show. **Scope and scale** Major attraction. **When to go** Check *Times Guide* for schedule; arrive at least 15 minutes before showtime for the best seats. **Duration of show** 22 minutes. **Probable waiting time** 15 minutes.

DESCRIPTION AND COMMENTS This venue is a sophisticated amphitheater where concerts and elaborate stage shows are performed according to the daily entertainment schedule. Better productions that have played here include *Beauty and the Beast Live, Snow White,* and *The Spirit of Pocahontas,* all musical stage adaptations of the respective Disney-animated features.

Mickey and the Magical Map involves apprentice Mickey's accidental adventure into sorcerer Yen Sid's mysterious dream-controlling map. This 22-minute musical adventure combines new songs and classic tunes in a score that skips from India to Hawaii, with a stopover under the sea. Rapunzel, Pocahontas, Mulan, King Louie, Sebastian, and Stitch are among the Disney icons who appear, along with a platoon of dancing paintpots and brushes, but the show is stolen by a mischievous animated paint splotch (brought to life through high-tech video effects).

The opening number is less than memorable, and the computer-generated animation of Yen Sid is disappointingly chunky. On the whole, however, this is easily the best new musical production that Disneyland's parks have mounted in a decade. Live singing and energetic choreography influenced by drum corps enliven the somewhat overfamiliar songs, and a gospel-flavored riverboat finale (complete with streamers shot over the audience) brings down the house. Well worth watching once you've experienced the headliners, or on your second day at Disneyland.

TOURING TIPS Performance times are listed in the *Times Guide.* Arrive at least 15 minutes early for optimal seating. Though it's a stage show, the performances are complimented by three giant video screens, each of which spans almost the entire width of the stage, that form a raised platform on which much of the action takes place. For that reason, the best seats are the ones farther back and slightly raised, in the center of the theater. Avoid the seats up front or too far on the sides, where the images on the slanted screen will look distorted.

It's a Small World ★★★★

Thumbs Up for the Whole Family

What it is World brotherhood–themed indoor boat ride. **Scope and scale** Major attraction. **When to go** Anytime except after a parade. **Duration of ride** 14 minutes. **Average wait in line per 100 people ahead of you** 2½ minutes. **Assumes** Busy conditions with 56 boats operating. **Loading speed** Fast.

DESCRIPTION AND COMMENTS A happy and upbeat attraction with a world-brotherhood theme and a catchy tune that will stick in your head for weeks. Small boats convey visitors on a tour around the world, with singing and dancing dolls showcasing the dress and culture of each nation. Almost everyone enjoys It's a Small World (well, there are those jaded folks who are put off by the dolls' homogeneous appearance, especially in light of the diversity theme), but it stands, along with the *Enchanted Tiki*

Room, as an attraction that some could take or leave but that others consider one of the real masterpieces of Disneyland Park. More than 20 Disney and Pixar characters were integrated into the classic attraction in 2009; tastefully crafted in the style of original artist Mary Blair, the additions don't detract from the ride, except in the tacky U.S.A. tribute added to the end. A mom from Castleton, Vermont, commented:

It's a Small World at Fantasyland was like a pit stop in The Twilight Zone. They were very slow unloading the boats, and we were stuck in a line of about six boats waiting to get out while the endless chanting of that song grated on my nerves. I told my husband that I was going to swim for it just to escape one more chorus.

A dad from New Brunswick, Canada, gives this advice for surviving the Happiest Cruise That Ever Sailed:

Ask to sit at the back of the boat. Pull out your iPod with headphones once you're in the building, and blast some heavy metal. You'd be amazed how different and deceptively funny the ride becomes!

From November through New Year's, the attraction receives an annual holiday overlay inside the attraction as well as outside, featuring "Jingle Bells" and "Deck the Halls" instead of the usual earworm sound track. We particularly enjoy the light show and projection effects outside the attraction that happen every 15 minutes.

TOURING TIPS It's a Small World is a fast-loading ride that's usually a good bet during the busier times of the day. The boats are moved along by water pressure, which increases as boats are added. Thus, the more boats in service when you ride (up to a maximum total of 60), the shorter the duration of the ride (and wait). Small World is taken off-line in mid-October and reopened in November with a special Christmas holiday theme. Removal of the overlay also keeps the ride closed for several weeks after the holiday season. Two notes: While the loading can be very quick when many boats are running, the unloading can be very slow. Second, the attraction has two loading zones, one that has wheelchair access and one without. Unless you need wheelchair access, we recommend using the loading zone on the far side of the entrance by choosing the right side of the queue when it splits.

King Arthur Carrousel ★★★

APPEAL BY AGE	PRESCHOOL ★★★★½	GRADE SCHOOL ★★★★	TEENS ★★★★
YOUNG ADULTS ★★★	OVER 30 ★★★		SENIORS ★★★½

What it is Merry-go-round. **Scope and scale** Minor attraction. **When to go** Before 11:30 a.m. or after 5 p.m. **Special comments** A showpiece carousel; adults enjoy the beauty and nostalgia of this ride. **Duration of ride** A little more than 2 minutes. **Average wait in line per 100 people ahead of you** 8 minutes. **Assumes** Normal staffing. **Loading speed** Slow.

DESCRIPTION AND COMMENTS A merry-go-round to be sure, but certainly one of the most elaborate and beautiful you will ever see, especially when lit at night. For the 50th anniversary in 2005, a special horse was added in tribute to Julie Andrews and her iconic role in *Mary Poppins;* the white horse has bells all over—hence her name, Jingles. She's the horse closest to the handicapped ramp.

TOURING TIPS Unless you have small children in your party, we suggest that you appreciate this ride from the sidelines. If your children want to ride, try to get them on before 11:30 a.m. or after 5 p.m. While nice to look at, the carousel loads and unloads very slowly.

Mad Tea Party ★★

**APPEAL BY AGE PRESCHOOL ★★★★★ GRADE SCHOOL ★★★★½ TEENS ★★★½
YOUNG   ADULTS   ★★★½   OVER 30   ★★★   SENIORS   ★**

What it is Midway-type spinning ride. **Scope and scale** Minor attraction. **When to go** Before 11 a.m. or after 5 p.m. **Special comments** You can make the teacups spin faster by turning the wheel in the center of the cup; fun but not worth the wait. **Duration of ride** 1½ minutes. **Average wait in line per 100 people ahead of you** 8 minutes. **Assumes** Normal staffing. **Loading speed** Slow.

  DESCRIPTION AND COMMENTS Well done in the Disney style, but still just an amusement park ride. *Alice in Wonderland*'s Mad Hatter provides the theme, and patrons whirl around feverishly in big teacups. A rendition of this ride, sans Disney characters, can be found at every local carnival and fair.

TOURING TIPS This ride, besides not being particularly special, loads notoriously slowly. Skip it on a busy schedule if the kids will let you. Ride in the morning of your second day if your schedule is more relaxed. A warning for parents: Teenagers like to lure adults onto the teacups and then turn the wheel in the middle (which makes the cup spin faster) until the adults are plastered against the side of the cup and on the verge of throwing up.

Matterhorn Bobsleds ★★★½

**APPEAL BY AGE PRESCHOOL ★★★★½† GRADE SCHOOL ★★★★½ TEENS ★★★½
YOUNG   ADULTS   ★★★★   OVER 30   ★★★★   SENIORS   ★★★**

†*Some preschoolers love Matterhorn Bobsleds; others are frightened.*

What it is Roller coaster. **Scope and scale** Major attraction. **When to go** During the first 90 minutes the park is open or during the hour before it closes. **Special comments** Fun ride but not too scary. Must be 42″ tall to ride. **Duration of ride** 2½ minutes. **Average wait in line per 100 people ahead of you** 3½ minutes. **Assumes** Both tracks operating with 10 sleds per track with 23-second dispatch intervals. **Loading speed** Moderate.

    DESCRIPTION AND COMMENTS The Matterhorn is the most distinctive landmark on the Disneyland scene, visible from almost anywhere in the park. Open since 1959, the Matterhorn maintains its popularity and long lines year in and year out. Matterhorn Bobsleds is a roller coaster with an alpine motif. On the scary scale, the ride ranks about 6 on a scale of 10. The special effects don't compare to Space Mountain's, but they do afford a few surprises. In 2012 the Matterhorn completed its first top-to-bottom overhaul since the 1970s, receiving rehabilitated tracks and a more-realistic exterior paint job; that was followed in 2015 by enhancements to the lighting and effects, including a more menacing appearance for the mysterious yeti. You now first glimpse the yeti during the initial uphill climb as a menacing silhouette distorted by ice and then cruise

DISNEY DISH WITH JIM HILL

WILL THE MATTERHORN GET AN ICY NEW NEIGHBOR?
Disney's *Frozen* is now the highest-grossing animated feature of all time, and one of the more interesting ideas currently making the rounds at Walt Disney Imagineering involves replacing the park's old Motorboat Cruise with a re-creation of Elsa's ice castle. What's intriguing about this proposed attraction is that, on the very same day the Snow Queen opens her doors to visitors, all of the Disney princesses would then show up to welcome Elsa and Anna. So under one enormous roof, you'd have the ultimate royal meet and greet. That said, given the glacial pace that projects move through WDI these days, I wouldn't want to predict when the Snow Queen's palace will begin rising up next to the Matterhorn Bobsleds.

past an ominous collection of old ride vehicles (including vintage bobsleds and an antique Skyway bucket) that the beast has hoarded. Finally, you'll come face-to-face with the furry legend not once but twice; the encounters are brief, but he moves with a fluid ferocity that his frozen cousin in WDW's Expedition Everest can only dream of. More controversially, the 2012 refurb included three-passenger cars with individual seats (similar to Florida's Space Mountain) and seat belts, which replaced the old four-passenger vehicles with straddle seats. Children have been robbed of the traditional thrill of riding nestled between their parent's legs, and thankful fathers have been spared the traditional bruising of their family jewels. The revamped vehicles are also unfriendly to the long-legged. Tall riders are advised to ask for the middle or back rows, which have marginally more room, and slide their feet forward into the snug footwells on either side of the seat ahead. For the short-limbed, the front seat is usually the smoothest. But be warned that, wherever you sit, this is the bumpiest coaster in Disneyland's inventory. A Richboro, Pennsylvania, dad disagrees with our scary rating of the Matterhorn:

My biggest disappointment was the Matterhorn. I understand it's iconic, but the notion that it could rate a 6 out of 10 on the scare factor is pure insanity. I'd rate it a 1! After the steep climb in the dark, you basically just go down in circles until you are left baffled that the "roller coaster" ride is over.

TOURING TIPS Lines for the Matterhorn form as soon as the gates open and persist throughout the day. Ride first thing in the morning or just before the park closes. If you are a roller coaster person, ride Space Mountain and then hurry over and hop on the Matterhorn. If roller coasters are not the end-all for you, we recommend choosing one of the other coasters or saving this one for a second day. The Matterhorn's poorly marked single-rider line, which can save you an hour in the queue, is currently one of the park's best-kept secrets. Ask an employee at the Fantasyland side exit how to take advantage of it.

One of the things we like about the Matterhorn is that the entire queuing area is visible. This makes the lines look more oppressive than they actually are and also provides an opportunity to closely approximate the time of your wait. If the line extending toward Tomorrowland reaches a point across from the Picture Spot, your wait to ride the Matterhorn

Bobsleds will be about 16 minutes. Most people stay to the left when the queue splits, often leaving the right loading station with a shorter line. Though the two sides are similar, they are not identical; veterans say the Tomorrowland track is faster with steeper drops, while the Fantasyland side is slightly longer with sharper turns.

Mr. Toad's Wild Ride ★★½

APPEAL BY AGE	PRESCHOOL ★★★★	GRADE SCHOOL ★★★★	TEENS ★★★½
YOUNG ADULTS ★★★½		OVER 30 ★★★½	SENIORS ★★★★

What it is Track ride in the dark. **Scope and scale** Minor attraction. **When to go** Before 11 a.m. **Special comment** Past its prime. **Duration of ride** Almost 2 minutes. **Average wait in line per 100 people ahead of you** 9 minutes. **Assumes** 12 cars operating. **Loading speed** Slow.

Dark

DESCRIPTION AND COMMENTS Mr. Toad's Wild Ride is a twisting, curving ride in the dark that passes two-dimensional sets and props. There are a couple of clever effects, but basically it's at the technological basement of the Disney attraction mix. Though Mr. Toad doesn't compare well with newer high-tech attractions, many Disneyland veterans appreciate it because it's one of a handful of attractions remaining from the park's beginning. Hannah, an official Touring Plans Stunt Kid™, summed the ride's appeal up perfectly:

Mr. Toad's Wild Ride is awesome, and everyone should go on it because it's about a toad who goes to hell. I feel like that's a neglected topic in theme parks these days.

TOURING TIPS Not a great but certainly a popular attraction. Lines build early in the day and never let up. Catch Mr. Toad before 11 a.m. Parents beware: There are some loud sound effects as well as a spooky "hell" scene at the end of the attraction.

Peter Pan's Flight ★★★★

APPEAL BY AGE	PRESCHOOL ★★★★½	GRADE SCHOOL ★★★★	TEENS ★★★½
YOUNG ADULTS ★★★★		OVER 30 ★★★★	SENIORS ★★★½

Thumbs Up for the Whole Family

What it is Indoor fantasy-adventure ride. **Scope and scale** Minor attraction. **When to go** Before 10 a.m. or after 6 p.m. **Duration of ride** Just over 2 minutes. **Average wait in line per 100 people ahead of you** 11 minutes. **Assumes** 13 ships operating. **Loading speed** Slow.

DESCRIPTION AND COMMENTS Though it is not considered one of Disneyland Park's major attractions, Peter Pan's Flight is superbly designed and absolutely delightful, with a happy theme, a reunion with some unforgettable Disney characters, beautiful effects, and charming music. Tiny pirate ships suspended from an overhead track launch you from Wendy's window to fly over nighttime London and on to Never Land and an encounter with Captain Hook, Mr. Smee, and the ubiquitous crocodile. In 2015 Peter Pan celebrated the park's 60th anniversary with a refreshed exterior and brand-new special effects inside, including digital pixie dust projections and floating figures of Wendy and the Darling boys in the nursery scene. The colorful new London flyover and rippling water effects are especially lovely. Though not a major feature of Disneyland Park, we nevertheless classify it as the best attraction in Fantasyland.

TOURING TIPS This attraction has a consistent wait of at least 20 minutes after the first hour of park operation. On the busiest of days, we've seen the wait go up to more than 60 minutes at the extreme. Try to ride before 10 a.m. or after 6 p.m., during the afternoon or evening parade(s), or during a performance of *Fantasmic!*

Pinocchio's Daring Journey   ★★½

APPEAL BY AGE   PRESCHOOL ★★★½   GRADE SCHOOL ★★★½   TEENS ★★½
YOUNG ADULTS ★★★   OVER 30 ★★★½   SENIORS ★★★★

What it is Track ride in the dark. **Scope and scale** Minor attraction. **When to go** Before noon or after 3:30 p.m. **Special comment** A big letdown. **Duration of ride** Almost 3 minutes. **Average wait in line per 100 people ahead of you** 8 minutes. **Assumes** 15 cars operating. **Loading speed** Slow.

Dark

DESCRIPTION AND COMMENTS This is another twisting, curving track ride in the dark, this time tracing the adventures of Pinocchio as he tries to find his way home. The action is hard to follow, and it lacks continuity. Though the sets are three-dimensional and more visually compelling than, say, Mr. Toad, the story line is dull and fails to engage the guest. In the ride's defense, it features some deliciously trippy Pleasure Island imagery, a clever vanishing Blue Fairy effect, and almost always an empty queue.

TOURING TIPS The word must be out about Pinocchio because the lines are seldom very long. Still, the longest waits occur 11:30 a.m.–4:30 p.m.

Royal Hall at Fantasy Faire   ★★★

APPEAL BY AGE   PRESCHOOL ★★★★½   GRADE SCHOOL ★★★★★   TEENS ★★★★
YOUNG ADULTS ★★★½   OVER 30 ★★★½   SENIORS ★★★

What it is Princess meet and greet. **Scope and scale** Major attraction. **When to go** If meeting the princesses is important to your little ones, try to arrive 15 minutes before opening. **Special comment** Note that Royal Hall doesn't stay open late, even if the park does. **Duration of experience** 5 minutes. **Probable waiting time** 35–60 minutes.

DESCRIPTION AND COMMENTS Once a sleepy corner off the central hub, mainly known since the 1950s for weekend swing-dancing parties, Carnation Plaza Gardens was given a pink-and-purple princess makeover in 2013 and emerged as the Fantasy Faire, which is comprised of Royal Hall and Royal Theatre (see the next profile). Even if you aren't enamored of the princess marketing craze, you can't help but admire the loving details applied throughout this mini-land, from a snoozing animatronic Figaro kitty and crank-operated Clopin music box to the twinkling hair on the courtyard's *Tangled*-inspired tower. (Boogie and jive fans, don't get jumpy: The weekend swing-dancing parties return to Disneyland, on its original dance floor, on most Saturday nights; see **tinyurl.com/disneydanceband** for the schedule.)

This indoor meet and greet features three princesses always on duty (usually Ariel, Aurora, and Cinderella). The usual Disneyland queue (mercifully mostly shaded) must be endured to meet and be photographed, but this current incarnation typically sees somewhat shorter waits than the former Fantasy Faire location. The trick is that the Royal Hall's intimate wood-paneled interior actually houses two identical meeting areas with duplicate trios of princesses (perhaps the product of an Epcot cloning experiment?) for double the greeting capacity.

TOURING TIPS Little girls love the Royal Hall, as do boys age 6 and younger. Incidentally, you won't believe how many of the kids come in costume. If you do everything, you'll spend about an hour, not counting shopping time. On busy days, you may be barred from bringing your stroller into Fantasy Faire, unless your child is asleep in it, so teach your kid to play dead on command if you don't want to park.

Royal Theatre at Fantasy Faire *(seasonal FastPass only)*
★★★★

APPEAL BY AGE   PRESCHOOL ★ ★ ★ ★ ★   GRADE SCHOOL ★ ★ ★ ★ ½   TEENS ★ ★ ★ ★ ½
YOUNG ADULTS   ★ ★ ★ ★ ½   OVER 30   ★ ★ ★ ★ ½   SENIORS   ★ ★ ★ ★

What it is Interactive storytelling show. **Scope and scale** Minor attraction. **When to go** Check the *Times Guide* for showtimes. If it's FastPass only, go at your scheduled time. **Duration of show** 20 minutes. **Probable waiting time** 30 minutes if not using FastPass.

DESCRIPTION AND COMMENTS Royal Theatre, which once hosted jazz greats such as Dizzy Gillespie, now houses a rotating repertory of 20-minute stage shows dramatizing the tales of popular Disney royalty. *Tangled, Beauty and the Beast,* and (most recently) *Frozen* are the featured fables, with Rapunzel and Flynn Ryder, Belle, or Anna and Elsa joining in their respective reenactments, accompanied by narrators Mr. Smyth and Mr. Jones, milkmaid stagehands, and a live pianist. Rather than straightforward retellings, these fast-paced comic condensations capture the anarchic slapstick of a Renaissance fair trunk show. Witty enough to keep adults far outside the target demographic awake, the Royal Theatre's shows are the sleeper hits of Fantasy Faire. Stick around after the curtain falls for an autograph session with the stars.

The *Frozen* show, which displaced the other productions full-time during 2015's Frozen Fun promotion, is by far the best of the three, and far superior to the similar sing-along show at Disney California Adventure. When the other shows return to rotation, the *Tangled* show is usually performed at the first three showtimes of the day, with *Beauty and the Beast* typically taking the stage for the remainder. If you must pick between those two, *Tangled* has the better script.

TOURING TIPS The theater only seats a little more than 200 (with room for 50 kids on the floor up front), so you may want to line up 30 or more minutes before showtime or simply settle for standing right outside the theater.

During 2015's Frozen Fun promotion, the Royal Theatre was FastPass only. When FastPass is offered, tickets can be obtained in Disneyland's hub; look for a sign, cast members, and a FastPass machine. Specific showtimes cannot be selected when you obtain a FastPass; they are instead distributed for the next performance time that still has tickets available. Look for a list of showtimes in the *Times Guide* or on a sign near the attraction. Once all FastPass guests are seated for a performance, a limited number of standby guests may be allowed to enter the theater or stand immediately outside it.

Sleeping Beauty Castle   ★★★

APPEAL BY AGE   PRESCHOOL ★ ★   GRADE SCHOOL ★ ★ ★   TEENS ★ ★ ★ ★
YOUNG ADULTS   ★ ★ ½   OVER 30   ★ ★ ★   SENIORS   ★ ★ ★ ½

What it is Walk-through exhibit. **Scope and scale** Minor attraction. **When to go**

> ## DISNEY DISH WITH JIM HILL
>
>
>
> **FERAL CATS CAUSE IMAGINEERS TO FLEA ... ER ... FLEE**
> When Disneyland Park was originally being built in late 1954, Walt didn't have enough money to install an attraction inside of Sleeping Beauty Castle. So the iconic structure stood empty until the fall of 1956, when the theme park had better cash flow. But when a design team arrived to begin taking measurements for the soon-to-be-built Sleeping Beauty Castle walk-through, they discovered that someone had moved into this structure ahead of Princess Aurora—a family of feral cats. To make matters worse, the castle was now so badly infested with fleas from these cats that—after spending just a few minutes inside—the Imagineers were forced to retreat, itching and scratching all the way. It took several weeks to capture and then relocate the cats, not to mention thoroughly fumigate the enormous structure, which is why the grand opening of Disneyland's Sleeping Beauty walk-through was pushed back to late April 1957.

Anytime. **Special comment** Must be able to climb up and down two flights of stairs. **Duration of exhibit** Varies; about 10 minutes. **Average wait** Usually none.

DESCRIPTION AND COMMENTS Disneyland Park's most famous icon, Sleeping Beauty Castle is at the heart of Disneyland and serves as a stage for shows and special events. For the non-claustrophobic, the Sleeping Beauty Castle walk-through exhibit is a miniature 3-D series, arranged along a narrow passage inside the castle, that tells the story of Sleeping Beauty. Originally opened on April 29, 1957, to preview the upcoming 1959 movie *Sleeping Beauty,* and then closed for most of a decade after 9/11, the attraction reopened in 2008 with new dioramas reflecting the style of artist Eyvind Earle, who gave *Sleeping Beauty* its distinctive design. In this version there are animated scenes, interactive elements, and Pepper's Ghost projection effects (as also seen in The Haunted Mansion).

TOURING TIPS The entrance is on the Fantasyland side of the castle near the passageway to Fantasy Faire and Frontierland. The exhibit allows for one-way traffic only. It can get a bit crowded inside, but there should rarely be a line outside the attraction. For those guests unable to handle stairs, a small alcove to the left of the bridge to Tomorrowland contains a collection of the animations, as well as music, allowing you to experience the attraction's elements without walking. The viewing location runs on a loop, so you might have to watch it out of order.

Snow White's Scary Adventures   ★★★

APPEAL BY AGE	PRESCHOOL ★★½	GRADE SCHOOL ★★★½	TEENS ★★★
YOUNG ADULTS ★★½		OVER 30 ★★★	SENIORS ★★★½

What it is Track ride in the dark. **Scope and scale** Minor attraction. **When to go** Before 11 a.m. or after 5 p.m. **Special comments** Quite intimidating for preschoolers; worth seeing if the wait is not long. **Duration of ride** Almost 2 minutes. **Average wait in line per 100 people ahead of you** 9 minutes. **Assumes** 10 cars operating. **Loading speed** Slow.

DESCRIPTION AND COMMENTS Here, you ride in a mining car in the dark through a series of sets drawn from *Snow White*

and the Seven Dwarfs. The attraction has a *Perils of Pauline* flavor and features Snow White as she narrowly escapes harm at the hands of the wicked witch. The action and effects are a cut above Mr. Toad's Wild Ride but not as good as Peter Pan's Flight. High-tech projection effects enhance the magic mirror and rainstorm scenes.

TOURING TIPS Enjoyable but not particularly compelling. Experience it if the lines are not too long or on a second-day visit. Ride before 11 a.m. or after 5 p.m. if possible. Also, don't take the "scary" part too seriously. The witch looks mean, but most kids take her in stride. Or maybe not. A mother from Knoxville, Tennessee, commented:

The outside looks cute and fluffy, but inside, the evil witch just keeps coming at you. My 5-year-old, who rode Space Mountain three times [and took other scary rides] right in stride, was near panic when our car stopped unexpectedly twice during Snow White. After Snow White, my 6-year-old niece spent a lot of time asking, "Will a witch jump out at you?" before other rides. So I suggest that you explain a little more what this ride is about. It's tough on preschoolers who are expecting forest animals and dwarfs.

It really punches the buttons of the 6-and-under crowd, when other more traditionally scary rides don't. Many kids, once frightened by Snow White's Scary Adventures, balk at trying any other attractions that go into the dark, regardless of how benign they are.

Storybook Land Canal Boats ★★★

What it is Scenic boat ride. **Scope and scale** Minor attraction. **When to go** Before 10:30 a.m. or after 5:30 p.m. **Special comment** Pretty, tranquil, and serene. **Duration of ride** 6½ minutes. **Average wait in line per 100 people ahead of you** 16 minutes. **Assumes** 7 boats operating. **Loading speed** Slow.

Thumbs Up for the Whole Family

DESCRIPTION AND COMMENTS Guide-operated boats wind along canals situated beneath the same miniature landscapes visible from the Casey Jr. Circus Train. This ride—offering stellar examples of bonsai cultivation, selective pruning, and miniaturization—is a must for landscape-gardening enthusiasts. The landscapes include scenes from more recent Disney features—such as the kingdom of Arendelle and Elsa's ice palace from *Frozen,* added in 2014—in addition to those from such classics as *The Wind in the Willows* and *The Three Little Pigs.*

TOURING TIPS The boats are much more comfortable than the train, the view of the miniatures is better, and the pace is more leisurely. On the downside, the lines are long and, if not long, definitely slow moving. The ride itself also takes a lot of time. Our recommendation is to ride Casey Jr. if you have children or are in a hurry. Take the boat if your party is all adults or your pace is more leisurely. Best of all, the boats' pilots deliver live narration that (depending on the driver) can be delightfully droll. If you ride the boats, try to get on before 10:30 a.m. If the queue isn't prohibitive, this ride is especially appealing after sunset, when the creative lighting adds a whole new dimension. It's closed during parades.

MICKEY'S TOONTOWN

MICKEY'S TOONTOWN IS SITUATED across the Disneyland Railroad tracks from Fantasyland. Its entrance is a tunnel that opens into Fantasyland just to the left of It's a Small World. As its name suggests, Toontown is a fanciful representation of the wacky cartoon community where all of the Disney characters live. Mickey's Toontown was inspired by the Disney animated feature *Who Framed Roger Rabbit?*, in which humans were able to enter the world of cartoon characters.

If you want to see characters, Mickey's Toontown is the place to go. In addition to Mickey, who receives guests all day (except during parades) in his dressing room, and Minnie, who entertains in her house, you are likely to bump into such august personages as Goofy and Pluto lurking around the streets. From time to time, horns sound and whistles blow atop Toontown City Hall, followed by a fanfare rendition of *The Mickey Mouse Club* theme song. This indicates that some characters are about to appear.

Mickey's Toontown is rendered with masterful attention to artistic humor and detail. There is an explosion at the Fireworks Factory every minute or so, always unannounced. Across the street, the sidewalk is littered with crates containing strange contents addressed to exotic destinations. If you pry open the top of one of the crates (easy to do), the crate will emit a noise consistent with its contents. A box of "train parts," for example, broadcasts the sound of a racing locomotive when you lift the top. Next to Goofy's Playhouse is a Goofy-shaped impact crater marking the spot where he missed his swimming pool while high diving.

Most of the attractions in Mickey's Toontown are for kids, specifically smaller children. Attractions open to adults include a dark ride drawn from *Who Framed Roger Rabbit?* (sort of a high-tech rendition of Mr. Toad's Wild Ride) and a diminutive roller coaster.

Be forewarned that Mickey's Toontown is not very large, especially in comparison with neighboring Fantasyland. A tolerable crowd in most of the other lands will seem like Times Square on New Year's Eve in Mickey's Toontown. Couple this congestion with the unfortunate fact that none of the attractions in Mickey's Toontown are engineered to handle huge crowds, and you come face-to-face with possibly the most attractive traffic jam the Disney folks have ever created.

Mickey's Toontown opens 1 hour after the rest of the park. If you're touring with younger children, hit the Fantasyland attractions during the first hour the park is open, and then head for Toontown.

Finally, be aware that all of Toontown, including the Roger Rabbit's Car Toon Spin, will close early before every nighttime fireworks show. It seems that rockets are launched from a building behind the land, showering Mickey's city with fiery embers, which might prove inconvenient for anyone standing below. *Note:* At press time, rumors circulated that all of Toontown could close within the next year to make room for an all-new *Star Wars*–themed area. Check **touringplans.com** for updates.

Chip 'n Dale Treehouse ★★

What it is Imaginative children's play area. **Scope and scale** Diversion. **When to go** Anytime. **Special comment** Good exercise for the small fry.

DESCRIPTION AND COMMENTS The play area consists of a tree house with slides.

TOURING TIPS Located in the most remote corner of Mickey's Toontown and obscured by the crowd waiting to ride the roller coaster next door, the tree house is frequently overlooked. Of all the attractions in Mickey's Toontown, this is the easiest one to get the kids into without much of a wait. Most any child who can fit is allowed to rummage around in the tree house.

Disneyland Railroad

DESCRIPTION AND COMMENTS Mickey's Toontown and Fantasyland share a station on the Disneyland Railroad's route around the perimeter of the park. This station becomes fairly crowded on busy days. If you are interested primarily in getting there, it may be quicker to walk.

Gadget's Go Coaster ★★

What it is Small roller coaster. **Scope and scale** Minor attraction. **When to go** Before 10:30 a.m., during the parades or *Fantasmic!* in the evening, or just before the park closes. **Special comments** Great for little ones but not worth the wait for adults. Must be 35" to ride; expectant moms shouldn't ride. **Duration of ride** About 50 seconds. **Average wait in line per 100 people ahead of you** 10 minutes. **Assumes** Normal staffing. **Loading speed** Slow.

Rough   Lose Things

DESCRIPTION AND COMMENTS Gadget's Go Coaster is a very small roller coaster; the idea is that you are miniaturized and riding around in an acorn shell. The zippy ride is over so quickly that you hardly know that you've been anywhere. In fact, of the 52 seconds the ride is in motion, 32 seconds are consumed in exiting the loading area, being ratcheted up the first hill, and braking into the off-loading area. The actual time you spend careening around the track is a whopping 20 seconds.

TOURING TIPS Gadget's Go Coaster, a beginner roller coaster for young children, is the perfect attraction to gauge the pluckiness of your little ones before tossing them to the coyotes on Big Thunder Mountain Railroad. The coaster cars are not very comfortable for adults, and you can expect a fair amount of whiplash, but as noted, the ride takes less than a minute. The coaster is both slow-loading and visually attractive, so you can expect long waits except during the first 30 minutes that Mickey's Toontown is open.

Goofy's Playhouse ★★½

What it is A whimsical children's play area. **Scope and scale** Diversion. **When to go** Anytime.

DESCRIPTION AND COMMENTS Goofy's Playhouse is a small but nicely themed play area for the under-6 set. Usually not crowded, the playhouse is a pleasant place to let preschoolers ramble and parents relax while older sibs enjoy more adventurous attractions.

TOURING TIPS There's not a lot of shade, so visit early or late in the day.

Mickey's House and Meet Mickey ★★★

APPEAL BY AGE	PRESCHOOL ★★★★★		GRADE SCHOOL ★★★★		TEENS ★★★
YOUNG ADULTS ★★½		OVER 30 ★★★½			SENIORS ★★★

What it is Walk-through tour of Mickey's House and Movie Barn, ending with a personal visit with Mickey. **Scope and scale** Minor attraction. **When to go** Before 10:30 a.m. or after 5:30 p.m. **Duration of tour** 15–30 minutes (depending on the crowd). **Average wait in line per 100 people ahead of you** 20 minutes. **Touring speed** Slow.

DESCRIPTION AND COMMENTS Mickey's House is the starting point of a self-guided tour that winds through the famous mouse's house, into his backyard, past Pluto's doghouse, and then into Mickey's Movie Barn. This last stop harks back to the so-called "barn" studio where Walt Disney created a number of the earlier Mickey Mouse cartoons. Once in the Movie Barn, guests watch vintage Disney cartoons while awaiting admittance to Mickey's Dressing Room.

In small groups of one or two families, guests are ultimately conducted into the dressing room where Mickey awaits to pose for photos and sign autographs. The visit is not lengthy (2–4 minutes), but there is adequate time for all of the children to hug, poke, and admire the star.

TOURING TIPS The cynical observer will discern immediately that Mickey's House, backyard, Movie Barn, and so on are no more than a cleverly devised queuing area to deliver guests to Mickey's Dressing Room for the mouse encounter. For those with some vestige of child in their personalities, however, the preamble serves to heighten anticipation while providing the opportunity to get to know the corporate symbol on a more personal level. Mickey's House is well conceived and contains a lot of Disney memorabilia. You will notice that children touch everything as they proceed through the house, hoping to find some artifact that is not welded or riveted into the set (an especially tenacious child during one of our visits was actually able to rip a couple of books from a bookcase).

Meeting Mickey and touring his house are best done during the first 2 hours that Toontown is open or in the evening during *Fantasmic!* If meeting Mickey is at the top of your child's list, consider taking the Disneyland Railroad from Main Street to the Toontown/Fantasyland Station as soon as you enter the park. Some children are so obsessed with seeing Mickey that they cannot enjoy anything else until they get Mickey in the rearview mirror. (Mickey is not available during parades.)

Minnie's House ★★½

APPEAL BY AGE	PRESCHOOL ★★★★★		GRADE SCHOOL ★★★★	TEENS ★★
YOUNG ADULTS ★★½		OVER 30 ★★★		SENIORS ★★★★

What it is Walk-through exhibit and character-greeting opportunity. **Scope and scale** Minor attraction. **When to go** Before 11:30 a.m. or after 4:30 p.m. **Duration of tour** About 10 minutes. **Average wait in line per 100 people ahead of you** 12 minutes. **Touring speed** Slow.

DESCRIPTION AND COMMENTS Minnie's House consists of a self-guided tour through the various rooms and backyard of Mickey Mouse's main squeeze. Similar to Mickey's House, only predictably more feminine, Minnie's House likewise showcases some fun Disney memorabilia. Among the highlights of the short tour are the fanciful appliances in Minnie's kitchen. Like Mickey, Minnie is usually present to receive guests.

TOURING TIPS Minnie's House can't accommodate as many guests as Mickey's House can. See Minnie early and before Mickey to avoid waiting outdoors in a long queue. (Minnie is not available during parades.)

Miss Daisy, **Donald's Boat**   ★★

APPEAL BY AGE   PRESCHOOL ★★★★   **GRADE SCHOOL** ★★★★   **TEENS** ★½
YOUNG   ADULTS ★★½   **OVER 30** ★★½   **SENIORS** ★★

What it is Creative play area with a boat theme. **Scope and scale** Diversion. **When to go** Before 10:30 a.m. or after 4:30 p.m.

DESCRIPTION AND COMMENTS Another children's play area, this time with a tugboat theme. Children can climb nets, ring bells, survey Toontown from the captain's bridge, and scoot down slides. The idea is that Donald Duck (who, as everyone knows, lives in Duckburg) is visiting Toontown.

TOURING TIPS Kids more or less wander on and off the *Miss Daisy,* and usually there isn't any sort of organized line or queuing area. Enjoy this play area at your leisure and stay as long as you like.

Roger Rabbit's Car Toon Spin *(FastPass)*   ★★★½

APPEAL BY AGE   PRESCHOOL ★★★½   **GRADE SCHOOL** ★★★★   **TEENS** ★★★★
YOUNG   ADULTS ★★★½   **OVER 30** ★★★½   **SENIORS** ★★★★

What it is Track ride in the dark. **Scope and scale** Major attraction. **When to go** Before 10:30 a.m. or after 6:30 p.m. **Special comment** Ride with your kids, if you can stomach it. **Duration of ride** A little more than 3 minutes. **Average wait in line per 100 people ahead of you** 7 minutes. **Assumes** Full-capacity operation. **Loading speed** Moderate.

Dark   Rough   Queasy

DESCRIPTION AND COMMENTS A so-called dark ride where guests become part of a cartoon plot. The concept is that you are renting a taxicab for a tour of Toontown. As soon as your cab gets under way, however, weasels throw a slippery glop (known as dip) on the road, sending the cab into a more or less uncontrollable spin. This spinning continues as the cab passes through a variety of sets populated by cartoon and Audio-Animatronic characters and punctuated by simulated explosions. As a child of the 1960s put it, "It was like combining Mr. Toad's Wild Ride with the Mad Tea Party while tripping on LSD." The ride features an elaborate indoor queue and some of the best effects of any Disneyland cartoon dark ride, climaxing in a head-scratchingly effective "portable hole" gag that holds up under repeated viewing.

The main problem with the Car Toon Spin is that, because of the spinning, you are often pointed in the wrong direction to appreciate (or even see) many of the better visual effects. Furthermore, the story line is loose. The attraction lacks the continuity and humor of Splash Mountain or the suspense of The Haunted Mansion or Snow White's Scary Adventures.

The spinning, incidentally, can be controlled by the guests. If you don't want to spin, you don't have to. If you do elect to spin, you still will not be able to approach the eye-popping speed attainable on the teacups at the Mad Tea Party. Sluggish spinning aside, our advice for those who are at all susceptible to motion sickness is not to get near this ride if you are touring with anyone under 21 years of age.

A reader from Milford, Michigan, echoed our sentiments, lamenting:

The most disappointing ride to me was Roger Rabbit's Car Toon Spin. I stood in line for 45 minutes for a fun house ride, and the wheel was so difficult to operate that I spent most of my time trying to steer the bloody car and missed the point of the ride.

TOURING TIPS The ride is popular for its novelty, and it is one of the few Mickey's Toontown attractions that parents (with strong stomachs) can enjoy with their children. Because the ride stays fairly thronged with people all day long, ride in the first 90 minutes that Toontown is open, during parades or *Fantasmic!*, or in the hour before the park closes. The best move is to obtain FastPasses before 10:30 a.m., when the return time is an hour or less away, and then let your children enjoy the other Toontown attractions until it's time to ride.

TOMORROWLAND

LOCATED DIRECTLY TO THE RIGHT of the central hub is Tomorrowland. This themed area is a futuristic mix of rides and experiences that relates to technological development and what life will be like in the years to come.

Tomorrowland's design reflects a nostalgic vision of the future as imagined by dreamers and scientists in the 1920s and 1930s. Frozen in time, Tomorrowland conjures up visions of Buck Rogers (whom nobody under age 60 remembers), fanciful mechanical rockets, and metallic cities spread beneath towering obelisks. Disney refers to Tomorrowland as the "Future That Never Was." *Newsweek* dubbed it "retro-future." Since Disney acquired Marvel Comics and *Star Wars*, rumors have swirled about a major revamp of Tomorrowland focusing on those brands, but for now the land is a hodgepodge of unrelated intellectual properties vaguely linked by their sci-fi aesthetics.

Astro Orbitor ★★

APPEAL BY AGE	PRESCHOOL ★★★★½	GRADE SCHOOL ★★★★½	TEENS ★★★½
YOUNG ADULTS ★★★★½		OVER 30 ★★★	SENIORS ★

What it is Very mild midway-type thrill ride. **Scope and scale** Minor attraction. **When to go** Before 10 a.m. or during the hour before the park closes. **Special comment** Not worth the wait. **Duration of ride** 1½ minutes. **Average wait in line per 100 people ahead of you** 13 minutes. **Assumes** Normal staffing. **Loading speed** Slow.

Thumbs Up for the Whole Family

DESCRIPTION AND COMMENTS The Astro Orbitor is a visually appealing midway-type ride involving small rockets that rotate on arms around a central axis. Be aware that the Astro Orbitor flies higher and faster than Dumbo, and it frightens some small children.

Queasy

TOURING TIPS Astro Orbitor is slow to load and expendable on any schedule. If you want to take a preschooler on this ride, place your child in the seat first and then sit down yourself.

Autopia *(FastPass)* ★★½

What it is Drive-'em-yourself miniature cars. **Scope and scale** Minor attraction. **When to go** Before 10 a.m., after 5 p.m., or use FastPass. **Special comments** Boring for adults; great for preschoolers. Must be at least 32″ tall to ride, and at least one guest in car must be 54″. **Duration of ride** Approximately 4½ minutes. **Average wait in line per 100 people ahead of you** 6 minutes. **Assumes** 35 cars operating on each track. **Loading speed** Slow.

DESCRIPTION AND COMMENTS An elaborate miniature freeway with gasoline-powered cars that will travel at speeds of up to 7 miles per hour. The attraction design—with its sleek cars, auto noises, highway signs, and even an "off-road" section—is quite alluring. In fact, however, the cars poke along on a track that leaves the driver with little to do. Pretty ho-hum for most adults and teenagers, but at least it's much more visually stimulating than the unthemed Magic Kingdom version.

TOURING TIPS This ride is appealing to the eye but definitely expendable on a schedule for adults. Preschoolers, however, love it. If your preschooler is too short to drive, place the child behind the wheel and allow him or her to steer (the car runs on a guide rail) while you work the foot pedal.

A mom from North Billerica, Massachusetts, writes:

> *I was truly amazed by the number of adults in line. Please emphasize to your readers that these cars travel on a guided path and are not a whole lot of fun. The only reason I could think of for adults to be in line was an insane desire to go on absolutely every ride. The cars also tend to pile up at the end, so it takes almost as long to get off as it did to get on. Parents riding with their preschoolers should keep the car going as slow as it can without stalling. This prolongs the preschooler's joy and decreases the time you will have to wait at the end.*

FastPass is only offered on busier days and doesn't work very well at Autopia. It's typical for the wait in the FastPass return line to exceed 20 minutes. If Autopia ranks high on your pop chart, you might be better off riding the first hour the park is open and using the standby line. At press time, Autopia FastPasses were unavailable due to construction on the nearby Innoventions building.

Buzz Lightyear Astro Blasters *(FastPass)* ★★★★

What it is Space-travel interactive dark ride. **Scope and scale** Major attraction. **When to go** Before 10:30 a.m. or after 6 p.m. **Special comment** A real winner! **Duration of ride** About 4½ minutes. **Average wait in line per 100 people ahead of you** 3 minutes. **Loading speed** Fast.

DESCRIPTION AND COMMENTS Based on the space-commando character Buzz Lightyear from *Toy Story,* the marginal story line has you and Buzz trying to save the universe from the evil Emperor Zurg. The indoor ride is interactive—you can spin your car and shoot simulated laser cannons at Zurg and his minions.

A similar attraction at the Magic Kingdom at Walt Disney World is one of the most popular attractions in the park. The Disneyland version, situated across from Star Tours, is much the same except mobile guns allow more accurate aiming. Don't forget to smile! You can e-mail an in-ride photo to yourself for free from kiosks at the exit.

Praise for Buzz Lightyear is almost universal. This comment from a Massachusetts couple is typical:

Buzz Lightyear was the surprise hit of our trip! My husband and I enjoyed competing for the best score so much that we went on this ride several times during our stay. Definitely a must.

TOURING TIPS Each car is equipped with two laser cannons and a score-keeping display. Each score-keeping display is independent, so you can compete with your riding partner. A joystick allows you to spin the car to line up the various targets. Each time you pull the trigger, you'll release a red laser beam that you can see hitting or missing the target. Most folks' first ride is occupied with learning how to use the equipment (fire off individual shots as opposed to keeping the trigger depressed) and figuring out how the targets work. The next ride (as with certain potato chips, one is not enough), you'll surprise yourself by how much better you do. *Unofficial Guide* readers are unanimous in their praise of Buzz Lightyear. Some guests, in fact, spend several hours on the attraction, riding again and again. See Buzz Lightyear early in the morning after riding Peter Pan's Flight, Matterhorn Bobsleds, and Star Tours. At press time, Buzz Lightyear was offering FastPasses while Autopia's FastPass access is unavailable.

Disneyland Monorail System   ★★★

What it is Scenic transportation. **Scope and scale** Major attraction. **When to go** During the hot, crowded period of the day (11:30 a.m.–5 p.m.). **Special comments** Nice, relaxing ride with some interesting views of the park; take the monorail to Downtown Disney for lunch. **Duration of ride** 12–15 minutes round-trip. **Average wait in line per 100 people ahead of you** 10 minutes. **Assumes** 3 monorails operating. **Loading speed** Moderate–fast.

Thumbs Up for the Whole Family

DESCRIPTION AND COMMENTS The monorail is a futuristic transportation ride that affords the only practical opportunity for escaping the park during the crowded lunch period and early afternoon. Boarding at the Tomorrowland monorail station, you can commute to the Disneyland Resort hotels and Downtown Disney. The monorail provides a tranquil trip with a nice view of Downtown Disney, Disney California Adventure, Fantasyland, and Tomorrowland. The Mark VII monorails have a sleek, retro look but can get quite hot inside during the summer (no air-conditioning!).

TOURING TIPS We recommend using the monorail to commute to Downtown Disney for a quiet, relaxing lunch away from the crowds and the heat. If you only want to experience the ride, go whenever you wish; the wait to board is usually 15–25 minutes except in the 2 hours before closing when everyone tries to leave at once. Also note that during busy times, you may be required to disembark and then queue up to reboard at Downtown Disney. The monorail may suspend services from 1 hour before the Disneyland Park's evening fireworks until 45 minutes afterward, and it ceases to bring guests into the park 30 minutes before closing.

Disneyland Railroad

DESCRIPTION AND COMMENTS The Disneyland Railroad makes a regular stop at the Tomorrowland Railroad Station. The wait to board here is usually short.

Finding Nemo Submarine Voyage ★★★★

APPEAL BY AGE	PRESCHOOL ★★★★		GRADE SCHOOL ★★★★	TEENS ★★★
YOUNG ADULTS ★★★		OVER 30 ★★★		SENIORS ★★★½

What it is Simulated submarine ride. **Scope and scale** Headliner. **When to go** Before 10 a.m. or during evening parades or fireworks. **Duration of ride** 11½ minutes. **Average wait in line per 100 people ahead of you** 7½ minutes. **Assumes** All 8 subs operating. **Loading speed** Slow–moderate.

DESCRIPTION AND COMMENTS The Finding Nemo Submarine Voyage ride is based on the story line of the hit Disney-Pixar animated feature *Finding Nemo.* Here you board a submarine in a loading area situated below the Disneyland monorail station in Tomorrowland. After a quick lap of the open-air lagoon, the sub passes through a waterfall and inside to follow the general *Finding Nemo* story. Special effects center on a combination of traditional Audio-Animatronics and, once you're inside the dark interior of the building, what appear to be rear-projection screens, underwater, at a distance of 3–10 feet from the sub's windows. Encased in rock and shipwrecks, the screens are natural looking and allow the animated characters to appear three-dimensionally in the undersea world. Other elements include traveling through a minefield and a sea of jellyfish (very cool) and entering the mouth of a whale. The onboard sound system allows the story to "travel" from front to back of the sub, and the visual experience is different depending on what seat you're in.

The attraction is well done. You don't have to be a Nemo fan to be impressed by the scale and effects. It's not fast-paced but, rather, leisurely in the way that Pirates of the Caribbean is.

TOURING TIPS The attraction's capacity is only about 900 guests per hour, a shockingly small capacity for a headliner attraction. Further, owing to the low carrying capacity, the subs are not a good candidate for FastPass (all FastPasses would be gone before noon).

Though Finding Nemo isn't as immensely popular as when it first opened, a sizable percentage of the guests on hand at park opening head straight for the subs—only if you are literally among the first 70 people to enter the park and arrive at the subs will you be rewarded with a short wait. But here's the kicker: Adding the time it takes to reach the subs, wait to board, ride, and disembark, you will invest 35–70 minutes to ride Finding Nemo first thing in the morning, sacrificing in the process the most crowd-free touring period of the day for the other popular attractions. Loading is especially slow during early entry, as it often takes an hour before all the subs are brought into service.

We've determined that, taking the day as a whole, you make much better use of your time enjoying Space Mountain, Splash Mountain, Peter Pan's Flight, and other popular attractions during the first hour the park is open and saving the subs for later, when a parade, fireworks show, or *Fantasmic!* has siphoned a large number of guests from the line. Incidentally, arriving 15 minutes before a parade or other presentation is not an arbitrary suggestion—during this time window, the Finding Nemo line (or lines at other popular attractions) will be its shortest. The last 30 minutes before park closing is another good time to get in line.

Claustrophobes may not be comfortable with the experience, even though the sub doesn't actually submerge (we saw one 30-ish woman who started hyperventilating before the sub left the dock). Children may be scared of the same thing, or of the encounter with sharks (they keep their distance). The sharks here are a bit less menacing than in the movie too.

The bright-yellow subs use electric power to minimize noise and pollution. The subs fit 40 people. It's not easy to get 40 aboard, however, because the seats are narrow and a few guests take up two. Ideally, large guests should aim to be in one of the four seats at the front or back, but this may be difficult to negotiate.

Wheelchair-bound guests or those who can't get down the spiral staircase into the sub can view the experience from a special topside viewing room (seats about six able-bodied persons plus two wheelchairs). With the exception of one small animated effect, the visual is identical (perhaps faster), but despite a large monitor, the creatures appear smaller than when viewing them through a real porthole. The wait for the alternate viewing area is usually brief (ask a cast member how to bypass the standby line), and there are Mickeys hidden in the dive lockers inside.

A reader from Sydney, Australia, disagrees with our Finding Nemo rating, writing:

Finding Nemo was the most overrated ride. Perhaps it would rate high for those younger than 8 years old, but for our group it was one of the worst rides. It was boring, had rushing water, and moved slowly. What made it worse was that it had a high rating, and this raised expectations.

Jedi Training Academy ★★★½

APPEAL BY AGE	PRESCHOOL ★★★½	GRADE SCHOOL ★★★★★	TEENS ★★★★½
YOUNG ADULTS ★★★½		OVER 30 ★★★★	SENIORS ★★★★

What it is Live entertainment where young audience members are trained to be Jedis. **Scope and scale** Major diversion. **When to go** See *Times Guide* for performance times. **Duration of show** 25 minutes.

DESCRIPTION AND COMMENTS Staged at the Tomorrowland Terrace Theater, the *Jedi Training Academy* recruits 30 young volunteers and trains them to fight with a light saber (an elegant, if plastic, weapon). The training consists of practicing a surprisingly long set of fencing-style moves while the audience gets to enjoy the minimal comprehension by some of the youngest Jedis. Just when the training ends, Darth Vader and Darth Maul arrive with a couple of Stormtroopers, and the young recruits meet them in "battle," with each Jedi getting his or her turn to take a whack at a Darth. All volunteers are awarded a *Jedi Training Academy* diploma. It's a great photo op for parents and a major hoot for everyone else. For a London, England, mother, Jedi boot camp was a highlight of the trip:

My 8-year-old son literally cried with joy after participating in the Jedi expe-
rience in Tomorrowland. You advise sitting in the front two rows to be picked,
but actually, they picked my son only after my husband launched him onto
his shoulders to draw their attention. I noticed that they especially picked
other kids on their parents' shoulders.

TOURING TIPS There are two prime viewing locations: standing room on the
show floor underneath the overhang, and seating at the Tomorrowland
Terrace restaurant. Only 10–20 tables have decent views of the show, so
make sure to stake them out early. Otherwise, there is plenty of standing
room space around the sides of the stage.

To be chosen to participate, arrive 20–30 minutes early and seat your
child in the first couple of rows surrounding the stage. Jedis look for energetic and excited children to recruit; wearing a *Star Wars* T-shirt helps, but
don't bring your own light saber because those are supplied. While participation doesn't require rushing at rope drop to sign up like at Walt Disney
World, if you are used to that system (like this father from London, Ontario),
you might find Disneyland's selection system somewhat haphazard:

The way WDW handles distribution of spots for Jedi Training Academy *is*
better. You have a ticket, and you know what time to come back. At DLR you
have to go to the show and try, and try, and try again with no guarantee that
the Jedi Master will choose your child.

Marvel and Star Wars Exhibits

DESCRIPTION AND COMMENTS At press time, the circular Innoventions building was closed for renovation. No reopening date or new name had been
officially announced, but we expect it to reemerge in late 2015 with Marvel superhero meet and greets (with Thor and Captain America) on the
upper level and interactive displays of *Star Wars* memorabilia on the bottom floor. There shouldn't be much wait to enter the building, but certain
exhibits (especially the meet and greets) will draw long, slow queues.
Check **touringplans.com** for updates as they become available.

Space Mountain *(FastPass)* ★★★★½

APPEAL BY AGE	PRESCHOOL ★★★★★	GRADE SCHOOL ★★★★½	TEENS ★★★★½
YOUNG ADULTS ★★★★½	OVER 30 ★★★★½		SENIORS ★★★½

What it is Roller coaster in the dark. **Scope and scale** Super-headliner. **When to go**
Right after the park opens or use FastPass. **Special comment** Must be 40″ tall to
ride. **Duration of ride** 2¾ minutes. **Average wait in line per 100 people ahead of**
you 3½ minutes. **Loading speed** Moderate.

Dark   Scary   Lose Things   Queasy   Rough   Muss Your 'Do

DESCRIPTION AND COMMENTS
Space Mountain is an indoor
roller coaster with a theme of
high-speed interstellar travel.
Space Mountain is a designer version of the Wild Mouse, a midway ride
that's been around for at least 50 years. There are no long drops or
swooping hills as there are on a traditional roller coaster—only quick,
unexpected turns and small drops. Disney's contribution essentially was
to add a space theme to the Wild Mouse and put it in the dark. And this
does indeed make the Mouse seem wilder.

The most surprising thing about Space Mountain is its aesthetic beauty.
The vistas of the solar system and the stars, the distant galaxies, and

passing comets are intoxicating and very realistic. Because you can't see the track or anticipate where your vehicle will go, your eyes are free to feast on the rich visuals. Disney transforms Space Mountain into Ghost Galaxy for Halloween, adding atmospheric audio and video projections of an angry space ghost (no, not that Space Ghost) chasing you through the cosmos. The interstellar specter is more goofy than genuinely scary, but it makes a fun novelty for the spooky season. Nighttime video projections, which make the iconic conical building look like it's crumbling to dust or crackling with electricity, are the most impressive element of the overlay.

TOURING TIPS Space Mountain is one of the park's most popular attractions. Experience it immediately after the park opens or use FastPass.

Starcade

DESCRIPTION AND COMMENTS Starcade is nothing more than a moderately sized electronic-games arcade. The most interesting items here are a score of vintage arcade machines such as *TRON* and *Pac-Man*. Note the full-size versions of *Fix It Felix Jr.,* the fictional coin-op from the movie *Wreck-It Ralph*.

TOURING TIPS Enjoy your time in the area with a pocket full of tokens.

Star Tours—The Adventures Continue *(FastPass)* ★★★★

APPEAL BY AGE PRESCHOOL ★★★★   **GRADE SCHOOL** ★★★★★   **TEENS** ★★★★½
YOUNG ADULTS ★★★★½   **OVER 30** ★★★★½   **SENIORS** ★★★★★

What it is Space-flight simulation ride. **Scope and scale** Headliner. **When to go** Before 11 a.m. or use FastPass. **Special comments** A blast; not to be missed. Frightens many small children; expectant mothers advised against riding; must be 40″ tall to ride. **Duration of ride** Approximately 7 minutes. **Average wait in line per 100 people ahead of you** 6 minutes. **Assumes** 4 simulators operating. **Loading speed** Moderate.

Scary   Queasy   Rough

DESCRIPTION AND COMMENTS When Disney's first modern flight simulator ride debuted in 1987, guests lined up for hours for their hyperspace voyage into a galaxy far, far away. But time and technology march on, and Star Tours received a top-to-bottom overhaul in 2011 with cutting-edge digital 3-D screens (the sharpest and clearest that we've ever seen) and in-cabin Audio-Animatronic figures of C-3PO, your golden droid pilot. During your inevitably turbulent travels, you'll bump, twist, and dive into a who's who of *Star Wars* icons, with heroes Master Yoda and Admiral "It's A Trap!" Akbar on your side, and villains Darth Vader and Boba Fett on your back. Jedi junkies will want to know that the ride takes place between episodes III and IV, so you'll be visiting planets from both the classic trilogy—such as icy Hot and arid Tatooine—and the not-so-classic prequels, including Geonosis (home of the dreaded Death Star) and Naboo (home of the equally dreaded Jar Jar Binks).

The big twist is that the six possible cosmic destinations and five celebrity cameos are randomly combined into 54 different story variations, giving the attraction unprecedented re-ridability (though you may see all 11 potential ride elements in as few as three voyages). Fans of the former ride will be thrilled to find a wealth of references (along with hidden Disney characters and *Star Wars* inside jokes) inside the detailed queue, and those made uncomfortable by the old ride's jerkiness will be surprised at how smooth and well-synchronized the reprogrammed experience now is.

TOURING TIPS Demand for the ride has died down since its grand reopening. But with only two-thirds the carrying capacity of Walt Disney World's version, Disneyland's Star Tours still sees hour-plus waits on busy days, so ride as early in the day as possible or grab a FastPass. If you have young children (or anyone) who are apprehensive about this attraction, ask the attendant about switching off (see page 145). You can track the ride combinations you've seen on your phone at **startourspassport.net.**

Tomorrowland Theater ★★★

APPEAL BY AGE	PRESCHOOL ★★★	GRADE SCHOOL ★★★½	TEENS ★★★
YOUNG ADULTS ★★★½		OVER 30 ★★★½	SENIORS ★★★½

What it is 3-D film with special effects. **Scope and scale** Minor attraction. **When to go** Anytime. **Special comment** The loud, intense show with tactile effects frightens some young children. **Duration of show** Approximately 15 minutes. **Probable waiting time** 15 minutes.

Loud   Scary

DESCRIPTION AND COMMENTS The Tomorrowland Theater, located directly in front of Space Mountain, was originally enclosed to serve as a 3-D theater for the 1986 debut of *Captain EO,* a sci-fi music video starring Michael Jackson. *Captain EO* was replaced in 1987 by *Honey, I Shrunk the Audience,* a 3-D film with in-theater effects based on the Rick Moranis comedy franchise. Disney brought Jackson back for a limited engagement following the pop star's 2009 death and then pulled the plug on *EO*'s exploits for good in 2014.

Currently, the Tomorrowland Theater hosts previews of upcoming Disney cinematic releases, featuring extended film clips enhanced with 4-D tactile effects, such as wind, water, or moving seats.

The Tomorrowland Theater isn't on our must-do list. But if you are interested in the featured film, it makes a fine air-conditioned distraction, either on your second day in the park or when everything else has too long a line.

TOURING TIPS Shows usually begin on the hour and continue about every 20 minutes throughout the day. Even during busier times, you should be able to get into the next show without issue.

The sound level can be earsplitting, frightening some young children. Some adults report that the loud sound track is distracting, even uncomfortable. Avoid seats in the first several rows; if you sit too close to the screen, the 3-D images don't focus properly. If the bouncing floor bothers you, ask for a stationary seat in the last row.

LIVE ENTERTAINMENT *and* SPECIAL EVENTS

LIVE ENTERTAINMENT IN THE FORM OF BANDS, Disney character appearances, parades, singing and dancing, and ceremonies further enliven and add color to Disneyland Park on a daily basis. During the off-season, certain evening spectaculars (such as the fireworks and *Fantasmic!*) may be performed only on weekends. For specific information about what's happening on the day you visit, check the daily entertainment schedule in the *Times Guide.* Be forewarned, however, that if you are on a tight schedule, it is impossible to both see the park's featured attractions and take in the numerous and varied live performances offered. In our one-day touring plans, starting on page 265, we exclude the live performances in favor of seeing as much of the park as time permits. This is a tactical decision based on the fact that the parades and *Fantasmic!,* Disneyland Park's river spectacular, siphon crowds away from the more popular rides, shortening waiting lines.

The color and pageantry of live events around the park are an integral part of the Disneyland Park entertainment mix and a persuasive argument for second-day touring. Though live entertainment is varied, plentiful, and nearly continuous throughout the day, several productions are preeminent.

Fantasmic! (FastPass) ★★★★★

**APPEAL BY AGE   PRESCHOOL ★★★★   GRADE SCHOOL ★★★★½   TEENS ★★★★½
YOUNG ADULTS ★★★★   OVER 30 ★★★★½   SENIORS ★★★★★**

Loud   Scary

DESCRIPTION AND COMMENTS *Fantasmic!* is a mixed-media show presented one or more times each evening that the park is open late (10 p.m. or later). Staged at the end of Tom Sawyer Island opposite the Frontierland and New Orleans Square waterfronts, *Fantasmic!* was, at its debut, the most extraordinary and ambitious outdoor spectacle ever attempted in any theme park. Starring Mickey Mouse in his role as the sorcerer's apprentice from *Fantasia,* the production uses lasers, images projected on a shroud of mist, fireworks, lighting effects, and music in combinations so stunning that you can scarcely believe what you have seen.

The plot is simple: good versus evil. The story gets lost in all the special effects at times, but no matter—it is the spectacle, not the story line, that is so overpowering. While *beautiful, stunning,* and *powerful* are words that immediately come to mind, they fail to convey the uniqueness of this presentation, which includes a 45-foot-tall full-bodied fire-breathing dragon (nicknamed Murphy) for the finale. It could be argued, with some validity, that *Fantasmic!* alone is worth the price of Disneyland Park admission. Needless to say, we rate *Fantasmic!* as not to be missed.

TOURING TIPS After years of watching guests stake out prime viewing spots along the edge of the New Orleans Square and Frontierland waterfronts as much as 4 hours in advance, Disney implemented a FastPass-only policy for *Fantasmic!* that is very similar to the one enforced at DCA's *World of Color.* There are now a few ways to see *Fantasmic!,* none of which should require showing up more than an hour before showtime.

The easiest method is to grab a FastPass ticket early in the day. Distribution of *Fantasmic!* FastPass tickets takes place on Big Thunder Trail, across from the entrance to Big Thunder Ranch. That's the path to the left of Big Thunder Mountain Railroad as you approach Fantasyland from Frontierland. FastPass tickets are distributed until 1 hour before showtime or until they run out, whichever comes first. When *Fantasmic!* FastPass was first introduced, we were seeing tickets run out entirely by noon. But since the introduction of new 60th-anniversary entertainment, demand for *Fantasmic!* has died down a bit. Tickets for the first showing are often available until early afternoon, and the second show (when scheduled) can

The Smith family from East Wimple stakes out their viewing spot for Fantasmic!

sometimes be snagged until just an hour or so before showtime.

The general FastPass viewing sections (in the order they are distributed) are Yellow, the entrance of which is located near the petrified tree (across from The Golden Horseshoe) in Frontierland; Green, located on the bridge over Pirates of the Caribbean's entrance; and Blue, in front of The Haunted Mansion in New Orleans Square. The color of the viewing section is printed on the ticket, and that color is the only section the ticket holder is allowed to enter. Yellow, the largest section, watches from along the waterfront to the right of the center island. Guests in the front half of Yellow are required to sit on the ground during the show, as are all guests in the dining section, while all those in Blue (located in the center and left, directly behind the dining section) and on the bridge in Green must stand. You can't request a specific section; before pulling your pass, ask a cast member at the FastPass machines which section they are dispensing and which ones are gone.

Fantasmic! general FastPass return windows begin 1 hour before showtime and end when the show begins. If you need to stand right at the railing in the heart of the splash zone, you'll want to be the first inside the viewing pen when it opens. Otherwise, you're best off arriving about 20–30 minutes before curtain and watching from the rear, taking advantage of any available elevation. Entry can be a bit confusing, so pay careful attention to your kids; look for colored lights indicating your section's entrance, and follow the flashlight-wielding cast members' directions.

Fantasmic! FastPasses are disconnected from the rest of Disneyland's FastPass machines, meaning that if you obtain a *Fantasmic!* FastPass, you can also immediately get one for another attraction.

Fantasmic! dining packages are available at Blue Bayou ($66.96 for adults and $27 for children, including tax but not tip) and River Belle Terrace ($45.36 for adults and $23.76 for children, including tax but not tip). Dining packages include a three-course meal and a FastPass ticket for a special preferred viewing area. The Blue Bayou package also includes a *Fantasmic!* themed seat cushion; all guests in the full-service dining FastPass section must sit on the ground during the show. The dinner package at Blue Bayou begins at 4 p.m. and River Belle Terrace at 3 p.m. While the meals are certainly overpriced, especially in comparison to the similar *World of Color* packages next door, the ease of entry and expansive elbow room afforded by preferred FastPasses are almost worth the expense.

For those looking to spend a little less money, there is also the *Fantasmic!* On-the-Go Dining Package ($24.83 for adults and $15.11 for children, including tax) at Aladdin's Oasis in Adventureland. This package includes a boxed meal, dessert, bottled beverage, and a general FastPass ticket. On-the-Go Dining Packages can be purchased noon-7 p.m. Based on the quality of the food and the recent ease of securing free FastPasses, we can't recommend the On-the-Go package unless you arrive late on a busy day and all other options are sold out. Reservations for all *Fantasmic!* dining packages can be made online at **disneyland.disney.go.com/dining/disney land/fantasmic-dinner-packages** or by calling ☎ 714-781-3463.

Fantasmic! viewing spots are first come, first served for all guests, including those in the FastPass dining-experience viewing section, which is located along the waterfront from center stage to Tom Sawyer Island. You can enter the dining section near the Harbour Galley restaurant beginning 30 minutes before each showtime, and the earlier you get in, the better spot you will obtain.

Disney also offers limited standby viewing for all showings. Be warned that the standby viewing area is not the best spot to see the show due to its location at the far left end of the viewing area. You're going to be looking at the side of the show rather than the front of it. The standby line begins 1 hour before showtime and is located between the Harbour Galley restaurant and the Tom Sawyer Island raft dock. The standby viewing section is small and fills up quickly. Plan to get in line as soon as it opens 1 hour before showtime. If you do not have a FastPass ticket, you will be aggressively shooed away from every available vantage point outside the designated standby section.

No matter which method you use, you'll probably spend some time sitting around waiting. A mom from Lummi Island, Washington, dismantled her Disney stroller to make a nest:

We used the snap-off cover on the rental stroller to sit on during Fantasmic! *since the ground was really cold.*

Along similar lines, a middle-aged New York man wrote, saying:

Your excellent guidebook also served as a seat cushion while seated on the ground waiting for the show to begin. Make future editions thicker for greater comfort.

Rain and wind conditions sometimes cause *Fantasmic!* to be canceled. Unfortunately, Disney officials usually do not make a final decision about whether to proceed or cancel until just before showtime. Note that if you purchased a *Fantasmic!* dining package earlier in the day, you will not be refunded if a show is canceled.

If you see the first *Fantasmic!* showing, stay in place afterward for the nightly fireworks, which should start a few minutes later. If attending the second performance, you'll be prevented from entering the New Orleans waterfront until all the earlier guests have exited the viewing areas.

Finally, make sure to hang on to children during *Fantasmic!* and to give

them explicit instructions for regrouping in the event that you become separated. Be especially vigilant when the crowd disperses after the show.

Incidentally, if you invested in the Made with Magic light-up ears that
synchronize with Disney California Adventure's *World of Color* show (see
page 305), you'll find that they interact with *Fantasmic!* as well. At times,
an exclusive viewing area may be offered for hat holders, intensifying the
impact of the illumination effects.

PARADES

DISNEY THEME PARKS ARE FAMOUS THE WORLD OVER for
their parades. Currently, there is a parade every day in late afternoon or
early evening and another at night. On days when the park closes late
(10 p.m.–midnight), each parade may run twice. The parades are full-
blown Disney productions with some combination of floats, huge
inflated balloons of the characters, marching bands, old-time vehicles,
dancers, and, of course, dozens of costumed Disney characters. Themes
for the parades vary from time to time, and a special holiday parade is
always produced for Christmas. Mickey's Soundsational Parade,
Disneyland's latest daytime processional, features a whimsical marching
band theme with floats dedicated to *The Princess and the Frog, The
Little Mermaid,* and a Keith Moon–channeling Drummer Mickey. The
parade is well worth watching, from the stick-twirling drum-line kickoff
to the *Mary Poppins* finale. A brief *Frozen*-themed pre-parade prior to
the first Soundsational performance offers a glimpse of Anna and Elsa
minus the massive meet and greet queue.

Parades always draw thousands of guests from the attraction lines.
We recommend, therefore, watching from the departure point. With
this strategy you can enjoy the parade, and then while the parade is
continuing on its route, take advantage of the diminished lines at the
attractions. Watching a parade that begins in Fantasyland from Small
World Mall affords the greatest mobility in terms of accessing other
areas of the park when the parade has passed.

Main Street is the most crowded area from which to watch a parade
when the route begins at Town Square. The opposite is true when the
parade begins in Fantasyland. The upper platform of the Main Street
Station affords the best viewing perspective along the route. The best
time to get a position on the platform is when the parade begins in
Fantasyland. When this happens, good spots on the platform are available right up to the time the parade begins. When you are at the end
of the parade route, you can assume that it will take the parade 15–18
minutes to get to you.

Keep an eye on your children during parades and give them explicit
instructions for regrouping in the event that you get separated. Children constantly jockey for better viewing positions. A few wiggles
this way and a few wiggles the other, and presto, they are lost in the
crowd. Finally, be especially vigilant when the crowd starts dispersing
after the parade. Thousands of people suddenly strike out in different
directions, creating a perfect situation for losing a child or two.

PAINT THE NIGHT Disneyland's newest nightly parade, Paint the Night (★★★★★), is patterned after the processional that debuted at Hong Kong Disneyland in 2014 (with a few new additions) as part of Disneyland's Diamond Anniversary entertainment additions. Inspired in part by the original Main Street Electrical Parade, these brand-new floats are covered in 1.5 million LEDs. Each float represents a classic Disney or Pixar film, as scenes from *Monsters Inc., Cars, Toy Story, Beauty and the Beast, The Little Mermaid,* and (wait for it . . .) *Frozen* are brought to life by a cast of more than 75 performers, who bounce down the route to the upbeat sound track of *Wreck-It Ralph*'s "When Can I See You Again?" by pop artist Owl City (your kids will know who that is). Keep an ear out for musical nods to "Baroque Hoedown," the old Electrical Parade's synth-tastic theme song.

These superbright displays go far beyond earlier nighttime pageants and include character puppets with digitally animated faces, a tractor-trailer full of floating 3-D designs, and a kinetic Sorcerer's Apprentice sculpture whose twisting motion defies description. In our opinion, Paint the Night is one of Disney's best nighttime parades ever—not to be missed.

On nights with two scheduled Paint the Night parades, the first performance will start at It's a Small World, travel past the west side of Matterhorn Bobsleds, go around the Tomorrowland side of Central Plaza, head down Main Street, and then circle Town Square counterclockwise. The second performance will begin at Town Square and run the route in the opposite direction. Most guests watch from Central Plaza or Main Street. The viewing area in front of It's a Small World will fill up last, so we recommend checking there if you need a spot. Keep in mind that this is a new parade for the 60th anniversary celebration and has already proven very popular with guests. On busy days, you may need to devote more than an hour of time to make sure you secure a good spot for the parade.

The parade route will fill up a couple of hours early for the first showing, so we recommend grabbing a spot for the fireworks, and then immediately getting a spot for the second performance of Paint the Night. Any spot along the parade route will offer the same experience, so you shouldn't worry if you can't see the parade on Main Street. Once the parade has started, count on gridlock all along the route, especially on Main Street. Due to aggressive crowd-control restrictions on the sidewalks, you're best off entering or exiting the park via the backstage breezeways (if open) or Emporium shops.

LIVE ENTERTAINMENT THROUGHOUT THE PARK

PARADES AND *FANTASMIC!* MAKE UP only a part of the daily live-entertainment offerings at Disneyland Park. The following is an incomplete list of other performances and events that are scheduled with some regularity and that require no reservations.

DISNEY CHARACTER APPEARANCES Disney characters appear at random throughout the park but are routinely present in Mickey's Toontown, in Fantasyland, and on Main Street. Behind Frontierland's

Big Thunder Ranch petting zoo, you'll find an outdoor arena stage where jamborees are held throughout the day, featuring crafts, music, and meet and greets with often-obscure characters. An irregularly used greeting area that sometimes features Aladdin and Jasmine is located at Aladdin's Oasis in Adventureland (see the *Times Guide*). Disney princesses are on call daily at the Royal Hall at Fantasy Faire (see page 238). An elaborate character-greeting area, Pixie Hollow, situated on the path connecting Matterhorn Bobsleds to the central hub, accumulates substantial wait times to meet Tinker Bell and a squad of her buddies.

DISNEY CHARACTER MEALS   Disney characters join guests for breakfast each morning until 11 a.m. at the **Plaza Inn** on Main Street, **Disney's PCH Grill** at Paradise Pier Hotel, and **Storytellers Café** at the Grand Californian Hotel. Disney characters also join guests for breakfast and dinner at **Goofy's Kitchen** at the Disneyland Hotel. **Ariel's Grotto** at Disney California Adventure serves breakfast and lunch with Ariel and friends.

DISNEYLAND FOREVER   As part of its Diamond Anniversary celebration, Disneyland retired the popular *Remember . . . Dreams Come True* fireworks spectacular (originally created for the park's 50th birthday) in favor of the all-new *Disneyland Forever* (★★★★½) show. Created by extravaganza expert Steve Davison, who designed *Wishes* and *World of Color,* this latest production runs the full gamut of special effects: a rousing score, castle lighting, lasers, and an impressive flight from the fairy Tinker Bell—not to mention spectacular fireworks effects. After an introduction evoking the orange-tree groves that originally covered Anaheim, the show sails through memorable musical vignettes from beloved Disney movies.

A major feature of this fireworks show are the immersive projections mapped onto Sleeping Beauty Castle, the Main Street buildings, the facade of It's a Small World, and mist screens on the Rivers of America, creating amazing visual effects. Digital imagery paints landmarks around the park, transforming them into coral reefs, jungle forests, or an African savanna. Via the projections, Main Street buildings may be covered in honey during the Winnie the Pooh segment, or look like they're submerged in water during the Little Mermaid segment. It's a beautiful effect that works well.

This pyrotechnic tribute to Disney's films also features a flyby from Nemo the fish as he "swims" his way toward the Matterhorn, which appears as the smoldering volcano known as Mount Wanahakalugi. *Disneyland Forever* also features an obligatory upbeat theme song, "Live the Magic." A second original song, an inspirational ballad called "Kiss Goodnight," was composed by Disney Legend Richard Sherman; it was supposed to play as guests exited but seems to have been cut because crowds lingered too long listening to it.

Disneyland Forever is a fantastic finale to your day in the park, particularly if you can see it from the proper perspective (see discussion following). For some lifelong Disneyland devotees, it won't have quite the same resonance as the 50th-anniversary spectacular (watch *World of Color* next door if you want vintage attraction references), and a number of the featured songs are already overused around the resort. But if an eye-popping aerial extravaganza of Disney standards is what you seek, *Disneyland Forever* more than fits the bill.

We rate this show as not to be missed, but seeing it poses some serious challenges that you should be aware of. Without a doubt, the area around the central hub is the best vantage point for watching *Disneyland Forever*. For the most immersive impression from the projection mapping effects, you'll want to stand in the middle of Main Street, from the Carnation Café up to the Coke Corner. Get too close to the castle and you'll have to turn around to see the animated shop fronts; stand in Town Square at the flagpole or train station and the castle projections will be just postage stamps.

Unfortunately, every guest in the park won't fit in that sweet spot at the same time. Fortunately, the *Disneyland Forever* fireworks were specifically designed to look good from multiple locations throughout the park. If you want the ideal view, you'll need to camp out on the curb (possibly for hours) before the evening's first Paint the Night performance and then claim your fireworks position as soon as the parade passes. Alternatively, slowly browse through Main Street's candy shop while the parade is concluding or linger on the Adventureland side of the hub (where the parade does not pass) and then slip out the exit and into the street following the finale float. Be warned— the crushing crowds can make this aggravating for adults and almost impossible with stroller-bound kids in tow.

The same projections seen along Main Street, but on a smaller scale, can be seen when viewing the fireworks in front of It's a Small World. You can face the attraction facade and then turn around to catch the Matterhorn effects. You'll be missing out on the bevy of fireworks and flames that shoot out of Sleeping Beauty Castle. But It's a Small World will be your best option if Main Street is full.

Your third option is viewing from the Rivers of America. Fireworks similar to those launched around the castle are shot from Tom Sawyer Island, and projections are mapped onto the mist screens used in *Fantasmic!*, but they're not as sharp as the ones projected on the other two locations. You'll also miss most or all of the flames and flying figures. The benefit of viewing from Rivers of America is that, if you have a FastPass for the first showing of *Fantasmic!*, you can stay in your spot (seated even, if in the right section) through the fireworks. Though you get the least impressive view from here, it's the least stressful way to experience *Disneyland Forever* and can be very enjoyable if you haven't already seen it from a better location.

Finally, be forewarned that the *Disneyland Forever* fireworks may be canceled for safety reasons with only a few minutes' notice if there are stiff winds at upper altitudes, even if the air at ground level seems calm. During one of our weeklong visits, the fireworks were nixed a full 40% of the time, which is a fairly frustrating percentage; you've never heard a collective groan like 50,000 people learning they've waited for nothing. For this reason, we don't recommend that you build your night around the fireworks—as wondrous as they are—if you only have one night at the resort.

DISNEY ROCK GROUPS High-energy Disney rock groups perform seasonally in Tomorrowland according to the *Times Guide*.

FLAG RETREAT CEREMONY Daily at around sunset in Town Square, an honor guard lowers the flag as the Disneyland marching band plays patriotic tunes. Members of the armed forces are encouraged to participate in this respectful ceremony and are called up to be honored by branch.

STREET ENTERTAINMENT Various bands, singers, comics, and strolling musicians entertain in spontaneous (that is, unscheduled) street performances throughout the park. Musical styles include banjo, Dixieland, steel drum, marching, and fife and drum. You'll often find the Bootstrappers, a roving band of musical pirates, roaming the waterfront near New Orleans Square. For a respite from the rides, grab a snack and listen to the ragtime piano player outside the Refreshment Corner on Main Street. You don't want to miss the Dapper Dans, a slapstick barbershop quartet that has been performing on Main Street, U.S.A. in Disneyland since 1959. While the cast changes on a regular basis, the Dans really liven up the street.

UNHERALDED TREASURES *at* DISNEYLAND PARK

UNHERALDED TREASURES are special features found in all of the Disney theme parks that add texture, context, beauty, depth, and subtlety to your visit. Generally speaking, unheralded treasures are nice surprises that should be accorded a little time. Lani Teshima, Unofficial Guide friend and writer for **mouseplanet.com,** knows them all. Her list follows.

TREASURE Snow White's Grotto and Wishing Well | **LOCATION** The front right of Sleeping Beauty Castle

A SLOW STROLL AROUND THE SLEEPING BEAUTY CASTLE can be romantic, but sitting quietly to its right is Snow White's Grotto and Wishing Well. If you stop for a few moments, you can hear the voice of Snow White singing "I'm Wishing" in the area. The grotto includes a trickling waterfall framing statues of Snow White and the Seven Dwarfs, placed on three tiers to make Snow White appear to be off in the distance in an optical illusion that masks the fact that her statue is the same height as those of the dwarfs. Next to the grotto is a wishing well, where you can toss a coin and make a wish. This area is a popular place for Snow White to appear for photos, so don't be surprised to see a group of people milling around.

TREASURE Disneyland Railroad | **LOCATION** Stations in Main Street, U.S.A.; New Orleans Square; Mickey's Toontown/Fantasyland; and Tomorrowland

AFTER A LONG DAY, the Disneyland Railroad offers a nice way to get from one end of the park to another. But trains held a special place in Walt Disney's heart, and the railroad offers much more than just a ride back to the park gates. Pause and turn around before you enter Main Street Station for a beautiful view of the entire length of Main Street, U.S.A. Inside the station, you can enjoy looking at model trains and other little exhibits. If you get off at the New Orleans Square Station, stop and listen— that beeping sound you hear is Walt Disney's 1955 Disneyland Park opening speech in landline telegraphic code. And don't forget to ride from Tomorrowland back to Main Street so you can enjoy an unexpected treat: two large indoor dioramas inside the train tunnel, one depicting the Grand Canyon and another depicting a primeval world, complete with large-scale dinosaurs!

TREASURE Windows on Main Street | **LOCATION** Main Street, U.S.A.

THE NAMES ON THE MAIN STREET WINDOWS represent very special people who have had a profound influence on the park in some way, like guardian angels looking over park guests. The names are also often associated with "professions" related to what the person used to do when he or she worked for Disney. For example, the inscription for a window dedicated to the person who modeled Disneyland's waterways reads, DECORATIVE FOUNTAINS AND WATERCOLOR BY FRED JOERGER. Disneyland still occasionally bestows this window honor in official dedication ceremonies in the park.

TREASURE Frontierland Shootin' Exposition | **LOCATION** Frontierland

SMACK IN THE MIDDLE OF FRONTIERLAND is the shooting gallery where cowpokes can close an eye and squeeze the trigger to try to get their target to ping, ting, move, or light up. Don't discount the Frontierland Shootin' Exposition as just another arcade gimmick. Everything about this well-themed attraction is dusty and rustic—except the laser-powered guns, which are both safe and cause little wear on the targets. About the only things missing are blowing tumbleweeds.

TREASURE Edible Plants | **LOCATION** Tomorrowland

THE DISNEY THEME PARKS are known for their magnificent landscaping, but did you know that many of the plants in Tomorrowland are edible, emphasizing the practicality of a future where the garden plants do double-duty as your vegetable garden? For example, the entryway to Tomorrowland is lined with orange trees, and the bushes along the walkways are planted with leafy vegetables such as lettuce, kale, and rhubarb, as well as herbs such as sage, chives, rosemary, and basil.

TREASURE Flag Retreat Ceremony | **LOCATION** Main Street Square

EVERY DAY IN THE AFTERNOON, THE DISNEYLAND BAND or Dapper Dans vocal group marches to the front of Main Street to perform a number of Americana tunes. Park security guards then lower the American flag as the band plays "The Star-Spangled Banner" in this very respectful ceremony.

TREASURE *Partners* statue | **LOCATION** Central Hub

AT THE CASTLE END OF MAIN STREET, in the center of the circular hub, is a bronze statue of Walt Disney holding the hand of Mickey Mouse. The statue, simply called *Partners,* pays homage to the two original ambassadors of Disneyland. If you stand in front of the statue, you can get a nice shot of it with Sleeping Beauty Castle in the background. The spot is encircled by a bench, and it's a great place to meet should your family decide to split up to visit different lands. Smaller statues of other popular Disney figures such as Dumbo, Goofy, and Pluto form a ring around this garden oasis in the middle of the park.

QUIET PLACES AT DISNEYLAND PARK

PEACE AND QUIET are anything but the norm at Disneyland. Yet sometimes when you're overwhelmed by it all, a place to decompress is worth a lot, as a reader from Culver City, California, points out:

I confess that I can't tolerate the hyperstimulation as well as my husband and kids. Sometimes when I'm on my ninth nerve, I'd give anything to put myself in time-out and just collapse for a while. Are there any nice out-of-the-way places in the park where this is possible?

Actually, there are a few. A **pier** with a canopy and benches, opposite the Matterhorn Bobsleds loading area, overlooks a quiet pool. There's still ambient noise, of course, but the pier is far enough removed from the action to afford both tranquility and a lovely setting. The **Hungry Bear Restaurant** in Critter Country offers upper and lower covered outdoor decks overlooking the Rivers of America. In between major feeding periods, the decks are decidedly low-key. **Snow White's Grotto and Wishing Well** (see page 261) is also very pleasant, though it does have a modest but continuous flow of pedestrian traffic. Finally, the alfresco dining area of **Troubadour Tavern,** adjacent to Fantasyland Theatre, is relaxing between shows.

TRAFFIC PATTERNS
at DISNEYLAND PARK

WHEN WE BEGAN our research on Disneyland, we were very interested in traffic patterns throughout the park, specifically these issues:

1. WHAT ATTRACTIONS AND WHICH SECTIONS OF THE PARK DO VISITORS HEAD FOR WHEN THEY FIRST ARRIVE? When guests are admitted, the flow of people to Tomorrowland (Space Mountain, Buzz Lightyear Astro Blasters, Star Tours, and Finding Nemo Submarine Voyage) is heaviest. The next most crowded land is Fantasyland, though the crowds are distributed over a larger number of attractions. Critter Country is likewise crowded with its small area and only two attractions (Splash Mountain and The Many Adventures of Winnie the Pooh). Adventureland, Frontierland, and New Orleans Square fill more slowly, with Mickey's Toontown not really coming alive until later in the morning. As the park fills, visitors appear to head for specific favored attractions that they wish to ride before the lines get long. This, more than any other factor, determines traffic patterns in the mornings and accounts for the relatively equal distribution of visitors throughout Disneyland.

ATTRACTIONS HEAVILY ATTENDED IN EARLY MORNING
ADVENTURELAND Indiana Jones Adventure | Jungle Cruise
CRITTER COUNTRY Splash Mountain
FANTASYLAND Alice in Wonderland | Dumbo the Flying Elephant | Matterhorn Bobsleds | Peter Pan's Flight
TOMORROWLAND Buzz Lightyear Astro Blasters | Finding Nemo Submarine Voyage Space Mountain | Star Tours—The Adventures Continue

2. HOW LONG DOES IT TAKE FOR THE PARK TO REACH PEAK CAPACITY FOR A GIVEN DAY? HOW ARE THE VISITORS DISPERSED THROUGHOUT THE PARK? A surge of early birds arrives before or around opening time but is quickly dispersed throughout the empty park. After the initial onslaught is absorbed, there is a bit of a lull that lasts until about an hour after opening. Following the lull, the park is inundated with arriving guests for about 2 hours, peaking 10–11 a.m. Guests continue to arrive in a steady but diminishing stream until around 2 p.m.

Sampled lines reached their longest length noon–3 p.m., indicating more arrivals than departures in the early afternoon. For general touring purposes, most attractions develop substantial lines 9:30–11 a.m. In the early morning, Tomorrowland, Critter Country, and Fantasyland fill up first. By late morning and into early afternoon, attendance is fairly equally distributed throughout all of the "lands." Mickey's Toontown, because it is comparatively small, stays mobbed from about 11:30 a.m. on. By midafternoon, however, we noted a concentration of visitors in Fantasyland, New Orleans Square, and Adventureland, and a slight decrease of visitors in Tomorrowland.

In the late afternoon and early evening, attendance continues to be more heavily distributed in Tomorrowland, Critter Country, and Fantasyland. Though Space Mountain, Buzz Lightyear Astro Blasters, Splash Mountain, and Star Tours remain inundated throughout the day, most of the other attractions in Tomorrowland and Critter Country have reasonable lines. In New Orleans Square, The Haunted Mansion, Pirates of the Caribbean, and the multitudes returning from nearby Critter Country keep traffic brisk. Frontierland (except Big Thunder Mountain Railroad) and Adventureland (except Indiana Jones Adventure) become less congested as the afternoon and evening progress.

3. HOW DO MOST VISITORS GO ABOUT TOURING THE PARK? IS THERE A DIFFERENCE IN THE TOURING BEHAVIOR OF FIRST-TIME VISITORS AND REPEAT VISITORS? Many first-time visitors accompany friends or relatives who are familiar with Disneyland and who guide their tour. These tours sometimes do and sometimes do not proceed in an orderly (clockwise or counterclockwise) touring sequence. First-time visitors without personal touring guidance tend to be more orderly in their touring. Many first-time visitors, however, are drawn to Sleeping Beauty Castle on entering the park and thus commence their rotation from Fantasyland. Repeat visitors usually proceed directly to their favorite attractions or to whatever is new.

4. WHAT EFFECT DO SPECIAL EVENTS SUCH AS PARADES, FIREWORKS, AND *FANTASMIC!* HAVE ON TRAFFIC PATTERNS? Special events such as parades, fireworks, and *Fantasmic!* pull substantial numbers of visitors from the lines for rides. Unfortunately, however, the left hand taketh what the right hand giveth. A parade or *Fantasmic!* snarls traffic flow throughout Disneyland so much that guests find themselves captive wherever they are. Attraction lines in Tomorrowland, Mickey's Toontown, Adventureland, and Fantasyland (behind the castle) diminish dramatically, making Space Mountain, Finding Nemo Submarine

Voyage, Buzz Lightyear Astro Blasters, Star Tours, Jungle Cruise, Indiana Jones Adventure, Peter Pan's Flight, and Snow White's Scary Adventures particularly good choices during the evening festivities. The remainder of the park (Critter Country, New Orleans Square, Frontierland, Main Street, and Small World Plaza in Fantasyland) is so congested with guests viewing the parade or *Fantasmic!* that it's almost impossible to move.

5. WHAT ARE THE TRAFFIC PATTERNS NEAR TO AND AT CLOSING TIME? On our sample days, which were recorded in and out of season, park departures outnumbered arrivals beginning in midafternoon, with a substantial number of guests leaving after the afternoon parade. Additional numbers of visitors departed during the late afternoon as the dinner hour approached. When the park closed early, there were steady departures during the 2 hours preceding closing, with a mass exodus of remaining visitors at closing time.

When the park closed late, departures were distributed throughout the evening hours, with waves of departures following the evening parade(s), fireworks, and *Fantasmic!* Though departures increased exponentially as closing time approached, a huge throng was still on hand when the park finally shut down. The balloon effect of this last throng at the end of the day generally overwhelmed the shops on Main Street, the parking lot, trams, and the hotel shuttles, as well as the exits onto adjoining Anaheim streets. In the hour before closing in the lands other than Main Street, touring conditions were normally uncrowded except at Indiana Jones Adventure in Adventureland and Splash Mountain in Critter Country.

DISNEYLAND PARK TOURING PLANS

THE DISNEYLAND PARK TOURING PLANS are step-by-step plans for seeing as much as possible with a minimum of time wasted standing in line. They are designed to assist you in avoiding crowds and bottlenecks on days of moderate to heavy attendance. On days of lighter attendance (see "Selecting the Time of Year for Your Visit," page 23), the plans will still save you time but will not be as critical to successful touring.

Choosing the Right Touring Plan

If you have two days to spend at Disneyland Park, the two-day touring plans are by far the most relaxed and efficient. The Two-Day Touring Plan A takes advantage of early-morning touring, when lines are short and the park has not yet filled with guests. This plan works well all year and is particularly recommended for days when Disneyland Park closes before 8 p.m. On the other hand, Two-Day Touring Plan B combines the efficiencies of early-morning touring on the first day with the splendor of Disneyland Park at night on the second day. This plan is perfect for guests who wish to sample both the attractions and the special magic of Disneyland Park after dark, including *Fantasmic!,* parades, and fireworks. The Two-Day Touring Plan for Adults with Small Children spreads the experience over two more-relaxed days and incorporates more attractions that both children and parents will enjoy.

For readers who have requested a Three-Day Park-Hopper Touring Plan, we recommend using the Two-Day Disneyland Park Touring Plan of your choice and mixing it with the One-Day Disney California Adventure Touring Plan as you see fit. Enter Disneyland Park first, and then send a runner across the Esplanade to DCA with your entire group's tickets. Because the FastPass systems of the two parks are disconnected, you can collect FastPasses for *World of Color* and Radiator Springs Racers with any you've already claimed in Disneyland Park (such as Space or Splash Mountains). Just keep an eye on your return windows when juggling cross-park FastPasses, as attendants enforce the expiration times.

If you have only one day but wish to see as much as possible, use the One-Day Touring Plan for Adults. This plan will pack as much into a single day as is humanly possible, but it is pretty exhausting. If you prefer a more relaxed visit, try the Author's Select One-Day Touring Plan. This plan features the best that Disneyland Park has to offer (in the author's opinion), eliminating some of the less impressive attractions.

If you have small children, you may want to use the Dumbo-or-Die-in-a-Day Touring Plan for Adults with Small Children. This plan includes most of the children's rides in Fantasyland and Mickey's Toontown and omits roller coasters and other attractions that small children cannot ride (because of Disney's age and height requirements), as well as rides and shows that are frightening for small children. Because this plan calls for adults to sacrifice many of the better Disney attractions, it is not recommended unless you are touring Disneyland Park primarily for the benefit of your children. In essence, you pretty much stand around, sweat, wipe noses, pay for stuff, and watch the children have fun. It's great.

An alternative to the Dumbo plan is the One-Day Touring Plan for Adults or the Author's Select One-Day Touring Plan, taking advantage of switching off, a technique whereby children accompany adults to the loading area of rides with age and height requirements but do not actually ride (see page 145). Switching off allows adults to enjoy the wilder rides while keeping the whole group together.

For guests who really want to burn the candle at both ends (and a bunch of money) by buying a single-day Park Hopper, we now offer a one-day/two-park touring plan that touches on the highlights of Disney California Adventure in the morning and Disneyland in the afternoon. See page 314 for details.

Park-Opening Procedures

Your progress and success during your first hour of touring will be affected by the particular opening procedure the Disney people use that day.

A. All guests are held at the turnstiles until the park opens (which may or may not be at the official opening time). On admittance, all "lands" are open. If this is the case on the day you visit, blow right past Main Street and head for the first attraction on whatever touring plan you are following.

B. Guests are admitted to Main Street 30 minutes–1 hour before the remaining "lands" open. Access to the other lands is blocked by rope barriers blocking access to the various lands from the central hub on these days. On admittance, move to the rope barrier and stake out a position as follows:

(1) If you are going to Indiana Jones Adventure or Splash Mountain first, take up a position in front of Jolly Holiday Bakery at the central-hub end of Main Street on the left. Wait next to the rope barrier blocking the walkway to Adventureland. When the rest of the park opens, proceed quickly to Adventureland for Indiana Jones, or Critter Country by way of Adventureland and New Orleans Square for Splash Mountain.

(2) If you are going to Finding Nemo Submarine Voyage, Star Tours, or Space Mountain first, wait on the right side of the central hub. When the rope drops at opening time, bear right and zip into Tomorrowland.

(3) If you are going to Fantasyland or Frontierland first, proceed as far forward in the central hub as allowed and line up at the rope, to the left of Walt and Mickey's central statue.

PRELIMINARY INSTRUCTIONS FOR ALL DISNEYLAND PARK TOURING PLANS

ON DAYS OF MODERATE to heavy attendance, follow the touring plans exactly, deviating only when you do not wish to experience a listed show or ride. For instance, the touring plan may direct you to go next to Big Thunder Mountain Railroad, a roller coaster. If you do not like roller coasters, simply skip that step and proceed to the next activity.

1. Buy your admission in advance (see "Admission Options" on page 19).

2. Call ☎ 714-781-7290 the day before you go for the official opening time.

3. Become familiar with the park-opening procedures (described on page 266) and read over the touring plan of your choice, so you will have a basic understanding of what you are likely to encounter as you enter the park.

DISNEYLAND PARK ONE-DAY TOURING PLAN FOR ADULTS *(page 363)*

FOR Adults without small children. **ASSUMES** Willingness to experience all major rides (including roller coasters) and shows.

If you have only one day but wish to see as much as possible, use this touring plan. It packs as much into a single day as is humanly possible, but it is pretty exhausting. Be forewarned that this plan requires a lot of walking and some backtracking; this is necessary to avoid long waits in line. A little extra walking coupled with some hustle in the morning will save you 2–3 hours of standing in line. Note that you might not complete the tour. How far you get will depend on the size of your group, how quickly you move from ride to ride, how many times you pause for rest or food, how quickly the park fills, and what time the park closes.

ABOUT EARLY ENTRY If you are eligible for early entry, arrive at the turnstiles 45–60 minutes before the early-entry period begins on

Tuesday, Thursday, or Saturday (days subject to change) with admission in hand. Upon admission to the park, experience (1) Peter Pan's Flight, (2) Alice in Wonderland, (3) Matterhorn Bobsleds, (4) Star Tours, and (5) Buzz Lightyear Astro Blasters, and then obtain FastPasses for Space Mountain, in that order. If you're not able to enjoy all of the above during the early-entry hour, see as many as you can. When the park opens to the general public, begin the touring plan, skipping any attractions you've already seen.

If you are not eligible for early entry, use the plan on a non-early-entry day (currently Sunday, Monday, Wednesday, or Friday). Do not attempt to use the plan on an early-entry day—Disneyland Park will be packed with early-entry guests before you even make it past the turnstiles. If you wish to tour on an early-entry day but are not eligible for early entry, visit Disney California Adventure and save Disneyland Park for a non-early-entry day.

Note: The success of the touring plan hinges on you entering the park when it first opens. Arrive at the entrance 40 minutes before official opening time.

AUTHOR'S SELECT DISNEYLAND PARK ONE-DAY TOURING PLAN *(page 364)*

FOR Adults touring without small children. **ASSUMES** Willingness to experience all major rides (including roller coasters) and shows.

This touring plan is selective, including only attractions that, in the author's opinion, represent the best that Disneyland Park has to offer. Be forewarned that this plan requires a lot of walking and some backtracking; this is necessary to avoid long waits in line. A little extra walking coupled with some hustle in the morning will save you 2–3 hours of standing in line. Note that you might not complete this tour. How far you get will depend on the size of your group, how quickly you move from ride to ride, how many times you pause for rest or food, how quickly the park fills, and what time the park closes. With a little zip and some luck, it is possible to complete the touring plan even on a busy day when the park closes early.

ABOUT EARLY ENTRY If you are eligible for early entry, arrive at the turnstiles 45–60 minutes before the early-entry period begins on Tuesday, Thursday, or Saturday (days subject to change) with admission in hand. Upon admission to the park, experience (1) Peter Pan's Flight, (2) Alice in Wonderland, (3) Matterhorn Bobsleds, (4) Star Tours, and (5) Buzz Lightyear Astro Blasters, in that order. If you're not able to enjoy all of the above during the early-entry hour, see as many as you can. When the park opens to the general public, begin the touring plan, skipping any attractions you've already seen.

If you are not eligible for early entry, use the plan on a non-early-entry day (currently Sunday, Monday, Wednesday, or Friday). Do not attempt to use the plan on an early-entry day—Disneyland Park will be packed with early-entry guests before you even make it past the turnstiles. If you wish to tour on an early-entry day but are not eligible for early entry, visit Disney California Adventure and save Disneyland Park for a non-early-entry day.

Note: The success of the touring plan hinges on your entering the park when it first opens. Arrive at the entrance 40 minutes before official opening time.

DUMBO-OR-DIE-IN-A-DAY TOURING PLAN
FOR ADULTS WITH SMALL CHILDREN *(page 365)*

FOR Parents with children under age 7 who feel compelled to devote every waking moment to the pleasure and entertainment of their small children. **ASSUMES** Periodic stops for rest, restrooms, and refreshment.

The name of this touring plan notwithstanding, this itinerary is not a joke. Regardless of whether you are loving, guilty, masochistic, truly selfless, insane, or saintly, this touring plan will provide a small child with about as perfect a day as is possible at Disneyland Park.

If this description has intimidated you somewhat or if you have concluded that your day at Disneyland Park is as important as your children's, use the One-Day Touring Plan for Adults, making use of the switching-off option (see page 145) at those attractions that impose height or age restrictions.

Because the children's attractions in Disneyland Park are the most poorly engineered in terms of handling large crowds, this touring plan is the least efficient of our touring plans. It does represent the best way to experience most of the child-oriented attractions in one day, if that is what you hope to do. We do not make recommendations in this plan for meals. If you can, try to hustle along as quickly as is comfortable until about noon. After noon, it won't make much difference if you stop to eat or take it a little easier.

ABOUT EARLY ENTRY Do not attempt to use the plan on an early-entry day if you're not eligible for early entry—Disneyland Park will be packed with early-entry guests before you even make it past the turnstiles. If you wish to tour on an early-entry day but are not eligible for early entry, visit Disney California Adventure and save Disneyland Park for a non-early-entry day.

If you are eligible for early entry, experience (1) Peter Pan's Flight, (2) Dumbo, and (3) Alice in Wonderland, in that order, and then begin the touring plan, skipping any attractions you've already seen.

Note: The success of this touring plan hinges on you being among the first to enter the park when it opens. Arrive at the entrance 40 minutes before official opening time.

DISNEYLAND PARK TWO-DAY TOURING PLAN
FOR ADULTS WITH SMALL CHILDREN *(pages 366–367)*

FOR Parents with children under age 7 who wish to spread their Disneyland Park visit over two days. **ASSUMES** Frequent stops for rest, restrooms, and refreshments.

This touring plan represents a compromise between the observed tastes of adults and the observed tastes of younger children. Included in this touring plan are many of the midway-type rides that your children may have the opportunity to experience at local fairs and amusement parks. These rides at Disneyland Park often require long waits in line, and they consume valuable touring time that could be better spent experiencing the many rides and shows found only at a Disney theme park and which best demonstrate the Disney genius. This touring plan is heavily weighted toward the tastes of younger children. If you want to balance it a bit, try working out a compromise with your kids to forgo some of the carnival-type rides (such as Mad Tea Party, Dumbo, King Arthur Carrousel, and Gadget's Go Coaster) or such rides as Autopia. All of the attractions are appropriate for children 40 inches and shorter.

Another alternative is to use one of the other two-day touring plans and take advantage of the switching-off option (see page 145). This technique allows small children to be admitted to rides such as Space Mountain, Indiana Jones Adventure, Big Thunder Mountain Railroad, Star Tours, and Splash Mountain. The children wait in the loading area as their parents ride one at a time; the nonriding parent waits with the children.

TIMING This two-day touring plan takes advantage of early-morning touring. On each day you should complete the structured part of the plan by 3 p.m. or so. We highly recommend returning to your hotel by midafternoon for a nap and an early dinner. If the park is open in the evening, come back to the park by 7:30 or 8 p.m. for the evening parade, fireworks, and *Fantasmic!*

ABOUT EARLY ENTRY Do not attempt to use day two of the touring plan on early-entry days if you are not eligible for early entry—Fantasyland will be packed with early-entry guests before you even make it past the turnstiles. Day one of the plan begins in Adventureland, which is not affected by early entry. Come back to Disneyland Park on the following non-early-entry day and proceed with day two. You can do day two first (the order makes no difference) as your travel plans dictate.

If you are eligible for early entry, experience (1) Peter Pan's Flight, (2) Alice in Wonderland, (3) Mr. Toad's Wild Ride, and (4) Dumbo, in that order, followed by the other Fantasyland attractions. At the end of the early-entry hour, begin day two of the touring plan, skipping any attractions you've already seen.

Note: Because the needs of small children are so varied, we have not built specific instructions for eating into the touring plan. Simply stop for refreshments or a meal when you feel the urge. For best results, however, try to keep moving in the morning. In the afternoon, you can eat, rest often, and adjust the pace to your liking.

DISNEYLAND PARK TWO-DAY TOURING PLAN A, FOR DAYTIME TOURING OR FOR WHEN THE PARK CLOSES EARLY *(pages 368–369)*

FOR Parties wishing to spread their Disneyland Park visit over two days and parties preferring to tour in the morning. **ASSUMES** Willingness to experience all major rides (including roller coasters) and shows.

TIMING This two-day touring plan takes advantage of early-morning touring and is the most efficient of all the touring plans for comprehensive touring with the least time lost waiting in line. On each day you should complete the structured part of the plan by 3 p.m. or so. If you are visiting Disneyland Park during a period of the year when the park is open late (after 8 p.m.), you might prefer our Two-Day Touring Plan B, which offers morning touring on one day and late afternoon and evening touring on the other day. Another highly recommended option is to return to your hotel around midafternoon for a well-deserved nap and an early dinner, and to come back to the park by 7:30 or 8 p.m. for the evening parade, fireworks, and live entertainment.

ABOUT EARLY ENTRY Do not attempt to use the plan on early-entry days if you are not eligible for early entry—Disneyland Park will be packed with early-entry guests before you even make it past the turnstiles. Do day one of the plan on a non-early-entry day. The next day will be an early-entry day, so visit Disney California Adventure on that day. Come back to Disneyland Park on the following non-early-entry day and proceed with day two.

If you're eligible for early entry, experience (1) Peter Pan's Flight, (2) Alice in Wonderland, (3) Mr. Toad's Wild Ride, and (4) Matterhorn Bobsleds, in that order. If you're not able to enjoy all of the above during the early-entry hour, ride as many as you can. When the park opens to the general public, begin day one of the touring plan, skipping any attractions you've already seen.

DISNEYLAND PARK TWO-DAY TOURING PLAN B, FOR MORNING AND EVENING TOURING OR FOR WHEN THE PARK IS OPEN LATE *(pages 370–371)*

FOR Parties who want to enjoy Disneyland Park at different times of day, including evenings and early mornings. **ASSUMES** Willingness to experience all major rides (including roller coasters) and shows.

TIMING This two-day touring plan is for those visiting Disneyland Park on days when the park is open late (after 8 p.m.). The plan offers morning touring on the first day and late afternoon and evening touring on the other day. If the park closes early, or if you prefer to do all of your touring during the morning and early afternoon, use the Two-Day Touring Plan A.

ABOUT EARLY ENTRY If you are not eligible for early entry, do not try to use day one of the plan on an early-entry day. Disneyland Park will be packed with early-entry guests before you even get past the turnstiles.

If you are eligible for early entry and want to use day one of the plan on an early-entry day, experience (1) Peter Pan's Flight, (2) Alice in Wonderland, (3) Matterhorn Bobsleds, (4) Space Mountain, and (5) Finding Nemo Submarine Voyage, in that order. If you're not able to enjoy all of the above during the early-entry hour, ride as many as you can. When the park opens to the general public, begin day one of the touring plan, skipping any attractions you've already seen.

THE DISNEYLAND NO RIDES, NO QUEUES, NO STRESS ANTI-TOURING PLAN

MOST OF OUR READERS are interested in touring plans to get them through as many attractions as possible in the most efficient manner. But, like the authors, some of you may have siblings, spouses, or other companions who are congenitally opposed to queuing for anything clanking or claustrophobic. What can Disney do to occupy your Aunt Gertie, who is dead set against standing in a line, or sitting in anything with a lap bar?

Disneyland Park is one of the few places where you can experience a full day of entertainment without getting on a ride faster than the railroad, and without waiting more than 15 minutes or so, even during the busiest season.

Yes, you can get your money's worth at Disneyland without sprinting to Space Mountain or spinning in a teacup. You just have to adjust your expectation of what constitutes an attraction. (A handful of sedate activities are available at Disney California Adventure, such as Disney Animation, the winery, and the bakery tour, but not enough to justify a full-price pass.)

Because this "anti-touring" plan is designed to eliminate stress, there is no strict order to follow the steps in, nor instructions to arrive before rope drop (though it doesn't hurt). Simply tour the park as your feet take you, skipping any suggested experiences that don't interest you. If there is more than a 15–20 minute wait for anything you want to do, simply move along and check back later. Most important, take a break after 4 or 5 hours and leave the park for a nap, meal, or swim. The key is to take your time and (literally) stop to smell the roses.

Main Street, U.S.A.

- Ride one of the vintage vehicles up Main Street to the hub, and then take a different one back.
- Look at the memorabilia in the Main Street train station, and then ride the rails for a round-trip or two around the park.
- Explore the Disneyana shop's collectible artwork inside the old Bank of Main Street.
- Peer in the Emporium's high-tech animated window displays.
- See *Great Moments with Mr. Lincoln,* arriving early enough to see the Steve Martin preshow and the lobby's Disney Gallery historical displays.
- Watch the classic short films inside the Main Street Cinema.
- Snoop on the antique party line telephones inside the Market House, and then sit outside at a table on Center Street, listening to the amusing sounds emanating from the windows above.
- Check out the primitive 3-D movie viewers in the Penny Arcade.
- Watch the chefs in the candy store whip up a batch of sweets. On select days during the holidays, the handmade supersize candy canes are a can't-miss. They are in short supply, so you'll need to line up early and receive a numbered wristband to buy one, but anyone can walk up and watch them being made.
- Catch a performance or three of the Dapper Dans, Main Street Marching

Band, or Coke Corner ragtime pianist. The daily flag retreat ceremony is not to be missed.

- Try to identify the names of Disney Legends and Imagineers honored on Main Street's windows.
- Stop and watch some artisans—such as the silhouette cutters, glass sculptors, and watch painters—work.
- Ask the prestidigitators at the Magic Shop to demonstrate some tricks for you, and stare at the creepy optical illusion in the window.
- On the right side of the street next to the silhouette shop, sit in the chairs on the porch.
- Take a picture with the *Partners* statue in the central hub, and appreciate the surrounding flora and fauna.

Adventureland

- See the *Enchanted Tiki Room,* arriving in time to buy a Dole Whip and watch the preshow.
- Jungle Cruise is gentle fun if the line isn't long.
- If stairs aren't an issue, climb Tarzan's Treehouse, or at least enter through the exit and watch the kids going wild on the playground.
- Consider walking through the Indiana Jones Adventure queue at least once, even if you aren't interested in riding; it's an impressive (if exhausting) example of scenic design. When the posted wait time is more than 15 minutes, get a FastPass to skip the boring exterior line. Before you climb the stairs near the loading bay, simply tell a cast member that you want to exit. If you are brave but impatient, Indy's single-rider line often has little to no wait.

New Orleans Square

- Haunted Mansion and Pirates of the Caribbean both move guests through quickly even on busy days, and neither is likely to disturb any but the most delicate constitutions.
- Seek out the jazz and pirate bands that play in the area.
- Poke around the lovingly detailed alleyways around the Pirates of the Caribbean exit.
- Sit outside Café Orléans with a plate of *pommes frites* and watch the crowds go by.

Critter Country

- Stand on the bridge near Splash Mountain and watch riders take the plunge. If you dare to get damp, the single-rider wait is usually bearable.
- Feed the ducks from the porch behind the Hungry Bear Restaurant.

Frontierland

- Take a raft to Tom Sawyer Island, and explore the island.
- Sail on the Sailing Ship *Columbia,* Mark Twain Riverboat, or both. You can usually step on board just before departure time without standing in line, or board early for the best seat at the top front.
- Grab some chili and a box seat for the show in The Golden Horseshoe.
- Get to know the pygmy goats and other animals at the Big Thunder Ranch petting zoo. Explore Miss Chris's cabin.
- Look for the petrified tree that was an anniversary gift from Walt to his wife;

she donated it to the park. Also try to spot the jumping fish and railroad tunnel remains from Mine Train Through Nature's Wonderland, across from Big Thunder Mountain.
- Pump some quarters into the Frontierland Shootin' Exposition.
- Walk through the Rancho del Zocalo patio, especially when decorated for Dia de Los Muertos.

Fantasyland

- Go through the Sleeping Beauty Castle walk-through, or watch the alternative experience video.
- Toss a wish into Snow White's well in front of the castle, and gaze at her grotto of handcrafted sculptures.
- Cruise Storybook Land Canal Boats or It's a Small World if lines are short.
- Try on some mouse ears in the Mad Hatter chapeau shop.
- Take a break with a vendor treat (such as an ear of corn) on the benches at the old motorboat dock across from the Matterhorn Bobsleds.
- Stick your head in the Fantasy Faire if a show is scheduled, but don't bother with the massive queue to meet a princess.
- The elevated mall near It's a Small World is a convenient spot to stand for the parade or fireworks show.
- Enjoy the stage musical inside Fantasyland Theatre.

Mickey's Toontown

- Play with the interactive doodads dotted around the building facades.
- Take a tour of Mickey's and Minnie's homes, but bail on the meet and greet if the line is out the door.
- Walk though the cleverly decorated children's playgrounds, being wary of bouncing babes.

Tomorrowland

- Take the Monorail to Downtown Disney for a bite or a drink, and then return (remember your park ticket!).
- Watch young Padawans battle Sith Lords on Tomorrowland Terrace in the *Jedi Training Academy* show. Check the schedule for other entertainment on this stage.
- Experience the 4-D film inside the Tomorrowland Theater. Ask for a nonmoving seat in the back to avoid bouncing.
- The line for Buzz Lightyear Astro Blasters moves swiftly, and almost everyone of all ages loves it.
- Browse the unique *Star Wars* merchandise (including build-your-own light sabers and droid action figures) in Star Traders with a life-size X-Wing overhead.
- Search for imaginatively groomed edible plants along the Tomorrowland walkways.
- Check out any exhibits or play an old-school arcade game in the Starcade.
- Explore the Marvel and Star Wars exhibits in the former Innoventions building.

PART SIX

DISNEY CALIFORNIA ADVENTURE

We enjoyed DCA much more than Disneyland. More fun, fewer strollers and little kids, more-adventurous people. Just a different feeling all the way around.

—Mom from Bend, Oregon

A MOST ANTICIPATED SEQUEL

DISNEY CALIFORNIA ADVENTURE held its grand opening on February 8, 2001. Now known as DCA among Disneyphiles, the park is a bouquet of contradictions conceived in Fantasyland, starved in utero by corporate Disney, and born into a hostile environment of Disneyland loyalists who believed they'd been handed a second-rate theme park. Its parts are stunningly beautiful yet come together awkwardly, failing to compose a handsome whole. And perhaps most lamentable of all, the California theme is impotent by virtue of being all-encompassing. But despite the long odds, just a little over a decade after its inauspicious debut, DCA emerged from a billion-dollar metamorphosis that finally made it an honorable companion to its storied older sibling across the Esplanade.

The history of the park is another of those convoluted tales found only in Robert Ludlum novels and corporate Disney. Southern California Disney fans began clamoring for a second theme park shortly after Epcot opened at Walt Disney World in 1982. Though there was some element of support within the Walt Disney Company, the Disney loyal had to content themselves with rumors and half-promises for two decades while they watched new Disney parks go up in Tokyo, Paris, and Florida. For years, Disney teasingly floated the "Westcot" concept, a California version of Epcot that was always just about to break ground. Whether it was a matter of procrastination or simply pursuing better opportunities elsewhere, the Walt Disney Company sat on the sidelines while the sleepy community of Anaheim became a sprawling city and property values skyrocketed. By the time Disney emerged from its Westcot fantasy and began to get serious about a second California

Disney California Adventure

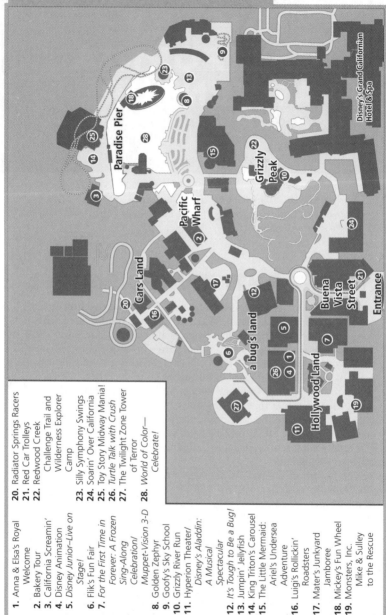

Paradise Pier

Pacific Wharf

Grizzly Peak

Cars Land

a bug's land

Buena Vista Street

Entrance

Hollywood Land

Disney's Grand Californian Hotel & Spa

park, the price tag—not to mention the complexity of integrating such a development into a mature city—was mind-boggling.

Westcot had been billed as a $2- to $3-billion, 100-plus-acre project, so that was what the Disney faithful were expecting when Disney California Adventure was announced. What they got was a park that cost $1.4 billion (slashed from an original budget of about $2.1 billion), built on 55 acres, including a sizable piece carved out for the Grand Californian Hotel. It's quite a small park by modern theme park standards, but $1.4 billion, when lavished on 55 acres, ought to buy a pretty good park.

Then there's the park's theme. Though flexible, California Adventure came off like a default setting, lacking in imagination, weak in concept, and without intrinsic appeal, especially when you stop to consider that two-thirds of Disneyland guests come from Southern California. As further grist for the mill, before the arrival of Cars Land, there was precious little new technology at work in Disney's newest theme park. Of the headliner attractions, only two—Soarin' Over California, a simulator ride, and Toy Story Midway Mania!, a "virtual dark ride"—broke new ground. All the rest are recycled, albeit popular, attractions from the Animal Kingdom and Disney's Hollywood Studios. When you move to the smaller-statured second half of the attraction batting order, it gets worse. Most of these attractions are little more than off-the-shelf midway rides spruced up with a Disney story line and facade.

From a competitive perspective, Disney California Adventure was an underwhelming shot at Disney's three Southern California competitors. The Hollywood section of DCA takes a hopeful poke at Universal Studios Hollywood, while Paradise Pier offers midway rides à la Six Flags Magic Mountain. Finally, the whole California theme has for years been the eminent domain of Knott's Berry Farm. In short, there's not much originality in DCA, only Disney's now-redundant mantra that "whatever they can do, we can do better."

Finally, after more than eight years of basically being in denial about Disney California Adventure, The Walt Disney Company seemed willing to admit that this theme park (which pulled in only about a third of Disneyland's attendance annually) needed some help. On June 15, 2012, The Mouse held a grand reopening to celebrate the completion of a $1.1 billion effort, originally announced in 2007, to address DCA's problems.

Starting at the park entrance, the Imagineers scoured every inch of DCA, injecting charm, character, and ride capacity wherever they could. The current entryway embraces the legacy of Disneyland's founder with a nostalgic re-creation of 1920s Los Angeles. That freshly poured-on theming flows all the way to Paradise Pier, where the tacky seaside amusements were softened with new-old Victorian-era stylings. An original family-friendly dark ride based on a popular Piscean princess was added, and the central lagoon now sports a Vegas-quality water show designed expressly to keep crowds in

DCA after dark. The final element of DCA's transformation fell into place with 2012's opening of Cars Land, an entire area dedicated to the best-selling Pixar property. Cars Land shaped up to be the biggest project to hit theme parks since Universal Orlando's Wizarding World of Harry Potter, and appears to be the final puzzle piece needed to rehabilitate DCA's poor reputation. While the park spent its first decade as a punch line, DCA is now a legitimate destination in its own right and finally rivals its older brother for turnstile entry bragging rights on busy days—something that was once almost unimaginable.

Mind you, the rest of Disneyland Resort has experienced its own gussying up. Downtown Disney added shops and restaurants, including a spiffy Starbucks Coffee and the popular Earl of Sandwich, to its lineup. Likewise, Disneyland Hotel completed a face-lift in 2012, which folded festive new furnishings and up-to-date amenities into the then-56-year-old resort. Disneyland Park also received new night-time entertainment and enhancement to some of its classic attractions in time for its 60th anniversary in 2015, and there's at least one new hotel (plus another Disney Vacation Club property) on the long-term drawing board. The rumor mill has been rumbling for several years about a third theme park, possibly to be built on an outlying parking lot, but Disney CEO Bob Iger has publicly downplayed any such plans, hinting instead at further expansion of the two existing parks.

Some Disneyholics may never forgive DCA's dire beginnings, dismissing recent additions as expensive attempts to patch over a flawed foundation. The rest of us will have some fun enjoying the park for what it is: the theme park equivalent of a jukebox musical, featuring a greatest hits collection of attractions also found in WDW's Epcot, Hollywood Studios, and Animal Kingdom, along with just enough exclusive E tickets to give DCA a unique personality all its own.

ARRIVING *and* GETTING ORIENTED

THE ENTRANCE TO DISNEY CALIFORNIA ADVENTURE faces the entrance to Disneyland Park across a palm-shaded pedestrian plaza called the **Esplanade.** If you arrive by tram from one of the Disney parking lots, you'll disembark at the Esplanade. Facing east toward Harbor Boulevard, Disneyland Park will be on your left and DCA will be on your right. In the Esplanade are ticket booths, the group sales office, and resort information.

Seen from overhead, Disney California Adventure is roughly arrayed in a fan shape around the park's central visual icon, **Grizzly Peak.** At ground level, however, the park's layout is not so obvious.

There are six themed "lands" at DCA, not including **Buena Vista Street.** A left turn at the hub leads you to **Hollywood Land,** celebrating California's history as the film capital of the world. **Grizzly Peak**

DISNEY CALIFORNIA ADVENTURE SERVICES

Baby Care Center In Pacific Wharf, near the Ghirardelli Soda Fountain

Banking Services/Currency Exchange At the Chamber of Commerce at Buena Vista Street, immediately to your left upon entering

Disneyland and Local Attraction Information At the Chamber of Commerce

First Aid At the Chamber of Commerce

Live Entertainment and Parade Information At the Chamber of Commerce

Lost Adults and Messages At the Chamber of Commerce

Lost and Found Lost and Found for the entire resort is located west of the entrance to Disneyland Park

Lost Children In Pacific Wharf next to the Baby Care Center

Storage Lockers Immediately to your right upon entering

(which absorbed the former Condor Flats area) is reminiscent of the Pacific Northwest woods, while **Pacific Wharf** nods to Monterey's Cannery Row. You'll find Grizzly Peak by taking the first right as you approach the hub, though you must walk two-thirds of the way around the mountain to reach its namesake raft ride. Pacific Wharf is situated along a kidney-shaped lake and can be accessed by following the walkway emanating from the hub at 7 o'clock and winding around Grizzly Peak. A fourth land, **A Bug's Land,** is situated opposite the Golden Vine Winery and can be reached by taking the same route. The fifth land, **Paradise Pier,** recalls seaside amusement parks of the Victorian era. It is situated in the southwest corner of the park, around the large lake. **Cars Land** is the sixth land, claiming a former parking lot behind the Pacific Wharf and A Bug's Land, with its primary entrance across from the Golden Vine Winery.

SINGLE-RIDER LINES

YOU CAN OFTEN SAVE TIME WAITING in line by taking advantage of single-rider lines, a separate line for people who are alone or don't mind riding alone or with a stranger. The objective of single-rider lines is to fill odd spaces left by groups who don't quite fill the entire ride vehicle. Because there aren't many singles and most groups aren't willing to split up, single-rider lines are usually much shorter than the regular line. Five attractions at DCA offer single-rider lines: California Screamin', Goofy's Sky School, Grizzly River Run, Radiator Springs Racers, and Soarin' Over California.

PARK-OPENING PROCEDURES

DISNEYLAND RESORT HOTEL GUESTS get a 1-hour jump on the public four or more mornings each week through the Extra Magic Hours program (see page 26). You'll be required to show a hotel key card before being allowed through. This entrance is often overwhelmed,

NOT TO BE MISSED AT DISNEY CALIFORNIA ADVENTURE
• **A BUG'S LAND** *It's Tough to Be a Bug!*
• **CARS LAND** Radiator Springs Racers
• **GRIZZLY PEAK** Grizzly River Run	Soarin' Over California
• **HOLLYWOOD LAND** Hyperion Theater	*Muppet-Vision 3-D* (if showing) The Twilight Zone Tower of Terror
• **PARADISE PIER** California Screamin'	Toy Story Midway Mania!	*World of Color*

especially on early-entry days, so you may save time by walking to the front gate. All other guests will be allowed through the main entrance onto Buena Vista Street up to 1 hour early and held there until after a brief "rope drop" musical fanfare at the official opening time. Guests wishing to ride Radiator Springs Racers first (or retrieve a FastPass) will gather to the right of Carthay Circle, while those headed to The Twilight Zone Tower of Terror or Anna & Elsa's Royal Welcome line up to the left outside Hollywood Land. The crowd will be walked toward their destination at the appointed hour to avoid a stampede.

BUENA VISTA STREET

FROM THE ESPLANADE, where huge block letters spelling CALIFOR-NIA originally stood, you now pass through a Streamline Modern entrance facade, designed after Los Angeles's fabled Pan Pacific Auditorium. (If it looks familiar, that's because it can also be recognized as the entrance to Disney's Hollywood Studios park in Florida.)

Once past the turnstiles, you'll find yourself on **Buena Vista Street,** a re-creation of 1920s Hollywood as Walt saw it when he first arrived. Immediately upon entering, to your left you'll find **Oswald's Filling Station** (a souvenir shop with a snazzy antique car parked outside) and the **Chamber of Commerce.** The street leading to the central plaza is lined on both sides with a variety of shops and eateries with backstories referring to Disney's early biography. Among the shops on the east side is **Elias & Company Department Store** (the park's largest shop, named after Walt's father). The west side of the street features an indoor shopping arcade that leads to **Kingswell Camera Shop** (a PhotoPass printing location) and the **Trolley Treats** candy shop (check out the Big Rock Candy Mountain model in the window), among others.

The hub area, called Carthay Circle, is home to the *Storytellers* statue (depicting a young Walt Disney with an early version of Mickey Mouse) and a replica of the **Carthay Circle Theater,** where *Snow White and the Seven Dwarfs* premiered in 1937; in this incarnation, it encloses an upscale restaurant and bar.

Winding past the shops and facades, the **Red Car Trolley** transports guests from the park entrance to The Twilight Zone Tower of Terror and back again.

Together, Buena Vista Street and Carthay Circle don't simply serve as a point of departure for the park's other various themed areas. They bring much-needed charm and warmth to DCA's opening act, forming a fantastic improvement over the flat cartoon-postcard facades that framed the former entryway.

Red Car Trolleys ★★★

APPEAL BY AGE	PRESCHOOL ★★★★½	GRADE SCHOOL ★★★★	TEENS ★★★½
YOUNG ADULTS ★★★★		OVER 30 ★★★★	SENIORS ★★★★★

What it is Scenic in-park transportation. **Scope and scale** Minor attraction. **When to go** The first or last 2 hours the park is open. **Duration of ride** About 11 minutes. **Average wait in line per 100 people ahead of you** 12 minutes. **Assumes** Both cars in operation. **Loading speed** Very slow.

DESCRIPTION AND COMMENTS Much like the vintage vehicles that travel up and down Main Street, U.S.A., at Disneyland Park, these trolley cars add visual interest to DCA's entrance area but not much entertainment value. Modeled after the Pacific Electric Railway that served the Los Angeles area in the 1920s and 1930s (as seen in *Who Framed Roger Rabbit?*), the trolleys boast authentic details such as narrating conductors who share historical tidbits during your travels, retro-styled interior advertisements, and realistic overhead power lines—unelectrified, as the eco-friendly cars are actually battery-powered. More transportation than attraction, the Red Car Trolleys ferry guests on a one-way trip between Buena Vista Street near the park entrance and The Twilight Zone Tower of Terror (or back the other way), making stops in Carthay Circle and Hollywood Land along the way.

TOURING TIPS It is usually faster to walk the route than to wait for the next Red Car Trolley, but if you wish to experience this nostalgic transportation, do so in the morning. Hop on at the station near the Tower of Terror exit; it should be less crowded than the station on Buena Vista Street near the park entrance.

The Red Car briefly stops serving guests several times daily so it can be commandeered as a stage for the Red Car News Boys show (see show schedule for details).

▌■ HOLLYWOOD LAND

HOLLYWOOD LAND OFFERS attractions and shopping that are inspired by California's (and Disney's) contribution to television and cinema. Visually, the land is themed as a studio back lot with sets, including an urban street scene, soundstages, and a central street with shops and restaurants that depict Hollywood's golden age.

Anna & Elsa's Royal Welcome *(FastPass only)* ★★★

APPEAL BY AGE	PRESCHOOL ★★★★★	GRADE SCHOOL ★★★★½	TEENS ★★★★
YOUNG ADULTS ★★★½		OVER 30 ★★★½	SENIORS ★★★½

What it is Character greeting with the *Frozen* sisters. **Scope and scale** Minor attraction. **When to go** Get a FastPass immediately after opening. **Special comments** FastPass required; located inside Disney Animation. **Duration of experience** 3–5 minutes. **Probable waiting time** 30–60 minutes.

DESCRIPTION AND COMMENTS After coping with overwhelming crowds at their tiny Fantasyland meet and greet cottage for more than a year,

Disney relocated the insanely popular ladies of Arendelle, Queen Elsa and Princess Anna, to DCA's Disney Animation building as part of 2015's Frozen Fun promotion. Much like Fantasy Faire's Royal Hall, the *Frozen* character encounter is richly appointed and has multiple meeting rooms to increase capacity without ruining the magic.

TOURING TIPS There is no standby queue: Royal Welcome is FastPass-only. FastPass return tickets (with a 20-minute return window) are distributed on a first-come, first-serve basis. During off-season, passes may last into the afternoon, but on busy days, we have observed tickets running out in as little as 1 hour after park opening. Disney does not grant requests for specific times. FastPass distribution is offered at park opening on days when early entry is offered (the only attraction in the resort to do so) or at the beginning of regular park hours on non-early-entry days. Fortunately, having a FastPass ticket for Royal Welcome does not impact your ability to use FastPass at other attractions.

If your party would like to meet Anna or Elsa, you need to be ready to dedicate a significant amount of time. The total time spent in line can be an hour or more, even with the FastPass procedures Disney has put in place. The line starts to the left of Carthay Circle Theater (look for a Disney cast member holding a *Frozen* sign) before park opening. As soon as the park opens for the day, the line of guests waiting for Royal Welcome Fast-Passes will be led to the ticket machines on the sidewalk outside the Disney Animation building. When the time on your FastPass arrives, expect to wait another 30–60 minutes in line before you actually meet the sisters. Obviously, meeting Anna and Elsa is not a part of any efficient touring plan.

Disney Animation ★★★½

What it is Behind-the-scenes look at Disney animation.
Scope and scale Major attraction. **When to go** Any-time. **Special comment** Quite amusing, though not very educational. **Duration of experience** 35–55 minutes. **Probable waiting time** None.

Thumbs Up for the Whole Family

DESCRIPTION AND COMMENTS The Disney Animation building houses a variety of shows, galleries, and interactive exhibits that collectively provide a sort of crash course in animation. Moving from room to room and exhibit to exhibit, you follow the Disney animation process from concept to finished film, with a peek at each of the steps along the way. Throughout, you are surrounded by animation, and sometimes it's even projected above your head and under your feet!

Because DCA's Animation building is not a working studio, the attraction does not showcase artists at work on real features, and the interactive exhibits are more whimsical than educational. "Sorcerer's Workshop," for example, is an interactive exhibit where you can use a book-shaped touch screen to discover which Disney character you most resemble.

The Animation Academy, hosted by a Disney cartoonist, teaches you how to draw a Disney character; if you have any artistic inclination, you may consider it DCA's best-kept secret and find yourself taking the class repeatedly, as a Salt Lake City reader suggests:

Animation Academy turned out to be one of my absolute favorite things. I did it four times in a row and would have gone more if I wasn't starving. I plan to devote quite a bit of time to it on my next trip. I don't think you give it enough credit in your book.

And from a Sammamish, Washington, mom:

You do not give enough emphasis to the Animation Academy drawing classes. I took three, and they were the highlight of the trip. I have no drawing ability whatsoever, but following along with the instructor I was able to make a pretty decent Donald, a passable Mickey, and a Pooh Bear, though he looked like he was in a car accident. My 4-year-old loved drawing along, my husband loved it, and my 2-year-old loved scribbling on her paper and drawing board. It was fun for the whole family.

The Animation Academy classes normally rotate during the day through a dozen-odd different classic and current Disney characters, but at times it may be devoted to a single theme. During 2015's Frozen Fun event, the class became all-Olaf, all the time.

Both "Sorcerer's Workshop" and Animation Academy provide a good foundation on the animation process and will enhance your appreciation of the other exhibits. *Turtle Talk with Crush* is also located here (see page 287).

TOURING TIPS On entering the Animation building, you'll step into a lobby where signs mark the entrances of the various exhibits. Look up in the lobby for a moment at the ultra-high-definition oversize projections of animations in process, including Disney's and Pixar's latest hits. It takes 40–55 minutes to do all the interactive stuff and see everything. You probably won't experience much of a wait for the Disney Animation offerings except on weekends and holidays. Even then, the Animation building clears out considerably by late afternoon.

Disney Junior—Live on Stage! ★★★★

APPEAL BY AGE	PRESCHOOL ★★★★½	GRADE SCHOOL ★★★	TEENS ★★
YOUNG ADULTS ★★★	OVER 30 ★★★½		SENIORS ★★★★

What it is Live show for children. **Scope and scale** Minor attraction. **When to go** Per the daily entertainment schedule. **Special comments** Audience sits on the floor. A must for families with preschoolers. **Duration of show** 20 minutes. **Probable waiting time** 25 minutes.

DESCRIPTION AND COMMENTS The show features characters from the Disney Channel's *Sofia the First, Mickey Mouse Clubhouse, Jake and the Never Land Pirates,* and *Doc McStuffins,* plus other Disney Channel characters. Refreshed in 2013, *Disney Junior* uses elaborate puppets instead of live characters on stage. A simple plot serves as the platform for singing, dancing, some great puppetry, and a great deal of audience participation. The characters, who ooze love and goodness, rally throngs of tots and preschoolers to sing and dance along with them. All the jumping, squirming, and high-stepping is facilitated by having the audience sit on the floor so that kids can spontaneously erupt into motion when the mood strikes. Even for adults without children, it's a treat to watch the tykes rev up. However, solo adults might feel creepy amid this extremely youthful exuberance, especially if they lack familiarity with any of the characters. If you have a younger child in your party, all the better: Just stand back and let the video roll.

For preschoolers, *Disney Junior* will be the highlight of their day, as a Thomasville, North Carolina, mom attests:

It was fantastic! My 3-year-old loved it. The children danced, sang, and had a great time.

Disney Junior is the second iteration of the stage show since 2007. Both versions replaced live characters with puppets, a fact that has left some parents less than enthralled. These comments from a Virginia Beach, Virginia, couple are typical:

We were disappointed with the updated show. This did not consist of live characters, and I think the level of excitement from the kids was lower because of this. I mean, the kids enjoyed it, but you would think they would be more excited when it's a show with some of their favorite characters.

TOURING TIPS The show is headquartered to the right of the entrance to Hollywood Land and has an Art Deco marquee. Because the tykes just can't get enough, it has become a hot ticket. Arrive earlier on Sundays, when all showings sometimes fill to capacity. If you arrive to find a line that extends out of the main queuing area and onto the sidewalk, you might not get into the show. Count two palm trees to the left of the theater entrance; if the line extends to the left of the second palm, you probably won't make the cut. If the line hasn't extended past the second palm tree, go ahead and get in line—chances are about 90% that you'll be admitted to the next show. Once inside, pick a spot on the floor and take a breather until the performance begins.

For the First Time in Forever: A Frozen Sing-Along Celebration (FastPass) ★★★
Muppet-Vision 3-D ★★★★

APPEAL BY AGE	PRESCHOOL ★★★★½	GRADE SCHOOL ★★★★½	TEENS ★★★★
YOUNG ADULTS ★★★½	OVER 30 ★★★		SENIORS ★★★

Thumbs Up for the Whole Family

What it is Sing-along stage show/ 3-D movie featuring the Muppets. **Scope and scale** Minor attraction. **When to go** Get a FastPass before noon; see *Muppet-Vision 3-D* (if showing) before noon or after 4 p.m. **Special comments** *For the First Time in Forever* replaced *Muppet-Vision 3-D*; 3-D effects and loud noises of *Muppet-Vision* frighten many preschoolers. **Duration of show** 25 minutes for *For the First Time in Forever*; 17 minutes for *Muppet-Vision 3-D*. **Probable waiting time** 30 minutes.

DESCRIPTION AND COMMENTS Lately, *Muppet-Vision 3-D* has been preempted in favor of *For the First Time in Forever: A Frozen Sing-Along Celebration.* Disney officially insists that Kermit and the gang will return one day, but we're skeptical—keep an eye on DCA's menus for frog legs and pork ribs. The venue has been transformed into the Crown Jewel Theatre, with satirical show posters adorning the redecorated lobby.

FOR THE FIRST TIME IN FOREVER: A FROZEN SING-ALONG CELEBRATION This show uses live actors and video clips to tell the story of *Frozen*. *For the First Time in Forever: A Frozen Sing-Along Celebration* is hosted by two presenters known as royal historians of Arendelle, who take the audience through the events of the film. Songs from the film such as "Do You Want to Build a Snowman?," "Love Is an Open Door," and "Let It Go" are played on the screen behind them. The songs and film clips shown in this attraction are the exact ones from the film, with the addition of lyrics at the bottom of the screen. The audience is encouraged to sing along, with help from a snowflake that bounces along with the lyrics.

The production is enhanced with falling "snow" and lighting effects that make the theater walls appear to frost over. Each performance culminates with an appearance of Anna and Elsa on stage, where they lead the crowd in a second rendition of "Let It Go." Unfortunately, the script for this show isn't nearly as witty as the one used in the identically named show at Walt Disney World's Hollywood Studios park, making this sing-along more of a slog for adults than it needs to be. For a much funnier take on the same material, see the *Frozen* show at Fantasy Faire's Royal Theatre in Disneyland Park (see page 238).

Note that there is no meet and greet with Anna and Elsa during or after this show. To do that, you must head over to Anna & Elsa's Royal Welcome in the Animation building (see page 281).

MUPPET-VISION 3-D *Muppet-Vision 3-D* provides a total sensory experience, with wild 3-D action augmented by auditory, visual, and tactile special effects. If you're tired and hot, this show will make you feel brand-new. Arrive early to catch the subversively snarky preshow. Clips featuring the criminal Constantine, a Kermit look-alike, were added to the preshow in concert with *Muppets Most Wanted*'s 2014 theatrical release. A father of four from New Brunswick, Canada, praises *Muppet-Vision*, writing:

I think Muppet-Vision 3-D *is a godsend for five reasons: 1. It NEVER has a line (even on our visit on New Year's Day). 2. Everyone, ages 1–100, gives the show high marks. 3. Between the preshow and the movie, it's half an hour seated comfortably in an air-conditioned theater. 4. Between the live actors and animatronics, it's so much more than just another silly 3-D movie. And 5. IT'S THE MUPPETS! Who doesn't love these hysterical creatures and their 3-D shenanigans?*

TOURING TIPS *For the First Time in Forever* offers FastPass, which is distributed for the next showtime for which FastPass has not sold out. There is also a standby line. We usually see plenty of standby seats available, even for shows where all FastPass tickets have been distributed. Be sure to get in line at least 30 minutes early if you are going to use the standby line.

Muppet-Vision 3-D handles crowds exceedingly well. If showing, your wait should not last longer than 20 minutes except on days when the park is jampacked. Special effects and loud noises may frighten some preschoolers.

Hyperion Theater / *Disney's Aladdin: A Musical Spectacular*
★★★★

Thumbs Up for the Whole Family

What it is Venue for live shows. **Scope and scale** Major attraction. **When to go** After experiencing DCA's rides. **Special comments** Great venue; not to be missed. **Duration of show** 50 minutes. **Probable waiting time** 30 minutes.

DESCRIPTION AND COMMENTS This 2,000-seat theater is DCA's premier venue for live productions, many of which are based on Disney-animated films and feature Disney characters. Shows exhibit

Broadway quality in every sense, except duration of the presentation, and alone are arguably worth the price of park admission. For now, *Disney's Aladdin—A Musical Spectacular* is continuing its run as the most elaborate show staged at any stateside Disney theme park. A breezy stage version of the *Aladdin* story, it features familiar film tunes ("Friend Like Me" and "Prince Ali") plus one newly written ballad, along with jaw-dropping overhead flying carpet effects. We rate it not to be missed, thanks largely to the actors playing the Genie, who are given remarkably long leashes to ad lib up-to-the-minute pop-culture references that sail right over younger audience members' heads. In the evening the Hyperion is sometimes used as a stage for separate-admission concerts and special events.

TOURING TIPS The lavish productions hosted by the Hyperion Theater are rightly very popular and commonly sell out on busier days. Presentations are described, and showtimes listed, in the park *Times Guide.* The theater is multilevel. Though all the seats provide a good line of sight, we recommend that you sit on the ground level relatively close to the entrance doors (if possible) to facilitate an easy exit after the performance. Finally, be forewarned that the sound volume for Hyperion Theater productions would give heavy metal concerts a good run for the money.

DISNEY DISH WITH JIM HILL

BACK LOT'S URBAN RENEWAL PLAN BACKED UP Virtually every corner of Disney California Adventure received a major face-lift, as well as a significant new attraction, as part of the theme park's $1.4 billion redo in 2012—every part of DCA except Hollywood Land. And why is that, exactly? Well, Hollywood Land had been booked years in advance by corporate groups holding their annual conventions in and around Anaheim. And these folks just love to hold their after-hours corporate parties in this part of DCA, if only so they can experience what it's like to stroll down the red carpet at a big Hollywood premiere. But the Imagineers do have some pretty elaborate plans in the works for this section of the park, which may involve pulling down most of the attractions and shops located on Hollywood's north side to make room for a huge new coaster set inside the Door Vault building from Monsters, Inc. But none of that can happen until Disneyland Resort honors every one of the private corporate parties previously booked for DCA.

Monsters, Inc. Mike & Sulley to the Rescue ★★★½

APPEAL BY AGE	PRESCHOOL ★★★★	GRADE SCHOOL ★★★★	TEENS ★★★½
YOUNG ADULTS ★★★½	OVER 30 ★★★★		SENIORS ★★★★½

What it is Dark ride. **Scope and scale** Major attraction. **When to go** Before 11 a.m. **Special comment** Disney's best dark ride in years. **Duration of ride** 3¾ minutes. **Average wait in line per 100 people ahead of you** 4 minutes. **Assumes** 23 cars in operation. **Loading speed** Moderate.

DESCRIPTION AND COMMENTS Based on characters and the story from the Disney-Pixar film *Monsters, Inc.,* the ride takes you through child-phobic Monstropolis as Mike and Sulley try to return baby Boo safely to her bedroom. If you haven't seen the film, the story line won't make much sense. In a nutshell, a human baby gets loose in a sort of parallel universe populated largely by amusing monsters. Good monsters Mike and Sulley try to return Boo to her home before the bad monsters get their hands on her.

The Disney Imagineers did a very good job on the Monsters, Inc. ride, recreating the humor, characters, and setting of the film in great detail. The section of the attraction where you ride through the Door Vault with all of its lifts and conveyors is truly inspired. Special effects are first-rate, and lots of subtle and not-so-subtle jokes are worked into the whole experience. As in the Tower of Terror, you'll have to ride several times to catch them all. Before disembarking, be sure to banter with sluglike supervisor Roz, an animatronic "living character" that can see and interact with riders.

TOURING TIPS You can usually ride without too much of a wait. Because it's near several theater attractions, the ride is subject to experiencing a sudden deluge of guests when the theaters disgorge their audiences.

Monsters, Inc. is an iffy attraction for preschoolers: Some love it and some are frightened. Increase your odds for a positive experience by exposing your little ones to the movie before leaving home.

Turtle Talk with Crush ★★★★

| APPEAL BY AGE | PRESCHOOL ★★★★ | GRADE SCHOOL ★★★★ | TEENS ★★★★½ |
| YOUNG ADULTS ★★★★½ | | OVER 30 ★★★½ | SENIORS ★★★½ |

What it is An interactive animated film. **Scope and scale** Minor attraction. **When to go** After you see the other attractions in the Animation building. **Duration of show** 17 minutes. **Probable waiting time** 10–20 minutes.

DESCRIPTION AND COMMENTS *Turtle Talk with Crush* is an interactive theater show starring the 150-year-old surfer-dude turtle from *Finding Nemo*. Though it starts like a typical Disney theme park movie, *Turtle Talk* quickly turns into a surprise interactive encounter as the on-screen Crush begins to have actual conversations with guests in the audience. Real-time computer graphics are used to accurately move Crush's mouth when forming words.

A mom from Henderson, Colorado, has a crush on Crush:

> Turtle Talk with Crush *is a must-see. Our 4-year-old was picked out of the crowd by Crush, and we were just amazed by the technology that allowed one-on-one conversation. It was adorable and enjoyed by everyone from Grammy and Papa to the 4-year-old!*

TOURING TIPS The animation is brilliant, and guests of all ages list *Crush* as their favorite Animation building feature. By late afternoon, the building has usually cleared out. Save this for your last stop there.

The Twilight Zone Tower of Terror *(FastPass)* ★★★★½

| APPEAL BY AGE | PRESCHOOL ★★★½ | GRADE SCHOOL ★★★★½ | TEENS ★★★★½ |
| YOUNG ADULTS ★★★★½ | | OVER 30 ★★★★★ | SENIORS ★★★★ |

What it is Sci-fi-themed indoor thrill ride. **Scope and scale** Super-headliner. **When to go** The first hour the park is open or use FastPass. **Special comments** Not to be missed. Must be 40" tall to ride; switching-off option provided (see page 145). **Duration of ride** About 4 minutes plus preshow. **Average wait in line per 100 people ahead of you** 4 minutes. **Assumes** All elevators operating. **Loading speed** Moderate.

Dark   Scary   Rough   Lose Things   Queasy   Muss Your 'Do

DESCRIPTION AND COMMENTS The Twilight Zone Tower of Terror is a unique species of Disney thrill ride, though it borrows elements of The Haunted Mansion at Disneyland Park. The story is that you're touring a once-famous Hollywood hotel gone to ruin. As at Star Tours, the queuing area integrates guests into the adventure as they pass through the hotel's once-opulent public rooms. From the lobby, guests are escorted into the hotel's library, where Rod Serling, speaking on an old black-and-white television, greets the guests and introduces the plot.

The Tower of Terror is a whopper at 13-plus stories tall. It breaks tradition in terms of visually isolating themed areas. The entire park is visible from the top, but you have to look quickly!

The ride vehicle, one of the hotel's service elevators, takes guests to see the haunted hostelry. The tour begins with a startling fiber-optic star field effect, and from there things quickly get seriously weird. You have entered The Twilight Zone. Guests are subjected to a full range of special effects as they encounter unexpected horrors and optical illusions. The climax of the adventure occurs when the elevator reaches the 13th floor and the cable snaps.

DCA's Tower of Terror is very similar to the Walt Disney World version, but they are definitely not clones. In Florida, you start by slowly approaching the tower through mood-setting decayed gardens, while in DCA you simply step off the street and through the hotel's front door. From there, the adventure begins the same way—you pass through the hotel lobby and into the library for the preshow, after which you enter the boarding area. DCA's boiler room is much bigger with colorful (that is, less creepy) lighting, and it's decorated with additional insider nods to the original TV series.

Once you're on the elevator, however, the two attractions really part company. In the Disney World version, the elevator stops at a couple of floors to reveal some eerie visuals, but then actually moves out of the shaft onto one of the floors. The effects during this brief sojourn are remarkable, and more remarkable still is that you don't know that you've reentered the shaft until the elevator speeds skyward. In the DCA Tower of Terror, the elevator never leaves the shaft. The visuals and special effects are equally compelling, especially the unique ghostly mirror not found in Orlando, but there's never that feeling of disorientation that distinguishes the Florida attraction. The DCA Tower of Terror is more straightforward, and consequently a little less mysterious. Once the elevator dropping ensues, both versions are similar, but Florida features multiple randomized drop profiles, making each re-ride a surprise, while every stay in DCA's hotel is the same. Regardless of which version you try, unless you're already fanatically familiar with the superior original, you're unlikely to be disappointed.

The Tower has great potential for terrifying young children and rattling more mature visitors. If you have teenagers in your party, use them as experimental probes—if they report back that they really, really liked it, run as fast as you can in the opposite direction. Seriously, avoid assuming that this attraction isn't for you. A senior from the United Kingdom tried The Tower of Terror and liked it very much, writing:

I was thankful I read your review of The Tower of Terror, or I would certainly have avoided it. As you say, it is so full of magnificent detail that it is worth riding, even if you don't fancy the drops involved.

On the flip side, a Shelton, Connecticut, reader strongly disagrees:

I am fine with rides like Matterhorn Bobsleds and Big Thunder Mountain Rail-road, but I have always avoided The Tower of Terror, as it sounded awful. However, on this trip, I read the quote by an older person saying they were glad they went, as the details were worth it "even if you don't fancy the drops involved." I am here to tell you that there is NO detail on that ride that is worth the multiple stomach-jolting drops. After the first drop, all I could do was hang on and pray that it would be over soon. My legs were shaking as we walked out.

TOURING TIPS Because of its height, the tower is a veritable beacon, visible from outside the park and luring curious guests as soon as they enter. Because of the attraction's popularity with schoolkids, teens, and young adults, you can count on a footrace to get there when the park opens. The tower used to be mobbed most of the day, but newer attractions at Cars Land have siphoned away some of the lines.

To access The Tower of Terror, bear left from the park entrance into Hollywood Land. Continue straight to the Hyperion Theater and then turn right. To save time, when you enter the library waiting area, stand in the far back corner across from the door where you entered and at the opposite end of the room from the TV. When the doors to the loading area open, you'll be one of the first admitted.

A **BUG'S LAND**

THIS LAND IS DISNEY'S RESPONSE to complaints that DCA lacked appeal for younger children with a bug's-eye world of giant objects, children's rides, and the *It's Tough to Be a Bug!* movie.

Flik's Fun Fair ★★★

APPEAL BY AGE	PRESCHOOL ★★★★½	GRADE SCHOOL ★★★★	TEENS ★★
YOUNG ADULTS ★★★		OVER 30 ★★½	SENIORS ★★★

What it is Children's rides and play areas. **Scope and scale** Minor attraction. **When to go** Before 11:30 a.m. for the rides; anytime for the play areas. **Special comment** Preschool heaven. **Duration of tour** About 50 minutes for a comprehensive visit.

DESCRIPTION AND COMMENTS Flik's Fun Fair is a children's park as seen through the eyes of an insect. Children can wander among 20-foot-tall blades of grass, tunnel-size garden hoses, an enormous anthill, and the like. Princess Dot's Puddle Park is a kid's water-maze play area fashioned from giant-size garden sprinklers (we're not making this up). Kiddie rides include Flik's Flyers, with a balloon-ride theme; a drive-it-yourself car ride called Tuck and Roll's Drive 'Em Buggies; Heimlich's Chew Chew Train, a miniature train ride; and a mini–Mad Tea Party ride titled Francis' Ladybug Boogie, where you can spin your own "ladybug."

TOURING TIPS Though they're colorful and magnetically alluring to the under-8 crowd, the rides are low capacity, slow loading, and ridiculously brief. Our advice is to ride them before 11 a.m. if you visit on a weekend or during the summer. The play areas can be enjoyed anytime, but then you're faced with the prospect of the kids caterwauling to get on the rides. Following is the relevant data on the kiddie rides (note that waiting times are per 50 people ahead of you as opposed to the usual 100 people):

FLIK'S FLYERS ★★½ *(suspended "baskets" swing around a central axis)*
- **RIDE TIME** Almost 1½ minutes
- **AVERAGE WAIT IN LINE PER 50 PEOPLE AHEAD OF YOU** 6 minutes

FRANCIS' LADYBUG BOOGIE ★★★ *(adaptation of Mad Tea Party)*
- **SPECIAL COMMENTS** Unlike most teacup-style rides, turning the center wheel won't spin you faster. Instead, squeeze together on one side of the car and lean your weight into the turns.
- **RIDE TIME** 1 minute
- **AVERAGE WAIT IN LINE PER 50 PEOPLE AHEAD OF YOU** 8 minutes

HEIMLICH'S CHEW CHEW TRAIN ★★★½ *(train ride)*
- **SPECIAL COMMENTS** Adults as well as children can ride and should enjoy the surreal narration and scent effects.
- **RIDE TIME** Almost 2 minutes
- **AVERAGE WAIT IN LINE PER 50 PEOPLE AHEAD OF YOU** 5 minutes

TUCK AND ROLL'S DRIVE 'EM BUGGIES ★★ *(bumper cars)*
- **SPECIAL COMMENTS** Adults as well as children can ride. Cars are much slower than on normal bumper car rides.
- **RIDE TIME** Almost 2 minutes
- **AVERAGE WAIT IN LINE PER 50 PEOPLE AHEAD OF YOU** 12 minutes

It's Tough to Be a Bug!   ★★★★

APPEAL BY AGE	PRESCHOOL ★★★½	GRADE SCHOOL ★★★★	TEENS ★★★½
YOUNG ADULTS ★★★½		OVER 30 ★★★★	SENIORS —

What it is 3-D movie. **Scope and scale** Major attraction. **When to go** After experiencing DCA's better rides. **Special comment** 3-D effects and loud noises frighten many preschoolers. **Duration of show** 8½ minutes. **Probable waiting time** 20 minutes.

Dark   Scary   Loud

DESCRIPTION AND COMMENTS *It's Tough to Be a Bug!* is an uproarious 3-D film about the difficulties of being a very small creature. It features some of the characters from the Disney-Pixar film *a bug's life*. *It's Tough to Be a Bug!* is similar to *Muppet-Vision 3-D* in that it combines a 3-D film with an arsenal of tactile and visual special effects. In our view, the special effects are a bit overdone and the film somewhat disjointed. Even so, we rate the *Bug* as not to be missed.

TOURING TIPS Because this attraction is situated in one of the sleepier themed areas, *Bug* is not usually under attack from the hordes until late morning. This should make *It's Tough to Be a Bug!* the easiest of the park's top attractions to see. Lately, *It's Tough to Be a Bug!* has periodically been preempted in favor of 4-D feature-film previews promoting Disney's latest potential blockbusters, *Cinderella* and *Ant-Man*. Check it out if you're interested in a supersized trailer of an upcoming movie, accompanied by bursts of wind and water.

Be advised that *It's Tough to Be a Bug!* is very intense and that the special effects will do a number on young children as well as anyone who is squeamish about insects. First, from a mother of two from Mobile, Alabama:

It's Tough to Be a Bug! was too intense for any kid. Our boys are 5 and 7, and they were scared to death. They love bugs, and they hated this movie. All of the kids in the theater were screaming and crying. I felt like a terrible mother for taking them into this movie. It is billed as a bug movie for kids, but nothing about it is for kids.

But a Williamsville, New York, woman had it even worse:

We almost lost the girls to any further Disney magic due to the 3-D movie It's Tough to Be a Bug! *It was their first Disney experience, and it was almost their last. The story line was nebulous and difficult to follow—all they were aware of was the torture of sitting in a darkened theater being overrun with bugs. Total chaos, the likes of which I've never experienced, was breaking out around us. The 11-year-old refused to talk for 20 minutes after the fiasco, and the 3½-year-old wanted to go home—not back to the hotel room, but home.*

Most readers, however, loved the movie, including this mom from Brentwood, Tennessee:

It's intense like Honey, I Shrunk the Audience *but mostly funny. The bugs are cartoonlike instead of realistic and icky, so I can't understand what all the fuss is about. Disney has conditioned us to think of rodents as cute, so kids think nothing of walking up to a mouse the size of a portable toilet but go nuts over some cartoon bugs. Get a grip!*

PARADISE PIER

WRAPPED AROUND THE SOUTHERN SHORE of the kidney-shaped lake, Paradise Pier is Disney's version of a seaside amusement park from the Victoria era. It covers about one-third of Disney California Adventure and contains almost one-third of the attractions.

Paradise Pier's original tacky mid-20th-century theme at DCA was ironic, and in a perverse way it brought the story of Walt Disney and Disneyland full circle. Walt, you see, created Disneyland Park as an alternative to parks such as this—parks with a carnival atmosphere, simple midway rides, carny games, and amply available wine, beer, and liquor. Amazingly, corporate Disney had made just such a place the centerpiece of Disneyland's sister park, slaughtering in effect one of the last of Walt's sacred cows. The 2012 refurb's clapboard buildings and retro carnival games gave the area much-needed charm, but not everything is perfect in Paradise; the now-removed Maliboomer tower was supposed to become a lush park, but it turned out to be a few benches on concrete and a patch of green behind barricades to gaze at longingly. The foregoing notwithstanding, Paradise Pier is spotlessly clean, exciting during the day, and eye-popping in the evening with all its colorful lights.

Incidentally, those aforementioned carnival games aren't as avaricious as their unfair fair ancestors. If you and a companion play together, you can win a modest stuffed animal for only $5 (less than you'd pay in the park's gift shops). Some games let you combine multiple wins for an impressive prize. The fishing and racehorse games seem easiest to win.

World of Color, an evening show synchronized to music and Disney film clips, complete with more than a thousand water fountains shooting water hundreds of feet into the sky, was overhauled in 2015 for Disneyland's 60th anniversary. *Note:* Most of the attractions (except Toy Story Midway Mania!) in Paradise Pier will close early for *World of Color* performances.

DISNEY DISH WITH JIM HILL

NOW THAT'S AN INTERESTING HOOK FOR AN ATTRACTION When the Imagineers were originally working on their major redo of Disney California Adventure, all sorts of ideas were on the table. And one of the wildest was giving guests a really good reason to scream as they rode California Screamin'. For a time, WDI toyed with retheming this thrill ride around the Disney villains. The concept was that California Screamin' would wind in and around enormous icons representing Disney's biggest baddies, such as the Evil Queen's crown, Jafar's cobra-shaped staff, and Maleficent's horns. And, in one particularly tight turn in the track, your coaster car would zoom by a supersize Captain Hook's hook. Unfortunately, this Disney villains coaster idea didn't (Peter) pan out.

California Screamin' *(FastPass)* ★★★★

| APPEAL BY AGE | PRESCHOOL — | GRADE SCHOOL ★★★★½ | TEENS ★★★★★ |
| YOUNG ADULTS ★★★★½ | | OVER 30 ★★★★½ | SENIORS ★★★ |

What it is Big, bad roller coaster. **Scope and scale** Super-headliner. **When to go** Ride first thing in the morning, or use FastPass. **Special comments** Long and smooth; may induce motion sickness. Must be 48″ tall to ride; switching-off option provided (see page 145). **Duration of ride** 2½ minutes. **Average wait in line per 100 people ahead of you** 2½ minutes. **Assumes** 24-passenger trains with 36-second dispatch interval. **Loading speed** Moderate–fast.

Scary   Lose Things   Queasy   Muss Your 'Do

DESCRIPTION AND COMMENTS This apparently antiquated wooden monster is actually a modern steel coaster, and at 6,072 feet, it's the third longest steel coaster in the United States. California Screamin' gets off to a 0-to-55-mph start by launching you up the first hill like a jet fighter plane off the deck of a carrier (albeit with different technology). From here you will experience tight turns followed by a second launch that sends you over the crest of a 110-foot hill with a 107-foot drop on the far side. Next, you bank and complete an elliptical loop. A diving turn followed by a series of camelbacks brings you back to the station. Speakers play a synchronized sound track complete with recorded canned screaming and a carnival barker cameo by actor Neil Patrick Harris.

We were impressed by the length of the course and the smoothness of the ride. From beginning to end, the ride is about 2½ minutes, with 2 minutes of actual ride time. En route the coaster slows enough on curves and on transition hills to let you take in the nice view. On the scary-o-meter, Screamin' is certainly worse than Space Mountain but doesn't really compare with some of the steel coasters at nearby Magic Mountain. What Screamin' loses in fright potential, however, it makes up for in variety. Along its course, Disney has placed every known curve, hill, dip, and loop in roller coaster design.

A Carlsbad, California, woman found the ride to be a smooth operator:

California Screamin' was WONDERFUL, and I am a 57-year-old mom, not an adrenaline-crazed young adult! It was my first ever upside-down ride, but it was so smooth and quick that I only felt a gentle pressure pushing me into the seat. It was so fun that I went again! Don't miss this one, at any age!

A Texas woman agrees, writing:

I hate roller coasters, and I love California Screamin'. Very smooth.

TOURING TIPS California Screamin' is a serious coaster, one that makes Space Mountain look like Dumbo. Secure any hats, cameras, eyeglasses, or anything else that might be ripped from your person during the ride. Stay away completely if you're prone to motion sickness.

Engineered to run several trains at once, California Screamin' does a better job than any roller coaster we've seen at handling crowds, at least when the attraction is running at full capacity. The coaster is sometimes shut down two or more times a day for technical problems. Early in the morning, however, it's usually easy to get two or three rides under your belt in about 15 minutes. Ride in the first hour the park is open or use FastPass or the single-rider line (enter up the ramp to the left of the queue). Note that FastPass here is sometimes disconnected from the rest of the park's attractions, meaning that you can hold a pass for this and another ride at the same time.

Golden Zephyr   ★★

APPEAL BY AGE	PRESCHOOL ★★★★	GRADE SCHOOL ★★★½	TEENS ★★★
YOUNG ADULTS ★★★½		OVER 30 ★★★½	SENIORS —

Queasy

What it is Zephyrs spinning around a central tower. **Scope and scale** Minor attraction. **When to go** The first 90 minutes the park is open or just before closing. **Special comment** Can't operate on breezy days. **Duration of ride** 2 minutes. **Average wait in line per 100 people ahead of you** 8½ minutes. **Assumes** Normal operations. **Loading speed** Slow.

DESCRIPTION AND COMMENTS First, a *zephyr* is a term often associated with blimps. On this attraction, the zephyrs look like open-cockpit rockets. In any event, each zephyr holds about a dozen guests and spins around a central axis with enough centrifugal force to lay the zephyr partially on its side. As it turns out, the Golden Zephyrs are very touchy, as zephyrs go: They can't fly in a wind exceeding about 10 miles per hour. Needless to say, the attraction is shut down much of the time.

TOURING TIPS This colorful attraction is another slow-loading cycle ride. Go during the first 90 minutes the park is open or prepare for a long wait.

Goofy's Sky School *(FastPass)*   ★★★

APPEAL BY AGE	PRESCHOOL ★★★★★	GRADE SCHOOL ★★★★½	TEENS ★★★½
YOUNG ADULTS ★★★★		OVER 30 ★★★½	SENIORS —

What it is Disney's version of a Wild (or Mad) Mouse ride. **Scope and scale** Major attraction. **When to go** During the first hour the park is open. **Special comments** Space Mountain with the lights on. May induce motion sickness; must be 42″ tall to ride; switching-off option provided (see page 145). **Duration of ride** About 1½ minutes. **Average wait in line per 100 people ahead of you** 6¼ minutes. **Assumes** 15-second dispatch interval. **Loading speed** Slow–moderate.

Scary

Lose Things

Queasy

Muss Your 'Do

DESCRIPTION AND COMMENTS Themed as Goofy teaching a bunch of new pilots how to fly, Goofy's Sky School is a designer Wild Mouse (sometimes also called a Mad Mouse). If you're not familiar with the genre, it's a small, convoluted roller coaster where the track dips and turns unexpectedly, presumably reminding its inventor of a mouse tearing through a maze. To define it more in Disney terms, the ride is similar to Space Mountain, only outdoors and therefore in the light. Goofy's Sky School is an off-the-shelf midway ride in which Disney has invested next to nothing in spiffing up. In other words, fun but nothing special.

TOURING TIPS A fun ride but also a slow-loading one, and one that breaks down frequently. Ride during the first hour the park is open, or use FastPass or the single-rider line (when open).

Jumpin' Jellyfish ★½

APPEAL BY AGE	PRESCHOOL ★★★★	GRADE SCHOOL ★★★★	TEENS ★★★
YOUNG ADULTS ★★		OVER 30 ★★½	SENIORS —

What it is Parachute ride. **Scope and scale** Minor attraction. **When to go** The first 90 minutes the park is open or just before closing. **Special comments** All sizzle, no meat; can't operate on breezy days. Must be 40″ tall to ride. **Duration of ride** About 45 seconds. **Average wait in line per 100 people ahead of you** 20 minutes. **Assumes** Both towers operating. **Loading speed** Slow.

DESCRIPTION AND COMMENTS On this ride, you're raised on a cable to the top of the tower and then released to gently parachute back to earth. Mostly a children's ride, Jumpin' Jellyfish is paradoxically off-limits to those who would most enjoy it because of its 40-inch minimum-height restriction. For adults, the attraction is a real snore. Oops, make that a real bore—the paltry 45-second duration of the ride is not long enough to fall asleep.

TOURING TIPS The Jellyfish, so called because of a floating jellyfish's resemblance to an open parachute, is another slow-loading ride of very low capacity. Get on early in the morning or prepare for a long wait.

King Triton's Carousel ★★★

APPEAL BY AGE	PRESCHOOL ★★★★½	GRADE SCHOOL ★★★½	TEENS ★★★★
YOUNG ADULTS ★★★		OVER 30 ★★★½	SENIORS ★★★★

What it is Merry-go-round. **Scope and scale** Minor attraction. **When to go** Before noon. **Special comment** Beautimus. **Duration of ride** A little less than 2 minutes. **Average wait in line per 100 people ahead of you** 8 minutes. **Assumes** Normal staffing. **Loading speed** Slow.

DESCRIPTION AND COMMENTS On this elaborate and stunningly crafted carousel, dolphins, sea horses, seals, and the like replace the standard prancing horses.

TOURING TIPS Worth a look even if there are no children in your party. If you have kids who want to ride, try to get them on before noon.

The Little Mermaid: Ariel's Undersea Adventure ★★★½

APPEAL BY AGE	PRESCHOOL ★★★★½	GRADE SCHOOL ★★★★	TEENS ★★★½
YOUNG ADULTS ★★★½		OVER 30 ★★★½	SENIORS ★★★★

What it is Track ride in the dark. **Scope and scale** Headliner. **When to go** First thing in the morning or after 4 p.m. **Duration of ride** 6¼ minutes. **Average wait in line per 100 people ahead of you** 3 minutes. **Assumes** Normal operations. **Loading speed** Fast.

DESCRIPTION AND COMMENTS The Palace of Fine Arts dome was incorporated into an impressive lagoon-facing facade modeled on early-20th-century aquariums. The seafoam-trimmed building, topped by a statue of King Triton, conceals Disney's newest old-school attraction. The basics of The Little Mermaid: Ariel's Undersea Adventure are similar to

Disneyland's Haunted Mansion: a continuously loading ride system transports you through a series of elaborately themed, darkened scenes with sophisticated special effects. In this case, The Little Mermaid attraction takes you to the bottom of the ocean in clam shell cars, where the ride recaps Ariel's journey from her father's undersea kingdom to marrying Prince Eric. After Scuttle the seagull recaps the backstory for you, your vehicle descends backward beneath the simulated sea surface with a spritz of cool air. Assuming that you haven't drowned, you'll then meet a cutting-edge animatronic Ariel (featuring "floating" hair); party down "Under the Sea" with Sebastian the crab; and be menaced by a 12-foot-wide, 7½-foot-tall undulating figure of Ursula, the evil sea witch. The adventure is all set to newly orchestrated versions of Alan Menken and Howard Ashman's classic songs, and original animator Glen Keane and actress Jodi Benson both returned to lend their talents.

The ride greatly benefited from a 2014 upgrade, which added more figures and enhanced the "Under the Sea" scene with vibrant black light. However, though the ride is colorful and kinetic, it still suffers from shortchanged storytelling, especially in the unsatisfyingly abrupt finale. While it's a welcome addition to DCA's short roster of kid-friendly indoor rides, anyone expecting a modern-day classic to compete with Haunted Mansion and Pirates of the Caribbean may come away somewhat disappointed. But this family from Arvada, Colorado, thinks the ride serves its supporting role well:

Head for The Little Mermaid ride when you need a break. It's well done, it's air-conditioned, and there's never a wait.

TOURING TIPS As one of the park's newer attractions and one that's suitable for most small children, The Little Mermaid can attract long lines as soon as the park opens on peak days. (On a positive note, this should reduce some of the early-morning demand for Toy Story Midway Mania! and Cars Land.) This attraction does not have FastPass. However, the Omnimover ride system is capable of efficiently handling more than 2,000 guests per hour, keeping lines moving swiftly even on busy days. If you find the line prohibitive, check back in the late afternoon, when you will often be able to walk on with little wait.

Mickey's Fun Wheel ★★½

APPEAL BY AGE	PRESCHOOL ★★★★★	GRADE SCHOOL ★★★½	TEENS ★★★½
YOUNG ADULTS ★★★★		OVER 30 ★★★½	SENIORS —

What it is Ferris wheel. **Scope and scale** Major attraction. **When to go** The first 90 minutes the park is open or just before closing. **Special comments** The world's largest chicken coop; may induce motion sickness. **Duration of ride** 9 minutes. **Average wait in line per 100 people ahead of you** 6¼ minutes. **Assumes** All 24 cabins in use. **Loading speed** Slow.

DESCRIPTION AND COMMENTS Higher than the Matterhorn Bobsleds at Disneyland Park, this whopper of a Ferris wheel tops out at 150 feet. Absolutely spectacular in appearance, with an enormous Mickey in the middle of its wheel, the aptly named Mickey's Fun Wheel offers stunning views in all directions. Unfortunately, however, the view is severely compromised by the steel mesh that completely encloses the passenger compartment. In essence, Disney has created the world's largest revolving chicken coop. As concerns the ride itself, some of the passenger buckets move laterally from side to side across the Fun Wheel in addition to rotating around with the wheel. Because it feels like your bucket has become unattached from the main structure, this lateral movement can be a little disconcerting if you aren't expecting it. If the movement proves too disconcerting, motion sickness bags are thoughtfully provided in each swinging car.

TOURING TIPS Ferris wheels are the most slow loading of all cycle rides, but the Fun Wheel has a platform that allows three compartments to be loaded at once. The lateral sliding buckets are loaded from the two outside platforms, while the stationary compartments are loaded from the middle platform. Loading the entire wheel takes about 6½ minutes, following which the Fun Wheel rotates for a single revolution. And speaking of the ride, the Fun Wheel rotates so slowly that the wonderful rising and falling sensations of the garden-variety Ferris wheel are completely absent. For our money, the Fun Wheel is beautiful to behold but terribly boring to ride. If you decide to give it a whirl, ride the first hour the park is open or in the hour before the park closes.

Silly Symphony Swings ★★★

APPEAL BY AGE	PRESCHOOL ★★★★	GRADE SCHOOL ★★★★	TEENS ★★★
YOUNG ADULTS —	OVER 30 ★★★		SENIORS ★★★★

What it is Swings rotating around a central tower. **Scope and scale** Minor attraction. **When to go** The first 90 minutes the park is open or just before closing. **Special comments** Simple but fun. Must be 40″ tall to ride (48″ tall to ride solo). **Duration of ride** Less than 1½ minutes. **Average wait in line per 100 people ahead of you** 6 minutes. **Assumes** Normal staffing. **Loading speed** Slow.

Lose Things   Queasy   Muss Your 'Do

DESCRIPTION AND COMMENTS The theme pays tribute to the 1935 Mickey Mouse cartoon *The Band Concert,* the first color Mickey cartoon released to the public, with guests seated in swings flying around a tower. In the scary department, it's a wilder ride than Dumbo, but SSS is still just swings going in circles. A number of tandem swings are available to allow children 40–48 inches to ride with a parent; look for a separate tandem line to the left as you approach the attraction.

TOURING TIPS This is a fun and visually appealing ride, but it's also one that loads slowly and occasions long waits unless you ride during the first hour or so the park is open. Be aware that it's possible for the swing chairs to collide when the ride comes to a stop—the author once picked up a nice bruise when an empty swing smacked him during touchdown.

Toy Story Midway Mania! ★★★★½

APPEAL BY AGE	PRESCHOOL ★★★★★	GRADE SCHOOL ★★★★½	TEENS ★★★★½
YOUNG ADULTS ★★★★½	OVER 30 ★★★★½		SENIORS ★★★★★

What it is 3-D ride through indoor shooting gallery. **Scope and scale** Headliner. **When to go** First thing after the park opens. **Special comment** Not to be missed. **Duration of ride** About 6½ minutes. **Average wait in line per 100 people ahead of you** 4½ minutes. **Assumes** Both tracks operating. **Loading speed** Fast.

DESCRIPTION AND COMMENTS Toy Story Midway Mania! ushered in a whole new generation of Disney attractions: virtual dark rides. Since Disneyland opened in 1955, ride vehicles had moved past two- and three-dimensional sets often populated by Audio-Animatronics (AA); these detailed sets and robotic figures literally defined the Disney creative genius in attractions such as Pirates of the Caribbean, The Haunted Mansion, and Peter Pan's Flight. Instead, Toy Story Midway Mania! has long corridors, totally empty, covered with reflective material. There's almost nothing there . . . until you put on your 3-D glasses. Instantly, the corridor is full and brimming with color, action, and activity, thanks to projected computer-graphic imagery (CGI).

Conceptually, this is an interactive shooting gallery much like Buzz Lightyear Astro Blasters (see page 247), but in Toy Story Midway Mania!, your ride vehicle passes through a totally virtual midway, with booths offering such games as ring tossing and ball throwing. You use a cannon on your ride vehicle to play as you move along from booth to booth. Unlike the laser guns in Buzz Lightyear, however, Toy Story Midway Mania's pull-string cannons take advantage of CGI technology to toss rings, shoot balls, and even throw eggs and pies. Each game booth is manned by a *Toy Story* character who is right beside you in 3-D glory cheering you on. In addition to 3-D imagery, you experience various smells, vehicle motion, wind, and water spray. The ride begins with a training round to familiarize you with your cannon and the nature of the games and then continues through a number of "real" games in which you compete against your riding mate. The technology has the ability to self-adjust the level of difficulty so that every rider is challenged, and there are plenty of easy targets for small children to reach. *Tip:* Let the pull-string retract all the way back into the cannon before pulling it again. If you don't, the cannon won't fire.

Also of note, a 6-foot-tall Mr. Potato Head interacts with and talks to guests in real time in the preshow queuing area of Toy Story.

TOURING TIPS Much of the queuing area for Toy Story Midway Mania! is across the pedestrian walkway from the attraction's entrance. The queuing is covered, which is good, but it's not air-conditioned, which is very bad, with temperatures escalating into the 90s and higher. Not roasting in this oven is a great incentive to experience Toy Story Midway Mania! in the early morning, before it gets crowded.

As you might expect, Toy Story Midway Mania! is addictive, and though it's great fun right off the bat, it takes a couple of rides before you really get the hang of the pull-string cannon and the way the targets are presented. To rack up a high score, you must identify and shoot at high-value targets: High-value targets are small and often moving, while low-value targets are larger and easier to hit. Toward the end of the ride, the top score of the day and the top scores of the month are posted. If you're a newbie and you'd like to ride several times to gain experience and get your skill level up, consider making the attraction your first stop after the park opens.

The challenge of seeing Toy Story Midway Mania! without a horrendous wait was a hot topic among *Unofficial Guide* readers. But since Cars Land's debut, waits have become much more manageable, especially in the early morning. If you've experienced the extreme waits that always accompany the Orlando clone of this ride, rest assured that Anaheim's operations keep the line here moving much more swiftly. As a father from London, Ontario, wrote us:

The lines for Toy Story Midway Mania! at DCA are so much more manageable, never being longer than about 40 minutes. It was great to not deal with the insanity experienced at the Florida version.

CARS LAND

CARS LAND IS THE CROWNING CAPSTONE on DCA's transformation, and the first major "land" in an American Disney theme park devoted solely to a single film franchise. Tucked in the park's southeast corner on 12 acres of repurposed parking lot, Cars Land's main entrance is across from the Golden Vine Winery, though there are secondary gateways in A Bug's Land and in Pacific Wharf (the vista through the latter's stone archway entrance is especially scenic). A massive mountainous backdrop topped with 125-foot-high peaks patterned after 1950s Cadillac Pinnacle tail fins, known as the Cadillac Range, cradles Ornament Valley, home to a screen-accurate re-creation of Radiator Springs. That's the sleepy single-stoplight town along Route 66 populated by Pixar's anthropomorphized automobiles. Along its main drag, in addition to three rides, you'll find eateries themed to the film's minor characters and souvenir shops selling *Cars*-themed and Route 66 merchandise.

Cars Land represents a considerable investment in capital and creativity for the Disney company, resulting in a rare example of complete entertainment immersion. Walking through the aesthetically astounding area is uncannily like stepping into the cinematic universe, and well worth the wait even if you weren't particularly enamored of the merchandise-moving movies. Since opening, the area has attracted massive crowds all day and has dramatically increased DCA's overall attendance. As striking as Cars Land is by daylight, it is even more stunning after sunset; the nightly neon-lighting ceremony set to the doo-wop classic "Life Could Be a Dream" is a magical must-see (showtimes are not publicized but occur promptly at sundown, so ask a Cars Land cast member and arrive early). Finally, a word to the wise from a Dallas, Texas, family:

Tip: *Cars Land has NO shade. Literally none. Wear a hat.*

Luigi's Rollickin' Roadsters *(opens 2016)*

What it is Outdoor "dancing" car ride. **Scope and scale** Minor attraction. **When to go** During the first or last hours of the day.

DESCRIPTION AND COMMENTS When Cars Land opened in 2012, one of its three new attractions was Luigi's Flying Tires, a reincarnation of the Disneyland Park's short-lived Flying Saucers, a Tomorrowland attraction that lasted five years in the early 1960s. Imagineers retreaded the concept of hovercraft bumper cars, using a system similar to an air hockey table, as the basis for a tribute to the Radiator Springs resident Ferrari fanatic.

Luigi's Flying Tires turned out to be an example of nostalgia being better than reality; the tires accelerated very gradually and were tricky for first-time riders to control. Word got out that Luigi's was less than life-changing, and lines dwindled substantially in the years after the tires debuted, despite how glacially slow the attraction was to load.

In early 2015, Disney shuttered Luigi's to reimagine the attraction, which should reopen in 2016 as Luigi's Rollickin' Roadsters. Guests will still first queue inside the Casa Della Tires shop (where memorabilia from Luigi's and Guido's careers is on display), and then pass through a garden of automotive-inspired topiaries before approaching the attraction itself, which will occupy the same outdoor arena. However, instead of giant tires, small open-top cars (with the franchise's signature cartoon faces) will serve as the ride vehicles. And instead of controlling their destiny, this time, passengers are just along for the ride, as the cars spin and "dance" autonomously around each other in unpredictable patterns, thanks to trackless GPS technology. For an idea of what the new attraction might look like, search YouTube for "DisneySea Aquatopia" and imagine something similar on dry land instead of water.

TOURING TIPS Luigi's is sure to draw a crowd when it reopens, and even if it is more efficient than its predecessor, capacity will still be limited. If it is open during your visit, try to ride during the first or last hours of the day.

Mater's Junkyard Jamboree ★★★

APPEAL BY AGE **PRESCHOOL** ★★★★★ **GRADE SCHOOL** ★★★★ **TEENS** ★★★½
YOUNG ADULTS ★★★½ **OVER 30** ★★★½ **SENIORS** ★★★★

What it is Midway-type whip ride. **Scope and scale** Minor attraction. **When to go** Before noon. **Special comment** Must be 32" tall to ride. **Duration of ride** About 1½ minutes. **Average wait in line per 100 people ahead of you** 10 minutes. **Assumes** Both sides operating. **Loading speed** Slow.

Queasy

DESCRIPTION AND COMMENTS On the outskirts of town sits the junkyard home of Mater, the redneck tow truck voiced by Larry the Cable Guy. In his yard sit 22 baby tractors, each towing an open-air two-seater trailer. While Mater's voice emerges from a jury-rigged jukebox singing one of seven specially composed square-dancing tunes (plus one hilarious hidden song that plays only once per hour), the tractors travel in overlapping figure eight patterns along interlocking turntables. The vehicles are transferred from one revolving turntable to another, creating near-miss moments much like Francis' Ladybug Boogie. The difference is that Mater's trailers swing freely from side to side, creating a centripetal snapping sensation similar to vintage whip carnival rides. Mater's may look like a simple kiddie ride, but it supplies an unexpected kick that draws us back for repeated spins. This London, Ontario, dad echoed our assessment:

Mater's Junkyard Jamboree was surprisingly good. It doesn't look like much, but you have to ride it. We saw a woman lose her sunglasses because she wasn't prepared for how it swings around. The mechanically inclined adults exiting the ride were impressed with the engineering that allowed for the figure eight movement.

TOURING TIPS Mater is the breakout hit character of the *Cars* franchise, and his namesake ride is visually attractive but slow loading. Still, it typically has the shortest queue of the three Cars Land attractions.

Radiator Springs Racers *(FastPass)* ★★★★★

APPEAL BY AGE **PRESCHOOL** ★★★★½ **GRADE SCHOOL** ★★★★★ **TEENS** ★★★★★
YOUNG ADULTS ★★★★★ **OVER 30** ★★★★★ **SENIORS** ★★★★½

What it is Automotive dark ride with high-speed thrills. **Scope and scale** Super-headliner. **When to go** The first 30 minutes the park is open or use FastPass. **Special comments** Not to be missed. Must be 40" tall to ride; switching-off option provided (see page 145). **Duration of ride** About 4 minutes. **Average wait in line per 100 people ahead of you** 4 minutes. **Assumes** Normal operations. **Loading speed** Moderate–fast.

Dark Scary Lose Things Muss Your 'Do

DESCRIPTION AND COMMENTS To the right of the Radiator Springs Courthouse at the end of Route 66 lies the entrance to the most ambitious attraction built at Disneyland Resort in more than a decade. Disney's Imagineers wedded an enhanced version of the high-speed slot cars developed for Epcot's Test Track with immersive sets and elaborate animatronics. The ride, which covers nearly 6 of Cars Land's 12 acres, mixes slow indoor sections with thrilling open-air acceleration in a way that appeals to every end of the demographic spectrum.

You begin your road trip by walking through Stanley's Oasis, the town's original 1909 settlement, and end up in a cavernous loading station. There you board a six-passenger convertible, each with a smiling face on its front grill, and you're off on a scenic tour of stunning Ornament Valley, on your way to compete in today's big race.

After a leisurely drive past massive rock formations and a majestic waterfall, you enter the show building for a series of indoor scenes depicting the residents of Radiator Springs. These environments don't quite match the awe-inspiring scale of scenes in Pirates of the Caribbean or Indiana Jones Adventure, but they are a big step up from the old-fashioned Fantasyland dark rides and feature movie-accurate animatronics with impressively expressive eyes and mouths (achieved through a combination of digital projections and practical effects). Along your tour, you'll be sidetracked by a tractor-tipping expedition with Mater, which leads to a run-in with an angry harvester. Before reaching the starting line, you'll need some new tires or a fresh coat of paint. Then it's time to line up alongside another carload of guests as you await Luigi's countdown. The last third of the ride is a flat-out race over camelback hills, under outcrops, and around banked curves, with a randomly chosen car crossing the finish line first. Radiator Springs Racers's top speed of 40 miles per hour falls short of Test Track's 60-plus peak, but the winding turns and airtime-inducing humps supply an exhilarating rush. After a final swing past the glowing stalactites of Tail Light Cavern and some parting praise from Lightning McQueen and Mater, you'll exit your vehicle and inspect your obligatory on-ride photo.

TOURING TIPS Radiator Springs Racers is a massive draw from the minute the park opens every day. With a carrying capacity of about 1,500 riders per hour, the attraction regularly sees standby waits of 2–3 hours, and FastPasses may all be claimed for the day within an hour of opening; even the single-rider queue can run 45 minutes or more. Your best options are to arrive at least 30 minutes before the park officially opens and position yourself to hustle for a FastPass (see page 280), or step into the standby queue shortly before closing. If time permits, try to ride once by day and again after dark; evening illumination makes the outdoor portions especially enchanting.

Note that FastPasses for Radiator Springs Racers are distributed outside of Cars Land proper, near *It's Tough to Be Bug!*, with a queue for tickets forming from Carthay Circle before the park officially opens. You may be tempted to rush to the standby queue at rope drop instead of getting a FastPass, but be warned that the ride regularly opens late due to daily maintenance, potentially wasting your valuable morning touring time. The ride also shuts down for long periods after any substantial rainstorm. Hotel guests using early-entry privileges should look for an exclusive FastPass queue just outside the kiosk corral and step into it shortly before regular park hours start. Day guests are currently only allowed into the FastPass queue after official park opening, with guests gathering in a disorganized blob to the right of Carthay Circle before rope drop. This can cause quite a traffic jam as hundreds of people rush to get in line. Send one member of your party with all the tickets to get FastPasses, and keep your kids clear of the mob. Don't be scared off by the size of the crowd queuing for FastPasses, says a Superior, Colorado, reader:

The FastPass line for RSR was amazingly efficient. A cast member at every kiosk was shoving tickets in and getting FastPasses out—none of that "which-way-do-I-put-these-in" thing. The line wove down the street, but I was out in less than 5 minutes!

PACIFIC WHARF

THIS LAND INCORPORATES a Cannery Row–inspired eatery area adjacent to Paradise Bay with a diminutive winery, situated at the base of Grizzly Peak and across from A Bug's Land, making it the smallest of the Golden State–themed areas. It would be a stretch to call it an attraction, much less a themed area.

Bakery Tour   ★★½

APPEAL BY AGE	PRESCHOOL —	GRADE SCHOOL ★★★½	TEENS ★★★½
YOUNG ADULTS ★★★½		OVER 30 ★★★½	SENIORS —

What it is Free bread! (Plus a short film and walking tour.) **Scope and scale** Diversion. **When to go** Anytime. **Special comment** Visitors get a free bite-size sample of fresh sourdough bread. **Duration of tour** 9 minutes. **Probable waiting time** None.

DESCRIPTION AND COMMENTS The Bakery Tour (hosted by Boudin Bakery) is a walk-through attraction featuring hosts Rosie O'Donnell and Colin Mochrie via video. It takes visitors through the history of the Boudin Bakery and also explains how the bread is baked for various restaurants across Disneyland Resort.

TOURING TIPS There's never any wait to enter this attraction, and you get a small bread sample as soon as you walk in. The tour is a great way to kill 10 minutes. See this when you have some downtime, perhaps after a meal, while on the way back to Paradise Pier, or before watching *Disney's Aladdin.*

If the bread sample whets your appetite, you can buy a full-size loaf (including ones shaped like Mickey) at the café adjoining the exit. Next door is the Ghirardelli Soda Fountain and Chocolate Shop, where you can indulge in diabetes-inducing ice cream sundaes (or snag a free sample of candy) while admiring an animated diorama of San Francisco.

GRIZZLY PEAK

GRIZZLY PEAK, a huge mountain shaped like the head of a bear, is home to **Grizzly River Run,** a whitewater raft ride, and the **Redwood Creek Challenge Trail,** an outdoor playground that resembles an obstacle course. In 2015, Grizzly Peak absorbed the adjacent area originally known as Condor Flats, rechristening the area around **Soarin' Over California** as Grizzly Peak Airfield and adding woodsy theming appropriate to a national park in the High Sierras, as opposed to its former desolate desert look.

Grizzly River Run *(FastPass)* ★★★★½

| APPEAL BY AGE | PRESCHOOL ★★★★½ | | GRADE SCHOOL ★★★★½ | TEENS ★★★★★ |
| YOUNG ADULTS ★★★★½ | | OVER 30 ★★★★½ | | SENIORS ★★★½ |

What it is Whitewater raft ride. **Scope and scale** Super-headliner. **When to go** First hour the park is open, or use FastPass. **Special comments** Not to be missed; you are guaranteed to get wet, and possibly soaked. Must be 42″ tall to ride. **Duration of ride** 5½ minutes. **Average wait in line per 100 people ahead of you** 5 minutes. **Assumes** 32 rafts operating. **Loading speed** Moderate.

Scary Wet Lose Things Rough Muss Your 'Do

DESCRIPTION AND COMMENTS Whitewater raft rides have been a hot-weather favorite of theme park patrons for decades. The ride consists of an unguided trip down a man-made river in a circular rubber raft, with a platform mounted on top seating six to eight people. The raft essentially floats free in the current and is washed downstream through rapids and waves. Because the river is fairly wide with numerous currents, eddies, and obstacles, there is no telling exactly where the raft will go. Thus, each trip is different and unpredictable. The rafts are circular and a little smaller than those used on most rides of the genre. Because the current can buffet the smaller rafts more effectively, the ride is wilder and wetter.

What distinguishes Grizzly River Run from other theme park raft rides is Disney's trademark attention to visual detail. Where many raft rides essentially plunge down a concrete ditch, Grizzly River Run winds around and through Grizzly Peak, the park's foremost visual icon, with the great rock bear at the summit. Featuring a 50-foot climb and two drops—including a 22-footer where the raft spins as it descends—the ride flows into dark caverns and along the mountain's precipitous side before looping over itself just before the final plunge. Period-appropriate props support the mid-century national parks theme.

When Disney opened the Kali River Rapids raft ride at the Animal Kingdom theme park at Walt Disney World, it was roundly criticized (and rightly so) for being a wimpy ride. Well, we're here to tell you that Disney learned its lesson. Grizzly River Run is a heart thumper, one of the best of its genre anywhere. And at 5½ minutes from load to unload, it's also one of the longest. The visuals are outstanding, and the ride is about as good as it gets on a man-made river. While it's true that theme park raft rides have been around a long time, Grizzly River Run has set a new standard, one we don't expect to be equaled for some time.

TOURING TIPS This attraction is hugely popular, especially on hot summer days. Ride the first hour the park is open, after 4:30 p.m., or use FastPass or the single-rider line. Make no mistake—you will certainly get wet on this ride. Our recommendation is to wear shorts to the park and bring along a jumbo-size trash bag, as well as a smaller plastic bag. Before boarding the raft, take off your socks and punch a hole in your jumbo bag for your head. Though you can also cut holes for your arms, you will probably stay drier with your arms inside the bag. Use the smaller plastic bag to wrap around your shoes. If you are worried about mussing your hairdo, bring a third bag for your head.

A Shaker Heights, Ohio, family who adopted our garbage-bag attire, however, discovered that staying dry on a similar attraction at Walt Disney World is not without social consequences:

The Disney cast members and the other people in our raft looked at us like we had just beamed down from Mars. We didn't cut armholes in our trash bags because we thought we'd stay drier. The only problem was that once we sat down, we couldn't fasten our seat belts. The Disney person was quite put out and asked sarcastically whether we needed wet suits and snorkels. After a lot of wiggling and adjusting and helping each other, we finally got belted in and off we went, looking like sacks of fertilizer with little heads perched on top. It was very embarrassing, but I must admit that we stayed nice and dry.

If you forget your plastic bag, ponchos are available at the adjacent Rushin' River Outfitters. Depending on the day, all or half of the Grizzly River Run FastPass booths are taken over by *World of Color* FastPass distribution. The booths then slowly return to becoming Grizzly River Run booths as the *World of Color* FastPasses have been fully distributed. The effect of *World of Color* has generally made Grizzly River Run more popular of an attraction, as well as getting a FastPass a generally harder position, especially earlier in the day.

Redwood Creek Challenge Trail and Wilderness Explorer Camp ★★★½

**APPEAL BY AGE   PRESCHOOL ★★★★½   GRADE SCHOOL ★★★★½   TEENS ★★★½
YOUNG ADULTS ★★½   OVER 30 ★★★   SENIORS ★★★★**

What it is Elaborate playground and obstacle course. **Scope and scale** Minor attraction. **When to go** Anytime. **Special comments** Very well done; plan to spend about 20 minutes here. Must be 42" tall.

DESCRIPTION AND COMMENTS An elaborate maze of rope bridges, log towers, and a cave, the Redwood Creek Challenge Trail is a scout camp combination of elements from Tarzan's Treehouse and Tom Sawyer Island. Built into and around Grizzly Peak, the Challenge Trail has eye-popping appeal for young adventurers. A mom from Salt Lake City writes:

Most underrated . . . If this were a city park, it would be packed every day. In Disneyland it seems to be the least popular thing. The kids, young and older, just loved it. The adults were able to run for FastPasses, change diapers, get snacks for all the kids, and sit down while the kids had a great time.

Russell and Dug from Pixar's *Up* appear here daily to lead kids in a short but sweet Wilderness Explorer ceremony. Grab a map near the entrance and complete the self-guided activities to earn your own merit badge sticker.

TOURING TIPS The largest of several children's play areas in the park, and the only one that is dry (for the most part) and relatively shady, the Challenge Trail is the perfect place to let your kids cut loose for a while. Though the Challenge Trail will be crowded, you should not have to wait to get in. Experience it after checking out the better rides and shows. Be aware, however, that the playground is quite large; you will not be able to keep your children in sight unless you tag along with them.

Soarin' Over California *(FastPass)* ★★★★½

APPEAL BY AGE	PRESCHOOL ★★★★½	GRADE SCHOOL ★★★★½	TEENS ★★★★½
YOUNG ADULTS ★★★★½	OVER 30 ★★★★½		SENIORS ★★★★★

What it is Flight-simulation ride. **Scope and scale** Super-headliner. **When to go** The first 30 minutes the park is open, or use FastPass. **Special comments** The park's best ride for the whole family. Must be 40" tall to ride; switching-off option provided (see page 145). **Duration of ride** 4½ minutes. **Average wait in line per 100 people ahead of you** 4 minutes. **Assumes** 2 concourses operating. **Loading speed** Moderate.

Thumbs Up for the Whole Family

DESCRIPTION AND COMMENTS Soarin' is a thrill ride for all ages, as exhilarating as a hawk on the wing and as mellow as swinging in a hammock. If you've ever experienced flying dreams, you'll have a sense of how Soarin' feels. Once you enter the main theater, you're secured in a seat not unlike the ones used on inverted roller coasters (in which the coaster is suspended from above). Once everyone is in place, you are suspended with your legs dangling. Thus hung out to dry, you embark on a hang glider tour of California with IMAX-quality images projected below you, and with the simulator moving your seat in sync with the movie. The immersive images are well chosen and slapdab beautiful, though scene transitions are jarringly abrupt. Soarin' Over California's celluloid projectors were replaced in 2015 with cutting-edge 4K digital models, and we expect the new Soarin' movie debuting at Shanghai Disneyland in 2016 (including a new finale filmed in 2014 over the Disneyland Resort) to eventually migrate across the Pacific. Special effects include wind, sound, and even olfactory stimulation. The ride itself is thrilling but perfectly smooth, exciting, and relaxing simultaneously. We think Soarin' Over California is a must-see for guests of any age who meet the 40-inch minimum-height requirement. And yes, seniors we interviewed were crazy about it. But a North Carolina mom says, "Wait a minute!"

Soarin' was VERY cool but definitely on the scary side for people afraid of heights or who don't like that "unsteady" feeling. While we were "soaring" up, I was fine, but when we were going down, I had to continually say to myself, "This is only an illusion, I cannot fall out, this is only an illusion . . . "

TOURING TIPS Aside from being a true technological innovation, Soarin' Over California also happens to be located near the entrance of the park, thus ensuring heavy traffic all day. Soarin' should be your very first attraction in the morning, or, alternatively, use FastPass or the single-rider line. If you arrive later and elect to use FastPass, obtain your FastPass before noon. Later than noon you're likely to get a return period in the hour before the park closes, or worse, find that the day's supply of FastPasses is gone. Interestingly, while this ride is virtually identical to Soarin' at Epcot, the line for DCA's version moves much more efficiently.

PARADES *and*
LIVE ENTERTAINMENT

World of Color—Celebrate!
The Wonderful World of Walt Disney (FastPass) ★★★★

APPEAL BY AGE	PRESCHOOL ★★★★½	GRADE SCHOOL ★★★★	TEENS ★★★★½
YOUNG ADULTS ★★★★½		OVER 30 ★★★★½	SENIORS ★★★★★

What it is Fountain show with special effects. **Scope and scale** Super-headliner. **When to go** See *Times Guide* for showtimes; FastPass only. If there's only one show, get your FastPass within the first 30 minutes the park is open. **Duration of show** 22 minutes. **Probable waiting time** Up to an hour if you want the best view.

Thumbs Up for the Whole Family

Muss Your 'Do   Wet

DESCRIPTION AND COMMENTS The 1,200 high-pressure water nozzles installed under the surface of DCA's Paradise Bay are the infrastructure for Disney's $75-million attempt to keep guests in the park (and spending money) until closing time. If you've seen or heard about the spectacular fountain show at the Bellagio in Las Vegas, *World of Color—Celebrate!* is similar but larger, with more special effects and themed to Disney movies.

Though the original version of *World of Color* was still wildly popular, in honor of Disneyland's Diamond Anniversary, it was completely overhauled and given the new subtitle *Celebrate! The Wonderful World of Walt Disney.* This new special edition of *World of Color* is explicitly a tribute to Walt Disney, the man and his "dreams of Disneyland," and incorporates classic animated images with live-action footage of Uncle Walt and a new musical score, along with clips from dozens of Disney films, attractions, and characters in its 22-minute performance.

The show's backdrop includes Mickey's Fun Wheel, fitted with special lighting effects for use in the show. Giant projection surfaces sculpted by sprayed water—even larger than those used in *Fantasmic!*—display custom-made animations, and flamethrowers spew almost enough heat to dry off guests standing in the splash zones. What's most remarkable about the show is how the flashing colored lights and pulsating fountains combine to look like low-level fireworks. The effects are astounding, and the colors are vibrant and deep.

World of Color—Celebrate! is hosted by stage and screen star Neil Patrick Harris, and boy, did Disney get their money's worth with him. NPH (as he's known to his fans) is in almost every scene of the show. If we had to rank the top four things you'll see and hear in the show, it's 1) water, 2) color, 3) Neil Patrick Harris, and 4) the word *celebrate*. Unfortunately, even if you're a huge fan of his work as Doogie Howser, Barney Stinson, and/or Hedwig, Harris's presence crosses the line from conducive host to obtrusive interloper, as he's awkwardly inserted into stiffly animated sequences and made to sing a mediocre new theme song that isn't nearly as catchy as the old "Wonderful World of Color" tune.

Rather than individual films getting their own segments as in the original *World of Color*, this version of the show is broken up into thematic sections including "It Was All Started by a Mouse," "The Golden Age of Animation," "Dream of Disneyland," and "A Celebration for Years to Come." The show starts strongly with representations of the early Mickey Mouse cartoons *Fantasia* and *Snow White* before detouring into *Frozen* territory with the Diamond Anniversary's third reprise of "Let It Go" (provoking equal parts groans and cheers from the assembled masses). A sing-along medley of theme park attraction tunes—from "The Tiki, Tiki, Tiki Room" to "Yo Ho"—culminates in a *Force Awakens*-flavored *Star Wars* tribute; you haven't teared up until you've heard Han Solo say, "Chewie, we're home," while skyscraper-high flames singe your eyebrows off. Just as it's gaining momentum, the production derails with a saccharine Disney Parks advertisement full of frolicking families from central casting, set to an insipid arrangement of Bob Dylan's "Forever Young." Harris returns, natch, to wrap everything up with a musical reprise, and while the finale fountain frenzy is certain to silence (or at least soak) the staunchest critic, the new show never quite matches the emotional through line of the original incarnation, which was itself admittedly a bit flawed. While *World of Color—Celebrate!* is a not-to-be-missed element of any first-time visitor's day, we're looking forward to the hopeful return of the original *World of Color*, perhaps with some new upgrades, at the end of the Diamond Anniversary celebration.

Disney may temporarily swap in new sequences from time to time, depending on what Mickey's media machine needs to market at the moment. For example, for the 2014 holiday season, a special *Winter Dreams* edition of *World of Color* was shown, hosted by Olaf the Snowman and featuring songs from *Frozen*. The presentation's highlights—Olaf's "follow-the-bouncing-butt" sing-along, an uproarious *Toy Story* reinterpretation of the "Nutcracker Suite"—made this seasonal spin on *World of Color* a worthy substitute for the standard show.

TOURING TIPS Entertainment value aside, *World of Color—Celebrate!* is an operational nightmare. The effects were expressly designed to be viewed from Paradise Park, the tiered area along the lagoon in front of The Little Mermaid attraction. Unfortunately, only about 4,500 people—barely a quarter of the park's average daily attendance—are permitted to stand there for each show. Getting a decent view for *World of Color* requires time, planning, and/or money, and therefore can almost seem to be more trouble to see than it's worth, but we still consider it not to be missed. A couple from San Jose writes:

Though the World of Color *FastPass line was horrible and waiting for the show was horrible, the show itself was simply amazing.*

An Austin, Texas, mom found *World of Color* challenging:

World of Color is fantastic but hard for kids and shorter adults to see unless they are standing right in front facing Mickey's Fun Wheel. My son could not see the preshow at all, and I had to put him on my shoulders for the 22-minute production. My back has not recovered. They need amphitheater reserved seating. We arrived 90 minutes prior to DCA opening to get a Fast-Pass and waited 90 minutes for the show to start when admitted.

If you want anything approaching a decent view of *World of Color*, you'll need a special FastPass, the securing of which can be an annoying adventure in and of itself. Here are your options for obtaining FastPass tickets, beginning with the easiest (and most expensive) method:

World of Color—Celebrate! meal packages are offered by Wine Country Trattoria, Ariel's Grotto, and Carthay Circle Restaurant. The fixed-price dinner runs $48.60 per adult ($27 for kids) at Wine Country Trattoria and Ariel's Grotto, and $66.96 per adult ($27 for kids) at Carthay Circle Restaurant. Lunch packages (not available at Ariel's) are $34.56 per adult ($22.68 for kids) at Wine Country Trattoria, and $44.28 per adult ($23.76 for kids) at Carthay Circle. (The above prices include tax but not tip.)

All viewing-package meals include an appetizer, your choice of entrée, dessert, and nonalcoholic beverage; selections are from a limited list that is separate from the restaurant's à la carte menu. After your meal, you'll receive special FastPasses for each member of your party, permitting entry into a preferred viewing area reserved for dining-package patrons. Note that you don't actually watch the show from the restaurant, so you'll want to eat early enough to make it to the viewing area. The viewing section for premium-dining patrons is dead center along the waterline. Those standing at the front railing are likely to get soaked; we recommend finding an elevated step in the rear of the dining section (just in front of the Blue section), which will afford a better (and drier) view. To enter the dining FastPass area, look for the illuminated white entrance signs between the Blue and Yellow sections, directly across from The Little Mermaid ride. Though expensive, this is the only way to be guaranteed a central viewing spot with minimal crowding. On nights when there are multiple *World of Color—Celebrate!* performances, early eaters receive passes to the first show, while those eating later get tickets to the later viewing; be sure to confirm when booking your meal which showing you'll be scheduled to attend.

Free FastPasses are distributed on a first-come, first-serve basis from the Grizzly River Run FastPass machines (tickets are available early to Disneyland Resort hotel guests during Extra Magic Hour). Make sure that you get passes for your whole party at once, or you may end up in different sections or showings. These machines are disconnected from the rest of the park's FastPass system, so your *World of Color—Celebrate!* ticket won't interfere with other attractions. On busy days, they may all be claimed by early afternoon. If seeing the first *World of Color—Celebrate!* show of the night is a priority for you, we suggest getting a FastPass within the first 30 minutes the park is open. When a second show is scheduled, FastPasses for the late performance can often be had well into the afternoon.

Once you have your FastPass, you'll notice that you've been assigned one of two color-coded sections. Yellow stretches from the center to the right side (near the Golden Zephyr), and Blue includes the left side and bridge to Paradise Pier. A special section is available on request for disabled guests, and a prime area in the middle is reserved for VIPs and dining-package purchasers.

Your FastPass also includes a return-time window. You won't be allowed into Paradise Park before the start time, but the best viewing spots will all be claimed shortly after opening, so don't be surprised to see people lining up an hour before the area opens. Once inside the viewing area, try to move to the front of an elevated area. You're best off at the front of an elevated tier farther back, rather than at the rear of a lower section, as these readers from Langley, British Columbia, discovered:

World of Color *was great, but even with FastPass, it was hard for me to see (wearing flat shoes and being 5'5"). My husband, who is 6'4", also found himself bobbing around trying to see. When we got there, we had good line of sight, but as people stood up and put their kids on their shoulders, it became difficult.*

A word to the wise: The new *World of Color* is even wetter than the original. If you stand anywhere near the railing, pay attention to the splash zone signs; on a calm night, you'll be seriously spritzed. When the wind blows the wrong way (which is pretty much always), even those several steps back will get soaked.

If all else fails, it's theoretically possible to view the show from various points around the park, but employees with flashlights will vigorously shoo you away from all the obvious vantage points. The best ticketless viewing spot is next to the Golden Zephyr, to the right of the Yellow section. Unticketed viewing is also available immediately in front of The Little Mermaid attraction. You can see many of the fountain and lighting effects from the opposite side of Paradise Pier, near the bases of Mickey's Fun Wheel and Silly Symphony Swings, but the mist projections are illegible from that angle, so we can't recommend it for first-time viewers. On nights when there are multiple performances, you have better odds finding a good spot for the last show.

You can also watch *World of Color—Celebrate!* from the Cove Bar. The view of the projections is less than ideal, but no reservations are required, and you can sit down with an adult beverage during the show, provided you can secure a perch in this popular watering hole.

If you choose to invest $25 in Made with Magic merchandise (mouse ear hats, headbands, gloves, wands, and sipper cups), their lights will illuminate in sync with the show. Better yet, stand toward the rear and freeload by eyeballing others who bought them.

While waiting for the show to start, connect your smartphone to the park's free "PierGames" Wi-Fi network and launch any Web browser to join in the Fun Wheel Challenge. Follow the pattern of flashing colored lights on Mickey's Fun Wheel, and duplicate them Simon-style on your device; points are awarded for speed and accuracy, with the winner of each round awarded 30 seconds of control over the giant wheel's light display. The games start 45 minutes prior to the evening's first *World of Color* show and stop about 7 minutes before the performance.

After the show, if you are headed to the hotels or Downtown Disney, you can bypass the crowd at the main entrance by exiting through the Grand Californian Hotel.

By the way, it is possible (if extremely exhausting) to experience all three of Disneyland Resort's Diamond Anniversary nighttime spectaculars in one evening, provided you have a Park-Hopper ticket, and both *World of Color* and Paint the Night are giving multiple performances. First, secure FastPasses for the later *World of Color* show. Then stake out a spot along Main Street for the first parade. Watch the parade and the fireworks, and then immediately exit Disneyland for DCA in time to find your *World of Color* viewing section.

AFTERNOON AND EVENING PARADES **Pixar Play Parade** features characters from *a bug's life; Cars; Finding Nemo; Monsters, Inc.; The Incredibles;* and *Toy Story*. Lively, very funny, and as varied as the Pixar characters, Pixar Play Parade should be on your must-see list.

The parade route runs from a gate to the left of The Twilight Zone Tower of Terror, through Hollywood Land toward the fountain in Carthay Circle, around Grizzly Peak past A Bug's Land and Cars Land, and through Pacific Wharf toward Paradise Pier, where it disappears backstage through a gate to the left of Boardwalk Pizza & Pasta. Note that for the second parade or on other occasions, the direction may be reversed. On days when the crowds are light, any place along the parade route will suffice. On days of heavy attendance, try to score a viewing spot on the elevated courtyard or steps of the Golden Vine Winery. The upstairs Alfresco Tasting Terrace offers an excellent bird's-eye perspective.

MAD T PARTY DCA turns Hollywood Land over to high-energy dance parties on select evenings. The current version, which has been running since 2012 (aside from a brief Frozen Fun hiatus in 2015), is a Mad T Party that takes stylistic cues from Tim Burton's take on *Alice in Wonderland*. This soirée centers on house techno-spinning DJs (many with authentic club cred) and alcoholic beverages in collectible cups. There's a "rabbit hole" entry portal and a live band clad in garishly "hip" garb loosely based on *Wonderland* characters. Weekend crowds seem to go crazy for the high-energy set list, which includes everything from Alicia Keys and The Killers to "The Unbirthday Song." Between the Day-Glo stilt-walking flamingos flocking among the revelers and the neon Nok-Hockey tables in the streets, the aesthetic resembles an over-the-top Bar Mitzvah party on acid. If you really want to get into the psychedelic spirit, the Made with Magic ears introduced for *World of Color* will also blink in sync with the Mad T Party's light display. If you're looking to get your dance and drink on without heading out to Downtown Disney, look no further. And if you aren't, the adult cocktails and oversize armchairs may provide comfort.

HOLLYWOOD BACKLOT STAGE This open-air stage, one of our favorite venues in the park, features small productions and Disney characters. Recently, visiting school bands, glee clubs, and dance teams have used this stage. Check the *Times Guide* to see what's playing.

STREET ENTERTAINMENT You'll frequently find a period-appropriate klezmer, Irish, or other ethnic band playing outside Paradise Garden Grill. On Buena Vista Street, a gang of singing **Red Car News Boys** (and one newsgirl), loosely inspired by the cult film and Tony-winning Broadway musical *Newsies,* uses the Red Car Trolleys as a roving stage for exuberant song-and-dance performances (look for the high-tech talking Mickey Mouse to make an extended cameo appearance). Also on Buena Vista Street, the **Five and Dime** musical sextet (accompanied by a zoot suit–clad Goofy) sings jazz standards of the 1920s and 1930s, such as "Toot, Toot, Tootsie," "Red, Red Robin," and "Bye, Bye, Blackbird"; this is one of the best street shows in Disney's repertoire. You may also bump into interactive improvisation actors portraying police officers, bicycle messengers, or other eccentric **Citizens of Buena Vista,** a troupe similar to the popular Streetmosphere characters at Disney's Hollywood Studios in Orlando. Along Cars Land's main drag, **Red the Firetruck** shows up in the morning with sirens blazing to spray down the crowds, and **DJ's Dance and Drive** features the "ultimate party car" hosting afternoon oldies dance parties with the help of interactive carhop waitresses. The **Mariachi Divas** is a fabulous all-female mariachi musical group that plays sets in the Pacific Wharf area, walking between the seating areas of the counter-service restaurants. They are probably the only multiple Grammy Award–winning recording artists (most recently Best Regional Mexican Music Album of 2014) with a regular theme park gig. We particularly enjoy the Divas' rendition of "It's a Small World."

DISNEY CHARACTERS Character appearances are listed in the daily *Times Guide.* In addition, Flik and Atta can usually be found at A Bug's Land; Russell and Dug from Pixar's *Up!* hang out around the Redwood Creek Challenge Trail; Olaf from *Frozen,* as well as pals from *The Incredibles* and *Monsters, Inc.,* make appearances in Hollywood Land; and Ariel's Grotto restaurant at Paradise Pier offers character dining featuring Ariel and her princess friends. Oswald the Lucky Rabbit (an old-school Disney cartoon from before Mickey's creation) sometimes greets guests on Buena Vista Street. Mater and Lightning take turns posing for photos near the Cozy Cone Motel; these life-size vehicles can deliver quips recorded by the original voice actors to grinning guests.

UNHERALDED TREASURES *at* DCA

TREASURE: Cove Bar | **LOCATION:** On the bridge to Paradise Pier

ARIEL'S GROTTO IS A FIXED-PRICE character-meal restaurant on the span connecting Paradise Pier to the Pacific Wharf. Instead of heading downstairs to the restaurant from the entrance, though, go around the walkway. There, you'll find the Cove Bar, where you can enjoy a full-service bar and a small selection of food. For some, the thought of a cocktail at the end of a long day might be enticement enough, but this is a good spot even for teetotalers—it's one of the best places to enjoy the view. It's a bit too sunny during the day, but as the sun sets and the evening lights come on, the Cove turns into a mellow hideaway where you can enjoy a beautiful view of Paradise Pier. In the background, you hear music, laughter, and the occasional sounds of a roller coaster, while watching small waves lapping against the pier that houses a brightly lit carousel—enough to make you forget that you're sitting in the middle of a completely artificial environment.

TREASURE: Redwood Creek Challenge Trail | **LOCATION:** Opposite Grizzly Peak

MAYBE A VISIT TO A THEME PARK was your kid's idea, and you prefer going on a quiet walk in the woods or enjoying a hike in a national park. If you just want to take a break from the hectic rush of a trip to DCA, hop over to the Redwood Creek Challenge Trail. Looking at the park map, you probably assume that this is just a playground designed for little kids, but the area is actually a good representation of a wilderness park. OK, so you don't really need to bring your bird-watching book, but there are various nooks and crannies, as well as a few "ranger buildings," that are very well themed (down to the wildlife books on the shelves). You could easily spend a portion of your day just enjoying the decidedly rustic feel of Redwood Creek.

TRAFFIC PATTERNS *at* DISNEY CALIFORNIA ADVENTURE

ONE OF THE PROBLEMS Disney had at DCA early on was that there was no traffic to create patterns. Attendance figures were far less than projected. On the relatively few crowded days (mostly weekends), the park didn't handle crowds particularly well. If Disney's gate projections had panned out, the park would have been in gridlock much of the time.

The opening of Cars Land at DCA significantly changed the park's traffic patterns. As soon as the park opens, most guests head straight for Radiator Springs Racers or the Racers FastPass machines. A slightly smaller number will head to Hollywood Land for Anna & Elsa's Royal Welcome FastPasses.

On days of lighter attendance, waits of more than an hour will form within a few minutes at Racers; waits of 2 hours or more appear on holidays and other days of peak attendance. FastPasses for Radiator Springs Racers will typically be gone within an hour or two of park opening on any day.

Of the other attractions in Cars Land, waits for Luigi's Rollickin' Roadsters will typically be 25–40 minutes as soon as the park opens, while Mater's Junkyard Jamboree's waits will be low for the first hour or two that DCA is open.

Cars Land's attractions' wait times will usually peak 11 a.m.–2 p.m. Radiator Springs Racers will have consistent 75- to 120-minute waits throughout the day, possibly higher if the attraction has to shut down for unscheduled maintenance, a common occurrence. Waits for Mater's Junkyard Jamboree will start to drop by 4 p.m., and lines at Luigi's Rollickin' Roadsters will start to diminish around dinnertime.

Our advice for Cars Land is to obtain FastPasses for Radiator Springs Racers as soon as the park opens. If FastPasses are all gone, consider using the single-rider line for RSR. If possible, wait until the last 2 hours the park is open to try Luigi's and Mater's.

As crowded as Cars Land is, the good news is that traffic to the rest of DCA is relatively light for the first hour the park is open. When DCA opens before 10 a.m., lines for Soarin' Over California, The Twilight Zone Tower of Terror, California Screamin', and Toy Story Midway Mania! are usually less than 20 minutes, even during holidays.

At Grizzly Peak, Soarin's wait times start to climb about an hour after the park opens and peak 11 a.m.–2 p.m. Once the crowds are in the park, Soarin' will have waits of at least 30–35 minutes for the rest of the day during most times of year. Next door, wait times at Grizzly River Run are relatively low for the first hour the park is open. During summer and warm holidays, lines grow quickly about an hour after the park opens, peaking at around noon. Waits grow more slowly when the weather is cooler but still peak around noon. Expect waits to start dropping around 4 p.m. regardless of the time of year.

In Hollywood Land, waits at The Twilight Zone Tower of Terror and Monsters, Inc. Mike & Sulley to the Rescue usually peak 11 a.m.– noon. Tower of Terror's waits drop off after 4 p.m., while the wait times at Monsters, Inc. typically drop off at 4 p.m. most days and 6 p.m. on holidays. *Disney Junior—Live on Stage!, Disney's Aladdin,* and *For the First Time in Forever* each draw good-size crowds throughout the late morning and afternoon.

Lines at A Bug's Land typically do not exceed 10–15 minutes at any time, except on the most crowded days of the year.

Toward the back of the park, long waits develop fastest at Toy Story Midway Mania!—still about an hour after the park opens—and peak by 11 a.m. Like Soarin' Over California, Toy Story will remain popular for the rest of the day, regardless of season. Secondary attractions, including Goofy's Sky School and California Screamin', won't usually be too crowded until about 2 hours after the park opens. Like the attractions at Hollywood Land, most lines at B-list Paradise Pier attractions start to drop after 4 p.m. Lines at The Little Mermaid seem to be low throughout the day and on any day of the year.

Park departures begin around 3 p.m., when families with small children start heading home. However, 9-to-5 workers with Annual Passes start coming into the park around 6 p.m. and generally stay for the evening. It's common to see waits hold steady or even rise from early evening until the park closes, undoubtedly because of Cars Land and *World of Color*.

World of Color FastPasses are now generally available until 11 a.m. or noon most days, though the new special edition has made it a popular ticket once again. Guests with *World of Color* FastPasses will begin queuing in the Pacific Wharf, Grizzly Peak, and Paradise Pier walkways an hour or more before showtime. The largest wave of departing guests occurs at the end of *World of Color*. Just before closing, crowd levels are thin except, of course, at Cars Land, Soarin' Over California, and The Tower of Terror.

CALIFORNIA ADVENTURE TOURING PLANS

PRELIMINARY INSTRUCTIONS FOR ALL DISNEY CALIFORNIA ADVENTURE TOURING PLANS

ON DAYS OF MODERATE to heavy attendance, follow the touring

plans exactly, deviating only when you do not wish to experience a listed show or ride.

1. Buy your admission in advance (see "Admission Options" on page 19).

2. Call ☎ 714-781-7290 the day before you go for the official opening time.

3. Become familiar with the park-opening procedures (described on page 279) and read over the touring plan of your choice, so you will have a basic understanding of what you are likely to encounter as you enter the park.

DCA ONE-DAY TOURING PLAN FOR ADULTS
(page 372)

FOR Adults without small children. **ASSUMES** Willingness to experience all rides and shows.

Height and age requirements apply to many attractions. If you have kids who aren't eligible to ride, try switching off (see page 145) or use the One-Day Touring Plan for Parents with Small Children. This touring plan includes most of the amusement park rides on Paradise Pier. If you're short on time or wish to allocate more of the day to DCA's theatrical attractions, forgo a few of the rides in A Bug's Land. Crowds are smaller at DCA on Tuesday, Thursday, and Saturday when Disneyland Park has early entry.

ABOUT EARLY ENTRY If you are eligible for early entry, experience Luigi's Rollickin' Roadsters (if open), Mater's Junkyard Jamboree, and Toy Story Midway Mania!, in that order, followed by The Twilight Zone Tower of Terror and Soarin' Over California (time permitting). Position yourself near the Radiator Springs Racers FastPass kiosks a few minutes before official park opening. Pick up the plan after picking up your FastPasses, skipping any attractions you've already seen, and return to ride Radiator Springs Racers once your FastPass window starts.

DCA normally hosts early entry on Sunday, Monday, Wednesday, and Friday. Unlike Disneyland, DCA's early entry is for hotel guests only; Magic Morning ticket holders may not enter early. If you are not eligible for early entry, try not to use the plan on an early-entry day. Cars Land will be packed with early-entry guests before you even get past the turnstiles.

DCA ONE-DAY TOURING PLAN FOR ADULTS WITH SMALL CHILDREN *(page 373)*

FOR Adults with small children who wish to experience all major rides and shows. **ASSUMES** Willingness to experience all rides and shows.

Height and age requirements apply to many attractions. If you have kids who aren't eligible to ride, try switching off (see page 145). This touring plan includes most of the amusement park rides on Paradise Pier. If you're short on time or wish to allocate more of the day to DCA's theatrical attractions, forgo a few of the rides in A Bug's Land. Crowds are smaller at DCA on Tuesday, Thursday, and Saturday when Disneyland Park has early entry.

ABOUT EARLY ENTRY If you are eligible for early entry, experience Luigi's Rollickin' Roadsters and Mater's Junkyard Jamboree, in that order, followed by Toy Story Midway Mania!, The Twilight Zone Tower of Terror, and/or Soarin' Over California (time permitting). Position yourself near the Radiator Springs Racers FastPass kiosks a few minutes before official park opening. Pick up the plan after picking up your FastPasses, skipping any attractions you've already seen, and return to ride Radiator Springs Racers once your FastPass window starts.

DCA normally hosts early entry on Sunday, Monday, Wednesday, and Friday. Unlike Disneyland, DCA's early entry is for hotel guests only; Magic Morning ticket holders may not enter early. If you are not eligible for early entry, try not to use the plan on an early-entry day. Cars Land will be packed with early-entry guests before you even get past the turnstiles.

THE BEST OF DISNEYLAND RESORT IN ONE DAY
(pages 374–375)

FOR Guests who really want to burn the candle at both ends (and a bunch of money) by buying a single-day Park Hopper. **ASSUMES** Willingness to experience all major rides (including roller coasters) and shows in both parks and to walk a lot.

This plan is for groups who wish to visit both Disneyland and Disney California Adventure in one day. Most of the major, must-see attractions are included for each park. The plan starts in DCA with Radiator Springs Racers, switching over to Disneyland in the afternoon, and finishes the night with Disneyland's fireworks spectacular. This plan is only recommended on days when the parks open early and stay open late.

ABOUT EARLY ENTRY If you are eligible for early entry, experience (1) Luigi's Rollickin' Roadsters (if open), (2) Mater's Junkyard Jamboree, and (3) Toy Story Midway Mania!, in that order, followed by The Twilight Zone Tower of Terror and Soarin' Over California (time permitting). Position yourself near the Radiator Springs Racers FastPass kiosks a few minutes before official park opening. Pick up the touring plan after picking up your FastPasses, skipping any attractions you've already seen, and return to ride Radiator Springs Racers once your FastPass window starts.

DCA normally hosts early entry on Sunday, Monday, Wednesday, and Friday. Unlike Disneyland, DCA's early entry is for hotel guests only; Magic Morning ticket holders may not enter early. If you are not eligible for early entry, try not to use the plan on an early-entry day. Cars Land will be packed with early-entry guests before you even get past the turnstiles.

PART SEVEN

UNIVERSAL STUDIOS HOLLYWOOD

UNIVERSAL STUDIOS HOLLYWOOD was the first film and TV studio to turn part of its facility into a modern theme park. By integrating shows and rides with behind-the-scenes presentations on moviemaking, Universal Studios Hollywood created a new genre of theme park, stimulating a number of clone and competitor parks. First came Disney-MGM Studios (now Disney's Hollywood Studios) at Walt Disney World, followed shortly by Universal Studios Florida, also near Orlando. Where Universal Studios Hollywood, however, evolved from an established film and TV venue, its cross-country imitators were launched primarily as theme parks, albeit with some production capability on the side. Disney is also challenging Universal in California with Disney California Adventure. While DCA does not have production facilities, one of its themed areas focuses on Hollywood and the movies.

Located just off US 101 north of Hollywood, Universal Studios operates on a scale and with a quality standard rivaled only by Disney, SeaWorld, and Busch Gardens parks. Unique among American theme parks for its topography, Universal Studios Hollywood is tucked on top of, below, and around a tall hill. The studios consist of an open-access area and a controlled-access area. The latter contains the working soundstages, back lot, wardrobe, scenery, prop shops, postproduction facility, and administration offices. Guests can visit the controlled-access area by taking the Studio Tour. The open-access area, which contains the park's rides, shows, restaurants, and services, is divided into two sections. The main entrance provides access to the upper section, the Upper Lot, on top of the hill. Four theater shows and three rides (more by the end of 2016, with the addition of The Wizarding World of Harry Potter), as well as the loading area for the Studio Tour, are located in the Upper Lot. The Lower Lot, at the northeastern base of the hill, is accessible from the Upper Lot via escalators. There are three rides and a walk-through exhibit in the Lower Lot.

In 2013 Universal received governmental approval to implement its ambitious Evolution plan, which will dramatically reshape its complex

Universal Studios Hollywood

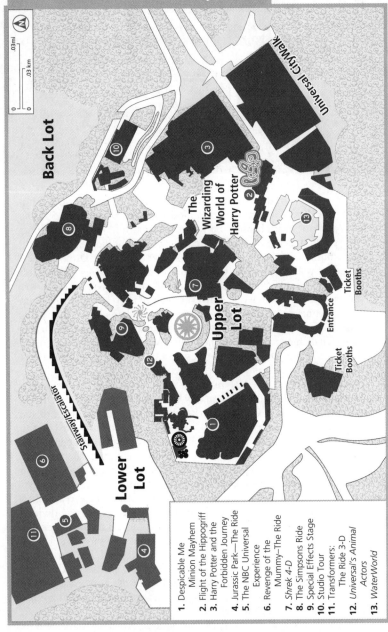

Back Lot

The Wizarding World of Harry Potter

Universal CityWalk

Upper Lot

Entrance

Ticket Booths

Ticket Booths

Stairway/Escalator

Lower Lot

1. Despicable Me
   Minion Mayhem
2. Flight of the Hippogriff
3. Harry Potter and the
   Forbidden Journey
4. Jurassic Park—The Ride
5. The NBC Universal
   Experience
6. Revenge of the
   Mummy—The Ride
7. *Shrek 4-D*
8. The Simpsons Ride
9. Special Effects Stage
10. Studio Tour
11. Transformers:
    The Ride 3-D
12. *Universal's Animal
    Actors*
13. *WaterWorld*

over the next decade. Two 500-room on-site hotels are planned, and CityWalk will expand into the current front entryway, accompanied by new parking structures. Inside the park, several new attractions are proposed for the Upper Lot, and three additional points of interest will be installed along the tram tour. And all of that is in addition to a West Coast annex of the wildly popular Wizarding World of Harry Potter found at Orlando's Islands of Adventure park. Opening mid-2016, the "land" will include the Flight of the Hippogriff children's roller coaster and a near-clone of the fantastic Harry Potter and the Forbidden Journey dark ride, though now in 3-D, plus opportunities to go broke on exclusive merchandise and food, such as wands and delicious Butterbeer. The parapets of Hogwarts Castle already tower over the Upper Lot, forming a beacon visible for miles around. Casualties of the expansions have included the old Wild West arena, the tram tour's Mummy tunnel, the Curious George playground, and Gibson Amphitheater, with the Special Effects Stage and *WaterWorld* show still potentially on the chopping block.

The park offers all standard services and amenities, including stroller and wheelchair rental, lockers, diaper-changing and nursing facilities, car assistance, and foreign-language assistance. Most of the park is accessible to disabled guests, and TDDs are available for the hearing impaired. Almost all services are in the Upper Lot, just inside the main entrance.

GATHERING INFORMATION

THE MAIN UNIVERSAL STUDIOS information number is ☎ 818-622-3801. To short-circuit the operating-hours litany, dial 3. If you have problems, try calling ☎ 818-622-3735 or 818-622-3750. Universal Studios' website, **universalstudioshollywood.com,** is easy to navigate.

WHAT MAKES UNIVERSAL STUDIOS HOLLYWOOD DIFFERENT

WHAT MAKES UNIVERSAL STUDIOS HOLLYWOOD different is that the attractions, with a couple of exceptions, are designed to minimize long waits in line. The centerpiece of the Universal Studios experience is the Studio Tour. While on the tram, you experience an earthquake and come face-to-face with King Kong, among other things. In other parks, including Universal's sister park in Florida, each of these spectacles is presented as an individual attraction, and each has its own long queue. At Universal Studios Hollywood, by contrast, you suffer only one wait to board the tram and then experience all of these events as part of the tour.

In addition to the time saving and convenience provided by the tram tour, most of the live shows at Universal Studios Hollywood are performed in large theaters or stadiums. Instead of standing in line outside, guests are usually invited to enter the theater and wait in seated comfort for the production to begin.

TIMING *Your* VISIT

CROWDS ARE LARGEST IN THE SUMMER (Memorial Day–Labor Day) and during specific holiday periods during the rest of the year. December 25–January 1 is extremely busy, as are Thanksgiving weekend, the week of George Washington's birthday, spring break for schools and colleges, and the two weeks bracketing Easter. The least busy time is from after Thanksgiving weekend until the week before Christmas. The next slowest times are September through the weekend preceding Thanksgiving, January 4 through the first week of March, and the week following Easter to Memorial Day weekend.

SELECTING THE DAY OF THE WEEK FOR YOUR VISIT

WEEKENDS ARE MORE CROWDED than weekdays year-round. Saturday is the busiest day. Sunday, particularly Sunday morning, is the best bet if you have to go on a weekend, but it is still extremely busy. During the summer, Friday is very busy; Monday, Wednesday, and Thursday are usually less so; Tuesday is normally the slowest of all. During the off-season (September–May, holidays excepted), Tuesday is usually the least-crowded day, followed by Thursday.

HOW MUCH TIME TO ALLOCATE

THOUGH THERE'S A LOT TO SEE and do at Universal Studios Hollywood, you can (unlike at Disneyland) complete a comprehensive tour in one day. If you follow our touring plan, which calls for being on hand at park opening, you should be able to check out everything by mid- to late afternoon, even on a crowded day.

Never mind that Universal Studios Hollywood claims to cover 400 acres; the area you will have to traverse on foot is considerably smaller. In fact, you will do much less walking and, miracle of miracles, much less standing in line at Universal Studios than at Disneyland.

Once the Harry Potter attractions open, increased attendance will likely make spending a full day in the park mandatory. If Orlando's attendance patterns hold, Hogsmeade will be mobbed from opening until afternoon, but crowds should be more manageable in the evening.

UNIVERSAL STUDIOS HOLLYWOOD FOR YOUNG CHILDREN

WE DO NOT RECOMMEND UNIVERSAL STUDIOS HOLLYWOOD for preschoolers. Of 11 major attractions, all but 2 (*Universal's Animal Actors* and *Shrek 4-D*) have the potential for flipping out sensitive little ones. See the Small-Child Fright-Potential Table on page 337.

All Universal rides with a height requirement offer child switch, which is similar to Disney's rider swap; most attractions allow everyone to wait in line together and have a quiet room where the non-riding parent can wait with the kids while his or her partner rides. Ask the greeter at each attraction's entrance how to take advantage of child switch.

COST

ONE-DAY TICKETS ARE AVAILABLE for $95 ($85 if purchased online) for people age 3 and up. A pass that allows you to skip to the front of the line at all attractions runs $169–$189 (depending on season) for adults and children, including admission. Season passes cost $119 with blackout dates, or $169 without blackout dates (save $10 by buying online). None of Universal's season passes include parking; make sure to check the expiration date of your pass before purchasing. Admission is free for those under age 3. Universal used to frequently run ticket promotions, such as "Buy One Day, Get the Rest of the Year Free" (blackout dates apply), but has largely discontinued those discounts (as well as annual passes) in anticipation of Potter's popularity. You can print your tickets for $1 fee at the Universal website.

For Hollywood-happy high rollers, USH offers a $329 (admission and valet parking included) VIP Experience that includes escorted queue-cutting at all attractions, off-tram walking tours of sets and soundstages, light breakfast and gourmet lunch, and amenities such as ponchos and bottled water. The quality of service provided by the VIP touring guides is exceptional, and you'll get to explore places—like Universal's gargantuan prop warehouse or the *War of the Worlds* airliner crash site—that are otherwise inaccessible to guests. Best of all, you travel in style, in a luxury air-conditioned bus that beats the heck out of the standard Studio Tour trams. If you have the spare dough, it's undoubtedly a better deal than Disney's pay-per-hour VIP guides, and once The Wizarding World opens, this service should be worth it's weight in goblin gold. Reservations are required; call ☎ 818-622-8477 to book.

In addition to the website discounts, admission discounts are sometimes offered in area freebie publications available in hotels. Admission discounts are also periodically offered to AAA members. Vacation packages including lodging and park admission are available from Hilton and Sheraton hotels, both of which offer accommodations nearby.

In a groundbreaking initiative, Universal Studios Hollywood will issue you a rain check good for 30 days if it rains more than one-eighth of an inch by 2 p.m. They'll also keep you warm with complimentary coffee and cocoa. And when rides at Universal Studios Hollywood break down (as they inevitably seem to do), the operators hand out free jelly beans to guests stuck in the queue, a policy we wish every park would adopt.

THE SHUTTLE

UNIVERSAL CITY is on the Red Line of **Los Angeles Metro Rail,** which makes it relatively easy to commute by light rail from downtown LA and many other places, though not from Anaheim. Across the street from the subway station and the bus stop, at Lankershim Boulevard and Universal Hollywood Drive, is a free Universal Studios shuttle bus that will conveniently take you to the main entrances of Universal Studios Hollywood and CityWalk. The bus runs daily, beginning at 7 a.m., with pickups about every 10–15 minutes; service continues until about 2 hours after the theme park closes. Refer to the posted times at each shuttle stop for information on the last departing shuttle. For rail and bus schedules and additional public transportation information, call the Los Angeles Metropolitan Transportation Authority at ☎ 323-GO-METRO (466-3876), or visit **metro.net.**

ARRIVING *and* GETTING ORIENTED

MOST FOLKS ACCESS UNIVERSAL STUDIOS by taking US 101, also called the Hollywood Freeway, and following the signs to the park. If the freeway is gridlocked, you can also get to the Studios by taking Cahuenga Boulevard and then turning north toward Lankershim Boulevard. If you are coming from Burbank, take Barham Boulevard toward US 101, and then follow the signs.

Universal Studios has a big, multilevel parking garage at the top of the hill. Signs directing you to the garage are a bit confusing, so pay attention and stay to the far right when you come up the hill. Even after you have made it to the pay booth and shelled out $17 to park, it is still not exactly clear where you go next. (Preferred parking cost $25, $40 for even closer front-gate parking; parking is $19 if your RV is more than 15 feet long. The cost for general parking is only $10 after 3 p.m.) Drive slowly, follow other cars proceeding from the pay booths, and avoid turns onto ramps marked EXIT. You may become a bit disoriented, but ultimately you will blunder into the garage. Once parked, make a note of your parking level and the location of your space. Valet parking ($15 for the first 2 hours, $30 more than 2 hours) is located inside the Frankenstein parking structure and is even more bewildering to navigate to.

Walk toward the opposite end of the garage from where you entered and exit into Universal CityWalk, a shopping, dining, and entertainment complex (no admission required) situated between the parking structure and the main entrance of the park. As an aside, CityWalk is much like Downtown Disney at Disneyland. Some of Universal's better restaurants and more interesting shops are at City-Walk, and it's so close to the theme park entrance that you can conveniently pop out of the park to grab a bite (don't forget to have your hand stamped for reentry).

Universal Studios' ticket booths and turnstiles are about 100 yards from the main parking garage. If you need cash, an ATM is outside and to the right of the main entrance. There is also an ATM inside the park next to the Cartooniversal store. Nearby is a guest-services window. As you enter the park, be sure to pick up a park map and a daily entertainment schedule.

THE UPPER LOT

THE UPPER LOT is essentially a large, amorphous pedestrian plaza. In-park signage (which is inordinately confusing) references street names such as New York Street and Baker Street and place names such as Cape Cod and Moulin Rouge, but on foot these theme distinctions are largely lost and placement of buildings appears almost random. An iconic Art Deco tower serves as a central "weenie" to navigate by, but outside of The Wizarding World of Harry Potter, don't expect any sort of thematic integrity.

Inside the main entrance, stroller and wheelchair rentals are on the right, as are rental lockers. Straight ahead is a TV Audience Ticket Booth, where you can obtain free tickets to join the audience for any TV shows that are taping during your visit (subject to availability).

Attractions in the Upper Lot are situated around the perimeter of the plaza. Near The Simpsons Ride (straight ahead) are the escalators and stairs that lead to the Lower Lot.

THE LOWER LOT

THE LOWER LOT IS ACCESSIBLE ONLY via the escalators and stairs descending from the back left section of the Upper Lot. Configured roughly in the shape of the letter T, the Lower Lot is home to Transformers, Jurassic Park, and Revenge of the Mummy, all headliner attractions at Universal Studios Hollywood.

UNIVERSAL STUDIOS HOLLYWOOD ATTRACTIONS

UPPER LOT ATTRACTIONS

Despicable Me Minion Mayhem ★★★★

APPEAL BY AGE	PRESCHOOL ★★★★	GRADE SCHOOL ★★★★★	TEENS ★★★★★
YOUNG ADULTS ★★★★		OVER 30 ★★★★	SENIORS ★★★

What it is Motion simulator with 3-D projection. **Scope and scale** Major attraction. **When to go** The first hour the park is open or after 4 p.m. **Special comment** Must be 40″ tall to ride. **Duration of ride** 5 minutes, plus 10-minute preshow. **Average wait time per 100 people ahead of you** 3½ minutes. **Loading speed** Moderate–slow.

DESCRIPTION AND COMMENTS Despicable Me Minion Mayhem is a 3-D motion simulator ride similar to The Simpsons Ride and Disneyland's Star Tours. You're seated in a ride vehicle that faces a large video screen, on which the attraction's story is projected. When the story calls for you to drop down the side of a mountain, your ride vehicle tilts forward as if you were falling; when you need to swerve left or right, your ride vehicle tilts the same way. The main difference between Minion Mayhem and other simulators is that most other simulators usually provide one video screen per ride vehicle, while Minion Mayhem arranges all of its eight-person vehicles in front of one large IMAX-size video screen. The ride vehicles are set on raised platforms, which get slightly higher toward the back of the theater, affording good views for all guests.

The preshow area is inside the home of adorably evil Gru (voiced by Steve Carell), where you see his unique family tree and other artifacts. The premise of the ride is that you're turned into one of Gru's chattering yellow minions. Once converted you must navigate the minion training grounds, where your "speed, strength, and ability not to die" is tested. Something soon goes amiss, though, and your training turns into a frenetic rescue operation.

The ride is a fast-paced series of dives, climbs, and tight turns through Gru's Rube Goldberg–esque machines. Like The Simpsons Ride, there are more sight gags and interesting things to see here than anyone possibly could in a single ride. Guests exiting the ride may find the opportunity for a short dance with one of the minions.

TOURING TIPS Minion Mayhem, a hit import from Universal Studios Florida, arrived in Hollywood in 2014, replacing the long-running *Terminator 2* show. The Hollywood version features a much more elaborate facade (try ringing doorbells on the homes neighboring the attraction entrance) than the Orlando ride; this version is also blessed with a second theater and preshow, effectively doubling the attraction's capacity. Unfortunately, unlike Orlando's version, Hollywood's ride lacks stationary seating, making the attraction inaccessible to those who don't meet the height requirement or can't handle the shaking simulators. Even so, it can accrue a long queue thanks to the franchise's popularity. Ride it immediately after experiencing the Lower Lot attractions, or first thing if you are skipping the bigger thrill rides. If the line for Despicable Me exceeds 30 minutes, try late afternoon or the hour before the park closes. Adjacent to the ride's exit, the Super Silly Fun Land area should help small tykes burn off some steam, with wet and dry playgrounds, carnival midway games, and Silly Swirly (★★½), a simple Dumbo-style spinning ride sporting wacky bug-shaped vehicles and Minion-ized disco music.

Shrek 4-D ★★★½

APPEAL BY AGE	PRESCHOOL ★★★★	GRADE SCHOOL ★★★★½	TEENS ★★★★½
YOUNG ADULTS ★★★★½		OVER 30 ★★★★½	SENIORS ★★★★

What it is 3-D theater show. **Scope and scale** Headliner. **When to go** The first hour the park is open or after 4 p.m. **Duration of show** About 20 minutes, plus 5-minute preshow video. **Probable waiting time** About 20 minutes.

DESCRIPTION AND COMMENTS *Shrek 4-D* is based on characters from the hit movie *Shrek*. A preshow presents the villain from the movie, Lord Farquaad, as he appears on various screens to describe his posthumous plan to reclaim his lost bride, Princess Fiona, who married Shrek. Lord Farquaad died in the movie, and it's his ghost making the plans, but never mind. Guests then move into the main theater, don their 3-D glasses, and recline in seats equipped with "tactile transducers" and "pneumatic air propulsion and water-spray nodules." As the 3-D film plays, guests are also subjected to smells relevant to the on-screen action (oh, boy).

Technicalities aside, *Shrek* is a mixed bag. It's irreverent, frantic, laugh-out-loud funny, and iconoclastic. Concerning the latter, the film takes a good poke at Disney with Pinocchio, the Three Little Pigs, and Tinker Bell (among others) all sucked into the mayhem. But the video quality and 3-D effects are dated by today's 4K standards, the story line is incoherently disconnected from the clever preshow, and the franchise's relevance has faded since the lackluster fourth film. As a plus, in contrast to Disney's *It's Tough to Be a Bug!*, *Shrek 4-D* doesn't generally frighten children under 7 years of age.

TOURING TIPS Universal claims that they can move 2,400 guests an hour through *Shrek 4-D*. You should be able to attend almost any time without waiting longer than the next showtime.

The Simpsons Ride ★★★★

APPEAL BY AGE	PRESCHOOL ★★★½	GRADE SCHOOL ★★★★	TEENS ★★★★
YOUNG ADULTS ★★★★		OVER 30 ★★★★	SENIORS ★★★½

What it is Mega-simulator ride. **Scope and scale** Super-headliner. **When to go** After the Lower Lot rides and Despicable Me Minion Mayhem. **Special comment** Must be 40" tall to ride; not recommended for pregnant women or people prone to motion sickness; switching-off option provided (see page 145). **Duration of ride** 4⅓ minutes, plus preshow. **Average wait time per 100 people ahead of you** 5 minutes. **Loading speed** Moderate.

Queasy

DESCRIPTION AND COMMENTS This ride is based on the Fox animated series that is TV's longest-running sitcom. Featuring the voices of Dan Castellaneta (Homer), Julie Kavner (Marge), Nancy Cartwright (Bart), Yeardley Smith (Lisa), and other cast members, the attraction takes a wild and humorous poke at thrill rides, dark rides, and live shows "that make up a fantasy amusement park dreamed up by the show's cantankerous Krusty the Clown."

Two preshows involve *Simpsons* characters speaking sequentially on different video screens around the line area. Their comments help define the characters for guests who are unfamiliar with the TV show. The attraction is a simulator ride similar to Star Tours at Disneyland Park, but with a larger domed Omnimax-type screen more like that of Soarin' at Disney California Adventure.

The story line has the conniving Sideshow Bob secretly arriving at Krustyland, the aforementioned amusement park, and plotting his revenge on Krusty and Bart, who, in a past *Simpsons* episode, revealed that Sideshow Bob had committed a crime for which he'd framed Krusty. Sideshow Bob gets even by making things go wrong with the attractions that the Simpsons (and you) are riding.

Like the show on which it's based, The Simpsons Ride definitely has an edge, and more than a few wild hairs. There will be jokes and visuals that you'll get but will fly over your children's heads—and most assuredly vice versa. A mom from Huntington, New York, had this to say:

The ride is lots of fun and suitable for all guests. I'm not a fan of wild motion simulators, but I was fine on this ride.

TOURING TIPS Expect large crowds all day. We recommend arriving at the park before opening and making the ride your first stop after experiencing the Lower Lot attractions. Though not as rough and jerky as its predecessor, it's a long way from being tame. Several families we interviewed found the humor a little too adult for their younger children. Don't miss the neighboring Simpson-ized carnival games and Kwik-E-Mart gift shop for more snarky Simpsons sight gags, and an expansive strip of Springfield-inspired shops and eateries (partially patterned after Universal Studios Florida's wildly popular Fast Food Boulevard) was added in 2015. Featured destinations include Krusty Burger, Luigi's Pizza, Phineas Q. Butterfat's 5600 Flavors Ice Cream Parlor, Moe's Tavern, and Duff's Brewery. You'll also find funny facades of iconic cartoon locations such as Springfield's police station, elementary school, and nuclear power plant.

Special Effects Stage ★★★

| APPEAL BY AGE | PRESCHOOL ★★½ | GRADE SCHOOL ★★★ | TEENS ★★★½ |
| YOUNG ADULTS ★★★½ | | OVER 30 ★★★ | SENIORS ★★★½ |

What it is A theater presentation on special effects. **Scope and scale** Major attraction. **When to go** Anytime. **Special comments** Predictable but still interesting; may frighten young children. **Duration of show** 30 minutes. **Probable waiting time** 15 minutes.

DESCRIPTION AND COMMENTS Guests view a fast-paced presentation on special effects, with elements borrowed from both the old Special Effects Stages (formerly on the park's Lower Lot) and the *Horror Make-Up Show* and *Disaster!* attraction found in Universal Studios Florida. Audience members participate in demonstrations of green screens, computer-generated imagery (CGI), and motion capture. For the finale, a volunteer is apparently attached to a flying rig (left over from the short-lived *Creature of the Black Lagoon* musical that once occupied this space) and sent sailing above the crowd. The educational content will already be familiar to anyone who has ever watched a DVD making-of documentary, and the thin through line about a youthful digital-era director upstaging an aging analog artist may mildly offend viewers who still appreciate old-fashioned films that don't look like video games.

TOURING TIPS The best seats seem to be in the center of the theater, not directly up front. Or try the seats to the left of the stage.

Studio Tour, including *Fast & Furious: Supercharged* ★★★★★

| APPEAL BY AGE | PRESCHOOL ★★★ | GRADE SCHOOL ★★★★ | TEENS ★★★★ |
| YOUNG ADULTS ★★★★ | | OVER 30 ★★★★ | SENIORS ★★★★ |

What it is Indoor-outdoor tram tour of soundstages and back lot. **Scope and scale** Headliner. **When to go** After experiencing the other rides. **Duration of tour** About 42 minutes. **Average wait time per 100 people ahead of you** 2½ minutes. **Loading speed** Fast.

Loud   Scary

DESCRIPTION AND COMMENTS The Studio Tour is the centerpiece of Universal Studios Hollywood and is one of the longest attractions in American theme parks. The tour departs from the tram boarding facility to the *right* of The Simpsons Ride and down the escalator. (Note that there's also an escalator to the left of The Simpsons Ride, so don't get confused.)

Tonight Show host and former *Saturday Night Live* star Jimmy Fallon is the tour's prerecorded host. (We dare you to get Fallon's "Tram-Tastic" tune out of your head.) All trams are equipped with high-definition monitors showing clips from actual movies that demonstrate how the various sets and soundstages were used in creating the films.

The tour circulates through the various street scenes, lagoons, special effects venues, and storage areas of Universal's back lot. The tram passes several soundstages where current films and TV shows such as *CSI* are in production and actually enters three soundstages where action inspired by *Earthquake* and *King Kong* is presented. Other famous sets visited include those from *Psycho, Jaws, War of the Worlds,* and *The Grinch Who Stole Christmas.* A simulated flash flood, long a highlight of the tour, has been enhanced with new sound effects. A 2008 fire destroyed the New York Street section of the back lot, including the huge animatronic King Kong, who returned in 2010 in a very different form. Instead of rebuilding the classic banana-breathing robotic monkey based on the 1976 version, the award-winning *King Kong 360/3-D* is a virtual experience inspired by Peter Jackson's 2005 remake. Guests enter a darkened tunnel where tram-length curved projection screens transform into the jungles of Skull Island. A family of hungry V-Rexes decide to dine on your tour group, and Kong himself swings to save you, with hydraulic lifts under the cars simulating the sensations of their tug-of-war. The experience is visceral and visually stunning, especially when seen from the middle of a row (sitting on the outside exposes the top of the screen, spoiling the illusion). At only about 90 seconds, *King Kong* is too short to be a satisfying stand-alone attraction, but it's a terrific addition to the overall tour.

In 2015 Universal debuted *Fast & Furious: Supercharged,* a new finale to the tram tour, featuring Vin Diesel (Dominic "Dom" Toretto), Dwayne Johnson (Luke Hobbs), Michelle Rodriguez (Letty Ortiz), Tyrese Gibson (Roman Pearce), and Luke Evans (Owen Shaw) from the long-running car-racing franchise. Inside a 50,000-square-foot soundstage built on the site of the old avalanche-effect tunnel, the "3D-HD thrill ride" uses hydraulic platforms, 400-foot-long screens, and 34 4K 3-D projectors to make it appear as if your tram is in the midst of a high-stakes car chase, pursuing an international crime cartel at 100-plus miles per hour through the streets of Los Angeles. The *Fast & Furious* finale begins when your tram driver spots Dom's iconic Dodge Charger along your path, prompting the revelation that a member of your party is a crime witness being sought by both the bad guys and the FBI. Your tram shelters in an industrial warehouse, where a rave is in full swing until the feds crash the party. The *F&F* crew come to your rescue and escort you on a virtual high-speed highway chase filled with CGI car crashes and simulated explosions. The dialogue and visual effects are shockingly cheesy (even by theme park standards), but it all goes by in such a nitro-fueled blur that audiences emerge applauding.

To mark the Studio Tour's 50th anniversary, seasonal nighttime tram tours were also introduced in summer 2015, with extended operating hours, new lighting on the back lot sets, and live encounters with "celebrities" such as Frankenstein's monster and Marilyn Monroe.

The great thing about the Studio Tour is that you see everything without leaving the tram—essentially experiencing four or five major attractions with only one wait.

TOURING TIPS Though the wait to board might appear long, do not be discouraged. Each tram carries several hundred people and departures are frequent, so the line moves quickly. We recommend taking the tram tour after experiencing the other rides.

Including your wait to board and the duration of the tour, you will easily invest an hour or more at this attraction. Remember to take a restroom break before queuing up. Though the ride as a whole is gentle, some segments may induce vertigo or motion sickness—especially the *Kong* encounter and *Fast & Furious* finale. Finally, be aware that several of the scenes may frighten small children.

Universal's Animal Actors ★★★½

APPEAL BY AGE PRESCHOOL ★★★★½ GRADE SCHOOL ★★★★ TEENS ★★★½
YOUNG ADULTS ★★★½ OVER 30 ★★★½ SENIORS ★★★½

Thumbs Up for the Whole Family

What it is Trained animals stadium performance. **Scope and scale** Major attraction. **When to go** After you have experienced all rides. **Special comment** Warm and delightful. **Duration of show** 20 minutes. **Probable waiting time** 15–20 minutes.

DESCRIPTION AND COMMENTS *Universal's Animal Actors* features various critters, including some rescued from shelters, demonstrating behaviors that animals often perform in the making of motion pictures. The live presentation is punctuated by clips from films and TV shows. Of course, the animals often exhibit an independence that frustrates their trainers while delighting the audience.

TOURING TIPS Presented five or more times daily, the program's schedule is in the daily entertainment guide. Go when it's convenient for you; queue about 20 minutes before showtime.

WaterWorld ★★★★

APPEAL BY AGE PRESCHOOL ★★★ GRADE SCHOOL ★★★★ TEENS ★★★★
YOUNG ADULTS ★★★★ OVER 30 ★★★½ SENIORS ★★★½

Thumbs Up for the Whole Family

What it is Arena show featuring simulated stunt-scene filming. **Scope and scale** Major attraction. **When to go** After experiencing all the rides and the tram tour. **Duration of show** 15 minutes. **Probable waiting time** 15–30 minutes.

DESCRIPTION AND COMMENTS Drawn from the film *WaterWorld*, this outdoor theater presentation features stunts and special effects performed on and around a small man-made lagoon. The action involves various watercraft and, of course, a lot of explosions and falling from high places into the water. Fast-paced and well adapted to the theater, the production is in many ways more compelling than the film that inspired it. The show was revamped in 2014 with a restructured climax featuring additional stunts and pyrotechnics, making for an even more rousing finale.

TOURING TIPS Wait until you have experienced all the rides and the tram tour before checking out *WaterWorld*. Because the show is located near the main entrance, most performances are filled to capacity. Arrive at the theater about 30 minutes before the showtime listed in the daily entertainment schedule. Be careful if you sit in on a green bench; when this show says "splash zone," it means it.

THE WIZARDING WORLD OF HARRY POTTER

UNIVERSAL STUDIOS HOLLYWOOD'S Wizarding World of Harry Potter, a close copy of the original "land" at Orlando's Islands of Adventure, is an amalgamation of landmarks, creatures, and themes that are faithful to the films and books. You access the area through an imposing gate that leads to The Wizarding World's primary shopping and dining area, **Hogsmeade,** a village depicted in winter and covered in snow. Exiting Hogsmeade, you first glimpse the towering castle housing **Hogwarts School of Witchcraft and Wizardry,** flanked by the **Flight of the Hippogriff** kiddie coaster and **Hagrid's Hut.** The grounds and interior of the castle contain part of the queue for the super-headliner **Harry Potter and the Forbidden Journey.** Universal went all out on the castle, with the intention of creating an icon even more beloved and powerful than Sleeping Beauty Castle at Disneyland.

Let's begin our exploration at The Wizarding World's main entrance, adjacent to the *Shrek 4-D* theater. Passing beneath a stone arch, you enter the village of Hogsmeade. The **Hogwarts Express** locomotive sits belching steam on your right. The village setting is rendered in exquisite detail: Stone cottages and shops have steeply pitched slate roofs, bowed multipaned windows, gables, and tall, crooked chimneys. Add cobblestone streets and gas streetlamps, and Hogsmeade is as reminiscent of Sherlock Holmes as it is of Harry Potter. Your first taste—literally—of the Harry Potter universe comes courtesy of **Honeydukes.** Specializing in Potter-themed candy such as Acid Pops (no flashbacks, guaranteed), Tooth Splintering Strong Mints, and Fizzing Whizzbees, the sweet shop offers no shortage of snacks that administer an immediate sugar high. There's also a small bakery inside; while we highly recommend the Cauldron Cakes, the big draw is the elaborately boxed Chocolate Frogs. The chocolate inside isn't anything special, but the packaging looks as if it came straight from a Harry Potter film, complete with lenticular wizard trading card. Attached to Honeydukes is **Zonkos's Joke Shop,** selling toys such as Fanged Flyers (Frisbees with teeth) and adorable Pygmy Puff dolls.

Next door to Honeydukes and set back from the main street is **Three Broomsticks,** a rustic tavern serving English staples such as fish-and-chips, shepherd's pie, Cornish pasties, and turkey legs. To the rear of the tavern is the **Hog's Head** pub, which serves a nice selection of beer and is the quickest place to get The Wizarding World's signature nonalcoholic brew, **Butterbeer** (vanilla soda with butterscotch-marshmallow foam, available cold or frozen).

On the far side of the pub is **Ollivanders Wand Shop,** where young wizards are matched with magic wands ($37–$45) in a brief but charming show. Adjoining the wand show (where you can browse without queuing for the show) is **Wiseacre's Wizarding Equipment,** where you can buy binoculars or telescopes.

Roughly across the street from the pub, you'll find benches in the shade at the **Owlery,** where animatronic owls (complete with lifelike poop) ruffle and hoot from the rafters. Next to the Owlery is the **Owl Post,** where you can have mail stamped with a Hogsmeade postmark before dropping it off for delivery. The Owl Post also sells stationery, toy owls, and magic wands. Here, once again, a nice selection of owls preens on the timbers overhead. The Owl Post is attached to **Dervish and Banges,** a magic supplies shop selling brooms and Quidditch equipment, and **Gladrags Wizardwear,** ground zero for getting outfitted in fashionable school robes.

Finally, at the exit of Hogwarts Castle is **Filch's Emporium of Confiscated Goods,** which offers all manner of Potter-themed gear, including Marauder's Maps, magical creature toys, film-inspired chess sets, and, of course, Death Eater masks (breath mints extra). In keeping with the stores depicted in the Potter films, the shopping venues in The Wizarding World of Harry Potter–Hogsmeade are small and intimate—so intimate, in fact, that they feel congested when they're serving only 12–20 shoppers. USH also sells some Potter merchandise, including wands, at an easily accessible store near the park entrance.

Flight of the Hippogriff *(opens 2016)* ★★★

APPEAL BY AGE	PRESCHOOL ★★★½	GRADE SCHOOL ★★★★	TEENS ★★★
YOUNG ADULTS ★★½		OVER 30 ★★★½	SENIORS ★★★

What it is Kiddie roller coaster. **Scope and scale** Minor attraction. **When to go** First 90 minutes the park is open or after 4 p.m. **Special comment** Must be 36″ tall to ride. **Duration of ride** 1 minute. **Average wait time per 100 people ahead of you** 14 minutes. **Loading speed** Slow.

DESCRIPTION AND COMMENTS Below and to the right of Hogwarts Castle, next to Hagrid's Hut, the Hippogriff is short and sweet but not worth much of a wait. This outdoor, elevated coaster is designed for children old enough to know about Harry Potter but not yet tall enough to ride Forbidden Journey. The ride affords excellent views of the area within Wizarding World and of Hogwarts, and the theming is also very good, considering that this isn't a major attraction. As a children's coaster only slightly taller and longer than Gadget's Go Coaster in Disneyland, there are no loops, inversions, or rolls: It's just one big hill and some mild turns, and almost half of the 1-minute ride time is spent going up the lift hill.

For fans of Harry Potter, there are two gorgeous items in this attraction that you will want to see. The first is a faithful re-creation of Hagrid's Hut in the queue (complete with the sound of Fang howling) while the second is an incredible animatronic of Buckbeak that you pass by while on the ride. Remember that when Muggles (also known as humans) encounter hippogriffs like Buckbeak, proper etiquette must always be maintained to avoid any danger. Hippogriffs are extremely proud creatures and must be shown the proper respect by bowing to them and waiting for them to bow in return.

TOURING TIPS Have your kids ride soon after the park opens while older siblings enjoy Forbidden Journey.

Harry Potter and the Forbidden Journey *(opens 2016)*
★★★★★

APPEAL BY AGE	PRESCHOOL ★	GRADE SCHOOL ★★★★½	TEENS ★★★★★
YOUNG ADULTS ★★★★★		OVER 30 ★★★★★	SENIORS ★★★★★

What it is Motion-simulator dark ride. **Scope and scale** Super-headliner. **When to go** Immediately after park opening or just before closing. **Special comments** Expect long waits in line. Must be 48" tall to ride. **Duration of ride** 4¼ minutes. **Average wait time per 100 people ahead of you** 4 minutes. **Loading speed** Fast.

Queasy   Lose Things

DESCRIPTION AND COMMENTS This ride provides the only opportunity at Universal to come close to Harry, Ron, Hermione, and Dumbledore as portrayed by the original actors. Half the attraction is a series of preshows, setting the stage for the main event, a thrilling dark ride. You can get on the ride in only 10–25 minutes using the singles line, but everyone should go through the main queue at least once. The characters are incorporated into the queue and serve as an important element of the overall experience, not merely something to keep you occupied while you wait for the main event.

From Hogsmeade you reach the attraction through the imposing Winged Boar gates and progress along a winding path. Entering the castle on a lower level, you walk through a sort of dungeon festooned with various icons and prop replicas from the Potter flicks, including the Mirror of Erised from *Harry Potter and the Sorcerer's Stone.* You later emerge back outside and in the Hogwarts greenhouses. The greenhouses compose the larger part of the Forbidden Journey's queuing area, and despite some strategically placed mandrakes, there isn't much here to amuse. If you're among the first in the park and in the queue, you'll move through this area pretty quickly. Otherwise . . . well, we hope you like plants. The greenhouses are not air-conditioned, but fans move the (hot) air around. Blessedly, there are water fountains but, alas, no restrooms.

Having finally escaped horticulture purgatory, you reenter the castle, moving along its halls and passageways. One chamber you'll probably remember from the films is a multistory gallery of portraits, many of whose subjects come alive when they take a notion. You'll see for the first time the four founders of Hogwarts: Helga Hufflepuff holding her famous cup, Godric Gryffindor and Rowena Ravenclaw nearby, and the tall, moving portrait of Salazar Slytherin straight ahead. The founders argue about Quidditch and Dumbledore's controversial decision to host an open house at Hogwarts for Muggles (garden-variety mortals). Don't rush through the gallery—the effects are very cool, and the conversation is essential to understanding the rest of the attraction.

Next up, after you've navigated some more passages, is Dumbledore's office, where the wizard principal appears on a balcony and welcomes you to Hogwarts. The headmaster's appearance is your introduction to Musion Eyeliner technology—a high-definition video-projection system that produces breathtakingly realistic, three-dimensional, life-size moving holograms. After his welcoming remarks, Dumbledore dispatches you to the Defence Against the Dark Arts classroom to hear a presentation on the history of Hogwarts.

As you gather to await the lecture, Harry, Ron, and Hermione pop out from beneath an invisibility cloak. They suggest that you ditch the lecture in favor of joining them for a proper tour of Hogwarts, including a Quidditch match. After some repartee among the characters and a couple of special effects surprises, it's off to the Hogwarts Official Attraction Safety Briefing and Boarding Instructions Chamber—OK, it's actually the Gryffindor common room, but you get the picture. The briefing and instructions are presented by animated portraits, including an etiquette teacher. Later on, even the famed Sorting Hat gets into the act. All this leads to the Room of Requirement, where hundreds of candles float overhead as you board the ride.

After all the high-tech stuff in your queuing odyssey, you'll naturally expect to be wowed by your ride vehicle. Surely it's a Nimbus 3000 turbo-broom, a phoenix, a hippogriff, or at least the Weasleys' flying car. But no, what you'll ride on the most technologically advanced theme park attraction in America is . . . a bench? Yep, a bench.

unofficial **TIP**

Even if your child meets the height requirement, consider carefully whether Forbidden Journey is an experience he or she can handle—because the seats on the benches are compartmentalized, kids can't see or touch Mom or Dad if they get frightened.

A bit anticlimactic, perhaps, but as benches go, this one's a doozy, mounted on a Kuka robotic arm. When not engaged in Quidditch matches, a Kuka arm is a computer-controlled robotic arm similar to the kind used in heavy manufacturing. If you think about pictures you've seen of automotive assembly plants, Kuka arms are like those long metal appendages that come in to complete welds, move heavy stuff around, or fasten things. With the right programming, the arms can handle just about any repetitive industrial tasks thrown at them (see **kuka-robotics.com** for more info).

High-tech hijinks aside, is the attraction itself ultimately worthy of the hype? In a word, yes! Your 4¼-minute adventure is a headlong sprint through the most thrilling moments from the first few Potter books: You'll soar over Hogwarts Castle, narrowly evade an attacking dragon, spar with the Whomping Willow, get tossed into a Quidditch match, and fight off Dementors inside the Chamber of Secrets. Scenes alternate between enormous physical sets (complete with animatronic creatures), elaborate lighting effects, and high-definition video-projection domes that surround your field of view, similar to Soarin' Over California or The Simpsons Ride. Those Kuka-powered benches really do "levitate" in a manner that feels remarkably like free flight, and while you don't go upside down, the sensation of floating on your back or being slung from side to side is certainly unique.

Following in the footsteps of Universal Studios Japan, USH's Forbidden Journey will be the first version in America to feature 3-D visuals in the ride, including cute Quidditch-themed glasses that securely strap to your skull. The seamless transitions between screens and sets, and the way the domes appear to remain stationary in front of you while actually moving (much like Dreamfinder's dirigible in the original Journey into Imagination with Figment at Epcot), serve to blur the boundary between actual and virtual better than any attraction before it. The greatest-hits montage plotline may be a bit muddled, but the ride is enormously effective at leaving you feeling as though you just survived the scariest scrapes from the early educational career of The Boy Who Lived.

To understand the story line and get the most out of the attraction, you really need to see and hear the entire presentation in each of the pre-show rooms. This won't happen unless, contrary to the admonishments of the team members, you just park yourself and watch a full run-through of each preshow. Try to find a place to stop where you can let those behind you pass and where you're as far away from any staff as possible.

As long as you're not creating a logjam, the team members will leave you alone as often as not.

Another alternative is to tell the greeter at the castle entrance that you want to take the castle-only tour. This self-guided experience lets guests who don't want to ride view the features of the castle via a different queue. You can pause as long as you desire in each of the various chambers and savor the preshows without being herded along. At the end, if you decide to ride, ask to be guided to the singles line—using this strategy, you'll maximize your enjoyment of the castle while minimizing your wait for the ride. Note that the castle-only tour is often unavailable on peak attendance days.

The dialogue in the preshows is delivered in English accents of varying degrees of intelligibility, and at a very brisk pace. Add an echo effect owing to the cavernous nature of the preshow rooms, and it can be quite difficult for Yanks to decipher what's being said. This is especially evident in the staccato repartee between Harry, Ron, and Hermione in the Defence Against the Dark Arts classroom.

TOURING TIPS Harry Potter and the Forbidden Journey will quickly became the most popular attraction at USH. The best way to ride Forbidden Journey with a reasonable wait is to be one of the first through the turnstiles in the morning or to visit in the final hours of the evening.

Upon approaching Forbidden Journey's front gates, those who have bags or loose items and therefore require a free locker may be directed into an extended outdoor queue. Our wait-time research has shown that in some cases, not needing a locker can save you as much as 30 minutes of standing in line. If you do need to stow your stuff, be aware that the Forbidden Journey locker area is small, crowded, and confusing. Alternatively, have one member of your party hold your bags for you in the child swap area.

Universal warns you to secure or leave behind loose objects, which most people interpret to mean eyeglasses, purses, ball caps, and the like. However, the ride makes a couple of moves that will empty your trousers faster than a master pickpocket—ditto and worse for shirt pockets. When these moves occur, your stuff will clatter around like quarters in a slot-machine tray. Much better to use the small compartment built into the seat back for keys, coins, phone, wallet, and pocket Bible. Be prepared, however: Team members don't give you much time to stow or retrieve your belongings.

The single-rider line is unmarked, so relatively few guests use it. Whereas on most attractions the wait in the singles line is one-third the wait in the standby line, at Forbidden Journey it can be as much as one-tenth. Because the individual seating separates you from the other riders whether your party stays together or not, the singles line is a great option, as this wife from Edinburgh, Scotland, discovered:

Trust me, sitting next to hubbie on Forbidden Journey, romantic though it may be, is not as awesome as having to wait only 15 minutes as a single rider.

To get there, enter the right (no-bags) line and keep left all the way into the castle. Past the locker area, take the first left into the singles line.

If you see a complete iteration of each preshow in the queue and then experience the ride, you'll invest 25–35 minutes even if you don't have to wait. If you elect to skip the preshows (the Gryffindor Common Room, where you receive safety and loading directions, is mandatory) and use the singles line, you can get on in about 10–25 minutes at any time of day. At a time when the posted wait in the regular line was 2 hours, we rode and were out the door in 15 minutes using the singles line.

We recommend that you not ride with a full stomach. If you start getting queasy, fix your gaze on your feet and try to exclude as much from your peripheral vision as possible.

If you have a child who doesn't meet the minimum height requirement of 48 inches, a child-swapping option is provided at the loading area.

The end seats on each flying bench are designed to accommodate a wider variety of body shapes and sizes. Though these modified seats allow many more people to ride, it's still possible that guests of size can't fit in them. The best way to figure out whether you can fit in a regular seat or one of the modified ones is to sit in one of the test seats outside the queue or just inside the castle. After you sit down, pull down on the safety harness as far as you can. One of three safety lights will illuminate: A green light indicates that you can fit into any seat, a yellow light means that you should ask for one of the modified seats on the outside of the bench, and a red light means that the harness can't engage enough for you to ride safely.

In addition, USH team members select guests of all sizes "at random" to plop in the test seats, but they're really looking for large people or those who have a certain body shape. Team members handle the situation as diplomatically as possible, but if they suspect you're not the right size, you'll be asked to sit down for a test. For you to be cleared to ride, the overhead restraint has to click three times; once again, it's body shape rather than weight (unless you're over 300 pounds) that's key. Most team members will let you try a second time if you don't achieve three clicks on the first go. Passing the test by inhaling sharply is not recommended unless you can also hold your breath for the entire 4-plus minutes of the ride.

LOWER LOT ATTRACTIONS

Jurassic Park—The Ride ★★★★

APPEAL BY AGE	PRESCHOOL ★★★	GRADE SCHOOL ★★★★½	TEENS ★★★★½
YOUNG ADULTS ★★★★		OVER 30 ★★★★	SENIORS ★★★★

What it is Indoor-outdoor adventure ride based on the movie *Jurassic Park*. **Scope and scale** Super-headliner. **When to go** Before 10:30 a.m. **Special comments** Must be 46″ tall to ride; switching-off option provided (see page 145). **Duration of ride** 6 minutes. **Loading speed** Fast.

Scary   Wet   Lose Things   Queasy   Rough

DESCRIPTION AND COMMENTS Guests board boats for a water tour of Jurassic Park. Everything is tranquil as the tour begins; the boat floats among large herbivorous dinosaurs such as apatosaurus and stegosaurus. Then word is received that some of the carnivores have escaped their enclosure, and the tour boat is accidentally diverted into Jurassic Park's water-treatment facility. Here the boat and its riders are menaced by an assortment of hungry meat-eaters led by the ubiquitous *T. rex*. At the climactic moment, the boat and its passengers escape by dropping over a waterfall.

Jurassic Park is impressive in its scale, but the number of dinosaurs is a little disappointing. The big herbivores are given short shrift to set up the plot for the carnivore encounter, which leads to floating around in what looks like a brewery. When the carnivores make their appearance, though, they definitely get your attention. The final drop down a three-story flume to safety is a dandy, though not as impressive as its Orlando sibling.

TOURING TIPS You can get very wet on this ride, and extra jets enabled during hot weather practically ensure a soaking. Once the ride is under way, there's a little splashing but nothing major until the big drop at the end. When you hit the bottom, enough water will cascade into the boat to extinguish a three-alarm fire. Bring along an extra-large garbage bag and (cutting holes for your head and arms) wear it like a sack dress. If you forget to bring a garbage bag, you can purchase a poncho at the park for about $10.

Young kids must endure a double whammy. First, they are stalked by giant, salivating reptiles and then are catapulted over the falls. Wait until your kids are fairly stalwart before you spring Jurassic Park on them, or let them sit out the ride inside the fossil-themed playground near the entrance.

Jurassic Park stays jammed most of the day. Ride early in the morning after Revenge of the Mummy.

The NBC Universal Experience ★★★

| APPEAL BY AGE | PRESCHOOL ★ | GRADE SCHOOL ★★ | TEENS ★★★ |
| YOUNG ADULTS ★★★ | | OVER 30 ★★★ | SENIORS ★★★ |

What it is Interactive walk-through exhibit. **Scope and scale** Diversion. **When to go** Anytime. **Duration of tour** 15–40 minutes. **Probable waiting time** None.

DESCRIPTION AND COMMENTS This exhibit features authentic props and costumes from many of Universal's most famous films—*Gladiator, To Kill a Mockingbird, Jurassic Park, E.T., The Sting, Psycho,* and *Coraline,* just to name a few. Cinephiles will love it. Recently added highlights include artifacts and interactive videos chronicling the park's first 50 years (including pieces of lost rides like E.T.) and the meticulously restored time-traveling DeLorean used in the *Back to the Future* trilogy.

TOURING TIPS Never crowded—visit after you've experienced all the rides.

Revenge of the Mummy—The Ride ★★★½

| APPEAL BY AGE | PRESCHOOL — | GRADE SCHOOL ★★★½ | TEENS ★★★★½ |
| YOUNG ADULTS ★★★★½ | | OVER 30 ★★★★ | SENIORS ★★★½ |

What it is High-tech dark ride. **Scope and scale** Super-headliner. **When to go** The first hour the park is open or after 4 p.m. **Special comments** Must be 48" tall to ride; switching-off option provided (see page 145). **Duration of ride** About 2 minutes. **Loading speed** Slow.

Dark   Scary   Lose Things   Queasy   Rough

DESCRIPTION AND COMMENTS Revenge of the Mummy is an indoor dark ride based on the *Mummy* flicks, where guests fight off "deadly curses and vengeful creatures" while flying through Egyptian tombs and other spooky places on a high-tech roller coaster.

The queuing area serves to establish the story line: You're in a group touring a 1944 archeological dig of an Egyptian tomb when evil Imhotep decides to make another comeback. The theming includes authentic hieroglyphics as the queue makes its way to the loading area, where you board a somewhat clunky, jeep-looking vehicle. The ride begins as a slow, elaborate dark ride passing through various chambers, including one where golden treasures are offered in exchange for your soul. Suddenly you're shot at high speed straight forward into a minute of pitch-black hills and tight curves, dead-ending in an encounter with leg-tickling scarab beetles. We don't want to divulge too much, but the roller coaster part of the ride has no barrel rolls or any upside-down stuff.

After an all-too-brief backward section, the attraction anticlimaxes in a darkened dome, where the mummy moans and then blinds you with a strobe. Compared to Universal Studios Florida's ride of the same name, this abbreviated attraction severely disappoints with shorter drops, simpler Audio-Animatronics, and no pyrotechnics.

TOURING TIPS Revenge of the Mummy has a very low riders-per-hour capacity for one of the park's top draws. Your only prayer for a tolerable wait is to be on hand when the park opens and sprint to the Mummy immediately after riding Transformers. If you can ride Space Mountain without getting sick, you should be fine on this.

Transformers: The Ride 3-D ★★★★★

| APPEAL BY AGE | PRESCHOOL ★★★ | GRADE SCHOOL ★★★★★ | TEENS ★★★★★ |
| YOUNG ADULTS ★★★★★ | | OVER 30 ★★★★★ | SENIORS ★★★ |

What it is Multisensory 3-D dark ride. **Scope and scale** Super-headliner. **When to go** The first 30 minutes the park is open or after 4 p.m. **Special comments** Must be 40″ tall to ride; single-rider line is available. **Duration of ride** 4½ minutes. **Average wait time per 100 people ahead of you** 3 minutes. **Loading speed** Moderate–fast.

Dark   Loud   Scary   Rough

DESCRIPTION AND COMMENTS Hasbro's Transformers—those toy robots from the 1980s that you turned and twisted into trucks and planes—have been around long enough to go from commercial to kitsch to cool and back again. Thanks to director Michael Bay's recent movies, "Robots in Disguise" are again a blockbuster global franchise. Recruits to this cybertronic war enlist by entering the N.E.S.T. Base (headquarters of the heroic Autobots and their human allies) beneath a massive dimensional mural depicting Optimus Prime and his nemesis Megatron locked in mortal metal combat. Inside an extensive, elaborately detailed queue, video monitors catch you up on the backstory. Basically, the Decepticon baddies are after the Allspark, source of cybernetic sentience. We're supposed to safeguard the shard by hitching a ride aboard our friendly Autobot ride vehicle EVAC, presumably without getting "smooshed" like a Lincoln in a souvenir penny press when he shifts into android form. Needless to say, Megatron and his pals Starscream and Devastator won't make things easy, but you'll have Sideswipe and Bumblebee (sadly, the modern Camaro version instead of an old-school VW Beetle) backing you up. For the ride's 4½ minutes, you play human Ping-Pong ball in an epic battle between these Made in Japan behemoths. To do justice to this Bay-splosion–packed war of good versus evil, Universal has harnessed the same ride system behind Islands of Adventure's Amazing Adventures of Spider-Man ride, blending motion simulation and live effects with 3-D.

Transformers ups the ante with photo-realistic high-definition imagery, boosted by dichroic 3-D glasses (the same kind used in the upgraded Star Tours) that produce remarkably sharp, vivid visuals. The plot amounts to little more than a giant game of keep-away, and the uninitiated will likely be unable to tell one meteoric mass of metal from another, but you'll be too dazzled by the debris whizzing by to notice. Fanboys will squeal with delight at hearing original cartoon actors Peter Cullen and Frank Welker voicing the pugilistic protagonists, and then spill into the post-ride gift shop to purchase armloads of exclusive merchandise, while the rest of us might need a bench on which to take a breather afterward. We'll admit slight disappointment at not getting to see an actual four-story-tall anima-tronic transform, but the ride's mix of detailed (though largely static) set pieces and video projections was likely a much more maintenance-friendly solution for bringing these colossi to life. Either way, this is one of the most intense, immersive thrill rides found in any theme park and makes a credi-ble claim on the title "best attraction in California." If you visit Universal and only ride this and the Studio Tour, you'll get your money's worth.

TOURING TIPS Transformers draws heavy crowds to the Lower Lot from the moment the park opens, so ride immediately upon park opening. The single-rider entrance will often let you walk on the attraction, even when the standby wait is an hour, but its queue lacks any theming, so be sure to take at least one trip through the regular line. It can be diffi-cult for your eyes to focus on the fast-moving imagery from the front row; center seats in the second and third rows provide the best per-spective. And be sure to say hello to the towering robots posing for photos outside the entrance; they can talk back to you!

LIVE ENTERTAINMENT *at* UNIVERSAL STUDIOS HOLLYWOOD

THE THEATER ATTRACTIONS operate according to the entertain-ment schedule available with handout park maps. The number of daily performances of each show varies from as few as 3 a day during less busy times of year to as many as 10 a day during the summer and holi-day periods. Look for the Doo Wop Singers belting out 1950s and 1960s harmonies near Mel's Diner during peak seasons. Cartoon characters like Shrek, Gru's Minions, and The Simpsons can be spotted hanging out near their respective rides, while others (SpongeBob SquarePants, Dora the Explorer, and Scooby-Doo) frequent the Universal Plaza in the middle of the Upper Lot. Don't miss bantering with the New York apartment dwellers leaning out of the second-story windows above the candy shop. Near the Jurassic Park ride, you can take a selfie with a real-life velociraptor (actually an actor inside an impressive full-body puppet) and her wry wrangler.

DINING *at* UNIVERSAL STUDIOS HOLLYWOOD

THE COUNTER-SERVICE FOOD at Universal Studios runs the gamut from burgers and hot dogs to pizza, fried chicken, crêpes, and Mexican specialties. We rank most selections marginally better than fast food. Prices are comparable to those at Disneyland.

If you are looking for full-service dining, try **Wolfgang Puck Bistro, Buca di Beppo, Wasabi,** or the **Hard Rock Cafe** in Universal City-Walk just outside the park entrance. Our favorites in the park are the gourmet sandwiches at **Palace Theatre Café,** and the **Hollywood Grill** pizza and burger joint across from *WaterWorld*. **Gru's Lab Café** (near Despicable Me Minion Mayhem) serves grilled cheese sandwiches with pulled pork, "El Macho" nachos, fried mac and cheese, and banana-flavored desserts to mollify your Minions' munchies. The new Simpsons eateries are a great bet; give Cletus's chicken and waffles, Bumblebee Man's tacos, or a Krusty burger a try, with a Duff beer to wash it down. If you leave the park for lunch, be sure to have your hand stamped for reentry. To service your caffeine addiction, there are now **Starbucks** outlets on both the Upper and Lower Lots.

UNIVERSAL STUDIOS HOLLYWOOD ONE-DAY TOURING PLAN *(page 376)*

THIS PLAN IS FOR GROUPS OF ALL SIZES and ages and includes thrill rides that may induce motion sickness or get you wet. If the plan calls for you to experience an attraction that does not interest you, proceed to the next step. The plan calls for minimal backtracking.

Before You Go

1. Call ☎ 818-622-3801 the day before your visit for the official opening time. If you can't get through, call ☎ 818-622-3735 or 818-622-3750. On all numbers, press 3 for a live attendant.

2. If you have young children in your party, consult the Universal Studios Hollywood Small-Child Fright-Potential Table on the following page.

UNIVERSAL STUDIOS HOLLYWOOD
SMALL-CHILD FRIGHT-POTENTIAL TABLE

DESPICABLE ME MINION MAYHEM Loud with some intense 3-D effects.

FLIGHT OF THE HIPPOGRIFF Frightens a small percentage of preschoolers.

HARRY POTTER AND THE FORBIDDEN JOURNEY Extremely intense special effects and macabre visuals with wild simulated movement that may frighten and discombobulate guests of any age.

JURASSIC PARK—THE RIDE Intense water-flume ride. Potentially terrifying for people of any age.

REVENGE OF THE MUMMY—THE RIDE Scares guests of all ages.

SHREK 4-D Special effects may frighten preschoolers.

THE SIMPSONS RIDE Motion simulator too intense for many children age 7 and younger tall enough to ride.

SPECIAL EFFECTS STAGE Some intense special effects. Shows how bloody fake wounds are created.

STUDIO TOUR Certain parts of the tour are too frightening and too intense for many preschoolers.

TRANSFORMERS: THE RIDE 3-D Too intense for children younger than age 7, and potentially terrifying for visitors of any age.

UNIVERSAL'S ANIMAL ACTORS Not frightening in any way.

WATERWORLD Fighting, gunplay, and explosions may frighten children age 4 and younger.

APPENDIX

READERS' QUESTIONS *to the* AUTHORS

QUESTION:

When you do your research, are you admitted to the park for free? Do the Disney people know you are there?

ANSWER:

We pay the regular admission, and usually the Disney people do not know we are on-site. Both in and out of Disneyland, we pay for our own meals and lodging.

QUESTION:

How often is The Unofficial Guide to Disneyland *revised?*

ANSWER:

We publish a new edition once a year but make corrections every time we go to press.

QUESTION:

I have an older edition of The Unofficial Guide to Disneyland. *How much of the information in it is still correct?*

ANSWER:

Veteran travel writers will acknowledge that 5%–8% of the information in a guidebook is out of date by the time it comes off the press! Disneyland is always changing. If you are using an old edition of *The Unofficial Guide to Disneyland,* the descriptions of attractions existing when the guide was published should still be generally accurate. Many other things, however—particularly the touring plans and the hotel and restaurant reviews—change with every edition. Finally, and obviously, older editions of *The Unofficial Guide to Disneyland* do not include new attractions or developments.

QUESTION:

Do you write each new edition from scratch?

ANSWER:

We do not. With a destination the size of Disneyland, it's hard enough keeping up with what is new. Moreover, we put great effort into communicating the most salient and useful information in the clearest possible language. If an attraction or hotel has not changed, we are very reluctant to tinker with its coverage for the sake of freshening up the writing.

QUESTION:

Do you stay at Disneyland hotels? If not, where do you stay?

ANSWER:

We do stay at Disneyland-area hotels from time to time, usually after a renovation or management change. Since we began writing about Disneyland in 1984, we have stayed in more than 55 different properties in various locations around Anaheim.

QUESTION:

How many people have you interviewed or surveyed for your age-group ratings on the attractions?

ANSWER:

Since the publication of the first edition of the *Unofficial Guide* in 1985, we have interviewed or surveyed more than 19,500 Disneyland patrons.

QUESTION:

How are your age-group ratings determined? I am 42 years old. During Star Tours, I was quite worried about hurting my back. If the senior citizens rating is determined only by those brave enough to ride, it will skew the results.

ANSWER:

The reader makes a good point. Unfortunately, it's impossible to develop a rating unless the guest (of any age group) has actually experienced the attraction. So yes, all age-group ratings are derived exclusively from members of that age group who have experienced the attraction. Health problems, such as a bad back, however, can affect guests of any age, and Disney provides more-than-ample warnings on attractions that warrant such admonitions. But if you are in good health, our ratings will give you a sense of how much others your age enjoyed the attraction.

QUESTION:

I have heard that when there are two lines to an attraction, the left line is faster. Is this true?

ANSWER:

In general, no. We have tested this theory many times and usually have not gained an advantage of even 90 seconds by getting in one line versus another. The few rare exceptions are noted in the ride descriptions. What *does* occasionally occur, however, is that after a second line has *just been opened,* guests ignore the new line and persist in standing in the established line. Generally, if you encounter a two-line waiting configuration with no barrier to entry for either and one of the lines is conspicuously less populated than the other, get in it.

AND FINALLY . . .

To end on a high note, consider this compliment from a Redding, California, reader:

> *Thanks to your book, this trip turned out much better than our last, so much in fact that I required only half as much Valium.*

And so it goes . . .

ACCOMMODATION INDEX

Note: Page numbers in **boldface** type indicate profiles.

RESTAURANT INDEX

Note: Page numbers in **boldface** type indicate a profile.

SUBJECT INDEX

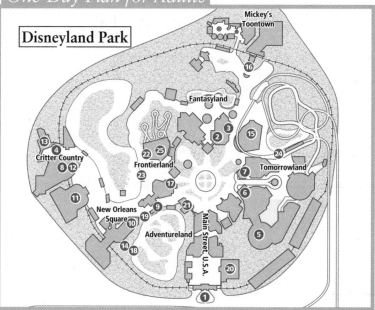

One-Day Plan for Adults

Disneyland Park

Mickey's Toontown

Fantasyland

Critter Country

Frontierland

Tomorrowland

New Orleans Square

Adventureland

Main Street, U.S.A.

1. Arrive at the entrance 40 minutes before official opening time.
2. Ride Peter Pan's Flight in Fantasyland.
3. Ride Alice in Wonderland.
4. Go to Big Thunder Trail and get FastPasses for *Fantasmic!*
5. Ride Space Mountain in Tomorrowland.
6. Ride Star Tours—The Adventures Continue.
7. Try Buzz Lightyear Astro Blasters.
8. Obtain FastPasses for Splash Mountain.
9. Take the Jungle Cruise in Adventureland.
10. Experience Pirates of the Caribbean in New Orleans Square.
11. Visit The Haunted Mansion.
12. Return to ride Splash Mountain in Critter Country using the FastPasses obtained earlier.
13. Ride The Many Adventures of Winnie the Pooh.
14. Get FastPasses for Indiana Jones Adventure.
15. Ride the Matterhorn Bobsleds in Fantasyland.
16. Ride It's a Small World.

17. Grab lunch and a show at The Golden Horseshoe in Frontierland.
18. Experience Indiana Jones Adventure in Adventureland using the FastPasses obtained earlier.
19. Explore Tarzan's Treehouse nearby.
20. See *The Disneyland Story,* presenting *Great Moments with Mr. Lincoln,* on Main Street, U.S.A.
21. See *Enchanted Tiki Room* in Adventureland.
22. Obtain FastPasses for Big Thunder Mountain Railroad in Frontierland.
23. Experience the Sailing Ship *Columbia* or the *Mark Twain* Riverboat.
24. Ride Finding Nemo Submarine Voyage in Tomorrowland.
25. Ride Big Thunder Mountain Railroad in Frontierland, using the FastPasses obtained earlier.
26. Eat dinner.
27. Check the *Times Guide* for parades, fireworks, and *Fantasmic!*

Author's Select One-Day Plan

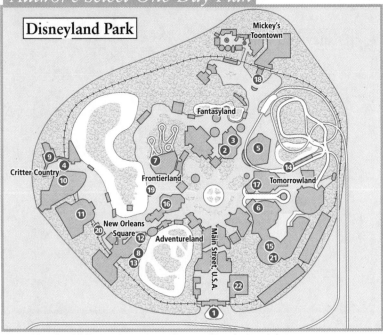

1. Arrive at the entrance 40 minutes before official opening time.
2. Ride Peter Pan's Flight in Fantasyland.
3. Ride Alice in Wonderland.
4. Go to Big Thunder Trail and get FastPasses for *Fantasmic!*
5. Experience the Matterhorn Bobsleds.
6. Ride Star Tours—The Adventures Continue in Tomorrowland.
7. Ride Big Thunder Mountain Railroad in Frontierland.
8. Obtain FastPasses for Indiana Jones Adventure.
9. See The Many Adventures of Winnie the Pooh in Critter Country.
10. Ride Splash Mountain.
11. See The Haunted Mansion in New Orleans Square.
12. Experience Pirates of the Caribbean.
13. Experience Indiana Jones Adventure in Adventureland using the FastPasses obtained earlier.
14. Take the Finding Nemo Submarine Voyage in Tomorrowland.
15. Obtain FastPasses for Space Mountain.
16. Eat lunch and grab a show at The Golden Horseshoe in Frontierland.
17. Try Buzz Lightyear Astro Blasters in Tomorrowland.
18. Ride It's a Small World in Fantasyland.
19. Experience the Sailing Ship *Columbia* or the *Mark Twain* Riverboat in Frontierland.
20. Take a round-trip on the Disneyland Railroad from the New Orleans Square Station.
21. Ride Space Mountain using the FastPasses obtained earlier.
22. See *The Disneyland Story*, presenting *Great Moments with Mr. Lincoln*, on Main Street, U.S.A.
23. Check the *Times Guide* for parades, fireworks, and *Fantasmic!*

Dumbo-or-Die-in-a-Day Plan

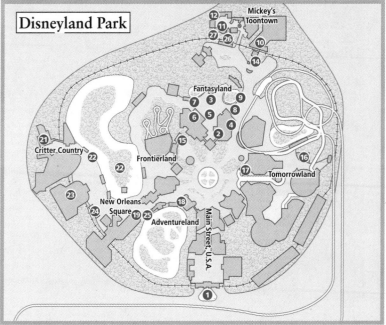

Disneyland Park

1. Arrive at the entrance 40 minutes before official opening time.
2. Ride Peter Pan's Flight in Fantasyland.
3. Ride Dumbo the Flying Elephant.
4. Ride Alice in Wonderland.
5. Ride the King Arthur Carousel.
6. Take Pinocchio's Daring Journey.
7. Ride the Casey Jr. Circus Train.
8. Take a spin on the Mad Tea Party.
9. Ride the Storybook Land Canal Boats.
10. In Mickey's Toontown, ride Roger Rabbit's Car Toon Spin. Obtain FastPasses if the wait exceeds 30 minutes.
11. Ride Gadget's Go Coaster.
12. Tour Minnie's House.
13. Let the kids blow off some steam at Goofy's Playhouse.
14. Take the It's a Small World boat ride in Fantasyland.
15. Experience the Royal Hall princess meet and greet.
16. In Tomorrowland, ride Autopia.
17. Try Buzz Lightyear Astro Blasters.
18. See the *Enchanted Tiki Room* in Adventureland.
19. Ride Pirates of the Caribbean in New Orleans Square.
20. Eat lunch.
21. Take The Many Adventures of Winnie the Pooh ride in Critter Country.
22. Take a raft to explore the Pirate's Lair on Tom Sawyer Island.
23. See The Haunted Mansion in New Orleans Square.
24. Take a round-trip on the Disneyland Railroad from the New Orleans Square Station.
25. Explore Tarzan's Treehouse in Adventureland.
26. If time permits, let the kids play at *Miss Daisy*, Donald's Boat, in Mickey's Toontown.
27. Also check out the Chip 'n Dale Treehouse.
28. Eat dinner.
29. Visit any attractions you may have missed earlier.
30. Check the *Times Guide* for parades, fireworks, and *Fantasmic!*

Two-Day Plan for Adults with Children: Day One

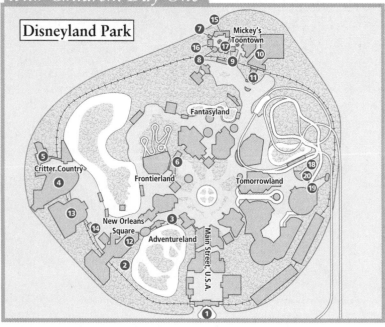

1. Arrive at the entrance 40 minutes before official opening time.
2. As soon as the park opens, ride Indiana Jones Adventure in Adventureland.
3. Take the Jungle Cruise.
4. Try Splash Mountain in Critter Country.
5. Ride The Many Adventures of Winnie the Pooh.
6. Experience the Royal Hall princess meet and greet in Fantasyland.
7. In Mickey's Toontown, tour Mickey's House.
8. Ride Gadget's Go Coaster.
9. Let the kids blow off some steam at Goofy's Playhouse.
10. Try Roger Rabbit's Car Toon Spin. Obtain Fast-Passes if the wait exceeds 30 minutes.
11. In Fantasyland, ride It's a Small World.
12. Ride Pirates of the Caribbean in New Orleans Square.
13. See The Haunted Mansion. If you're visiting between mid-September and New Year's, and

Haunted Mansion is distributing FastPasses, obtain FastPasses if the wait exceeds 30 minutes.
14. Eat lunch and take the Disneyland Railroad from New Orleans Square to Toontown.
15. In Mickey's Toontown, see Minnie's House.
16. Try the Chip 'n Dale Treehouse.
17. Check out *Miss Daisy*, Donald's Boat.
18. Obtain FastPasses for Autopia in Tomorrowland.
19. If time permits, take a round-trip on the Disneyland Monorail.
20. Ride Autopia using the FastPasses obtained earlier.
21. Eat dinner.
22. Visit any attractions you may have missed earlier.
23. Check the *Times Guide* for parades, fireworks, and *Fantasmic!*

Two-Day Plan for Adults with Children: Day Two

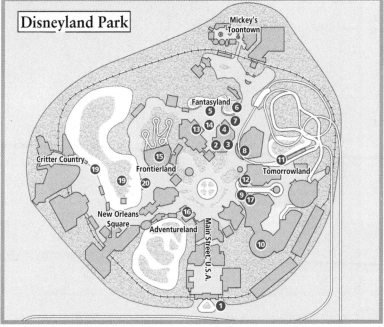

Disneyland Park

1. Arrive at the entrance 40 minutes before official opening time.
2. As soon as the park opens, ride Peter Pan's Flight in Fantasyland.
3. Ride Alice in Wonderland.
4. Take Mr. Toad's Wild Ride.
5. Experience Dumbo the Flying Elephant.
6. Try the Storybook Land Canal Boats.
7. Take a spin on the Mad Tea Party.
8. Ride the Matterhorn Bobsleds.
9. In Tomorrowland, send one member of your party to obtain FastPasses for Star Tours—The Adventures Continue.
10. Ride Space Mountain.
11. Take the Finding Nemo Submarine Voyage.
12. Try Buzz Lightyear Astro Blasters.
13. In Fantasyland, ride Pinocchio's Daring Journey.
14. Take a spin on the King Arthur Carousel.
15. Ride Big Thunder Mountain Railroad in Frontierland.
16. See the *Enchanted Tiki Room* in Adventureland.
17. Ride Star Tours in Tomorrowland, using the FastPasses obtained earlier.
18. Eat lunch.
19. Take a raft to Tom Sawyer Island, and let the kids run around the island's Pirate's Lair.
20. If time permits, try the Sailing Ship *Columbia* or the *Mark Twain* Riverboat.
21. Visit any attractions you may have missed earlier.
22. Check the *Times Guide* for parades, fireworks, and *Fantasmic!*

Two-Day Plan A: Day One

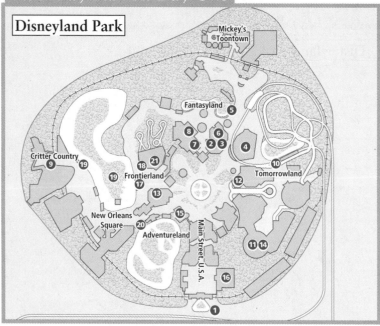

Disneyland Park

1. Arrive at the entrance 40 minutes before official opening time.
2. As soon as the park opens, ride Peter Pan's Flight in Fantasyland.
3. Experience Alice in Wonderland.
4. Ride the Matterhorn Bobsleds.
5. Take a cruise on the Storybook Land Canal Boats.
6. Take Mr. Toad's Wild Ride.
7. Ride Snow White's Scary Adventures.
8. Take Pinocchio's Daring Journey.
9. Go to Big Thunder Trail and get FastPasses for *Fantasmic!*
10. In Tomorrowland, take the Finding Nemo Submarine Voyage.
11. Obtain FastPasses for Space Mountain.
12. Ride Buzz Lightyear Astro Blasters.
13. Eat lunch and grab a show at The Golden Horseshoe in Frontierland.
14. Return to Tomorrowland and ride Space Mountain using the FastPasses obtained earlier.
15. See the *Enchanted Tiki Room* in Adventureland.
16. See *The Disneyland Story*, presenting *Great Moments with Mr. Lincoln* on Main Street, U.S.A.
17. Ride the Sailing Ship *Columbia* or the *Mark Twain* Riverboat, whichever is boarding first.
18. Send one member of your party to obtain FastPasses for Big Thunder Mountain Railroad in Frontierland.
19. Take a raft to the Pirate's Lair on Tom Sawyer Island.
20. Climb through Tarzan's Treehouse in Adventureland.
21. Ride Big Thunder Mountain Railroad using the FastPasses obtained earlier.
22. Eat dinner.
23. Visit any attractions you may have missed earlier.
23. Check the *Times Guide* for parades, fireworks, and *Fantasmic!*

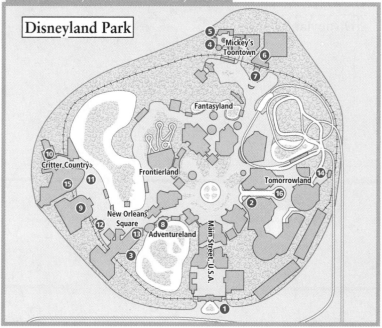

Two-Day Plan A: Day Two

Disneyland Park

1. Arrive at the entrance 40 minutes before official opening time.
2. As soon as the park opens, ride Star Tours—The Adventures Continue in Tomorrowland.
3. Take the Indiana Jones Adventure in Adventureland.
4. In Mickey's Toontown, visit Mickey's House.
5. See Minnie's House.
6. Try Roger Rabbit's Car Toon Spin. Use FastPass if the wait exceeds 30 minutes.
7. Ride It's a Small World in Fantasyland.
8. Take the Jungle Cruise in Adventureland.
9. Ride The Haunted Mansion in New Orleans Square.
10. Experience The Many Adventures of Winnie the Pooh in Critter Country.

11. Obtain FastPasses for Splash Mountain.
12. Take a round-trip on the Disneyland Railroad from the New Orleans Square Station.
13. Ride Pirates of the Caribbean.
14. Take the monorail from Tomorrowland to Downtown Disney, and eat lunch.
15. Ride Splash Mountain in Critter Country using the FastPasses obtained earlier.
16. See the *Jedi Training Academy* in Tomorrowland.
17. Revisit any favorite attractions or visit any attractions you may have missed earlier.
18. Check the *Times Guide* for parades, fireworks, and *Fantasmic!*

Two-Day Plan B: Day One

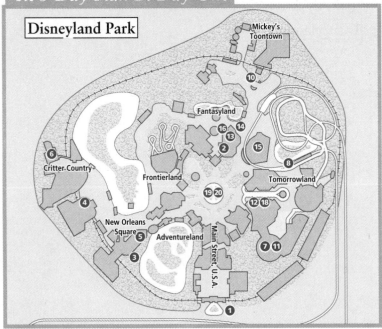

1. Arrive at the entrance 40 minutes before official opening time.
2. Ride Peter Pan's Flight in Fantasyland.
3. Ride Indiana Jones Adventure in Adventureland.
4. See The Haunted Mansion in New Orleans Square.
5. Ride Pirates of the Caribbean.
6. See The Many Adventures of Winnie the Pooh in Critter Country.
7. Obtain FastPasses for Space Mountain in Tomorrowland.
8. Ride the Finding Nemo Submarine Voyage.
9. Eat lunch.
10. See It's a Small World in Fantasyland.
11. Ride Space Mountain in Tomorrowland using the FastPasses obtained earlier.
12. Obtain FastPasses for Star Tours—The Adventures Continue.
13. Ride Alice in Wonderland in Fantasyland.
14. Take a spin on the Mad Tea Party.
15. Ride the Matterhorn Bobsleds.
16. Try Mr. Toad's Wild Ride.
17. Eat dinner.
18. Ride Star Tours—The Adventures Continue in Tomorrowland using the FastPasses obtained earlier.
19. Watch the *Disneyland Forever* fireworks. Find a spot on Main Street or near Sleeping Beauty Castle to watch the fireworks.
20. Enjoy the Paint the Night parade.

Two-Day Plan B: Day Two

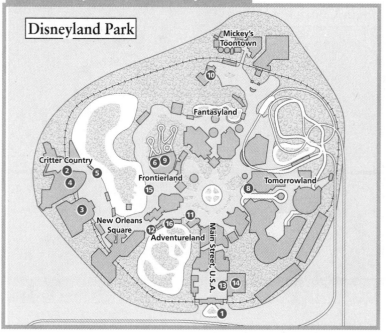

Disneyland Park

Mickey's Toontown

10

Fantasyland

Critter Country

2 5

4

3

Frontierland

6 9

15

New Orleans Square

12 16

Adventureland

11

Tomorrowland

8

Main Street U.S.A.

13 14

1

1. Arrive at Disneyland Park around noon.
2. Go to Big Thunder Trail and get FastPasses for *Fantasmic!*
3. See The Haunted Mansion in New Orleans Square.
4. Ride Splash Mountain in Critter Country.
5. Take Davy Crockett's Explorer Canoes around Tom Sawyer Island.
6. Obtain FastPasses for Big Thunder Mountain Railroad.
7. Eat a late lunch. A good choice is Jolly Holiday Bakery.
8. Try Buzz Lightyear Astro Blasters in Tomorrowland.
9. Ride Big Thunder Mountain Railroad in Frontierland using the FastPasses obtained earlier.
10. See *Mickey and the Magical Map* in Fantasyland.
11. See the *Enchanted Tiki Room* in Adventureland.
12. Explore Tarzan's Treehouse.
13. Enjoy Mickey's Soundsational Parade.
14. On Main Street, U.S.A., see *The Disneyland Story*, presenting *Great Moments with Mr. Lincoln.*
15. Ride the *Mark Twain* Riverboat or Sailing Ship *Columbia,* whichever boards first.
16. Take the Jungle Cruise in Adventureland.
17. Eat dinner. The Plaza Restaurant is a good choice.
18. Check the *Times Guide* for parades, fireworks, and *Fantasmic!*

One-Day Plan for Adults

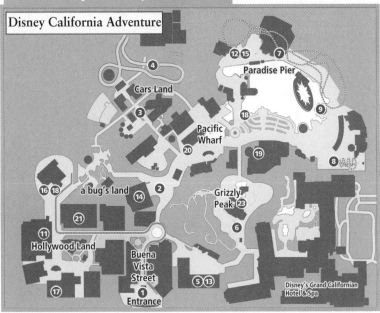

Disney California Adventure

1. Arrive at the entrance 40 minutes before official opening time.
2. As soon as the park opens, obtain FastPasses for Radiator Springs Racers in Cars Land. FastPasses are distributed outside of Cars Land near *It's Tough to Be a Bug!*
3. Ride Mater's Junkyard Jamboree in Cars Land.
4. Ride Radiator Springs Racers using the Fast-Passes obtained earlier.
5. Obtain FastPasses for Soarin' Over California in Grizzly Peak.
6. Obtain FastPasses for *World of Color—Celebrate!* FastPasses are distributed near the entrance to Grizzly River Run.
7. Try Toy Story Midway Mania! in Paradise Pier.
8. Ride Goofy's Sky School.
9. Try the Silly Symphony Swings.
10. Eat lunch.
11. Check the daily entertainment schedule for the next showing of *Disney's Aladdin—A Musical Spectacular*. Work in this show around lunch.
12. Get FastPasses for California Screamin' in Paradise Pier.
13. Ride Soarin' Over California in Grizzly Peak using the FastPasses obtained earlier.
14. See *It's Tough to Be a Bug* in A Bug's Land.
15. Ride California Screamin' in Paradise Pier using the FastPasses obtained earlier.
16. Obtain FastPasses for The Twilight Zone Tower of Terror in Hollywood Land.
17. Ride Monsters, Inc. Mike & Sulley to the Rescue!
18. Ride The Twilight Zone Tower of Terror using the FastPasses obtained earlier.
19. Ride The Little Mermaid: Ariel's Undersea Adventure in Paradise Pier.
20. Take the Bakery Tour in the Pacific Wharf.
21. See the Disney Animation exhibit, including Animation Academy and *Turtle Talk with Crush*, in Hollywood Land.
22. Eat dinner.
23. Ride Grizzly River Run in Grizzly Peak.
24. Repeat any favorite attractions or see any missed attractions.
25. Check your daily entertainment schedule for parades, and check your *World of Color—Celebrate!* FastPass for the performance time.

One-Day Plan for Adults with Small Children

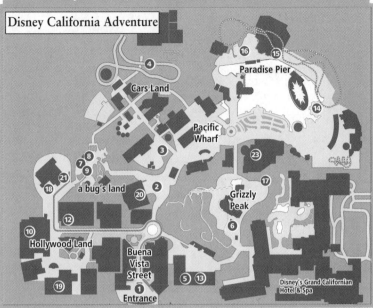

Disney California Adventure

1. Arrive at the entrance 40 minutes before official opening time.
2. As soon as the park opens, obtain FastPasses for Radiator Springs Racers in Cars Land. FastPasses are distributed outside of Cars Land near *It's Tough to Be a Bug!*
3. Ride Mater's Junkyard Jamboree.
4. Ride Radiator Springs Racers using the Fast-Passes obtained earlier.
5. Obtain FastPasses for Soarin' Over California in Grizzly Peak.
6. Obtain FastPasses for *World of Color—Celebrate!* FastPasses are distributed near the entrance to Grizzly River Run.
7. Try Francis' Ladybug Boogie in A Bug's Land.
8. Ride Tuck and Roll's Drive 'Em Buggies.
9. Ride Flik's Flyers.
10. Check the daily entertainment schedule for the next showing of *Disney's Aladdin—A Musical Spectacular* in Hollywood Land. Work in this show around lunch.
11. Eat lunch.

12. See the Disney Animation exhibit, including Animation Academy and *Turtle Talk with Crush.*
13. Ride Soarin' Over California in Grizzly Peak using the FastPasses obtained earlier.
14. Try the Silly Symphony Swings in Paradise Pier.
15. Try Toy Story Midway Mania!
16. Experience King Triton's Carousel.
17. Explore the Redwood Creek Challenge Trail in Grizzly Peak.
18. Obtain FastPasses for The Twilight Zone Tower of Terror in Hollywood Land.
19. Ride Monsters, Inc. Mike & Sulley to the Rescue!
20. See *It's Tough to Be a Bug!* in A Bug's Land.
21. Ride The Tower of Terror in Hollywood Land using the FastPasses obtained earlier.
22. Eat dinner.
23. Ride The Little Mermaid: Ariel's Undersea Adventure in Paradise Pier.
24. Repeat any favorite attractions or see any missed attractions.
25. Check your daily entertainment schedule for parades, and check your *World of Color—Celebrate!* FastPass for the performance time.

The Best of Disneyland Resort in One Day

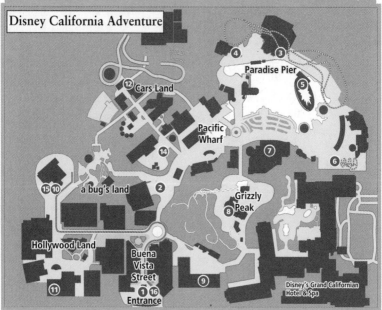

1. Arrive at the entrance 40 minutes before official opening time.
2. As soon as the park opens, obtain FastPasses for Radiator Springs Racers; the FastPass machine is located outside of Cars Land near *It's Tough to Be a Bug!*
3. Try Toy Story Midway Mania! in Paradise Pier.
4. Ride California Screamin'.
5. Ride Mickey's Fun Wheel (non-swinging).
6. Ride Goofy's Sky School.
7. Ride The Little Mermaid: Ariel's Undersea Adventure.
8. Ride Grizzly River Run in Grizzly Peak.
9. Experience Soarin' Over California.
10. Obtain FastPasses for The Twilight Zone Tower of Terror.
11. In Hollywood Land, ride Monsters, Inc. Mike & Sulley to the Rescue!
12. Ride Radiator Springs Racers in Cars Land using the FastPasses obtained earlier.
13. Eat lunch. A good choice nearby is Flo's V8 Cafe.
14. Ride Mater's Junkyard Jamboree.
15. Ride The Twilight Zone Tower of Terror in Hollywood Land using the FastPasses obtained earlier.
16. Leave DCA and head to Disneyland Park.

(continued on next page)

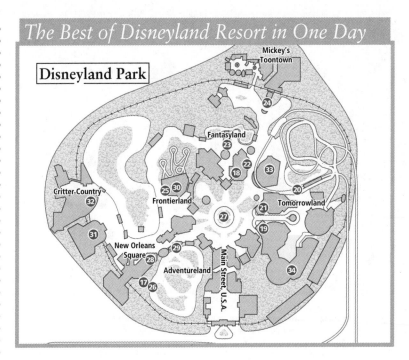

The Best of Disneyland Resort in One Day

Disneyland Park

Mickey's Toontown

Fantasyland

Critter Country

Frontierland

Tomorrowland

New Orleans Square

Adventureland

Main Street, U.S.A.

(continued from previous page)

17. Get FastPasses for Indiana Jones Adventure in Adventureland.
18. Ride Peter Pan's Flight in Fantasyland.
19. Ride Star Tours—The Adventures Continue in Tomorrowland.
20. Ride the Finding Nemo Submarine Voyage.
21. Try Buzz Lightyear Astro Blasters.
22. Ride Alice in Wonderland in Fantasyland.
23. Ride Dumbo the Flying Elephant.
24. See It's a Small World.
25. Obtain FastPasses for Big Thunder Mountain Railroad in Frontierland.
26. Ride Indiana Jones Adventure in Adventureland using the FastPasses obtained earlier.

27. Watch the *Disneyland Forever* fireworks. Find a spot on Main Street or near Sleeping Beauty Castle to watch the fireworks.
28. Ride Pirates of the Caribbean in New Orleans Square.
29. Take the Jungle Cruise in Adventureland.
30. Ride Big Thunder Mountain Railroad in Frontierland using the FastPasses obtained earlier.
31. See The Haunted Mansion in New Orleans Square.
32. Ride Splash Mountain in Critter Country.
33. Ride the Matterhorn Bobsleds in Fantasyland.
34. Ride Space Mountain in Tomorrowland.

Universal Studios One-Day Touring Plan

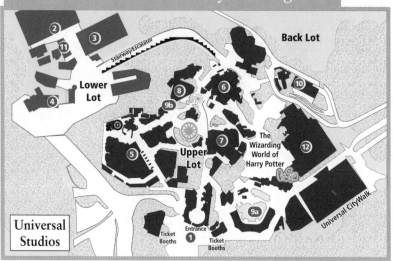

1. Arrive 20 minutes before opening time.
2. Ride Transformers: The Ride 3-D in the Lower Lot.
3. Ride Revenge of the Mummy—The Ride.
4. Check out Jurassic Park—The Ride.
5. In the Upper Lot, ride Despicable Me Minion Mayhem.
6. Experience The Simpsons Ride.
7. See *Shrek 4-D.*
8. See the Special Effects Stage.
9. Check your daily entertainment schedule for a) *WaterWorld* and b) *Universal's Animal Actors* showtimes.

10. Eat lunch and take the Studio Tour. Allocate an hour and 10 minutes for the tour.
11. Return to the Lower Lot and check out The NBC Universal Experience. Return to the Upper Lot.
12. Explore Hogsmeade Village, and experience Harry Potter and the Forbidden Journey, along with any other attractions in the Wizarding World (if open).
13. Revisit your favorites or see attractions you missed. Check your daily entertainment schedule for live performances that interest you.